Youth Cou

Youth Court Guide

Sixth Edition

Pakeeza Rahman LLB, Barrister
Magdalen Chambers, Exeter

and

Tony Rendell LLB, Barrister
Deputy Justices' Clerk,
HMCTS Avon, Somerset and Gloucestershire

Bloomsbury Professional

Bloomsbury Professional
An imprint of Bloomsbury Publishing Plc

Bloomsbury Professional Ltd	Bloomsbury Publishing Plc
41–43 Boltro Road	50 Bedford Square
Haywards Heath	London
RH16 1BJ	WC1B 3DP
UK	UK

www.bloomsbury.com

**BLOOMSBURY and the Diana logo are trademarks of
Bloomsbury Publishing Plc**

British Library Cataloguing-in-Publication Data

A catalogue record for this book is available from the British Library.

ISBN:	PB:	978 1 78451 695 6
	ePDF:	978 1 78451 697 0
	ePub:	978 1 78451 696 3

Typeset by Compuscript Ltd, Shannon
Printed and bound by CPI Group (UK) Ltd, Croydon, CR0 4YY

To find out more about our authors and books visit www.bloomsburyprofessional.com. Here you will find extracts, author information, details of forthcoming events and the option to sign up for our newsletters

Contents

Foreword

As the Operation's Manager of a Youth offending Team (YOT), in a time where there have been so many changes, and with many uncertainties ahead, it is reassuring to see this invaluable guide coming to its sixth edition.

Since its first publication this guide has been an essential point of reference for YOT staff. The guide systematically considers the sentencing ladder that young people can ascend, from police diversions and out of court disposals, through to trials and appeals including everything in between. Staff like the way that it is laid out and disentangles very complex law and process in a way that is user friendly. It has been and will be, particularly helpful in unpicking sentencing guidelines. This is vitally important for practitioners in the construction of court reports, especially in the consideration of sentencing options.

The role of the YOT Court Duty Officer (CDO) is a complex one, managing the competing demands of supporting the court itself whilst also managing young people and those attending with them. This guide is an integral part of the tool kit we provide for our CDO's to prepare themselves and others for appearance and to assist the management of situations as they arise on court days themselves. It is vitally important that court appearances provide all those that work within them the very best opportunity to get the right outcomes for the young people attending.

For new staff joining the YOT, the Youth Court Guide is an integral part of any induction programme and continues to assist staff with their continual development and often also provides the reference point when internal training is facilitated for staff. Having so much interwoven and relevant information to hand in one place is really important and it is clear that the authors, with their considerable experience, really understand the requirements of those this book is aimed at supporting.

When informed that Somerset YOT had been asked if it would provide a foreword for this book, staff were very keen to recommend this guide as the definitive point of reference for Youth Court work to their colleagues from other YOT's and to other Youth Court using professionals. I would fully endorse this recommendation.

Mike Stevens
Operations Manager
Somerset Youth Offending Team

May 2017

Preface

The reforms introduced by the Legal Aid Sentencing and Punishment of Offenders Act 2012 (LASPO 2012) soon became embedded in the practice of Youth Courts. Subsequent legal changes have interfered little with the main provisions of LASPO 2012. The Anti-social Behaviour, Crime and Policing Act 2014 abolished the anti-social behaviour order and introduced in their place the criminal behaviour order and anti-social behaviour injunction. These are covered in Chapter 14. The law surrounding reporting restrictions has received legislative attention. The court now has the option of providing lifetime anonymity for witnesses of all ages in relation to their involvement as a witness. The scope of the reporting restrictions has, under certain of the provisions, been extended to include social media. Section 39 of the Children and Young Persons Act 1933 is no longer applicable to criminal proceedings. It is now confined to civil and family proceedings. In the adult court the relevant provision is s 45 of the Youth Justice and Criminal Evidence Act 1999. In addition to the impact on reporting, the Criminal Justice and Courts Act 2015 has made changes to sentences for dangerous offenders as well as providing even greater flexibility regarding referral orders. Perhaps of most significance to the day to day operation of the Youth Court has been the amendment of s 3B of the Powers of Criminal Courts (Sentencing) Act 2000 which now allows that court to commit grave crimes to the Crown Court for sentence following trial and conviction in the Youth Court. Those and other reforms in CJC 2015 have been incorporated into this edition. The Sentencing Council's definitive guideline *Sentencing Children and Young People* was published in March 2017. Although the general approach is similar to the guideline which it replaces, *Overarching Principles - Sentencing Youths* there are a number of key differences which should make a real difference to outcomes for children and young people appearing before the courts. There are, therefore, many references and extracts from the new guideline throughout this book. Appendix I contains the new guidelines as they relate to robbery and sexual offences. The Policing and Crime Act 2017 came into force on 3 April 2017 and introduces judicial oversight of new limits on the length of pre charge bail. These are covered in Chapter 7. The Judiciary, and Her Majesty's Courts and Tribunal Service (HMCTS) are engaged in a process of transformational change. In the Youth Court arena this has so far led to the deregulation of the way Youth Court Panels are governed. The Youth Court (Constitution of Committees and Right to Preside) Rules 2007 have been replaced by a protocol between the Senior Presiding Judge and HMCTS. The requirement for mixed gender benches has gone.

The Youth Court Guide continues to feature extensive case law references and a sentencing compendium at Appendix J which reaches those offences which the Sentencing Council guidelines do not cover.

Preface

We would like to thank DJ(MC) David Taylor for casting his expert eye over Chapter 15.

We have attempted to state the law as it stood on 3 April 2017 unless otherwise indicated in the text.

Pakeeza Rahman and Tony Rendell

Somerset

April 2017

Table of Cases

Table of Statutes

[References are to paragraph number and appendices]

Table of Statutory Instruments

Abbreviations of Statutes, Rules and Regulations

ASBA 2003	=	Anti-social Behaviour Act 2003
ASBCPA 2014	=	Anti-Social Behaviour, Crime and Policing Act 2014
BA 1976	=	Bail Act 1976
CA 1989	=	Children Act 1989
CA 2003	=	Courts Act 2003
CAA 1968	=	Criminal Appeal Act 1968
CDA 1971	=	Criminal Damage Act 1971
CDA 1998	=	Crime and Disorder Act 1998
CEA 1968	=	Civil Evidence Act 1968
CEA 1995	=	Civil Evidence Act 1995
CJA 1982	=	Criminal Justice Act 1982
CJA 1987	=	Criminal Justice Act 1987
CJA 1988	=	Criminal Justice Act 1988
CJA 1991	=	Criminal Justice Act 1991
CJA 2003	=	Criminal Justice Act 2003
CJA 2009	=	Coroners and Justice Act 2009
CJIA 2008	=	Criminal Justice and Immigration Act 2008
CJPOA 1994	=	Criminal Justice and Public Order Act 1994
CPIA 1986	=	Criminal Procedure and Investigations Act 1996
CPR 2005	=	Criminal Procedure Rules 2005
CPR 2010	=	Criminal Procedure Rules 2010
CPR 2012	=	Criminal Procedure Rules 2012
CPR 2015	=	Criminal Procedure Rules 2015
CSA 2010	=	Crime and Security Act 2010
CYPA 1933	=	Children and Young Persons Act 1933
CYPA 1963	=	Children and Young Persons Act 1963
CYPA 1969	=	Children and Young Persons Act 1969
DVCVA 2004	=	Domestic Violence, Crime and Victims Act 2004
FA 1968	=	Firearms Act 1968
FSA 1989	=	Football Spectators Act 1989
HRA 1998	=	Human Rights Act 1998
LASPOA 2012	=	Legal Aid, Sentencing and Punishment of Offenders Act 2012
MCA 1980	=	Magistrates' Courts Act 1980
MC Rules 1981	=	Magistrates' Courts Rules 1981
MC (CYP) Rules 1992	=	Magistrates' Courts (Children and Young Persons) Rules 1992
MHA 1983	=	Mental Health Act 1983

MHA 2007	=	Mental Health Act 2007
MSA 2015	=	Modern Slavery Act 2015
OAPA 1861	=	Offences Against the Person Act 1861
PACE 1984	=	Police and Criminal Evidence Act 1984
PCA 2009	=	Policing and Crime Act 2009
PCC(S)A 2000	=	Powers of Criminal Courts (Sentencing) Act 2000
PFA 2012	=	Protection of Freedoms Act 2012
PHA 1997	=	Protection from Harassment Act 1997
PJA 2006	=	Police and Justice Act 2006
POA 1985	=	Prosecution of Offences Act 1985
ROA 1974	=	Rehabilitation of Offenders Act 1974
RTA 1988	=	Road Traffic Act 1988
RTOA 1988	=	Road Traffic Offenders Act 1988
SCA 1981	=	Senior Courts Act 1981
SOA 1956	=	Sexual Offences Act 1956
SOA 1993	=	Sexual Offences Act 1993
SOA 2003	=	Sexual Offences Act 2003
SOCPA 2005	=	Serious Organised Crime and Police Act 2005
VCRA 2006	=	Violent Crime Reduction Act 2006
YJCEA 1999	=	Youth Justice and Criminal Evidence Act 1999
Youth Court (Constitution etc) Rules 2007	=	Youth Courts (Constitution of Committees and Rights to Preside) Rules 2007

Chapter 1   Before charge

The framework of the system

1.01   The underlying philosophy of the legislation relating to persons under the age of 18 years who come before the courts is embodied in the Children and Young Persons Act 1933 (CYPA 1933). Section 44 of this Act provides that every court in dealing with a child or young person who is brought before it, either as an offender or otherwise, shall have regard to his or her welfare. The 1933 Act has been amended frequently and may be overridden completely by the Crown Court imposing detention for life under s 226 of the Criminal Justice Act 2003 (CJA 2003). Section 37 of the Crime and Disorder Act 1998 (CDA 1998) provides that the principal aim of the youth justice system shall be to prevent offending by children and young persons.

The Sentencing Council's definitive guideline *Sentencing Children and Young People* makes a number of references to the objectives of sentencing. (see **9.01**).

The Crime and Disorder Act 1998 introduced a new range of police and court powers to help to achieve that aim and deliver a faster and more effective youth justice system while at the same time overhauling the management of the agencies working within the system. The Government published a framework document on the principal aim in 1998 that set out a number of key objectives on how it was intended that this aim should be achieved. These were:

(a)   the swift administration of justice so that every young person accused of breaking the law has the matter resolved without delay;

(b)   confronting young offenders with the consequences of their offending, for themselves, their family, their victims, and their community, and helping them to develop a sense of personal responsibility;

(c)   intervention which tackles the particular factors (personal, family, social, educational or health) that put young persons at risk of offending and which strengthens 'protective factors';

(d)   punishment proportionate to the seriousness and persistence of the offending;

(e)   encouraging reparation to victims by young offenders; and

(f)   reinforcing the responsibilities of parents.

In addition to any other duty to which they are subject, it is the duty of all persons carrying out functions in relation to the youth justice system to have regard to the principal aim: CDA 1998, s 37(2).

Youth Justice Board

1.02   The Youth Justice Board was established on 30 September 1998 by CDA 1998, s 41. The Board reports to the Secretary of State for Justice and is required to monitor the operation of the youth justice system and set national standards for the provision of youth justice services and custodial accommodation.

CDA 1998, s 38(1) places a duty on local authorities to ensure the availability of all youth justice services for their area. It is the duty of the chief officers of police, police authorities, probation committees and health authorities within the local authority's area to co-operate in discharging the local authority's duty.

Every local authority is required to formulate a youth justice plan each year: CDA 1998, s 40.

Youth offending teams

1.03   Under CDA 1998, s 39 local authorities were charged with the creation of Youth Offending Teams (YOTs). These were created in co-operation with other agencies and include:

(a)   a probation officer;

(b)   a social worker of a local authority social services department;

(c)   a police officer;

(d)   a person nominated by a health authority any part of whose area lies within the local authority's area;

(e)   a person nominated by the chief education officer.

Youth Offending Teams were created in all areas in April 1999. In addition to the above objectives the YOTs must conduct their processes in accordance with the Youth Justice Board National Standards. All their work is governed by a policy ensuring it is free from discrimination and subject to monitoring and evaluation.

Unless charged with an offence of homicide, juveniles should be tried summarily, that is before magistrates. The courts dealing with their cases are known as Youth Courts and these courts must, in addition to the principal aim, have regard to the welfare of the persons appearing before them (see **1.01** above).

Persons under the age of 18 are known as 'juveniles' or simply as 'youths'. Important divisions of age exist within the 1933 Act and the amending legislation. They are listed below.

Under 10 years

1.04   A child below the age of 10 years is under the age of criminal responsibility and cannot be guilty of any offence in law (CYPA 1933, s 50). However, a juvenile, whether under the age of 10 or not, may be the subject of care proceedings brought under the Children Act 1989. Care proceedings are civil applications brought by a local authority or the NSPCC, whenever they believe that a court order is needed to ensure the juvenile's proper care and control. Such applications are made to a Family Proceedings Court, together with Child Safety Orders under CDA 1998, s 11 and are therefore outside the scope of this Guide.

Between 10 and 14 years

1.05   A juvenile within the age group of 10 to 13 inclusive is referred to as a child (CYPA 1933, s 107).

Between 14 and 18 years

1.06   A juvenile who has attained the age of 14 but is under 18 years is referred to as a young person (CYPA 1933, s 107 as amended by Criminal Justice Act 1991 (CJA 1991), Sch 8). However, there are specific exceptions where 'young person' means someone who has attained the age of 14 but is under 17 years. These exceptions are now quite rare and referred to at the appropriate parts of the text.

Throughout the text, the description 'juvenile' is used to include both children and young persons, unless it is necessary to differentiate between them.

Aged 16 and 17 years

1.07   Although this age group are not specifically referred to in any legislation, they are set apart from other juveniles in a number of important respects. First, they may attend court without a parent. Second, a number of orders and sentences can only be made in respect of them. These differences are dealt with fully in the following chapters.

Powers of arrest

1.08   Any person other than a police constable may arrest without a warrant anyone who is in the act of committing an indictable offence or anyone whom he has reasonable grounds for suspecting to be committing such an offence.

When an indictable offence has been committed, any person other than a constable may arrest without a warrant another who is guilty of that offence or anyone whom he has reasonable grounds for suspecting to be guilty of it (Police and Criminal Evidence Act 1984 (PACE 1984), s 24A(2)).

3

A police officer has wider powers of arrest than an ordinary citizen, in addition to the powers outlined above, he may arrest without a warrant anyone who is about to commit an offence or anyone whom he has reasonable grounds for suspecting to be about to commit an offence.

Further, where a constable has reasonable grounds for suspecting that an offence has been committed, he may arrest without a warrant anyone whom he has reasonable grounds for suspecting to be guilty of the offence. A juvenile should not be arrested or interviewed at his place of education unless this is unavoidable. In this case the principal or his nominee must be informed and agree to any interview (PACE 1984, Code of Practice C11.16; Note 11D).

The power of summary arrest mentioned above is only exercisable if a constable has reasonable grounds for believing that it is necessary to arrest the person because:

(a)   the name of the relevant person is unknown to, and cannot be readily ascertained by, the constable; or

(b)   the constable has reasonable grounds for doubting whether a name furnished by the relevant person as his name is his real name;

(c)   correspondingly as regards the person's address;

(d)   the arrest is necessary to prevent the relevant person:

   (i)   causing physical harm to himself or any other person;

   (ii)   suffering physical injury;

   (iii)   causing loss of or damage to property;

   (iv)   committing an offence against public decency (where members of the public going about their business cannot reasonably be expected to avoid the person in question); or

   (v)   causing an unlawful obstruction of the highway;

(e)   it is necessary to protect a child or other vulnerable person from the relevant person;

(f)   in order to allow the prompt and effective investigation of the offence or because of the conduct of the person in question;

(g)   it is necessary to prevent a prosecution from being hindered by the disappearance of the person in question; PACE 1984, s 24.

Juveniles involved in criminal matters are sometimes reported for summons. A summons is a direction in writing to the juvenile to attend the Youth Court on a given day and time and is normally sent to him by post. Where a juvenile is under 16 a parent or guardian should also be summoned. Alternatively there may be a written charge and requisition to attend court (see **3.10**).

Representing juvenile suspects at the police station

1.09   PACE 1984 and the Codes of Practice for detention, treatment and questioning of persons by the police apply to both juveniles and adults. The responsibility for the detained person is that of the custody officer, usually a police sergeant appointed by the chief officer of police to a police station designated for the purposes of and suitable for detaining arrested persons.

Code C covers the detention, treatment and questioning of persons by police officers. The provisions for the detention of arrested adults apply equally to juveniles, but extra duties and responsibilities are placed on the police in respect of persons under 18 years of age. In the police station anyone who appears to be under 18 is to be treated as a juvenile in the absence of clear evidence that they are older. Persons aged 18 or over are to be treated as adults. It is the age that the detained person appears to be that is relevant and not his actual age. Thus if he is over18 but the evidence available to the custody officer points to him being under that age, he is to be treated as a juvenile. Likewise if the police treat as an adult someone who is under 18 but appears to be older, they are acting properly (PACE 1984, s 37(15) and Code C1.5A).

Any arrested person must be informed by the custody officer of his rights which may be exercised at any time during his detention. Those rights are:

(a)   the right to have someone informed of his arrest;

(b)   the right to consult privately with a solicitor (the detained person must be told that independent legal advice is available free of charge); and

(c)   the right to consult the Codes of Practice (Code C3.1).

In addition, where a juvenile suspect is detained the police have a duty to identify specified people and notify them, as soon as is practicable, of the juvenile's arrest (CYPA 1933, s 34). The custody officer must if it is practicable ascertain the person responsible for the juvenile's welfare. That person may be his parent or guardian or, if he is in care, the care authority or voluntary organisation or any other person who has for the time being assumed responsibility for his welfare. That person must be informed as soon as practicable that the juvenile has been arrested, why he has been arrested, and where he is being detained (Code C3.13 and CYPA 1933, s 34(2), (3) and (4)). This applies even if the offences being investigated are terrorism offences (CYPA 1933, s 34(10)). If it appears that at the time of his arrest the child or young person is being provided with accommodation by or on behalf of the local authority under the Children Act 1989, s 20 the local authority should also be informed of the matters referred to above as soon as it is reasonably practicable (CYPA 1933, s 34(7A)). The notes for guidance to the Codes of Practice suggest that if the juvenile is in the care of the local authority or voluntary organisation but is living with his parents or other adults responsible for his welfare then (although there is no legal obligation on the police to inform them) they, as well as the authority or organisation, should normally be contacted unless suspected of involvement in the offence concerned. Even if a juvenile in care is not living with his parents, consideration is to be given to informing them (C: Note 3C)

In the case of a juvenile who is known to be subject to a court order under which a person or an organisation is given any degree of statutory responsibility to supervise or otherwise monitor him, reasonable steps must also be taken to notify that person or organisation (the 'responsible officer'). The responsible officer will normally be a member of a Youth Offending Team, apart from where there is a curfew order which requires electronic monitoring when the contractor providing the monitoring will be the responsible officer (Code C3.14 and CYPA 1933, s 34(7)).

Appropriate adult

1.10   The 'appropriate adult' in the Codes of Practice means:

(a)   parent or guardian or if he is in care, the care authority or voluntary organisation;

(b)   a social worker;

(c)   failing either of the above, another responsible adult aged 18 or over who is neither a police officer nor employed by the police (Code C1.7).

Police support volunteers and detention or escort officers employed by a contractor (C1.7(a)(iii),(b)(ii) and Note 1F) cannot act as appropriate adults under the new PACE Codes C, D and H which were published on 23 February 2017.

Local authorities, together with Youth Offending Team managers, have a duty to supply sufficient appropriate adults for their area.

The custody officer must as soon as practicable inform the appropriate adult (who may or may not be the person responsible for the juvenile's welfare) of the grounds for his detention and his whereabouts, and ask the appropriate adult to attend the police station straightaway to see the detained person (Code C3.15).

Where the detainee is a ward of court the police are required to notify the parent or foster parent with whom the ward is living or other appropriate adult and, if practicable, the reporting officer if one has been appointed. The reporting officer should be invited to attend the interview or nominate a representative to attend on his behalf. A copy of the tape of the interview should be provided to the reporting officer. If the interview has taken place in the absence of the reporting officer he should be notified of it and told of any further interviews that are proposed and invited to attend (*Practice Direction* [2002] 3 All ER 904).

The definition of appropriate adult amounts to a hierarchy. The police in arranging for the attendance of the appropriate adult should start with the parent or guardian and move on to the other categories only if they are not available. So far as category (c) is concerned, in the case of *R v Palmer* [1991] Legal Action 21 it was held that for a

16-year-old detainee, a 17-year-old could not be the appropriate adult because he was under 18 and probably too close in age.

Even when a parent has been present this can lead to difficulties. In *R v Morse* [1991] Crim LR 195 the court said that the juvenile suspect's father was not suitable. He was nearly illiterate, had a low IQ and was probably incapable of appreciating the gravity of the situation. However in *R v W* [1994] Crim LR 130, CA, the Court of Appeal refused to interfere with the finding of the first instance judge that the appellant's mother, who was mentally handicapped and therefore would have needed an appropriate adult herself if she had been arrested, was capable of fulfilling the appropriate adult's role. The court commented that at the time she was acting as appropriate adult she was experiencing a 'lucid interval'.

The notes for guidance to the Codes of Practice (C: Note 1B) make it clear that a person including the parent or guardian of a juvenile may be the appropriate adult unless he is suspected of involvement in the offence, is a victim, is a witness, is involved in the investigation or has received admissions prior to attending at the police station. In such circumstances it will be desirable for the appropriate adult to be some other person. If the parent of the juvenile is estranged from the juvenile the Notes for Guidance state that he should not be asked to be the appropriate adult if the juvenile expressly and specifically objects to his presence. The determining factor is the attitude of the juvenile and whether he or she expressly and specifically objects. In *DPP v Blake* [1989] 1 WLR 432 a confession was excluded where it had been obtained in the presence of the juvenile's father whom she had specifically rejected in favour of a named social worker who proved to be unavailable. The question of whether the child and parent are estranged is difficult and will eventually be a question of fact for the court to determine.

If a social worker or member of the Youth Offending Team is suspected of involvement, or is a witness, or has received admissions prior to attending at the police station he or she should not be the appropriate adult (C: Note 1B and C). A social worker who has called the police should not act as the appropriate adult because the detainee would see him or her as being on the side of the police (*DPP v Morris* (8 October 1990, unreported)).

A solicitor who is present at the police station in a professional capacity should not be the appropriate adult nor should an independent custody visitor (formerly lay visitor) present in that capacity (C: Note 1F).

The Home Office *Guidance for Appropriate Adults* (2011) and Code C11.17 state that the appropriate adult's role is:

'To support, advise and assist the detained person particularly during interview;

to observe whether the police are acting properly, fairly and with respect for the rights of the detainee and to tell them if he thinks they are not;

to assist communication between the detainee and the police;

to ensure that the detained person understands their rights and that the appropriate adult has a role in protecting their rights.'

The Home Office Guidance specifically states that it is not the appropriate adult's role to advise on the law.

The juvenile should be advised by the custody officer that the appropriate adult is there to advise and assist him and that he may consult with the appropriate adult privately at any time (Code C3.18).

Code C6.5A indicates that the appropriate adult can ask for advice on behalf of the juvenile. If the juvenile does not wish to have a solicitor but the appropriate adult does the solicitor should then treat the appropriate adult as the client. The solicitor may not force himself onto an unwilling juvenile, nor can the juvenile be forced to see the solicitor.

Code C11.15 requires the presence of the appropriate adult in the interview and requires the police to explain the appropriate adult's role to him or her. In *H and M v DPP* [1998] Crim LR 653, CA, the Court of Appeal refused to overturn the justices' decision to admit the accused's confession, even though the person present in interview whom the court deemed to be the appropriate adult was unaware of that expression and had not known the reason for his presence in the interview. It was also decided in this case that more than one person, for example, both parents, may be present as an appropriate adult. Although there had been a technical failure to follow the Codes of Practice, the protection envisaged had been provided.

An interview will not necessarily be deemed inadmissible if an appropriate adult intervenes too much. In *R v Jefferson* [1994] 1 All ER 270, CA, this happened but the detainee's denials were not altered and so the Court of Appeal upheld the decision to admit the evidence. In reviewing such a set of facts now, a court would have regard to Article 6 of the ECHR and the effect the evidence would have on the overall fairness of the trial.

However, an appropriate adult can be removed from an interview 'if their conduct is such that the interviewer is unable properly to put questions to the suspect' (C11.17A).

The independence of the appropriate adult from the police was underlined in *Leach v Chief Constable of Gloucestershire Constabulary* [1999] 1 All ER 215, CA, where it was held that the police had no duty of care to prevent psychological harm to the appropriate adult.

The right to legal advice

1.11   PACE 1984, s 58 and the Terrorism Act 2000, Sch 8, para 7 give a right to all persons arrested and held in custody to consult a solicitor in private at any time. This right applies equally to juveniles. If a juvenile wishes to exercise this right the request should be acted upon immediately, even though the appropriate adult has not arrived at the police station (PACE 1984, s 58(4)).

The Code of Practice provides that a detained person who does not know the name of a solicitor should be told of the availability of the local duty solicitor scheme and be provided with a list of such solicitors who are available to provide advice and assistance to detained persons. A duty solicitor should usually be available to provide advice at the police station under the duty solicitor scheme.

If a solicitor is told in the initial telephone call that the suspect is a juvenile, he should speak to him straightaway. In the case of a direct referral from the Criminal Defence Service a duty solicitor must give initial advice on the telephone unless they can advise the client in person without delay. Additionally under the old General Criminal Contract first contact with the client took place within 45 minutes of the solicitor being informed that the client was in custody. This is still good practice in relation to a juvenile client. It is not necessary to wait for the appropriate adult to arrive. If the appropriate adult arrives and considers that a duty solicitor should attend the police station then this must be arranged (Code C: 6.5A). In some circumstances the Legal Services Commission limit advice to that given over a telephone from a criminal defence call centre. Where the detained suspect is entitled to an appropriate adult then this forms an exception to that rule and in those circumstances, a solicitor should attend the police station (C: Note 6B2). The solicitor representing a juvenile both in the police station and in any subsequent proceedings must not lose sight of the fact that it is the juvenile who is the client and no other person, whether that other person is a parent or social worker. The solicitor should explain this to the appropriate adult at an early stage to reduce the possibility of any misunderstanding later. The Law Society document *Youth Court Guide – Defence Good Practice* (Law Society Criminal Practitioners Newsletter April 2002 available at www.thelawsociety.org.uk), emphasised that the solicitor's primary duty is to the client and that this is the child or young person. No one else, whether parent or social worker, should be allowed to give instructions. The Law Society's advice makes it clear that instructions should be taken from the juvenile and goes on to say that working with the family and appropriate adult is ancillary but should be approached with respect to their anxiety. Code C: Note1E makes it clear that the juvenile detainee has the right to see the solicitor in private. It is often more prudent for the solicitor to see the juvenile in private. If the consultation is to be in the absence of the appropriate adult then steps should be taken by the solicitor to ensure that the appropriate adult understands, particularly if he or she is a parent, what the reasons are for this. If the solicitor speaks to the juvenile alone, he may tell the appropriate adult what was said if the juvenile consents.

The solicitor representing the juvenile in the police station must take steps to be aware of the appropriate adult's attitude to information given in private consultation. The British Association of Social Workers and The Association of Directors of Social Services have both indicated that social workers have a duty to assist in the prevention and detection of crime and if asked they should pass on relevant information to the police. The Department of Health has issued guidance where it contemplates that disclosure will take place if the social worker considers that the juvenile suspect presents a danger to another person or the general public: LAC (88)17. The Law Society Criminal Law Committee has stated that the suspect should be advised in the absence of the appropriate adult about the risk of disclosure and then a decision should be taken by the client about admitting the appropriate adult to the consultations between the lawyer and the client. The Law Society's advice in *Youth Court Cases – Defence Good Practice* is for the solicitor to talk to the juvenile client alone both at the outset and at the various stages of the process.

The solicitor owes a duty of confidentiality to all clients including juveniles. This should be carefully explained to a juvenile client who may well see the solicitor as just another authority figure. The only exception to this is where there is a substantial fear that the juvenile may be in danger of abuse (*The Guide to Professional Conduct of Solicitors*).

If the appropriate adult is already at the police station when information is given to the detained juvenile about his rights then this should be done in the appropriate adult's presence. If the appropriate adult is not present at the police station when the information is given then the information should be repeated to the detainee when the appropriate adult attends (Code C3.17).

The Law Society Good Practice Guide (*Youth Court Cases – Defence Good Practice*) advised solicitors when dealing with juveniles to have regard to the following:

'To start, when taking instructions, by seeking basic details about the client and his circumstances;

to be aware of learning disabilities, ascertain details of school attended and ask if appropriate if anyone helps with their reading;

to take time to prepare the client for interview and to tell him how it will be conducted;

to carefully explain the caution and its consequences;

to consider conducting a practice interview with the client if the advice is to make no comment.'

The custody record

1.12   The custody record is a log kept by the custody sergeant recording all that happens to or concerning the detained person whilst in police custody.

In the case of a juvenile detainee the custody officer is to note the following in the custody record:

(a)   details of special action taken in respect of a juvenile detainee under Code C3.12 to C3.20 (Code C3.24);

(b)   where a juvenile is kept in a cell the reason for this (Code C8.10);

(c)   the grounds for interviewing a detained juvenile in the absence of the appropriate adult (Code C11.20).

These are in addition to the many other matters that have to be noted for all detainees.

The appropriate adult has the right to inspect the custody record, as has the detainee and his solicitor.

Interviews

1.13   A person under 18 years must not be interviewed or asked to provide or sign a written statement in the absence of the appropriate adult. This applies whether the juvenile is suspected of committing an offence or not. The only exception to this is where an officer of the rank of superintendent or above considers that delay will lead to one of the following consequences:

(a)   interference with or harm to evidence connected with an offence or physical harm to other people or serious loss or damage to property; or

(b)   the alerting of other people suspected of having committed an offence but not yet arrested for it; or

(c)   hindering the recovery of property obtained in consequence of the commission of an offence, and a superintendent is satisfied that the interview would not significantly harm the juvenile's physical or mental state (Code C11.18).

In those circumstances interviewing may not continue once sufficient information to avert the immediate risk has been obtained. A record has to be made of the grounds for any decision to interview without the appropriate adult and the notes of guidance state that this should only be done in urgent cases of need (Code C11.19).

The police are required to inform the appropriate adult present at an interview that he is not expected to act simply as an observer but also to advise the person being questioned; to observe whether the interview is being conducted properly and fairly; and to facilitate communication with the person being interviewed (Code C11.17).

Juveniles may only be interviewed at school in exceptional circumstances and only where the principal or his nominee agrees. Every effort should be made to notify either both parents or the other persons responsible for the juvenile's welfare and the appropriate adult (if a different person) that the police want to interview the juvenile, and reasonable time should be allowed to enable the appropriate adult to be present at the interview. Where waiting for the appropriate adult would cause unreasonable delay (unless the interviewee is suspected of an offence against the educational establishment), the principal or his nominee can act as the appropriate adult for the purposes of the interview (Code C11.16).

The notes for guidance remind the police that although juveniles are often capable of providing reliable evidence they may, without knowing or wishing to do so, be particularly prone in certain circumstances to provide information which is unreliable, misleading, or self incriminating. Special care is therefore to be exercised in questioning juveniles. Because of the risk of unreliable evidence, it is also important to obtain corroboration of any facts admitted whenever possible (C: Note 11C).

If a juvenile is a ward of court, the police can interview him without getting permission from the court, provided they follow the rules for interviewing juveniles. Those having care of the juvenile must notify the court of what has happened at the earliest opportunity (*Re G (minors)* [1990] 2 All ER 633).

Juvenile suspects have the same right to remain silent that adults have. The police must caution the juvenile. The words of the caution are:

> 'You do not have to say anything. But it may harm your defence if you do not mention now something which you later rely on in court. Anything you do say may be given in evidence.'

It is important to ensure that the juvenile understands the meaning of the caution and particular care must be taken to explain it in language that he or she will understand. Criminal Justice and Public Order Act 1994 (CJPOA 1994), ss 34, 36 and 37 apply to juveniles and a court may draw proper inferences from a failure to answer questions.

Identification procedures

1.14   Any procedure involving the participation of a juvenile (whether as a suspect or a witness) must take place in the presence of the appropriate adult. Any procedure requiring information to be given to or sought from a juvenile suspect must be given or sought in the presence of the appropriate adult, and if he has not arrived it must be repeated in his presence when he arrives (Code D2.14). Thus identification procedures including video identification when the juvenile is present, identification parades, group identifications or confrontations must always take place in the presence of the appropriate adult.

It is generally necessary for a suspect to consent to taking part in a video identification or an identification parade. However, under PACE 1984, s 64A an officer may photograph a detainee at a police station with consent, or without if it is withheld or it is not practicable to obtain consent. D: Note 5Ed gives as one example of impracticability the situation where the parent or guardian cannot be contacted in sufficient time to allow the photograph to be taken. A juvenile suspect's consent is valid only if given in the presence of the appropriate adult and the consent of the parent or guardian is required as well as his own (unless he is under 14 in which case the consent of the parent or guardian alone is sufficient (Code D2.12)). For the purposes of Code D2.12 in the case of a juvenile in the care of the local authority the consent may be given by the authority (D: Note 2A). However the consent of, for example, a social worker present as appropriate adult will not suffice if the juvenile is not in care. If the only obstacle to an identification procedure is that a juvenile's parent or guardian refuses consent or reasonable efforts to obtain it have failed the identification officer may arrange a video identification in accordance with Code D, Annex A. The parent or guardian who is asked to consent does not have to be at the police station, but they must be given an opportunity to speak to the juvenile detainee and the appropriate adult if they so wish before giving their consent. The consent, if given, must be informed consent (D: Note 2A).

Video identification parades electronic recording (VIPER) is a speedier process than the old-fashioned method of holding identification parades involving volunteers. A short video film of the suspect with other volunteers of a similar age and appearance is prepared and shown to witnesses. The witness will attend to look at the film with an identification officer and the suspect's legal representative, whose role is to observe the procedure and the manner in which it is conducted. The witness will watch the film at least twice and be asked if they can make a positive identification. The identification officer may then ask some questions for the purposes of clarification.

Where a suspect refuses to take part in a video identification or an identification parade, a group identification can be held or a witness can be shown a moving video made for the purposes of an identification. The suspect should be asked for his consent in the presence of the appropriate adult, but even if he refuses the group identification can still proceed and the video can still be made. The suspect, the appropriate adult and the suspect's solicitor should all be shown the film to enable objections to be made before it is shown to witnesses.

Searches

Initial search

1.15   A search on initial detention at the police station under PACE 1984, s 54 and Code C4 does not have to be carried out in the presence of an appropriate adult. This will normally involve no more than emptying of pockets and rubbing down over clothing, or removal of outer clothing.

Search to establish identity

1.16   A police officer of the rank of inspector or above may authorise a search or examination for the purposes of ascertaining whether a mark would tend to identify the detained person as being involved in the commission of an offence or for the purpose of establishing their identity: PACE 1985, s 54A(1)(a) and (b). Authorisation may only be given where consent has been withheld or it has been impracticable to obtain. In the case of a juvenile this might be applied where the parent or guardian could not be contacted in sufficient time to allow the search, examination or photograph to be carried out.

Strip search

1.17   This is a search involving the removal of more than outer clothing. A strip search should normally be conducted by a police officer of the same sex as the juvenile or take place in the presence of the appropriate adult of the same sex. The juvenile's consent to a search is only valid if their parents or guardians consent is also obtained, unless the juvenile is under 14, in which case their parents or guardians consent is sufficient in its own right. The search may proceed in the appropriate adult's absence in cases of urgency where there is a risk of serious harm to the person being searched or others. (*PD v Chief Constable of Merseyside Police* [2015] EWCA Civ 114). In the case of *PD v Chief Constable of Merseyside Police* the court expressed concern 'that it should have been thought appropriate immediately to remove the clothes of a distressed and vulnerable 14 year old girl without thought for alternative and less invasive measures to protect her from herself'. Alternative measures could include placing the child in a monitored CCTV room and checking them at regular intervals; or sitting with the child until the appropriate adult arrives. The juvenile may signify that he or she does not wish the appropriate adult present during the search or that he or she wishes an appropriate adult of the opposite sex who is readily available to be present and if this is done the appropriate adult need not be present. This must however be signified in the appropriate adult's presence and must be recorded and signed by the appropriate adult.

Intimate search

1.18   This consists of the examination of the person's bodily orifices other than the mouth. It must only be carried out by, medical practitioner or a nurse (Code C, Annex A, para 2) unless an officer, of at least the rank of inspector, considers it is not practicable, in which case a police officer may carry out the search (Code C, Annex A, Notes A1 to A5). Such a search must always be carried out in the presence of an appropriate adult of the same sex. The juvenile may signify that he or she wishes the search to take place without an appropriate adult or in the presence of an appropriate adult of the opposite sex who is readily available. This must however be signified in the appropriate adult's presence and must be recorded and signed by the appropriate adult.

Intimate samples

1.19   An appropriate adult of the same sex must be present during the taking of intimate samples involving the removal of clothing in circumstances likely to lead to embarrassment. The juvenile may signify that he or she wishes this to take place without an appropriate adult or in the presence of an appropriate adult of the opposite sex who is readily available. This must however be signified in the appropriate adult's presence and must be recorded and signed by the appropriate adult.

DNA and fingerprinting

1.20   The police can take fingerprints without the suspect's consent if he or she has been arrested for, charged with, informed he or she will be reported for or convicted of a recordable offence. Fingerprints may only be taken with the authorisation of an officer of at least the rank of inspector where he is satisfied that the taking of the fingerprints is necessary to assist in the prevention or detection of crime. Since 7 March 2011 the Serious Organised Crime and Police Act 2005 (SOCPA 2005), s 117 has amended PACE 1984, s 61 giving a police constable the power to take a person's fingerprints without their consent where the person is unknown to the officer and their name cannot reasonably be ascertained, or where an officer has reasonable grounds for doubting the validity of the name given.

In *S and Marper v United Kingdom* [2009] Crim LR 355, fingerprints and DNA samples had been taken from S, an 11-year-old boy who was acquitted of robbery, and from Michael Marper, a man against whom proceedings for harassment of his partner had been discontinued. The European Court of Human Rights found that data in the case of persons whose prosecutions had been discontinued, was a violation of Article 8 of the ECHR and the 'blanket and indiscriminate' nature of the power of retention could not be sufficiently justified.

The Protection of Freedoms Act 2012 (PFA 2012), ss 1–18 introduced a new retention regime reflecting the judgment in *S and Marper v United Kingdom* [2009]. This inserted into PACE 1984, ss 63D to 65B which provide, with some exceptions, that fingerprints and DNA will not be retained where a suspect is arrested for a minor offence but not charged or convicted. However where a suspect is arrested for but not charged with a serious offence, the police are only permitted to retain fingerprints and DNA in very tightly controlled circumstances. Where the suspect is arrested for and charged with a serious offence but not convicted, fingerprints and DNA can be retained for three years, with the option of a single two year extension by a court. Fingerprints and DNA data can still be retained indefinitely where an adult is convicted of a recordable offence.

Where the suspect is under 18 and is convicted of a serious offence the juvenile's fingerprints and DNA will be retained indefinitely. If the juvenile is convicted of a minor offence the data will be retained for five years on a first conviction (plus the length of any custodial sentence) and then indefinitely following a second conviction.

Cautions for adults and youth cautions and youth conditional cautions for those under 18 are treated as convictions for DNA and fingerprint retention. In relation to those persons who receive a penalty notice for disorder, their fingerprints and DNA will be retained for two years.

The responsible Chief Officer of police can order retention for two years on national security grounds. This can be renewed every two years. There are separate retention provisions in terrorism legislation.

Police detention of juveniles

1.21   A juvenile should not be placed in a police cell unless there is no other secure accommodation available and the custody officer considers that it is not practicable to supervise him if he is not placed in a cell, or the custody officer considers that a cell provides more comfortable accommodation than other secure accommodation within the police station. A juvenile may not be placed in a cell with a detained adult. If a juvenile is placed in a cell the reason must be recorded on the custody record (Code C8.8 and C8.10).

All detainees should be visited every hour but juveniles should be visited more often wherever possible (C: Note 9B).

After charge

1.22   The custody officer is required by PACE 1984, s 37 to decide whether there is sufficient evidence to charge a detained person, although it is for the Crown Prosecution Service (CPS) to decide whether a suspect should be charged and with what they should be charged. If the detained person is charged, he must be cautioned, the charge must be read to him and he must be given a written notice showing particulars of the offence with which he is charged. This must include the name of the officer in the case, his police station and the reference number for the case. The charge is to be stated in simple terms but the particulars should also show the precise offence in law with which the defendant is charged. Where a juvenile is charged an appropriate adult must be present and the notice is to be given to the appropriate adult. A record must be kept of anything said at the time of charging.

The general duties of the custody officer, before charge, are set out in PACE 1984, s 38. The custody officer shall order the release of a juvenile from detention either on bail or without bail, unless:

(a)

    (i)   his name or address cannot be ascertained or the custody officer has reasonable grounds for doubting whether a name or address furnished by him is his real name or address;

    (ii)   the custody officer has reasonable grounds for believing that the person arrested will fail to appear in court to answer bail;

    (iii)   in the case of a person arrested for an imprisonable offence the custody officer has reasonable grounds for believing that the detention of the person arrested is necessary to prevent him from committing an offence;

    (iv)   in the case of a person arrested for an offence which is not an imprisonable offence, the custody officer has reasonable grounds for believing that the detention of the person arrested is necessary to prevent him causing physical injury to any other person or causing loss or damage to property;

(v) the custody officer has reasonable grounds for believing that the detention of the person arrested is necessary to prevent him interfering with the administration of justice or with the investigation of the offences or of a particular offence; or

(vi) the custody officer has reasonable grounds for believing that the detention of the arrested person is necessary for his own protection;

(b) additionally, an arrested juvenile may be detained if the custody officer has reasonable grounds for believing that he ought to be detained in his own interests (PACE 1984, s 38(1)); or

(c) where drug test procedures are in place a detention of a juvenile between the ages of 14 and 17 inclusive may be authorised where it is necessary to enable the sample to be taken: PACE ss 38 and 63B.

'Own interests' is not defined and thus the custody officer has a wide discretion.

In taking the decisions required by (a) and (b) above (except (a)(i) and (vi) and (b)) the custody officer is required to consider whether there are substantial grounds for believing that the defendant, if released on bail, would:

(a) fail to surrender to custody; or

(b) commit an offence while on bail; or

(c) interfere with witnesses or otherwise obstruct the course of justice, whether in relation to himself or any other person (PACE 1984, s 38(2A)).

Where a custody officer authorises an arrested juvenile to be kept in police detention the custody officer shall ensure that the arrested juvenile is moved to local authority accommodation. The exceptions to this are where the custody officer certifies that:

(a) by reason of such circumstances as are specified in the certificate, it is impracticable for him to do so (see *R v Chief Constable of Cambridgeshire, ex parte M* [1991] 2 QB 499); or

(b) in the case of the arrested juvenile who has attained the age of 12 years that no secure accommodation is available and that keeping him in other local authority accommodation would not be adequate to protect the public from serious harm from him (PACE 1984, s 38(6)(b)).

R v Chief Constable of Cambridgeshire, ex parte M, which was decided both before the revision to Code C in April 1991 and before the Criminal Justice Act 1991, is sometimes interpreted to mean that a custody officer would be justified in deciding that the transfer would not be practicable if he believed that the accommodation would not be secure. Home Office Circular 78/1992 *'Criminal Justice Act 1991: Detention of Juveniles'* states that the construction of s 38(6)(a):

> 'makes it clear that the type of accommodation in which the local authority proposes to place the juvenile is not a factor which the custody officer may take into account in considering whether the transfer is impracticable. In particular the unavailability of local authority secure accommodation does not make the transfer impracticable.'

The circular indicates that 'impracticable' means circumstances where transfer would be physically impossible by reason of, for example, floods, blizzards, or the impossibility despite repeated efforts of contacting the local authority. Code C: Note16D provides that:

> 'Neither a juvenile's behaviour nor the nature of the offence provides grounds for the custody officer to decide it is impracticable to arrange the juvenile's transfer to local authority care.'

Where the juvenile is charged with a violent or sexual offence, 'protecting the public from serious harm from him' is to be construed as a reference to protecting members of the public from death or serious personal injury, whether physical or psychological, occasioned by further such offences committed by him (PACE 1984, s 38(6A)).

Where the arrested juvenile is moved to local authority accommodation, it is lawful for any person acting on behalf of the local authority to detain him (PACE 1984, s 38(6B)). The Children Act 1989 (CA 1989), s 21(2) stipulates that every local authority shall receive and provide accommodation for children who are referred under PACE 1984, s 38(6).

The custody officer is under a duty to do everything practicable to ensure that the place of detention for the juvenile is in local authority accommodation and not the police station. In para (b) specific reference is made to taking the lack of secure accommodation into account for young persons who have attained the age of 12 years when deciding whether to transfer them to local authority accommodation.

The certificate (Juvenile Detention Certificate) under these provisions made in respect of an arrested juvenile shall be produced to the court to which he was first brought. The Juvenile Detention Certificate given to the court in accordance with PACE 1984, s 38(7) must show why the juvenile was kept in the police station and their case must be monitored and supervised by an officer of inspector rank or above (C16.7). Although the certificate must be produced to the court, the statute neither provides any sanction for non compliance nor gives the court any powers to act on its non production where the custody officer certifies under PACE 1984, s 38(6). Neither the juvenile's unruliness, nor the nature of the offence with which he is charged, provide grounds for the custody officer to fail to arrange this transfer. The requirement to transfer to local authority accommodation applies to a juvenile charged during daytime as it does to a juvenile to be held overnight. A pragmatic approach can, however, be taken so that if the transfer is likely to mean that the juvenile's sleep is likely to be substantially disturbed due perhaps to the time required to find a placement and then to transport them there, with an early rise to attend court in the morning, then it may not be practicable (*R (on the application of BG) v The Chief Constable of the West Midlands Constabulary and Birmingham City Council* [2014] EWHC 4374 (Admin). PACE 1984, s 39(4) makes it clear that upon such a transfer to local authority accommodation the custody officer's duties cease in relation to custody records and ensuring that the juvenile is treated in accordance with police codes of practice for detained persons.

It should be noted that there is no duty to transfer to local authority accommodation where the juvenile has been arrested on a warrant not backed for bail or for breach of bail conditions or breach of remand conditions. This is because PACE, s 38 refers to persons who are charged with an offence and excludes those arrested on warrants without bail.

Arrangements should be made for preventing a child or young person under 18 while detained in a police station or being conveyed to or from any criminal court from associating with an adult (not being a relative) who is charged with any offence other than an offence with which the child is jointly charged. Arrangements should also be made to ensure that a girl should be in the care of a woman (CYPA 1933, s 31, *R (on the application of BG) v The Chief Constable of the West Midlands Constabulary and Birmingham City Council* [2014] EWHC 4374 (Admin)).

Breaches of codes of practice

1.23   A breach of the Codes can lead to evidence obtained as a result of the breach being treated as inadmissible (PACE 1984, ss 76, 76A and 77), or excluded (PACE 1984, ss 78 and 82). In *R v Hassan* [2007] EWCA Crim 1140, it was held that although breaches of Code A were important it had been right to allow the case to go before the jury, where the judge had given a clear direction about the serious issue of the credibility of the police officers. A breach of the PACE Codes of Practice may also lead to disciplinary action being taken against the police officer. Such action may only be instigated by the police, that is, not by a civilian or a solicitor.

Confessions

1.24   PACE 1984, s 76(2) states that:

'If, in any proceedings where the prosecution proposes to give in evidence a confession made by an accused person, it is represented to the court that the confession was or may have been obtained:

(a)   by oppression of the person who made it; or

(b)   in consequence of anything said or done which was likely, in the circumstances existing at the time, to render unreliable any confession which might be made by him in consequence thereof,

the court shall not allow the confession to be given in evidence against him except in so far as the prosecution proves to the court beyond reasonable doubt that the confession (notwithstanding that it may be true) was not obtained as aforesaid.'

PACE 1984, s 76A contains similar provisions to allow a court to exclude the confession of a co-accused sought to be adduced against another in the same proceedings.

'Confession' includes any statement wholly or partly adverse to the person who made it, whether made to a person in authority or not and whether made in words or otherwise (PACE 1984, s 82(1)). 'Oppression' includes torture, inhuman or degrading treatment, and the use or threat of violence (whether or not amounting to torture) (PACE 1984, s 76(8)).

An example of conduct found to be 'unsporting' but not oppressive is the case of *R v Fulling* [1987] QB 426. The facts involved the interviewing of a 34-year-old woman who was questioned 'persistently' about her involvement in an offence of obtaining insurance money by the deception that her home had been burgled. She exercised her right to silence until informed that her lover (also implicated in the offence) had been having an affair, whereupon she became so distressed that (she alleged) she made a statement simply in order to be released from custody. However in *R v Beales* [1991] Crim LR 118 where a defendant was hectored and bullied from first to last, the interview was said to have stepped into the realm of oppression. The Court of Appeal held in *R v Cox* [1991] Crim LR 276 that a trial judge should have excluded a confession that was obtained by oppression, even when the defendant accepted that it was true.

The Court of Appeal held that:

(a)   The 1984 Act was not intended to follow the common law. The modern law is to be ascertained by interpreting the Act, not by 'roaming over a vast number of authorities'.

(b)   The definition in s 76(8) is not all embracing, but is to be extended to cover anything within the ordinary dictionary meaning of the word. The particular definition relied upon was 'exercise of authority or power in a burdensome, harsh, or wrongful manner, or unjust or cruel treatment, or the imposition of unreasonable or unjust burdens'.

(c)   Oppression implies some impropriety on the part of the interrogator, which leads to the confession. If the defendant would have confessed in any event s 76(2) will not apply. Section 76(2)(b) is potentially wider since it covers not only threats, but also promises. This could apply, for example, where a defendant is offered favourable treatment in return for a confession, such as a promise not to oppose bail. Note, Code C11.5 also prohibits such behaviour.

The effect of s 76(2) is that in summary proceedings justices should, before the end of the prosecution case:

(a) hold a 'trial within a trial' if it is represented to them by the defence that a confession was, or might have been, obtained either by 'oppression', or in circumstances which might render the confession 'unreliable';

(b) in such a 'trial within a trial' allow the defendant to give evidence confined to the question of admissibility, and the justices will not then be concerned with the truth or otherwise of the confession;

(c) give the defendant a ruling on the admissibility of a confession before or at the end of the prosecution case, in case he should wish to make a submission of no case to answer at the end of the prosecution evidence and ask that the case be dismissed at that point;

(d) not allow the prosecution evidence relating to the obtaining of the confession to be called twice (*R v Liverpool Juvenile Court, ex parte R* [1988] QB 1).

It is worth noting that even where a confession is not excluded under s 76(2) it does not prevent it being excluded under s 78(1) on the basis that it would adversely affect the fairness of the proceedings (see **1.25**).

Evidence unfairly obtained

1.25   The Police and Criminal Evidence Act 1984, s 78 provides that:

'(1)   In any proceedings the court may refuse to allow evidence on which the prosecution proposes to rely to be given if it appears to the court that, having regard to all the circumstances, including the circumstances in which the evidence was obtained, the admission of the evidence would have such an adverse effect on the fairness of the proceedings that the court ought not to admit it.

(2)   Nothing in this section shall prejudice any rule of law requiring a court to exclude evidence.'

These provisions apply just as much to juveniles as they do to adults.

An example of how the section works can be found in *R v Deacon* [1987] Crim LR 404. Admissions made to the police were ruled inadmissible by the judge on the grounds that the police had wrongly refused the defendant access to his solicitor. It was said that to have allowed the evidence to go before the jury would have had an adverse effect upon the fairness of the trial. Technical breaches of the Code of Practice (defendant not allowed eight hours of continuous rest and failure to record the time the interview ended) weighed little in the decision, but nonetheless were to be taken into account. The jury was accordingly directed to acquit the defendant.

However, where the question of unfairness is raised under PACE 1984, s 78 there is no general requirement to conduct a 'trial within a trial' to be held (*Vel v Owen* [1987] Crim LR 496).

With specific reference to a juvenile court case the Divisional Court in *DC (a juvenile) v DPP* (9 November 1987, unreported) confirmed that there is no obligation upon a magistrates' court to hold a 'trial within a trial' where it is represented to the court that it should use its discretion under PACE 1984, s 78 to exclude evidence of a confession in circumstances where it is not represented that such evidence was or might have been obtained in breach of PACE 1984, s 76(2) or indeed in breach of the ECHR articles: see *Halawa v Federation Against Copyright Theft* [1995] 1 Cr App R 21.

Any magistrates' court has power to make a binding ruling before the start of a trial where it believes it to be in the interests of justice to do so: MCA 1980, s 8A(1) and (3).

Such a ruling could include the admission of a confession and would involve representations from both parties. The effect of such a ruling is that it is binding from the time it is made until the case is disposed of: MCA 1980, s 8B(1).

There is power to vary a binding ruling under MCA 1980, s 8B(3) and (5), but no application to do so may be made, unless there has been a material change in circumstances or fresh evidence since the ruling was made: *R (on the application of the CPS) v Gloucester Justices* [2008] All ER (D) 197 (Jun).

In general terms no report may be made for a hearing involving a pre-trial binding ruling: MCA 1980 s 8C(1) and (2).

Chapter 2   Prosecution and the constitution of the court

Introduction

2.01   The belief that a court appearance by a juvenile will not prevent, and indeed may induce further, offending was encapsulated in the Government's White Paper, *Young Offender*, published in 1980 where it was stated that:

> 'All the available evidence suggests that juvenile offenders who can be diverted from the criminal justice system at an early age in their offending are less likely to re-offend than those who become involved in judicial proceedings.'

Cautioning as a means of diversion was replaced in the Crime and Disorder Act 1998 (CDA 1998) by a reprimand and final warnings scheme. In terms of re-offending diversion is as effective as other disposals: Home Office statistics show that four out of five young people aged 14 to 20 cautioned for a standard list of offences are not re-convicted within two years of the caution. The reprimand and final warnings scheme was later abolished and replaced within the Crime and Disorder Act by youth cautions and youth conditional cautions (CDA 1998, ss 66ZA–66H). (see **2.03** and **2.04**).

Diversion means that a juvenile neither has to appear in court, nor is he convicted or sentenced. A juvenile who is dealt with in this manner avoids the damaging stigma of criminal proceedings. Broadly, the choices available are to take informal action, to offer community resolutions such as a youth restorative disposal, to give a caution or a youth conditional caution, or to bring proceedings before the Youth Court.

Where a restorative approach or a rehabilitation programme is contemplated the police may involve the Youth Offending Team for assistance in carrying out a prior assessment of the young offender. The assessment is conducted by the Youth Offending Team within 10 working days. The assessment is based upon the 'ASSET' Plus tool and this may involve a visit to the young person, his family and, where relevant, the victim. In addition to the core assessment there are a number of Asset Plus self-assessment tools for juveniles and their parents/carers. The Home Office guidance specifies the purpose of a prior assessment as being an exploration of the young offender's attitude to intervention and an assessment of the likelihood of his engaging with a rehabilitation or change programme.

Community Resolutions

2.02   Community resolutions are informal disposals which are delivered locally by police forces. These include youth restorative disposals (YRD). Community resolutions are measures for diverting a juvenile from the formal criminal justice system. YRDs have been introduced by the Home Office as a way of providing instant justice for both the victim and offender. Typically a meeting will be arranged between the youth and the victim with a view to resolving the harm which has been done, and helping the juvenile understand the consequences of his actions. It can only be used where the victim agrees and the offender is willing to participate. It cannot be given where the youth has previously offended, nor is it appropriate for offences involving anti-social behaviour, crossbows, cruelty, deaths, drugs, firearms, football grounds and sporting events offences, interference with the course of justice, offensive weapons, road traffic, road traffic documents and sexual offences. YRDs are recorded locally by police forces and are not entered on the police national computer. Details of any community resolutions may be disclosed on an enhanced Disclosure and Barring Service (previously CRB) check. A juvenile should only be given one YRD. More information can be found on the Youth Justice Board website at www.gov.uk.

Youth cautions

2.03   The police are given power to caution juveniles under CDA 1998, s 66ZA. The power may be exercised if there is sufficient evidence to charge, the juvenile admits the offence and the police officer does not consider the juvenile should be prosecuted or given a youth conditional caution. A caution must be administered in the presence of an appropriate adult. The Secretary of State has been given authority to provide guidance to the police in connection with the use and recording of youth cautions. There is no statutory bar on giving a youth caution to a juvenile who has a previous conviction. The police must refer juveniles who have been cautioned to the Youth Offending Team. If the juvenile has not previously been cautioned or given a youth conditional caution the YOT may complete an assessment and must arrange a rehabilitation programme for the offender unless they consider it inappropriate. Following any further cautions the YOT must make an assessment and provide a rehabilitation programme. There is no statutory limit to the number of cautions which may be given, although guidelines may be issued. A court may only impose a conditional discharge on a juvenile for an offence committed within two years of a second caution if there are exceptional circumstances relating to the offence or offender. The court has to explain in open court what the exceptional circumstances are. The restriction also applies where the juvenile has previously received a youth conditional caution followed by a youth caution. Reprimands and final warnings which have been issued under CDA 1998, s 65 are to be treated as youth cautions for these purposes. Cautions and any failure to comply with a rehabilitation programme may be cited in court. If an adult offender commits a minor offence within two years of receiving a youth caution they can only be given a caution for that offence if there are exceptional circumstances relating to the offender or either offence (CJCA 2015, s 17).

Youth conditional cautions

2.04   The Criminal Justice and Immigration Act 2008, s 48 and Sch 6 gives the prosecution an additional option, of imposing a youth conditional caution. A youth conditional caution (YCC) can be given where the juvenile has previous convictions.

A youth conditional caution is a caution in respect of an offence committed by the offender to which conditions are attached with which the offender must comply. Any condition attached must have the objective of facilitating the rehabilitation of the offender and/or ensuring that the offender makes reparation for the offence and/or punishing the offender. A financial penalty may be imposed as a condition but only for a prescribed offence and in an amount of no more than £100. Payment of such an order is to a designated officer for a local justice area: CDA 1998, ss 66B and 66C. www.gov.uk/government/uploads/system/uploads/attachment_data/file/329810/ Code_of_practice_for_youth_conditional_cautions.pdf.

Before making a conditional caution the authorised person, who may be the constable, investigating officer or a person authorised by the relevant prosecutor, must satisfy five requirements, as follows:

(a)   there is evidence that the offender has committed an offence;

(b)   there is sufficient evidence to charge the offender with the offence and that a youth conditional caution should be given in respect of that offence;

(c)   the offender admits to the authorised person that he committed the offence;

(d)   the authorised person explains the effect of the youth conditional caution to the offender and warns him that failure to comply with any of the conditions attached may result in his being prosecuted for the offence (if the offender is 17 or under this must be done in the presence of an appropriate adult);

(e)   the offender signs a document containing details of the offence, his admission, his consent to being given a youth conditional caution and details of the conditions attached to that caution.

The authorised person must refer the juvenile to the Youth Offending Team as soon as practicable after the youth conditional caution has been given. If the offender fails, without reasonable excuse, to comply with any of the conditions attached to the youth conditional caution, criminal proceedings may be instigated against him for the offence in question. He may be arrested without warrant in order to be charged (CJA 2003, s 24A(1)). The document mentioned above may be admissible in such proceedings, and on the commencement of the proceedings the conditional caution ceases to have effect. As with youth cautions, reprimands and warnings, if a person who has been given a conditional caution is convicted of an offence committed within two years of the caution the court so convicting him may not make a conditional discharge in respect of the offence unless it is of the opinion that there are exceptional circumstances relating to the offence or the offender which justify its doing so: CDA 1998, s 66F. The Code of

Conduct provides guidance. The maximum financial penalties are prescribed according to age and category of offence. Those aged 10–13 years at the time the YCC is given can have a penalty of up to £15 for a summary only offence, £25 for an either way offence and £35 for an indictable only offence. The amounts for the 14–17 year olds are £30, £50 and £75 respectively. (The Crime and Disorder Act 1998 (Youth Conditional Cautions: Financial Penalties) Order 2013). In addition, the CPS Director's guidance sets out mitigated levels for use in practice. That guidance also includes compensation levels for typical injuries. The authority for imposing compensation conditions comes under the heading reparation, and not the financial penalty provisions.

If an adult offender commits a minor offence within two years of receiving a youth conditional caution they can only be given a caution for that offence if there are exceptional circumstances relating to the offender or either offence (CJCA 2015, s 17).

In *R (on the applications of G) v Chief Constable of Surrey Police and Others* [2016] EWIIC 295 (Admin) the High Court held the statutory regime that required disclosure of historic reprimands to potential employers seeking enhanced disclosure was, in the absence of procedural safeguards to assess relevance and proportionality, incompatible with art 8 of the ECHR.

Prosecution

2.05   The decision to charge or summons a juvenile in practice rests with the police and the CPS, although a prosecution may be commenced by any person, unless the statute under which the prosecution is brought states otherwise. It is worth noting however, that where the Crown have administered a formal warning and the offender is told that he will not have to go to court, it will be an abuse of process to allow a private prosecution in those circumstances: *Jones v Walley* [2006] All ER (D) 369 (Jul).

However, as soon as proceedings are instituted, the Crown Prosecution Service is under a duty to take over the conduct of these proceedings (Prosecution of Offences Act 1985 (POA 1985), s 3(2)).

The Director of Public Prosecutions also has the right at any stage to take over the conduct of criminal proceedings if he thinks it appropriate, even though he may be under no duty to do so (POA 1985, s 6(2)).

The Crown Prosecutor may decide during the preliminary stages that the prosecution should be discontinued. Discontinuance has nothing to do with the philosophies behind diversion from prosecution but is based upon a Code of Practice published on behalf of the Director of Public Prosecutions.

The Crown Prosecutor's discretion to discontinue proceedings will therefore be exercised on the basis of such questions as whether or not the evidence against the defendant is sufficient to provide a realistic prospect of a conviction, whether it is in the public interest to continue the prosecution, the likely penalty, the age of the defendant and the complainant's attitude to the offence. The Crown Prosecution Service 'Code for Crown Prosecutors' stresses that Crown Prosecutors should not avoid going to court simply because of the juvenile's age. In *R (on the application of CM) v Crown Prosecution Service* [2014] EWHC 4457 (Admin) the High Court confirmed that it was rare for a case challenging the decision to prosecute (in this case a 10-year-old) to succeed. However, this is a useful case which reviews the case law in this area, and confirms that the courts will take a different approach when the defendant is a child.

There have been concerns that young people in the care of local authorities are being unfairly criminalised for their behaviour in care homes. There is a CPS guidance document, *Offending Behaviour in Children's Homes*, which prosecutors must consider in conjunction with their code when deciding whether to prosecute. The guidance balances the right of all people to feel safe in the place that they live, and the needs of the child or young person whose behaviour is in question. The care homes (private or local authority owned) also have to provide evidence that their written behaviour-management plans were followed. The guidance is reproduced at **Part 2** in **Appendix D**.

Furthermore, the new CPS guidance document, *Guidelines on prosecuting cases involving communications sent via social media*, suggests 'sexting' between children or sharing of 'youth produced sexual imagery' should not be routinely prosecuted. The guidance advises that it would not usually be in the public interest to prosecute the consensual sharing of sexual images between children which suggests most of these incidents will be dealt with informally. However, whilst it would not usually be in the public interest to prosecute the consensual sharing of an image between two children of a similar age in a relationship, a prosecution may be appropriate in other scenarios, such as those involving exploitation, grooming or bullying. When assessing whether a prosecution is required in the public interest prosecutors must follow the approach set out in these guidelines as well as the wider principles set out in the Code for Crown Prosecutors. One factor that may warrant particular consideration is the involvement of younger or immature perpetrators. Children may not appreciate the potential harm and seriousness of their communications and as such the age and maturity of suspects should be given significant weight, particularly if they are under the age of 18.

Where proceedings are discontinued the Crown Prosecutor will give the defendant notice of his decision and, where the Youth Court is already seized of the case, the court shall also be served with a discontinuance notice. Discontinuance takes effect from the time the discontinuance notice is given. It should be noted that the prosecutor's power to discontinue is in addition to his powers to offer no evidence or withdraw the case, with or without the consent of the court (*R v DPP, ex parte Cooke* (1991) 95 Cr App R 233).

If the accused wishes the proceedings to continue (where for instance he wishes to clear his name publicly) he must send notice to the court within 35 days of the date when proceedings were discontinued requiring the court to re-list the case.

Once the decision to prosecute has been taken, the police or other informants have a duty to notify the local authority and the probation service of their decision (CYPA 1969, ss 5(8) and 34(2)). In effect this is notification to the Youth Offending Team. In the case of *DPP v Cottier* [1996] 3 All ER 126, it was held that such notification was directory and not mandatory and, as such would not jeopardise proceedings where the prosecution had omitted to make such notification.

Having been so notified, the local authority and probation service via the Youth Offending Team have a duty to provide information to the court as to home surroundings, school record and health and character of the person being prosecuted unless they are of the opinion that it is not necessary to do so (CYPA 1969, s 9). Reports are usually provided by a Youth Offending Team after a conviction has been recorded and a specific request made for a report.

Although the CPS guidance suggests that the circumstances will be rare, a prosecutor reviewing a case may decide that a youth conditional caution may be appropriate. The prosecutor should consult the Youth Offending Team. If they remain of the view that the caution should be offered they can direct the police to administer the caution together with any conditions the prosecutor considers necessary (CPS – Director's Guidance).

The Youth Court panel

2.06   The general rule under CYPA 1933, s 46 is that no charge against a juvenile may be heard in a magistrates' court other than a Youth Court unless the juvenile is jointly charged with an adult, when the case must be directed in the first instance to the adult court and may be so directed if the juvenile is in some other way connected with an adult's case. An adult court may also deal with a juvenile's remand status (CYPA 1933, s 46(2)).

For this reason, offenders under 18 are generally dealt with in specially constituted courts of summary jurisdiction called Youth Courts.

The panel of specially appointed magistrates who deal with juvenile criminal cases is referred to throughout the text as the Youth Court panel to avoid confusion with other youth panels such as the Youth Offender Panels which operate referral orders.

The Youth Courts (Constitution of Committees and Rights to Preside) Rules 2007 were revoked on 30 July 2016 as part of a move to deregulate Magistrates' Courts. They have been replaced by the Justices of the Peace Rules 2016 and a youth panel protocol issued by the Senior Presiding Judge and HM Courts and Tribunals Service. Each youth panel has a youth panel area. Existing areas were preserved on the transfer from the 2007 Rules to the 2016 Rules. The new youth panel protocol allows for youth panel areas to be changed. Applications must be made to the Senior Presiding Judge. Such applications can be made by the chair of a Youth Court panel, or the Judicial Business Group.

Each Youth Court must be chaired by a justice who is an approved Youth Court chairman. Exceptions to this rule are made so that a chairman who is undergoing training may chair. Also where ,due to some illness, or circumstances unforeseen when the justices to sit were chosen, or other emergency, an approved qualified chairman is not available then those youth magistrates present may appoint one of their number to take the chair. If possible the magistrate selected should have completed or be in the process of training to take the chair. (Justices of the Peace Rules 2016, r 5) The revocation of the 2007 Rules means that there is no longer a statutory requirement for a youth court of magistrates to be comprised of a man and a woman.

A district judge (magistrates' courts) is qualified to sit as a member of a Youth Court without being a panel member and may sit alone.

The Youth Court panel shall meet at least twice a year, but more often if necessary. The panel members must elect a chairman and one or more deputy chairmen of the panel. Terms of office last for one year at a time. When the Justices' Clerk indicates there is a vacancy, individual members of the panel may give notice of their candidacy. If there are more notices than vacancies a secret ballot will be held either by post or electronically.

The Youth Court

2.07   The Youth Court is a court of summary jurisdiction specially constituted for the purpose of hearing any charge against a child or young person and for the purpose of exercising any other jurisdiction conferred on Youth Courts (CYPA 1933, s 45). It is required to sit as often as necessary for the purpose of exercising any jurisdiction conferred on it (CYPA 1933, s 47(1)). The Youth Court is not an open court, those persons who may be present are:

(a)   members and officers of the court. This category includes the justices, their legal adviser and any members of the court staff;

(b)   parties to the case before the court, their solicitors and counsel, and witnesses and other persons directly concerned in the case. This category includes the parents of the juvenile but not, for example, the juvenile's sisters, brothers, cousins, aunts or uncles; if they wish to be present the justices must specifically consider whether or not to allow this. The court may also be faced with the attendance of a parent's co-habitee who has no implicit right to be present but who may be permitted to remain if the court feels it to be desirable;

(c)   *bona fide* representatives of the press, who are restricted in what they may report in Youth Court proceedings, and may not reveal the name, address or school, or include any particulars calculated to lead to the identification of the juvenile, except where the court or the Secretary of State specifically authorises such disclosure;

(d)   such other persons as the court may specifically authorise to be present (CYPA 1933, ss 47 and 49).

The justices thus have a general discretion as to who they allow into the Youth Court. Persons they specifically authorise to be present will often be trainee solicitors, social work students, trainee YOT workers and researchers with an interest in the Youth Court. The victims of crime may occasionally wish to sit in on Youth Court proceedings. Unless attending as a witness they have no absolute right to do so, although the court should normally accede to a request to be present so long as the victim's motivation in wishing to be present is a proper one. The joint Home Office/Lord Chancellor's department circular, *Opening up Youth Court Proceedings*, encouraged Youth Courts to exercise this discretion particularly so far as the victim is concerned. The circular made it clear that the court could balance the desirability of allowing the victim into the court against the desirability of doing so where the defendant is very young or where there are a number of charges and therefore a number of victims. It is not desirable for the court to be crowded with such people and the justices must limit the number of visitors to ensure that the purpose of having specially constituted Youth Courts is not defeated.

Arrangements must be made to prevent a juvenile, while waiting before or after attendance in any criminal court, from associating with an adult (not being a relative) who is charged with any offence other than an offence with which the juvenile is charged. This segregation is to prevent the contact of juveniles with adult offenders (CYPA 1933, s 31). Where separate juvenile facilities are available in police or court cells they must be used. Reasonable action should be taken to comply with s 31 where there are no separate cells or court waiting areas for this purpose. This might mean reviewing listing practices or taking measures to prevent youths seeing or hearing adult offenders (*R (on the application of BG) v The Chief Constable of the West Midlands Constabulary and Birmingham City Council* [2014] EWHC 4374 (Admin) and *R (T) v Secretary of State for Justice* [2013] EWHC 1119 (Admin)).

Each Youth Court must be constituted of not more than three justices; it may consist of two justices only, (unless a district judge is sitting). A district judge may sit alone. Having only two justices is acceptable for dealing with an admission but where the court has to decide the question of guilt or innocence it is desirable to have three justices hearing the case, a point emphasised by both a former Lord Chancellor and Lord Chief Justice. Three justices sitting as a bench have a duty to reach a decision having heard all the evidence and may not order the case to be reheard. If there is reasonable doubt then it is their obligation to acquit (*R v Bromley Justices, ex parte Haymill (Contractors) Ltd* [1984] Crim LR 235).

In the event of two justices failing to agree on a verdict a retrial before a fresh bench would have to be ordered, with the consequential expense and waste of court time (*R v Redbridge Justices, ex parte Ram* [1992] 1 All ER 652). It would also mean putting the juvenile and witnesses through the ordeal of a second contested hearing. If at any sitting of a Youth Court an approved Youth Court chairman is unexpectedly not available, any member of the panel may be appointed by those magistrates present to act as chairman, but wherever possible this should be a person who has completed the chairmanship training course (Justices of the Peace Rules 2016, r 5).

It should be noted that a justice is not prevented by the rules relating to Youth Courts from exercising the powers of a single justice. This means that a single justice may hear and determine an application to adjourn and remand in custody or on bail, even though the application relates to a juvenile offender.

Warrant of further detention

2.08 The normal procedure is that an arrested juvenile must be charged within 24 hours or released, unless a police officer of the rank of superintendent or above authorises the detention of a person without charge for up to 36 hours if the investigation is for 'an indictable offence', such as an assault occasioning actual bodily harm. The superintendent must also be satisfied that the detention of the subject is necessary to secure or preserve evidence relating to the offence, or to obtain such evidence by questioning him, and that the investigation is being conducted diligently and expeditiously (PACE 1984, s 42).

Applications may be made by the police to a magistrates' court for an authorisation to detain a suspect for a maximum of a further 72 hours before charge, up to a total of 96 hours (PACE 1984, ss 43 and 44). The time for the purposes of either a superintendent's extension or the application to court is calculated from the 'relevant time', which in most cases will be the point when the arrested person arrives at the police station. Any time during which the defendant is on police bail in connection with the investigation is not to be counted, but previous periods of detention in relation to the offence must be counted. (PACE 1984, s 47(6) as inserted by the Police (Detention and Bail) Act 2011).

Application to the court

2.09 An application for a warrant of further detention may be made, even though no application has been made under s 42 to a superintendent. This may happen where a superintendent is not available, or where it is obvious that detention for more than 36 hours is going to be necessary, ie in a case requiring forensic examination of evidence.

The application must be made before the expiry of 36 hours after 'the relevant time'. In a case where it is not practicable for the magistrates' court (to which the application will be made) to sit at the expiry of 36 hours after the relevant time, but where the court will sit during the six hours following the end of that period, the application may be made before the expiry of that extra six hours.

However, if an application is made after the expiry of the 36-hour period and it appears to the court that it would have been reasonable to make it before the expiry of that period, the court shall dismiss the application (*R v Slough Magistrates' Court, ex parte Stirling* [1987] Crim LR 576).

The procedure

2.10   Application to the court should where possible be made within normal court hours because of the difficulties in convening special court sessions. The Code of Practice under PACE provides that it may be impracticable for courts to sit other than between the hours of 10am and 9pm (C: Note 15D).

Before a court is convened, a number of steps must be taken by the police. An information must be prepared stating:

(a)   the nature of the offence for which the person to whom the application relates has been arrested;

(b)   the general nature of the evidence on which that person was arrested;

(c)   what inquiries relating to the offence have been made by the police and what further inquiries are proposed by them;

(d)   the reason for believing the continued detention of that person to be necessary for the purposes of such further inquiries (PACE 1984, s 43(14)).

The hearing

2.11   The court must be composed of at least two justices who, in the case of a juvenile, need not be on the Youth Court panel as the application is being made before a charge has been preferred and thus not specifically assigned to a Youth Court under CYPA 1933, s 46.

A district judge may sit alone for these purposes.

The court is not an open court and no persons other than the parties and the court officers should be present. Before the court can hear an application the arrested person must have been given a copy of the written information and must have been brought before the court for the hearing.

If the arrested person is not legally represented but wishes to be so represented, the court must adjourn the hearing to enable him to obtain such representation. He may be kept in police detention during such an adjournment (PACE 1984, s 43).

The application commences when a constable appears before the court and gives evidence on oath or affirmation supported by his written information (*R v Slough Magistrates' Court, ex parte Stirling* [1987] Crim LR 576). This is a small but important point because of the provision in PACE 1984, s 43(7) which requires the court to dismiss an application for a warrant of further detention, no matter what the grounds, if it appears to the court that the application could reasonably have been made within the 36-hour period. In such a case, the detained person must be released immediately unless charged.

If the application is in order, the court will hear the evidence of the police and also any representations or evidence on behalf of the detained person.

A court's decision to issue a warrant of further detention is based on the court being satisfied that there are reasonable grounds for believing that the further detention of the arrested person is justified. If not so satisfied the court must:

(a)   refuse the application; or

(b)   adjourn the hearing of it until a time not later than 36 hours after the relevant time.

The detained person may be kept in police custody during the adjournment (PACE 1984, s 43(8) and (9)).

If the court refuses the application, the person to whom it relates shall forthwith be charged or released either on bail or otherwise. However he need not be released before the expiry of 24 hours after the relevant time, or before the expiry of any longer period for which his continued detention is or has been authorised (PACE 1984, s 42(10)).

If an application is refused no further application may be made unless supported by fresh evidence which has come to light since the refusal (PACE 1984, s 43(17)).

The burden of proof

2.12   It is clearly for the police to satisfy the court that the necessary criteria are fulfilled and many commentators have argued that this must be on the criminal standard of proof, ie beyond reasonable doubt. That standard of proof is used in English criminal law as part of an adversarial system to evaluate two sets of conflicting evidence. In the circumstances of an application for a warrant of further detention there may only be the confirmation of the written information on oath. There is no statutory provision for the detained person to call evidence, though in practice it should be allowed.

Further, it appears that the general scheme set up under the statute to review police detention does comply with Article 5(3) of the European Convention on Human Rights. The words 'reasonable suspicion' have been interpreted as meaning facts or information which would satisfy an objective observer that the detained person may have committed the offence (*Fox, Campbell and Hartley v United Kingdom* (1990) 13 EHRR 157).

In the Bail Act 1976 similar wording is used: 'The defendant need not be granted bail if the court is satisfied that there are substantial grounds for believing that one of the exceptions in Sch I of the Act applies.' *Re Moles* [1981] Crim LR 170, makes it clear that the strict rules of evidence applicable in a criminal trial are inappropriate when the court's duty is to consider whether substantial grounds for believing a particular state of affairs exist.

Whilst the matter has yet to be tested in the High Court the authors' views are that magistrates must make these decisions based on the balance of probabilities. The purpose of PACE 1984, s 43 is to allow the police to secure, preserve, or obtain that very evidence. Alternatively, the words of the statute simply require a judgment as to whether the application is made out or not.

The lack of rules of court may cause other problems to the court in making its decision. The police may wish to submit the detained person's criminal record to the court to assist or support their application for a warrant of further detention. It is submitted that this should not normally be allowed by the court, on the basis that such information will be irrelevant to the application and the prejudicial value of the previous convictions will outweigh any probative value they may have. However, it may well be that where an offence is strikingly similar in its method of commission to a recorded offence or offences committed by the detained person then a criminal record may indeed go a long way towards satisfying the justices that detention is necessary to secure or preserve evidence relating to the offence in question. It may be argued that CJA 2003, s 101 allows for evidence of bad character to be admitted in criminal proceedings, however that term was defined in the case of *R v Bradley* [2005] EWCA Crim 20 to include any trial or *Newton* hearing, so although the point was not specifically argued before the court it seems likely that the statute does not apply to detention applications and that the relevance of such convictions may be the determining factor.

Inferences from silence or a failure to explain evidence may not be drawn by the court as a detention application is not included within the ambit of CJPOA 1994, s 34(2) or s 37(2).

Length of further detention

2.13   If the court accedes to the police application the warrant must state the time at which it was issued and the length of time for which the person to whom it relates may be detained. The period may be any period the court thinks fit but shall not exceed 36 hours.

If it is proposed to transfer the person to another police area the court is required to have regard to the distance and the time the journey would take (PACE 1984, s 43(12) and (13)).

If an application for further detention is refused in circumstances where the original 24-hour period, or 36-hour period with a superintendent's permission, has not run out then the police may continue to hold the suspect until the expiry of the relevant period. The court also has power to adjourn the hearing until some later stage in the 36-hour period.

If a warrant of further detention is refused or the period authorised in the warrant runs out, the detained person must be charged or released either on bail or not. It is however possible to apply for an extension of the warrant.

Whether a court grants or refuses a warrant of further detention it must give its reasons for doing so. Any warrant extending the time of detention must be proportional to the needs of the police to secure evidence, the seriousness of the offence and the possible consequences of an early release.

Extension of warrant of further detention

2.14   Applications may be made for extensions of the period of detention allowed. Again the application must be on oath and supported by an information containing the matters specified in PACE 1984, s 43(14). The court must be satisfied that there are reasonable grounds for believing that the further detention of the person to whom the application relates is justified (PACE 1984, s 44(1)). The overall period of detention may not exceed 96 hours. No single extension may exceed 36 hours. Where an application for extension is refused the detained person must be charged or released either with or without bail. Where an extension is granted the court is to endorse this on the original warrant and not issue a fresh warrant (PACE 1984, s 44).

A person released at the expiry of a warrant of detention may not be re-arrested without a warrant for the offence or new evidence justifying a further arrest which has come to light since his release (PACE 1984, s 43(19)).

Chapter 3   Attendance at court

Youth Court time limits

Commencing proceedings

3.01   In the magistrates' courts adults may be dealt with for summary offences (offences which may only be heard in a magistrates' court), or either way offences (which may be heard either in the magistrates' court or in the Crown Court before a judge and jury). Offences which are triable either way, are not generally subject to a time limit during which they must be brought before the court. However, purely summary proceedings must have the information laid or requisition issued by the prosecution within six months of the date of the commission of the offence or such other time limit as may be expressly provided for in individual statutes (Magistrates' Courts Act 1980 (MCA 1980), s 127). Laying an information is one method by which criminal proceedings are commenced, giving in writing details of the offender and the offence alleged (see **3.08**). It has been decided in the case of *R v Dartford Justices, ex parte Dhesi* [1983] 1 AC 328, HL, that an information is laid on the date on which it is received in the office of the clerk to the justices. An alternative procedure is for the prosecuting authority to issue a requisition direct to the alleged offender. In such cases any issues regarding jurisdiction, compliance with time limits, or defects in the way the allegation has been presented are dealt with at the first or subsequent hearings.

Custody time limits

3.02   The Prosecution of Offences Act 1985 (POA 1985), s 22 provides for restrictions on the period which a person charged with an offence may be remanded in custody. Custody for these purposes includes remands made under CYPA 1969, s 23, to local authority or other accommodation.

The maximum period of a remand to custody is 56 days from first court appearance to the start of summary trial (Prosecution of Offences (Custody Time Limits) Regulations 1987 as amended). Where an offence is sent to the Crown Court for trial the defendant cannot be remanded in custody before the trial for more than 182 days (which includes any time remanded in custody before the offence is sent). A custody time limit may be extended by application (CPR 2012, r 19.16). The application may be heard by a court presided over by two lay justices or a district judge (magistrates' courts). The court cannot however extend a custody time limit after it has already expired.

Reasons to extend the custody time limit: POA 1985, s 22(3) states that the court shall not grant an extension unless it is satisfied that:

(a)   the need for the extension is due to

   (i)   the illness or absence of the accused, a necessary witness, a judge or a magistrate;

   (ii)   a postponement which is occasioned by the ordering by the court of separate trials in the case of two or more accused or two or more offences; or

   (iii)   some other good and sufficient cause; and

(b)   the prosecution has acted with all due diligence and expedition.

The matters to be considered by the court in deciding whether to extend a custody time limit are set out in *R v Crown Court at Manchester, ex parte McDonald* [1999] 1 All ER 805. The seriousness of the charge or the need to protect the public will not amount to a good and sufficient cause in itself (*R v Crown Court at Sheffield, ex parte Headley* [2000] Crim LR 374). There are a number of cases which were decided under the now repealed POA 1985, s 22A. That section provided for time limits within which youth cases must be completed. These cases are still relevant to extension of custody time limits, as they provide guidance on what can amount to a 'good and sufficient cause' and where it can be said that the 'prosecution has acted with all due diligence and expedition'. Thus if the prosecution have failed in the early stages to provide primary and initial disclosure to the defence thereby delaying the trial date, their application for an extension of time will fail (*R v Crown Court at Kingston and Sutton Youth Court, ex parte Bell* [2000] All ER (D) 1191).

In *R v Croydon Youth Court, ex parte C* [2000] All ER (D) 985 a juvenile trial was listed together with other trials in the Youth Court. It was not given priority in the list and when it transpired that there was insufficient time to hear the complete trial the magistrates decided that there was just and sufficient cause to enable them to extend the time limit under the POA 1985, s 22A(3). On appeal, the High Court decided that the magistrates had addressed themselves to the right issue. Faced with a late start and a disinclination to go part heard, the magistrates' decision to extend the time limits was not in any way perverse.

Similarly, where delays are caused by pressure on the court's list, the custody time limits may be extended. In *R (on the application of Kalonji) v Wood Green Crown Court* [2007] All ER (D) 283 (Oct), the judge was held to have acted properly in finding exceptional circumstances, having examined the steps taken to alleviate the listing problems and concluded that they were not systematic.

The recent case of *R (on the application of McAuley) v Coventry Crown Court* [2012] EWHC 680 (Admin) deals with extension of custody time limits due to lack of court resources and sets out the procedure to be followed in 'routine cases'. It clearly states that lack of money or resources will rarely, if ever, provide any justification for the extension of custody time limits and 'the court has no option but to apply the present custody time limits and HMCTS must find the necessary money or face the prospect of a person who may represent a danger to the public being released pending trial'.

Where the court extends, or further extends, a time limit or refuses to extend the time limit the accused or prosecution may appeal against the decision to the Crown Court (CPR 2015, r 14.19). There is no right of appeal against an extension applied for by the police before charging the person (POA 1985, s 22A(8)).

Attendance of the parents or guardians

3.03   Although the juvenile remains responsible for any criminal act committed over the age of criminal responsibility, it is desirable that the parent or guardian should attend court during criminal proceedings for a number of reasons. The court has a duty to consider making a parental bind over and in appropriate circumstances a parenting order. Should the court impose financial penalties it may wish to make the parent responsible for payment. For these reasons section 3 of the SC's *Sentencing Children and Young People* reinforces the responsibilities of parents and guardians and of the Youth Court to make every effort to ensure their attendance.

The law makes a distinction between a child or young person under the age of 16, where the court must require a parent to be present, and a young person of 16 or 17 where it may require the attendance of a parent (CYPA 1933, s 34A). This provision applies during all stages of the proceedings, unless and to the extent that the court is satisfied that it would be unreasonable to require such attendance having regard to the circumstances of the case. In some circumstances, it may be obvious to the court that a parent should not be required to attend all stages of the proceedings, for example where the victim of the alleged offence is the juvenile's parent. Less clear is the situation where a parent feels unable to attend court because of pressures brought to bear by employment or the need to care for other younger children in the family. It must be a matter of judgment as to whether this forms part of the circumstances of the case and whether the court would be satisfied that it would be unreasonable in such circumstances to require the attendance of the parent. In order to avoid delay, many courts will wish to send a notice or request that a notice is served on juveniles at the time they are charged at the police station. Where a juvenile is summoned to court following the laying of an information, a parent may be summoned or requisitioned at the same time in accordance with CYPA 1933, s 34A and Criminal Procedure Rules 2015 (CPR 2015), r 7.4(9). A subsequent failure to attend can be enforced by the issue of a warrant (r 18). Generally when a parent fails to attend, a letter making clear the court's powers will usually be sufficient to ensure attendance at the next hearing.

The term 'parent' is not defined in the Children and Young Persons Acts. The rules of court however state that parent means a parent who has parental responsibility under the Children Act 1989.

The position of children in care or accommodation provided by the local authority

3.04   The definition of parent or guardian is expanded in CYPA 1933, s 34A(2) to include a local authority where the local authority has parental responsibility for the child or young person and the child or young person is either in their care or is being accommodated by them in the exercise of any functions (particularly those under the Children Act 1989).

Parental responsibility

3.05   Parental responsibility is defined as all the rights, duties, powers, responsibilities and authority which by law a parent of a child has in relation to the child and his property (Children Act 1989, s 3). Therefore, where a child's father and mother were married to each other at the time of his birth, they shall each have parental responsibility for the child. Where they were not so married, then the mother alone shall have parental responsibility although the father may acquire parental responsibility under the provisions of the Children Act 1989, s 2 and since 1 December 2003 where the birth is registered jointly (Children Act 1989, s 4). A local authority has parental responsibility for a child in respect of whom a care order has been made to that authority. The local authority also has the power to determine the extent to which a parent or guardian of a child may meet his parental responsibility for him. A juvenile for whom the local authority have parental responsibility and are looking after, should be accompanied to court by a representative of the social services department who will stand in loco parentis. In such circumstances, it would be unreasonable to require the attendance of the parent unless the child or young person was in fact living with that parent whilst being 'looked after' by the local authority. The lack of the clear definition of 'parent' in any of the pieces of legislation relating to children may leave courts in some difficulty. There is a definition contained in the Family Law Reform Act 1987, s 1(1) which indicates that a parent shall include a father and mother who have not been married to each other. Thus, the father of an illegitimate child would be a parent for these purposes. As indicated the provisions are wide enough to allow for a continuing variation in practice from court to court as to whether or not parents are summoned to attend. Some areas may require only a father or mother to attend, some may require both. In practice, where both parents are available, they should in the case of a young person under the age of 16 be required to attend court. If they failed to do so, the court would make enquiry into the circumstances of the case to decide whether it would be unreasonable to require such an attendance.

The role of a parent or guardian in court

3.06   At the hearing, parents have a vital role to play. It is good practice to involve the parents or guardian in the proceedings as much as possible. Following the availability of free professional representation, and the consequent increase in the numbers of solicitors appearing in Youth Courts, it is important that the chairman of the bench or the clerk to the court explain to the parents how proceedings will be conducted, who the parties are and what roles they are expected to play during the hearing. Of course, where a juvenile is not represented then the parent or guardian should be allowed to conduct the case on their behalf. Communication between the chairman, the young offender and his parents or guardian, which focuses on the consequences of offending, is to be encouraged. Magistrates should recognise however that some young offenders may be physically/mentally unable to engage in dialogue or may simply decline to do so. Young people with various learning difficulties may find it hard to follow complex or multi-faceted questions. No adverse inference should be drawn from a failure to engage in this way.

Charges, warrants, summonses and requisitions

3.07   Once an initial decision to prosecute has been taken, the next step is to secure the juvenile's attendance at the Youth Court.

Charges

3.08   Where a juvenile has been arrested for a criminal offence, such as robbery, theft, or assault, he may be charged at the police station and bailed to appear in court at a date and time specified. Alternatively, where the investigation is incomplete, he may be bailed to reappear at a police station without charge. In such instances, there is a limit of 28 days on the duration of the bail. This may be extended by an officer of at least the rank of superintendent for up to three months. Applications for further extension may be made to the court before the expiry of the current time limit. The court may then extend the time limit by further periods of three month at a time (or six months where justified). Each renewal application would need to be made before expiry of the latest extension. These limits were introduced with effect from 3 April 2017 by the Policing and Crime Act 2017, s 63 which amends PACE 1984. Applications for extensions will be dealt with in the first instance under the single justice powers but may be referred to a court of two or more Magistrates if appropriate. The court can only grant extensions where it is satisfied that there are reasonable grounds to believe that the investigation is being conducted diligently and expeditiously, and reasonable grounds for believing that the release on bail of the person in question is necessary and proportionate in all the circumstances (having regard, in particular, to any conditions of bail which are, or are to be, imposed).

Under the Bail Act 1976, a person bailed to court is not required to enter into a recognisance (a sum of money that may be forfeited on non-attendance at court). However, bail by the police or by the court does place an obligation upon a person bailed to attend court and failure to attend at the time and place stated without reasonable excuse is an offence punishable with a level five fine, three months' imprisonment or both in the case of an adult convicted summarily (Bail Act 1976, s 6(2) and (7)).

The maximum fine that can be imposed upon a juvenile is limited by virtue of the Magistrates' Courts Act 1980, s 24. This means that a juvenile offender over the age of 14 could be made subject to a fine up to a maximum of £1,000. In the case of a child found guilty of an offence under the Bail Act, the maximum fine is £250.

Where a juvenile is to be charged with an offence, the procedure is the same as for an adult except that everything should be carried out in the presence of an 'appropriate adult'. 'Appropriate adult' is defined by PACE 1984, Code of Practice C1.7 (see **1.10**).

Further guidance is found in Code C Notes for guidance as follows:

1B   The parent or guardian of a juvenile should not be the appropriate adult if they are suspected of involvement in the offence concerned, a victim, a witness, involved in the investigation or have received admissions. In such circumstances, it will be desirable for the appropriate adult to be some other person. The estranged parent of a juvenile should not be asked to act as the appropriate adult if the juvenile expressly and specifically objects to his presence.

1C   If a child in care admits an offence to a social worker, or member of a YOT (other than during their period as appropriate adult) another social worker should be appointed in the interest of fairness.

1E   A detainee should always be given an opportunity to consult privately with a solicitor in the presence of an appropriate adult should they so wish.

1F   A solicitor or independent custody visitor who is present in that capacity may not act as the appropriate adult.

The rules for the charging of detained persons are found in Code C16 which states:

'16.1   When an officer reasonably believes that there is sufficient evidence to provide a realistic prospect of the detainee's conviction, he should without delay (and subject to the following qualification) bring him before the custody officer who shall then be responsible for considering whether or not he should be charged. When a person is detained in respect of more than one offence, it is permissible to delay bringing him before the custody officer until the conditions are satisfied in respect of all the offences. Any resulting action should be taken in the presence of the appropriate adult if the person is a juvenile or mentally ill or mentally vulnerable.

16.1B   Where in compliance with the DPP's charging guidance the custody officer decides that the case should be immediately referred to the CPS to make the charging decision, consultation should take place with a Crown Prosecutor as soon as is reasonably practicable. Where the Crown Prosecutor is unable to make the charging decision on the information available at the time, the detainee may be released without charge and on bail (with conditions if necessary) under PACE 1984 s 37(7)(a). In such circumstances, the detainee should be informed that they are being released to enable the Director of Public Prosecutions to make a decision following consultation, PACE 1984 s 37B(1).

16.2   When a detained person is charged with or informed that he may be prosecuted for an offence, he shall be cautioned.

The caution shall be in the following terms:

"*You do not have to say anything. But it may harm your defence if you do not mention now something which you later rely on in court. Anything you do say may be given in evidence.*"

Minor deviations do not constitute a breach of this requirement provided that the sense of the caution is preserved. If it appears that the juvenile does not understand what the caution means, the officer who has given it should go on to explain it in his own words.

16.3   At the time the person is charged, he should be given a written notice showing the particulars of the offence with which he is charged and including the name of the officer in the case, and the reference number for the case. So far as possible, the particulars of the charge shall be stated in simple terms but they shall also show the precise offence in law with which he is charged. The notice shall begin with the following words:

"*You are charged with the offence(s) shown below. You do not have to say anything. But it may harm your defence if you do not mention now something which you later rely on in court. Anything you do say may be given in evidence.*"

If the person is a juvenile or is mentally ill or mentally vulnerable the notice should be given to the appropriate adult.'

Conditional bail from the police station

3.09   When a custody officer releases a juvenile on bail he may impose conditions on that bail but only when it appears to him necessary to prevent him:

(a)   failing to surrender to custody; or

(b)   committing an offence whilst on bail; or

(c)   interfering with witnesses or otherwise obstructing the course of justice; or,

(d)   for his own protection, or, in the case of a juvenile, his welfare or his own interests (Bail Act 1976, s 3A(5)).

A custody officer who imposes conditional bail must give his reasons for doing so; those reasons must be noted in the custody record and a copy given to the juvenile and the appropriate adult. A court may, on application, review bail granted by the custody officer and may remand in custody or bail with the same or more onerous conditions. In either case bail conditions must be reasonable, able to be complied with, proportionate to the need to impose them, clear and enforceable. While it is not possible to set out all permissible conditions, see **7.07** and the criteria set out in the Bail Act 1976, s 3A.

Summons

3.10   In some cases the police may prefer to require attendance at court of the juvenile and his parents by the issue of a summons. Although in the adult court it is common for summary cases to be dealt with in a defendant's absence, compliance with the Rules of Court make such a procedure unusual in the Youth Court. Instead of a summons the prosecutor may commence proceedings by way of a written charge and a requisition requiring the person to appear before a magistrates' court (CJA 2003, ss 28 to 31).

The police may institute criminal proceedings against a person by issuing a document (a 'written charge') that charges the person with an offence.

When they issue a written charge, they must at the same time issue a document (a 'requisition') that requires the person to appear before a magistrates' court to answer the written charge.

The written charge and requisition must be served on the person concerned, and a copy of both must be served on the court named in the requisition: CJA 2003, s 29(1) and (3).

As a consequence of sub-ss (1) and (3), the police do not have the power to lay an information for the purpose of obtaining the issue of a summons under s 1 of the Magistrates' Courts Act 1980.

Warrants of arrest

3.11   The issue of a warrant is a serious step for any court to take as it involves a command to the police to arrest the person named in the warrant (CPR 2015, r 13.2). This means that any constable in possession of the warrant may arrest the offender and bring him before the court. A warrant should not be issued where a summons would be equally effective, except where the charge is of a serious nature (*O'Brien v Brabner* (1885) 49 JP Jo 227). This case involved what was called 'a trifling assault' by one woman on another and resulted in the defendant being arrested on a Saturday morning and kept in custody until the Monday following. It was stressed that there seemed to be no reason for the justices to have believed that a summons would not have been equally effective in securing the appearance of the accused person and this was really a case for the issue of a summons instead of a warrant.

A warrant of arrest issued by a justice remains in force until it is either executed or withdrawn (MCA 1980, s 125(1)). Any such warrant must name or otherwise identify the person for whose arrest it is issued and must include a brief reference to the reason why it was issued (CPR 2015, r 13.4). Any warrant for the arrest of a person may command that he be brought before the next available court, or that he be arrested and released on bail with a duty to surrender to court on the date and time specified in the warrant.

Warrants with bail

3.12   The Bail Act 1976 allows conditions to be imposed where bail is granted in criminal proceedings. Section 1(1) defines criminal proceedings as including: 'bail grantable in connection with an offence to a person ... for whose arrest for the offence a warrant (endorsed for bail) is being issued'. Therefore, where the court issues a warrant endorsed for bail, it may make conditions which must be complied with by the defendant before and after his release.

Conditions may be imposed:

(a)   to ensure his attendance, for example the juvenile may be required to reside with his parents until the court appearance;

(b)   to prevent the commission of further offences, for example the court may require the juvenile to stay indoors between specified times;

(c)   to prevent interference with the course of justice, for example a condition that the juvenile does not contact named witnesses in the case;

(d)   to ensure co-operation after conviction with the making of any report or inquiries which will assist the court in dealing with him, for example a condition to report to the Youth Offending Team before the court hearing; or

(e)   for the defendant's own protection or, in the case of a juvenile, his welfare or his own interests (Bail Act 1976, s 3(6); MCA 1980, s 117).

Although the insertion of conditions on a warrant endorsed for bail is permissible, it is rare. This is because the court issuing a warrant will not usually have sufficient information to enable it to comply with the Bail Act 1976, s 5(3) which requires the court to give reasons for the imposition of conditions.

Warrant in the first instance

3.13   Instead of instituting proceedings by way of a charge or a summons, the prosecution may ask a justice of the peace to issue a warrant for the arrest of the juvenile. This is called a warrant in the first instance. No warrant shall be issued under this section unless the information is in writing (MCA 1980, s 1(3)). An example of a warrant in the first instance being issued for a juvenile might be where the juvenile has run away from home and cannot be found for the purpose of serving a summons. MCA 1980, s 1(4) imposes restrictions on the issue of a first instance warrant, 'for the arrest of any person who has attained the age of 18'.

The restrictions are that no warrant shall be issued unless:

(a)   the offence to which the warrant relates is an indictable offence or is punishable with imprisonment; or

(b)   the person's address is not sufficiently established for a summons to be served on him.

These restrictions do not apply to juveniles. However it is submitted that a magistrate, in exercising a discretion to issue the warrant or not, may consider these restrictions as guidelines in cases where the offender is a juvenile. Where the offence charged is an indictable offence, a warrant in the first instance may be issued at any time notwithstanding that a summons has previously been issued (MCA 1980, s 1(6)).

Warrant for arrest – summons having been served

3.14   Where the juvenile has failed to attend in answer to a summons or requisition, the court should first consider whether it is in the interests of justice to proceed in his absence (MCA 1980, s 11(1)(b)). If it is not the court may issue a warrant for his arrest. In either case the court must be satisfied that the summons has been served in accordance with CPR 2015, r 4. Depending on the seriousness of the offence alleged, the court may also cause a letter to be served on the juvenile's parents warning of the court's powers to issue a warrant. In *R (on the application of R) v Thames Youth Court* [2002] All ER (D) 356 (Jul), a youth failed to attend his trial having been arrested and detained by the police on another matter. The High Court quashed a decision to proceed in his absence, saying that where a defendant had not voluntarily absented himself from the trial any conviction was likely to be quashed. The court also commented that where a defendant is a juvenile he or she may not have the same development and understanding as an adult.

It should be noted that MCA 1980, s 13(3A) as substituted by CJA 2003 contains restrictions on issuing warrants for any person who has not attained the age of 18, namely that no warrant shall be issued unless:

(a)   the offence to which the warrant relates is punishable, in the case of a person who has attained the age of 18, with imprisonment; or

(b)   the court, having convicted the accused, proposes to impose a disqualification on him.

Failure to attend by a juvenile who has been bailed

3.15   Where the juvenile has been charged and bailed to court and fails to attend, the court may issue a warrant for his arrest (Bail Act 1976, s 7). The warrant may be without bail or endorsed for bail, with or without conditions. Failure to attend court in answer to bail is an offence punishable by a magistrates' court with a level 5 fine or three months' imprisonment in the case of an adult (Bail Act 1976, s 6(1), (2) and (7)).

Where a juvenile has been released on bail from a police station with a duty to attend the police station at a later date and fails to attend, a constable may arrest that juvenile without a warrant and take him to the appointed police station (PACE 1984, s 46A); but see also **3.08** above.

Chapter 4   The Youth Court and Human Rights Act

4.01   The purpose of this chapter is to give the reader an insight into the operation of the Human Rights Act 1998 and to examine some of the areas which practitioners and the courts may come across in their everyday dealings in the Youth Court. Detailed examinations of human rights points cannot be undertaken without reference to European case law and specialist texts on the subject.

History

4.02   The European Convention for the Protection of Human Rights and Fundamental Freedoms was drawn up within the Council of Europe following the Second World War. The Convention was an attempt at collective enforcement of some of the rights stated in the United Nations Universal Declaration of Human Rights 1948. Not only were the numerous rights and freedoms set down in the Convention but it also set up a system of enforcement of the obligations entered into by the various contracting states. The right to petition the European Commission of Human Rights (set up in 1954) was given to individual citizens (see below) and contracting states.

The United Kingdom and UK lawyers were in the forefront of both the drafting and the setting up of the Convention but declined to contract in, giving citizens the right to petition the commission until 1966. Until 1998, a violation complaint was dealt with by a two-tier system. First, the matter went before the Commission which decided upon the admissibility of the complaint. If the Commission decided that the complaint was admissible and no settlement had been reached, the matter proceeded before the European Court. This system was changed by Protocol No 11 and in 1998 the newly constituted European Court of Human Rights came into being.

Finally in October 2000 the Human Rights Act 1998 (HRA 1998) came into force in England and Wales.

Convention rights

4.03   The effect of the HRA 1998 is to require public authorities to deal with individuals in such a way that their rights are protected by the Convention and not breached. It is important to note that individuals cannot act in breach of the Convention, only states or public authorities. The Convention rights are set out conveniently in the table below.

Article no	Subject	Summary
Article 2	Right to life	Protects human life subject to lawful exceptions.
Article 3	Prohibition on torture etc	An absolute prohibition on torture, inhuman or degrading treatment or punishments.
Article 4	Prohibition on slavery and forced labour	An absolute prohibition on slavery and servitude. Forced or compulsory labour is excluded from protection in specified circumstances.
Article 5	Right to liberty and security	Everyone has the right to liberty and security except in limited circumstances. Sets out the rights of a person who is arrested or detained.
Article 6	The right to a fair trial	Lists the requirements of a fair trial, the minimum rights of the accused. Confirms the presumption of innocence.
Article 7	No punishment without law	A prohibition against retrospective criminal legislation.
Article 8	The right to respect for individual private and family life	Protects private and home life and correspondence from unlawful and unnecessary interference.
Article 9	Freedom of thought, conscience freedom of thought, conscience and religion	Everyone has the right to and religion and a qualified right to exercise them subject to society's needs.
Article 10	Freedom of expression	Everyone has a qualified right to a freedom of expression, which includes publishing books, articles or leaflets, and the spoken word subject to the needs of society.
Article 11	Freedom of assembly and association	Qualified rights of assembly and free association, including for example the right to join a trade union and take part in peaceful demonstrations.
Article 12	The right to marry	Absolute right which includes the founding of a family
Article 14	Prohibition from discrimination within the Convention	A limited right ensuring the enjoyment of Convention rights avoiding discrimination by sex, race, colour, language, religion, political or other opinion national or social origin, association with a national minority, property, birth or status.

The First Protocol

| Article 1 | Protection of property | A qualified right to peaceful enjoyment of possessions. |
| Article 2 | The right to education | States must respect the rights of parents to ensure education is in line with their religion and philosophy. |

| Article 3 | The right to free elections | States that free elections to the legislature must be held at regular intervals by secret ballot. |

The Sixth Protocol

| Articles 1 and 2 | Abolition of death penalty | An absolute prohibition in peacetime but qualified in time of war. |

The Human Rights Act 1998

4.04   The HRA 1998 has a two-fold purpose, first to ensure that domestic legislation and its application is compatible with the rights set out in the Convention and secondly to give citizens the right to enforce Convention rights in the domestic courts by providing remedies for breaches. This means that juveniles may rely upon the Convention rights at any point during the youth justice process, from arrest through trial to sentence. The Act itself is a relatively short piece of legislation and an examination of the major sections will help put into context the effect of its provisions.

HRA 1998, s 1 sets out the Convention rights referred to, and s 2 governs the standing of Convention rights. By its provisions the courts must take into account decisions of the European Court of Human Rights, including past opinions of the now defunct Commission of Human Rights. In making a decision upon a point of law the court must ensure that it is acting lawfully within the terms of Convention law. In doing so, decisions of the European Court of Human Rights must be given precedence over domestic decisions, no matter what level they were made at. It should be noted however that where domestic law provides a higher level of protection to the citizen, the Act does not require the domestic courts to lower standards to meet any minimum guarantees provided by European jurisprudence.

HRA 1998, s 3 deals with the important topic of interpretation of legislation. The Act states that, so far as is possible, legislation must be read and given effect to in a manner so as to be compatible with the Convention rights whenever it is possible to do so. This section embodies what is referred to as the 'purposive approach', that is to say a requirement that the courts should always aim to interpret legislation so that the objects of the Convention are upheld: namely the protection of rights with minimal interference from the state and proportionate with those objectives. The Youth Court, as with other courts, will treat *primary* legislation slightly differently from *secondary* legislation. Primary legislation refers to Acts of Parliament debated and passed in both the House of Commons and House of Lords. Secondary legislation flows from primary legislation and includes orders, rules, regulations and byelaws. All courts, including the Youth Court, are bound by primary legislation if they are unable to interpret it in a manner which is compatible with the Convention. The court is not allowed to refuse to enforce primary legislation if it has found it to be incompatible with the Convention. It must work from the premise that the legislation should be read in a manner compatible with the Convention and this may mean reading in or reading out words from the statute. The court must interpret legislation so as to uphold Convention rights unless it is impossible to do so because the statute itself is clear and unambiguous.

HRA 1998, ss 4 to 5 deal with declarations of incompatibility. It is clear that the Youth Court will not be bound by a previous construction given to legislation by a higher court if the Youth Court is clear that this construction would lead to a decision incompatible with Convention rights. In the case of secondary legislation if the court finds it incompatible with the Convention the court will interpret those provisions so as to give effect to Convention rights. This may in effect mean ignoring part of the domestic legislation in order to give effect to the Convention rights. An exception to this is the instance where secondary legislation and its primary legislation are closely interdependent with each other that a 'striking down' of the secondary legislation would inevitably compromise the primary legislation. The courts may not strike down primary legislation and so the Act makes provision for a declaration of incompatibility by the High Court.

Where a court finds it impossible to interpret primary legislation compatibly with the Convention it has a duty to follow the legislation giving effect to the will of Parliament. However, the High Court may make a declaration of incompatibility. This has the effect of curing the violation or incompatibility by allowing the relevant minister to introduce a fast-track procedure through Parliament amending the legislation and bringing it into line with the Convention. In practice this should be a very rare event.

HRA 1998, s 6 defines a crucial concept within the Act, that is, of a 'public authority'. Under this provision it is unlawful for a public authority to act in a way which is incompatible with a Convention right. This will not apply to actions done as a result of one or more provisions of primary legislation (or provisions made under primary legislation) which could not be read or given effect to in a way that was compatible with Convention rights, so that the authority could not have acted differently.

The definition of a public authority specifically includes a court or tribunal and any person or persons whose functions are of a public nature (excluding either House of Parliament). The Youth Court acts as a public authority as do its legal advisers, police officers and members of Youth Offending Teams. The definition of public authority is consequently wide and potentially complex. The Home Office has provided guidance on specific areas of interest. This can be found on their website: www.homeoffice.gov.uk.

Remedies

4.05 It is important to note that whilst HRA 1998, s 6 makes it unlawful for a public authority to act in a way which is incompatible with the Convention this will not give rise to any claim for damages in respect of a judicial act done in good faith (HRA 1998, s 9(3)). So far as the Youth Court is concerned it will normally be the provider of the remedy so long as it acts compatibly with the Convention.

HRA 1998, s 8 provides that in relation to any act of a public authority which the court finds unlawful, it may grant such relief, remedy, or make such order within its powers as it considers just and appropriate. In relation to criminal proceedings, this may mean excluding evidence, allowing a submission of no case to answer, or a stay of proceedings. An example might be where the court found evidence had been obtained from a child in breach of the Police and Criminal Evidence Act Codes of Practice. The effective remedy here may be to exclude that evidence under PACE 1984, s 78. A potential breach of Article 6 (the right to a fair trial) because the prosecution have failed to provide disclosure may be remedied by the court granting an adjournment with a direction that the appropriate disclosure be given.

A structured approach to human rights

4.06   Under the provisions of the Criminal Procedure Rules 2015, before raising a Convention point an advocate should be prepared to identify the nature of the alleged breach, the article of the Convention that is engaged and the remedy sought.

After the court has identified that a Convention right is engaged it must define to which class of article it belongs. *Absolute rights*, including the prohibition against torture, inhuman or degrading treatment, are fundamental rights and where a breach occurs this will be a violation of the Convention regardless of the reason for the breach.

Limited rights are limited in scope by the Convention itself. This means that if a breach of the Convention falls within one of the permitted limitations in the article there will have been no violation. A good example of a limited right is the right to liberty and security guaranteed by Article 5. This states that no person shall be deprived of his liberty save in the following cases and in accordance with a procedure described by law, for example the detention of a minor by lawful order for the purpose of educational supervision, or lawful detention for the purpose of bringing him before the competent legal authority. However, if detention falls outside the limitations allowed by the article, it is likely that there will have been a violation of the Convention right.

Qualified rights set out in the article conditions or qualifications when a Convention right may be breached. These conditions are as follows:

(a)   The breach is prescribed by national law. Such law must be clear and accessible to the public.

(b)   The breach pursues a legitimate aim. These aims are set out in the qualified rights. For example, the right to a private and family life is qualified where it is necessary in a democratic society to interfere with the right, for example for the prevention of crime or disorder.

(c)   The action taken is proportionate. This essentially means that any breach of a qualified right may be a violation unless the action taken is the least intrusive necessary to fulfil the legitimate aim set out in the article.

Can the violation be avoided?

Primary legislation

- A court must attempt to interpret the legislation in a way which is compatible with the Convention. If this is not possible, the domestic law must be applied.

Secondary legislation

- A court must attempt to interpret the legislation in a way that is compatible with the Convention (subject to the effect on primary legislation). If this is not possible, the court must disregard the domestic law and give effect to the Convention right.

Precedent

- A court must attempt to interpret the precedent in a way that is compatible with the Convention. If this is not possible, the court must disregard the domestic law and give effect to the Convention right.

Is a Convention right engaged?

- If no Convention right is engaged, the case must be decided on the basis of domestic law.

- If the Convention is engaged, the relevant article must be identified

What class of article is engaged?

- The application of the Convention is dependent upon the class of article or protocol engaged.

  Absolute rights:

  - Article 3: prohibition of torture, inhuman or degrading treatment;

  - Article 4(1): prohibition of slavery or servitude;

  - Article 7: prohibition against punishment without law.

  Limited rights:

  - Article 2: right to life;

  - Article 4(2): prohibition of forced or compulsory labour;

  - Article 5: right to liberty;

  - Article 6: right to a fair trial.

  Qualified rights:

  - Article 8: right to respect for private and family life;

  - Article 9: freedom of thought, conscience and religion;

  - Article 10: freedom of expression;

  - Article 11: freedom of assembly and association.

Absolute rights

•   The threshold is high but if breached for any reason, a violation is established.

Limited rights

•   The articles contain definitive statements of the circumstances, which permit a breach of the right. If the restrictions are not complied with, there has been a violation of the article.

Qualified rights

•   The articles contain general exemptions. If the measures taken are justified under an exemption then there will be no violation. The exemptions are in the form of specified 'legitimate aims'. To fall within an exemption the measures must be allowed under domestic law. That law must itself be clear and accessible. Finally, the measures must be proportionate.

Human rights issues and young offenders

Issues at trial

4.07   The Youth Court is not an open and public court but nevertheless complies with a requirement of Article 6 (the right to a fair trial). This limited right clearly recognises that the press and public may be excluded from all or part of a trial in the interests of, amongst other things, juveniles. However, juveniles are not always tried in the Youth Court as proceedings begun by way of a complaint; for example, applications under the Dangerous Dogs Act 1991 are not assigned to the Youth Court and must be heard in a magistrates' court.

Some commentators suggested that the old anti-social behaviour order was in fact a criminal order as opposed to a civil one.

The importance of defining whether a matter is civil or criminal is that it will determine whether it is heard in the Youth Court or the magistrates' court. Additionally, the rules of evidence applicable to criminal proceedings would have to be complied with and those proceedings would be subject to the additional protection provided by Article 6 of the European Convention in relation to criminal proceedings.

The criminal charge provisions of Article 6 do not apply to procedures for determining whether a mentally ill defendant 'did the act' as these proceedings cannot result in a conviction (*R v M* [2001] EWCA Crim 2024) and neither does a final warning involve the determination of a criminal charge against a juvenile such as to engage the right to a fair trial under Article 6 (*R (on the application of R) v Durham Constabulary* [2005] 2 All ER 369).

It should also be noted that legal representation is available by way of the duty solicitor. Civil legal aid is not available. However, a breach of an order is a criminal offence and legal assistance is therefore normally available under the Access to Justice Act 1999.

In *V v United Kingdom (Application 24888/94)* and *T v United Kingdom (Application 24724/94)* [2000] Crim LR 187 the European Court was asked to consider if the killers of James Bulger had received a fair trial and whether the trial itself amounted to inhumane and degrading treatment in violation of Article 3. Although the court found that Article 3 was not contravened, it was held that the juveniles had not received a fair trial because of the intense media and public interest prior to the trial, the media and public presence in court during the trial and because insufficient adjustments had been made to the Crown Court trial procedure to allow the juveniles to participate fully in the trial bearing in mind their ages, level of maturity and intellectual and emotional capacity. The European Court did not rule that youth trials in the Crown Court are unfair *per se*.

Following this case a Practice Direction was delivered by the Lord Chief Justice Bingham titled *Trial of Children and Young Persons in the Crown Court* (2000). Although not specifically aimed at the adult magistrates' courts it will be good practice to employ this Practice Direction when children and young people are tried in the magistrates' court. The Practice Direction sets out that the trial process should not in itself expose the young person to avoidable intimidation, humiliation or distress. Account must be taken of the age, maturity, intellectual and emotional development, of the defendant. The Practice Direction also gives advice on the layout of the courtroom, appropriate dress (in the Crown Court), timetabling and the need to explain procedures and involve young people in the trial process at all times (*R v Devizes Youth Court ex parte A and others* [2000] All ER (D) 24; *R v C (a Minor)* TLR 5/7/2000).

Practical steps that the court may wish to take include: (a) keeping the defendant's level of cognitive functioning in mind; (b) using concise and simple language; (c) having regular breaks; (d) taking additional time to explain court proceedings; (e) explaining and being proactive in ensuring the defendant understands the ingredients of the charge; (f) explaining the possible outcomes and sentences; (g) ensuring that cross-examination is carefully controlled so that questions are short and clear and frustration is minimised. Further the minimum requirements for a fair hearing at a criminal trial are set out in *R (on the application of Wotton) v Central Devon Magistrates' Court* [2003] EWHC 146 (Admin).

Both the European Court and the High Court in the past have followed similar reasoning in relation to the requirement to register under the Sex Offenders Act 1997 (now repealed by the Sexual Offences Act 2003), namely that it is civil in nature and preventative, not punitive (*Ibbotson v United Kingdom* [1999] Crim LR 153). Nor is the failure to advise that a warning for a sexual offence would result in a requirement to register on the sex offenders register a breach of Article 6 (*R (on the application of R) v Durham Constabulary* [2005] 2 All ER 369). It should be noted that the Sexual Offences Act 2003 repealed the Sex Offenders Act 1997 on 1 May 2014 and defendants would now be subject to notification requirements. See **13.06** for notification requirements.

As normal practice is for children under 18 years to give evidence by live link there will have to be special reasons for departing from that practice. However, there is nothing inconsistent in the special measures provisions with Article 6, since the defendant has every opportunity to challenge and question the prosecution witnesses despite the absence of face-to-face confrontation: *R v Camberwell Green Youth Court ex parte D (a minor)* [2005] 1 All ER 999.

In relation to hearsay evidence and whether a statement from a witness who could not be called might be adduced in evidence, the only question should be whether its admission was compatible with a fair trial, and this would depend on the facts of the particular case (*R v Cole* [2007] EWCA Crim 1924). The Grand Chamber of the European Court of Human Rights has ruled in *Al-Khawaja and Tahery v UK (Applications nos 26766/05 and 22228/06)* that convictions based on statements from witnesses who could not be cross-examined in court did not violate the applicants' rights under Article 6. The general right to a fair trial under Article 6 requires the court to ascertain whether the proceedings as a whole are fair. See **13.11** to **13.13** for hearsay provisions.

The right to silence

4.08   The issue as to whether a Youth Court should draw an adverse inference in circumstances where a juvenile has refused to answer questions during police interview, is one which affects the overall fairness of the trial process. In *Murray v United Kingdom* (1996) 22 EHRR 29 the European Court considered whether the drawing of adverse inferences following the exercise of the right to silence was a violation of Article 6. The court said that by providing the accused with protection against improper compulsion by the authorities, these immunities contributed to avoiding miscarriages of justice and to securing the aims of Article 6. In the *Murray* case guilt was decided by a judge sitting alone who demonstrated by his reasons that careful consideration had been given to the weight given to the adverse inference. Subsequently, the Youth Justice and Criminal Evidence Act 1999 amended ss 34, 36 and 37 of the Criminal Justice and Public Order Act 1994 to prevent adverse inferences being drawn from silence before the defendant receives legal advice.

The matter was further tested in the case of *Condron v United Kingdom* (2000) 31 EHRR 1. The European Court expressed dissatisfaction with the Appeal Court's finding that the conviction was safe despite an unsatisfactory direction on the right to silence by the judge. They took the view that the only appropriate test was whether the trial was fair; the safety of the conviction was not the right test:

> 'In the court's opinion, as a matter of fairness, the jury should have been directed that unless it was satisfied that the applicant's silence at the police interview could not sensibly be attributed to their having no answer or none that would stand up to cross-examination, it should not draw an adverse inference.'

In *Condron* it was suggested that the fact that the defendant had been advised to remain silent was a factor that the jury should consider when assessing the validity of the defendant's silence, but it was not the only factor. An assertion that the defendant remained silent on the advice of his solicitor would not carry much weight. However, for the jury to assess the extent to which the solicitor's advice influenced the defendant's actions, the jury would need to have some information about why the solicitor advised silence in the first place.

The Youth Court must apply this judgment, and having weighed all the issues and circumstances of the case, give very clear reasons if it decides to draw an adverse inference from silence.

Youth detention accommodation

4.09   The use of youth detention accommodation when remanding a young person under the Legal Aid, Sentencing and Punishment of Offenders Act 2012 (LASPOA 2012), s 98 makes a useful study when considering if Article 3 is engaged (the prohibition against torture, inhuman or degrading treatment). This is an absolute right and as such the courts have set the threshold at a high level. If any ill treatment or suffering does not reach that minimum level of severity then it falls outside the scope of Article 3. It is unlikely then that the article is engaged at all and, even if it were, LASPOA 2012, ss 91 and 92 make provision to allow juveniles who might fall within the scope of Article 3 to be remanded to local authority accommodation rather than in youth detention accommodation (and therefore outside the scope of Article 3).

It could be argued that Article 8 (the right to private and family life) was engaged by remanding a young person into a secure environment away from their home. Article 8 is a qualified right and as such any breach needs to be described by domestic law which is clear and accessible. In this instance the law is set out clearly and accessibly in LASPOA 2012, s 91. Does the breach pursue a legitimate aim, which is set out in the article? In this case one of the qualifications to Article 8 is that:

> 'There shall be no interference by a public authority with the exercise of this right except such as is in accordance with the law and is necessary in a democratic society in the interests of … public safety … for the prevention and disorder or crime …, or for the protection of the rights and freedoms of others.'

Once again the clear purpose of LASPOA 2012, s 98 accords with the qualification in Article 8, that is 'to protect the public from death or serious personal injury' from him.

The next and probably most obvious breach of the Convention could be Article 5. Article 5 is a limited right in that it sets out and guarantees the right to liberty and security of the person and then provides exceptions or limitations to the right. One of those limitations is 'the detention of a minor by unlawful order … for the purpose of bringing him before a competent legal authority'. Once again this is clearly within the scope of the domestic legislation. In *R (on the application of Davies) v South Devon Magistrates' Court and Another* [2004] All ER (D) 330 (Dec) it was decided that requirements to live in a bail hostel for three months and not to leave the premises except with an approved escort or the express consent of hostel staff of a Young

Offender Institution licence did not amount to a deprivation of liberty, under Article 5. In any event the court found that each condition served an important purpose, namely preventing the offender committing further offences.

Prior to the LASPOA 2012 being brought into force, another possible breach may have been Article 14 of the Convention which prohibits discrimination in the enjoyment of the rights and freedoms set forth in the Convention. The objection would be that Article 5 was used in a discriminatory way as between males and females, due to 15- and 16-year-old males being remanded to prison accommodation, while females in the same age group were always held in local authority accommodation. The statute treated males and females in exactly the same way as regards the grounds to restriction of liberty; it was only the accommodation where they were detained which was different. In fact this point was tested in *R (on the application of SR) v Nottingham Magistrates' Court* [2001] EWHC 802 (Admin). The Appeal Court said that given the particular difficulties in providing secure placements for females, legislation which gives them priority to local authority accommodation was legitimate in its aims and a proportionate response to the problem. This is no longer an issue as LASPOA 2012, s 102 does not make such a distinction.

Parenting orders and parental bind overs

4.10   Both parental bind overs and parenting orders may be in breach of Article 7 of the Convention if they are not made in clear and specific terms. Article 7 is often paraphrased as meaning that there should be no punishment without law. This encompasses both the prohibitions against retrospective legislation concerning criminal behaviour and a requirement that criminal provisions should be neither vague nor uncertain. In the case of *Hashman and Harrup v United Kingdom* [2000] Crim LR 185 the European Court held that a bind over to be of good behaviour was too imprecise to be complied with and therefore Article 7 was violated. The court did accept however that a bind over to keep the peace was both understandable and enforceable.

The lesson from this case is that parental bind overs, which are aimed at ensuring parents take proper care and exercise proper control over their children, must be clear in their expectations of parents. Parents should know what is expected from them in order to avoid a forfeiture of the recognisance. In the same way parenting orders must be sufficiently clear in their requirements for counselling, guidance etc so that parents are able to comply with the orders.

Parenting orders also impinge upon private and family life as provided for in Article 8. However, Article 8 is a qualified right and as such the state is permitted to intervene in an individual's private and family life so long as that interference is prescribed by law, clear and accessible, necessary in a democratic society and its provisions are proportionate to the harm it seeks to avoid. In *R (on the application of M) v Inner London Crown Court and Another* [2003] All ER (D) 104 (Feb), the High Court held that parental training was necessary in a democratic society and proportionate but the seriousness of the offence would be a relevant factor in the court's decision. Although the legislation is both clear and accessible, a challenge under Article 6 was not without merit and indeed emphasises that the requirements made should be those which the court considers desirable in the interests of preventing repetition of offending or anti-social behaviour. It will readily be seen that one of the legitimate aims in Article 8 is for protection from disorder or crime, or the protection of rights and freedoms of others.

It should be clear from this brief analysis that these orders in the Youth Court pertaining to parents should not be in violation of the Convention. However, the court must be careful to follow the statutory provisions, clearly specify the requirements in its orders and give its reasons for doing so.

Reasons for decisions

4.11   There are many statutory requirements to give reasons in the Youth Court. Examples are where the court imposes a detention and training order or where it orders the removal of press restrictions normally applicable in the court. Such requirements are outlined throughout the text of this work. Article 6(1) states:

> '…everyone is entitled to a fair and public hearing within a reasonable time by an independent and impartial tribunal established by law. Judgment shall be pronounced publicly …'

Essentially, the usual safeguards require the court to give reasons for its decisions. The giving of reasons enables an aggrieved person to understand the decision and make an informed decision on his right to appeal. It also provides an explanation for the public at large and those observing the proceedings in court.

This obligation to give reasons for decisions does not transform the Youth Court, nor alter what should be current good practice. In *McKerry v Teesside and Wear Valley Justices* [2000] All ER (D) 140 the then Lord Chief Justice Lord Bingham said:

> '… the justices did announce that they were acceding to the request to dispense to the extent to which they did because they considered that the appellant constituted a serious danger to the public and had shown a complete disregard for the law. That was, in my judgement, enough to indicate the basis of the decision … justices are not obliged to state reasons in the form of a judgement or to give reasons in any elaborate form.'

That is not to say that a reasoned judgment at the end of a trial which covers the major issues in dispute, any legal submissions, and the justices' findings should in any way be discouraged.

The *McKerry* case involved the issue of the partial lifting of the normal reporting restrictions in the Youth Court in respect of a young person aged 15. This is exactly the sort of decision which will require the court to give reasons. The judgment of the

Lord Chief Justice was that the reasons of the court depended on both the matter to be decided and the court by which the matter was to be decided. A similar view can be found in the European Court of Human Rights in the case of *Toriga (Ruiz) v Spain* (1994) 19 EHRR 553. The court stated:

> 'The court reiterates that Article 6(1) obliges the courts to give reasons for their judgements, but cannot be understood as requiring a detailed answer to every argument. The extent to which this duty to give reasons applies may vary according to the nature of the decision.'

Following a trial the reasons should demonstrate that the justices have applied their minds to the ingredients of the offence and the defendant's state of mind so as to be able to inform the defendant in a few sentences why he has been found guilty (*R (on the application of McGowan) v Brent Justices* [2001] EWHC 814 (Admin)).

One area where it is clear that the court will have to give reasons is where there is any suggestion that an inference from the exercise of the right to silence is to be drawn: *Condron v United Kingdom* (2000) 31 EHRR 1.

One other qualification is that the courts must not resort to formatted or standard reasons. It is interesting to compare the High Court's criticism of the lower court for pre-preparing bail notices in *R v Mansfield Justices, ex parte Sharkey* [1985] QB 613 and subsequent European case law such as *Yagci and Sargin v Turkey* (1995) 20 EHRR 505 in which the European Court disapproved of the use of stereotyped reasons when refusing bail. The Youth Court must be able to demonstrate that each case has been considered on its individual merits and that the reasons given for withholding bail or imposing conditions apply specifically to the facts of the individual case.

In conclusion, the Youth Court like all other tribunals and public authorities must act compatibly with the European Convention on Human Rights. In general a rigorous approach to giving reasons for a decision will normally alert the court to any human rights issues. A structured approach to those issues should lead to a successful resolution of the majority of human rights problems.

Chapter 5   Venue of proceedings

The type of court in which the proceedings should commence

5.01   In this chapter the term 'adult court' will be used to identify a magistrates' court which is not sitting as a Youth Court. All criminal cases against a juvenile will be commenced in either the Youth Court or the adult court.

Youth Court

The General rule

5.02   The Youth Court may only deal with matters that have been specifically assigned to it by virtue of CYPA 1933, s 46, namely: criminal charges (against a child or young person); and applications involving juveniles which are specifically assigned to the Youth Court by rules made under the CYPA 1933, s 46(1).

It is arguable that this section does not exclusively define the jurisdiction of the court but simply assigns certain matters to it. For example applications for secure accommodation under the Children Act 1989, s 25 may be heard by the Youth Court but are not assigned to it by s 46. Instead CYPA 1969, s 23 and CJA 1991, s 60(3) rather than s 46 gives the Youth Court jurisdiction in that instance.

With certain specific exceptions, the Youth Court hears all criminal charges against juveniles. 'Charge' in this context includes all informations and requisitions laid against juveniles. Broadly speaking, 'informations' and 'requisitions' are laid to commence criminal proceedings and 'complaints' are made to commence civil proceedings.

Applications

5.03   This refers to civil matters, and for the Youth Court to deal with applications they have to be specifically assigned by virtue of rules made pursuant to CYPA 1933, s 46(1).

It is interesting to note that no civil matters have been assigned to the Youth Court. Again it is arguable that as s 46 does not define the jurisdiction of the court it would be permissible and more desirable to hear such cases before the Youth Court. However, the Youth Court is a magistrates' court specially constituted for the purpose of hearing any charge against a child or young person and for the purpose of exercising any other jurisdiction conferred on Youth Courts (CYPA 1933, s 45). Following the wording of s 45 the power to hear proceedings under MCA 1980, s 115 or Dogs Act 1871, s 2 is not 'conferred' on the Youth Court by any statutory provision or by any rules. It would appear therefore that the Youth Court would not have jurisdiction to hear such applications. The same argument would apply to breaches of parental bind overs which are dealt with later.

Exceptions

5.04 Please see the paragraphs below which set out the circumstances in which an adult court can usually deal with juveniles in the first instance.

Adult court

Civil applications

5.05 The adult court must hear civil applications, usually commenced by the making of a complaint. For example, complaints for binding over (MCA 1980, s 115), dangerous dog applications (Dogs Act 1871, s 2).

Juvenile charged with an adult

5.06 Where adults and juveniles are alleged to have been involved together in criminal activities then their charges are likely to be heard at first in the adult court. The various provisions are set out below:

(a) Where a child or young person and an adult are charged jointly with an offence, a court other than a Youth Court (CYPA 1933, s 46(1)(a)) shall hear the charge. In *R v Rowlands* [1972] 1 All ER 306, it was held that it was not necessary to use the words 'together' or 'jointly' to make a charge a joint one. Similarly in *R v Peterborough Magistrates' Court, ex parte Allgood* (1994) 159 JP 627, it was held that in the case of taking without the owner's consent or aggravated vehicle taking, the driver and passengers charged with allowing themselves to be carried are jointly charged.

(b) Where a child or young person is charged with an offence, the charge *may* be heard by a court other than a Youth Court if an adult is charged at the same time with aiding and abetting, causing, procuring, allowing or permitting that offence (CYPA 1933, s 46(1)(b)).

(c) Where a child or young person is charged with aiding, abetting, causing, procuring, allowing or permitting an offence with which an adult is charged at the same time, the charge *may* be heard by the adult court (CYPA 1963, s 18).

(d) Where a child or young person is charged with an offence arising out of circumstances which are the same as or connected with those giving rise to an offence with which an adult is charged at the same time, the charge *may* be heard by the adult court (CYPA 1963, s 18).

In the case of (a) above the Youth Court clearly still has jurisdiction to hear such charges, or the adult magistrates' court may remit the case to it for trial or sentence: *R v Coventry City Magistrates' Court, ex parte M* (1992) 156 JP 809. In (b) to (d) there is discretion as to whether the case starts in the magistrates' court or the Youth Court.

Remand hearing where no Youth Court available

5.07   In many areas there is not a Youth Court sitting each weekday. The adult court is given a general power to hear an application for a remand or bail (CYPA 1933, s 46(2)). See **Chapter 7.**

Movement between different types of court

Youth Court to adult court

Before trial

5.08   Under CDA 1998, s 47 the Youth Court can remit a young person who has attained 18 years of age to the adult court for trial (provided no evidence has been heard). The adult court can then deal with the defendant in any way in which it could if all the proceedings had been before it. By analogy with the case of *R (on the application of Denny) v Acton Justices (DPP, interested party)* [2004] All ER 961 it would be ill-advised to remit an indictable only offence to the adult court under CDA 1998, s 47 (see below).

After conviction

5.09   PCC(S)A 2000, ss 9 and 10 provide the Youth Court with a discretionary power to remit a convicted juvenile to an adult magistrates' court in the same area, for sentence. This power arises once the juvenile reaches the age of 18. The intention of the legislation is to permit the courts to ensure that young people are dealt with in the most appropriate way, according to their age, maturity, attitude and offending history, whilst avoiding unnecessary delay. There is no power to appeal such a remittal. The remitting court simply adjourns proceedings and applies the provisions of the Bail Act 1976 as normally operated. There would appear to be no reason why the adult court should not remit to another adult court under PCC(S)A 2000, s 10 should this prove necessary. In *R (on the application of Denny) v Acton Justices (DPP, interested party)* [2004] All ER 961 it was held that the Youth Court has no power to remit a person who becomes 18 during the proceedings to the adult court for sentence for a purely indictable offence because that court would have no power to impose any sentence for such an offence.

Youth Court to Crown Court

5.10 The court's powers to refer a case to the Crown Court are quite complicated and much detail is given in this chapter. For a simple overview please see the flow charts at **5.44**.

A suggested step by step approach to sending for trial/committal for sentence can be found at **Appendix L**.

The Sentencing Council's definitive guideline *Sentencing Children and Young People* states at para 2.1:

> 'Subject to exceptions....., cases involving children and young people should be tried in the youth court. It is the court which is best designed to meet their specific needs. A trial in the Crown Court with the inevitably greater formality and greatly increased number of people involved (including a jury and the public) should be reserved for the most serious cases. The welfare principles in this guideline apply to all cases, including those tried or sentenced in the Crown Court.'

Cases which for a juvenile can only be tried in the Crown Court

Homicide

5.11 A juvenile charged with homicide cannot be tried summarily in the Youth Court (MCA 1980, s 24(1) and CDA 1998, s 51A(12)). Such offences will be brought before the Youth Court in the first instance and sent to the Crown Court for trial.

Homicide is commonly understood to mean any offence of unlawful killing, for example murder, manslaughter, infanticide, child destruction. Although MCA 1980, s 24(1) and CDA 1998, s 51A(12) provides the authority for excluding homicide from summary trial in the Youth Court, the Act does not define exactly what homicide means in this context. This leaves open the question of how offences of attempted murder should be dealt with in the Youth Court. There is a distinct lack of any statutory definition of homicide which is of general application. CJPOA 1984, s 25 does include attempted murder under the heading 'homicide or rape' as being an offence for which bail can only be granted in exceptional circumstances (if the person has a previous conviction for that or another listed offence). In relation to a charge of murder, s 115 of the Coroners and Justice Act 2009 (CJA 2009) requires the court to commit the juvenile to the Crown Court in custody for a decision to be made about bail. For further detail on bail in murder cases see **7.06**. In practice a Youth Court may be minded to deal with a charge of attempted murder as an offence of homicide and send it to the Crown Court for trial under CDA 1998, s 51A(3)(a). If grave crime mode of trial was applied and a not guilty plea indicated, summary jurisdiction would no doubt be declined by the court. The case would then be sent to the Crown Court for trial under CDA 1998, s 51A(3)(b). If a guilty plea were indicated then the case would surely in all but truly exceptional cases be committed to the Crown Court for sentence under PCC(S) A 2000, s 3B. Alternatively, if the circumstances of the alleged offence and offender clearly demonstrate that the juvenile is dangerous then the case must be sent for trial under CDA 1998, s 51A(3)(d). Attempted murder is a serious specified offence for the purpose of dangerousness provisions (CJA 2003, Sch 15, para 65). Murder is not included in schedule 15 presumably because the sentence is fixed by law.

Section 51A of the Firearms Act 1968 and s 29(3) of the Violent Crime Reduction Act 2006

5.12   Where a juvenile of 16 years or older commits an offence to which either of the sections apply then the case cannot be tried summarily. The case will therefore have to be sent to the Crown Court for trial under CDA 1998, s 51A(3)(a) and (12). If the juvenile is convicted at the Crown Court a minimum three-year sentence of long-term detention (PCC(S)A 2000, s 91) applies unless there are exceptional circumstances relating to the offence or the offender. Section 29(3) of the Violent Crime and Reduction Act 2006 (VCRA 2006) relates to using someone else to look after, hide or transport a dangerous weapon where possession of the weapon/ammunition would be an offence attracting a minimum three-year term under the Firearms Act 1968, s 51A. The offences referred to in the Firearms Act 1968, s 51A and VCRA 2006, s 29 all relate to prohibited weapons or ammunition listed in the Firearms Act 1968, s 5. These include shortened shot guns, pump-action guns and rocket launchers.

Sending to the Crown Court for trial

5.13   When the court allocates an offence to the Crown Court it will immediately send the defendant on bail or in custody to the Crown Court for trial. The court does not consider the sufficiency of the evidence for these purposes. Instead the court makes directions for the provision of prosecution papers and management of the case as required under the Criminal Procedure Rules 2015.

Where the court sends or has previously sent the juvenile to the Crown Court for trial, it may subject to the indication of plea procedure also send him for trial for any other related indictable offence (ie one which could be included in the same indictment) or any related summary only offence which is imprisonable or carries a possible disqualification, provided that the offence arises out of circumstances which are the same as or connected with those giving rise to the sent offence (CDA 1998, s 51A(4) and (5)).

Where the offence sent to the Crown Court is one which is indictable in the case of an adult, then a purely summary offence of taking a motor vehicle without the owner's consent, driving whilst disqualified, common assault or criminal damage may be included in the indictment at the Crown Court. This may only happen if the charge is founded on the same facts or evidence as the indictable offence or is part of a series of offences of the same or similar character as the indictable offence. The facts of the summary offence must be disclosed in the material served on the defence in accordance with the Criminal Procedure Rules 2015 relating to offences sent for trial to the Crown Court (CJA 1988, s 40).

Sending dangerous offenders to the Crown Court for trial

5.14   A dangerous juvenile must either be sent to the Crown Court for trial under CDA 1998, s 51A(d), or committed to the Crown Court for sentence under PCC(S)A 2000, s 3C. At the Crown Court sentences of detention for life (where the offence is punishable with life imprisonment in the case of an adult), or extended sentences of detention may be imposed. An extended sentence carries an additional period for which the offender will remain on licence. This extension period may not exceed five years for a specified violent offence or eight years for a specified sexual offence (CJA 2003, ss 226B and 228).

When a person is sent to the Crown Court under CDA 1998, s 51A this should be done at the first hearing. The plea before venue procedure does not apply to the offence which satisfies the dangerousness provisions, but it does apply to any related offences which could also be sent to the Crown Court to be included within the indictment. There is no requirement for the magistrates to consider the evidence. If the juvenile is charged with any related offences which do not themselves satisfy the criteria for dangerousness (perhaps because they are not specified offences – see below) then those offences can also be sent to the Crown Court for trial provided either no plea or a not guilty plea is indicated and they fulfil certain criteria. The criteria are that the offences are indictable (in the case of an adult) or if summary only are punishable with imprisonment or involve obligatory/discretionary disqualification. The offences may only be considered 'related' if for indictable offences they could be included in the same indictment or if summary only if they arose out of circumstances which are the same as or connected with those giving rise to the indictable offence. The magistrates will decide any applications for a remand in custody or on bail. Any remand will last until the hearing at the Crown Court.

Where a juvenile is committed to the Crown Court for sentence under the dangerousness provisions (PCC(S)A 2000, s 3C) then the court will usually set a date for the sentencing hearing by liaison with the Crown Court listing office. The Crown Court will have power to impose any sentence it could if it had just convicted the juvenile on indictment (PCC(S)A 2000, s 5A). The Youth Court may also commit to the Crown Court for sentence any other offences which the juvenile has been convicted of (see PCC(S)A 2000, s 6). The sentencing powers of the Crown Court in relation to those offences committed under s 6 are limited to those of a magistrates' court. It is interesting to note that if the juvenile attains 18 then the Crown Court would be restricted to a maximum of a six-month custodial sentence for an indictable only offence which had been tried summarily in the Youth Court (PCC(S)A 2000, s 7(4)). The juvenile may be remanded in custody or on bail until his appearance at the Crown Court.

The criteria for determining whether a juvenile should be dealt with as a 'dangerous offender' are as follows:

(a)   the offender must be charged with or convicted of a 'specified offence or serious specified offence'. A specified offence is one listed in Sch 15 of the Criminal Justice Act 2003. The schedule contains lists of violent offences in Part 1 and sexual offences in Part 2. Where a specified offence is punishable with at least 10 years' imprisonment in the case of an adult it is classified as a 'serious offence'; and

(b)   the offence justifies a determinate term of at least four years' custody; and

(c)   the court must be of the opinion that there is a significant risk to members of the public of serious harm caused by the commission of further specified offences by the offender (CJA 2003, ss 226B and 228(2A)).

'Serious harm' means 'death or serious personal injury, whether physical or psychological.'

The criteria (CJA 2003, ss 226B(1)(d) and 228(2A)) remove the possibility of committing to the Crown Court specified offences that have a maximum penalty of less than four years, such as affray or racially aggravated common assault.

Making the assessment

5.15   Section 229(2) of the Criminal Justice Act 2003, as amended, details how the court is to assess whether there is a significant risk to members of the public of serious harm occasioned by the commission of further specified offences and the factors which the court can take into account in assessing whether the offender is dangerous.

The court:

(a)   **must** take into account all such information as is available to it about the nature and circumstances of the offence;

(b)   **may** take into account all such information as is available to it about the nature and circumstances of any other offences of which the offender has been convicted by a court anywhere in the world;

(c)   **may** take into account any information which is before it about any pattern of behaviour of which the offence forms part; and

(d)   **may** take into account any information about the offender which is before it.

Significant risk

5.16 Significant risk is not defined in the statute and is therefore a matter for the court to assess in each individual case. The Sentencing Council's definitive guideline *Sentencing Children and Young People* at paras 2.3–2.7 provides guidance on dangerousness. It underlines the importance of obtaining a pre-sentence report before making the decision. It states that 'in anything but the most serious cases it may be impossible to form a view ... (on dangerousness)... in those circumstances jurisdiction for the case should be retained in the youth court. If following a guilty plea or finding of guilt, the dangerousness criteria appear to be met then the child or young person should be committed for sentence.' The guideline appears to be a distillation of following case law.

The Court of Appeal in *R v Lang* [2006] 2 All ER 410 set out a detailed list of considerations to be borne in mind, when the court is assessing significant risk. These include:

(a) The fact that *significant* has a higher threshold than a mere possibility of occurrence, and could be taken as meaning 'noteworthy, of considerable amount or importance'.

(b) In assessing the risk of further offences being committed the court had to take into account the nature and seriousness of the instant offence; the defendant's history of offending, including not just this kind of offence, but its circumstances and the sentences passed (details of which the prosecution had to have available); information in relation to the defendant's social and economic circumstances including his accommodation, education, associations and relationships, together with his attitude towards offending and supervision that will be derived, largely, from antecedents, pre-sentence reports and medical reports. (See: *R v Beesley* [2011] EWCA Crim 1021).

(c) A serious specified offence does not necessarily mean there is a significant risk of serious harm. Robbery is a serious offence, but can be committed in a variety of ways many of which do not give rise to a significant risk of serious harm. The court must guard against making assumptions. A pre-sentence report should usually be obtained before a sentence is passed based upon a significant risk of serious harm.

(d) Where a specified offence is not serious, there would be comparatively few cases in which a risk of serious harm could properly be regarded as significant. As to whether the defendant demonstrated any pattern of offending, repetitive violent or sexual offending at a relatively low level without serious harm will not in itself give rise to a significant risk of serious harm in future.

(e) It is necessary to bear in mind in relation to offenders under 18 that within a short period of time they will be adults and they may change and develop. Their level of maturity may be highly pertinent when assessing their future conduct and whether it might give rise to a significant risk of serious harm.

(Note *R v Williams* [2009] EWCA Crim 107 reinforced this point by adding that a young offender was far more susceptible to change than an adult, and if influenced to the good, more likely to reform.)

Although for young offenders there has never been a presumption of dangerousness even where there are previous convictions for specified offences, it is nevertheless important that previous convictions are considered by the court. Equally, it is not a prerequisite to a finding of dangerousness that the offender should be an individual with previous convictions; a man of good character could qualify for a sentence under the dangerousness provisions: *R v Johnson, Attorney General's Reference No 64 of 2006* [2007] All ER 1237.

When considering 'a pattern of behaviour' and 'information about the offender' the court may also take into account any previous acquittals and complaints which were not pursued or prosecuted: *R v Considine and Davis* [2007] EWCA Crim 1166. Also, specified offences committed before the implementation of the dangerous offender provisions would still be relevant in the overall assessment of dangerousness according to *R v Robert Michael S and Others* [2007] EWCA Crim 1633. A finding of guilt in service disciplinary proceedings and a conviction of a service offence within the meaning of the Armed Forces Act 2006 can also be taken into account (CJA 2003, s 229(2A)).

Further consideration to the issue was given in *R v Johnson, A-G's Reference (No 64 of 2006)* [2007] 1 All ER 1237. Looking at a number of specific issues surrounding the dangerousness provisions, the Appeal Court concluded by stating that it will not normally interfere with the conclusions reached by a sentencer who has accurately identified the relevant principles, and applied his mind to the relevant facts.

The court in accordance with CJA 2003, s 174 should give reasons for all its conclusions, in particular whether there is or is not a significant risk of further offences or serious harm and identify the information which has been taken into account (*R v Lang* [2006] 2 All ER 410).

Procedure where dealing with a 'specified offence' which is capable of being a 'grave crime'

5.17   Where a juvenile is charged with an offence that is both a specified offence and capable of being a grave crime (see below) the court must bear in mind the following factors considered in *CPS v South East Surrey Youth Court* [2005] EWHC 2929 (Admin):

(a)   The policy of the legislature is that those under 18 should, wherever possible, be tried in a Youth Court, which is best designed for their specific needs.

(b)   Where a non-serious specified offence is charged, an assessment of dangerousness will not be appropriate until after a finding of guilt has been made. At that stage, if the dangerousness criteria are met, following receipt of an appropriate pre-sentence report, the defendant can be committed to Crown Court for sentence as a dangerous offender.

(c)   If it is appropriate to consider the dangerousness provisions at the outset of the case, a defendant can be sent to the Crown Court for trial immediately, if it is in the interests of the youth to be tried on indictment (CDA 1998, s 51A(3)(d)). However, it is unlikely that the court will be in a position to make this decision in the absence of a formal risk assessment undertaken by the Youth Offending Team.

(d)   In the case of a joint charge with an adult the magistrates must assess the need for a joint trial against the presumption that the Youth Court trial will be most appropriate.

(e)   Where the defendant is not deemed dangerous the court should go on to consider whether grave crimes provisions apply; if they do he can then be committed to the Crown Court for trial.

In *R (on the application of B) v Barking Youth Court* [2006] EWHC 2121 (Admin), the Court of Appeal declined to interfere with the decision of the Youth Court at the first hearing in the proceedings to send for trial at the Crown Court a young offender charged with a *serious* specified offence, despite the lack of reports of any kind. The court relied on the facts of the offence and the young person's record of similar offences. The court suggested that at the first appearance defence lawyers should be in a position to assist the court with material on which dangerousness could be assessed.

The juvenile plea before venue procedure does not appear to apply to potential dangerous offences which are not also potential grave crimes (MCA 1980, s 24A(1)(b) and (5)(b).

When neither the dangerousness nor the grave crime provisions apply the court will proceed to a summary trial in the Youth Court.

It must be remembered that there is no general power to commit to the Crown Court for sentence in the Youth Court. There is however a power to commit a juvenile to the Crown Court for an extended sentence or sentence of detention for life under PCC(S)A 2000, s 3C where the dangerousness criteria are met. See below for the power to commit grave crimes to the Crown Court for sentence under PCC(S)A 2000, s 3B.

Grave crime mode of trial

5.18   Please refer to the paragraph above where the offence is a specified violent or sexual offence.

For certain very serious offences the charges against juveniles aged 10 to 17 years inclusive may be sent to the Crown Court for trial even where no adult offender is involved. In particular, the court may send the case to the Crown Court for trial if it considers that the offence is one for which the Crown Court judge may wish to order long-term detention under PCC(S)A 2000, s 91(3).

The sentence under PCC(S)A 2000, s 91 may be for any period up to the maximum for the offence. An example would be 14 years for burglary. The order made by the Crown Court is for the offender to be detained in such place and on such conditions as the Secretary of State may direct. The juvenile could be held in any suitable accommodation as is felt appropriate from an ordinary local authority children's home to a prison. This is at the discretion of the Home Secretary. This discretion is illustrated by the case of *R v Secretary of State for the Home Department, ex parte J* (1999) 96(1) LSG 23, CA. The juvenile had been placed in a Young Offender Institution and it was argued that he should have been placed in a care establishment. It was held that in deciding upon the appropriate place of detention for an offender under PCC(S)A 2000, s 91, the Secretary of State is bound to have regard to the welfare of the individual. He is also to take account of the need for punishment and the need to maintain confidence in the criminal justice system. He is also entitled to have regard to the finite number of places in childcare establishments. The court fixes the term of the order but the offender may be released by the parole board.

Potential 'grave crimes'

5.19   The power of the Crown Court under PCC(S)A 2000, s 91 to order long-term detention applies to juveniles from 10 to 17 inclusive. The provisions apply to:

(a)   all offences which in the case of an adult carry a maximum term of imprisonment of 14 years or more;

(b)   various forms of sexual assault of either male or female, including an offence under s 3 (sexual assault), s 13 (child sex offences committed by children or young persons), s 25 (sexual activity with a child family member) or s 26 (inciting a child family member to engage in sexual activity) of the Sexual Offences Act 2003;

(c)   16 and 17 year olds guilty of firearms offences under Firearms Act 1968 s 5(1) and (1A) who but for the fact that exceptional circumstances apply in their case, would be liable to a minimum of three years detention (under Firearms Act 1968, s 51A or VCRA 2006, s 29). Such offences which attract the minimum three-year custodial sentence for a 16 or 17 year old can only be tried on indictment (see **5.12** above). In practice, all offences which fall within Firearms Act 1968, s 51A or VCRA 2006, s 29 should be sent to the Crown Court for trial under CDA 1998, ss 51A(3)(a) and (12) and leave that Court to determine whether there are exceptional circumstances.

Some of the more common examples of offences punishable by 14 years or more are:

(a)   arson (criminal damage by fire) (Criminal Damage Act 1971, s 1);

(b)   aggravated burglary (burglary with a weapon of offence, firearm, imitation firearm or explosive) (Theft Act 1968, s 10);

(c)   blackmail (demanding money with menaces) (Theft Act 1968, s 21);

(d)   burglary, including burglary with intent to commit rape, inflict injury on any person, attempt to inflict serious bodily harm therein or unlawfully damage the building or steal anything in the building (but excluding non-dwelling house burglary which carries a maximum term of 10 years' imprisonment) (Theft Act 1968, s 9);

(e)   handling stolen goods (Theft Act 1968, s 22);

(f)   rape and assault by penetration (Sexual Offences Act 2003, s 2);

(g)   robbery (Theft Act 1968, s 8);

(h)   assault with intent to rob (Theft Act 1968, s 8(2));

(i)   sexual activity with a child (Sexual Offences Act 2003, s 9);

(j)   wounding with intent to do grievous bodily harm or causing grievous bodily harm with intent (Offences Against the Person Act 1861, s 18);

(k)   production of class A or B drugs (Misuse of Drugs Act 1971 (MDA 1971), s 4(2));

(l)   supplying class A, B or C drugs (MDA 1971, s 4(3));

(m)   possessing class A or B drugs with intent to supply (MDA 1971, s 5(3));

(n)   cultivating cannabis (MDA 1971, s 6(2));

(o)   possession of firearm with intent to endanger life (Firearms Act 1968, s 16);

(p)   causing death by dangerous driving, causing death by careless driving whilst intoxicated, causing death by aggravated vehicle-taking (maximum penalties increased by CJA 2003, s 285).

The above list is not exhaustive.

The tests to be applied when deciding grave crime mode of trial for allocation purposes

5.20   The tests to be applied by the magistrates in determining whether a defendant should be committed to the Crown Court are now set out in the Sentencing Council's document *Sentencing Children and Young People* at paras 2.8 to 2.10:

'The test to be applied by the court is whether there is a **real prospect** that a sentence in excess of two years' detention will be imposed.... the court should hear submissions from the prosecution and defence. As there is now a power to commit grave crimes for sentence the court should no longer take the prosecution case at its highest when deciding whether to retain jurisdiction. In most cases it is likely to be impossible to decide whether there is a real prospect that a sentence in excess of two years' detention will be imposed without knowing more about the facts of the case and the circumstances of the child or young person. In those circumstances the youth court should retain jurisdiction and commit for sentence if it is of the view having heard more about the facts and the circumstances of the child or young person, that its powers of sentence are insufficient.

Where the court decides that the case is suitable to be dealt with in the youth court it must warn the child or young person that all available sentencing options remain open and, if found guilty, the child or young person may be committed to the Crown Court for sentence.

Children and young people should only be sent for trial or committed for sentence to the Crown Court when charged with or found guilty of an offence of such gravity that a custodial sentence substantially exceeding two years is a realistic possibility. For children aged 10 or 11, and children/young people aged 12–14 who are not persistent offenders, the court should take into account the normal prohibition on imposing custodial sentences.'

In the case of *R (on the application of the DPP) v South Tyneside Youth Court* [2015] EWHC 1455 (Admin) the District Judge had not realised that the new powers to commit those convicted of a grave crime to the Crown Court for sentence under s 3B(1) of the PCC(S)A 2000 were not yet in force. The High Court therefore had to quash the decision and remit the matter back to the Youth Court. In this case Sir Brian Leveson made some observations which are now embodied in the Sentencing Council's *Sentencing Children and Young People* (see above). He said that new power (s 3B(1)) revises the 'real prospect' test:

'Because s. 3B (as amended) of the 2000 Act means that the youth court is not making a once and for all decision at the point of allocation, the "real prospect" assessment requires a different emphasis and taking the prosecution case at its highest is no longer necessary; to that extent, the observations of Langstaff J in *Oldham Youth Court* no longer apply. For the future, there will, of course, be cases in which the alleged offending is so grave that a sentence of or in excess of two years will be a "real prospect" irrespective of particular considerations in relation either to the offence or the offender's role in it: such cases are, however, likely to be rare.' [para 31]

The judgment approved the observations in *R (on the application of H, A and O) v Southampton Youth Court* [2004] that a Crown Court trial for a youth 'should be reserved for the most serious cases'. When deciding allocation and determination of venue, the views of the prosecution and defence should be taken into account; these views could include representations as the value of privacy of the proceedings or, alternatively, the desire for a jury trial

It is interesting to note that the Sentencing Council has again not expressly preserved the exception for under 15-year-olds whereby an unusual feature of the case could be relied upon for justifying committal for trial where the offence would not justify a term of more than two years' custody. The authors are not aware of any reported case where an unusual feature had been the basis of a committal for trial. It was decided that the fact that the juvenile could not otherwise be given a custodial sentence (because the defendant is under 15 years of age and not a persistent offender) did not constitute such a feature *(R (on the application of H, A and O) v Southampton Youth Court* [2004] EWHC 2912 (Admin) – see below). It would appear however, that it might still be open to a court to find that some unusual feature justified committal to the Crown Court as by their nature the guidelines cannot deal with exceptional cases.

Under the Sentencing Council's definitive guideline it is necessary for the court to be satisfied that the offence justifies substantially more than two years' custody. There is no definition of what term might be the lowest which could be classed as *substantially more than two years*. The intention is however clear that a juvenile should not be committed for trial if the likely sentence is only slightly greater than the two-year detention and training order available to the Youth Court. It may be instructive in this context to consider that the final steps in the length of detention and training orders are each six months (12 months; 18 months; 24 months).

It was held in *R (on the application of FS) v Wakefield Magistrates' Court* [2010] EWHC 3412 (Admin) that a district judge had not erred in concluding that there was a real prospect of a sentence of two years or more being imposed on a defendant (aged 15) of attempted rape. The district judge had therefore been justified in upholding an earlier decision made by the magistrates that the defendant should be committed for trial in the Crown Court. The right test had been used and the decision was not unreasonable.

Gauging the likely sentence

Using Sentencing Council's guidelines for adults and scaling down

5.21   This approach to determining the appropriate length of a custodial sentence for a juvenile may be of assistance at the stage of deciding grave crime mode of trial. The Sentencing Council's *Sentencing Children and Young People* suggests that, where there are no specific offence guidelines which contain guidance for dealing with youths, the appropriate SC offence guidelines for adult offenders should be used as a starting point for setting the length of the term. The appropriate adult sentencing starting point should be scaled down according to the age and immaturity of the young offender. It is indicated that a reduction of between 33% and 50% may be appropriate for 17- to 15-year-olds, with further reductions for those children under 15. It is emphasised that this approach is only a rough guide and must not be applied mechanistically.

Sentencing Council's guidelines relevant to Crown Court sentencing

5.22   Section 2 of the Sentencing Council's *Sentencing Children and Young People* which deals with the trial and sentencing of cases in the Crown Court opens with a statement that summarises the relevant statutory provisions and case law.

At paragraph 2.1 reference is made to the previous guideline case on the imposition of long-term detention under PCC(S)A 2000, s 91 of *R (on the application of H, A and O) v Southampton Youth Court* [2004] EWHC 2912 (Admin), in which Leveson J set out the position in the Youth Court as follows:

(a)   The general policy of the legislature is that those who are under 18 years of age and in particular children under 15 years of age should, wherever possible, be tried in the Youth Court. It is that court that is best designed to meet their specific needs. A trial in the Crown Court with the inevitably greater formality and greatly increased number of people involved (including a jury and the public) should be reserved for the most serious cases.

(b)   It is further policy of the legislature that, generally speaking, first-time offenders aged 12 to 14 and all offenders less than 12 years old should not be detained in custody and decisions as to jurisdiction should have regard to the fact that the exceptional power to detain for grave offences should not be used to water down that general principle. Those under 15 years old will rarely attract a period of detention and, even more rarely, those who are under 12.

(c)   In each case the court should ask itself whether there is a real prospect, having regard to his or her age, that the defendant whose case they are considering might require a sentence of, or in excess of, two years or, alternatively, whether, although the sentence might be less than two years, there is some unusual feature of the case that justifies declining jurisdiction, bearing in mind that the absence of a power to impose a detention and training order because the defendant is under 15 is not an unusual feature.

The SC guidelines have however, as noted earlier, developed the test outlined in paragraph (c) above.

In both *R (on the application of B) v Norfolk Youth Court and Another* [2013] EWHC 1459 (Admin) and *R (on the application of T) v Bromley Youth Court* [2014] EWHC 577 (Admin) the defendants challenged the decision of the Youth Court who had declined jurisdiction to determine allegations of robbery. *Norfolk Youth Court* [2013] concerned a defendant who was 13-years-old at the time of the offence and had no previous convictions or reprimands or warnings recorded against him and in *Bromley Youth Court* [2014] the defendant was 14-years-old and she was also of previous good character. The High Court quashed the decision of the Youth Court in both cases on the basis that in the light of the age and previous good record a sentence exceeding two years would be manifestly excessive and the Youth Court had failed to take account of all the relevant sentencing principles. It is hoped that the new guidelines, in addition to these authorities, will assist the Youth Court in determining which court the defendant should be tried.

Sentencing Council's specific offence guidelines

5.23   There are Sentencing Council guidelines for robbery and sexual offences within the 2017 definitive guideline *'Sentencing Children and Young People'* which replace the previous guidance on those offences. (see **Appendix I**).

Case law

5.24 There are a number of offences for which there are no definitive Sentencing Council guidelines. Arson is an example. The SC Magistrates' Court Sentencing Guidelines do not provide any starting points beyond six months imprisonment. In these circumstances it may be necessary to refer to sentencing case law.

PCC(S)A 2000, s 3B does, however, provide that the magistrates can commit the juvenile to the Crown Court for sentence if they are convicted after trial or a guilty plea of an offence mentioned in PCC(S)A 2000, s 91(1). This power applies to a juvenile who first appears for the offence or is brought before a magistrates' court in those proceedings on or after 13 April 2015. The case of *R v S* [2014] EWCA Crim 2062 was decided before the most recent amendment to s 3B. The 17-year-old defendant had not been asked to indicate his plea before the youth court accepted jurisdiction on a charge of robbery. He then entered a not guilty plea which he changed on the day of trial to guilty. It was decided that the court could not then commit him to the Crown Court under s 3B as that power was simply not available at that point. The latest wording is sufficient to allow such a committal in those circumstances.

There is a series of sentencing cases at **Appendix J** which may be of relevance to mode of trial decisions.

The Sexual Offences in the Youth Court Protocol

5.25 Following the Sexual Offences Act 2003, the definition of rape was widened and a Protocol was issued in November 2007 by the Senior Presiding Judge dealing with 'Rape cases in the Youth Court'. Although historically the position was that the Youth Court should never accept jurisdiction in a rape case (*R v Billam* [1986] 1 All ER 985), recent authorities have suggested that in the case of very young defendants it may be appropriate in exceptional circumstances to accept jurisdiction (*R (on the application of B) v Richmond on Thames Youth Court* [2006] EWHC 95 (Admin)). The determination of venue is still governed by MCA 1980, s 24. When considering whether the Youth Court should retain jurisdiction in a rape case, the court should apply the principles and guidelines in the ordinary way. If the decision is taken to accept jurisdiction then the protocol provided a procedure for allocating a Circuit Judge authorised to try serious sexual cases to hear the case in the Youth Court. 'The Rape Protocol' has been superseded with effect from 31 March 2010 by the 'Sexual Offences in the Youth Court' Protocol issued by the Senior Presiding Judge. It does not change the test for deciding whether a serious sexual offence should be committed to the Crown Court, but it does affect the procedure. The new protocol provides that wherever possible the grave crime mode of trial decision should be made by a District Judge (Magistrates' Courts) (DJ) authorised to hear such cases. If this is not practicable and the case is retained in the Youth Court then a full report about the case must be sent to an authorised DJ for him or her to decide whether an authorised DJ should hear the trial. If the case involves actual or alleged penetrative behaviour then an authorised DJ must hear the case. The current protocol is reproduced at **Appendix M**. (See also **13.06** and **J.2** at **Appendix J** for range of sentences in sexual offences cases.)

Procedure in potentially grave crime cases

5.26   There is now a statutory procedure for some aspects of the grave crimes mode of trial decision process (MCA 1980, s 24A). It is necessary to conduct a plea before venue procedure for any potential grave crime offence. This involves the court legal adviser putting the charge to the juvenile and explaining that if a guilty plea is indicated then the court would start to consider sentence and that the court does have a power to commit the juvenile to the Crown Court if it believes that a sentence of more than 2 years detention is necessary (MCA 1980, s 24A(5)). If the juvenile indicates a not guilty plea (or no plea) then a full determination of grave crime mode of trial must take place. Unlike the position with adults there is no statutory provision to allow the juvenile to ask for an indication of sentence and to review his indication of plea in the light of such an indication (see CPR 2015, r 9.13).

It is then incumbent upon the prosecutor and the legal adviser to bring to the attention of the bench that a matter is potentially one to which the grave crime provisions could apply so that the court may consider the matter.

The magistrates can make a decision as to venue after hearing representations. There is no requirement to hear evidence (*R v South Hackney Juvenile Court, ex parte RB (a minor) and CB (a minor)* (1983) 77 Cr App R 294).

Additional principles have been set out in the case of *R (on the application of W) v Brent Youth Court; R (on the application of B) v Richmond on Thames Youth Court* [2006] EWHC 95 (Admin):

(a)   The principles already set out in *R (on the application of H, A and O) v Southampton Youth Court* [2004] as modified by the SC's *Sentencing Children and Young People* should be applied.

(b)   The Youth Court should expect to be assisted by both its legal adviser and the advocates.

(c)   In order to make a satisfactory decision, the court must have all the necessary information before it, namely:

(i)   the factual allegation (which must be assumed to be true, unless manifestly not so), it being the duty of the advocates to ensure that the summary is both scrupulously fair and balanced;

(ii)   any undisputed mitigation (see *R (on the application of C and D) v Sheffield Youth Court* [2003] EWHC 35 (Admin)), including any indication of an intention to plead guilty;

(iii)   the defendant's previous record (if any and if relevant). The leading case on whether previous convictions can be taken into account at a grave crime mode of trial is *R (on the application of Tullet) v Medway Magistrates' Court* [2003] EWHC 2279 (Admin). In that case a juvenile aged 17 appeared before the court charged with a dwelling house burglary, described as an opportunistic, daytime walk-in burglary of unlocked premises. He had five previous convictions for dwelling house burglaries. The court held that taking previous convictions into account was appropriate;

(iv) the correct approach as set out in the authorities; and

(v) any relevant sentencing guidelines. Where there are no guidelines from the Sentencing Council, any relevant published advice by the Sentencing Advisory Panel, provided that the court recognises that such advice does not carry legal force.

Where several defendants are charged together, the position of each of them is to be considered separately. In *R (on the application of W and another) v Oldham Youth Court* [2010] EWHC 661 (Admin) the following words of Smith LJ in *R (on the application of) v The Brent Youth Court* [2006] EWHC 95 (Admin), were quoted with approval:

'. . .the need mentioned by Leveson J for the court to consider the position of each Defendant separately. Where all the Defendants are under the age of 18 there is no power to commit (for trial as a grave crime) a young person to the Crown Court in the interests of justice, as there is where one Defendant is over the age of 18 and must be committed to the Crown Court. If all are under 18, the court must make an appropriate decision for each Defendant, even if this results in one Defendant being tried in the Youth Court and others in the Crown Court.'

There is also some debate over whether the court which has to consider venue in relation to potentially grave crimes has to look at each offence individually, or whether it is able to aggregate the seriousness of a number of offences charged at the same time, thus pushing all of the offences into the grave crime bracket. The orthodox view is that each offence should be considered individually and PCC(S)A 2000, s 91 refers to 'the offence'. It is at least arguable that this is an illogical approach. It is established that at the sentencing stage the persistence of offending aggravates the sentence (*R v Simmons* (1995) 16 Cr App R (S) 801, CA). The grave crime procedure is a sentencing prediction and nothing more. Why should it not be possible to look at the totality of all of the offences charged together? This point has never been considered judicially. It was argued in *R v Hammersmith Juvenile Court, ex parte O* (1988) 86 Cr App R 343, but the court chose not to rule on it. When deciding whether a juvenile who has been convicted of a grave crime following an indication of a guilty plea should be committed to the Crown Court for sentence, the court is entitled to look at all associated offences (PCC(S)A 2000, s 3B(2)). The thrust of the SC's guideline *Sentencing Children and Young People* is that generally such decisions should be made after a finding of guilt. In such a situation the court will be actively considering all the offences.

A sentence passed under PCC(S)A 2000, s 91 ('long term detention') is a custodial sentence for the purposes of CJA 2003, s 152 (PCC(S)A 2000, s 76(1)(b) as applied by

CJA 2003, s 305). This means that before the Crown Court can pass a sentence under s 91 it has to be of the opinion that the offence, or the combination of the offence and one or more offences associated with it, is so serious that neither a fine alone nor a community sentence can be justified for the offence. It follows that an adult court or a Youth Court, when determining whether an offence falls to be committed to the Crown Court as a grave crime, must also have regard to these provisions.

Where a Youth Court sends a child or young person for trial at the Crown Court for a grave crime under MCA 1980, s 24A and CDA 1998, s 51A it may also send him for trial at the same time, or on a subsequent occasion for any related offence to which an indication of a not guilty plea or no indication has been given. The CDA 1998 removed the presumption that cases which are not sent to the Crown Court for trial should be postponed until after the more serious matter has been dealt with. This reversed the decision in *R v Khan* (1994) 158 JP 760.

Where the defendant is charged with more than one offence, or an offence could fall within a number of provisions dealing with sending for trial, the Crime and Disorder Act 1998 does provide some guidance about the order for dealing with the offences or provisions. If an offence satisfies any of the main criteria for being sent to the Crown Court for trial (youth indictable only, notices under CDA 1998, ss 51B or 51C; grave crime; dangerousness) then it should be sent under CDA 1998, s 51A(2) and not under any other provision of CDA 1998, ss 51 or 51A. Only related offences which do not meet those requirements are therefore to be dealt with under CDA 1998, s 51(7) or (8) or s 51A(4) or (5).

Reviewing mode of trial decisions

5.27   There is a statutory power to review allocation decisions for adult offenders under MCA 1980, s 25. This allows the court to change from summary trial and send the case to the Crown Court for trial. The prosecutor must make the application before the trial has begun and before any other application or issue in relation to the summary trial is dealt with. The sole ground for approving the application is that sentence which a magistrates' court would have power to impose for the offence would be inadequate. This power does not apply to juveniles.

There is a great deal of case law about whether there is a general discretion for magistrates to review a grave crime mode of trial decision made earlier in the proceedings. This is considered in more detail in **Chapter 13** at **13.25** to **13.29**. In summary, the prevailing view appears to be that there is no such general discretion.

Powers of the Crown Court following sending for trial

5.28   Once a juvenile has been sent to the Crown Court for trial, if he is convicted, the restrictions placed on the Youth Court regarding the imposition of a detention and training order, or length of sentence do not apply to the Crown Court where it imposes a sentence of long-term detention under PCC(S)A 2000, s 91. In *R v Jenkins-Rowe and Glover* [2000] Crim LR 1022, a 14–year-old was sentenced to long-term detention under s 91. It was argued that he was not a persistent offender for the purpose of making a detention and training order and therefore should not have received long-term detention. The Court of Appeal rejected this argument saying that the provisions relating to detention and training orders did not affect long-term detention. Thus if a defendant under 15 who is not a persistent offender is sent for trial under CDA 1998, s 51A(3)(b) because the Youth Court believes the offending deserves two years or more, the Crown Court is not restrained from passing a long-term detention sentence regardless of whether that sentence is more or less than two years. The Crown Court can impose any sentence it considers appropriate where the offence is convicted on indictment. This can include a detention and training order, and any other youth sentence with the exception of a referral order. It is arguable that the judge could also impose a referral order (where the various conditions are satisfied) by using the powers of a district judge (magistrates' court) under the Courts Act 2003, s 66. This use of s 66 has, however, been disapproved of (see *Frimpong v CPS* [2015] EWCA 1933 and *R(W) v Crown Court at Leeds* [2011] EWHC 2326). In the case of *X v R* [2012] EWCA Crim 1610 the benefits and dangers of the practice are outlined.

Committal to the Crown Court for sentence

5.29   Where a juvenile is convicted following a guilty plea (or indicated guilty plea) then the Youth Court powers to commit to the Crown Court for sentence arise where:

(a)   The offence is a specified sexual or violent offence and the dangerousness criteria are satisfied (see **5.14** (a)-(c) above) PCC(S)A 2000, s 3C. The Crown Court can then deal with the offender in any way it could have dealt with him if he had just been convicted on indictment (PCC(S)A 2000, s 5A).

(b)   The offence is a grave crime and the court is satisfied that the offence, or the combination of the offence and one or more offences associated with it are such that the Crown Court should have the power to deal with the offender as if the provisions of PCC(S)A 2000, s 91(3) (long term detention) applied (PCC(S)A 2000, s 3B). The court can take into account all associated offences when making this decision. The Crown Court can then deal with the offender in any way it could have dealt with him if he had just been convicted on indictment (PCC(S) A 2000, s 5A).

(c)   The offence is a potential grave crime and the offender has been sent to the Crown Court for trial for what the court considers to be a related offence (PCC(S) A 2000, s 4A). If the court could have committed the offence for sentence under PCCC(S)A 2000, s 3B instead then it should certify this, otherwise the Crown Court will be restricted to the powers of a magistrates' court unless the defendant is convicted on indictment of a related offence (PCC(S)A 2000, s 5A and s 4A(4) and (5)). So, even where the court has not certified that it could have committed the offence to the Crown Court under PCCC(S)A 2000, s 3B for long-term detention (s 91(3)), the Crown Court is still able to impose such detention for the offence if the defendant is convicted of a related offence which has been sent to the Crown Court for trial.

(d) The offender is committed for sentence under any of the provisions referred to above (PCC(S)A 2000, ss 3B, 3C and 4A) or for breach of a Crown Court conditional discharge. If the offence committed for sentence under any of those provisions is an indictable offence then the court can also commit any other convicted offence to the Crown Court for sentence. If that offence is summary only then any imprisonable or endorseable offences can be committed to the Crown Court for sentence (PCC(S)A 2000, s 6). The Crown Court is limited to the sentencing powers of the magistrates' court (PCC(S)A 2000, s 7). If the offence to be sentenced is an indictable only offence then a maximum custodial sentence of 6 months is provided for by PCC(S)A 2000, s 7(4).

(e) The offender is in breach of a Crown Court Youth Rehabilitation Order either for failure to comply with a requirement or by committing an offence whilst subject to the Youth Rehabilitation Order (see **11.05** and **11.06**).

Where a juvenile is convicted following a not guilty plea and trial, then the Youth Court powers to commit to the Crown Court for sentence arise where:

(a) The offence is a specified sexual or violent offence and the dangerousness criteria are satisfied (see **5.14** (a)–(c) above) PCC(S)A 2000, s 3C. The Crown Court can then deal with the offender in any way it could have dealt with him if he had just been convicted on indictment (PCC(S)A 2000, s 5A).

(b) The offence is a grave crime and the court is satisfied that the offence, or the combination of the offence and one or more offences associated with it are such that the Crown Court should have the power to deal with the offender as if the provisions of PCC(S)A 2000, s 91(3) (long-term detention) applied (PCC(S)A 2000, s 3B). The court can take into account all associated offences when making this decision. The Crown Court can then deal with the offender in any way it could have dealt with him if he had just been convicted on indictment (PCC(S) A 2000, s 5A).

(c) The offence is a potential grave crime and the offender has been sent to the Crown Court for trial for what the court considers to be a related offence (PCC(S) A 2000, s 4A). If the court could have committed the offence for sentence under PCCC(S)A 2000, s 3B instead, then it should certify this, otherwise the Crown Court will be restricted to the powers of a magistrates' court unless the defendant is convicted on indictment of a related offence (PCC(S)A 2000, s 5A and s 4A(4) and (5)). So, even where the court has not certified that it could have committed the offence to the Crown Court under PCCC(S)A 2000, s 3B for long-term detention (s 91(3)), the Crown Court is still able to impose such detention for the offence if the defendant is convicted of a related offence which has been sent to the Crown Court for trial.

(d) The offender is committed for sentence under any of the provisions referred to above (PCC(S)A 2000, ss 3B, 3C and 4A) or for breach of a Crown Court conditional discharge. If the offence committed for sentence under any of those provisions is an indictable offence then the court can also commit any other convicted offence to the Crown Court for sentence. If that offence is summary only then any imprisonable or endorseable offences can be committed to the Crown Court for sentence (PCC(S)A 2000, s 6). The Crown Court is limited to the sentencing powers of the magistrates' court (PCC(S)A 2000, s 7). If the offence to be sentenced is an indictable only offence then a maximum custodial sentence of six months is provided for by PCC(S)A 2000, s 7(4).

(e)   The offender is in breach of a Crown Court Youth Rehabilitation Order either for failure to comply with a requirement or by committing an offence whilst subject to the Youth Rehabilitation Order (see **11.05** and **11.06**).

Adult court to Crown Court

Juveniles charged with adults on indictable only offences

5.30   Where the youth is jointly charged with an adult they will appear before the adult magistrates' court in the first instance. If the adult is charged with an indictable only offence (such as robbery), he will be sent to the Crown Court for trial under CDA 1998, s 51(1) and the youth under CDA 1998, s 51(7)(b) provided the juvenile indicates a not guilty plea or no plea and the court is satisfied that it is necessary in the interests of justice to do so. This applies even if the juvenile is not jointly charged with the adult in respect of the indictable only offence, provided that he is jointly charged with an indictable offence (which term includes either way offences) which appears to be related to the indictable only offence.

If the juvenile is charged with an offence which for a youth cannot be tried summarily (such as a homicide offence) and the adult is linked only by an either way offence related to the juvenile's charge then the adult court should also send the adult to the Crown Court for trial under CDA 1998, s 51A(6). If however the adult appears on a subsequent occasion, after the juvenile has been sent, then the court has a discretion whether or not to send the case for trial in the Crown Court. If the adult is not sent then the adult plea before venue mode of trial procedures would apply to the adult. If the adult indicates a guilty plea then he can only be committed to the Crown Court for sentence if the magistrates' sentencing powers are insufficient.

Dangerous juveniles charged with adults

5.31   If the adult court determines that the juvenile is a dangerous offender and sends him to the Crown Court for trial in relation to the specified offence(s) and any related offence for which a not guilty plea or no plea has been indicated, (provided that if the related offence is a summary only that it is imprisonable or endorseable) under CDA 1998, s 51A(3)(d), then an adult who has linked either way charges may be sent for trial under s 51A(6) of that Act for those offences and for any related offences. Indeed if the adult appears before the adult court on the same occasion that the juvenile is sent then he *shall* also be sent. If the adult appears before the adult court on a subsequent occasion then he *may* be sent to the Crown Court for trial. The adult's offences qualify whether they are related to the juvenile's specified dangerous offence(s) or the adult's other sent offence(s).

Either way offences are treated as related if they could be joined in the same indictment. Summary offences are related if they arise out of circumstances which are the same as or connected with those giving rise to the indictable offence (CDA 1998, s 51E).

Juveniles charged with adults on either way offences

No 'grave crime' involved

5.32   If the offences are either way in the case of an adult, but there is not an offence in respect of the juvenile which is potentially a 'grave crime', then the mode of trial for the adult should be considered first. This will only apply where the adult, at the plea before venue stage, either refuses to intimate a plea or indicates a plea of not guilty. The criteria applied by the court are different as between the adult and the juvenile. In relation to the adult, the court will consider the Sentencing Council Guidelines and MCA 1980, ss 17A to 23. If the adult is directed to the Crown Court or elects to be dealt with by that court the magistrates then move on to consider the juvenile's case. If the juvenile indicates a not guilty plea or no plea the criterion that the court should consider is whether it is necessary in the interests of justice to send the offence to the Crown Court for trial (CDA 1998, s 51(7)).

The Sentencing Council's definitive guideline *Sentencing Children and Young People* provides at paras 2.11–2.14 that:

> 'The proper venue for the trial of any child or young person is normally the youth court. Subject to statutory restrictions, that remains the case where a child or young person is jointly charged with an adult. If the adult is sent to the Crown Court, the court should conclude that the child or young person must be tried separately in the youth court unless it is in the interests of justice for the child or young person and the adult to be tried jointly.

> Examples of factors that should be considered when deciding whether to send the child or young person to the Crown Court (rather than have a trial in the youth court) include:

> *   whether separate trials will cause injustice to witnesses or to the case as a whole (consideration should be given to the provisions of sections 27 and 28 of the Youth Justice and Criminal evidence Act 1999 – recorded evidence)

> *   the age of the child or young person; the younger ... the greater the desirability that child or young person be tried in the youth court;

- the age gap between the child or young person and the adult; a substantial gap in age militates in favour of the child or young person being tried in the youth court;

- the lack of maturity of the child or young person;

- the relative culpability of the child or young person compared with the adult and whether the alleged role played by the child or young person was minor, and/or

- the lack of previous findings of guilt on the part of the child or young person.'

The court should bear in mind that the youth court now has a general power to commit for sentence (NB only for grave crimes)... 'in appropriate cases this will permit a sentence to be imposed by the same court on adults and children and young people who have been tried separately.'

In *Re C (a minor)* (2000) *The Times*, 5 July, it was held that neither Article 3 (prohibition of inhuman or degrading treatment or punishment), nor Article 6 (right to a fair trial) precluded the committal of an 11-year-old defendant to the Crown Court under similar provision. If at plea before venue stage the adult pleads guilty then the court does not have to commit the juvenile to the Crown Court, but instead should normally take a plea from the juvenile and remit for trial or sentence.

'Grave crime' involved

5.33   However, in the case of a 'grave crime' (see below) the magistrates' court should still consider whether the charge should be sent to the Crown Court for trial as a grave crime under MCA 1980, ss 24 and 24A and PCC(S)A 2000, s 91(3). *R v Tottenham Youth Court, ex parte Fawzy* [1998] 1 All ER 365 makes it clear that in the case of an either way offence the adult court must conduct a mode of trial (allocation) hearing first before deciding whether a remittal to the Youth Court is appropriate, even when the proceedings against the adult have been discharged. If the charge is found to be one to which PCC(S)A 2000, s 91 applies then, if the powers of the adult and Youth Court respectively are insufficient, the adult if he has pleaded guilty may be committed to the Crown Court for sentence and the juvenile's case, if he has indicated a not guilty plea, be sent to the Crown Court for trial. If the juvenile has indicated a guilty plea then he may be committed to the Crown Court for sentence. If the adult does not indicate a plea or indicates a not guilty plea, the court will have to decide whether the case is more suitable for trial in the adult or Crown Court. If the adult is sent to the Crown Court for trial then the juvenile should also be sent if he has indicated a not guilty plea or no plea and it is the interests of justice to do so (CDA 1998, s 51(7)). The factors listed by the Sentencing Council (see **5.32** above) will be relevant in making that decision. An additional and preliminary consideration will be whether there is a real prospect that the juvenile will be sentenced to substantially more that two years detention if he is convicted. In view of the SC's definitive guideline *Sentencing Children and Young People* it is likely to be a rare case where this view will be reached in advance of any trial. If the court decides that the adult's offence is suitable for summary trial and he consents to being tried in a magistrates' court and pleads not guilty, then if the juvenile indicates a not guilty plea (or no plea) and after full consideration the juvenile's offence is not considered a 'grave crime' a plea should be taken and if the plea is not guilty the juvenile should be tried with the adult in the adult court (MCA 1980, s 29).

Must the adult and youth appear together?

5.34   In the old case of *R v Doncaster Crown Court, ex parte Crown Prosecution Service* [1987] Crim LR 395, it was held that when justices were considering whether it was in the interests of justice that a juvenile who was charged jointly with an adult should be sent to the Crown Court it was necessary that they both appeared before the court at the same time (but see *R v Coventry City Magistrates, ex parte M* [1992] Crim LR 810 (below)). Once that decision had been taken it was not necessary that they should appear together in subsequent committal proceedings. The facts of this case were that on 19 March 1986 the defendant, then aged 16, appeared before the Doncaster justices charged with offences of burglary together with six other defendants. His co-defendants included two juveniles and four adults. On that day the justices considered the mode of trial. They decided that the adults should go to the Crown Court and, having heard representations from both sides, decided that it was in the interests of justice for the juveniles also to be committed to the Crown Court for trial. They then adjourned for the committal proceedings to take place. On 30 April they committed all of the defendants except one juvenile who had been arrested for other offences. He was committed to the Crown Court the next day. The Crown Court judge declined to deal with the defendant who had been committed subsequently and referred his case back to the justices. The Divisional Court overturned the judge's ruling, saying that what mattered was that the juveniles and the adults should appear together at the mode of trial stage.

In the case of *R v Coventry City Magistrates, ex parte M*, it was held that a juvenile court (now Youth Court) could commit a juvenile to be tried at the Crown Court with an adult with whom he had been jointly charged pursuant to MCA 1980, s 24(1)(b) when the adult had already been committed for trial by a different bench, as it was not a requirement of the section that the adult should be before the court at the same time the juvenile was committed. In this case the juvenile was charged with aiding and abetting rape. The court considered *R v Doncaster Crown Court* but found that it was not correct to interpret that case, as saying that both juvenile and adult defendant had to appear together at the mode of trial stage.

Committal to the Crown Court for sentence

5.35   Please refer to **5.29** above for information concerning the adult court's powers to commit for sentence where a youth appears with an adult.

Note that a juvenile who appears in the adult court but is not linked with an adult may not be sent to the Crown Court for trial by the adult court nor committed by the Crown Court for sentence. The case must be remitted to the Youth Court (see **5.39** below).

Adult court to Youth Court

Juveniles charged with adults

5.36   Before an adult court can remit a juvenile (who is jointly charged with an adult) to the Youth Court the juvenile must enter a plea.

Juvenile pleading not guilty

5.37   Where an adult and youth who have linked charges are going to be tried summarily then unless the charges can properly be heard separately according to general principles, the trial should be heard in the adult court. If the adult (or all the adults) then enters a guilty plea, before any evidence is heard the juvenile may be remitted for trial to either the Youth Court for the same area or that for the area where the juvenile 'habitually resides' (MCA 1980, s 29).

If the adults are to be sent to the Crown Court but the adult court has decided that it is not in the interests of justice for the juvenile also be tried in the Crown Court, or it is not possible for the youth's case to be tried at the Crown Court then before any evidence is heard the adult court may remit the juvenile for trial to either the Youth Court for the same area or that for the area where the juvenile 'habitually resides' (MCA 1980, s 29).

Juvenile pleading guilty

5.38   Where an adult and youth who have linked charges are going to be tried summarily, then if the juvenile pleads guilty in the adult court he should be remitted for sentence to the Youth Court acting for the same area or the area where the juvenile 'habitually resides' (PCC(S)A 2000, s 8). The adult court can only impose sentence itself if a discharge, fine or mandatory referral order is appropriate (it can also impose a parental bind over) (PCC(S)A 2000, s 8(6) to (8)).

Juveniles not charged with adults

5.39   The adult court may simply remand the juvenile to the Youth Court. In practice this is likely to be to a Youth Court for the same area but this is not required by the Children and Young Persons Act 1933, s 46. In practice the court may be able to reconstitute itself as a Youth Court if a District Judge with youth authorisation is sitting or there is at least one Youth Court magistrate sitting. The power to send a youth for trial can be exercised by a single (Youth Court) magistrate (CDA 1998, ss 51(13) and 51A(11).

From the Crown Court to the Adult or Youth Court for trial

5.40   The Crown Court cannot remit a juvenile who has already been arraigned to a magistrates' court for trial where the adult co-defendants have pleaded guilty.

This is the case even if the offence is not a grave crime and the only reason why the juvenile was committed to the Crown Court is to be tried with an adult under section 24(1)(b) of the Magistrates' Courts Act 1980. The only option is for the Crown Court to hear the trial (*R on the application of W) (a minor) v Leeds Crown Court* [2011] EWHC 2326 (Admin). Where the juvenile has not been arraigned by the Crown Court then it is possible to remit him or her back to the (Adult or) Youth Court for trial. CDA 1998, Sch 3, para 13 provides, that where for any reason such as amendment the juvenile is not charged on the indictment with an offence which can only be tried at the Crown Court, that he or she should be remitted back to a Magistrates' Court for trial unless either (i) the juvenile is charged with a grave crime and a sentence of long-term detention is a possibility or (ii) the juvenile is charged jointly with an adult, with an offence triable either way and the Crown Court considers it necessary in the interests of justice that they both be tried for the offence in the Crown Court. If, for example, the case against the adult is withdrawn then this provision would allow the juvenile to be remitted to the Youth Court for trial, subject to the proviso that the juvenile has not been arraigned.

Where the juvenile has appealed to the Crown Court, that court may refer the case back to the Youth Court with directions. This might include where a guilty plea is considered equivocal by the Crown Court.

From the Crown Court or the Adult Court to the Youth Court for sentence

5.41   Where any court finds a juvenile guilty of an offence other than homicide, it may (and if not a Youth Court shall) remit the case to a Youth Court where the offender habitually resides (or if he had been committed or sent for trial to a Youth Court for the same area as the committing/sending court, unless it is undesirable to do so. The receiving Youth Court may then deal with him in any way in which it might have dealt with him if he had been tried and found guilty by that court. The court remitting the juvenile is empowered to bail the juvenile or remand him in custody. It must send a certificate to the clerk of the receiving Youth Court setting out the nature of the offence, and stating that the offender has been found guilty and has been remitted for the purpose of being dealt with (PCC(S)A 2000, s 8).

In *R v Allen and Lambert* [1999] All ER (D) 654, the defendants had been committed to the Crown Court on charges of arson, burglary and attempted burglary under the 'grave crimes' provisions. The arson charge was dismissed and guilty pleas entered to the burglary charges, which were then remitted by the Crown Court to the Youth Court for sentence. The Youth Court then purported to commit back to the Crown Court for sentence on all matters. On appeal, it was held that the power of remittal gives the Youth Court authority to deal with the defendant in any way that it might have dealt with him having been tried and found guilty by that court. This included committal for sentence (when available) but not committal for trial. It was also said that where justices found offences to be grave crimes and committed them to the Crown Court it was undesirable for the Crown Court to exercise its power to remit to the Youth Court for sentence. This judgment follows the judgment in *R v Lewis* (1984) 79 Cr App R 94.

The SC's definitive guideline *Sentencing Children and Young People* provides that in considering whether the Crown Court should remit the juvenile to the Youth Court for sentence, it should balance the needs for expertise in the sentencing of young offenders with the benefits of sentence being imposed by the court which had determined guilt. The guideline also states that particular attention should be given to children and young people who are appearing before the Crown Court only because they have been charged with an adult offender; referral orders are generally not available in the Crown Court but may be the most appropriate sentence.

Where a serious sexual offence is remitted for sentence from the Crown Court to the Youth Court it must be listed before a District Judge (Magistrates' Courts) authorised to hear such cases. (See **Appendix M** for the 'Sexual Offences in the Youth Court' Protocol issued by the Senior Presiding Judge with effect from 31 March 2010 which is now subsumed into Annex 2 of the Criminal Practice Direction Part XIII).

Where any case is remitted, the offender has the same right of appeal against any order of the court to which the case is remitted as if he had been found guilty by that court, but has no right of appeal against the order of remission.

Between Youth Courts

Before conviction

5.42   There may be power under MCA 1980, s 27A to transfer a juvenile to any other Youth Court in England and Wales. That section allows transfer of cases between magistrates' courts at any stage before conviction. Subsection (4) states that 'The power of the court under this section to transfer any matter must be exercised in accordance with any directions given under s 30(3) of the Courts Act 2003'.

It may be noted that although magistrates are assigned to a Youth Court panel for an area, there are no geographical restrictions on where offences may be heard, following the introduction of the Courts Act 2003.

After conviction

5.43   There is a clear and accepted statutory power for a Youth Court to remit a juvenile for sentence to the area where he 'habitually resides'. There is no obligation on a Youth Court to remit a juvenile to his 'home court', however it can make for a better informed decision and make it easier for him to attend (PCC(S)A 2000, s 8(2)). The court to which the juvenile is remitted for sentence may allow a change of plea from guilty to not guilty (*R v Stratford Youth Court, ex parte Conde* [1997] 1 WLR 113). It is doubted whether there is power to remit back to the original court that remitted for sentence.

Venue decisions in the Youth Court

5.44

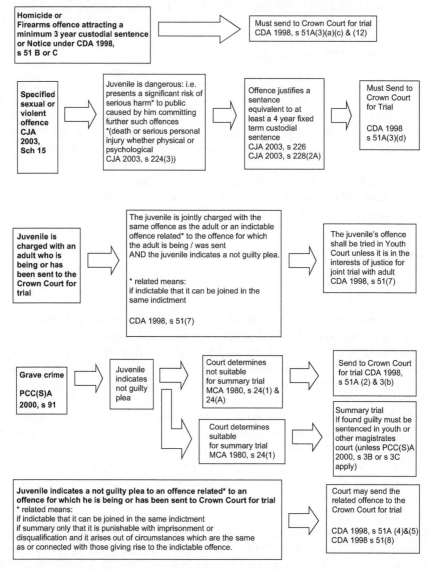

ALLOCATION TO CROWN COURT OF OFFENCES ALLEGED AGAINST JUVENILES

Homicide or Firearms offence attracting a minimum 3 year custodial sentence or Notice under CDA 1998, s 51 B or C	Must send to Crown Court for trial CDA 1998, s 51A(3)(a)(c) & (12)

Specified sexual or violent offence CJA 2003, Sch 15 → Juvenile is dangerous: i.e. presents a significant risk of serious harm* to public caused by him committing further such offences *(death or serious personal injury whether physical or psychological CJA 2003, s 224(3)) → Offence justifies a sentence equivalent to at least a 4 year fixed term custodial sentence CJA 2003, s 226 CJA 2003, s 228(2A) → Must Send to Crown Court for Trial CDA 1998 s 51A(3)(d)

Juvenile is charged with an adult who is being or has been sent to the Crown Court for trial → The juvenile is jointly charged with the same offence as the adult or an indictable offence related* to the offence for which the adult is being / was sent AND the juvenile indicates a not guilty plea. * related means: if indictable that it can be joined in the same indictment CDA 1998, s 51(7) → The juvenile's offence shall be tried in Youth Court unless it is in the interests of justice for joint trial with adult CDA 1998, s 51(7)

Grave crime PCC(S)A 2000, s 91 → Juvenile indicates not guilty plea →
- Court determines not suitable for summary trial MCA 1980, s 24(1) & 24(A) → Send to Crown Court for trial CDA 1998, s 51A (2) & 3(b)
- Court determines suitable for summary trial MCA 1980, s 24(1) → Summary trial If found guilty must be sentenced in youth or other magistrates court (unless PCC(S)A 2000, s 3B or s 3C apply)

Juvenile indicates a not guilty plea to an offence related* to an offence for which he is being or has been sent to Crown Court for trial * related means: if indictable that it can be joined in the same indictment if summary only that it is punishable with imprisonment or disqualification and it arises out of circumstances which are the same as or connected with those giving rise to the indictable offence. → Court may send the related offence to the Crown Court for trial CDA 1998, s 51A (4)&(5) CDA 1998 s 51(8)

COMMITTALS OF JUVENILES TO THE CROWN COURT FOR SENTENCE

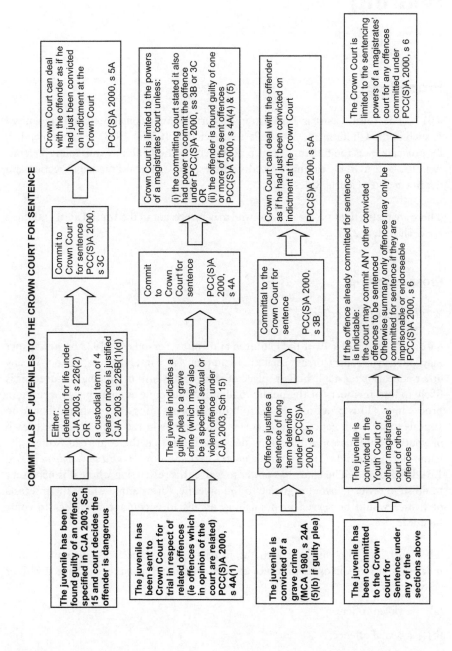

The juvenile has been found guilty of an offence specified in CJA 2003, Sch 15 and court decides the offender is dangerous

Either:
detention for life under CJA 2003, s 226(2)
OR
a custodial term of 4 years or more is justified CJA 2003, s 226B(1)(d)

Commit to Crown Court for sentence PCC(S)A 2000, s 3C

Crown Court can deal with the offender as if he had just been convicted on indictment at the Crown Court

PCC(S)A 2000, s 5A

The juvenile has been sent to Crown Court for trial in respect of related offences (ie offences which in opinion of the court are related) PCC(S)A 2000, s 4A(1)

The juvenile indicates a guilty plea to a grave crime (which may also be a specified sexual or violent offence under CJA 2003, Sch 15)

Commit to Crown Court for sentence

PCC(S)A 2000, s 4A

Crown Court is limited to the powers of a magistrates' court unless:

(i) the committing court stated it also had power to commit the offence under PCC(S)A 2000, ss 3B or 3C
OR
(ii) the offender is found guilty of one or more of the sent offences PCC(S)A 2000, s 4A(4) & (5)

The juvenile is convicted of a grave crime (MCA 1980, s 24A (5)(b) if guilty plea)

Offence justifies a sentence of long term detention under PCC(S)A 2000, s 91

Committal to the Crown Court for sentence

PCC(S)A 2000, s 3B

Crown Court can deal with the offender as if he had just been convicted on indictment at the Crown Court

PCC(S)A 2000, s 5A

The juvenile has been committed to the Crown court for Sentence under any of the sections above

The juvenile is convicted in the Youth Court or other magistrates' court of other offences

If the offence already committed for sentence is indictable:
the court may commit ANY other convicted offences to be sentenced
Otherwise summary only offences may only be committed for sentence if they are imprisonable or endorseable PCC(S)A 2000, s 6

The Crown Court is limited to the sentencing powers of a magistrates' court for any offences committed under PCC(S)A 2000, s 6

Chapter 6   The Youth Court hearing

Procedure

6.01   The Youth Court is a magistrates' court specially constituted and recognised as such in the Children and Young Persons Act 1933 (CYPA 1933), s 45 as amended. Its procedures at the hearing are also governed by the Children and Young Persons Act 1933 and by the Criminal Procedure Rules, the Criminal Practice Direction and the Magistrates Courts Rules 1981.

There are restrictions on the persons who may be present in the Youth Court and these are dealt with at **2.07**.

Press reporting

Youth Court proceedings

6.02   By virtue of s 49 of the Children and Young Persons Act 1933 no newspaper may publish a report of any matter, including the name, address, school or any other educational establishment, place of work or any still or moving picture if it is likely to lead members of the public to identify a juvenile as someone concerned in proceedings. This provision relates to criminal proceedings in youth courts and to appeals from youth courts. It also covers proceedings in the adult court for breach of youth rehabilitation orders. This does not mean that the court can protect the name of a dead child: *R v Central Criminal Court, ex parte Crook and Goodwin* [1995] 1 All ER 537, CA. The court has power to waive this restriction where it is necessary to do so in order to avoid injustice to the juvenile, for example where the interests of justice would be served in publishing details to encourage witnesses to come forward.

The court may also dispense with the restrictions in respect of a juvenile who is unlawfully at large, in order to secure his apprehension if he has been charged with or convicted of:

(a)   a violent offence;

(b)   a sexual offence;

(c)   an offence punishable with 14 years' imprisonment or more in the case of a person aged 21 or over.

The power may be exercised by a single justice, but only on the application of the DPP and only after notice has been given to any legal representative of the juvenile (CYPA 1933, s 49(8)).

Additionally, the court may of its own motion dispense with all or part of the restrictions applying to a juvenile who has been convicted of an offence if it is satisfied it is in the public interest to do so (CYPA 1933, s 49(4A)). The court may not exercise this power without affording the parties an opportunity to make representations. In *McKerry v Teesside and Wear Valley Justices* [2000] All ER (D) 140, Bingham LJ said that the court had to be satisfied that it was in the public interest to dispense with reporting restrictions and that would very rarely be the case.

Other criminal proceedings

6.03   An adult magistrates' court or Crown Court dealing with a juvenile or before whom a juvenile witness appears may make an order in proceedings under YJCE 1999, s 45. This restricts the press as if the court were a Youth Court. If this is done, the chairman of the court should make an announcement in open court so that the restriction may be made effective. It is important that the direction is framed carefully to ensure that it does not have a broader effect than intended or justified. If no warning is given the press are free to publish such details as they wish. Article 10 of the European Convention guarantees the right to freedom of expression. However, the article also recognises that such a freedom carries with it duties and responsibilities, which may be subject to restrictions or penalties prescribed by law and necessary in a democratic society among other things for the protection of the rights of others. In this instance the other rights to be balanced are the juvenile's right to private and family life and possibly the rights of the victim or victims who may not welcome publicity. Additional factors highlighted for consideration in *McKerry* were the importance of the principle that justice should be administered in public, that great weight is given to the welfare of youths in court proceedings and on no account should publicity be used as a punishment. However, when a juvenile attains the age of 18 reporting restrictions will cease.

Unlike CYPA 1933, s 49 where the restriction is automatic, an order under YJCE 1999, s 45 may only be imposed where there is good reason. A member of the press who is aggrieved by the making of a s 45 order should go back to the court which made the order if the media were not afforded the opportunity to make representations or there has been a material change in circumstances. Alternatively, a defendant or the press may make an appeal against the order (or the withholding or discharging of the order) by proceedings for judicial review in the Divisional Court (*R v Lee* [1993] 1 WLR 103, CA).

In England and Wales there are no automatic restrictions on the publication of a juvenile's details during the investigation of an offence. Section 44 of the Youth Justice and Criminal Evidence Act 1999 is not in force. Section 46 of that Act has been implemented so that a court can prohibit the identification of an adult witness where this would improve the quality of the witness's evidence or encourage that witness to give evidence in a situation where the witness fears publicity connecting him or her with the case. Section 45A now provides the same option in respect of juvenile witnesses. Both ss 46 and 45A allow the witness lifelong anonymity in respect of their involvement as a witness. Neither sections extend that protection to a defendant. Section 49 makes it an offence to publish a report of the proceedings which contravenes the press direction. Liability is limited to editors, proprietors and publishers (*Aitken v DPP* [2015] EWHC 1079 (Admin). Section 50 provides statutory defences.

Civil and family courts

6.04   Section 39 of the Children and Young Persons Act 1933 continues to be available in civil and family courts. It also can be used in connection with anti-social behaviour injunction and criminal behaviour order proceedings. Any direction made under s 39 will not last beyond the juvenile concerned attaining 18 years of age (*DPP v Todd* [2003] EWHC 240 (Admin)). The section has been extended to cover online publications as well as other media. Any person who publishes any matter in contravention of s 39 shall, on summary conviction, be liable on each offence to a fine not exceeding level 5. Anyone who publishes can be liable. There are no statutory defences included in the CYPA 1933.

Trial in the Youth Court

Criminal proceedings

6.05   The proceedings begin with the court, usually through its legal adviser, identifying the juvenile, ascertaining his age and whether or not a parent accompanies him. A parent or guardian of a juvenile under the age of 16 years is required to be in court. A parent of 16- and 17-year-old youths may be required to attend (CYPA 1933, s 34A). The charge and the nature of the proceedings are then explained to the child or young person in simple language suitable to his age and understanding (CPR 2015, r 24.2). These Rules are reproduced at **Appendix C**.

For example, a charge of theft involving an appropriation and a dishonest intention permanently to deprive the owner of the property might be explained to a 14-year-old thus: 'The police say you stole a pedal cycle, that means that it did not belong to you, that you were going to keep it as your own, and you knew that it was wrong to do that. Do you understand?'

In the case of *R v Blandford Justices, ex parte G (infant)* [1967] 1 QB 82, which involved a 15-year-old charged with the theft of jewellery, it was said that although it would be good sense and desirable to ensure that the legal elements of the charge are explained, the rule does not impose a duty on the court to give a detailed or elaborate explanation of the legal constituents of the charge.

If the court is satisfied that the juvenile understands the charge he should be asked if he pleads guilty or not guilty to the charge. Every effort should be made to ensure that the plea entered by a juvenile is unqualified. In *R v Blandford Justices*, above, the plea entered before the magistrates was equivocal, that is to say the juvenile admitted the offence and then went on to say she intended to replace the jewellery. The court failed to take the proper course of entering a 'not guilty' plea on the juvenile's behalf on hearing the evidence. The conviction was subsequently quashed in the High Court.

Not guilty trial

6.06   Sometimes a magistrate may know a witness or the defendant in some way. It will depend on the nature and extent of that knowledge whether it is appropriate for the magistrate to hear the trial. In the case of *R (on the application of B) v Wolverhampton Youth Court* [2009] All ER (D) 149 (Oct), the court chairman was a teacher at a school which the 15-year-old defendant had attended. She recognised the boy's name but had never taught or had any dealings with him personally. The Divisional Court held that the fair-minded and informed observer would not have concluded that there was a real possibility that the chairman of the court had been biased. Where a not guilty plea is entered, this will involve the witnesses being called to give evidence. On the basis of that evidence the magistrates must decide if the case has been proved beyond reasonable doubt.

If the juvenile fails to attend his trial the court may proceed in the absence of the accused but shall not do so if it considers that there is an acceptable reason for his failure to appear (MCA 1980, s 11 as amended by CJIA 2008, s 54). See also CPR 2015, r 24.12 which states that the general rule that a court should proceed as if the defendant were present does not apply to a juvenile.

The juvenile must be able to participate effectively in the trial and therefore the trial must be conducted in a manner which makes allowance for the juvenile's age, level of maturity and intellectual and emotional capabilities. In *R (on the application of TP) v West London Youth Court* [2005] EWHC 2583 (Admin), it was held that the trial of a juvenile, who was aged 15 but had the mental age of eight, did not necessarily involve a breach of Article 6 as steps could be taken during the trial to ensure participation and fairness. These steps will include the use of concise and simple language, regular breaks, explanation of the proceedings and possible outcomes. After each prosecution witness has given his evidence in chief, the defence solicitor is given the opportunity to cross-examine. If the juvenile is unrepresented, the court may assist. If the juvenile makes assertions such as 'I did this' or, 'he did that', the court shall then put to the witness such questions as it thinks necessary on behalf of the juvenile. It may, for this purpose, question the juvenile in order to bring out or clear up any point arising from any such assertion. This is a function which may be carried out by an experienced chairman, but it may be delegated to the legal adviser, thus avoiding the justices entering the arena (CPR 2015, r 24.15). In *Simms v Moore* [1970] 3 All ER 1, a case in which the legal adviser assisted an unrepresented party in examination of witnesses, Lord Parker CJ said:

> 'Where, however, the unrepresented party, whoever he may be, is not competent, through a lack of knowledge of court procedure or rules of evidence or otherwise, to examine the witnesses properly, the court can at its discretion permit the clerk [*sic*] to do so. Fortunately, this is a relatively rare occurrence as most juveniles will be represented in a not guilty trial.'

This is now embodied in the Criminal Practice Directions 2015 Division VI 24A: 'Role of the justices' clerk/legal adviser. Indeed, it is the duty of the legal adviser to assist unrepresented defendants (CPR 2015, r 24.3 and 24.15).

At the conclusion of the prosecution case the magistrates must decide whether or not the prosecution has made out a prima facie case which the juvenile should be called on to answer. The High Court has provided guidance as to the circumstances in which the court may rule there is no case to answer:

> 'How then should the judge approach a submission of "no case"? If there is no evidence that the crime alleged has been committed by the defendant, there is no difficulty. The judge will of course stop the case. The difficulty arises where there is some evidence but it is of a tenuous character, for example because of inherent weakness or vagueness or because it is inconsistent with other evidence. (a) Where the judge comes to the conclusion that the Crown's evidence, taken at its highest, is such that a jury properly directed could not properly convict on it, it is his duty, on a submission being made, to stop the case. (b) Where however the Crown's evidence is such that its strength or weakness depends on the view to be taken of a witness's reliability, or other matters which are generally speaking within the province of the jury and where on one possible view of the facts there *is* evidence on which a jury could properly come to the conclusion that the defendant is guilty, then the judge should allow the matter to be tried by the jury.' (*R v Galbraith* [1981] 2 All ER 1060, CA, per Lord Lane).

Although revoked, a former Practice Note remains good advice to magistrates, namely that, apart from these two situations (above) a tribunal should not in general be called on to reach a decision as to conviction or acquittal until the whole of the evidence which either side wishes to tender has been placed before it. If, however, a submission is made that there is no case to answer, the decision should depend not so much on whether the adjudicating tribunal (if compelled to do so) would at that stage convict or acquit but on whether the evidence is such that a reasonable tribunal might convict. If a reasonable tribunal might convict on the evidence so far laid before it, there is a case to answer (per Lord Parker CJ, *Practice Note* [1962] 1 All ER 448).

The court may of its own motion find that there is no case for the juvenile to answer. However, it is more common for a juvenile's solicitor to make a submission of no case to answer, and where this is done the prosecution should be afforded an opportunity to reply to the submission (*R v Barking and Dagenham Justices, ex parte DPP* [1995] Crim LR 953). (See also CPR 2015, r 24.3(3)(c)). Occasionally, a juvenile may ask to change his plea from guilty to not guilty. In such circumstances the court has discretion to exercise. This discretion must be exercised reasonably, taking account of the circumstances of the case and the legal advice received by the juvenile (*R (on the application of S) v Sheffield Youth Court* [2000] All ER (D) 2373). The Criminal Procedure Rules 2015 (r 24.10) require any application to change a plea of guilty to be in writing and sets out the information required for the application.

Where the court finds that there is a case to answer the juvenile must be told that he may address the court or that he may give evidence (CPR 2015, r 24.3(e)). The juvenile and his parents should be told that he has the right to remain silent or to give sworn evidence, and to call any witnesses they may have. The juvenile and his parent should also be told that if he refuses to answer any questions the court may draw such inferences as appear proper from his failure (Criminal Justice and Police Order Act 1994 (CJPOA 1994), s 35). The choice and its effect should be explained in clear and simple language. This section does not prevent a defendant from addressing the court on the admissibility of evidence, making a submission of no case to answer or making a closing speech. Prior to the defendant making a closing speech the prosecutor may make final representations in support of the prosecution case, but only where the defendant is represented by a legal representative, or where he has introduced evidence other than his own (CPR 2015, r 24.3).

The onus is on the prosecution to prove its case beyond reasonable doubt, not for the defendant to prove his innocence. A conviction may never be reached on the basis of inferences from silence alone (CJPOA 1994, s 38(3)).

Whether the juvenile gives evidence or not, he may call witnesses to assist his defence and, if he is not represented, and has difficulty framing questions, the court should assist him by putting relevant questions to the witness. This function might properly be assigned to the legal adviser provided that care is exercised to avoid an appearance that the legal adviser is acting as an advocate for the juvenile. The criminal procedure rules state that a justices' legal adviser or the court may (a) ask a witness questions; and in particular (b) where the defendant is not represented, ask any question necessary in the defendant's interests (CPR 2015, r 24.4(6)). The Criminal Practice Direction at division VI part 24A.16 provides that a legal adviser is under a duty to assist unrepresented parties, whether defendants or not, to present their case, but must do so without appearing to become an advocate for the party concerned. The legal adviser should also ensure that members of the court are aware of obligations under the Victims' Code. At part 24A.13 the Practice Direction states that a justices' clerk or legal adviser may ask questions of witnesses and the parties in order to clarify the evidence and any issues in the case. A legal adviser has a duty to ensure that every case is conducted justly. The case of *Hobby v Hobby* [1954] 2 All ER 395, is the case where the parties are represented. Despite the age of the case, and an increasingly active role in case management required of Justices and Magistrates' court legal advisers, the words of Sachs J continue to apply:

> 'Both parties were represented at the trial by solicitors. Accordingly, neither of them was in need of assistance as to how to present the case to court. Both parties were entitled, within the limits of relevancy and reasonableness, so to conduct their case as seemed best to their legal representatives in court. In those circumstances a justices' clerk is no more entitled to step into the arena and conduct a litigant's case for him than is a justice himself. Indeed, it is important in the interests of justice that the clerk should not give even the appearance of seeking himself to conduct the case of either party or to limit the way in which that case is conducted.'

The magistrates hearing the trial will follow a structured decision-making approach to reach their decision and will need to give sufficient reasons to explain their decision (CPD VI 24A.5). The Justices' Clerks' Society in June 2012 issued guidance on 'Magistrates Returning to Sentence following Conviction after a Trial'. They said that where the juvenile has been convicted after trial and the case is adjourned for the preparation of a pre-sentence report, the magistrates need not return to sentence if the trial was uncomplicated, did not involve making significant findings of fact and the information on the verdict form is sufficient to enable a differently constituted court to properly sentence the juvenile. However, where the magistrates have made significant findings of fact it will be appropriate for the convicting magistrates to return to sentence if the case is adjourned. In such a scenario, the sentencing court should only be composed of those magistrates who heard the evidence and who made the findings. If a single member of the convicting bench were to return to sentence, that magistrate would be joined by others who had not heard the evidence. This could result in the single magistrate having a disproportionate influence on the decision. Therefore the JCS Guidance makes it clear that unless two magistrates of the convicting bench can return to sentence at a resumed hearing, then no magistrate should return and a differently constituted bench should sentence on the basis of the findings made by the convicting court.

Procedure after a finding of guilt

6.07   Where the juvenile admits the charge or he is found guilty, a number of procedural points should be borne in mind:

(a)   Before the court passes sentence it must give the defendant an opportunity to make representations and introduce evidence relevant to sentence, and where the defendant is under 18, give the juvenile's parents, guardian or other supporting adult, if present, such an opportunity as well; and the justices' legal adviser or the court must elicit any further information relevant to sentence that the court may require.

It is of importance that the juvenile and the parent be made aware that the court is prepared to hear them while still observing the propriety of affording the advocate his proper role. Many functions may be delegated to the legal adviser but it is preferable that the chairman conducts communication with the juvenile and his parents, after a finding of guilt. It is worth noting that legal representatives speak on behalf of the juvenile and not the parents. Nevertheless, the court should attempt to engage with the young person in an attempt to address his attitude to offending and the consequences of his offending behaviour.

Effective communication at this level is an art requiring considerable skill and clarity of expression.

(b)   The court shall take into consideration information as to the juvenile's general conduct. This may include previous findings of guilt and warnings, reprimands or conditional cautions previously administered by the police.

Where previous findings of guilt are to be placed before the court they should be shown to and agreed by the juvenile and his parent or guardian. The juvenile's legal representative may indicate the acceptance of previous findings of guilt.

Where previous findings of guilt are disputed then they must be proved by the prosecution either by producing the court register or an extract thereof certified by the court to be a true extract, or by producing a record of the previous findings and by proving the identity of the offender to be the same as that of the person appearing in the antecedent record to have been found guilty.

(c)   The court shall also consider information as to home surroundings, school record and medical history of the juvenile such as is necessary to deal with the case in his best interests. This refers particularly to reports provided by the Youth Offending Team (YOT). Legally the school and the probation service or the local authority social services department have a duty to supply information under CYPA 1969, s 9. It is now usual for most of the relevant information to be contained in a pre-sentence report prepared by the YOT.

Pre-sentence reports

6.08   A pre-sentence report (PSR) means a report in writing which contains information as to such matters prescribed by rules and prepared with a view to assisting the court in determining the most suitable method of dealing with an offender (CJA 2003, s 158). National Standards provided by the Youth Justice Board require reports to be prepared within the timescales set by the court.

A juvenile will require a different approach from that which would be adopted in relation to an adult and the maturity of a juvenile will be at least as important as the chronological age. The court will need to assess the culpability of the juvenile and the harm caused (intended or foreseeable) taking into account the aggravating and mitigating factors in relation to the offence. Once the court has determined the threshold (ie the most serious penalty that can be imposed for the offence), it will then need to go on to consider any mitigating factors that apply to the juvenile. If the Youth Offending Team does not have sufficient information about the defendant to assist the court, the court may decide to adjourn the case to obtain a pre-sentence report.

Before preparing a report the YOT will complete an ASSET Plus assessment report. This process will help the YOT officer assess the risk of re-offending and any risk of serious harm. Those assessments will be reviewed by the YOT in the context of all other available information and the report will identify a level of intervention according to the Scaled Approach. This sets out three intervention levels: a standard level, for those who show a low likelihood of re-offending or a low risk of serious harm; or enhanced level, for those who show a medium likelihood of re-offending or a medium risk of serious harm; or intensive level, for those with a high likelihood of re-offending or a very high/high risk of serious harm. This approach will enable the writer of the pre-sentence report to make proposals that match the obligations on the court to balance the various factors involved. (See also **9.04**)

A written pre-sentence report must contain standard headings: sources of information; offence analysis (including what is known about the impact of the offence on any victim); offender assessment (including the offender's awareness of the consequences of his offending upon himself, his family and any victim); assessment of risk to the community (which should include the risk of re-offending (see above)). The need for any parenting support should also be identified. Finally, the report should have a conclusion with proposals. The nature of any suggested requirements should be given. The level of any intervention and supervision envisaged under the Scaled Approach should be made clear so that both the magistrates and offender are clear about what is planned should the recommendation be accepted. The report writer should have particular regard to the individual's maturity and consider which sentence available to the Youth Court is most suitable for the offender.

Not all sentences require a full risk assessment and a full PSR. A specific sentence report can be prepared quickly for less serious offending where the court has indicated a disposal such as a reparation order (see **8.09**). The Powers of Criminal Courts (Sentencing) Act 2000 (PCC(S)A 2000), s 73(5) provides that before making a reparation order the court shall obtain and consider a written report indicating the type of work that is suitable and the attitudes of the victim(s) to the requirements proposed as part of the reparation.

A court may receive an oral pre-sentence report except when the court is considering a reparation order or a youth rehabilitation order with either intensive supervision and surveillance or fostering, or a custodial sentence, in which case it must be in writing: CJA 2003, s 158(1A) and (1B). Where custody is not being considered, the use of stand down reports (verbal or written) is encouraged by YJB to achieve a prompt conclusion to the proceedings, where a recent ASSET report is available (ie no more than three months old) and any other relevant information or reports are to hand.

In criminal cases the court shall arrange for copies of any written report before the court to be made available to:

(a)   the juvenile or his legal representative, if any;

(b)   any parent or guardian of the relevant minor who is present at the hearing; and

(c)   the prosecutor, who has conduct of the proceedings in respect of the offence (CJA 2003, s 159).

In *R v Kirkham* [1968] Crim LR 210, the Court of Appeal stated that reports should be received by the court before any statement in mitigation. The case is as relevant to the Youth Court as to adult courts, and the practice has advantages in that it precludes the necessity for the advocate to go into detail about home background, schooling or personal factors as these should be dealt with fully in the pre-sentence reports.

CPR 2015, r 24.11(7) provides that before the court passes sentence it must give the defendant an opportunity to make representations and introduce evidence relevant to sentence, and where the defendant is under 18, give the juvenile's parents, guardian or other supporting adult (if present) such an opportunity as well. The justices' legal adviser or the court must elicit any further information relevant to sentence that the court may require.

The court should no longer give an indication of sentence when requesting a PSR as per the Senior Presiding Judge's guidelines. These guidelines were introduced in light of the decisions in cases such as *R v Jones* [2007] EWCA Crim 1956, *Nicholas v Chester Magistrates' Courts* [2009] EWHC 1504 (Admin) and *Thornton v Crown Prosecution Service* [2010] EWHC 346 (Admin) all of which deal with the issue of legitimate expectation as to sentence. In *R v Jones* [2007] the judge ordered an all options report but appeared to favour a community sentence. The case returned before a different judge, who imposed a DTO despite a favourable report. The Appeal Court substituted a 12-month community order on the basis that the first judge indicated that a community sentence would be imposed if there was a favourable report, which gave the offender reason to suppose that he would be dealt with in that way. In *Nicholas v Chester Magistrates' Courts* [2010] the practice of one bench giving a sentencing indication before adjourning the case to another date and not reserving sentence to itself was deprecated. A similar view was taken in *R (on the application of C) v Stratford Magistrates' Courts* [2012] All ER (D) 87 (Jan). In this case it was held that despite the magistrates having given a clear indication that a non custodial sentence was appropriate, the district judge had been entitled to disregard the indication on the grounds that it was perverse. The Appeal Court based their decision on the fact that if the magistrates had followed the guidelines they could not have ruled out custody, even for a 16-year-old. In *Thornton v Crown Prosecution Service* [2009] it was held that the sentencing court was not bound by the indication given by the previous bench because the magistrates had clearly not followed the guidelines properly and therefore there could be no legitimate expectation by the defendant that a non-custodial sentence would be imposed. In light of these constant issues it was decided by the Senior Presiding Judge that the courts should no longer give sentencing indications.

The court has a duty to give reasons for the sentence and explain the effect of the sentence (CJA 2003, s 174). The court must identify any definitive sentencing guidelines relevant to the juvenile's case and where the court does not follow any such guidelines because it is of the opinion that it would contrary to the interests of justice to do so, it must state why it is of that opinion.

The court on passing sentence will have to give credit for a guilty plea where appropriate (see **6.09** below). On making any order, the court shall, in simple language, suitable to his age and understanding, explain to the juvenile the general nature and effect of the order unless it appears to it impracticable so to do having regard to his age and understanding and shall give such an explanation to the offender's parent or guardian, if present (CJA 2003, s 144).

Credit for guilty plea

6.09   CJA 2003, s 144 provides that, in determining what sentence to pass on a juvenile who has pleaded guilty to an offence, the court must take into account the stage in the proceedings at which the plea was entered and the circumstances in which the plea was given. The purpose of giving credit is to encourage those who are guilty to plead at the earliest opportunity, which avoids the need for a trial thereby saving victims and witnesses from having to give evidence and saves considerable cost. The Sentencing Council's definitive guideline, *Sentencing Children and Young People*, sets out the position in some depth at s 5. It notes that a further benefit of an early guilty plea is that this normally reduces the impact on victims. At the same time it is made clear that the purpose of the guidance is to encourage those who are going to plead guilty to do so as early as possible in the process and that nothing in the guidance should be used to put pressure on a child or young person to plead guilty. The greatest credit is to be given to those who plead guilty at the earliest possible stage. It is notable that factors such as admissions in interview, co-operation with the investigation and demonstrations of remorse should not be taken into consideration as part of the reduction for a guilty plea but should be considered separately as potential mitigating factors, prior to any guilty plea reduction. Guilty plea credit should only be applied to punitive elements of a sentence and not to any ancillary orders, including disqualification from driving.

The amount of the reduction for a guilty plea depends on the stage in the proceedings when it is entered. At the first stage a reduction of one-third should be given. The first stage is the first hearing in the adult/youth court where a plea is sought. A guilty plea indicated after the first stage will attract a reduction of a quarter with a sliding scale to a maximum of 10% where the plea is given on the first day of a trial – and reduced further, even to zero if the plea comes during the course of the trial.

There are exceptions where the normal rules are adjusted. If the case has been adjourned for a juvenile to receive assistance or advice before indicating a plea then they may still be allowed full credit if it was unreasonable to expect them to enter the plea sooner than was done. Here a distinction is drawn between cases where advice/sight of the evidence was necessary to help understand whether they are in fact guilty of the offence charged. In those cases the credit should be given. In contrast where the juvenile has delayed guilty pleas in order to assess the strength of the prosecution evidence and the prospects of a finding of guilt then the court will not allow full credit.

The strength of the evidence should not be taken into account when determining the level of the reduction for a guilty plea. The fact that the juvenile was caught in the act of committing the offence cannot prevent them from receiving a one-third reduction if they plead guilty at the first hearing.

In Newton hearings and special reasons hearings there is a guilty plea but the court is required to decide between the prosecution and the defence version of events. If the defence version is rejected then the guilty plea credit should normally be halved. Where witnesses were called in the hearing the reduction in sentence due to the qualified guilty plea may even less than half that otherwise due.

If a juvenile is found guilty of a lesser offence to which they had earlier indicated an unequivocal plea the court should give the level of reduction appropriate to the stage at which that indication was given.

When a detention and training order (DTO) is to be imposed and the reduction for a guilty plea places the length of the provisional sentence in between two of the prescribed periods for DTOs (4, 6, 8, 12, 18, 24 months) the court must impose the lesser of those terms. This may result in a reduction of greater than one third but that is necessary to ensure that the full reduction is given and a lawful sentence imposed. This could mean, for example, that where a court is considering a 24-month DTO and full guilty plea credit of one third is due, that the sentence after reduction for a guilty plea would be 16 months (one third of 24 is 8, 24 minus 8 is 16). This period of 16 months falls between the prescribed DTO lengths of 12 months and 18 months. The court would therefore have to impose a DTO of 12 months. The Youth Court can still impose the maximum 24-month DTO in a case where it would otherwise have committed the case to the Crown Court for a PCC(S)A 2000, s 91 sentence of long term detention.

In *R v T* [2011] EWCA Crim 2345, it was held that a judge had been wrong to withhold credit for a guilty plea in the case of a juvenile who had caused grievous bodily harm to a stranger on the basis that an adult would have faced a sentence of up to three years' imprisonment. Although applying a discount would have meant imposing an 18-month instead of a 24-month DTO, there had been no justification for departing from the general principle that an offender was to be given a discount for his guilty plea.

Paragraph 5.15 of the Sentencing Council's definitive guideline, *Sentencing Children and Young People* refers to a situation where the court may be dealing with a number of summary only offences and is considering custody. The maximum sentence for a summary offence is effectively six months. The guideline notes that the aggregate sentence is also limited to a maximum of six months. It continues that 'allowing for a reduction for each guilty plea might result in the imposition of the maximum six-month sentence'. Where this is the case, the court may make a modest additional reduction to the overall sentence to reflect the benefits derived from the guilty plea. It is difficult to see how this might be applied in the Youth Court because of the restrictions on the length of DTOs. If credit for a guilty plea is given for each offence then each sentence can only be four months which is the minimum term for a DTO. The sentences could therefore not be made consecutively because the aggregate sentence would exceed the overall six-month maximum for multiple summary only offences. This guidance would therefore seem to be more relevant to a PCC(S)A, s 91 detention which the Crown Court can impose. There are no prescribed terms for such sentences.

However, when the total sentence in the Youth Court for all of the offences (including either way offences) is 24 months' DTO, a court may determine to impose consecutive sentences which, even allowing for a reduction for a guilty plea where appropriate on each offence, would still result in the imposition of the maximum sentence available. In such circumstances, in order to achieve the purpose for which the reduction principle has been established, some modest allowance should normally be given against the total sentence for the entry of a guilty plea. If there were four indictable offences and each is given a six-month DTO (after receiving a guilty plea reduction from a starting point of 10 months) consecutive to the others, this would total 24 months. One of the offences could be reduced to a four-month sentence so that the overall sentence becomes 22 months' DTO.

Credit for pleading guilty can justify a reduction in the level of a sentence. This means that a court might be persuaded to impose a youth rehabilitation order (YRO) rather than a DTO. Alternatively, if the provisional sentence is a YRO the guilty plea could lead to a fine/reparation order/referral order or discharge. If the court has imposed a different type of sentence because of a guilty plea there should normally be no further reduction on account of the guilty plea.

If the court does not change the level/type of sentence due to a guilty plea it can reduce the length or severity of any punitive elements in a community sentence. The court should be careful to ensure that the sentence is an effective one which meets the aim of the youth justice system – to prevent offending by children and young people.

The guideline indicates that because referral orders are only available where there is a guilty plea that there should be no further reduction to reflect the guilty plea.

The discount for a guilty plea should be applied after a provisional sentence has been arrived at by taking into account aggravating and mitigating factors relevant to the offence and the offender.

A court departing from a guideline must state the reasons for doing so. A court cannot remedy perceived defects (ie level of charge or maximum penalty) by refusal of the appropriate discount.

When pronouncing the sentence the court should usually state what the sentence would have been if there had been no reduction as a result of the guilty plea.

Chapter 7 Adjournments and remands

7.01   A magistrates' court may at any time whether before or after beginning to try an information in a criminal case adjourn the matter, and may do so when only composed of a single justice (MCA 1980, s 10(1)). If the juvenile appears in response to a summons or requisition the case can be adjourned, for example to enable the juvenile or his parents to obtain legal representation or to a trial date for witnesses to attend. When granting an adjournment the court may fix the time and place when the hearing is to resume, or leave the time and place to be determined later. The court cannot resume the hearing unless it is satisfied that the parties have had adequate notice (MCA 1980, s 10(2)). If the parties have attended court, notice should be given in court in a clear and unequivocal manner. If they have not attended court, a notice of adjournment should be sent to the address on the summons in accordance with the Criminal Procedure Rules 2015, r 4.

The overriding objective in the Criminal Procedure Rules 2015 (see **Appendix C** for extracts) is that criminal cases be dealt with justly. This involves all aspects of adjournments and case management and includes:

(a)   acquitting the innocent and convicting the guilty;

(b)   dealing with the prosecution and the defence fairly;

(c)   recognising the rights of a defendant, particularly those under Article 6 of the European Convention on Human Rights;

(d)   respecting the interests of witnesses, victims and jurors and keeping them informed of the progress of the case;

(e)   dealing with the case efficiently and expeditiously;

(f)   ensuring that appropriate information is available to the court when bail and sentence are considered; and

(g)   dealing with the case in ways that take into account the gravity of the offence alleged, the complexity of what is in issue, the severity of the consequences for the defendant and others affected, and the needs of other cases (CPR 2015, r 1.1).

Each party must actively assist the court in fulfilling its duty under r 3.2, with or without a direction; and apply for a direction if needed to further the overriding objective. Rule 3.2 places a duty on the court actively to manage the case. This includes the early identification of the real issues, achieving certainty as to what must be done, by whom, and when and in particular by the early setting of a timetable for the progress of the case. The court must also make any direction appropriate to the needs of that case as early as possible and monitor the progress of the case and compliance with directions (CPR 2015, rr 3.2 and 3.2(3)).

At every hearing, if a case cannot be concluded there and then the court must give directions so that it can be concluded at the next hearing or as soon as possible after that. The court must, where relevant, if the defendant is absent, decide whether to proceed. It must take the defendant's plea (unless already done), or if no plea can be taken then find out whether the defendant is likely to plead guilty or not guilty and set, follow, or revise a timetable for the progress of the case, which may include a timetable for any hearing including the trial.

The court must, in giving directions, ensure continuity in relation to the court and to the parties' representatives where that is appropriate and practicable; and where a direction has not been complied with, find out why, identify who was responsible, and take appropriate action (CPR 2015, r 3.9(2)(e)).

The Judiciary have been very active in promoting a robust approach to case management in order to achieve the objectives within the Criminal Procedure Rules. When Lord Justice Leveson was Senior Presiding Judge he led the 'Simple, Speedy, Summary Justice' initiative. As the title suggests this was aimed at reducing delays and keeping the process of criminal justice in the magistrates' courts simple. Central to the approach was the need for all involved in the proceedings to concentrate on the real issues rather than to treat criminal litigation as a game between advocates. The concept of proportionality was introduced into the preparation of prosecution files so that less paperwork is required for cases where it is anticipated that the defendant will plead guilty. Another feature of the new system was a reduction in the number of hearings per case. Where guilty pleas are entered there should only be one hearing unless a full written pre-sentence report is necessary. Where a not guilty plea is entered there should be only two hearings; the first hearing where the plea in taken, the real issues identified, a case management form completed and a trial date set and the second hearing where the trial takes place. A third hearing should only be appropriate if the defendant is convicted and a full written pre-sentence report is necessary. The expectation is that further case progression should take place outside the courtroom between the first hearing and the trial date. The initiative has been further strengthened in the magistrates' courts by 'Stop Delaying Justice' led by the Senior District Judge following the guidance from the Lord Chief Justice. The effect has been to focus more on the need to avoid the unnecessary attendance of witnesses and to keep the presentation of cases as short and simple as possible. These initiatives and the Criminal Procedure Rules themselves are built on a large body of case law which has steadily grown since the year 2000. In the Youth Court there has long been an emphasis on reducing delay. 'Simple, Speedy, Summary Justice' and 'Stop Delaying Justice' have both given added impetus and provided very clear practical guidance on how this can be achieved. There is perhaps only one proviso in the Youth Court; that compared to other magistrates' courts it has power to deal with more serious offences, including indictable only offences such as robbery, and the Youth Court has greater powers of punishment (2 years custody as opposed to 6 months for a single offence). In relation to the most serious cases dealt with in a Youth Court, the Criminal Procedure Rules justify an approach which is commensurate to the seriousness of the offence and the severity of the consequences for the defendant and others (CPR 2015, r 1.1(g)).

The most recent development of case management practice has been the Transforming Summary Justice initiative led by the Senior Judiciary, Crown Prosecution Service and Her Majesty's Courts and Tribunal Service. A key element in this is the importance of following the legal framework regarding disclosure of unused material. In December 2013, the Lord Chief Justice issued a Judicial Protocol on the Disclosure of Unused Material in Criminal Cases and the Attorney General published Guidelines on Disclosure for investigators, prosecutors and defence practitioners.

In the case of *R (on the application of A) v Thames Youth Court* [2012] EWHC 1822 (Admin) the Divisional Court said it was established law that in considering an adjournment application a criminal court should closely scrutinise the application and unless it was satisfied that the adjournment was necessary the application should be refused. In this case, the Youth Court granted the CPS an adjournment when the prosecution witnesses failed to attend to give evidence at a trial. The Divisional Court said it was unacceptable for the juvenile to have had the charge hanging over him for nearly two years; and in light of the fact that the prosecution had failed to proceed on two previous occasions the Youth Court's decision to grant the adjournment was quashed.

Some staff including legal advisers working for Her Majesty's Courts and Tribunals Service (HMCTS) have delegated case progression powers, including to the power to adjourn cases. In the case of *R (on the application of Director of Public Prosecutions) v Lancaster Magistrates' Court* [2010] EWHC 662 (Admin), a legal adviser had refused to vacate the trial of a persistent young offender because the prosecution did not have accurate witness availability when the trial date was fixed and in fact the alleged victim was on a pre-booked holiday on the relevant date. It was conceded for the purpose of the appeal that this decision was unreasonable. The Divisional Court was asked to comment on the suggestion that all applications to adjourn were dealt with by legal advisers. Mr Justice Foskett observed 'I am anxious not to go beyond what is appropriate because I am unaware of practices in other courts and I have not received submissions on behalf of the court... since questions of adjournment essentially involve the exercise of a judicial discretion, it seems to me that where there is no agreement about adjourning a case, the application for the adjournment should be listed before the Magistrates for consideration before the date of trial'.

Remands

7.02   When adjourning the hearing of a criminal case, the court may remand the defendant (MCA 1980, s 10(4)). Where the juvenile appears on a criminal charge and has been bailed to attend court, then the court will remand the juvenile, either on bail or in custody, and in either case the remand must be to a fixed date. Where a person is remanded in custody before a finding of guilt, it must not, subject to exceptions dealt with below, be for more than eight clear days, and where he is remanded on bail the court may remand him for a longer period if both parties agree (MCA 1980, s 128(6)). A court may remand him in custody for more than eight clear days if it has previously remanded him in custody for the same offence and he is before the court (MCA 1980, s 128A). However, the court has to have given the parties an opportunity to make representations and must have set a date on which it expects the next stage in the proceedings to take place. This remand may not exceed 28 clear days (MCA 1980, s 128A). If the defendant is present and consents he may be remanded in custody for up to 28 days. This will apply, for example, where he is being remanded for the first time or the court is not able to set a date for the next stage. If the court is satisfied that any person who has been remanded is unable by reason of illness or accident to appear or be brought before the court at the expiration of the period of remand the court may remand him for a further time in his absence (MCA 1980, s 129). The court must have been given solid grounds on which to form a reliable opinion (*R v Liverpool City Justices, ex parte Grogan* (1990) 155 JP 450).

Remands for reports

7.03   After a finding of guilt the court may adjourn for the purpose of enabling inquiries to be made or of determining the best method of dealing with the offender. After the finding of guilt but before making any order, the court may adjourn for a maximum of four weeks, unless the offender is remanded in custody when the maximum is three weeks (MCA 1980, s 10). The four-week time limit on the remand period when the court requires reports on bail is discretionary and not mandatory (*R v Manchester City Justices, ex parte Miley and Dynan* (1977) 141 JP Jo 248). Consequently, failures by the court to comply with the time limit will not affect the validity of the proceedings. Where a case is adjourned for inquiries or a report, the defendant need not be granted bail if it appears to the court that it would be impracticable to complete the inquiries or make the report without keeping the defendant in custody (Bail Act 1976 (BA 1976), Sch 1, para 7). Reports in this context may include pre-sentence, specific sentence, school, medical, psychological or psychiatric reports.

When remanding to local authority accommodation or youth detention accommodation after a finding of guilt, the court is limited to a remand of three weeks.

It must be emphasised that the power to adjourn after a finding of guilt must be exercised judicially and for a proper purpose. Courts must not therefore remand after a finding of guilt purely for punitive purposes. In *R v Toynbee Hall Juvenile Court Justices, ex parte Joseph* [1939] 3 All ER 16, the Divisional Court quashed the remand of a juvenile found guilty of riding on the railway without paying the fare. The juvenile court's chairman gave the reasons for the remand saying that 'the boy was a liar and had to learn not to defraud the railway company … and that for his own good the boy ought to go to a remand home'.

Custody time limits

7.04 The Prosecution of Offences (Custody Time Limits) Regulations 1987 are regulations made by the Secretary of State under the power granted to him by POA 1985, ss 22 and 29.

A time limit is set for the time spent in custody between the accused's first appearance and commencement of summary trial, namely 56 days. Where a juvenile is sent to the Crown Court for trial then the custody time limit is 182 days (including any custodial remands in the magistrates' court prior to the case being sent under CDA 1998, s 51).

The regulations apply in Youth Courts by virtue of the definition of 'custody' inserted into POA 1985, s 22 by CJA 1988, Sch 11 and LASPOA 2012, Sch 12, namely that it includes local authority accommodation or youth detention accommodation to which a person is remanded.

The regulations apply to indictable, either way and summary offences. They reflect the general rights of the detained person under Article 5(3) of the ECHR. As Lord Bingham said in *R v Manchester Crown Court, ex parte McDonald* [1999] Cr App R 409: 'Everyone arrested or detained (for trial) shall be entitled to trial within a reasonable time or to release pending trial.' Where the prosecution fails to commence trial or committal to the Crown Court within the time limit set, the accused is automatically entitled to bail. If the time limit is unlikely to be adhered to the prosecution may apply for an extension of the limit. This application must be made before the expiry date and may only be granted where the court is satisfied that there is good and sufficient cause for doing so and that the prosecution has acted with all due diligence and expedition.

Either way offences include those which must be tried summarily in the Youth Court by virtue of MCA 1980, s 24 – *R v Stratford Youth Court, ex parte S* [1998] 1 WLR 1758. In that case the question was whether the custody time limit regulations applied to a 14-year-old charged with robbery. The defendant was at that time too young to be committed to the Crown Court for such an offence. It was held that the offence of robbery was effectively an either way offence for juveniles and that the defendant was entitled to the protection of the 56-day time limit. It was stated that the 56-day time limit applied to all indictable cases heard in the Youth Court other than homicide. It would seem that the 70-day time limit applies to homicide. The judgment does not make reference to other offences for which a juvenile can only be tried in the Crown Court, nor is reference made to cases where the court directs trial on indictment. It would seem to follow from the regulations as currently framed that in any case where the Youth Court or magistrates' court declines jurisdiction that the 70-day custody time limit would apply. The regulations were subsequently amended to extend their scope to include offences which can only be tried summarily (reg 4A).

The regulations provide that an application to extend may be made orally or in writing. Although not a requirement of reg 7, it is good practice to give the grounds for the application in the notice (*R v Central Criminal Court, ex parte Marrota Crown* Office Digest 13).The prosecution is required to give written notice of its intention to apply not less than five days beforehand in the Crown Court and not less than two days beforehand in a magistrates' court. The requirement to give notice is directory and not mandatory, however failure to give notice will be a factor for the court in considering whether the prosecution has acted with all due diligence and expedition. The accused may waive his right to notice and the court (if satisfied that it is not practicable in all the circumstances for the prosecution to give the notice required) may abridge the period.

Procedure regarding appeals against a court's decision to extend a custody time limit can be found in CPR 2015, r 14.19.

In *R v Sheffield Justices, ex parte Turner* [1991] 2 QB 472, it was held that a defendant was unlawfully detained in custody after the expiry of the 70-day remand time limit. However, that did not prevent the justices committing him in custody for trial at the Crown Court, as that was a fresh stage in proceedings and a different time limit applied.

Police bail

7.05   The police may require an arrested person to return to the police station and may bail that person to do so (PACE 1984, s 47(3)(b)). There is a limit of 28 days on the duration of the bail. This may be extended by an officer of at least the rank of superintendent for up to three months. Applications for further extension may be made to the court before the expiry of the current time limit. The court may then extend the time limit by further periods of three months at a time (or six months where justified). Each renewal application would need to be made before expiry of the latest extension. These limits are introduced with effect from 3 April 2017 by the Policing and Crime Act 2017, s 63 which amends PACE 1984. Applications for extensions will be dealt with in the first instance under the single justice powers but may be referred to a court of two or more Magistrates if appropriate. The court can only grant extensions where it is satisfied that there are reasonable grounds to believe that the investigation is being conducted diligently and expeditiously, and reasonable grounds for believing that the release on bail of the person in question is necessary and proportionate in all the circumstances (having regard, in particular, to any conditions of bail which are, or are to be, imposed).

On charging a defendant with an offence the police may grant bail to attend court: PACE 1984, s 47(3)(a). A charged person has the right to bail unless exceptions set out in the schedule to the Bail Act 1976 are satisfied: these are dealt with in the next section. If the custody sergeant grants bail with conditions the defendant should be given a record of those conditions. The sergeant may impose any conditions that a court could impose except a condition specifically excluded by s 3A, such as a condition of residence in a probation hostel: Bail Act 1976, s 3A(2) or an electronically monitored curfew condition. The custody sergeant may vary such conditions at any time before the first court appearance (Bail Act 1976, s 3A(4)).

Bail – the general principles

7.06   Most of the general principles apply equally to juveniles as to adults. The most notable exceptions include the welfare of the young person being a ground for withholding bail and the added restrictions which make it more difficult to impose an electronically monitored curfew as a condition of bail. The rules which govern the grant of bail depend in part on where the offence can be tried. In relation to adults, a magistrates' court is not required to allow a bail application after the second hearing unless there has been a change in circumstances or there are fresh considerations. The remand status of juveniles should however be considered afresh at each hearing given the need to take into account their welfare (*R (on the application of B) v Brent Youth Court* [2010] EWHC 1893 (Admin)).

There are 3 main categories here: either way/indictable imprisonable offences (BA 1976, Sch 1, Part1), summary imprisonable offences (BA 1976, Sch 1, Part 1A), non imprisonable offences, (BA 1976, Sch 1, Part 2).

In cases involving allegations of criminal damage MCA 1980, s 22 requires the court to determine in the mode of trial hearing for defendants aged 18 and above whether the value of the offence of criminal damage exceeds £5,000. If the value is accepted as less than £5,000 the case is to be tried summarily and will fall under Part 1A of the Bail Act 1976. In order to enable the court to determine if the bail decision on a juvenile charged with an offence of criminal damage is to be made under Part 1A, the court is required to consider whether the value of any offence of criminal damage is less than £5,000 (Bail Act 1976, s 9A). If the value of the damage is clearly less than that amount, the charge will be subject to Bail Act 1976, Part 1A (see **7.14** below).

A juvenile has a general right to unconditional bail. It is perhaps worth noting that the restrictions on granting bail to adults charged with offences carrying life imprisonment (Bail Act 1976, Sch 1, Part 1, para 2A) do not apply to those under the age of 18. A magistrates' court may not grant a person bail in relation to a charge of murder. The case must be committed to the Crown Court in custody for a decision to be made about bail (Coroners and Justice Act 2009, s 115).

This applies even where there is to be no bail application. The Crown Court must determine whether bail should be granted within the period of 48 hours which begins the day after the date on which the defendant appears or is brought before the magistrates' court. If for any reason the case is returned to a magistrates' court it is thereafter restricted either to continuing the remand in custody or re-imposing the same bail conditions as ordered by the judge. If the juvenile is remanded in custody by the judge and at any subsequent hearing in the magistrates' court the juvenile wishes to apply for bail then that court should again commit the defendant to the Crown Court in custody under s 115 following the same procedure.

Where a juvenile is on bail granted by a judge pending a committal hearing in the Youth Court or other magistrates' court, any application for a variation of the bail conditions cannot be considered by the magistrates and the matter must be returned to the Crown Court.

The Senior Presiding Judge has directed in accordance with the Consolidated Criminal Practice Direction that only High Court judges or Crown Court judges authorised to sit on murder cases may decide the issue of bail in murder cases. If such a judge is not available within the 48-hour time limit, a resident judge may, with the approval of the relevant presiding judges, nominate a sufficiently experienced circuit judge to determine bail under CJA 2009, s 115(3). Unless the defence indicate that there will not be a bail application at the Crown Court hearing arranged under s 115 then the magistrates must order that the juvenile is produced to the Crown Court. When calculating the 48-hour time limit Saturdays, Sundays, Christmas Day, Good Friday and bank holidays are to be excluded.

The Coroners and Justice Act 2009 does not specify what is meant by 'custody' in the context of a juvenile being committed to custody under s 115. A custodial remand for a juvenile is generally considered to include any of the custodial forms of remand which become available once bail is withheld. This view was confirmed by the High Court in *R (on the application of A) v Lewisham Youth Court* [2011] EWHC 1193 (Admin). In practice the remand under CJA 2009, s 115 could therefore be to either local authority accommodation or youth detention accommodation.

In the exceptional case where a magistrates' court at the first hearing does not send the murder charge for trial in the Crown Court and the magistrates' court indicates to the Crown Court what the next suitable date is for the proceedings to be resumed in the Youth Court or other magistrates' court it should be careful to avoid exceeding the time limits placed on the duration of remands in custody under MCA 1980, ss 128 and 128A. This is by analogy with the position relating to prosecution appeals against the grant of bail as set out in *Remice v Governor of Belmarsh Prison* [2007] EWHC 936 (Admin).

Bail under the Bail Act 1976 does not involve a recognisance or surety when it is unconditional. Bail by the police either to report back to the police station or to attend court may have conditions attached to it.

Unconditional bail imposes a duty on the offender to surrender to custody at a time and place appointed, which may be either the police station or the court. Failure to surrender without reasonable excuse is an offence in itself punishable in the case of an adult convicted summarily by three months' imprisonment or a level 5 fine (Bail Act 1976, s 6(7)). Even surrendering late to the court provides the court with discretion whether or not to put a Bail Act charge (*R v Scott* [2007] All ER (D) 191 (Oct)). A juvenile who fails to surrender to custody could be made subject to any of the orders available to the court (other than a detention and training order) or a fine not exceeding £1,000 (£250 in the case of a child).

Bail may be subject to conditions or may be refused if certain criteria set out in the Bail Act 1976 are satisfied.

Bail conditions

7.07   The court or custody sergeant may impose conditions on bail where it appears to be necessary to ensure that an offender:

(a)   surrenders to custody;

(b)   does not commit an offence while on bail;

(c)   does not interfere with witnesses or otherwise obstruct the course of justice;

(d)   for his own protection or, if he is a child or young person, for his own welfare or in his own interests.

The court may additionally impose conditions to ensure that an offender:

(e)   makes himself available for the purpose of enabling inquiries or a report to be made to assist the court in dealing with him for the offence;

(f)   attends an interview with an authorised advocate or authorised litigator, as defined by s 119(1) of the Courts and Legal Services Act 1990.

He may be required to comply with such conditions as are imposed either before or after release on bail (Bail Act 1976, s 3(6)).

Where a court or custody sergeant imposes conditions of bail, reasons must be stated and a record of the decision kept. A copy of that note must be given to the person in relation to whom the decision was taken (Bail Act 1976, s 5(4)).

Conditions, imposed by the police or the court, may be as follows:

(a)   To ensure attendance at court. The most common conditions imposed under this exception to unconditional bail are:

(i)   To report to a police station at times specified by the court during the adjournment period. This is an unpopular condition with police forces due to staffing and administrative difficulties.

(ii)   Residence at an address specified by the court. In the case of a juvenile this is usually his parents' address. However, situations can arise where the court imposes a condition of residence at the address of a relative, for example where the juvenile is estranged from his immediate family.

(iii)   That sureties be provided. This involves persons agreeing to secure the attendance of the juvenile at court by pledging a sum of money that may be forfeit if they fail to ensure that attendance. No money is actually deposited with the court. The court must be satisfied, however, that any person standing surety has the financial resources to pay the amount set by the court in the event of non-attendance by the juvenile and the subsequent forfeiture of the monies: *R v Birmingham Crown Court, ex parte Rashid Ali* [1999] Crim LR 504. The court, in considering the suitability of a person to stand surety, may also have regard to his character and any previous convictions, and his proximity to the person for whom he is to be surety. Proximity in this sense may mean either geographically or in terms of kinship.

(b)   To prevent the commission of offences. The most common conditions imposed are:

(i)   Curfew: that the juvenile remains indoors between specified hours. Usually this involves the hours of darkness.

(ii)   Not to associate with co-accused. This embraces the case where offenders are alleged to have acted in unison in the commission of an offence and it is believed that if they associate they will commit further offences.

(iii)   Not to contact the complainant. This is sometimes imposed where the charge is, for example, one of assault and there is still bad feeling between the parties.

(c)   To prevent interference with witnesses or the obstruction of the course of justice. The most common condition is not to contact prosecution witnesses where the court fears that the offender may attempt to prevent these witnesses giving evidence.

(d)   To ensure the availability of the offender if necessary for the purpose of enabling inquiries if a report is to be made to assist the court in dealing with him for the offence. This condition may be worded to involve co-operation with a doctor, probation officer or social worker where the court believes he would otherwise be uncooperative.

(e)   To ensure he attends for interview with a solicitor before the next hearing.

Conditions (d) and (e) may only be imposed by a court and if the police feel an electronic monitoring condition, residence at a hostel or medical reports in a murder case are required then the case must go before a court for such conditions to be attached.

An offender may be required to comply with such conditions as are imposed either before or after release on bail. For example, the offender may be remanded into local authority accommodation until suitable sureties are found. In addition, a parent may stand surety for his child to ensure that the juvenile (under 17 years old) shall comply with any conditions imposed on him under the Bail Act 1976, s 3(6), (6ZAA) or (6A) as mentioned above. The parent may only stand surety to guarantee those conditions to which he consents, and the sum shall not exceed £50. If the young person is likely to attain the age of 17 years before the date fixed for his surrender to custody a parent may not stand surety to ensure compliance with conditions (Bail Act 1976, s 3(7)).

Although it is rare in the context of the Youth Court, if it appears that the juvenile is unlikely to surrender to custody, he may be required to give security for his surrender to custody. The security may be given by him or on his behalf. This involves the deposit of a sum of money with the appropriate officer.

Before imposing conditions on bail, the court or custody sergeant must be satisfied that there is a genuine need for each condition imposed and that they are both precise and workable. For example, in a case of theft from a city store the justices may be tempted to impose a condition that the juvenile stays away from the city centre to prevent the commission of further offences. Objections to this condition are that the city centre is not identifiable, the offender's solicitor may have his office in the city centre and the Youth Court itself may be situated near the main shopping centre. In human rights terms, bail conditions should be proportionate to the mischief which they aim to prevent.

Electronic monitoring of conditions of remand

7.08   A juvenile aged between 12 and 17 inclusive may be made the subject of a remand condition that he or she is subjected to electronic tagging (Bail Act 1976, s 3(6ZAA)). The criteria to be satisfied are:

(a)   he or she is being charged with or convicted of a specified violent or specified sexual offence or an offence punishable in the case of an adult with 14 years' imprisonment or more; or

(b)   he or she is charged with or has been convicted of one or more imprisonable offences which together with any other imprisonable offences of which he or she has been convicted in any proceedings:

(i)   amount to, or

(ii)   would, if he or she was convicted of the offences with which he or she is charged, amount to

a recent history of repeatedly committing imprisonable offences whilst remanded on bail, remanded to local authority accommodation, or remanded to youth detention accommodation.

The court has to have been notified by the Secretary of State that electronic monitoring arrangements are available and the Youth Offending Team must have informed the court that in its opinion the imposition of such a condition will be suitable in that defendant's case (Bail Act 1976, s 3AA(4) and (5); CYPA 1969, ss 23(7) and 23AA).

A defendant may be made the subject of a condition that he or she complies with the terms of an intensive supervision and surveillance programme. Such a programme involves 25 hours of supervision per week and additional surveillance. It can be combined with a condition of electronic monitoring. (see **7.17**).

Failure to surrender

7.09   If a defendant, who has been released on bail, fails without reasonable excuse to surrender to the custody of the court he is guilty of an offence (Bail Act 1976, s 6(1)). Alternatively, if the defendant, having had a reasonable excuse for failing to surrender to custody at the appointed time, fails to surrender to custody as soon after the appointed time as is reasonably practicable he is also guilty of a criminal offence (Bail Act 1976, s 6(2)). Such an offence is punishable at the magistrates' court in the case of an adult with a fine not exceeding level 5, or imprisonment not exceeding three months. It would appear that custody is not available for this offence in the Youth Court as the minimum detention and training order sentence available is four months: see *P v Leeds Youth Court* [2006] EWHC 2527 (Admin).

Such an offence is only triable in the court at which proceedings are to be heard in respect of which bail has been granted. The case will normally be heard immediately in accordance with the Criminal Practice Direction 2015 Division III 14 C.5 as amended and not adjourned until the end of the substantive hearing.

The actions which qualify as surrendering to the court include booking in at a desk in the courthouse where this is the practice of the court, entering the dock in the courtroom or identifying himself in the courtroom when his case is called (*R v Evans* [2011] EWCA 2842).

Where the bail in question was granted by a police officer, proceedings for failure to surrender should be started by a charge or the laying of an information within six months of the time of the commission of the relevant offence or an information laid no later than three months from the occurrence of the first of the following events to occur after the commission of the relevant offence:

(a)   the person surrenders to custody at the appointed place;

(b)   the person is arrested, or attends at a police station, in connection with the relevant offence or the offence for which he was granted bail;

(c)   the person appears or is brought before a court in connection with the relevant offence or the offence for which he was granted bail (Bail Act 1976, s 6(12) to (14)).

Where the bail was granted by a court, the court may initiate proceedings following an express invitation by the prosecutor. The prosecutor must consider that proceedings are appropriate in all the circumstances (Practice Direction (Criminal Consolidated) 2002 as amended Part 1.13.9).

Breach of bail conditions

7.10   Breach of bail conditions is not a criminal offence. It does however give a constable having reasonable grounds for believing that the person is likely to break or has broken the bail condition a power of arrest. Following arrest the defendant must be brought before a magistrates' court, except where he was arrested within 24 hours of the time appointed for him to surrender to custody to a particular court. In such a case he must be brought as soon as practicable, and in any event within 24 hours after his arrest, before a justice of the peace for the area in which he was due to appear. If he had been due to appear before a Crown Court within 24 hours of the arrest then he must be taken before the Crown Court instead.

Where the person is charged with murder and has been arrested for alleged breach of bail conditions he must be produced before a judge of the Crown Court and not a magistrate (Bail Act 1976, s 7(8), as inserted by the Coroners and Justice Act 2009).

The 24-hour period shall not be taken to include Christmas Day, Good Friday or any Sunday. Detention, solely for a breach of bail conditions, beyond the 24-hour time limit may be an unlawful imprisonment. A defendant need not be granted bail if he is arrested under s 7 of the Bail Act 1976 and the court is satisfied that there are substantial grounds for believing that he will fail to surrender, interfere with witnesses or commit offences.

Where a person is charged with murder and has been arrested for alleged breach of bail conditions he must be produced before a judge of the Crown Court (and not a magistrate) within 24 hours (Bail Act 1976, s 7(8) as inserted by the Coroners and Justice Act 2009). The 24-hour period shall not be taken to include Saturdays, Sundays, Christmas Day, Good Friday and bank holidays. If however the arrest is within 24 hours of the time when the juvenile was due to surrender to a magistrates' court he is to be brought before that magistrates' court instead (Bail Act 1976, s 7(4)). The magistrates' court would then be required to commit the juvenile to the Crown Court in custody for a bail decision under CJA 2009, s 115 without consideration of whether the bail condition was breached. It remains to be decided whether the Crown Court would be bound to resolve within 24 hours of the arrest whether the bail condition had been breached as is required by the terms of Bail Act 1976, s 7(4). If the operation of the time limit in that section is taken to be superseded by CJA 2009, s 115 then it would still be open to the Crown Court to hear such information or evidence as it considers appropriate in relation to the alleged breach of bail condition which led to the arrest, when deciding on the issue of bail.

Procedure on breach of bail conditions

7.11   Non-compliance with bail conditions is not in itself an offence, but a person released on bail may be arrested without warrant and brought before the court:

(a)   if a constable has reasonable grounds for believing that that person is not likely to surrender to custody; or

(b)   if a constable has reasonable grounds for believing that that person is likely to break any of the conditions of his bail or has reasonable grounds for suspecting that that person has broken any of these conditions; or

(c)   in a case where that person was released on bail with one or more surety or sureties, if a surety notifies a constable in writing that that person is unlikely to surrender to custody and that for that reason the surety wishes to be relieved of his obligations as a surety (Bail Act 1976, s 7(3)).

A person arrested in breach of bail conditions may be remanded in custody on the grounds specified in the Bail Act, or he may be released on the same or amended conditions.

Proceedings under the Bail Act 1976, s 7(5) can be held before a single justice. Where an allegation that a defendant is in breach of his bail conditions is denied there is no power to adjourn the case and a decision must be taken on the occasion when the defendant is produced to the court (*R v Liverpool City Magistrates' Court, ex parte DPP* [1993] QB 233). In *R (on the application of Culley) v Dorchester Crown Court* [2007] EWHC 109 (Admin), it was made clear that once the 24-hour limit had elapsed the court no longer had jurisdiction to deal with the matter. It followed that everything done after the expiration of the 24-hour period was *ultra vires* and unlawful. Courts therefore need to be vigilant to ensure that breach of bail applications are concluded within the 24-hour period. Doubt has been expressed about this approach in the case of *McElkerney v Highbury Corner Magistrates' Court* [2009] EWHC 2621 (Admin) where although the point did not arise for determination by the Divisional Court, Lord Justice Richards commented 'the statutory requirement is that the person be brought before a justice as soon as practicable and in any event within 24 hours after his arrest. It is not on the face of it a requirement that the justice's decision be reached within that 24-hour period.'

Where a defendant does not accept an alleged breach of bail condition, it is unnecessary to have a hearing in which evidence on oath is called. Section 7 provides:

'a simple and expeditious procedure for dealing with the situation where a constable believes that a person bailed is unlikely to surrender to custody or alternatively, that a person bailed is likely to breach a condition of his bail, or has broken a condition of his bail.'

The structure of s 7 clearly contemplates the constable who has arrested the person bailed bringing him before the justice of the peace and stating his grounds for believing that the defendant has broken a condition of his bail. That may well involve the giving of 'hearsay evidence'. No doubt the justice of the peace will in fairness give the defendant an opportunity to respond to what the constable is saying. The justice will then either form one of the opinions set out in subs (5) and, if he does so, go on to decide whether to remand the defendant in custody or on bail on the same or more stringent conditions; or, if the justice feels unable to form one of the opinions set out in the subsection, he will order the defendant to be remanded on bail on the same terms as were originally imposed (*R v Liverpool City Magistrates, ex parte DPP* [1993] QB 233).

The effect of the Human Rights Convention on the procedure set down by the High Court in the *Liverpool case* was reviewed in *R (on the application of the DPP) v Havering Magistrates' Court* [2001] 3 All ER 977. The court held that Article 6 had no direct relevance where justices were exercising their judgment on whether or not to commit a person to custody following a breach of bail conditions.

The court said that it was clear that Article 5 did have direct relevance. Where a decision was taken to deprive somebody of his liberty that should only be done after he had been given a fair opportunity to answer the basis upon which such an order was sought. In testing whether or not such an opportunity had been given, it was essential to bear in mind the nature and purpose of the proceedings in question. To this end the procedures set out in domestic law were entirely compatible with the requirements of the article. The fact of a breach of conditions was evidence of a relevant risk arising, but it was no more than one of the factors that the justices had to consider in exercising their discretion.

The court had to ensure that the defendant had a full and fair opportunity to comment on, and answer, any material before the court. If a prosecution witness attends court and gives evidence, the accused has to be given an opportunity to cross-examine that person. Similarly, if he also wishes to give oral evidence he should be entitled to do so.

The fact that, under domestic law there is no power to adjourn the hearing once a defendant has been brought before the court under the Bail Act 1976, s 7(4), does not result in a breach of Article 5. A person arrested under s 7(4) must be dealt with by the court and released on bail or remanded in custody (*R (on the application of Ellison) v Teesside Magistrates' Court* [2001] EWHC 11 (Admin)).

If any person who is bailed fails to attend at the time and place appointed, the court may issue a warrant for his arrest (Bail Act 1976, s 7(1); see *R v Evans* [2011] EWCA 2842 above at **7.09**).

Reconsideration of bail on application of the prosecution

7.12   Where a magistrates' court (including a Youth Court) or a constable has granted bail for an indictable or either way offence the prosecutor may apply to:

(a)   vary the conditions of bail;

(b)   impose conditions in respect of bail which has been granted unconditionally;

(c)   withhold bail.

These provisions do not apply to bail granted by a constable to return to a police station under PACE 1984, s 37 (as amended by CJA 2003, Sch 2).

Such an application may only be made where it is based on information in the hands of the prosecutor, which was not available to the court or constable when the decision was taken. Procedural requirements under r 14.7 of the CPR 2015 must be complied with. Where the decision of the court is to withhold bail from the person to whom it was originally granted it must, if that person is before the court, remand him in custody. If he is not before the court it must order him to surrender himself forthwith into the custody of the court. When he surrenders himself, the court must remand him in custody. If he fails to surrender he may be arrested without warrant and must then be taken before a justice of the peace for the petty sessions area in which he was arrested as soon as practicable and in any case within 24 hours (Bail Act 1976, s 5B).

Prosecution right of appeal

7.13   Where bail is granted to a person charged with an offence punishable in the case of an adult with imprisonment the prosecution may appeal to a Crown Court judge. They may only appeal if they made representations against the granting of bail. The prosecution must give oral notice at the end of the remand proceedings and written notice within two hours. It is not necessary for the prosecution to give oral notice the moment that the last word is said in the proceedings; it has been held that giving oral notice to the proper officer five minutes after the conclusion of the proceedings and after the justices have left the court building is sufficient (*R v Isleworth Crown Court, ex parte Clarke* [1998] 1 Cr App R 257). The bailed juvenile must then be remanded to local authority accommodation or youth detention accommodation until the appeal is heard and the appeal hearing must be commenced within 48 hours from the date on which the notice was given (Bail Amendment Act 1993, s 1(6) and (8)). *R v Crown Court at Middlesex Guildhall, ex parte Okali* [2001] 1 Cr App R 1 provides that the appeal must be commenced within two working days of the date of decision of the magistrates' court, rather than literally within 48 hours of the moment upon which oral notice had been given by the prosecutor. It is for the magistrates' court to decide the type of 'custodial' remand it will impose pending the appeal (*R (on application of A) v Lewisham Youth Court* [2011] EWHC 1193 (Admin). The starting point is that the remand will be to local authority accommodation unless the court is satisfied that the grounds are made out for a remand to youth detention accommodation and it considers such a remand to be appropriate. Given that the magistrates' court had already granted bail before the prosecution appeal against that decision, then in most cases the remand is likely to be to local authority accommodation, albeit with any conditions which had been considered necessary.

Refusal of bail

7.14   Every person who appears or is brought before a court accused of an offence has the general right to bail (Bail Act 1976, s 4). No person may be remanded in custody unless the court finds that one or more of the specific exceptions found in the Bail Act 1976, Sch 1 applies. In the context of the European Convention on Human Rights, Article 5(3) requires that a person charged with an offence be released pending trial unless the prosecution can show that there are *relevant and sufficient* reasons to justify his continued detention. The role of the court in considering bail is to examine all the facts both for and against the existence of a genuine public interest requirement justifying departure from the presumption of individual liberty. In the case of a juvenile the court is required to consider whether the welfare of the defendant requires a fresh consideration of bail at each hearing (*R (on the application of B) v Brent Youth Court* [2010] EWHC 1893 (Admin)). In the case of **indictable only or either way imprisonable offences**, the following reasons may justify refusal of bail:

(a)   there are substantial grounds for believing that the defendant if released on bail would:

    (i)   fail to surrender; or

    (ii)   commit fresh offences; or

    (iii)   interfere with witnesses or obstruct justice;

(b)   the court is satisfied that the defendant should be kept in custody for his own protection; or

(c)   if he is a child or young person, for his own welfare or in his own interests;

(d)   the defendant is a serving prisoner;

(e)   the court is satisfied that it has not been practicable to obtain sufficient information for the purpose of making a bail decision for want of time since the institution of proceedings against him;

(f)   the defendant having been released on bail in, or in connection with, the proceedings for the offence for which he has been arrested is in breach of conditions of that bail; or

(g)   where his case is adjourned for inquiries or a report and it appears that it would be impracticable to complete the inquiries or complete the report without keeping the defendant in custody.

Where a person under 18 years of age has failed to surrender already in the proceedings for an offence committed on or after 1 January 2007 which carries a maximum sentence of life imprisonment, the court shall give particular weight to that fact when considering whether (a)(i) above applies (Bail Act 1976, Sch 1, para 9AB and the Criminal Justice Act 2003 (Commencement No 14 and Transitional Provision) Order 2006).

Where a person under 18 years of age was on bail when it is alleged that he committed on or after 1 January 2007 an offence which carries a maximum sentence of life imprisonment the court shall give particular weight to that fact when considering whether (a)(ii) above applies (Bail Act 1976, Sch 1, para 9AA and the Criminal Justice Act 2003 (Commencement No 14 and Transitional Provision) Order 2006).

In the case of **summary only offences punishable with imprisonment**, or criminal damage cases where the value is less than £5,000, Part 1A of the Bail Act 1976 (as amended by CJIA 2008, s 52 and Sch 12) contains more restrictive grounds for withholding bail with effect from 14 July 2008. In such circumstances bail may be withheld if:

(a)   it appears to the court that, having been previously granted bail in criminal proceedings, he has failed to surrender to custody in accordance with his obligations under the grant of bail and the court believes, in view of that failure, that the defendant, if released on bail (whether subject to conditions or not), would fail to surrender to custody;

(b)   it appears to the court that the defendant was on bail in criminal proceedings on the date of the offence and the court is satisfied that there are substantial grounds for believing that the defendant, if released on bail (whether subject to conditions or not), would commit an offence while on bail;

(c)   there are substantial grounds for believing that the defendant, if released on bail (whether subject to conditions or not), would commit an offence while on bail by engaging in conduct that would, or would be likely to, cause physical or mental injury to any person associated with the defendant; or any person associated with the defendant to fear physical or mental injury. A person associated with the defendant includes relatives or partners (see Family Law Act 1996, s 62);

(d)   the defendant should be kept in custody for his own protection or, if he is a child or young person, for his own welfare;

(e)   he is in custody in pursuance of a sentence of a court or a sentence imposed by an officer under the Armed Forces Act 2006;

(f)   having been released on bail in or in connection with the proceedings for the offence, he has been arrested in pursuance of s 7 of this Act and the court is satisfied that there are substantial grounds for believing that the defendant, if released on bail (whether subject to conditions or not) would fail to surrender to custody, commit an offence while on bail or interfere with witnesses or otherwise obstruct the course of justice (whether in relation to himself or any other person);

(g)   it has not been practicable to obtain sufficient information for the purpose of making a bail decision for want of time since the institution of the proceedings.

In the case of all juveniles charged with **non-imprisonable offences**, the following reasons apply:

(a)   it appears to the court that, having previously been granted bail in criminal proceedings, the defendant has failed to surrender to custody and the court believes, in view of that failure, that the defendant would fail to attend;

(b)   the court is satisfied that the defendant should be kept in custody for his own protection or, if he is a child or young person, for his own welfare;

(c)   the defendant is in custody in pursuance of the sentence of the court or of any authority acting under any of the armed services Acts (ie the Army Act 1955, the Air Force Act 1955 and the Naval Discipline Act 1957);

(d)   having been released on bail or in connection with the proceedings for the offence, the defendant has been arrested as being in breach of any of the conditions of his bail and the court is satisfied that there are substantial grounds for believing that the defendant, if released on bail (whether subject to conditions or not) would fail to surrender to custody, commit an offence on bail, or interfere with witnesses, or otherwise obstruct the course of justice (whether in relation to himself or any other person) (Bail Act 1976, Sch 1, Part 2).

When withholding bail the court must give reasons, include a note of those reasons in the court register and give a copy of that note to the defendant (Bail Act 1976, s 5).

In deciding whether to grant or refuse bail the court is required to have regard to such of the following considerations as appear to it to be relevant:

(a)   the nature and seriousness of the offence, or default (and the probable method of dealing with the defendant for it);

(b)   the character, antecedents, associations, and community ties of the defendant;

(c)   the defendant's record in respect to the fulfilment of his obligations under previous grants of bail in criminal proceedings;

(d)   (except in the case of a defendant whose case is adjourned for inquiries or a report) the strength of the evidence of his having committed the offence or having defaulted, as well as any other things which appear to be relevant (Bail Act 1976, Sch 1, Pt 1, para 9).

The above provisions apply strictly in the Youth Court as they do in the adult court. At each remand hearing, the court, before it may withhold bail must be satisfied that there are substantial grounds for believing one or more of the exceptions to the general right to bail apply, and that there are adequate reasons to support that finding. Having found that an exception to the right to unconditional bail exists based on supporting reasons, the court should then consider whether or not the imposition of conditions would be sufficient to remove the grounds for withholding bail. Where the juvenile has previously been remanded to local authority or youth detention accommodation the issue of bail should be considered afresh even where applications for bail have previously been made on more than one occasion (*R (on the application of B) v Brent Youth Court* [2010] EWHC 1893 (Admin)).

Where the Crown Court refuses bail for murder at a hearing within 48 hours of the first appearance and the case is still within the Youth Court or other magistrates' court pending being sent to the Crown Court for trial, the juvenile would be entitled to a second full bail application but this must be made before the Crown Court judge. Therefore at the second hearing in the Youth Court the juvenile would have to be committed back to the Crown Court in custody for his second full bail application: see **7.06** above and CPR 2015, r 14.10.

Remands to police custody

7.15   On refusing bail the court may remand to police custody for a period of up to 24 hours if the defendant is 17 or younger. Such a remand may only be ordered if it is necessary for the purpose of making enquiries for other offences. The defendant should be brought back before the court as soon as the need for the remand has been satisfied. The court must be satisfied that the exceptions to the right to bail are satisfied (MCA 1980, s 128(7) and (8)).

Remands to local authority accommodation

7.16   Where a court remands a child charged or convicted of one or more offences, sends him for trial, or commits him for sentence and refuses him bail, the remand is to local authority accommodation (LASPOA 2012, ss 91(3) and 92). In this context 'child' means someone who has attained 10 years and is under 18 years. The period of remand before conviction is for a maximum of eight clear days. If the remand is after conviction, the maximum period is three weeks. When remanded to local authority accommodation the juvenile will live wherever the social services department direct and this can include a residential children's home, remand foster placements or the juvenile living at home or with other members of his or her family. The remanding court must designate the local authority that is to receive the defendant. In the case of a juvenile being looked after by a local authority it will be that local authority. Otherwise it will be the local authority in whose area it appears to the court that he habitually resides, or where the offence or one of the offences was committed.

It is important to note that a remand to the care of the local authority does not confer parental responsibility on the authority. This may have ramifications when the court decides issues as to who pays a compensation order (*North Yorkshire County Council v Selby Youth Court Justices* [1994] 1 All ER 991).

On remanding a person to local authority accommodation, the court may require the defendant to comply with conditions as if he had been granted bail (LASPOA 2012, s 93). These conditions could include conditions of electronic tagging or intensive supervision and surveillance programmes (see 7.17). If such conditions are imposed the court is required to explain to the defendant in open court why those conditions are imposed. Those reasons are to be specified in the warrant of commitment and in the court register. If a court remands a person to local authority accommodation it may impose requirements on that authority for securing compliance with the conditions or stipulations that he may not be placed with a named person. The court may only impose such conditions and requirements after consultation with the local authority. The court has no power to direct that a child or young person who was remanded to local authority accommodation reside at a specific place (*Cleveland County Council v DPP* (1995) LSGaz 37).

If the court wishes to impose an electronic tagging condition it must ensure that the criteria are satisfied. A juvenile aged 12 or over may be made the subject of a condition that he or she is subjected to electronic tagging (Bail Act 1976, s 3AA and s 3(6ZAA)). The criteria to be satisfied are:

(a)   he or she is being charged with or convicted of a specified violent or a specified sexual offence or an offence punishable in the case of an adult with 14 years' imprisonment or more; or

(b)   he or she is charged with or has been convicted of one or more imprisonable offences which together with any other imprisonable offences of which he or she has been convicted in any proceedings:

   (i)   amount to, or

   (ii)   would, if he or she was convicted of the offences with which he or she is charged, amount to

   a recent history of committing imprisonable offences whilst remanded on bail or while remanded to local authority accommodation or youth detention accommodation.

The court has to have been notified that electronic monitoring arrangements are available in their local justice area and the Youth Offending Team must have notified the court that in its opinion the imposition of such a condition will be suitable in that defendant's case (Bail Act 1976, s 3AA(4) and (5); LASPOA 2012, s 94). There are similar provisions for extradition proceedings (see LASPOA 2012, s 95).

Intensive supervision and surveillance and local authority remand

7.17   A defendant may be made the subject of a condition of a remand to local authority accommodation that he or she complies with the terms of an intensive supervision and surveillance programme. Such a programme involves 25 hours of supervision per week and additional surveillance and can be combined with a condition of electronic monitoring.

The police have power to arrest a juvenile who breaches a condition of his remand to local authority accommodation where the constable has reasonable grounds of suspecting that the juvenile has broken any of the conditions imposed (LASPOA 2012, s 97). Breach of such conditions is not an offence in itself but may trigger an application for a remand to youth detention accommodation.

The court may impose conditions on a defendant remanded to local authority accommodation on application by the local authority and where it does so may impose requirements on the local authority for securing compliance with conditions. The court may vary or revoke such conditions on the application of the local authority or the defendant.

This should not be confused with the common bail condition to reside as directed by the local authority. Such a condition does not remand a juvenile into local authority accommodation.

Remands to youth detention accommodation

7.18   The removal of a juvenile's liberty whilst on remand must always be a last resort. Alternatives must be considered and reasons given by the court which demonstrate that the statutory criteria are satisfied.

The criteria include firstly the grounds for withholding bail under the Bail Act 1976 and secondly a set of conditions imposed by the Legal Aid, Sentencing and Punishment of Offenders Act 2012.

There are 2 sets of conditions for remands to youth detention accommodation (LASPOA 2012, ss 98 and 99). If either set is satisfied then the juvenile can be so remanded. The first set is based on the seriousness of the offence. The second set is based on a history of offending or absconding. There is a proviso to the second set of criteria that a custodial sentence must be a realistic outcome if the juvenile is found guilty.

The first set of conditions for remands to youth detention accommodation are:

(a)   The juvenile is 12 years or older.

(b)   He is charged with either –

    (i)   a specified violent or specified sexual offence, or

    (ii)   an offence punishable in the case of an adult with imprisonment for a term of 14 years of more.

(c)   Only a remand to youth detention accommodation would be adequate to either –

(i)   protect the public from death or serious personal injury (whether physical or psychological) occasioned by further offences committed by the juvenile, or

(ii)   to prevent the commission by the juvenile of imprisonable offences.

(d)   The juvenile is –

(i)   legally represented before the court, or

(ii)   representation was provided to the juvenile for the purposes of the proceedings, but was withdrawn because of the juvenile's conduct, or because it appeared that the juvenile's financial resources were such that the juvenile was not eligible for such representation, or

(iii) the child applied for such representation and the application was refused because it appeared that the juvenile's financial resources were such that the juvenile was not eligible for such representation, or

(iv)   having been informed of the right to apply for such representation and having had the opportunity to do so, the juvenile refused or failed to apply (LASPOA 2012, s 98).

The second set of conditions for a remand to youth detention accommodation are:

(a)   The juvenile is 12 years or older.

(b)   There is a real prospect that the juvenile will be sentenced to a custodial sentence for the offence or one or more of those offences.

(c)   The offence, or one or more of those offences, is an imprisonable offence.

(d)   Either –

(i)   the juvenile has a recent history of absconding while remanded to local authority accommodation or youth detention accommodation, and the offence, or one or more of those offences, is alleged to be or has been found to have been committed while the juvenile was remanded to local authority accommodation or youth detention accommodation, or

(ii)   the offence or offences together with any other imprisonable offences of which the juvenile has been convicted in any proceedings, amount or would, if the juvenile were convicted of that offence or those offences, amount to a recent history of committing imprisonable offences while on bail, remanded to local authority accommodation, or remanded to youth detention accommodation.

(e)   Only a remand to youth detention accommodation would be adequate to either –

    (i)   protect the public from death or serious personal injury (whether physical or psychological) occasioned by further offences committed by the juvenile, or

    (ii)   to prevent the commission by the juvenile of imprisonable offences.

(f)   The juvenile is –

    (i)   legally represented before the court, or

    (ii)   representation was provided to the juvenile for the purposes of the proceedings, but was withdrawn because of the juvenile's conduct, or because it appeared that the juvenile's financial resources were such that the juvenile was not eligible for such representation, or

    (iii)   the juvenile applied for such representation and the application was refused because it appeared that the juvenile's financial resources were such that the juvenile was not eligible for such representation, or

    (iv)   having been informed of the right to apply for such representation and having had the opportunity to do so, the juvenile refused or failed to apply (LASPOA 2012, s 99).

The court must state in open court and explain to the juvenile in ordinary language why it is of the opinion, after considering all the options for the remand of the child, that only remanding the juvenile to youth detention accommodation would be adequate –

(a)   to protect the public from death or serious personal injury (whether physical or psychological) occasioned by further offences committed by the juvenile, or

(b)   to prevent the commission by the juvenile of imprisonable offences.

The explanation given must be specified on the warrant and entered in the court register (LASPOA 2012, s 102 (4) and (5)).

CYPA 1969, s 23(13)(c) indicates that in relation to sexual and violent offences 'serious harm' means death and/or serious physical or psychological injury occasioned by further such offences committed by the young person. Serious harm is not defined in relation to other offences. However, the definition for sexual and violent offences gives an indication of the gravity of the harm to which the public would need to be exposed from a juvenile in other circumstances before the test was likely to be satisfied.

In relation to (d)(i) above it is significant that the absconding will only qualify if this occurs whilst the defendant is remanded to local authority accommodation (or youth detention accommodation). Thus if a juvenile has been absconding whilst on bail with a condition to reside where directed by Children's Social Care or regularly been missing from home whilst on bail or wanted on warrant then these facts will not satisfy the statutory requirements. 'History of absconding' means at least one previous occasion of absconding (*R v Calder Justices, ex parte C* (4 May 1993, unreported)).

In respect of (d)(ii) above the words 'convicted of' have been held not only to apply to the present proceedings, but also to any such offences of which the juvenile has on previous occasions been convicted (*Re C* 22, October 1993, unreported, CO 2974/93).

When a juvenile is remanded to youth detention accommodation the court has to designate a local authority to look after him. Where the juvenile is already looked after by a local authority that authority will be designated for the purposes of the remand. In other cases it will be the authority where the juvenile habitually resides or where the offence was committed.

The court cannot direct where the juvenile will be placed whilst remanded to youth detention accommodation. There are various types of youth detention accommodation which may be used. These include secure children's homes, secure training centres, and young offender institutions. It is a matter for the Secretary of State to determine the placement. The Youth Offending Team will assist by providing information about the young person and the offence.

Video link hearings for those in youth detention accommodation or police custody centres

7.19   Many courts have facilities for linking with custodial institutions using audio and video equipment. The prisoner is taken to a room within the Police custody centre, Young Offender Institution or other youth detention accommodation where there are camera microphones and television screens which can be connected to those in a courtroom. In this way the members of the court and the advocates and defendant can see and talk to each other. This saves the costs and risks in transporting the prisoner to the court. When remanding a defendant into custody then a court may direct that the next hearing takes place over the video link. Indeed the court is required to give reasons in open court and record them in the register if it does not make a video link direction in a case where it has power to do so. Where the remanding court does not have a prison video link it may be appropriate for the court to remand the defendant to appear before another court which has the facilities. The court can make such a direction for any preliminary hearing and provided it is not contrary to the interests of justice also in relation to sentencing hearings (including committal for sentence hearings). The defendant is treated as being present at court whilst attending through a live link. See CDA 1998, ss 57A to 57E.

Youth detention accommodation in extradition proceedings

7.20   In relation to proceedings under the Extradition Act 2003 the 2 sets of conditions for remands to youth detention accommodation (see **7.18**) are the same as apply for non-extradition cases except that necessary modifications are made to allow the court to use an equivalent UK offence when considering whether offence based criteria are satisfied (LASPOA 2012, ss 100 and 101).

Secure accommodation

7.21   Where a juvenile is looked after by a local authority, the authority may keep that person in secure accommodation for up to 72 hours in any period of 28 consecutive days (Children (Secure Accommodation) Regulations 1991, reg 10). Apart from this power the local authority has to have an order of the court to keep the juvenile in secure accommodation for a maximum period of 28 days. The local authority may apply for permission to accommodate the juvenile securely under CA 1989, s 25. The maximum period for which a court could make a secure accommodation order of a juvenile who has been remanded to local authority accommodation is the period of the remand or 28 days, whichever is the shorter.

Application for secure accommodation order

7.22   A local authority may apply to the court for an authority to use secure accommodation for the purpose of restricting the liberty of a child who it is looking after. Applications are made under the Children Act 1989. They are excluded from the definition of specified proceedings by virtue of the Family Proceedings Courts (Children Act 1989) Rules 1991, r 2(2). Such applications can be made either to a Youth Court or a magistrates' court by virtue of the CJA 1991, s 60(3) in the case of youths who are remanded into local authority accommodation under LASPOA 2012, s 91(4). If the remand order was made by the Crown Court the application should be made to the Family Proceedings Court.

If the Youth Court made the remand, then any secure accommodation application should be made to that court. If the remand order was made in the adult magistrates' court, perhaps by virtue of the young person being jointly charged with an adult, then the application for a secure accommodation order should be made to that court.

Where a juvenile has been remanded into local authority accommodation by a Youth Court sitting outside that authority's boundary, the local Youth Court has jurisdiction to hear an application by the authority for a secure accommodation order (*Liverpool City Council v B* [1995] 1 WLR 505).

Generally a juvenile may not be placed in secure accommodation unless it appears to the court that:

(a)   he has a history of absconding and is likely to abscond from any other accommodation;

(b)   if he absconds, he is likely to suffer significant harm; or

(c)   if he is kept in any other accommodation he is likely to injure himself or other persons (Children Act 1989, s 25(1) and (3)).

One previous instance of absconding is sufficient for there to be a 'history of absconding' (*R v Calder Justices, ex parte C (a minor)* (4 May 1993, unreported)).

In the case of a juvenile who is remanded to local authority accommodation and is either:

(a)   charged with or convicted of an offence punishable in the case of a person of 21 or over with 14 years' imprisonment or more, or a violent or sexual offence; or

(b)   has a recent history of absconding while remanded to local authority accommodation, and is charged or convicted of an imprisonable offence committed while so remanded

the criteria is modified to allow the court to order detention in secure accommodation if it appears that any other accommodation is inappropriate because:

(a)   the juvenile is likely to abscond from such other accommodation; or

(b)   the juvenile is likely to injusre himself or other persons if he is kept in such other accommodation (Children (Secure Accommodation) Regulations 1991, reg 6).

These are the only provisions which would allow the criminal court to make a secure accommodation order in respect of a 10- or 11-year-old child. It is however necessary for the applicant to obtain the approval of the Secretary of State before making such an application (see below).

In *Re G (a child) (secure accommodation order)* [2001] 3 FCR 47, it was held that where a child had previously been remanded to local authority accommodation and had not committed a further offence, the conditions in reg 6 had not been met; but the Youth Court could nevertheless make a secure accommodation order if it was satisfied under s 25(3) that all the criteria of s 25(1) were met and indeed it was required to do so.

In this context the words 'convicted of' have been held not only to apply to the present proceedings but also to any such offences of which the juvenile has on previous occasions been convicted (*Re C* (22 October 1993, unreported, CO 2974/93)).

The local authority may apply for a secure accommodation order for a juvenile who it is looking after and who is residing in its accommodation. Thus in *Re C* [1994] 2 FCR 1153 the family proceedings court had jurisdiction to make a secure accommodation order for a girl who had been bailed with a condition to reside as directed by the social services and was being accommodated in local authority accommodation.

In *Re M (a minor)* [1995] 3 All ER 407, CA, it was held that it is the duty of the court to put itself in the position of a reasonable local authority and consider first, whether the criteria were satisfied and secondly, whether it would be in accordance with the local authority's duty under Children Act 1989, s 22(3) to safeguard and promote the welfare of the child by placing him or her in secure accommodation. Although the welfare of the child was a relevant consideration it could not be a paramount one, as the local authority was permitted to exercise its powers in relation to the child to protect members of the public from serious injury.

A child under 13 may not be placed in secure accommodation without the prior approval of the Secretary of State (Children (Secure Accommodation) Regulations 1991, reg 4). Such approval may be sought through the Department of Health duty service.

Procedure at the hearing

7.23   The hearing of an application for secure accommodation is as if it were by way of complaint and the Magistrates' Courts Act 1980, ss 56 and 57 apply. This means that if at the time of the hearing or the adjourned hearing the relevant minor appears but the complainant local authority fails to appear, the court may dismiss their application, or if evidence has been received on a previous occasion it may proceed in the absence of the applicant. Where neither the applicant nor the juvenile appears the court has power to dismiss the application.

Where the court proceeds with the application the procedure and order of evidence and speeches is governed by the Magistrates' Courts Act 1980, s 53 and MC Rules 1981, r 14. This means that the applicant may address the court outlining the application and will then call evidence in support of the application. At the conclusion of the evidence for the applicant the juvenile may address the court whether or not he afterwards calls evidence. At the conclusion of any evidence on behalf of the juvenile the applicant may call evidence to rebut that evidence. Either party may then, with the leave of the court, address the court a second time. Where the court grants leave to one party it must not refuse leave to the other. The parent or guardian of the juvenile is also entitled by the Magistrates' Courts (Children and Young Persons) Rules 1992 to make representations to the court and shall be allowed to do so at any such stage after the conclusion of the evidence at the hearing as the court considers appropriate (r 15).

As these are civil proceedings, the provisions of the Civil Evidence Act 1995 governing the admissibility of hearsay evidence may apply.

Before the hearing commences the court must inform the juvenile of the general nature of the proceedings and of the grounds on which they are brought. Such an explanation should be made in terms suitable to the juvenile's age and understanding. If for any reason the court is unable to give such an explanation to the juvenile because of his absence, age, or lack of understanding then the court must inform the parent or guardian present at the hearing giving a similar explanation as it would to the juvenile himself.

A court may not make an order for secure accommodation in the case of a juvenile who is not legally represented unless he has failed or refused to apply or had public funding withdrawn. Most juveniles will have the benefit of legal representation in applications for secure accommodation, but where this is not the case the court must allow his parent or guardian to conduct the case on his behalf. If the court thinks it appropriate, and subject to any request by the juvenile himself, it may allow a relative of his or some other responsible person to conduct the case on his behalf. One of the reasons that it is preferable that the juvenile should be legally represented is that the court has power under MC (CYP) Rules 1992, r 19 to hear evidence in the absence of the relevant minor, or to require his parent or guardian to withdraw. This should only be done where the court is of the opinion that it is in the interests of the relevant minor that the evidence should be received but without him being present or, in the case of the parent or guardian, that it is appropriate that they withdraw when certain evidence is heard. The court must however hear evidence relating to the character or conduct of the juvenile in his presence and if a parent or guardian is excluded then the court must inform that person of the substance of any allegations made against him by the relevant minor.

Oral evidence need not be adduced by either party if they agree that statements filed will constitute the evidence (*Re AS (secure accommodation order)* [1999] 1 FLR 103). If at the end of the applicant's case the court is satisfied that there is sufficient evidence upon which a reasonable tribunal could find the application proved, then it must tell the juvenile or the person conducting the case on his behalf of his right to give evidence or make a statement and call witnesses.

If having heard the juvenile's case the court finds the matter proved, it should so announce and go on to consider its disposal of the application. Before finally disposing of the case the court must inform the relevant minor, any person conducting the case on his behalf and his parent or guardian if present of the manner in which it proposes to deal with the case. This should be done in simple language and those persons informed should be allowed to make representations. The only exception to the court explaining its proposals to the relevant minor are if it considers it undesirable for some reason or having regard to his age and understanding it feels it would be impracticable to inform him. Having heard any such representations on its proposal the court must then make its order and shall in simple language suitable to the age and understanding of the juvenile explain the general nature and effect of the order. Again, the court may dispense with this explanation if it appears impracticable, having regard to the age and understanding of the juvenile. The court must in any case give such an explanation to the relevant minor's parent or guardian if they are present in court (MC (CYP) Rules 1992, r 17).

Youth Court remands where bail is refused

7.24

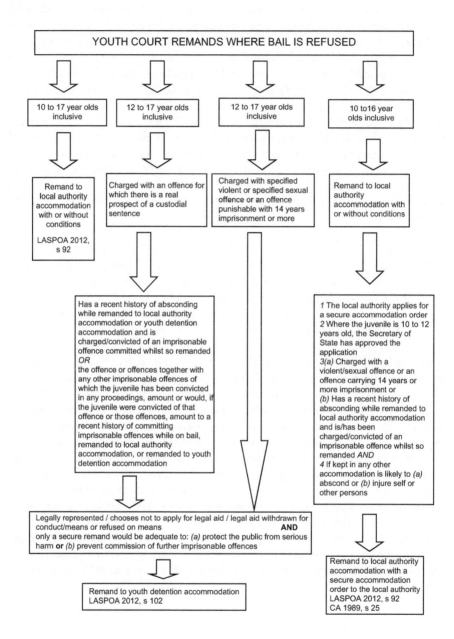

YOUTH COURT REMANDS WHERE BAIL IS REFUSED

10 to 17 year olds inclusive

12 to 17 year olds inclusive

12 to 17 year olds inclusive

10 to16 year olds inclusive

Remand to local authority accommodation with or without conditions

LASPOA 2012, s 92

Charged with an offence for which there is a real prospect of a custodial sentence

Charged with specified violent or specified sexual offence or an offence punishable with 14 years imprisonment or more

Remand to local authority accommodation with or without conditions

Has a recent history of absconding while remanded to local authority accommodation or youth detention accommodation and is charged/convicted of an imprisonable offence committed whilst so remanded *OR* the offence or offences together with any other imprisonable offences of which the juvenile has been convicted in any proceedings, amount or would, if the juvenile were convicted of that offence or those offences, amount to a recent history of committing imprisonable offences while on bail, remanded to local authority accommodation, or remanded to youth detention accommodation

1 The local authority applies for a secure accommodation order *2* Where the juvenile is 10 to 12 years old, the Secretary of State has approved the application *3(a)* Charged with a violent/sexual offence or an offence carrying 14 years or more imprisonment or *(b)* Has a recent history of absconding while remanded to local authority accommodation and is/has been charged/convicted of an imprisonable offence whilst so remanded *AND* *4* If kept in any other accommodation is likely to *(a)* abscond or *(b)* injure self or other persons

Legally represented / chooses not to apply for legal aid / legal aid withdrawn for conduct/means or refused on means   **AND** only a secure remand would be adequate to: *(a)* protect the public from serious harm **or** *(b)* prevent commission of further imprisonable offences

Remand to youth detention accommodation LASPOA 2012, s 102

Remand to local authority accommodation with a secure accommodation order to the local authority LASPOA 2012, s 92 CA 1989, s 25

Chapter 8   Referral orders, deferment of sentence, discharges, reparation orders and financial orders

Referral orders

Criteria for imposition

8.01   Where the offence was committed on or after the date when LASPOA 2012, s 79 came into force a defendant under the age of 18 years appears for sentence before a Youth Court or adult magistrates' court the court *must* make a referral order if:

(a)   the offence is imprisonable;

(b)   the offence or offences are not ones for which the sentence is fixed by law;

(c)   the defendant pleaded guilty to the offence and any connected offence;

(d)   the court is not proposing to impose a custodial sentence or make a hospital order, to grant an absolute or conditional discharge for the offence or any connected offence;

(e)   the defendant has never been convicted by a court in the United Kingdom or another member state of the European Union of any other offence. (A previous conviction for which the offender was given an absolute or conditional discharge does not count for these purposes (PCC(S)A 2000, s 14).

Where a defendant under the age of 18 years appears for sentence before a Youth Court or adult magistrates' court the court *may* make a referral order if:

(a)   the compulsory referral order conditions are not satisfied in relation to the offence and

(b)   the defendant pleaded guilty to the offence or any of the offences which are before the court to be dealt with.

General provisions

8.02   The Youth Court must specify the length of the order during which time the offender will have contact with the Panel. This must be not fewer than three and not more than 12 months and will be assessed on the basis of the seriousness of the offence.

The Sentencing Council's, definitive guideline *Sentencing Children and Young People* at paras 6.19–6.22 provides some guidance for setting the length of the order. The gist of this guidance is that for offences of relatively low seriousness the range should be three to five months; for medium seriousness five to seven months; for relatively high seriousness seven to nine months; and orders of ten to twelve months should be reserved for the most serious cases. Where the court is dealing with a first offence which is on the cusp of custody YOTs should be encouraged to set up a pre-panel to agree an intensive contract with the offender in order that the court can have confidence about what the juvenile will be required to do if it decides that a referral order is appropriate. This informal procedure is not designed to allow the court to determine or alter the content of the contract in any way. The complete Guidelines can be found at www. sentencingcouncil.org.uk.

Where the court makes a referral order it must *not* make a sentence that consists of or includes a youth rehabilitation order, impose a fine, grant a conditional discharge or make a reparation order for that offence. The court may not bind over a parent or the young offender (PCC(S)A 2000, s 19(5)), but may make a parenting order and a referral order on the same offence (CJA 2003, s 324 and Sch 34). A referral order may be accompanied by ancillary orders such as costs and compensation.

A discretionary referral order can be made irrespective of any previous convictions. There are no statutory bars or restrictions on the court making a second or subsequent referral orders for successive convictions. It is legally possible, for example, for a referral order to be imposed on a seventh conviction whatever orders have been made on the previous six convictions. Furthermore, a new referral order can be made whilst the juvenile is still subject to an existing referral order. In such a case the court may direct under PCCC(S)A 2000, s 18(3A) that the contract on the new order shall not take effect until the previous order is completed (revoked or discharged). The Sentencing Council's definitive guideline *Sentencing Children and Young People* positions referral orders between community disposals and fines. It suggests that second or subsequent referral orders may be appropriate where the offence is not serious enough for a Youth Rehabilitation Order (YRO) but some intervention is required. Or in cases where the offence is serious enough for a YRO but a referral order is considered to be the most effective way of preventing re-offending because the juvenile has responded well to an earlier order and the new offence is dissimilar. The referral order is seen by the Sentencing Council as the main sentence for delivering restorative justice. One feature of the referral order which may be beneficial to the offender is that a conviction which results solely in a referral order will become spent under s 5 of the Rehabilitation of Offenders Act 1974 (ROA 1974) as soon as the contract has been completed. If however any other order is imposed at the same time then the conviction will not become spent until the rehabilitation period which applies to that order has expired. Ancillary orders for costs, compensation, or even mandatory driving licence endorsements each carry separate rehabilitation periods. (See ROA 1974 as amended by LASPOA 2012). The rehabilitation period for a compensation order ends when the order is paid in full. The Sentencing Council's definitive guideline *Sentencing Children and Young People* sets out rehabilitation periods at page 23.

The order requires the offender to attend meetings with the Youth Offender Panel. The Panel will comprise at least one member of the Youth Offending Team and at least two lay people who are not members of the Youth Offending Team. The court must order the offender's parents or guardian to attend meetings where the offender is under 16 years of age and may do so in the case of a 16- or 17-year-old. Whatever the offender's age the court shall not order attendance by the parent if the court is satisfied that it would be unreasonable to do so or to an extent which the court is satisfied would be unreasonable. The parent or guardian will normally be required to attend at least the first meeting. The court may order the parent or guardian to attend the meetings of the panel in his or her absence in which case the court is required to send a notice to such a person. As indicated above, the court may make a parenting order at the same time as making a referral order. Before it does so it must consider a report by a probation officer, social worker or a member of the Youth Offending Team.

At the first meeting the Panel will reach an agreement with the youth on a programme aimed at preventing re-offending by the offender. The Panel can tailor the programme to the offender and the offending. The court is required to send to the Panel a statement of the offence for which the defendant has been made the subject of the referral order. Often a copy of the prosecution statements will be sent to the Panel. Defence advocates need to be alive to this and ensure that the statement from the court reflects any basis of plea.

The role of the Youth Offender Panels is outside the scope of this work but following a referral they will meet with the offender and devise programmes, participation and reparation in an attempt to address offending behaviour. Once the contract has been agreed and signed by the offender the compliance period for the referral order begins.

After the contract has taken effect, circumstances may arise (including the offender making good progress under the contract) in which it appears to the Youth Offender Panel to be in the interests of justice for the referral order to be revoked. In such circumstances the panel may refer the offender back to the Youth Court requesting it to revoke the order or alternatively to revoke the order and deal with the offender for the offence in respect of which the original order was made.

If the Youth Court decides not to exercise its power to revoke the referral order the Youth Offender Panel may not make a further application in the following three months except with the consent of the appropriate court (PCC(S)A 2000, s 27A).

Once a youth offender contract, for less than 12 months, has taken effect the panel may refer the offender back to the appropriate court requesting it to extend the length of the order (PCC(S)A 2000, s 27B and Sch 1, paras 9ZB to 9ZE). This can be done at any time so long as the period of the order has not ended and the request for the extension is not in excess of three months. The Panel shall make the referral by sending a report to the appropriate court explaining the circumstances that have arisen since the contract took effect and why the offender is being referred back to it for an extension of the period. If the offender is under 18 at the time of the referral back to court he will appear in a Youth Court; otherwise he will appear in a magistrates' court.

If the referral order is to be extended, the offender must appear before the court, the contract must be in force and any extension must not extend the order beyond the maximum 12 months. In determining whether to grant an extension the court shall have regard to the extent of the offender's compliance with the terms of the contract (PCC(S)A 2000, Sch 1, paras 9ZB to 9ZE).

Breach of the order and the commission of offences

Breaches

8.03   The Youth Court will deal with all breaches except where the juvenile is 18 years old at the date of the first hearing. In that event, the case must be heard in the adult court. Where the court decides that a failure to comply with the order has not been proved the offender will remain subject to referral unless the contract has by then expired. Even where the court is satisfied that there has been failure to comply with a referral order it can take no action in relation to a breach if for any reason it considers this appropriate. In this situation, the order will continue unless the contract has expired (PCC(S)A 2000, Sch1, para 7).

If the court concludes, contrary to the decision of the panel, that the offender's compliance has been such as to justify the conclusion that it has been satisfactorily completed then it can make an order declaring that the order has been discharged (PCC(S)A 2000, Sch1, para 8).

Paragraph 6(A) of PCC(S)A 2000, Sch 1 as amended by CJCA 2015, s 43 provides that where the referral panel refer the juvenile back to the court for breach, then provided that it is proved to the court's satisfaction that the offender has failed without reasonable excuse to comply with the terms of the contract, and that the failures to comply occurred on or after 13 April 2015, then if the court decides not to revoke the order it may:

(a)   impose a fine of up to £2,500 for the breach; or

(b)   extend the period for which the contract will have effect, up to the maximum 12 months. If the period has expired before the hearing date then it is not possible to extend the contract.

Any fine for the breach may be enforced as if imposed on conviction.

Where the court decides to revoke the order, it may resentence the juvenile for the offences for which the order had been imposed. The court must have regard to the circumstances of the referral back to the court and where the contract has taken effect between the offender and the panel and the extent of his or her compliance with the contract. It may re-sentence the juvenile in any way the court which imposed the referral order could, except that it may not impose a new referral order (PCC(S)A 2000, Sch1, para 5)

Further convictions

8.04   **Extension:** The court's sentencing powers on further convictions have been widened by the Criminal Justice and Courts Act 2015. It is no longer confined to extending a first referral order. Where a juvenile under the age of 18 is subject to a referral order when the court is dealing with them for a further offence, the court may sentence the offender for the further offence by imposing an extension to the referral order, provided this does not extend the overall referral compliance period to more than 12 months. This power to extend the compliance period does not apply if the court intends to impose any of the following sentences for the further offence:

(a)   absolute discharge;

(b)   conditional discharge;

(c)   a hospital order;

(d)   a custodial sentence or any sentence fixed by law.

(PCC(S)A 2000, Sch1, para 10)

Revocation: If the court imposes an absolute or conditional discharge for the further offence or extends the compliance period as in the paragraph above then it cannot revoke the existing referral order. In any other circumstances, it may revoke the order if it considers this is in the interests of justice. Where the referral order is revoked, the court may deal with the juvenile in any way they could have been dealt with by the court which made the order, other than imposing a new referral order. Regard should be had to the extent of the offenders' compliance where a contract was signed. An option now available to the court is to impose a new referral order for the further offence, even where it has left in place the pre-existing order. In that scenario, it may direct that the contract under the new order does not take effect until the earlier order is revoked or discharged (PCC(S)A 2000, s 18(3A)).

If the parent (or guardian) does not attend meetings of the Youth Offender Panel in accordance with the order then the panel can report this to the court and a summons or warrant can be issued for the parent to attend the Youth Court. If satisfied that the parent failed without reasonable cause to comply with the order the court can make a parenting order and/or deal with the parent under MCA 1980, s 63. (See PCC(S)A 2000, Sch 1, Part 1A.)

Deferment of sentence

8.05   A deferment of sentence is, strictly speaking, not a sentence at all. The court may, after a finding of guilt, defer dealing with the offender for the purpose of enabling it to have regard, in determining the method of disposal, to his conduct (including, where appropriate, the making by him of reparation for his offence) or to any change in his circumstances. Such a deferment may be for a period not exceeding six months.

The date must be fixed by the court at the point of deferment and the case adjourned without the imposition of bail upon the offender (PCC(S)A 2000, s 1(6), as substituted by CJA 2003, Sch 23). This power is exercisable only if the juvenile consents, and for these purposes he should be asked in open court for his consent. He or she must also undertake to comply with any requirements as to his conduct during the period of deferment that the court considers it appropriate to impose. Furthermore, the court should be satisfied, having regard to the nature of the offence and the character and circumstances of the offender that it would be in the interests of justice to exercise this power (PCC(S)A 2000, s 1(3) as inserted by CJA 2003, Sch 23).

The requirements as to his conduct may include reparative and other activities. The court can include requirements as to the defendant's residence. If the defendant is to undertake requirements the court may appoint a supervisor to monitor his or her compliance with the requirements. The supervisor must consent to acting and must also provide the court with such information as it requires about the defendant's compliance. If the offender fails to comply with the requirements he or she may be returned to court before the end of the period of deferment. The defendant may then be sentenced for the original offence. The court may issue a summons or warrant to ensure his or her attendance.

Should the offender commit a further offence during the period of deferment, the court which deals with that further offence may also deal with the deferred sentence, unless the deferred sentence was imposed by the Crown Court (see below). Where the court deals with the offender because of breach of requirements or because he has committed a further offence it has the same powers of sentence that it had when it decided to defer sentence. The court may not defer sentence if the compulsory referral conditions are satisfied.

It can be seen from the drafting of the statute and from the possible ramifications of a deferred sentence that this is not an order that the court will impose lightly. It is an option that should be used in very limited circumstances and reserved for the offender whose circumstances suggest a positive likelihood of altering his behaviour in any way clearly specified by the court.

The principles set out on deferment of sentence have been reinforced in the case of *R v George* [1984] 3 All ER 13, CA. Deferment of sentence should not be adopted without careful consideration of whether the sentencer's intentions could not best be achieved by other means. If deferment is decided upon, care must be taken to avoid the risk of misunderstanding and a risk of injustice when the defendant returns to court. Where the court has deferred sentence it must give a copy of the order deferring sentence and setting out the requirements to the offender and any person appointed as supervisor.

As a matter of principle, a substantial custodial sentence is said not to be appropriate after a deferment where the report on conduct and circumstances given to the court is not unfavourable. In many cases an order of conditional discharge can be as effective as deferring sentence.

Deferring sentence should be reserved for those cases in which the justices have reason to believe that the juvenile's lifestyle will change constructively over the period of deferment. The Sentencing Council makes it clear that the court should impose specific and measurable conditions that do not involve a serious restriction on liberty, give a clear indication of the type of sentence it would have imposed if it had decided not to defer and ensure that the offender understands the consequences of failure to comply with the court's wishes during the deferment period. For these reasons, it is recommended that the justices deferring sentence should return to make the final order.

If the juvenile is found guilty of any offence during the period of deferment the court, which deferred sentence on him, may deal with him for the deferred matter before the term of deferment expires. If the court that makes a finding of guilt for the subsequent events is the same court which deferred sentence then it may deal with both the deferred matter and the new offence. However, if the subsequent offence is dealt with by another Youth Court, that court may deal with the deferred matter as well as the new offence. Note, however, that this power is not exercisable by the Youth Court if the court that deferred passing sentence was the Crown Court. Where a court dealing with a subsequent offence, deals with another court's deferred sentence, it is not required to obtain that court's consent. As a matter of practice, inquiry should be made of the other court for details of the deferment. Where a Crown Court deals with a subsequent offence, it shall not pass any sentence in respect of the deferred offence which could not have been imposed by a Youth Court.

Absolute discharge

8.06   Where the court convicts a juvenile of an offence and it is of the opinion, having regard to the circumstances (including the nature of the offence and the character of the offender), that it is inexpedient to inflict punishment, it may discharge the defendant absolutely (PCC(S)A 2000, s 12(1)(a)). This power is generally reserved for cases where the defendant has committed a crime in law but can be said to be morally blameless.

An absolute discharge may also be applicable where a juvenile is being made subject to a custodial order and has other offences for which a custodial sentence would either not be lawful or would be inappropriate. In such circumstances the court may impose an absolute discharge, although some courts prefer to record no separate penalty for the offences not subject to the custodial order. Either course of action is preferable to the imposition of a financial penalty, which could be considered oppressive in addition to a custodial order.

Conditional discharge

8.07   This is an order discharging the offender on the condition that he commits no further offence during a specified period not exceeding three years. If he is found guilty of a subsequent offence during the period of the conditional discharge he may be dealt with not only for that offence, but also for the original offence for which he was conditionally discharged. As in the case of an absolute discharge the court should be of the opinion that it would not be expedient to inflict punishment, having regard to the nature and circumstances of the offence and the character of the offender.

It is good practice when making an order for conditional discharge for the court to explain the effect of the order to the juvenile in ordinary language. The court may delegate the explanation of a conditional discharge to a defendant's advocate. However, the case of *R v Wehner* [1977] 3 All ER 553, CA, makes it clear that the better practice is face-to-face communication from the magistrate to the defendant, thus ensuring that the juvenile before them has fully understood the order made.

The effect of a conditional discharge is that it is not deemed to be a conviction for any purpose other than the purpose of the proceedings in which the order is made and any subsequent breach of the order (PCC(S)A 2000, s 14(1)).

Unless there are exceptional circumstances the court may not impose a conditional discharge for an offence committed within two years of a youth caution or youth conditional caution. The exceptional circumstances must be related directly to the offence or the offender and the court must explain its reasons for believing there are exceptional circumstances (CDA 1998, ss 66 and 66F).

As noted elsewhere, a conditional discharge may not be imposed at the same time as a referral order, nor may it be given as a penalty for a breach of a criminal behaviour order.

Breach of conditional discharge

8.08   Where it is proved to the satisfaction of the court which made the order for conditional discharge that the juvenile subject to the order has been found guilty of an offence committed during the relevant period, the court may deal with him for the offence for which the order was made in any manner in which it could deal with him if he had just been found guilty by that court of that offence. If the juvenile subject to a conditional discharge is found guilty by another magistrates' court or Youth Court of any offence during the relevant period, that court may, with the consent of the court which made the order, deal with him for the original offence as if it had just found him guilty of that offence (PCC(S)A 2000, s 13(8) subject to restrictions imposed on an adult court by PCC(S)A 2000, s 8).

If a juvenile attains the age of 18 and is then found guilty of an offence committed during the currency of a conditional discharge made by the Youth Court, the Youth Court has jurisdiction to enforce his attendance and deal with him for the original offence. Where an offender attains the age of 18, and appears before a magistrates' court in breach of a conditional discharge made in the Youth Court in respect of an offence triable only on indictment in the case of an adult, the powers of the magistrates' court are to impose a fine of up to £5,000 and/or deal with the offender in any way a magistrates' court could deal with him or her if it had just convicted the offender of an offence punishable with imprisonment for a term not exceeding six months (PCC(S) A 2000, s 13(9)).

The Youth Court may issue a summons or warrant for the purposes of enforcing attendance. Before issuing a summons an information must be laid and where a warrant is issued that information must be in writing and substantiated on oath (PCC(S)A 2000, s 13(3)).

The correct procedure for dealing with an offender found guilty of an offence during the operational period of a conditional discharge is to put the alleged breach to the offender and ask him if it is admitted or denied. If it is denied the court must determine whether a further offence has been committed within the terms of the section. The admission or denial should be entered on the court register along with the adjudication when the case is finally dealt with. An obligation is placed on the prosecution to relate to the court the details of the original offence so that the court may deal with that offence in a fair and effective manner.

Reparation orders

8.09   A reparation order is a disposal requiring a young offender to make reparation to the victim of the offence or to the community at large. This is reparation other than the payment of compensation and may cover a variety of activities from simply writing a letter of apology to carrying out work to assist the local community.

There is a statutory presumption that the court will make such a reparation order if it has power to do so. If it does not make a reparation order it must give its reasons (PCC(S)A 2000, s 73(8)). In practice, this provision is only likely to come into play where the court imposes a discharge, fine or attendance centre order.

A reparation order may only be made if the court has been notified by the Secretary of State that arrangements for implementing such orders are available. The court shall not make a reparation order if it proposes:

(a)   to pass on him a custodial sentence; or

(b)   to make a youth rehabilitation order; or

(c)   to make a referral order.

The court may not make a reparation order where a youth rehabilitation order is in force in respect of the offender, unless when it makes a reparation order it revokes the youth rehabilitation order. See **Chapter 11** for revocation powers.

Before it makes an order the court is required to obtain a report by a probation officer, social worker, or member of a Youth Offending Team indicating:

(a)   the type of work that is suitable for the offender; and

(b)   the attitude of the victim.

The order shall not require the offender to work for more than 24 hours in aggregate and must be completed within three months. The requirements of the order shall, so far as is practicable, avoid conflict with the offender's religious beliefs or interference with schooling or work.

Fines

8.10   One common order made in dealing with criminal offences in the Youth Court is the fine. In the Youth Court (or adult court) where an offender under the age of 14 is fined, the maximum fine available is £250. When a juvenile over the age of 14 and under the age of 18 is fined in the Youth Court (or adult court), the maximum fine available is £1,000 (PCC(S)A 2000, s 135). Where the maximum fine that can be imposed on an adult is less than the appropriate limit for the juvenile, then the adult maximum will apply. There is no statutory maximum fine in respect of a juvenile who is sentenced before the Crown Court, although when dealing with an appeal or breach of a conditional discharge imposed by a lower court the lower courts' maxima apply.

General considerations

8.11   The basic principle of fines imposition is that the court must ensure that the financial penalty imposed reflects and is commensurate with the seriousness of the offence being punished. The aim is for the fine to have an equal impact on offenders with different financial circumstances. It may be a hardship but should not force the offender below a reasonable 'subsistence' level. The court will therefore go through its normal assessment of mitigating and aggravating factors to assess the gravity of the offence, and then proceed to look at the offender's financial circumstances and ability to pay the fine. The court has a duty to take into account the financial circumstances of the offender in so far as they are known or appear to the court. Normally, a fine should be of an amount that is capable of being paid within 12 months. In the Youth Court the offender will usually be before the court and a means enquiry can take place (CJA 2003, ss 162 and 164).

This requirement, to take the offender's financial circumstances into account in setting the amount of the fine, also applies to compensation orders and to the financial circumstances of a parent or guardian who is ordered to pay a fine on behalf of their child (see **8.13** and **8.14** below). If a parent or guardian is not before the court, the court has power to make an order requiring them to provide the court with a statement of means within a period specified. The court has the power to make such a determination as it thinks fit of the financial circumstances of an offender where he has been convicted in his absence, or in the case of a parent or guardian who has been ordered to pay the fine on behalf of the young offender when they fail to comply with the order to give a statement of financial circumstances.

It is worth noting that where the court has made a determination of financial circumstances in the absence of sufficient information, it may at a subsequent means enquiry remit all or part of the fine if as a result of its enquiry it finds that the original fine was disproportionate to the actual means of the offender.

If the court orders the juvenile to pay the fine then it is likely to be a fairly small fine repayable from pocket money or a part-time job, or if the offender is in the 16- to 17-year-old bracket, from wages if the offender is working. The parents, however, will pay the majority of financial penalties in the Youth Court.

Approach to the assessment of fines

8.12   Where financial circumstances are limited, priority should be given to compensation, victim surcharge, fines and then costs. Costs must not in any event exceed the amount of any fine where the juvenile is ordered to make payment (POA 1985, s 18(5)). It is the means of the payer which are used to determine the correct level of a financial payment and any payment terms. The maximum compensation which can be ordered by a Magistrates' Court (including a Youth Court) is £5,000 per offence (PCC(S)A 2000, s 131(A1)).

The Sentencing Council offers the following guidance at paras 6.17 and 6.18 of the definitive guideline *Sentencing Children and Young People*:

> 'The court may impose a fine for any offence (unless the criteria for a mandatory referral order are met)... If the child or young person is under 16 then the court has a duty to order parents or guardians to pay the fine; if the young person is 16 or over this duty is discretionary. In practice, many children and young people will have limited financial resources and the court will need to determine whether imposing a fine will be the most effective disposal.

> A court should bear in mind that children and young people may have money that is specifically required for travel costs to school, college or apprenticeships and lunch expenses.'

Parental responsibility for financial penalties

8.13   The courts have for many years had an obligation, now consolidated under PCC(S)A 2000, s 137, to order fines, etc to be paid by parents where this is thought to be appropriate. Section 137(3) is worded so that in the case of an offender who is under 16 years of age the court must order the parent or guardian to pay the fine unless it would be unreasonable in the circumstances of the case so to do, or the parent or guardian cannot be found. In the case of the 16- and 17-year-old, the court has a power to order the parent or guardian to pay the financial penalty rather than a duty to do so.

Provided a parent has been given the opportunity to attend court, an order for payment may be made against him in his absence. If the parent is present he must be given the opportunity to make representations as to whether he should be responsible for the payment of the financial penalty.

It may be said to be unreasonable, having regard to the circumstances of the case, to order the parent or guardian to pay a financial order where he satisfies the court either that he did not have charge or control of the juvenile at the time the offence was committed, or that he had not contributed to the commission of the offence by neglect or failure to exercise due care or control over the juvenile.

In *TA v DPP* [1997] 1 Cr App R (S) 1, a 16-year-old girl was accommodated in a local authority children's home under a voluntary arrangement. There was no care order in force. She kicked a police car and subsequently pleaded guilty to criminal damage. She was given a conditional discharge and ordered to pay £30 costs. Her mother was made responsible for payment of £100 compensation. The Divisional Court set this order aside saying it was unreasonable bearing in mind that the mother had had no opportunity to prevent her committing the offence as the girl was not living with her. The requirement to inquire into whether it would be reasonable to make the parent pay financial penalties and the need to give the parent the opportunity to be heard before making such an order were again underlined in *R v J-B* [2004] EWCA Crim 14. In this case the Court of Appeal held that it would be unreasonable to order a parent to pay where it was impossible to identify any fault on the part of the parent or guardian or anything done by him that may have caused the defendant to commit the offence. The court should not order the parent or guardian to pay a fine without considering his means (*Lenihen v West Yorkshire Metropolitan Police* (1981) 3 Cr App R (S) 42). Nor should the court rely on assertions made about the parent's attitude to the offending and to the prevention of that offending made in pre-sentence reports without checking the truthfulness of those comments with the parent (*R v Sheffield Crown Court, ex parte Clarkson* (1986) 8 Cr App R (S) 454). See also **12.14** for compensation orders and **12.33** for binding over parents to enforce financial penalties.

Local authority responsibility for financial penalties

8.14   Section 137 of the Powers of Criminal Courts (Sentencing) Act 2000 also makes local authorities responsible for the payment of fines, etc for offenders under the age of 18 where the authority has parental responsibility for the relevant juvenile, and that juvenile is in local authority care, or is being provided with accommodation by the authority in the exercise of any functions, in particular those under the Children Act 1989. The legislation was considered in *North Yorkshire County Council v Selby Youth Court Justices* [1994] 1 All ER 991. This was a case concerning a compensation order made against a local authority. It was held that an order made under CYPA 1969, s 23, remanding a young person to local authority accommodation did not confer parental responsibility on the local authority. Thus a local authority cannot be ordered to pay fines, victim surcharge, costs or compensation in relation to a juvenile remanded to its care.

In *D (a minor) v DPP* [1995] Crim LR 748, it was held that where a local authority was found to have done everything that it reasonably and properly could to protect the public from a young person in its care who was guilty of a criminal offence it would be unreasonable and unjust that it should be ordered to pay a compensation order. It followed from this case that if the local authority had breached a statutory duty then a compensation order could be made against it and the court would not need to consider the means of the local authority. This point was taken in *Bedfordshire County Council v DPP* [1995] Crim LR 962, where the council was ordered to pay compensation because it failed adequately to check on the juvenile's whereabouts. The sentencing court did not find that such checks would have prevented the offending. The Divisional Court held that to make a compensation order against the local authority the court must be satisfied of a causal link between the failure by the local authority and the offending. In *Marlowe Child and Family Services Ltd v DPP* [1998] Crim LR 594, where a local authority placed a juvenile with a company that specialised in looking after difficult children, the court could not make the company responsible for paying a compensation order because the company was not a guardian.

For the purpose of assessment of any such financial penalty in respect of the local authority, it will be fixed by reference solely to the circumstances and the seriousness of the offence. If the young person in local authority accommodation is ordered to pay the fine, it is the offender's means, and not those of the local authority, which are to be assessed for the purpose of the fine. See also **12.14** for compensation orders.

Chapter 9   Youth rehabilitation orders

General principles

9.01   The process of sentencing young people who appear before a Youth Court has never been a simple one. The difficulties in the past were largely rooted in the failure to implement the Children and Young Persons Act 1969 (CYPA 1969) in its entirety which would have resulted in a largely welfare-based system. Legislation has continued to amend and alter the sentencing process in the Youth Court and courts have continued to adapt and to apply the legislative imperative. Despite this there remains on the statute book an important consideration or duty which the court is bound to discharge, namely:

> 'Every court in dealing with a child or young person who is brought before it, either as an offender or otherwise, shall have regard to the welfare of the child or young person, and shall in a proper case take steps for removing him from undesirable surroundings, and for securing that proper provision is made for his education and training' (CYPA 1933, s 44, as amended).

This general welfare principle must be considered having regard to the principal aim of the youth justice system and the specified purposes of sentencing which are discussed below.

The Criminal Justice Act 1991 (CJA 1991) brought to the Youth Court a new philosophy of sentencing. The Act seeks (now embodied in the Criminal Justice Act 2003 (CJA 2003)) to ensure proportionality of sentencing so that the severity of the sentence should reflect the seriousness of the offence committed. Sentencing is seen in terms of a graduated restriction upon the offender's liberty, such restriction increasing with the seriousness of the offence.

This new legislative framework gives a clear and graduated approach to sentencing. It starts with fines and discharges at the lower end of the seriousness scale, moving through to community penalties where the offence is 'serious enough' to merit such a sentence and finally to custodial alternatives in cases where the offending is 'so serious that neither a community penalty nor a fine be justified for the offence'. The community sentence in the Youth Court is known as a 'Youth Rehabilitation Order' (YRO).

The Crime and Disorder Act 1998 (CDA 1998) introduced yet another layer to the sentencing principles to be applied in the Youth Court. The principal aim is in s 37 of the aforementioned Act. It reads:

> '(1) It shall be the principal aim of the youth justice system to prevent offending by children and young persons.

(2) In addition to any other duty to which they are subject, it shall be the duty of all persons and bodies carrying out functions in relation to the youth justice system to have regard to that aim.'

These two principles (welfare and preventing offending) have been recognised by the Sentencing Council's definitive guideline *Sentencing Children and Young People* at paragraph 1.1. No priority is given to either purpose in the guidelines. Section 142A of the CJA 2003 has not been implemented, so the statute setting out the purposes of sentencing do not apply to youths. The Sentencing Council's guidance indicates that the statutory sentencing purposes for adults (CJA 2003, s 142) only apply in the Youth Court where the juvenile attains 18 years of age during the proceedings.

The Sentencing Council make it clear that offence seriousness is the starting point for any sentencing exercise. The definitive guideline contains a section on available sentences which includes general guidance about the imposition of YROs (paras 6.23–6.36). There is a table setting out the type of requirements which might be appropriate depending on the level of risk of re-offending and/or causing serious harm. The Sentencing Council's definitive guideline *Sentencing Children and Young People* also has offence specific guidelines; at Part 2 for sexual offences and at Part 3 for robbery offences. Those guidelines incorporate guidance on available sentences, including YROs.

Although the legal restrictions and requirements are dealt with in detail in the following section, a few general considerations are noted here to put the concept of the community sentence into its proper context. A community sentence or order stands in its own right and should reflect the seriousness of the offence for which it is imposed.

General considerations before making a youth rehabilitation order

9.02   Youth rehabilitation orders (YROs) can only be made for offences committed on or after 30 November 2009. A court shall not pass a youth rehabilitation order on an offender unless it is of the opinion that the offence, or the combination of the offence and one or more offences associated with it, was serious enough to warrant that sentence. Even where an offence crosses this threshold, the Youth Court is not obliged to make a youth rehabilitation order (CJA 2003, s 148(5)).

The order and requirements forming the sentence must be the most suitable for the offender and the restrictions which they impose upon the offender's liberty must be such as in the opinion of the court are commensurate with the seriousness of the offence, or the combination of the offence and the other offences associated with it. In reaching this opinion, the court must take into account all information about the circumstances of the offence including any aggravating or mitigating factors, the offender's culpability and any harm the offence caused or may have caused. The court should also take account of all relevant information about the offender

147

which will include previous findings of guilt: CJA 2003, s 148. Previous convictions are treated as an aggravating factor depending on the nature of the offence and the time elapsed between offences. Offences committed whilst on bail are aggravated by that factor.

The Sentencing Council's definitive guideline *Sentencing Children and Young People* at section 4 sets out the individualistic approach which the Youth Court should take. There are non-exhaustive lists of possible aggravating and mitigating factors. The importance of a juvenile's age is a key factor in any sentencing exercise. Developmental and emotional age is to be considered at least as important as chronological age.

Before making the order, the court must obtain and consider information about the offender's family circumstances and the likely effect of such an order on those circumstances.

When deciding on the restrictions on liberty imposed by a community sentence the court may have regard to any period the offender has spent in custody in connection with the offence. This includes remands to youth detention accommodation (CJA 2003, ss 149 and 242(2) as amended by LASPOA 2012, Sch 12, para 51).

A court cannot impose a YRO if there is an existing YRO or reparation order. There is power however to revoke the existing YRO and then make a new YRO for all the offences. An existing reparation order can be revoked but the court cannot re-sentence the offences which had been subject to the reparation order. (See **Chapter 11**.)

Length of order

9.03   The overall length of a YRO must be set and may not exceed three years. Individual requirements can have varying lengths. The end date of the order must be the same as the date set for the completion of longest requirement. Once the end date has been passed then the order will no longer be in force except for the purpose on any outstanding hours of unpaid work. It is not possible to extend the length of the YRO after it has been imposed except on one occasion only and then by up to 6 months for the purpose of imposing a requirement for breach of the order, or on an application to amend the YRO. If the youth commits an offence during the order then the court can revoke the order and re-sentence him for the original offence(s). The primary intention when a juvenile breaches an order is to determine the most effective way of preventing the person re-offending. This may involve reviewing all the circumstances, including the support provided by the YOT and any other agency or individual. Amendments to the requirements may be appropriate. There is no duty to make the requirements more onerous. (See also **Chapter 11**.)

9.04   Pre-sentence reports must be obtained before the court makes a youth rehabilitation order in order that it can be satisfied that the restriction on liberty imposed is commensurate with the seriousness of the offending, and that requirements are the most suitable for the offender. Before preparing a report, the Youth Offending Team will complete an approved assessment such as ASSET Plus.

are required to follow the YJB 'scaled approach' to intervention with young offenders under any requirements or orders which include supervision. The general idea is that the level of intervention should be related to the risks presented by the young person. There are three levels of intervention; standard, enhanced and intensive. Both the degree of risk of re-offending and the risk of serious harm are taken into account when determining the appropriate level of intervention. This is a matter for the Youth Offending Team to assess and report on to the court. It is important that courts and YOTs work together to ensure that both have confidence in such assessments and any requirements imposed as a consequence. The actual level of intervention can change over the life of any relevant requirement. Reviews should be held at least once every three months. If the risks have reduced significantly then the extent of any intervention can be cut back. If the risks have increased significantly then the intervention should be increased.

The Sentencing Council's definitive guideline *Sentencing Children and Young People* provides the following guidance when determining the nature and extent of requirements:

'The requirements included within the order (and the subsequent restriction on liberty) and the length of the order must be proportionate to the seriousness of the offence and suitable for the child or young person. The court should take care to ensure that the requirements imposed are not too onerous so as to make breach of the order almost inevitable.

When determining the nature and extent of the requirements the court should primarily consider the likelihood of the child or young person re-offending and the risk of the child or young person causing serious harm. A higher risk of re-offending does not in itself justify a greater restriction on liberty than is warranted by the seriousness of the offence; any requirements should still be commensurate with the seriousness of the offence and regard must still be had for the welfare of the child or young person.

If a child or young person is assessed as presenting a high risk of re-offending or of causing serious harm but the offence that was committed is of relatively low seriousness then the appropriate requirements are likely to be primarily rehabilitative or for the protection of the public.

Likewise if a child or young person is assessed as presenting a low risk of re-offending or of causing serious harm but the offence was of relatively high seriousness then the appropriate requirements are likely to be primarily punitive.

• **Standard level** – for those who show a low likelihood of reoffending *and* a low risk of serious harm; in those circumstances, the order primarily will seek to repair the harm caused through, for example: reparation; unpaid work; supervision; and/or attendance centre.

- **Enhanced level** – for those who show a medium likelihood of reoffending *or* a medium risk of serious harm. The order will seek to repair harm caused and to enable help or change through, for example: supervision; reparation; requirement to address behaviour e.g. drug treatment, offending behaviour programme, education programme; and/or a combination of the above.

- **Intensive level** – for those with a high likelihood of reoffending *or* a high or very high risk of serious harm; in those circumstances, the order will seek to ensure the control of and enable help or change for the child or young person through, for example: supervision; reparation; requirement to address behaviour; requirement to monitor or restrict movement, e.g. prohibited activity, curfew, exclusion or electronic monitoring; and/or a combination of the above.'

The court need not have a pre-sentence report if in the circumstances of the case it is of the opinion that it is unnecessary to obtain one (CJA 2003, s 156(4)). In the case of a juvenile, the court shall not form this opinion unless there was a previous pre-sentence report obtained in respect of the offender and the court has had regard to information contained in that report or the most recent report (CJA 2003, s 156(5)). In practice, such a report should be current so as to deal with any significant changes that may have occurred in the young person's life.

The purpose of a pre-sentence report in relation to a youth rehabilitation order is to give the court information as to the suitability of the offender for one or more of the available requirements and create an order that will be most likely to address the offending behaviour. The failure of the court to obtain a pre-sentence report in the required case will not invalidate the court's order, but in the case of an appeal a report must be obtained and considered at the appeal hearing. The appellate court does not have to obtain a report if it is of the opinion that the Youth Court was justified in forming the opinion that it was unnecessary to obtain one or, although the Youth Court was not justified in forming that opinion, in the circumstances of the case at the time it is before the court, it is unnecessary to obtain such a report (CJA 2003, s 156(7)). In any event an appellate court would have to obtain a report or have regard to an existing report before forming the opinion in subs (7) (CJA 2003, s 156(8)).

Pre-sentence reports must comply with the requirements set out in the National Standards. A report may be received in an oral form unless the court is considering passing a custodial sentence.

General requirements on making a youth rehabilitation order

9.05 Before making an order, imposing two or more requirements, or making two or more youth rehabilitation orders in respect of associated offences, the court must consider whether, in the circumstances of the case, the requirements to be imposed are compatible with each other.

The court must ensure, as far as is practicable, that any requirements imposed in the order avoid conflicting with the offender's religious beliefs. Nor should requirements interfere with the offender's ability to attend work, school or other educational establishment.

In terms of its length a youth rehabilitation order must specify an end date, not more than three years after the date on which the order takes effect, by which time all the requirements in it must have been complied with. The court may set different dates for the completion of separate requirements, however the latest date must be the same as the end date for the order itself.

The order normally takes effect on the day the order is made. However, if a detention and training order is in force in respect of the offender at the time it makes the order it may order that it takes effect at the expiry of the term of the detention and training order or when the period of supervision begins following release from custody of the detention and training centre.

The court is not permitted to make a youth rehabilitation order when another youth rehabilitation order or a reparation order is already in force, unless it first revokes those earlier orders.

A youth rehabilitation order should specify who the responsible officer will be. This will usually be a Youth Offending Team. It is a matter for the court to decide which YOT will be specified in the order. Where the juvenile and family members all live within the same area as the court and YOT this will be straightforward. Where however the defendant has been placed away from his usual home or that of his family by a local authority then issues can arise as funding for YOTs does not 'follow the child'. In such circumstances, it may be appropriate to specify the YOT for the local authority who placed the child out of that authority's area.

It is also necessary for the court to specify in the order the local justice area where the offender resides or will reside (CJIA 2008, Sch 1, para 33). A consequence of specifying the local justice area in the order is that any application to amend an order must be made to a court within the specified local justice area. Proceedings for breach of an order may be started in that area if it is not known where the offender resides at the time breach proceedings are commenced. The specified local justice area can be changed where the juvenile moves address (CJIA 2008, Sch 2, para 13(2)).

If a requirement is made for the protection of a person from the defendant or for the defendant to reside with a person then the court must give that person notice of the requirement (CPR 2015, r 28.2(2)(d)).

Orders which can be made without a pre-sentence report are dealt with at **6.08** and in **Chapter 8**.

Concurrent and consecutive orders

9.06   Where an offender is convicted of two or more associated offences the court may make two or more youth rehabilitation orders. Where it does so it must direct in relation to requirements of the same kind whether those requirements are to be concurrent or consecutive to each other. Fostering requirements may not be directed to run consecutively. Where the court directs that two or more requirements of the same kind are to run consecutively, the number of hours, days or months specified in the order may run one after another, so long as the aggregate number does not exceed the maximum that may be specified in relation to any one of them.

Types of youth rehabilitation order

9.07   There are effectively three types of YRO:

(a)   a standard YRO with up to 15 substantive requirements (and two monitoring requirements);

(b)   a YRO with intensive supervision and surveillance;

(c)   a YRO with a fostering requirement.

The types of YRO in (b) and (c) above may only be imposed as a direct alternative to a custodial sentence. They will be looked at in more detail at the end of this chapter.

Standard youth rehabilitation order

9.08   A standard YRO can be imposed for any offence. In contrast to the adult court community order the offence does not have to be imprisonable.

The following requirements may be attached to a standard youth rehabilitation order. The details are found in Sch 1 of the Act and the relevant paragraph of the schedule is in brackets next to each of the requirements:

(a)   an activity requirement (paras 6 to 8);

(b)   a supervision requirement (para 9);

(c)   an unpaid work requirement (in a case where the offender is aged 16 or 17 at the time of the conviction) (para 10);

(d)   a programme requirement (para 11);

(e)   an attendance centre requirement (para 12);

(f)   a prohibited activity requirement (para 13);

(g)   a curfew requirement (para 14);

(h)   an exclusion requirement (para 15);

(i)   a residence requirement (para 16);

(j)   a local authority residence requirement (in a case where the offender is aged 16 or 17 at the time of conviction) (paras 17 and 19);

(k)   a mental health treatment requirement (para 20);

(l)   a drug treatment/drug testing requirement (paras 22 and 23);

(m)   an intoxicating substance treatment requirement (para 24);

(n)   an education requirement (para 25); and

(o)   an electronic monitoring requirement (para 26).

(a) Activity requirement

9.09   An activity requirement means that the offender must do any or all of the following:

(a)   participate, on such number of days as may be specified in the order, in activities at the place or places specified by presenting himself at the place specified or to a specified person in accordance with instructions given by the responsible officer and comply with instructions given by, or under the authority of, the person in charge of that activity;

(b)   participate in activity, or activities, specified in the order on such number of days so specified;

(c)   participate in one or more residential exercises for a continuous period or periods comprising such number of days as specified;

(d)   engage in activities in accordance with instructions of the responsible officer on such number of days as may be specified.

Where the order requires the offender to participate in a residential exercise, it must specify a place or an activity. Such a requirement may last for a period of no more than seven days and require him to:

(a)   present himself at the beginning of that period to a person or persons specified in the instructions at a place or places so specified and reside there for that period; or

(b)   participate for that period in activities specified in the instructions.

A requirement to participate in a residential exercise may not be given except with the consent of a parent or guardian of the offender.

The specified activities may consist of or include reparation, for example contact between the offender and victims affected by his offending behaviour as part of specified activities or as directed by the responsible officer.

A court may not include an activity requirement in a relevant order unless it has consulted either an officer of a local probation board or a member of a Youth Offending Team, and it is satisfied that the activities to be specified in the order can be made under arrangements that exist in the local justice area in which the offender resides and that it is feasible to secure compliance with those requirements.

A court may not include an activity requirement in a relevant order if compliance with that requirement would involve the co-operation of a person other than the offender and the offender's responsible officer, unless that other person consents to its inclusion.

The aggregate of the number of days specified must not exceed 90 unless the 'custody' criteria are satisfied as set down in CJIA 2008, s 1(4)(a) to (c) when the number of days permitted doubles to 180 days, within a youth rehabilitation order with intensive supervision and surveillance.

(b) Supervision requirement

9.10   A supervision requirement is a requirement that, during the relevant period, the offender must attend appointments with the responsible officer or another person determined by the responsible officer, at such time and place as may be determined by the officer. The purpose for which a supervision requirement may be imposed is that of promoting the offender's rehabilitation.

For these purposes the 'relevant period' means the period for which the youth rehabilitation order remains in force.

(c) Unpaid work requirement

9.11   This is a requirement that the offender must perform unpaid work in accordance with the number of hours specified in the order, at such times as he is instructed by the responsible officer. Unless revoked, a requirement imposing an unpaid work condition remains in force until the offender has worked under it for the number of hours specified in it.

The work required to be performed under an unpaid work requirement in a youth rehabilitation order ordinarily must be completed in a period of 12 months.

The number of hours that a person may be required to work under an unpaid work requirement must be specified in the relevant order and must be in the aggregate:

(a)   not less than 40, and

(b)   not more than 240.

The court may not impose an unpaid work requirement in respect of an offender unless, after hearing (if the courts thinks necessary) from an appropriate officer, the court is satisfied that the offender is a suitable person to perform work under such a requirement.

The court must also be satisfied that provision for the offender to work under this requirement can be made under arrangements that exist in the local justice area in which the offender resides.

Where the court makes orders in respect of two or more offences of which the offender has been convicted on the same occasion and includes unpaid work requirements in each of them, the court may direct that the hours of work specified in any of those requirements is to be concurrent or consecutive. However the total number of hours must not exceed the maximum of 240 hours.

An unpaid work requirement can only be imposed where the offender was 16 or 17 at the time of conviction.

(d) Programme requirement

9.12   This requirement involves the offender's participation in a systematic set of activities specified in the order, on such number of days as may be specified. The court may not include a programme requirement in the youth rehabilitation order unless:

(a)   the programme that the court proposes to specify in the order has been recommended to it as being suitable for the offender by an officer of a local probation board or by a member of a Youth Offending Team or an officer of a provider of probation services; and

(b)   the court is satisfied that the programme is available at the place proposed to be specified.

A court may not include a programme requirement in the youth rehabilitation order if compliance with that requirement would involve the co-operation of a person other than the offender and the offender's responsible officer, unless that other person consents to its inclusion.

A requirement to attend a programme operates to require the offender:

(a)   in accordance with instructions given by the responsible officer, to participate in the programme at the place specified in the order on the number of days specified in the order; and

(b)   while at that place, to comply with instructions given by, or under the authority of, the person in charge of the programme.

(e) Attendance centre requirement

9.13   An attendance centre requirement is a requirement to attend at an attendance centre for any period on any occasion at the beginning of the period and, during that period, to engage in occupations, or receive instruction, under the supervision of and in accordance with instructions given by, or under the authority of, the officer in charge of the centre.

The aggregate number of hours for which the offender may be required to attend at an attendance centre will depend on the age of the offender:

(a)   If the offender is aged 16 or over at the time of conviction, the hours must be:

    (i)   not less than 12, and

    (ii)   not more than 36.

(b)   If the offender is aged 14 or over but under 16 at the time of conviction, the hours must be:

    (i)   not less than 12, and

    (ii)   not more than 24.

(c)   If the offender is aged under 14 at the time of conviction, the hours must not be more than 12.

A court may not include an attendance centre requirement in a youth rehabilitation order unless it has been notified by the Secretary of State that an attendance centre is available for persons of the offender's description, and provision can be made at the centre for the offender.

Not all areas have an attendance centre in their locality. Some areas have access to a centre but only use it for older offenders, particularly if it is geographically remote from the juvenile's home. The statute requires that the court is satisfied that the attendance centre proposed to be specified is reasonably accessible to the offender, having regard to the means of access available to the offender and any other circumstances.

The first time at which the offender is required to attend at the attendance centre is a time notified to the offender by the responsible officer. The subsequent hours are to be fixed by the officer in charge of the centre in accordance with arrangements made by the responsible officer, having regard to the offender's circumstances. An offender may not be required to attend at the centre on more than one occasion on any day, or for more than three hours on any occasion.

(f) Prohibited activity requirement

9.14   This means a requirement that the offender must refrain from participating in activities specified in the order:

(a)   on a day or days so specified; or

(b)   during a period so specified.

156

A court may not include a prohibited activity requirement in a relevant order unless it has consulted either an officer of a local probation board (a provider of probation services) or a member of a Youth Offending Team.

The statute provides that one of the requirements that may be included in an order is that the offender does not possess, use or carry a firearm within the meaning of the Firearms Act 1968.

(g) Curfew requirement

9.15 A curfew requirement is a requirement that the offender must remain, for periods specified in the relevant order, at a place so specified. It may specify different places or different periods for different days, but may not specify periods which amount to fewer than two hours or more than 16 hours in any one day.

The order may not exceed a period of twelve months beginning with the day on which it first takes effect. The court must also make an electronic monitoring requirement (see **9.25**), unless it considers it inappropriate to do so in the particular circumstances of the case, or the court is prevented from including an electronic monitoring requirement because the requirements of para 26 of Sch 1 cannot be met (eg it is not practicable to secure the co-operation of a person other than the offender). Before making a relevant order imposing a curfew requirement, the court must obtain and consider information about the place proposed to be specified in the order (including information as to the attitude of persons likely to be affected by the enforced presence there of the offender).

(h) Exclusion requirement

9.16 An exclusion requirement is a provision prohibiting the offender from entering a place named in the order for a specified period of not more than three months. An exclusion requirement:

(a)   may provide for the prohibition to operate only during the periods specified in the order; and

(b)   may specify different places or areas for different periods or days.

The court must also make an electronic monitoring requirement (see **9.25**), unless it considers it inappropriate to do so in the particular circumstances of the case, or the court is prevented from including an electronic monitoring requirement because the requirements of para 26 of Sch 1 cannot be met (eg it is not practicable to secure the co-operation of a person other than the offender).

(i) Residence requirement

9.17 This requirement is only applicable to offenders aged 16 or over at the time of conviction.

The requirement means that, during a period specified in the relevant order, the offender must reside with an individual or at a place specified in the order. If the court wishes to specify residence with an individual, that individual has to consent to the requirement.

If the order makes specific provision for it, a residence requirement does not prohibit the offender from residing, with the prior approval of the responsible officer, at a place other than that specified in the order.

Before making a youth rehabilitation order containing a residence requirement, the court must consider the home surroundings of the offender.

A court may not specify a hostel or other institution as the place where an offender must reside, except on the recommendation of an officer of a local probation board, or provider of probation services, a local authority social worker or a member of a Youth Offending Team.

(j) Local authority residence requirement

9.18   The imposition of this requirement means that, during the period specified in the order, the offender must reside in accommodation provided by or on behalf of a local authority specified in the order.

A court may not include a local authority residence requirement in a youth rehabilitation order made in respect of an offence unless it is satisfied that the behaviour that constituted the offence was due to a significant extent to the circumstances in which the offender was living, and that the imposition of that requirement will assist in the offender's rehabilitation.

A court may not include a local authority residence requirement in a youth rehabilitation order unless it has consulted the local authority and a parent or guardian of the offender (unless it is impracticable to consult such a person) and the local authority that is to receive the offender. A youth rehabilitation order that imposes a local authority residence requirement may also stipulate that the offender is not to reside with a person specified in the order.

The order must specify the local authority in whose area the offender resides or is to reside.

Any period specified in the order as a period for which the offender must reside in accommodation provided by or on behalf of a local authority must not be longer than six months, and must not include any period after the offender has reached the age of 18.

It is worth noting that a local authority has power to place an offender with a local authority foster parent where a local authority residence requirement is imposed (CJIA 2008, Sch 1, Part 2, para 18(6)).

Pre-conditions to imposing local authority residence requirement

9.19 A court may not include a local authority residence requirement in a youth rehabilitation order in respect of an offender, unless the offender was legally represented at the relevant time in court, or either:

(a) the offender was granted a right to representation funded by the Legal Services Commission as part of the Criminal Defence Service for the purposes of the proceedings but the right was withdrawn because of the offender's conduct; or

(b) the offender was informed of the right to apply for such representation for the purposes of the proceedings and had the opportunity to do so, but nevertheless refused or failed to apply.

It is worth noting that a local authority has power to place an offender with a local authority foster parent where a local authority residence requirement is imposed (CJIA 2008, Sch 2, Pt 2, para 18(6)).

(k) Mental health treatment requirement

9.20 This requires the offender to submit, during periods specified in the order, to treatment by or under the direction of a registered medical practitioner or a chartered psychologist (or both, for different periods) with a view to the improvement of the offender's mental condition.

The treatment required must be one of the following kinds of treatment as may be specified in the relevant order:

(a) treatment as a resident patient in an independent hospital or care home within the meaning of the Care Standards Act 2000 or a hospital within the meaning of the Mental Health Act 1983, but not in hospital premises where high security psychiatric services within the meaning of that Act are provided;

(b) treatment as a non-resident patient at such institution or place as may be specified in the order;

(c) treatment by or under the direction of such registered medical practitioner or chartered psychologist (or both) as may be so specified;

but the nature of the treatment may not be specified in the order except as mentioned in (a), (b) or (c) above.

A court may not include a mental health treatment requirement in an order unless:

(a) the court is satisfied that the mental condition of the offender:

(i) is such as requires and may be susceptible to treatment, but

(ii) is not such as to warrant the making of a hospital order or guardianship order within the meaning of that Act;

(b)   the court is also satisfied that arrangements have been or can be made for the treatment intended to be specified in the order (including arrangements for the reception of the offender where he is to be required to submit to treatment as a resident patient); and

(c)   the offender has expressed his willingness to comply with such a requirement.

While the offender is under treatment as a resident patient in pursuance of a mental health requirement, his responsible officer shall carry out the supervision of the offender to such extent only as may be necessary for the purpose of the revocation or amendment of the order.

Mental health treatment at place other than that specified in order

9.21   Where the medical practitioner or chartered psychologist, treating the offender in pursuance of a mental health treatment requirement, is of the opinion that part of the treatment can be better or more conveniently given in or at an institution or place that:

(a)   is not specified in the relevant order; and

(b)   is one in or at which the treatment of the offender will be given by or under the direction of a registered medical practitioner or chartered psychologist;

he may, with the consent of the offender, make arrangements for him to be treated accordingly.

These arrangements may provide for the offender to receive part of his treatment as a resident patient in an institution or place notwithstanding that the institution or place is not one that could have been specified for that purpose in the relevant order.

Where any such arrangements are made for the treatment of an offender the medical practitioner or chartered psychologist by whom the arrangements are made shall give notice in writing to the offender's responsible officer giving details of the place and the treatment provided as it is deemed to be treatment to which the offender is required to submit to in pursuance of the order.

Detailed consideration to the mentally disordered juvenile is given in **Chapter 15**.

(l) Drug treatment requirement and drug testing requirement

9.22   A drug treatment requirement means a requirement that during a period specified in the order the offender must submit to treatment by or under the direction of a specified person having the necessary qualifications or experience with a view to the reduction or elimination of the offender's dependency on, or propensity to misuse, drugs.

During that period, he may be required to provide samples for the purpose of ascertaining whether he has any drug in his body (a drug-testing requirement) (CJIA 2008, Sch 2, para 23(1)).

A drug-testing requirement may not be made unless the court has been notified that arrangements for implementing drug-testing requirements are in force in the local justice area in which the offender resides. This additional requirement may only be imposed as part of a drug treatment requirement and the offender must express his willingness to comply with it.

Where it is imposed the court must specify the minimum numbers of occasions each month on which samples are to be provided. They may also specify times at which, and circumstances in which, the responsible officer or treatment provider may require samples and descriptions of the samples that may be so required.

A court may not impose a drug treatment requirement unless:

(a)   it is satisfied that:

(i)   the offender is dependent on, or has a propensity to misuse, drugs; and

(ii)   his dependency or propensity is such as requires and may be susceptible to treatment;

(b)   it is also satisfied that arrangements have been or can be made for the treatment intended to be specified in the order (including arrangements for the reception of the offender where he is to be required to submit to treatment as a resident);

(c)   the requirement has been recommended to the court as being suitable for the offender either by an officer of a local probation board (or provider of probation services) or by a member of a Youth Offending Team; and

(d)   the offender expresses his willingness to comply with the requirement.

The treatment and testing period is the period specified in the youth rehabilitation order and will be treatment as a resident in such institution or place as may be specified in the order, or treatment at a non-resident place, as may be so specified.

A youth rehabilitation order imposing a drug treatment requirement must provide that the results of tests carried out by a person other than the responsible officer on any samples provided by the offender in pursuance of the testing requirement are to be communicated to the responsible officer.

(m) Intoxicating substance treatment requirement

9.23   This is a requirement that the offender submits during a specified period or periods to treatment by or under the direction of a specified person having the necessary qualifications or experience with a view to the reduction or elimination of the offender's dependency on, or propensity to misuse, intoxicating substances.

Intoxicating substances are defined as alcohol or any other substance or product (other than a drug) which is, or the fumes of which are, capable of being inhaled or otherwise used for the purpose of causing intoxication.

Before making an order, the court must be satisfied that arrangements have been or can be made for the treatment intended and the requirement must have been recommended to the court as suitable for the offender by a member of the Youth Offending Team, an officer of the local probation board or a provider for probation services. The court may not impose an intoxicating substances treatment requirement in respect of an offender unless it is satisfied that he is dependent or has a propensity to misuse intoxicating substances, and his dependency is such as requires and may be susceptible to treatment.

Arrangements must be made for the treatment intended to be specified in the order (including arrangements for the reception of the offender where he is to be required to submit to treatment as a resident).

A court may not impose an intoxicating substance treatment requirement unless the offender expresses his willingness to comply with its requirements.

The treatment required by an intoxicating substance treatment requirement for a specified period must be:

(a) treatment as a resident in such institution or place as may be specified in the order;

(b) treatment as a non-resident in or at such institution or place, and at such intervals, as may be so specified; but the nature of the treatment shall not be specified in the order except as mentioned in paras (a) and (b) above.

(n) Education requirement

9.24 This is a requirement that the offender must comply, during a period or periods specified in the order, with approved education arrangements. These may be arrangements made for the offender's education by his parent or guardian and approved by the local education authority specified in the order. The authority should be the local education authority for the area in which the offender resides.

Before the court can include an education requirement in a youth rehabilitation order it must have consulted with the local education authority and be satisfied that arrangements exist for the offender to receive sufficient full-time education suitable for his age, ability, aptitude and special educational needs (if any).

The court must also be satisfied that the inclusion of the education requirement is necessary for securing the good conduct of the offender or for preventing the commission of further offences.

Any period specified in the youth rehabilitation order as a period during which the offender must comply with approved education arrangements must not include a period after the offender has ceased to be of compulsory school age.

(o) Electronic monitoring requirement

9.25 This requirement must be added to a curfew or exclusion requirement and may be added to other requirements. It entails the offender being 'tagged' with an electronic monitoring device that monitors his whereabouts during the hours specified in the order.

Before making the order the court must have been notified that arrangements for electronic monitoring of offences are available in the local justice area proposed to be specified in the order and they must include provision in the order for making a person responsible for the monitoring.

The period of monitoring of the offender's compliance with other requirements will be for a period specified in the order or determined by the responsible officer in accordance with the order.

Consequently, where an electronic monitoring requirement is to take effect, determined by the responsible officer, he must, before beginning that period, notify the offender, the person responsible for monitoring and any other person without whose co-operation it will not be practicable to secure that the monitoring takes place. The consent of any such person is required and the requirement may not be included in the order without that consent.

YRO with intensive supervision and surveillance

9.26 A court may only make an order for a youth rehabilitation order with intensive supervision and surveillance if:

(a) the court is dealing with the offender for an offence that is punishable with imprisonment;

(b) the court is of the opinion that the offence, or the combination of the offence and one or more offences associated with it, was so serious that, but for these provisions, a custodial sentence would be appropriate (or, if the offender was aged under 12 at the time of conviction, would be appropriate if the offender had been aged 12); and

(c) if the offender was aged under 15 at the time of conviction, the court is of the opinion that the offender is a persistent offender (see **10.07**).

The restrictions outlined above will not apply if the offender has failed to comply with an order for pre-sentence drug testing under s 161(2) of the Criminal Justice Act 2003 (however s 161 is not in force).

This requirement allows the court to make an extended activity requirement of no more than 180 days. If the court decides to make an extended activity requirement it must also impose a supervision requirement and a curfew requirement with electronic monitoring.

This order is known as an intensive supervision and surveillance requirement. It may also include one or more of the other requirements of a 'standard YRO' subject to it being proportionate to the seriousness of the offence. It is not possible to add a fostering requirement.

There are wider powers to make a YRO with intensive supervision and surveillance following breach, revocation or amendment of a YRO. These are outlined in **Chapter 11.**

YRO with fostering

9.27 A court may only make an order for a youth rehabilitation order with a fostering requirement if:

(a) the court is dealing with the offender for an offence that is punishable with imprisonment;

(b) the court is of the opinion that the offence, or the combination of the offence and one or more offences associated with it, was so serious that, but for these provisions, a custodial sentence would be appropriate (or, if the offender was aged under 12 at the time of conviction, would be appropriate if the offender had been aged 12); and

(c) where the offender was aged under 15 at the time of conviction, the court is of the opinion that the offender is a persistent offender (see **10.07**).

(d) the court is satisfied that the offender is legally represented at the relevant time in court, or either:

(i) the offender was granted a right to representation funded by the Legal Services Commission as part of the Criminal Defence Service for the purposes of the proceedings but the right was withdrawn because of the offender's conduct, or

(ii) he was informed of the right to apply for such representation for the purposes of the proceedings and had the opportunity to do so, but nevertheless refused or failed to apply.

(e) the court is satisfied that:

(i) the behaviour which constituted the offence was due to a significant extent to the circumstances in which the offender was living, and

(ii) that the imposition of a fostering requirement would assist in the offender's rehabilitation.

(f)   the court has consulted the offender's parents or guardians (unless it is impracticable to do so), and it has consulted the local authority which is to place the offender with a local authority foster parent.

A youth rehabilitation order which imposes a fostering requirement must also impose a supervision requirement. Other requirements of a 'standard YRO' can also be imposed, provided the order would not become disproportionate to the seriousness of the offence.

A fostering requirement means a requirement that, for a period specified in the order, the offender must reside with a local authority foster parent.

A period specified in a youth rehabilitation order as a period for which the offender must reside with a local authority foster parent must end no later than the end of the period of 12 months beginning with the date on which the requirement first has effect but must not include any period after the offender has reached the age of 18. An 18-month period may be substituted following breach proceedings (CJIA 2008, Sch 2, paras 6(9), 8(9) and 16(2)).

If at any time during that period the responsible officer notifies the offender that no suitable local authority foster parent is available, and that the responsible officer has applied or proposes to apply for the revocation or amendment of the order, the fostering requirement is, until the determination of that application, to be taken as requiring the offender to reside in accommodation provided by or on behalf of a local authority.

A youth rehabilitation order that imposes a fostering requirement must specify the local authority that is to place the offender with a local authority foster parent under s 23(2)(a) of the Children Act 1989.

The authority so specified must be the local authority in whose area the offender resides or is to reside.

A court may not include a fostering requirement in a youth rehabilitation order unless it has been notified by the Secretary of State that arrangements for implementing such a requirement are available in the area of the local authority that is to place the offender with a local authority foster parent.

The Sentencing Council's definitive guideline *Sentencing Children and Young People* provides the following advice:

'In order to impose this requirement the court must be satisfied that the behaviour which constituted the offence was due to a significant extent to the circumstances in which the child or young person was living, and that the imposition of fostering requirement would assist in the child or young person's rehabilitation. It is likely that other rights will be engaged (such as those under Article 8 of the European Convention on Human Rights) and any interference with such rights must be proportionate. It is unlikely that the statutory criteria will be met in many cases; where they are met and the court is considering making an order, care should be taken to ensure that there is a well developed plan for the care and support of the child or young person throughout the period of the order and following conclusion of the order. The court will need to be provided with sufficient information, including proposals for education and training during the order and plans for the child or young person on completion of the order.'

Youth rehabilitation order review

9.28   The Secretary of State may introduce powers for courts periodically to review the progress of juveniles on youth rehabilitation orders (CJIA 2008, Sch 1, para 35).

For a quick reference guide to sentencing orders see **Appendix H**.

Chapter 10   Custodial orders

10.01   In the context of the Youth Court, a custodial sentence means a detention and training order. The detention and training order replaced secure training orders and detention in the young offenders institute in the Youth Court in April 2000. Detention in a young offenders institute is still available for 18- to 21-year-olds in the magistrates' court. The Crown Court dealing with a young offender may also pass detention under Powers of Criminal Courts (Sentencing) Act 2000 (PCC(S)A 2000), s 91 or a sentence of custody for life under PCC(S)A 2000, ss 90 to 95 or an extended sentence under CJA 2003, s 226B. A 16 or 17-year-old convicted on an offence of threatening with a knife or offensive weapon on school premises or public place must be given a minimum four-month detention and training order unless it would be unjust to do so (LASPOA 2012, s 134, Prevention of Crime Act 1953, s 1A and CJA 1988, s 139AA). The circumstances of the offence and offender and the welfare of the child can be taken into consideration when deciding whether imposing the otherwise mandatory minimum sentence would be unjust. This concept of a four-month minimum custodial sentence was extended by the Criminal Justice and Courts Act 2015 to cover repeat offenders. The 2015 Act amends existing legislation to the effect that where a 16 or 17-year-old is convicted of an offence of possession of an offensive weapon (Prevention of Crime Act 1953, s 1) or possession of a knife/bladed article in a public place or on school premises (CJA 1988, s 139 and s 139A respectively) and the juvenile has a relevant previous conviction, then a minimum sentence of four months must be imposed unless it would be unjust. The new offence must have been committed on or after 17 July 2015 (Criminal Justice and Courts Act 2015 (Commencement No 1, Saving and Transitional Provisions) Order 2015 (SI 2015/778)) The defendant must also have attained 16 (or 17) years of age by the date of the offence. A previous conviction is relevant, whatever date it was committed, if it was an offence under any of the following provisions: s 1 or 1A of the Prevention of Crime Act 1953 Act, or ss 139, 139A or 139AA of the CJA 1988. The circumstances of the offender, offence, relevant previous offence(s) and the welfare of the child can be taken into consideration when deciding whether imposing the otherwise mandatory minimum sentence would be unjust.

A detention and training order (DTO) can be made for up to a maximum of 24 months. This gives the Youth Court concurrent jurisdiction with the Crown Court outside its powers related to grave crimes and dangerous offenders. The order is available for both males and females between the ages of 12 to 17. This power is not available for 10- and 11-year-olds. Additionally, in the case of a child or young person aged 12 but under 15 years the court must be of the opinion that he or she is a persistent offender, in order to pass such a sentence.

Permitted terms of detention and training order

10.02   The order is a two-part sentence, the first half being a period of detention and training served in youth secure detention accommodation, the second half being a period under supervision in the community. The court is restricted by statute to the term of the order which may be for 4, 6, 8, 10, 12, 18 or 24 months. In the case of *R v Shan* [2007] EWCA Crim 1861, it was suggested that these terms are only administratively convenient and a 15-month sentence was upheld as not being wrong in principle. However, this case does not fit easily with other authorities.

The term of a detention and training order may not exceed the maximum term of imprisonment that the Crown Court (in the case of an offender aged 21 or over) may impose for the offence (PCC(S)A 2000, s 101(2)). Concurrent and consecutive orders may be made where more than one principal offence is involved so long as the overall term does not exceed the 24-month maximum. In effect this means that if the court made consecutive orders for six months and eight months, a total of 14 months can lawfully be imposed even though it is not within one of the specified terms for a single period (*R v Norris* [2000] 2 Cr App R (S) 105, CA). It also means that terms less than four months cannot be imposed consecutively so as to aggregate to four months (*R v Ganley* [2001] 1 Cr App R (S) 60, CA). Section 133 of the Magistrates' Courts Act 1980 limits the maximum period of imprisonment or detention in a young offenders' institute that magistrates may impose. In the case of *LCC v DPP* [2001] EWHC (Admin) 453 it was decided that this section does not apply to detention and training orders and a Youth Court could therefore impose consecutive orders for summary offences to an aggregate that exceeds six months. In *B v Leeds Crown Court* [2016] EWHC 1230 (Admin) an opposite view was taken. In that case, a 17-year-old had been sentenced to a total of eight months made up of consecutive four-month DTOs for two summary only aggravated vehicle taking offences. An offence of handling stolen property committed on the same occasion as one of the other offences was given a concurrent four-month DTO. The decision of the magistrates was confirmed by the Crown Court but declared unlawful by the High Court. The principle applied was that a juvenile should not be given a more onerous sentence than they could have been given by a court if they were an adult. The absolute maximum which the adult court could have imposed would have been six months by virtue of MCA 1980, s 133. Leggatt J observed that the case of *LCC* had been decided on the correct interpretation of PCC(S)A 2000, s 101. The court in *LCC* drew a distinction between DTOs and adult custodial sentences. Since then the approach to sentencing youths had moved on, as evidenced by the definitive guideline issued by the Sentencing Guidelines Council which implicitly treated them as equivalents.

It is also wrong in principle to impose a greater sentence on a youth than is possible on an adult for a single offence. Consequently, a juvenile found guilty of criminal damage to a value of less than £5,000 is not liable to a custodial sentence as the maximum sentence on an adult is three months and the minimum period of a DTO is four months

(*Pye v Leeds Youth Court* [2006] EWHC 2527 (Admin)). The same principle will also apply to offences such as motor vehicle interference and obstructing a police constable in the execution of his duty. This is endorsed in the Sentencing Council's guideline *Sentencing Children and Young People* which provides that any case that warrants a detention and training order of less than four months must result in a non-custodial sentence (para 6.43).

The overall total period of detention and training of 24 months may, however, not be exceeded (*C v DPP* [2001] Crim LR 670). A court is not permitted to make a detention and training order consecutive to a long-term detention order under PCC(S)A 2000, s 91 (*R v Kent Youth Court, ex parte Kingwell* [1999] 1 Cr App R (S) 263).

Where a youth is already serving a detention and training order and the court wishes to impose a consecutive or wholly or partly concurrent detention and training order for a new offence, then the term of the detention and training order shall be treated as a single term and as if the orders were made on the same occasion (PCC(S)A 2000, s 101(13)).

Restrictions on the passing of custodial sentences

10.03 The following restrictions apply before the court may make an order of detention and training:

(a)   The court may not make an order for detention and training in respect of a person who is not legally represented unless:

(i)   he was granted a right to representation funded by the Legal Services Commission as part of the Criminal Defence Service but the right was withdrawn because of his conduct, or

(ii)   because he is financially ineligible; or

(iii) having been informed of his right to apply for such representation and having had the opportunity of doing so, he refused or failed to apply (PCC(S)A 2000, s 83(3)).

A person is treated as being legally represented if a solicitor or counsel represented him after a finding of guilt and before sentence (PCC(S)A 2000, s 83(4)).

(b)   The court may not pass a custodial sentence on the offender unless it is of the opinion:

(i)   that the offence or the combination of the offence and one or more offences associated with it, was so serious that neither a fine alone nor a community sentence (this includes a youth rehabilitation order (YRO) – CJA 2003, s 147(1)(c)) can be justified for the offence (CJA 2003, s 152(2)). The court must specifically be satisfied that a YRO with an intensive supervision and surveillance requirement or fostering requirement (where available) cannot be justified; and

(ii)   nothing in (i) above shall prevent the court from passing a custodial sentence on an offender who refuses to express his willingness to comply with a requirement in a community sentence which is proposed by the court and requires that consent (CJA 2003, s 152(2) and (3)). Essentially this second statement relates to a YRO with an intoxicating substance requirement, a drug treatment requirement or a mental health treatment requirement; and

(iii)   the court must explain in open court why it has reached the relevant opinion.

If CJA 2003, s 161 is brought into force then failure to provide samples for pre-sentence drug testing will enable the court to impose a custodial sentence irrespective of whether the conditions in (i) above are satisfied.

(c)   Before forming the opinion referred to in (b)(i) above the court must obtain and consider a pre-sentence report (CJA 2003, s 156(3)). The only exception to this is where the offender is under the age of 18, and the court is of the opinion that a pre-sentence report is unnecessary because it has had regard to a pre-existing PSR or, where there are more than one, the most recent (CJA 2003, s 156(4), and (5)). The statute envisages courts receiving pre-sentence reports in all cases where a custodial order is being considered. In the case of an offence triable on indictment which by its very nature is so serious as to make custody look inevitable, courts have, in the past, proceeded without a pre-sentence report; however, even this will be rare in practice. In *R v Massheder* (1983) 5 Cr App R (S) 442, the juvenile, who was aged 15, pleaded guilty to an offence of arson which involved deliberately starting a fire in a lift shaft at Kennett House, Southwark. Over £5,000 worth of damage was done. The judge passed a sentence of 18 months' detention under CYPA 1933, s 53(2) and did so without the benefit of a report. He gave two reasons for not having obtained a report, namely:

(i)   there was no report available due to an industrial dispute in the social services department of whom the report had been requested; and

(ii)   the offence was very serious and beyond anything in the nature of a community sentence.

In substituting a supervision order for two years, the Court of Appeal said that a report was necessary in a case of this nature and that indeed had been recognised by the judge at the first instance when he had made the initial request of the social services department. In the exceptional circumstances of a court not obtaining a pre-sentence report, it would be good practice for the court to give its reasons as to why it was unnecessary to obtain a pre-sentence report (a failure to give such reasons would in any event breach Article 6 of the Human Rights Convention). See also *R (on the application of Rees) v Feltham Justices* [2001] Crim LR 47.

As stated above the court may form an opinion that it is unnecessary to obtain a pre-sentence report but only:

(i)   if a previous pre-sentence report obtained in respect of the offender is available; and

(ii)   the court has had regard to the information contained in that report, or, if there is more than one report, the most recent.

(d)   Before forming the opinion that the offence is so serious that only a custodial sentence can be passed the court must take into account all information about the circumstances of the offence, including any aggravating or mitigating factors as are available to it. In the case of a violent or sexual offence the court may also take into account any information about the offender which is before it. In the event of a custodial sentence being passed without the benefit of a pre-sentence report, the sentence will not be invalidated by the failure of the court to comply with the statute. However, on appeal to the Crown Court from the Youth Court the appellate court must obtain a pre-sentence report if one was not previously obtained and must give due consideration to that report (CJA 2003, s 156(6)).

(e)   A pre-sentence report for a juvenile facing a custodial sentence must be in a written format (CJA 2003, s 158(1B)).

The Sentencing Council's guideline 'Sentencing Children and Young People', at paragraphs 11.5 to 11.9, offers the following guidance in approaching the threshold:

'Under both domestic and international law, a custodial sentence must only be imposed as a "measure of last resort;" statute provides that such a sentence may be imposed only where an offence is "so serious that neither a fine alone nor a community sentence can be justified." If a custodial sentence is imposed, a court must state its reasons for being satisfied that the offence is so serious that no other sanction would be appropriate and, in particular, why a YRO with intensive supervision and surveillance or fostering could not be justified.

The term of a custodial sentence must be the shortest commensurate with the seriousness of the offence; any case that warrants a DTO of less than four months must result in a non-custodial sentence. The court should take account of the circumstances, age and maturity of the child or young person.

In determining whether an offence has crossed the custody threshold the court will need to assess the seriousness of the offence, in particular the level of harm that was caused, or was likely to have been caused, by the offence. The risk of serious harm in the future must also be assessed. The pre-sentence report will assess this criterion and must be considered before a custodial sentence is imposed. A custodial sentence is most likely to be unavoidable where it is necessary to protect the public from serious harm.

The welfare of the child or young person must be considered when imposing any sentence but is especially important when a custodial sentence is being considered. A custodial sentence could have a significant effect on the prospects and opportunities of the child or young person and a child or young person is likely to be more susceptible than an adult to the contaminating influences that can be expected within a custodial setting. There is a high reconviction rate for children and young people that have had custodial sentences and there have been many studies profiling the effect on vulnerable children and young people, particularly the risk of self harm and suicide and so it is of utmost importance that custody is a last resort.'

Where the offence has crossed the custody threshold, the statutory tests are likely to be satisfied only where a custodial sentence will be more effective in preventing offending by children and young persons. The obligation to have regard to the welfare of the offender will require a court to take account of a wide range of issues including those relating to mental health, capability and maturity. Even where the threshold is crossed, a court is not required to impose a custodial sentence.

When a detention and training order is likely, it is important that the Youth Offending Team officer writing the pre-sentence report contacts the Youth Justice Board placement service to provide assessments to help ensure that decisions are made about placement on the best evidence available and that those looking after the juvenile whilst in custody has the information they need to address the offenders needs and address any risks.

The Youth Court itself should ensure that the agency providing prisoner transport is notified as soon as the court has made its decision.

The length of sentence

10.04   A custodial sentence shall be for such a term:

(a)   as in the opinion of the court is commensurate with the seriousness of the offence, or the combination of the offence and other offences associated with it; or

(b)   where the offence is of a violent or sexual offence, for such longer term as in the opinion of the court is necessary to protect the public from serious harm from the offender.

In both cases the maximum term of 24 months may not be exceeded (PCC(S)A 2000, s 101(4)).

Therefore, a court may only pass a detention and training order for a term longer than is commensurate with the seriousness of the offence, or the combination of the offence and other offences associated with it where it is of the opinion that the offence is of a violent or sexual nature and that the public need protection from serious harm from the offender. If it reaches this opinion, it must give its reasons in open court and explain to the offender in ordinary language why the sentence is for such a term (CJA 2003, s 174(1) and (2)).

The Sentencing Council's guideline '*Sentencing Children and Young People*' provides (paras 6.45–6.48):

> 'Only if the court is satisfied that the offence crosses the custody threshold, and that no other sentence is appropriate, the court may, as a preliminary consideration, consult the equivalent adult guideline in order to decide upon the appropriate length of the sentence.
>
> When considering the relevant adult guideline, the court may feel it appropriate to apply a sentence broadly within the region of half to two thirds of the adult sentence for those aged 15 – 17 and allow a greater reduction for those aged under 15. This is only a rough guide and must not be applied mechanistically. In most cases when considering the appropriate reduction from the adult sentence the emotional and developmental age and maturity of the child or young person is of at least equal importance as their chronological age.
>
> The individual factors relating to the offence and the child or young person are of the greatest importance and may present good reason to impose a sentence outside of this range. The court should bear in mind the negative effects a short custodial sentence can have; short sentences disrupt education and/or training and family relationships and support which are crucial stabilising factors to prevent re-offending.
>
> There is an expectation that custodial sentences will be particularly rare for a child or young person aged 14 or under. If custody is imposed, it should be for a shorter length of time than that which a young person aged 15 – 17 would receive if found guilty of the same offence. For a child or young person aged 14 or under the sentence should normally be imposed in a youth court.'

In practice, it may be difficult to justify imposition of a detention and training order for a juvenile who has pleaded guilty to a single summary only offence carrying six months' imprisonment for an adult. If the six months is reduced by a third for an early guilty plea to four months, then any further reduction for age or immaturity takes the length below the minimum allowed for a detention and training order.

The Sentencing Council guideline states that when dealing with more than one summary offence, the aggregate sentence is limited to a maximum of six months. Allowing for a reduction for each guilty plea, consecutive sentences might result in the imposition of the maximum six-month sentence. Where this is the case, the court may make a modest additional reduction to the overall sentence to reflect the benefits derived from the guilty plea.

It would appear that this guidance is most easily applied to a s 91 detention rather than DTOs. In relation to DTOs, multiple summary offences which cross the custody threshold might well justify a four-month DTO. It might be arguable that even where early guilty pleas have been entered to multiple summary only offences that a six-month DTO could be imposed on each offence concurrently provided that consecutive sentences of four months would otherwise be appropriate in principle and the overall sentence would not be greater than could be imposed on an adult for the same offences.

Taking into account period of remand

10.05   In determining the length of a detention and training order the court must take into account any period for which the offender has been remanded in custody in connection with the offence or in the case of multiple offences the total period he has been remanded in custody in connection with any of those offences (PCC(S)A 2000, s 101(8)). For these purposes, remand in custody is defined as including time spent in police detention, a remand to prison, a remand to youth detention accommodation, a remand under the Mental Health Act 1983 and/or time remanded on bail with an electronically monitored curfew of at least nine hours per day. Time spent on remand to local authority accommodation, where the placement is not a secure one, is eliminated from the court considerations in determining the length of sentence (PCC(S)A 2000, s 101(11)). Time spent on remand in custody is not subsequently offset against the term set by the court. This is an important consideration which can lead to potential injustice where it is overlooked (*R v Cassidy* [2000] All ER (D) 1200). It is worth noting that CJA 2003, ss 240 to 242 do not apply to detention and training orders.

It has also been made clear by the appellate courts that whilst time spent on remand is not automatically deducted from the period to be imposed it has to be taken into account by the court (*R v Ganley* [2001] 1 Cr App R (S) 60, CA). However, the requirement to take remand time into account does not inevitably require the court to reflect that time in some specific way in the sentence passed. It does not provide for a one-to-one discount. In *R v Inner London Youth Court, ex parte I* [2000] All ER (D) 612 the defendant had spent less than 24 hours in custody. It was held that the court was entitled to find that the time could make no difference to the sentence passed. The sentence was a four-month detention and training order. It was argued unsuccessfully that the 24 hours spent in custody should have been taken into account so that the court would be looking at a sentence of less than four months and not be able to pass a detention and training order. The case makes it clear that the requirement in the Act to 'take into account remand time' does not mean that there will be an automatic discount. The court may however be persuaded to adjust the length of DTO where the time spent on remand has been 'considerable'. *R v B* [2000] Crim LR 870, *ex parte I* was cited with approval. The Court of Appeal repeated that the requirement to take time on remand into account did not provide for a one-to-one discount. The reason given was that the periods to which a court was entitled to sentence by way of a DTO were specified in blocks and reducing a sentence by precisely the time spent on remand would be inconsistent with that provision: *R v Inner London Crown Court, ex parte N and S* [2000] Crim LR 871 reiterates these points.

In *R v Fieldhouse and Watts* [2000] Crim LR 1020, the Court of Appeal illustrated how the court might take periods on remand into account depending on the length of order being considered. The court took as an example the case of a defendant who had served four weeks on remand. This would be the equivalent of a two-month term. The court is likely to take such a period into account in different ways depending on the period of DTO it had in mind. If that period was four months a non-custodial sentence is likely.

If the period was 6, 8, 10 or 12 months then 4, 6, 8, and 10 months respectively might be appropriate. However, for 18- or 24-month sentences the court may well conclude that no reduction could properly be made.

The difficulties of this provision are illustrated in *R v Eagles* [2006] EWCA Crim 2368, where the Court of Appeal indicated that a 17-year-old who had spent 88 days on remand should have been given 176 days' credit against his 12 month DTO sentence so as properly to reflect the nature of that sentence. As a consequence, the Court of Appeal substituted a six-month sentence, this being the nearest permissible period, having given full credit for the time spent on remand.

The Sentencing Council's Guidance is clearly based on the above-mentioned case law and the position is summarised at paragraph 6.53 of Sentencing Children and Young People:

> 'A DTO can be made only for the periods prescribed – 4, 6, 8, 10, 12, 18 or 24 months. Any time spent on remand in custody or on bail subject to a qualifying curfew condition should be taken into account when calculating the length of the order. The accepted approach is to double the time spent on remand before deciding the appropriate period of detention, in order to ensure that the regime is in line with that applied to adult offenders. After doubling the time spent on remand the court should then adopt the nearest prescribed period available for a DTO.'

If a court is considering making a detention and training order it is good practice for it to indicate its intention in open court so that it may hear any representations from the defence and be informed of any time spent on remand. In most cases the court would expect to reduce the length of the order to reflect the period of remand. Where the court finds that it is not just to do so, it must say so and state what the circumstances were that led it to that opinion bearing in mind the statutory requirement to state in open court the reasons for and the effect of the court sentence (*R v Barber* [2006] All ER (D) 240 (Feb); *R v Haringey Youth Court, ex parte A* [2000] All ER (D) 611).

As stated above, the court must be alert to a juvenile who has been subject to a qualifying curfew condition whilst on bail as this *must* be taken into account when the period of the DTO is fixed. Consequently, where the offender has been on bail with a curfew condition and electronic monitoring with a requirement to remain at a specified place for at least nine hours in any given day, then half the time he has been on bail with that curfew condition must be taken into account by the court when setting the length of the DTO unless the court considers it just in all circumstances not to do so. In the latter case the court can order that a lesser period should be taken into account.

Early and late release

10.06 The first half of a detention and training order will normally be spent in detention and the second half under supervision in the community. Offenders should be made aware however that there is provision for early or late release depending on their behaviour and progress whilst in detention. There is no early or late release for sentences between four and six months, but for sentences between eight and 12 months' release may be one month before or one month after the halfway point. For sentences between 18 and 24 months, release may be one or two months before or all after the halfway point. Early release may be authorised by the Home Secretary, whilst delay beyond the halfway point can only be authorised by the Youth Court on application on behalf of the Home Secretary. There is a mechanism for appeal against a decision not to release early or a decision to apply for a delayed release. The Secretary of State may release an offender at any time if he is satisfied that exceptional circumstances exist which justify the offender's release on compassionate grounds.

The provisions for early release on home detention curfew (tagging) are different for those under 18 years. This should be borne in mind particularly in the Crown Court when sentencing adult and juvenile co-defendants (*R v D* [2000] All ER (D) 295).

Persistent offender (under 15 years old)

10.07 Whilst there is no statutory definition for the term 'persistent offender', the legislation provides that in the case of a child or young person under the age of 15 years at the time of conviction (and 12 years or more) the court must be of the opinion that he is a persistent offender before it can pass a detention and training order.

The Sentencing Children and Young People guidelines deal with the meaning of persistent offenders at paragraphs 6.4–6.10:

'The term persistent offender is not defined in statute but has been considered by the Court of Appeal. In general it is expected that the child or young person would have had previous contact with authority as a result of criminal behaviour. This includes previous findings of guilt as well as admissions of guilt such as restorative justice disposals and conditional cautions.

A child or young person who has committed one previous offence cannot reasonably be classed as a persistent offender, and a child or young person who has committed two or more previous offences should not necessarily be assumed to be one. To determine if the behaviour is persistent the nature of the previous offences and the lapse of time between the offences would need to be considered.

If there have been three findings of guilt in the past 12 months for imprisonable offences of a comparable nature (or the child or young person has been made the subject of orders ... in relation to an imprisonable offence) then the court could certainly justify classing the child or young person as a persistent offender.

When a child or young person is being sentenced in a single appearance for a series of separate, comparable offences committed over a short space of time then the court could justifiably consider the child or young person to be a persistent offender, despite the fact that there may be no previous findings of guilt. In these cases the court should consider whether the child or young person has had prior opportunity to address their offending behaviour before imposing one of the optional sentences available for persistent offenders only; if the court determines that the child or young person has not had an opportunity to address their behaviour and believes that an alternative sentence has a reasonable prospect of preventing re-offending then this alternative sentence should be imposed.

The court may also wish to consider any evidence of a reduction in the level of offending when taking into account previous offending behaviour. Children and young people may be unlikely to desist from committing crime in a clear cut manner but there may be changes in patterns of criminal behaviour (e.g. committing fewer and/or less serious offences or there being longer lengths of time between offences) that indicate that the child or young person is attempting to desist from crime.

Even where a child or young person is found to be a persistent offender, a court is not obliged to impose one of the optional sentences. The approach should still be individualistic and all other considerations still apply. Custodial sentences must be a last resort for all children and young people and there is an expectation that they will be particularly rare for children and young people aged 14 or under.'

The Sentencing Council has avoided being over-prescriptive, and has been careful to point out that the example given involving three previous disposals for imprisonable offences within the past 12 months is no more than a very clear illustration of what criminal conduct might make a youth be considered a 'persistent offender'. The case law which had built up around this subject is set out below and may still provide some useful pointers. If there is any conflict between the Sentencing Council's definitive guideline and the case law then the former should be followed.

In *R v Smith* [2000] Crim LR 613, a 14-year-old pleaded guilty in the Crown Court to a count of robbery, one of possessing an offensive weapon and one of false imprisonment. Originally sentenced to three years' long-term detention an appeal was lodged with the Court of Appeal. The court took the view that a detention and training order was appropriate and that as the defendant had committed a series of crimes over a period of two days this qualified him for the category of persistent offender even though he had no previous convictions. In *R v Charlton* [2000] 2 Cr App R (S) 102, CA, a 14-year-old was sentenced to a 12 months' detention and training order for two groups of offences of burglary and taking without consent. The Court of Appeal upheld the sentence noting that the Government's definition of persistent young offender referred to for the purposes of fast-track arrangements did not apply and indeed predated the Crime and Disorder Act 1998. The sentencing judge had based his decision on the evidence before him in the individual case and the Court of Appeal refused to interfere with that finding.

In *R v D* [2000] All ER (D) 1496, the Court of Appeal suggested that an offender with no previous convictions may still be classed as a persistent offender.

However, the offence involved was one of affray and the defendant had a caution, previous convictions for handling stolen goods, and was awaiting sentence for riding on a stolen motorcycle. This led the court to say that the different nature of the earlier offending meant that the defendant could not properly be regarded as a persistent offender.

The case of *R v AD* [2000] Crim LR 867, establishes that the sentencing court is entitled to have regard to previous cautions when deciding whether an offender is a persistent offender. The defendant had three previous cautions. The court said a caution could only be given if there was sufficient evidence to warrant a prosecution and the offender admitted the offence. The court was therefore entitled to take them into account in deciding whether the defendant was a persistent offender. However, in the very recent case of *R v L* [2012] EWCA Crim 1336, it was held that a 14-year-old who pled guilty to three offences of robbery and one of attempted robbery and had only two reprimands, for theft of a bicycle and possession of an imitation firearm in public, was not a 'persistent offender'. The Court of Appeal took the view that the juvenile did not satisfy the statutory criterion for the imposition of a detention and training order as the two reprimands and three robberies committed on a single occasion within a minute or so of each other could not be characterised as 'persistent offending'. Therefore the 10 months' detention and training order was quashed and replaced a 12 month youth rehabilitation order.

In the case of *R v LM* [2003] Crim LR 205, the court held that where a defendant crossed a relevant age threshold between the date of commission of the offence and the date of conviction the starting point should be the sentence the defendant was likely to receive if he had been sentenced at the time of the commission of the offence. In this case, the offender had been 14 at the time of the commission of the offence and therefore could not have received a detention and training order unless he had been a persistent offender. He was not a persistent offender and therefore a custodial sentence was not appropriate or available: the court substituted an 18-month supervision order. This approach was first followed by the Court of Appeal in *R v Ghafoor* [2002] EWCA Crim 1857, CA, where an offender was 17 at the time of commission and 18 at the time of sentence. The court held that he should have been sentenced by reference to his age at the time of commission of the offence and a detention and training order was substituted for a four-and-a-half-year young offenders institute sentence. However, in *R v Thomas* [2004] EWCA Crim 2199, another Court of Appeal case, it was held that PCC(S)A 2000, s 100(2)(a) was clear in that it stipulated a defendant convicted after they became 15 could be made the subject of a detention and training order and did not need to be a persistent offender.

Consequently, a defendant under the age of 15 who is not a 'persistent offender', and will therefore, not qualify for a detention and training order if convicted, should not normally be committed to the Crown Court for trial with a view to a term of detention under PCC(S)A 2000, s 91 unless, in the event of conviction, he is likely to receive a detention term in excess of two years (*R (on the application of M) v Waltham Forest Youth Court* [2002] EWHC 1252 (Admin)).

Mentally disordered offenders

10.08 The subject of the mentally disordered juvenile is dealt with more fully in **Chapter 15** but it should be noted at this point that before passing a custodial sentence on an offender who is or appears to be mentally disordered, the court must consider any information before it which relates to his mental condition such as a medical report or pre-sentence report and must consider the likely effect of a custodial sentence on his mental condition and on any treatment which may be available for it (CJA 2003, s 157).

Seriousness of the offence

10.09 The first restriction mentioned above (see **10.03**) is that the court shall not pass a custodial sentence unless it is of the opinion that the offence, or the combination of the offence and one or more offences associated with it, was so serious that neither a fine nor a community order can be justified for the offence. The principle here is that a number of offences tried together will generally make the offending more serious. An 'associated offence' is defined as an offence for which the offender is sentenced at the same time as he is sentenced for an offence of which he is convicted in the same proceedings, or it may be a matter which the offender wishes the court to take into consideration when sentencing him for the offence of which he has been convicted.

It should be noted that the Senior Presiding Judge has made it clear that a court must not give an indication as to sentence unless the same magistrates will be the sentencing bench. It is for this reason that courts are no longer using report request forms which include an indication of seriousness. See **6.08**.

The Sentencing Children and Young People definitive guideline sets out at section 4 the general approach to be taken when determining sentence:

'In determining the sentence, the key elements to consider are:

the principal aim of the youth justice system (to prevent re-offending by children and young people);

the welfare of the child or young person;

the age of the child or young person (chronological, developmental and emotional);

the seriousness of the offence;

the likelihood of further offences being committed; and the extent of harm likely to result from those further offences.

The seriousness of the offence

(This applies to all offences; when offence specific guidance for children and young people is available this should be referred to.)

The seriousness of the offence is the starting point for determining the appropriate sentence; the sentence imposed and any restriction on liberty must be commensurate with the seriousness of the offence. The approach to sentencing children and young people should always be individualistic and the court should always have in mind the principal aims of the youth justice system.

In order to determine the seriousness of the offence the court should assess the culpability of the child or young person and the harm that was caused, intended to be caused or could foreseeably have been caused.

In assessing culpability the court will wish to consider the extent to which the offence was planned, the role of the child or young person (if the offence was committed as part of a group), the level of force that was used in the commission of the offence and the awareness that the child or young person had of their actions and its possible consequences. There is an expectation that in general a child or young person will be dealt with less severely than an adult offender. In part, this is because children and young people are unlikely to have the same experience and capacity as an adult to understand the effect of their actions on other people or to appreciate the pain and distress caused and because a child or young person may be less able to resist temptation, especially where peer pressure is exerted. Children and young people are inherently more vulnerable than adults due to their age and the court will need to consider any mental health problems and/or learning disabilities they may have, as well as their emotional and developmental age. Any external factors that may have affected the child or young person's behaviour should be taken into account.

In assessing harm the court should consider the level of physical and psychological harm caused to the victim, the degree of any loss caused to the victim and the extent of any damage caused to property. (This assessment should also include a consideration of any harm that was intended to be caused or could foreseeably have been caused in the committal of the offence.)

The court should also consider any aggravating or mitigating factors that may increase or reduce the overall seriousness of the offence. If any of these factors are included in the definition of the committed offence they should not be taken into account when considering the relative seriousness of the offence before the court.

Aggravating factors

Statutory aggravating factors

Previous findings of guilt, having regard to a) the nature of the offence to which the finding of guilt relates and its relevance to the current offence; and b) the time that has elapsed since the finding of guilt

Offence committed whilst on bail

Offence motivated by, or demonstrating hostility based on any of the following characteristics or presumed characteristics of the victim: religion, race, disability, sexual orientation or transgender identity

Other aggravating factors (non-exhaustive):

    Steps taken to prevent the victim reporting or obtaining assistance

Steps taken to prevent the victim from assisting or supporting the prosecution

Victim is particularly vulnerable due to factors including but not limited to age, mental or physical disability

Restraint, detention or additional degradation of the victim

Prolonged nature of offence

Attempts to conceal/dispose of evidence

Established evidence of community/wider impact

Failure to comply with current court orders

Attempt to conceal identity

Involvement of others through peer pressure, bullying, coercion or manipulation

Commission of offence whilst under the influence of alcohol or drugs

History of antagonising or bullying the victim

Deliberate humiliation of victim, including but not limited to filming of the offence, deliberately committing the offence before a group of peers with the intention of causing additional distress or circulating details/photos/videos etc of the offence on social media or within peer groups

Factors reducing seriousness or reflecting personal mitigation (non-exhaustive)

No previous findings of guilt or no relevant/recent findings of guilt

Remorse, particularly where evidenced by voluntary reparation to the victim

Good character and/or exemplary conduct

Unstable upbringing including but not limited to:

   time spent looked after

   lack of familial presence or support

   disrupted experiences in accommodation or education

   exposure to drug/alcohol abuse, familial criminal behaviour or domestic abuse

   victim of neglect or abuse, or exposure to neglect or abuse of others

   experiences of trauma or loss

Participated in offence due to bullying, peer pressure, coercion or manipulation

Limited understanding of effect on victim

Serious medical condition requiring urgent, intensive or long-term treatment

Communication or learning disabilities or mental health concerns

In education, work or training

Particularly young or immature child or young person (where it affects their responsibility)

Determination and/or demonstration of steps taken to address addiction or offending behaviour

Age and maturity of the child or young person

There is a statutory presumption that no child under the age of 10 can be guilty of an offence.

With a child or young person, the consideration of age requires a different approach to that which would be adopted in relation to the age of an adult. Even within the category of child or young person the response of a court to an offence is likely to be very different depending on whether the child or young person is at the lower end of the age bracket, in the middle or towards the top end.

Although chronological age dictates in some instances what sentence can be imposed (see section six for more information) the developmental and emotional age of the child or young person should always be considered and it is of at least equal importance as their chronological age. It is important to consider whether the child or young person has the necessary maturity to appreciate fully the consequences of their conduct, the extent to which the child or young person has been acting on an impulsive basis and whether their conduct has been affected by inexperience, emotional volatility or negative influences.'

When considering possible offender mitigation the court must find out at what stage in proceedings the offender first indicated his intention to plead guilty and the circumstances in which this indication was given. An early guilty plea or admission should normally lead to a substantial reduction in sentence and where this happens the court must state in open court that it has imposed a less severe punishment by virtue of the plea (CJA 2003, s 144). Details can be found in the Sentencing Council's guideline *Sentencing Children and Young People* at section 5 (see also **6.09**).

In *R v March* [2002] EWCA Crim 551, the youth who was 17 years old and two others had assaulted and sexually abused family members who had learning difficulties. Despite spending eight months in custody on remand and entering a guilty plea the offender received a 24-month DTO. It was held that the judge should have given credit for the guilty plea. Had the offences attracted detention under PCC(S)A 2000, s 91 then the judge could have given a 24-month DTO, the credit being not sentencing under s 91. The facts of the case did not allow a sentence under s 91. At that time there was no statutory obligation for credit to be given for time spent on remand. The 24-month DTO was reduced to 18 months because of the guilty plea.

In the recent case of *R v T* [2011] EWCA Crim 2345, it was held that a judge had been wrong to withhold credit for a guilty plea in the case a juvenile who had caused grievous bodily harm to a stranger on the basis that an adult would have faced a sentence of up to 3 years. Although the general principle is that credit is to be given for a guilty plea, the sentencing guidelines do not preclude the court from withholding credit in a proper case. The exceptions to the general principle are set out in *R v March* [2002] but no reference was made to any of those exceptions in the instant case. Although there was every indication that *T* was a dangerous offender, it could not be said that a departure from the general principle was necessary in order to achieve what would be a comparatively short additional period of public protection. Therefore the 24-month DTO was quashed and replaced with 18 months' detention because of the guilty plea.

The Sentencing Council's Definitive guideline *Sentencing Children and Young People* at paragraphs 5.10–5.12 adds the following guidance:

> 'The reduction in sentence for a guilty plea can be taken into account by imposing one type of sentence rather than another, for example: by reducing a custodial sentence to a community sentence; or by reducing a community sentence to a different means of disposal. Alternatively the court could reduce the length or severity of any punitive requirements attached to a community sentence.

> The court must always have regard to the principal aim of the youth justice system, which is to prevent offending by children and young people. It is, therefore, important that the court ensures that any sentence imposed is an effective disposal.

> Where a court has imposed one sentence rather than another to reflect the guilty plea there should normally be no further reduction on account of the guilty plea. Where, however, the less severe type of sentence is justified by other factors, the appropriate reduction for the plea should be applied in the normal way.'

In the case of an offender convicted of a number of offences, the length of the sentence should be mitigated by applying the 'totality' principle. This effectively means bundling all the offences together and taking an overview of their collective seriousness rather than sentencing each individually and adding their seriousness together. Having assessed the seriousness of the offence in that light, the court is then still able to mitigate that sentence by taking into account any such matters as in the opinion of the court are relevant in the mitigation of sentence including previous good character.

The court is, however, empowered to take into account aggravating factors of an offence which are disclosed by the circumstances of other offences committed by the offender. (This may include previous offending or any failure by the defendant to respond to previous sentences.) The court may take those factors into account for the purpose of forming an opinion as to the seriousness of the offence (CJA 2003, s 143(2)) and the court must by statute treat the fact that an offence was committed while the offender was on bail as an aggravating factor (CJA 2003, s 143(3)).

Where the previous convictions reveal something in the way in which they were committed they may aggravate the seriousness of the current offence. For example, if their history shows a pattern of offending which convinces the sentencer that the court is dealing with a 'professional burglar', or if a juvenile consistently targets elderly victims, these will represent aggravating factors when assessing the seriousness of the current offence of dishonesty.

In *R v Osborne* (1990–91) 12 Cr App R (S) 55, CA, the case involved an appellant who had pleaded guilty to what was then reckless driving and driving with excess alcohol. The aggravating features included a consumption of four pints of lager, driving through a housing estate at high speed, mounting the pavement and hitting two lampposts. This was followed by a police chase at speeds of 60 to 70 mph and the appellant concealing himself to avoid arrest. The Court of Appeal said that it was correct to hold this offence as being so serious that a non-custodial sentence could not be justified.

Another example of a case where aggravating features were held to make the offence so serious as to justify a custodial sentence is that of *R v KB* (2000) 164 JP 714. A 12-year-old pleaded guilty to five sexual offences against two other boys. Reports suggested that his upbringing and childhood had produced a need for long-term support and therapy. Whilst on remand within a local authority residential care centre he was said to have made progress during his 11-month stay. The judge held that although a continuation of the remand placement would be a suitable method of treating the appellant, it would not deal with the seriousness of the offences which called for an immediate custodial sentence. A sentence of four years' detention (under what was then s 53 of the Children and Young Persons Act 1933) was upheld. However, in *R v W* [1999] 1 Cr App R (S) 488, CA, an eight-month detention order was reduced to an eight-month supervision order for a 13-year-old boy convicted of indecent assault on a 12-year-old girl. The assault consisted of touching the girl's private parts against her will and simulated sex by lying on top of her. In view of the slight age difference and the young age of the defendant the appeal was allowed. Sexual offences are subject to a definitive set of guidelines which form part of *Sentencing Children and Young People* from the Sentencing Council. The guidelines should be used in all cases involving sexual offences. These are reproduced in **Appendix I** and sentencing cases on sexual offences are at **J.2** in **Appendix J** and **13.06**.

Offences of arson with intent to endanger life have always been treated very seriously by the courts and will nearly always be treated as a grave crime under the provisions of PCC(S)A 2000, s 91. Arson in itself (criminal damage by fire) will not necessarily merit a custodial sentence as stated in *R v Dewberry and Stone* (1985) 7 Cr App R (S) 202, CA, in which a young man with no previous court appearances was convicted of setting fire to a coat in a school room causing £200 worth of damage. The Court of Appeal said that whilst arson was a very serious offence, the range of criminality was vast and the offence to which the appellant pleaded guilty came in the lower range of cases of arson and did not merit a custodial sentence. Dewberry's co-defendant, Stone, was convicted of a further count of arson resulting in damage of some £67,000. Both offences were committed after the appellant had consumed vodka. The court said that in cases of arson, attention should be focused on the intention with which the acts were done rather than the consequences which resulted. The aggravating feature in this case was that the appellant had gone to the school on a second occasion and started a fire deliberately making that offence so serious that a non-custodial sentence could not be justified. In the case of *R v Iles* [2012] EWCA Crim 1610 the Court of Appeal imposed a sentence of 30 months' detention for an offence of arson at a school. The juvenile was 16 years old. He had been caught by police running away from the scene having smashed 22 windows with a crowbar and by kicking. One of the windows had been prised open, and an attempt had been made to start a fire within the English block. That block was found to be full of smoke. A deodorant can was found in the corridor. It was wrapped in some kind of material and set alight. In interview, the juvenile admitted causing the damage and attempting to set fire to the school because he had been banned from attending the school prom. The charge referred to damage to walls and carpets to the value of £100. He had a number of previous convictions. He also had other associated offences but the Court of Appeal indicated that the 30 months was justified by the arson alone. He was living with his extended family after his mother died. He was misusing alcohol and had some psychiatric issues but not sufficient to justify a hospital order. He lacked victim empathy and had a history of aggressive behaviour.

Criminal damage itself may be so serious as to merit a custodial sentence. In *R v George* (1992) 14 Cr App R (S) 12, CA, a 16-year-old pleaded guilty to damaging a church at night to the value of £33,000. He had four previous offences, the last of which was the criminal damage. The Court of Appeal described this as a quite disgraceful offence, which merited 12 months' detention. This was reduced to 10 months on the basis of a discount for a guilty plea.

Offences of violence may fulfil the seriousness criteria. Again, this will depend on the aggravating features in the offending. In *R v Beddoes* (1990–91) 12 Cr App R (S) 363, CA, the appellant pleaded guilty to an offence of violent disorder. He was involved in a fight when a large group of young men attacked a group of soldiers with snooker cues and glasses. Two people were hospitalised as a result of the incident. The defendant received a custodial sentence on the basis of the seriousness of the offence. An offence of violence, however, which on the bare facts may fit the seriousness criteria, may nevertheless be subject to mitigating factors which will allow the court to pass a community sentence.

Offences of robbery are subject to Part 3 of the Sentencing Council's definitive guideline *Sentencing Children and Young People*. The guidelines should be used in all cases involving robbery. These are reproduced in **Appendix I** and sentencing cases on robbery are at **J.1** in **Appendix J**.

Burglary of a dwelling house may be so serious that a non-custodial sentence cannot be justified, although of course the discretion to impose a community penalty remains with the court. In *R v Winson and Poole* [1998] 1 Cr App R (S) 239, CA, a 15-year-old and a 13-year-old entered a dwelling house by an unlocked rear door and stole theft and cash. A sentence of 12 months' detention was reduced to nine months on appeal bearing in mind the guidelines laid down in the case of *R v Brewster* [1998] 1 Cr App R (S) 181, CA. A number of sentencing cases for offences of burglary can be found at **J.5** in **Appendix J**.

The general restrictions in CJA 2003, s 152 do not apply to sentences fixed by law, the offences carrying minimum sentences for juveniles or to dangerous offenders. In the case of adults, they do not apply to third-time drug traffickers and burglars of dwelling houses.

Reasons for imposing a custodial sentence

10.10   Where a court passes a custodial sentence, then it is under a duty to state in open court that it is of the opinion that the relevant criteria apply and why it is of that opinion. The court must explain to the offender in open court and in ordinary language why it is passing a custodial sentence on him and its reasons must be recorded in the court register and on the warrant of commitment.

When giving its reasons the court must include a statement that it is of the opinion that a sentence consisting of or including a youth rehabilitation order with intensive supervision and surveillance or fostering cannot be justified for the offence, together with its reasons for reaching that opinion (CJA 2003, s 174(8)).

Giving reasons in open court is a prerequisite of Article 6 of the European Convention on Human Rights and is embodied in the Criminal Justice Act 2003, s 174, which requires the court to give reasons for and explain the effect of its sentence. The court must identify any definitive sentencing guidelines which apply and explain how it has followed those guidelines. If departing from the guidelines the court must explain why it is in the interests of justice to do so. Similarly, when different types of sentence are imposed on defendants jointly charged there may again be a need for the court to give fuller reasons than normal. A structured approach to the sentencing decision in the Youth Court carried out in consultation by the magistrates and their legal adviser will generally provide sound reasons that can be given in open court.

Refusal to express a willingness to agree to a requirement in a community sentence

10.11   This criterion means that an offence that would not otherwise have fallen within the custody bracket may still result in a custodial sentence. Indeed, where custody is imposed due to the lack of an agreement to a requirement in any specified community sentence, the court does not have to justify its passing of such a sentence. Nor is it required to obtain a pre-sentence report, although it must still explain to the offender in ordinary language why it is passing a custodial sentence and record its reasons. In most cases a PSR will have been obtained in order to facilitate the making of the intended community sentence.

There are a number of youth rehabilitation order sentence requirements that need an offender's agreement, namely an order with the requirement of treatment for dependence on an intoxicating substance, a drug treatment requirement, a requirement for mental health treatment or, a failure to comply with an order for pre-sentence drugs testing.

Two points need to be considered. First, the offender should have a clear understanding of his choice as to whether or not to agree to the sentence proposed. In *R v Marquis* [1974] 2 All ER 1216, CA, it was said that a suggestion that a custodial sentence was the only alternative, when in fact this was not the case, could invalidate the consent given by the defendant. However, in *R v Barnett* (1986) 8 Cr App R (S) 200, CA, the point was made that where custody is a realistic alternative to the community sentence proffered, the offender's knowledge that this is so does not negate his consent to the making of a community sentence. The relevance of these cases is somewhat diminished due to the passage of time and greater focus on individualistic sentencing for juveniles.

Secondly, the offender may have reason for not wishing to agree to specific community sentence requirements, but this does not make a custodial order a foregone conclusion. The court has other community sentences requirements that may be equally appropriate to meet the seriousness of the offence and the needs of the offender and its overall aim to prevent further offending.

Supervision after release

10.12   The aim of the detention and training order is that it should be constructive and linked to the work to be done by the Youth Offending Team during the custodial part of the sentence. The Youth Offending Team must appoint a supervising officer who will meet with the detainee, his parents or carer. A training plan will be drawn up to meet the young offender's needs with respect to education, health and accommodation. In this way, it is anticipated that release back into the community subject to supervision will be part of a process rather than an abrupt change from custody to community.

Supervision will generally be carried out by the Youth Offending Team. The offender will be issued a supervision notice before release giving him details of the supervision. Under national standards, minimum levels of contact are set including the fact that the offender must be seen on the day of release and the supervising officer must make a home visit within five working days of that release. Thereafter contact must be at least monthly for the duration of the order. The supervision notice may include a requirement to comply with an intensive supervision and surveillance programme.

Breach of supervision and further offending

10.13   Where a breach of supervision requirement is alleged, an information will usually be laid in the local justice area where the juvenile lives. Where the detention and training order was imposed by the Crown Court, an information should be laid in the local justice area where the offender lives. The court will issue a summons and has the power to issue a warrant where necessary if the information is in writing and upon oath (PCC(S)A 2000, s 104(1)). At the hearing the supervising officer will present evidence to the court about the alleged breach and the juvenile will have an opportunity to challenge that evidence. If having heard evidence from both sides the Youth Court is satisfied that there has been a failure to comply with the supervision requirement of the detention and training order it may:

(a)   impose a fine not exceeding level 3 (£250 for a child), leaving the detention and training order in place, or

(b)   direct that the juvenile be returned to detention for a period of up to either three months or if shorter, a period equal to that from the failure to the end of the order. (PCC(S)A 2000, s 104(3A), or

(c)   direct that the juvenile be under supervision for up to the maximum length of detention it could impose under (b) above, or

(d)   return the juvenile to detention and impose supervision as in (b) and (c) above.

These periods of detention and supervision take effect immediately and may overlap with the original detention and training order or supervision. They cannot be ordered to run consecutively. A subsequent failure to comply with the new supervision period can be dealt with as if it were a breach of a detention and training order. Likewise, an imprisonable offence committed during the new supervision period makes the juvenile liable to be detained (see below).

If the juvenile is convicted of a further offence (punishable with imprisonment, in the case of a person aged 21 or over) during the supervised period, in addition to any other sentence it imposes, a court can order detention in custody for a period not greater than that from the date of the commission of the offence to the end of the detention and training order. Any such sentence may be ordered to be served concurrently or consecutively to any sentence imposed for a new offence. For the purpose of calculation, an offence committed during or over a period of time is treated as having been committed on the last of those days (PCC(S)A 2000, s 105(4)).

10.14   Where the offender is serving a fixed-term custodial sentence of less than 12 months imposed by the Crown Court under s 91 of the PCC(S)A 2000, they must be released after half the sentence imposed has been served, if on that date they are under 18 years (CJA 2003, s 243A). They will then be subject to a supervision period of three months. If any of the requirements of this supervision period are not complied with the offender can be prosecuted by the YOT. If the failure to comply is proved then the juvenile can be fined up to level 3 on the standard scale or committed to youth detention for a maximum of 30 days (CJA 2003, s 256B). If the offender is 18 years or older at the date of release the proceedings must be brought in the adult court rather than the Youth Court.

Chapter 11   Breach, revocation and amendment of youth rehabilitation orders and reparation orders

11.01   The Criminal Justice and Immigration Act 2008, Sch 2 contains the relevant provisions dealing with youth rehabilitation order breaches.

Reparation orders, although not community sentences, are dealt with later in this chapter. The relevant provisions are in PCC(S)A 2000, ss 73 to 75 and Sch 8.

Breach of youth rehabilitation orders

General considerations – powers of remand

11.02   The court is given powers to adjourn any of the proceedings dealt with under CJIA 2008, Sch 2. This includes breaches and applications to amend or revoke a YRO (CJIA 2008, Sch 2, para 22). Where the case is adjourned, the court can either release the offender or remand him until the next hearing. It would appear that MCA 1980, s 128 would then allow the court to either remand the defendant on bail or to local authority accommodation. (see CJIA 2008, Sch 2, para 21(9)).

Failure to comply with a requirement

11.03   Before any breach proceedings are taken the responsible officer has a duty to issue an initial warning to the offender.

If the responsible officer is of the opinion that the offender has failed without reasonable excuse to comply with any of the requirements of a YRO the officer must give him a warning unless:

(a)   the offender has within the previous 12 months been given a warning in relation to a failure to comply with any of the requirements of the order; or

(b)   during the period of a first warning he has been given another warning in respect of the failure to comply with the order; and

(c)   the responsible officer is of the opinion that, during that warned period, the offender has again failed without reasonable excuse to comply with the order.

A warning must:

(a)   describe the circumstances of the failure;

(b)   state that the failure is unacceptable; and

(c)   inform the offender that, if within the next 12 months (or if it is a second warning during the period of that warning) he again fails to comply with any requirement of the order, he will be liable to be brought before a court.

Breach proceedings

11.04   If at any time while a YRO is in force in respect of an offender it appears on information to a justice of the peace acting for the appropriate local justice area that the offender has failed to comply with any of the requirements of the order, the justice may:

(a)   issue a summons requiring the offender to appear at the place and time specified in it; or

(b)   if the information is in writing and on oath, issue a warrant for his arrest.

Any summons or warrant issued shall direct the offender to appear or be brought:

(a)   in the case of a YRO which was made by the Crown Court that does not include a direction that any failure to comply with any of the requirements of the order be dealt with by the magistrates' court, before the Crown Court; and

(b)   in the case of a relevant order that is not an order to which paragraph (a) above applies, before a magistrates' court acting for the appropriate local justice area.

The appropriate local justice area is the area where the offender resides at the time the information is laid. If it is not known where the offender resides then it will be the area originally specified in the YRO.

Where breach proceedings do not have to be heard in the Crown Court, if the offender is aged 18 or over breach proceedings will commence in a magistrates' court other than the Youth Court. Offenders under the age of 18 will appear before the Youth Court.

Where a summons issued above requires an offender to appear before the Crown Court and the offender does not appear in answer to the summons, the Crown Court may issue either a warrant or a further summons requiring the offender to appear at the place and time specified in it. If the offender does not appear in answer to a further summons, the Crown Court may issue a warrant for the arrest of the offender (CJIA 2008, Sch 2, para 5). Where a Crown Court warrant is executed but the detained person cannot be brought immediately before the Crown Court, then the defendant can be detained for up to 72 hours from the time of arrest and produced before a magistrates' court within that period. The magistrates' court can then either direct that the juvenile is released forthwith or remand him to local authority accommodation until he can appear before the Crown Court (CJIA 2008, Sch 2, para 21).

Powers of Youth or magistrates' courts

11.05 If it is proved to the satisfaction of a Youth Court or magistrates' court before which an offender appears that he has failed without reasonable excuse to comply with any of the requirements of a YRO the court may deal with the offender in respect of the failure in one of the following ways:

(a) by fining the offender an amount not exceeding £2500 (but note the restriction in PCC(S)A 2000, s 135 which limits the level of fines imposed on juveniles found guilty of offences to £1000 if under 18 years old and £250 if under 14);

(b) by amending the youth rehabilitation order requirements so as to add to or substitute any requirement already imposed by the order. However, this may not include an extended activity requirement or fostering requirement if the order does not already include such a requirement. Where the original order included a fostering requirement and this is substituted by a new fostering requirement the order may run for 18 months (as opposed to the original 12), beginning with the date on which the original requirement first took effect;

(c) by dealing with the offender, for the offence in respect of which the order was made, in any way in which the court could have dealt with the offender for that offence (had the offender been before that court to be dealt with for it) (CJIA 2008, Sch 2, para 6(2)(c)).

The Sentencing Council have indicated that it is not necessary for the court to take any action in respect of a breach of a YRO, nor is it necessary to make the order more onerous. The *Sentencing Children and Young People* definitive guideline at paras 7.12–7.19, includes the following:

> 'The primary objective when sentencing for breach of a YRO is to ensure that the child or young person completes the requirements imposed by the court.
>
> A court must ensure that it has sufficient information to enable it to understand why the order has been breached and should be satisfied that the YOT and other local authority services have taken all steps necessary to ensure that the child or young person has been given appropriate opportunity and the support necessary for compliance. This is particularly important if the court is considering imposing a custodial sentence as a result of the breach.
>
> Where the failure arises primarily from non-compliance with reporting or other similar obligations and a sanction is necessary, the most appropriate response is likely to be the inclusion of (or increase in) a primarily punitive requirement such as the curfew requirement, unpaid work, the exclusion requirement and the

prohibited activity requirement or the imposition of a fine. However, continuing failure to comply with the order is likely to lead to revocation of the order and re-sentencing for the original offence.'

When imposing any requirement imposed under (b) above the court can extend the end date for completion of the requirements by up to 6 months, even if this makes the order longer than 3 years. An end date can only be extended once. Where the original order does not contain an unpaid work requirement and the court imposes such requirement, the minimum number of hours that may be imposed is reduced to 20 from the normal 40.

As always when dealing with the original offence ((c) above) the court shall take into account the extent to which the offender has complied with the requirements of the relevant order. In such circumstances the court must revoke the original order if it is still in force

The meaning of CJIA 2008, Sch 2, para 6(2)(c) is open to different interpretations. The issue becomes particularly relevant when the offender, convicted of an indictable only offence, such as robbery for example, attains 18 years before the YRO is breached. The breach action must be commenced in the magistrates' court (see **13.24**). The magistrates' court has no power to sentence an adult for an indictable only offence. The Justices' Clerks' Society advice (produced at **Appendix K** with the kind permission of the Society) is that sub-paragraph (c) gives the magistrates' court power to deal with the offence as if it had the powers of the Youth Court, as at the hearing date when the order was first imposed. There may be occasions, therefore, where it would be appropriate for the magistrates' court to be comprised of Youth Court magistrates. They would have the requisite knowledge and experience to re-sentence in more complicated or serious cases.

In the case of an offender who has wilfully and persistently failed to comply with those requirements, and the court is dealing with him under (c) above, the court may impose a youth rehabilitation order with an intensive supervision and surveillance requirement without regard to the fact that the court is not dealing with the offender for an offence that is punishable with imprisonment; nor need it form the opinion that the offence is so serious that it would (but for the restrictions) merit a custodial sentence. Furthermore, where the court does make such an order, then if in a subsequent breach, the offender is found to have failed wilfully and persistently to comply with that order, the court has power to deal with the offender for the offence by imposing a custodial sentence, even if the offence is not in itself so serious that only custody can be justified. If the original offence is not imprisonable then the court can still impose a detention and training order (DTO) for a term not exceeding four months (CJIA 2008, Sch 2, paras 6(12) to (15)). It might be thought that this power to impose a four-month DTO for a non-imprisonable offence would apply to offences which carry a maximum of less than four months' imprisonment (such as vehicle interference, obstructing a police officer and in line with the case of *P v Leeds Youth Court* [2006] EWHC 2527 (Admin) an offence of criminal damage where the value is less than £5,000), as well as to offences which are not otherwise punishable with a custodial sentence (such as causing harassment, alarm or distress contrary to s 5 of the Public Order Act 1986).On closer examination however the legislation only allows the court to impose a 4 month DTO for offences which do not carry imprisonment at all in respect of an adult.

Those offences which carry less than four months for imprisonment for an adult do not fall within the definition of 'non imprisonable' for these purposes and hence a DTO cannot be imposed however many times the defendant wilfully and persistently fails to comply with the YRO.

In relation to YROs imposed for non imprisonable offences, an important question is what wilful and persistent means in this context. The Sentencing Council's definitive guideline *Sentencing Children and Young People* at para 7.17 provides that:

> 'A child or young person will almost certainly be considered to have "wilfully and persistently" breached a YRO where there have been three breaches that have demonstrated a lack of willingness to comply with the order that have resulted in an appearance before court.'

Again, it should be noted that the example given of an offender breaching an order three times is intended only to act as an illustration of a clear case, rather than setting a prescriptive definition.

An offender is not to be treated as having failed to comply with an order in respect of a mental health treatment requirement, a drug treatment requirement or an intoxicating substance treatment requirement, solely on the ground that the offender had refused to undergo any surgical, electrical or other treatment required by that requirement if, in the opinion of the court, the refusal was reasonable having regard to all the circumstances.

When the Youth Court or magistrates' court is dealing with a breach of a Crown Court YRO (in accordance with a certificate allowing for this) then the court does not have to commit the offender to the Crown Court even if it comes to the conclusion that the order should be revoked and the youth re-sentenced. The Youth or magistrates' court powers in this situation are to deal with the offender, for the offence in respect of which the order was made, 'in any way in which the court could have dealt with the offender for that offence (had the offender been before that court to be dealt with for it)'. The meaning of this phrase, contained in CJIA 2008, Sch 2, para 6(2)(c) is subject to debate. It appears to be a departure from the form of words previously employed by Parliamentary draftsmen where typically the choice would be either the power to deal with the offender in any way the original sentencing court could have, or power to sentence as if the offender had just been convicted by the breach court. The power for a magistrates' court to revoke the order and re-sentence following breach of a Crown Court order is however most unusual. The new formula means that the re-sentencing court may impose any order which it could have done had it been sentencing the offender on the occasion when the order was originally imposed. This limits the Youth or magistrates' court to those courts' own powers of sentence. If this were not the case and the re-sentencing court had the powers of the original sentencing court that would allow the Youth or magistrates' court to impose long-term detention. Where such a sentence is being contemplated, it is suggested that the Youth or magistrates' court uses the option to commit to the Crown Court for re-sentence.

Breaches dealt with at Crown Court

11.06   Where a relevant order was made by the Crown Court and a Youth or magistrates' court has power to deal with the offender for the breach, it may instead commit him to custody or release him on bail until he can be brought or appear before the Crown Court.

A Youth or magistrates' court that deals with an offender as above shall send to the Crown Court:

(a)   a certificate signed by a justice of the peace certifying that the offender has failed to comply with the requirements of the relevant order in the respect specified in the certificate; and

(b)   such other particulars of the case as may be desirable; and a certificate purporting to be so signed shall be admissible as evidence of the failure before the Crown Court.

Where the Youth or magistrates' court do not have power to deal with a breach of a Crown Court order, because the judge has not authorised this by certificate then the Crown Court proceedings are initiated in the magistrates' court by the issue of a summons directing the offender to appear before the Crown Court on a given date (see **11.04**).

The Crown Court has similar powers to the Youth Court in dealing with breaches; however, in proceedings before the Crown Court any question whether the offender has failed to comply with the requirements of the relevant order is determined by the court and not by the verdict of a jury. The Crown Court's powers on re-sentence are to deal with the offender, for the offence in respect of which the order was made, in any way in which the Crown Court could have dealt with the offender for that offence: CJIA 2008, Sch 2, para 8(2)(c).

Commission of further offences

11.07   If an offender is convicted of a further offence while a YRO (which is either made by the Youth Court or the Crown Court, but contains a direction that breaches may be dealt with in a magistrates' court), is in force in respect of him, the convicting court may revoke that order. Where it does revoke the order, it may deal with the offender, for the offence in respect of which the order was made, in any way in which a Youth Court could have dealt with the offender for that offence (had the offender been before that court to be dealt with for it) (see **11.05** above). If the court deals with him in this manner it must take into account the extent to which the offender has complied with the order.

The court cannot impose a YRO for the new offence if there is an existing YRO, unless it revokes the old order. When revoking the old order the court can then make a YRO for both the old and new offences (provided of course that the 'new' offences were not committed before 30 November 2009). Requirements can be made concurrent or consecutive, with some exceptions (see **9.06**).

The court may not revoke and re-sentence the offender unless it considers it would be in the interests of justice to do so, having regard to circumstances that have arisen since the youth rehabilitation order was made.

Where the Crown Court orders that the Youth Court is authorised to deal with breach proceedings, the Youth Court may nonetheless commit the offender back to the Crown Court in custody or on bail to be dealt with by the judge. The judge can then revoke the order and deal with the offender in any way the Crown Court could have. The further offence can also be sentenced at the Crown Court in any way the convicting court could have (CJIA 2008, Sch 2, para 19(6)).

In the case of a Crown Court YRO, where there is no such direction and the offender is subsequently convicted in a magistrates' court, he can be committed to the Crown Court on bail or in custody (CJIA 2008, Sch 2, para 18(10) and (11)). The Crown Court can then also deal with the further offence in any way in which the convicting court could have (CJIA 2008, Sch 2, para 19(6)).

Revocation of youth rehabilitation orders

Applications for revocation

11.08   The court which is to hear the application must issue a summons to secure the attendance of the offender, if he is not already before the court. If the offender fails to attend in answer to the summons, the court may issue a warrant of arrest (CJIA 2008, Sch 2, para 20). It is however not necessary to secure the defendant's attendance where the court proposes to revoke the order in full (without re-sentencing).

Powers of Youth or magistrates' courts

11.09   Where a YRO made by a Youth or magistrates' court, or Crown Court (where there is a certificate authorising breach proceedings in a magistrates' court), is in force and, on the application of the offender or the responsible officer, it appears to the appropriate Youth or magistrates' court that, having regard to circumstances that have arisen since the order was made, it would be in the interests of justice for the order to be revoked, or for the offender to be dealt with in some other way for the offence in respect of which the order was made, the appropriate court may:

(a)   revoke the order; or

(b)   revoke the order, and deal with the offender, for the offence in respect of which the order was made, in any way in which the appropriate court could have dealt with the offender for that offence (had the offender been before that court to be dealt with for it).

'Appropriate Court' in this context means:

(a)   if the offender is aged under 18 when the application under sub-paragraph (1) was made, a Youth Court acting in the local justice area specified in the youth rehabilitation order; and

(b)   if the offender is aged 18 or over at that time, a magistrates' court (other than a Youth Court) acting in that local justice area (CJIA 2008, Sch 2, para 11(8)).

Circumstances that may lead to a revocation include the offender making good progress or responding satisfactorily to supervision or treatment as the case may be.

Where an application to revoke an order is dismissed, then during the period of three months beginning with the date on which it was dismissed no further application may be made except with the consent of the appropriate court (CJIA 2008, Sch 2, Part 3, para 11(7)).

In dealing with an offender for the original offence, a court shall take into account the extent to which the offender has complied with the requirements of the relevant order. A person so sentenced may appeal to the Crown Court against that sentence.

Where a Youth or magistrates' court proposes to exercise its powers under this paragraph otherwise than on the application of the offender, it shall summon him to appear before the court and, if he does not appear in answer to the summons, may issue a warrant for his arrest.

No application may be made by the offender while an appeal against the relevant order is pending.

Powers of the Crown Court

11.10   The provisions for the Crown Court mirror those of the magistrates' courts (as above) except that the power to re-sentence is 'to deal with the offender, for the offence in respect of which the order was made, in any way in which the Crown Court could have dealt with the offender for that offence' (CJIA 2008, Sch 2, para 12(2)(b)(ii)).

Note also that the Crown Court has no jurisdiction under CJIA 2008, Sch 2, para 12 to deal with an application to revoke a YRO made by it where that court has authorised any subsequent proceedings for breach/revocation/amendment to be heard in a Youth or magistrates' court.

Amendment of youth rehabilitation orders

Applications for amendment

11.11 Applications should be made to the Youth Court if the offender is under 18 when the application is made and otherwise to the magistrates' court.

Powers of Youth or magistrates' courts

Amendment by reason of change of residence

11.12 If at any time while the order is in force, a Youth or magistrates' court acting for the local justice area specified in the order is satisfied that the offender proposes to change, or has changed, his residence from that area to another area, the court may and on the application of the responsible officer, must amend the relevant order by substituting the other local justice area for the area specified in the order.

Amendment of requirements of order

11.13 In connection with a YRO imposed in a Youth Court, or a Crown Court where there is a direction authorising subsequent proceedings to be heard in a magistrates' court, then a magistrates' court acting for the local justice area specified in the order may, on the application of an eligible person, amend an order by cancelling or replacing a requirement of the same kind which could have been included when the order was made. The stipulation that the replacement requirement must be of the same kind means that, for example, one programme requirement could be replaced by a requirement to complete a different programme. It is however not possible to replace a programme requirement with a curfew requirement (CJIA 2008, Sch 2, para 13(4)(b) and Sch 2, para 1(3)(a)).

The appropriate court will be a Youth Court if the offender is under 18 when the application is made, otherwise a magistrates' court (CJIA 2008, Sch 2, para 13(6)). If a Crown Court YRO does not contain a direction as above then the application must be made direct to the Crown Court under paragraph 14 of Sch 2 to the Criminal Justice and Immigration Act 2008. The Crown Court may then issue a summons or warrant (CJIA 2008, Sch 2, para 20).

In either case where the original order contains a specific area requirement (eg an activity requirement which contains elements which are not available to the Youth Offending Team in the new local justice area) or a programme requirement, the court must not make an amendment that would prevent the offender from complying with that requirement. In such circumstances the court must substitute a similar requirement within the new area.

Where the court replaces a requirement with a new requirement of the same kind, the new requirement must be capable of being complied with before the end of the order. The supervising officer or offender can however apply to the court to extend the duration of the order by up to 6 months even if this makes the youth rehabilitation order longer than 3 years. This power can only be exercised once. In the case of a fostering requirement that substitutes the original fostering requirement it may run for a period of 18 months beginning with the date on which the original requirement first had effect.

An order containing an unpaid work requirement may on the application of the offender or the responsible officer be amended to extend the period of 12 months during which time the order must be completed, if it would be in the interests of justice to do so having regard to circumstances that have arisen since the order was made.

The court may not impose a treatment requirement such as mental health treatment, drug treatment or drug testing by way of amendment unless the offender has expressed willingness to comply with the requirement. If an offender fails to express willingness to comply with such a requirement the court may revoke the youth rehabilitation requirement and deal with the offender, for the offence in respect of which the order was made, in any way in which that court could have dealt with the offender for that offence (had the offender been before that court to be dealt with for it) (CJIA 2008, Sch 2, para 16(4)). Also see **11.05** above for issues relating to offenders who have attained 18. If such circumstances arise the court must take into account the extent to which the offender has complied with the order.

Procedural requirements

11.14   The court which is to deal with the application for amendment must, where this is necessary to secure the attendance of the offender, issue a summons or warrant, unless the application is only cancelling a requirement of an order, reducing the period of any requirement, or substituting a new local justice area or place for the one specified in the order (CJIA 2008, Sch 2, para 20).

Breach of reparation orders

National standards

11.15   The manner in which all of the orders referred to in this chapter are managed by Youth Offending Teams is governed by the National Standards for Youth Justice Services. YOT practitioners must meet regularly with the child or young person to discuss progress and monitor compliance. They must ensure that all efforts are made to help the offender complete the order satisfactorily.

Disclosure

11.16 In order to ensure a fair trial in accordance with Article 6 of the European Convention, Youth Offending Teams should provide full disclosure of the circumstances surrounding the breach by way of a written statement or statements to the defendant or his legal representative.

Breach proceedings

11.17 Whilst a reparation order is in force for an offender of any age, the responsible officer may initiate breach proceedings in the Youth Court acting for the area where the offender is then living (or if it is not known where the offender resides the application must be made to a court acting for the area specified in the order). Note that the failure to comply must be proved within the three-month duration of the order. Where the court is satisfied of the failure to comply, it may fine the offender an amount not exceeding £1,000 (£250 in the case of a child). Any fine imposed shall be deemed to be a sum adjudged to be paid by conviction.

Where the order was made in a Youth Court any breach may be dealt with by revoking the order and dealing with the offender for the original offence. The court has the powers that it would have had where it was dealing with the offence at the time the offender was originally sentenced.

Where the order was made by the Crown Court, a Youth Court may commit the offender in custody or release him on bail to appear before the Crown Court. The court should also send particulars of the offender's failure to the Crown Court in a certificate signed by justice of the peace to the Crown Court. The Crown Court may deal with the offender for the original offence in any way in which it could have dealt with him for that offence had it not made the order, and if it does so it should revoke the reparation order if it is still in force.

Ensuring the attendance of the offender at court

11.18 Where the supervising or responsible officer commences breach proceedings, a summons will normally be issued by the court. However, where the application is substantiated on oath a warrant with or without bail may be issued and this can include circumstances where a summons cannot be served usually because the offender has left his address or has absconded. In such circumstances the Youth Offending Team manager must ensure that the police are given all the relevant information about the possible whereabouts of the offender. If a warrant is issued and a juvenile is arrested he must normally be brought before a Youth Court for the relevant local justice area. If no Youth Court is sitting the person having custody of the offender may arrange for his detention in a place of safety for up to 72 hours starting from the time of arrest. A place of safety will usually be local authority accommodation although this may include a police station. The juvenile must be brought before a Youth Court within that period. Where he is brought before a Youth Court other than the appropriate court, the Youth Court may direct his release or remand him to local authority accommodation. If the offender is aged 18 or over the remand should be to a remand centre if availability has been notified or alternatively prison accommodation. The schedule makes no mention of a power to bail either with or without conditions. As magistrates' courts have no powers outside those provided by statute it seems unlikely that they could claim to act under a common law power.

There is power to remand, or further remand, to local authority accommodation where the application is for revocation or amendment of the orders. No such powers are mentioned where there is a need to further remand in breach proceedings. A further remand to custody in such circumstances may not be lawful and as such would violate Article 5 of the European Convention on Human Rights. This sets out that no person shall be deprived of his liberty save in accordance with a procedure prescribed by law and limited by the terms of the article. The court's alternatives would appear to be a remand on bail, despite the lack of an express power, or a reliance on MCA 1980, s 55(5) which provides a general power to remand, in cases commenced by complaint or application, following an arrest under a warrant.

Variation or revocation of reparation orders

11.19   On the application of an appropriate officer or of the offender the court named in the order may amend or revoke a reparation order, or cancel or vary any provisions included in it (PCC(S)A 2000, Sch 8, para 5). Variation includes reference to inserting, as an additional or substitute requirement, any provision which could have been included in the order if the court had then power to make it and were exercising that power. This includes changing the name of the area specified in the order.

The court can revoke the order, cancel any requirement or change the responsible officer or area named in the order without the offender being present in court.

On varying or discharging a reparation order, the court must send a copy to the supervised person, and if the supervised person is a child, to his parent or guardian. The supervisor and local authority must also receive a copy.

Repeat applications

11.20   In the case of a reparation order where the application for revocation has been dismissed, no further application may be made except with the consent of the appropriate court.

Chapter 12   Additional powers and ancillary orders in the Youth Court

Introduction

12.01   In addition to the range of disposals considered in **Chapters 8** to **10**, there are many other orders available to the court that may be imposed at the same time. Some of these orders are in respect of parents, some are ancillary orders that are primarily intended for use in the adult court, but have a role to play in the Youth Court.

Due to their complexity and dual nature criminal behaviour orders and anti-social behaviour injunctions are dealt with in **Chapter 14**.

Binding over orders

12.02   A binding over order is a measure of preventive justice, by which the person entering into the order agrees to be of good behaviour or, in the case of parents, agrees to ensure the good behaviour of their child. When the order is made, the court fixes the duration of the order, which is at the court's discretion, and also a sum of money, called a recognisance, which may be forfeited if the order is not complied with during the period fixed. In all cases involving a bind over the court must follow directions in the *Criminal Consolidated Practice Direction Part VII, J as at November 2016*.

Parents and guardians

12.03   Where a juvenile is found guilty of an offence, the court may, as a preventive measure, and with the consent of the parent or guardian, bind over the parent or guardian. The recognisance may not exceed the sum of £1,000 for a period not exceeding three years or until the juvenile attains the age of 18 years, whichever is the shorter. The terms of the bind over are:

(a)   to take proper control of and exercise control over the offender; and

(b)   where a youth rehabilitation order has been passed to ensure that the offender complies with the requirements of that sentence.

The Practice Direction (VII, J.19 Nov 16) requires that the court specifies the actions which the parent or guardian is to take. Under PCC(S)A 2000, s 150, when a child or young person under 16 years is convicted of an offence the court is under a duty to bind over the parent or guardian if it is satisfied, having regard to the circumstances of the case, that it would be desirable in the interests of preventing the commission by him of further offences. Where it decides not to bind the parent or guardian over the court is required to state in open court why it is not satisfied that it would be so desirable. If the parent or guardian refuses to consent and the court considers that refusal unreasonable, the court may fine the parent or guardian up to £1,000.

In fixing the amount of the recognisance the court is required to take into account the means of the parent or guardian and reduce or increase the amount accordingly (PCC(S) A 2000, s 150(7)). Care should be exercised to involve parents in the proceedings and the court should perhaps consider explaining its obligation to bind over parents before it goes on to consider the substantive order of the court. Before the court makes an order binding over the parents, they should be given an opportunity to make representations as to why they should not enter into a recognisance if such reasons exist. The parent may wish to be represented by a solicitor in these circumstances.

The court may revoke an order under PCC(S)A 2000, s 150 on the application of the parent or guardian if it appears to be in the interests of justice to do so, having regard to any change of circumstances since the order was made.

A parent or guardian may appeal to the Crown Court against an order made under PCC(S)A 2000, s 150.

The juvenile

12.04   The juvenile offender may be bound over to keep the peace by way of complaint under MCA 1980, s 115 for a specific incident. Alternatively, the justices may use their powers to bind over under the Justices of the Peace Act 1361. This is not by reason of any offence having been committed but as a measure of preventive justice where the juvenile's conduct amounts to a breach of the peace involving violence or an imminent threat of violence or that there is a real risk of violence in the future. Such violence may be perpetrated by the individual who will be subject to the order, or by a third party as a natural consequence of the individual's conduct. (*Consolidated Practice Direction Part VII, J.2*).

The two provisions are quite separate, as stated in *R v Aubrey-Fletcher, ex parte Thompson* [1969] 2 All ER 846. In this case, a magistrates' court used its common law powers to bind over and the High Court on appeal held that this case was not a bind over under MCA 1980, s 115. In such cases there must be a complaint and the complaint must be adjudged to be true, in other words the case must be heard out completely. An order under the Act of 1361 can be made at any time during the proceedings.

A complaint under MCA 1980, s 115, is not a matter assigned to the Youth Court by CYPA 1933, s 46, and should therefore be heard in an adult magistrates' court.

The only way in which a juvenile may be bound over in the Youth Court is by virtue of the court's common law powers. In such circumstances it should be stressed that the person to be bound over must consent to the binding over order. Where an adult is concerned, the court may commit that person to prison until he consents to be bound over (MCA 1980, s 115(3)). In the case of a juvenile, imprisonment is not available to the court and therefore the court has no sanction to enforce consent to a binding over order. This point arose in the case of *Veater v Glennan* [1981] 2 All ER 304, where the police made a complaint for a binding over order against six juveniles aged 14 and 15 years. At the hearing the juveniles admitted disorderly behaviour but refused to consent to being bound over in the sum of £100 to keep the peace for one year. The magistrates took the view that they had no sanction to compel a binding over, nor could they impose a unilateral obligation to be bound over. The High Court agreed that this was the case (but see also *R v Lincoln Crown Court, ex parte Jude* [1997] 3 All ER 737).

Any bind over should avoid the terms 'to be of good behaviour' as this has been held to be too imprecise to be enforceable (*Hashman and Harrup v United Kingdom* [2000] Crim LR 185).

Although a juvenile may not be imprisoned for refusing to consent to a binding over order, the court still has the power to bind him over if he consents. This was decided in *Conlan v Oxford* (1983) 79 Cr App R 157, where the juvenile (youth) court had declined to bind over a juvenile because there was no sanction to enforce its order in the event of a refusal. Goff LJ held that this was incorrect and that the court did have the power to bind a juvenile over despite the absence of an enforcement sanction.

Estreatment of a recognisance

12.05   Where the power to bind over has been utilised, the juvenile having consented to be bound over, the recognisance may be forfeited on complaint to the court (MCA 1980, s 120). This will usually occur where there is an offence committed or a breach of the peace during the currency of the binding over order. The hearing of a complaint alleging breach of a binding over order is not a matter assigned by CYPA 1933, s 46 to the Youth Court and should thus be heard by the adult court. See **Chapter 5** for further discussion as to the jurisdiction of the Youth Court to hear such complaints. Where the complaint is denied the hearing will proceed by hearing the evidence of the complainant and of the juvenile. The court will decide whether the case is proved. The complaint may be admitted, thus rendering evidence unnecessary (*Berkhamsted RDC v Duerdin-Dutton* [1964] Crim LR 307), but the Practice Direction requires that representations are still heard. If contested, the court should be satisfied beyond reasonable doubt of the matters complained of before a binding over order may be imposed. Where the procedure has been commenced on complaint, the burden of proof rests on the complainant. In all other circumstances, the burden of proof rests upon the prosecution (*Consolidated Practice Direction Part VII, J.5*). Proceedings on complaint to forfeit a recognisance may result in the estreatment of the whole or part of the recognisance, and an additional order as to costs. Where the parent is the subject of the bind over he may be subject to proceeding to forfeit the recognisance by virtue of PCC(S)A 2000, s 150 and MCA 1980, s 120.

There is no statutory authority as to who commences a complaint to estreat a parental bind over should they fail to keep proper control over their child. However, whilst it is clearly inappropriate for the court to lay such a complaint where a juvenile offends, the police at the time of charge are in a position to do so both legally and practically. In the normal course of events the re-offending and its surrounding circumstances will be sufficient to enable the magistrates (in an adult court) to decide whether or not the complaint is proved, but see the remarks above.

Parenting orders

12.06   A parenting order is made against a parent or guardian of a child or young person.

Where a young person under the age of 16 is convicted of an offence the court must make a parenting order if satisfied that a parenting order would be desirable in the interests of preventing the commission of any further offence by the child or young person.

If it is not so satisfied, the court must state its reasons in open court, that a parenting order would not be desirable in the interests of preventing the commission of any further offence by the child or young person.

The Youth Court will make a parenting order against the parent or guardian of a child or young person:

(a)   where the juvenile has been convicted of an offence; or

(b)   where a court makes or deals with a failure to comply with a child safety order; or

(c)   where a court makes a sexual harm prevention order in respect of the juvenile; or

(d)   where a parental compensation order is made in relation to the child's behaviour; or

(e)   where a conviction is recorded for failure to ensure regular school attendance or comply with the school attendance order; or

(f)   where a referral order has been made or where a parent is referred back to court by a Youth Offender Panel after failing to attend panel meetings.

The prohibition on the making of a parenting order and a referral order for the same offence was removed by s 324 and Sch 34 of the Criminal Justice Act 2003.

This means that parenting orders may be made by all criminal courts (ie Youth Court, magistrates' court and Crown Court). They may also be made by a Family Proceedings Court and a magistrates' court exercising its civil jurisdiction.

Prior to making a parenting order the court shall obtain and consider information about the juvenile's family circumstances and the likely effect of the order on those circumstances and where the court is considering making both a referral order and a parenting order, this information shall be in a report.

The parenting order is made by the court of its own motion and the court's decision is one of judgment or evaluation. The court will need to act on all the relevant evidence before it, including information about the family circumstances and reach a judgment that is rational (*R (on the application of M) v Inner London Crown Court* [2003] EWHC 301 (Admin). The consent of a parent/guardian is not required although many courts recognise the importance of the willing participation of the parents in a parenting order. The order will last for a period not exceeding 12 months, and must require the parent or guardian to comply with requirements that the court considers desirable in the interests of preventing the commission of further offences. (Where the order was made in non-Youth Court proceedings the requirements are those which the court considers desirable to prevent the behaviour which led to the making of a particular order.).

The order must include a requirement to attend a parenting programme for a period not exceeding three months. All orders must include this unless the parent has previously received a parenting order. The court fixes the length of the parenting programme but must allow sufficient time for assessing parents and any work needed to prepare the parents for the programme.

Additional requirements

12.07 The court may wish to impose additional requirements to ensure or encourage the parent to prevent undesirable or offending behaviour. Such requirements may include making sure the juvenile is indoors between certain hours and ensuring that the juvenile is accompanied to school. There may be further requirements that the juvenile attends a programme or course to address relevant problems (eg anger management or drug or alcohol misuse; that the juvenile avoids contact with disruptive and possibly older children; or that the juvenile avoids unsupervised visits to certain places, such as shopping centres). Another common requirement is that the juvenile does not have contact with named co-defendants. Any such requirements shall, so far as practicable, avoid any conflict with a parent's religious beliefs and any interference with the times, if any, in which he normally works or attends an educational establishment (CDA 1998, s 9). As breach is a criminal offence, the requirements must be clear so that the parents or guardians know exactly what is required of them.

The parenting order may include a residential course if two conditions are satisfied. These are that the attendance by the parent or guardian on such a course where the court is satisfied that it is likely to be more effective than he or she attending a non-residential course in preventing the child or young person from re-offending, and that likely interference with family life is proportionate.

A parenting order must specify a responsible officer. This will often be a member of the Youth Offending Team but it may be a social worker, a probation officer, or a person nominated by the chief education officer such as an education welfare officer.

Variation

12.08   During the operational period of a parenting order the court that made it may, on application of the responsible officer or the parent, make an order discharging or varying the parenting order. This includes cancelling or inserting any provision within the court's existing powers. When application to discharge an order is dismissed no further application for its discharge shall be made by any person except with the consent of the court which made the order.

Breach

12.09   If the parent fails without reasonable excuse to comply with any requirement included in the order or specified in directions given by the responsible officer, he shall be liable on summary conviction to a fine not exceeding level 3. The prosecution of a parent for breach of a parenting order will take place in the magistrates' court and is conducted by the Crown Prosecution Service.

Deprivation orders and forfeiture

Deprivation

12.10   Where a juvenile is found guilty of an offence, the court by or before which he is found guilty may make an order depriving the offender of his rights to certain property (PCC(S)A 2000, s 143). The court must be satisfied that the property in his possession or under his control at the time of his apprehension was:

(a)   used for the purpose of committing or facilitating the commission of any offence; or

(b)   was intended by him to be used for that purpose.

An order may also be made depriving an offender of property where the offence or an offence taken into consideration consists of unlawful possession of property which:

(a)   has been lawfully seized from him; or

(b)   was in his possession or under his control at the time when he was apprehended for the offence of which he has been convicted or when a summons in respect of that offence was issued.

An example of this provision's most common use is the confiscation of keys used in the course of theft of cars or tools used in the course of burglary.

Where the court makes an order of conditional or absolute discharge under PCC(S) A 2000, s 12, a deprivation order may still be made, as such an order is deemed to be a conviction for the purposes of the proceedings in which it is made (PCC(S)A 2000, s 12(7)).

Forfeiture

12.11   Orders of forfeiture are rare in the Youth Court because of the nature of the offences from which the statutory powers of forfeiture arise. Where the statute gives a court a power of forfeiture, it may order property to be confiscated and either sold or destroyed as appropriate. For example, drugs found in a person's possession may be subject to a forfeiture order made under the Misuse of Drugs Act 1971, s 27. Another of the more common offences seen in the Youth Court is the possession of a knife, bladed article or weapon. Where such a case is proved the court may order the forfeiture of the knife or other article (Knives Act 1997, s 6 and Prevention of Crime Act 1953).

Perhaps the most common offences of all in the Youth Court where the question of forfeiture arises are those involving the possession of air weapons by juveniles. There is a general power to confiscate a firearm under the Firearms Act 1968, s 52, if the court has made a custodial order. Specific offences in relation to air weapons are those under s 22(4) of the 1968 Act (possession of an air weapon or ammunition by a minor under the age of 17 years). There is power on a finding of guilt to order confiscation by virtue of the Firearms Act 1968, Sch 6.

Effect of an order

12.12   The effect of a forfeiture order is to deprive the offender of his rights to property. The court may direct the property to be sold or disposed of in any other manner, for example by its destruction. The proceeds of sale of items forfeited are treated as a fine and sent to the Home Office, to be applied to public funds. The effect of a deprivation order is to deprive the offender of his rights (if any) to the property, and the property will be taken into the possession of the police (PCC(S)A 2000, s 143(3)). Subsequent claims to ownership of the property can be dealt with either by the civil courts or by an application under the Police (Property) Act 1897, s 1, to the magistrates' court.

Restitution orders

12.13   PCC(S)A 2000, s 148, provides for the making of restitution orders. Although orders for the restitution of goods against juveniles are rare, such an order may be made if the court is satisfied on the facts of the case, either having heard evidence during the trial or from documentary evidence. The court must have found the offender guilty:

(a)   of an offence involving goods which have been stolen, whether or not stealing is the gist of his offence; or

(b)   of any other offence and an offence under (a) above is taken into consideration.

The powers of the court in these circumstances are:

(a)   to order anyone having possession or control of the goods to restore them to any person entitled to recover them from him; or

(b)   on the application of a person entitled to recover from the person convicted any other goods, being the proceeds of any disposal or realisation of the whole or part of them, the court may order those other goods to be delivered or transferred to the applicant; or

(c)   the court may order that a sum not exceeding the value of the goods shall be paid out of the money of the person convicted which was taken out of his possession on his apprehension, to any person who, if those goods were in the possession of the person convicted, would be entitled to recover them from him.

Orders under (b) and (c) may be made at the same time, provided that a victim does not receive more than the value of the original goods.

A restitution order may be made notwithstanding the fact that sentence is deferred in all other respects.

Compensation orders

12.14   The criminal courts often deal with offences that result in the victim suffering loss in some form or another. Magistrates are given power to award compensation to be paid by the offender either at their own discretion or on the application of the prosecution. The power to award compensation is contained in PCC(S)A 2000, s 130, and by virtue of this provision the court may order the offender, after finding him guilty, to pay compensation:

> 'for any personal injury, loss or damage resulting from that offence or any other offence which is taken into consideration by the court in determining sentence or to make payments for funeral expenses or bereavement in respect of a death resulting from any such offence, other than a death due to an accident arising out of the presence of a motor vehicle on a road.'

If personal injury, loss or damage arises out of an accident caused by the presence of a motor vehicle on a road, a compensation order may be made (see below).

Section 130(2A) of the PCC(S)A 2000 states that a court must consider making a compensation order in any case where this section empowers it to do so. If the court does not make a compensation order it is required to give reasons on passing sentence.

A compensation order may be made instead of, or in addition to, dealing with the offender in any other way.

The amount of compensation which the court may order is limited to £5,000 for each offence. Where compensation is ordered for offences taken into consideration the court is still limited to a total compensation order of £5,000 for each offence that has actually been charged.

For example, an offender is charged with and admits three offences of theft and also asks the magistrates to take into consideration 20 other matters. Compensation is applied for on both the offences and the matters taken into consideration. A total of £300 is awarded as compensation on the offence charged, and therefore the court is limited to awarding compensation in total of £15,000, less the £300 awarded, that is £14,700, on the matters taken into consideration (PCC(S)A 2000, s 131).

The court must be satisfied that the injury, loss or damage which occurred is attributable to the offence in respect of which a compensation order is made.

A compensation order may only be made in respect of injury, loss or damage that was due to a road traffic accident involving the presence of a motor vehicle on a road, if:

(a) it is in respect of damage which is treated as resulting from an offence under the Theft Act 1968 (eg TWOC); or

(b) it is in respect of injury, loss or damage with regard to which the offender is uninsured in relation to the use of the vehicle; and compensation is not payable under the agreement between the Secretary of State and the Motor Insurers' Bureau.

A compensation order is to be of such amount as the court considers appropriate having regard to any evidence and to any representations that are made by or on behalf of the accused or the prosecutor (PCC(S)A 2000, s 130(4)). This subsection contemplates that the court can make assessments and approximations where the evidence is scanty or incomplete and then makes an order which is deemed 'appropriate'.

Where the basis for making any compensation order is challenged, the court must consider evidence and cannot act merely on representations. The position prior to the passing of the Criminal Justice Act 1982 was that before awarding compensation the court had to be satisfied that the amount to be ordered was either agreed or proved.

In *R v Vivian* [1979] 1 All ER 48, CA, £209 compensation was claimed for damage done to a car. It was asserted that the estimate was excessive because the damaged car was very old and had defects before the collision. The judge, without hearing any evidence on this disputed point and without hearing detailed representations, made a compensation order of £100. This was quashed on appeal. The Court of Appeal said that as there was neither agreement on, nor proof of the amount, which the owner of the damaged car was entitled to claim, a compensation order ought not to have been made. The words 'considers appropriate' in PCC(S)A 2000, s 131 are rather vague, but although there is no mention of a standard of proof it is submitted that the magistrates must at least be satisfied on the balance of probabilities that a particular amount is appropriate before making an order.

In *R v Horsham Justices, ex parte Richards* [1985] 2 All ER 1114, a compensation order was made by the justices. The application had been contested and the court made the order after hearing representations but without receiving any evidence. Neill LJ held that this approach was wrong and that the court had no jurisdiction to make a compensation order without receiving evidence where there were real issues raised as to whether the claimants had suffered any, and if so what, loss.

In *R v Miller* [1976] Crim LR 694, CA, the principles to be followed in making orders for compensation were considered. This was a case in which a defendant was convicted of theft of £6,100 from his employer. He was sentenced to 18 months' imprisonment and ordered to pay £6,100 compensation. The defendant obtained employment after his release from prison but could only offer payments of £5 per week. The following points extracted from the judgment in *Miller* are still of relevance when considering the making of a compensation order, both in the adult and Youth Court:

(a)   An order should only be made where the legal position is quite clear.

(b)   Regard must be had to the defendant's means.

(c)   The order must be precise, relate to an offence, and specify the amount and the instalments, if there is to be payment by instalments.

(d)   The order must not be oppressive.

(e)   There may be good moral grounds for making an order including payment by instalments to remind the defendant of the evil he has done.

(f)   The order must be realistic.

In considering the amount of compensation, the court must have regard to the means of the juvenile's parents or, if appropriate, the means of the juvenile himself. It is the duty of the court to order that any compensation awarded be paid by the parents of the juvenile unless the court is satisfied that the parent or guardian cannot be found or that it would be unreasonable, having regard to the circumstances of the case, to make such an order (PCC(S)A 2000, s 137). However, see below in relation to juveniles of 16 years or older and those accommodated in local authority accommodation.

In *R v Scott* (1986) 83 Cr App R 221, it was held that the compensation awarded to be paid should not be such that it would take an excessive period of time to pay. However, in *R v Olliver and Olliver* [1989] Crim LR 387, CA, it was stated that there was no reason in principle why an order should not be paid over two or three years. This case was decided on its particular facts and many Youth Courts prefer to work to a 12-month maximum period.

Where the court considers it appropriate to impose a fine, a victim surcharge (see **12.15**) and a compensation order, but the offender has insufficient means to pay all the orders, the compensation order must be given preference by the court (PCC(S) A 2000, s 130(12)). Where the offender's means are limited the court should make a compensation order, order the victim surcharge (see **12.15** for amounts) and reduce the fine so that the compensation can be paid. See below for principles in respect of costs.

Where the offence involved is one contrary to the Theft Act 1968 and the property involved is recovered in a damaged condition, then the court may order compensation for all the damage caused while out of the owner's possession, however and by whomsoever it was caused (PCC(S)A 2000, s 130(5)).

A victim's civil remedies remain the same whether or not a compensation order is made. However, any subsequent award will be reduced by any sum already awarded in criminal proceedings.

Where the juvenile has attained the age of 16 the court has a power rather than a duty to order the parent to pay (PCC(S)A 2000, s 137(3)). It would be unreasonable to make an order against a parent, where it was quite clear that the parent had done what he or she could to keep the juvenile from criminal ways (*R v Sheffield Crown Court, ex parte Clarkson* (1986) 8 Cr App R (S) 454). Also it may not be reasonable to hold a parent responsible for the juvenile's actions where the parent had no control over what the juvenile was doing at the time and could not take any steps to prevent the juvenile from committing the offence, due to the child being accommodated voluntarily by the local authority, with the parents' consent (*TA v DPP* [1997] 1 Cr App R (S) 1). See also **8.13** for further details on parental responsibility for financial penalties.

In relation to a child or young person for whom the local authority have parental responsibility and who is in their care, or is provided with accommodation by them, references to parent or guardian are to be construed as references to the local authority. Parental responsibility can only be acquired by a local authority where it is expressly conferred by statute, for example under a care order or emergency protection order made under the Children Act 1989. Consequently, where a juvenile had been remanded to the local authority under the provisions of CYPA 1969, s 23, (pre LASPOA 2012, s 91) this did not give parental responsibility and therefore a compensation order could not be made against the local authority in these circumstances (*North Yorkshire County Council v Selby Youth Court Justices* [1994] 1 All ER 991). See also **8.14** for a discussion of the power to order local authorities to pay financial orders.

The court is permitted to find that it would be unreasonable to make such an order having regard to the circumstances of the case. What would be regarded as 'unreasonable' by the courts remains to be seen. It is suggested that before a compensation order is made against a local authority, that authority should be given the opportunity of making representations (*Bedfordshire County Council v DPP* [1996] 1 Cr App R (S) 322). The court should normally find some causative link between any fault proved and the offences committed before considering whether to make a compensation order against a local authority. When making a compensation order the court is required to have regard to the offender's means. Where the parent or guardian is ordered to pay, it is the means of the parent or guardian which must be taken into account (PCC(S)A 2000, s 138). An order against the local authority is not restricted by the offender's means (PCC(S)A 2000, s 138(2)).

Victim surcharge

12.15   The imposition of a victim surcharge on sentence is a mandatory provision. The revenue from the imposition of victim surcharges goes towards assisting victims and witness services throughout England and Wales.

Previously for offences committed on or after 1 April 2007 (CJA 2003, s 161A) there was a duty on the court to impose a surcharge of £15 whenever it ordered an offender to pay a fine.

From 1st October 2012 (SI 2012/1696) for offences committed on or after this date a victim surcharge must be imposed whatever the sentence and not only where a fine is imposed. The amount of the victim surcharge imposed reflects the level of sentence. For juveniles, the amount of a victim surcharge for a conditional discharge is £10, for a fine, referral order or youth rehabilitation order is £15 and for a custodial sentence of any length (initially only imposed by a crown court) is £20.

Offences committed on or after 8 April 2016 will attract victim surcharges at the following rates: £15 for a conditional discharge, £20 for a fine, referral order or youth rehabilitation order and £30 for an immediate custodial sentence.

Where the juvenile is dealt with in different ways (such as a fine in relation to one offence and custody in relation to another) only one surcharge (whichever is the higher) will be imposed. Where an offender is dealt with by a court for more than one offence, and at least one of these was committed before 1 October 2012, the surcharge payable if the person is fined will be £15 as specified by the 2007 Order. Where a court deals with an adult offender for more than one offence, and at least one of those offences was committed when he was under 18, the surcharge will be payable at the rate for under 18 year olds.

Where a court is faced with imposing multiple financial orders a priority must be followed. Preference must be given to compensation, followed by the victim surcharge, followed by a fine and costs. In a situation where the juvenile has insufficient means to pay, the court may find that it can only make a compensation order. The same order of priority applies for payment of sums outstanding.

Costs

12.16   A magistrates' court convicting any person of an offence may make such order as to costs to be paid by the accused as it considers 'just and reasonable' (Prosecution of Offences Act 1985 (POA 1985), s 18). However, where any fine imposed is £5 or less, no order for costs may be made unless in the particular circumstances of the case the court considers it right to do so. If the juvenile himself is ordered to pay the costs the amount may not exceed the amount of any fine imposed on the same occasion (POA 1985, s 18(5)). This has been reinforced by paragraph 6.17 of the Sentencing Council's *Sentencing Children and Young People.* As with all monetary orders in the Youth Court, PCC(S)A 2000, s 137 places a duty on the court to order the parent or guardian to pay costs awarded unless he cannot be found or it would be unreasonable in the circumstances of the case to order him to do so. Where the juvenile has attained 16 years of age the court has a power rather than a duty to order the parent to pay and where the juvenile is accommodated by a local authority that authority could be ordered to pay (see earlier discussion on compensation orders at **12.14**). Whoever is ordered to pay the amount the order ought to be such that the defendant or parent is able to pay it off within one year (*R v Nottingham Magistrates' Court, ex parte Fohmann* (1986) 151 JP 49; and see *R v Northallerton Magistrates' Court, ex parte Dove* [2000] 1 Cr App R (S) 136). However, in the case of *R v Dickinson* [2010] EWCA Crim 2143 a Crown Court judge had been entitled to rely on the national scale of costs provided by the Crown Prosecution Service in deciding what was 'just and reasonable'. In principle there is no objection to an order for costs which is greater than the fine imposed for the offence, if the defendant has behaved in a manner which has inflated the costs incurred by the prosecution. The final question will be whether the defendant has the means, or will have the means, to pay the amount ordered within a reasonable time.

A Youth Court may order costs to be paid out of central funds in favour of a defendant in three situations:

(a)   where any information charging a person with an offence is not proceeded with;

(b)   where any information is dismissed at summary trial (POA 1985, s 16).

This is known as a defendant's costs order. If the court considers that that there are circumstances that make it inappropriate for the accused to recover the full amount, a defendant's costs order must be for the payment out of central funds of such lesser amount as the court considers just and reasonable. The amount of costs should either be specified by the court in the order or referred for determination by the HMCTS national costs taxation team with a description of how the amount should be reduced (see POA 1985, s 16(6A)). If the court considers that costs should be paid in full, the amount should be specified in the order if that amount is agreed by the defence, otherwise the issue must be referred to the HMCTS national costs taxation team. The limits on the rates payable are prescribed.

Normally a defendant should expect that costs will be awarded from central funds if he falls within one of these three categories (*R v Birmingham Juvenile Court, ex parte H* (1992) 156 JP 445). The court should only refuse to make such an order if it has positive reasons for doing so. This might be appropriate where the defendant was convicted of at least one offence or the defendant's conduct led the prosecutor reasonably to think the prosecution case stronger than it was (CPR 2015, r.45.4(5)). However, a court should not deny a defendant his costs order where it would undermine the presumption of innocence in the ECHR (*R v South West Surrey Magistrates' Court, ex parte James* [2000] Crim LR 690.

If the Crown Prosecution Service has served a notice of discontinuance pursuant to POA 1985, s 23, there is no need for a defendant to attend court simply to obtain an award of costs. An application for costs may be made in writing and then considered by the court on the paperwork before it. Home Office Circular, 13/1986, indicates that there should be a presumption in the defendant's favour so that he does not suffer financially due to a decision of the prosecution to discontinue proceedings. This was confirmed in the case of *DPP v Denning* [1991] 2 QB 532.

In many cases a defendant's costs order will not be requested as those costs are already covered by a representation order.

The court may award the costs of the prosecution from central funds in any proceedings that are purely indictable or triable either way in the case of an adult. However, no order may be made for prosecution costs from central funds in favour of a public authority. 'Public authority' includes a police force, the Crown Prosecution Service or any other local or national government department (POA 1985, s 17).

The courts may now order costs against a defendant for breach of a community sentence (or suspended sentence) under the Criminal Justice Act 2003 following an amendment to reg 14 of Costs in Criminal Cases (General) Regulations 1986 (Costs in Criminal Cases (General) (Amendment) Regulations 2008, SI 2008/2448).

Disqualification and endorsement of driving licences

12.17   Under the Road Traffic Acts, a juvenile under 17 years cannot hold a licence to drive a motor car, additionally a juvenile under 16 years cannot hold a licence to drive a motor cycle. Nevertheless, if a juvenile appears before the court charged with an offence which carries obligatory endorsement, the court is required to order that particulars of the finding of guilt be endorsed on any driving licence held by the defendant along with the number of penalty points awarded, unless the defendant is on that occasion disqualified from driving, when particulars of the disqualification must be endorsed on the driving licence. Where a person is convicted of more than one endorsable offence and these offences were committed on the same occasion, the court only endorses the licence with the number of points for the offence which carries the highest number of points (Road Traffic Offenders Act 1988 (RTOA 1988), s 28(4)). The court has discretion to determine that s 28(4) shall not apply, but if it does so determine the reasons must be stated in open court and recorded in the court register. Thus, if someone is convicted of speeding and careless driving on the same occasion the court could impose three points for the speeding and five for the careless driving. Normally only the highest number, in this example five, would be endorsed but if the court determines that RTOA 1988, s 28(4) should not apply it could endorse eight points.

The meaning of 'same occasion' for these purposes was clarified in *Johnson v Finbow* [1983] 1 WLR 879, where two offences of failing to stop after an accident and failing to report an accident were held on appeal to have been committed on the same occasion.

If a defendant does not hold a driving licence then the order of endorsement and penalty points should still be made, as it operates as an order that any licence he may hold or subsequently obtains should be so endorsed until he becomes entitled under s 45(5) of the Road Traffic Offenders Act 1988 to have a licence issued to him free from these particulars (RTOA 1988, s 45(1)).

Although endorsement, and in some cases disqualification, is obligatory, the statute allows the court a limited discretion to find 'special reasons' not to endorse or disqualify the defendant.

In *R v Wickins* (1958) 42 Cr App R 236, the Court of Criminal Appeal prescribed four requirements that a 'special reason' must fulfil:

(a)   it must be a mitigating or extenuating circumstance;

(b)   it must not amount in law to a defence to the charge;

(c)   it must be directly connected with the commission of the offence;

(d)   the matter must be one which the court ought properly to take into consideration when imposing punishment.

The concept was further reviewed and summarised in *DPP v O'Connor* [1992] RTR 66, which also emphasised that it was a two-stage process, first determining whether there are special reasons and then asking whether it is a case where in its discretion the court ought not to endorse or disqualify for the full period.

A simple example of a possible special reason might be where a juvenile had been actively misled by a parent into believing he was insured to drive. However, it is worth noting that special reasons may not be found in a case of aggravated vehicle taking (Theft Act 1968, s 12A) on the basis that the defendant was not the driver.

Most offences carrying penalty points and an endorsement give the magistrates a discretionary power to disqualify the offender from driving if the offence is thought to be a serious one of its kind. Offences of theft, or attempted theft, of a motor vehicle, taking a motor vehicle without the owner's consent, allowing oneself to be carried in a vehicle so taken and going equipped, carry a discretionary disqualification only. Some offences, such as causing death by dangerous driving, dangerous driving, causing death by careless driving, driving while under the influence of drink or drugs, driving with excess alcohol, failure to provide a specimen and aggravated vehicle taking, carry an obligatory disqualification for a minimum period set by statute. For some of these offences the disqualification period may be reduced if the offender attends a course approved by the Secretary of State (RTOA 1988, s 34A).

In addition, if an offender comes within what is often called the 'totting-up' system he must be disqualified for a minimum period of six months in the absence of mitigating circumstances. To fall within the totting-up provisions of RTOA 1988, s 35, the offender must have accumulated 12 points within a three-year period prior to the present offence. If he has a previous disqualification on his present driving record imposed within three years of the commission of the present offence, the minimum period of totting-up disqualification must be 12 months and, if there are two more relevant disqualifications, the minimum period is two years' disqualification.

A previous disqualification may only be taken into account for this purpose if it was for a fixed period of 56 days or more.

If an offender has accumulated sufficient points to be liable to disqualification he may plead mitigating circumstances amounting to exceptional hardship and ask the court not to disqualify him or to reduce the period of disqualification (RTOA 1988, s 35(1)). If such mitigating circumstances have been successfully pleaded and taken into account by a court on an occasion within a three-year period preceding the conviction for the present offence, they may not be used again (RTOA 1988, s 35(4)).

Newly qualified drivers are subject to a probationary period of two years beginning on the day on which a test of competence to drive is passed. If a person is convicted of (or accepts a fixed penalty or conditional offer for) an endorsable offence during this period with six or more penalty points being endorsed, the Secretary of State will revoke the driving licence and may not issue a full licence until a further driving test has been passed (Road Traffic (New Drivers) Act 1995). The Sentencing Council's *Magistrates' Courts Sentencing Guidelines* states that a short disqualification should not be used as a means of evading the normal consequences for a new driver of accruing six penalty points. Where the court is not proposing to disqualify for an offence which carries a range of penalty points and revocation of the licence may have a disproportionate effect on the individual it may be appropriate for the court to impose a lower number of penalty points which does not trigger the revocation. In *R v Edmunds* [2000] 2 Cr App R (S) 62, the court imposed five penalty points for an offence of careless driving to avoid the young defendant from having his new licence revoked. The court took into account the fact that he lived in a remote area and it would have been extremely difficult to arrange someone to supervise his driving.

Interim disqualification

12.18 In certain circumstances the court may order an interim disqualification. This only applies to offences which carry disqualification, and may only last for a maximum of six months. Normally the interim disqualification will last until the defendant is sentenced. This power is available on committal to the Crown Court for sentence to be dealt with (PCC(S)A 2000, s 6), where a magistrates' court remits to another magistrates' court (PCC(S)A 2000, s 10), where a court defers sentence and on adjournment after conviction and before sentence (RTOA 1988, s 26). This power is not specifically applied to remittal from the adult court to the Youth Court, although it is arguable that this is an adjournment after conviction and before sentence.

Principles applicable to disqualification

12.19 When disqualification is considered courts may have regard to the following principles:

(a)   A disqualification for life will rarely be appropriate. In *R v Buckley* [1994] Crim LR 387, CA, such a disqualification was upheld in a serious case of reckless driving where the defendant's record included 20 offences for taking vehicles without consent, 21 for driving whilst disqualified and five for what was then, reckless driving. The offender was also sentenced to five years in custody.

(b)   Extremely long periods of disqualification should be avoided if at all possible. In *R v Baptista* (2 May 1975, unreported), a defendant convicted of driving with excess alcohol was disqualified for 20 years. Kenneth Jones J expressed disapproval of long disqualifications such as this, saying that the court must balance the danger to the public represented by the defendant against the frustration he would feel in connection with obtaining possible future employment.

(c)   The effect of disqualification on the offender's prospects of obtaining employment in the future may be considered. This applies particularly in the case of juveniles who are about to leave school and start to look for work. In *R v Aspden* [1975] RTR 456, a defendant was disqualified for two-and-a-half years. On appeal this was reduced to 12 months, James LJ stating that this was because of the effect that a long period of disqualification would have on the defendant's employment.

(d)   Where the court proposes to impose any driving disqualification for an offence for which the defendant is to be given a detention and training order, the court must extend the disqualification by a period equivalent to half the term of that detention and training order. If an offence attracting disqualification is not dealt with by a detention and training order, but such a sentence will be imposed on other offences, or if there already is an existing DTO in force, then the court must have regard to the diminished effect of the disqualification as a distinct punishment during the time the defendant is in custody (RTOA 1988, ss 35A and 35B; PCC(S)A 2000, ss 147A and 147B; *R v Needham and Others* [2016] EWCA Crim 455).

A defendant who has been disqualified from driving may apply for that disqualification to be lifted. There are, however, the following restrictions on how soon after the imposition of the disqualification the defendant may apply:

(a)   If the disqualification is for less than four years he may apply after two years.

(b)   If the disqualification is for more than four years but less than 10 years he may apply after one half of the period.

(c)   In any other case he may apply after five years (RTOA 1988, s 42(3)).

In fixing the period of disqualification the magistrates should avoid reference to the above provisions. In the case of *R v Lobby* (1975, unreported) James LJ severely criticised a judge who had taken these provisions into account when disqualifying a person for four years and then alluded to the fact that he could apply for his licence to be restored to him after two years.

Disqualification for any offence

12.20   The court has power to disqualify a defendant from driving for any offence instead of or in addition to dealing with him in any other way (PCC(S)A 2000, s 146). Certain non-endorsable offences – kerb crawling, unlawful tipping and unlawful off-road driving – recommend themselves for such a penalty, although these are offences rarely seen in the Youth Court.

Restraining orders

12.21   Section 12 of the Domestic Violence, Crime and Victims Act 2004 (DVCVA 2004) has amended s 5 of the Protection from Harassment Act 1997 (PHA 1997) to allow the court to make a restraining order following a conviction or acquittal for any criminal offence. This applies to any offence convicted or acquitted after 30 September 2009 (DVCVA 2004, Sch 12, para 5), regardless of whether the offence was committed prior to 30 September 2009. A restraining order is intended to be a preventative and protective measure and the court can make such an order where there is a need to protect a person from conduct, which amounts to harassment or which will cause a fear of violence. 'Harassment' is not defined in the PHA 1997, except that it includes causing a person alarm or distress.

Unfortunately the Act does not specify the standard of proof that needs to be applied by the court. In any event the court will need to evaluate the evidence before it and determine whether there is sufficient evidence to enable it to form a view that an order is necessary. The order may have effect for a specified period or until further order. The defendant can be prohibited from doing any act, as described in the order.

The court can make a restraining order of its own volition. The court may have regard to any evidence it may have heard during a criminal trial in determining whether a restraining order is necessary. However, further evidence may be required especially where the defendant has been acquitted or especially in circumstances where the prosecution are offering no evidence to a charge on the agreement that the defendant will consent to a restraining order being imposed upon him. In *R v Major* [2010] EWCA Crim 3016, it was not accepted that a restraining order on acquittal may only be made on uncontested facts or used only rarely. It was said that s 5A(1) was inserted into the PHA 1997 to deal with those cases where there is clear evidence that the victim needs protection but there is insufficient evidence to convict of the particular charges before the court. The victim need not have been blameless and the court's added powers avoid the need for alternative proceedings to protect the victim, added costs and delay. Further it was said that PHA 1997, s 5A addresses future risk, the evidential basis for such an assessment being the conduct of the defendant. The evidence does not have to establish on the balance of probabilities that there has been harassment. It is enough if the evidence establishes conduct which falls short of harassment but which may well in the judgment of the court, if repeated, amount to harassment, so making an order necessary. Compliance by a defendant of bail conditions which prohibited contact with the victim, while a consideration, may not be a ground for not making an order.

Under PHA 1997, s 5(3A) both the prosecution and defence can lead evidence before the court and adduce evidence that would not normally be admissible in the criminal proceedings, such as previous convictions, hearsay evidence and live evidence not given at the trial. The procedural rules for making applications are set out in CPR 2015, Pt 31. *R v Kapotra* [2011] EWCA Crim 1843, states that where a judge, on his own initiative, is considering making a restraining order, he should consider adjourning the hearing in order for the procedural requirements to be met and, even if he was minded to exercise the discretion open to him under CPR 2010, r 50.9 (now CPR 2015, r 31.2) to dispense with some of these requirements, he had to bear in mind the fundamental principle that any person faced with the possible imposition of a restraining order should be given proper notice of what is sought, the evidential basis for the application and, in addition, be allowed a proper opportunity to address the evidence and make informed representations as to the appropriateness of such an order. The court should identify the factual basis for imposing an order and although not a sentence (as per CJA 2003, s 174(1)) or bind over order (*Consolidated Practice Direction Part III, 31.4*). *R v Major* provides that the court should state in open court, in ordinary language, its reasons for making the order.

The court must only impose prohibitions and not positive requirements on the defendant and the terms of the order must be clear, concise and easy to understand. The prohibitions must also be realistic, reasonable and proportionate.

R v Picken [2006] EWCA Crim 2194, held that there is provision within PHA 1997, s 5 for the court to hear representations from persons affected by the order. In *R v Picken* a sentencing judge made an order without hearing from the complainant and it was held that it was inappropriate to make a restraining order as the complainant wished to continue her relationship with the defendant. Further in *R v Brown* [2012] EWCA Crim 1152, a restraining order was quashed for similar reasons.

Although there is no such thing as an interim restraining order, PHA 1997, s 5(3) provides that the court can make a restraining order for a specified period.

Section 4A of the PHA 1997 also gives any person mentioned in a restraining order the right to make representations in court if an application is made to vary or discharge that order.

A restraining order made on acquittal can be appealed against in the same way as an order made on conviction. Also where a conviction is quashed on appeal, the Court of Appeal may remit the case to the Crown Court to consider the making of a restraining order if it is satisfied that it is necessary to do so to protect any person from harassment (PHA 1997, s 5A).

Breach

12.22   If without reasonable excuse the defendant does anything which he is prohibited from doing under the restraining order, then on summary conviction he is liable up to six months' imprisonment or a fine not exceeding level 5, or both.

Drinking banning orders

12.23   Drinking banning orders (DBOs) were replaced by Criminal Behaviour Orders in 2014. See **Chapter 14**.

Football banning orders

12.24   If an offender is convicted of a relevant offence (listed in schedule 1 of the Football Spectators Act 1989 (FSA 1989)) and the court is satisfied that there are reasonable grounds to believe that a football banning order (FBO) would help prevent violence or disorder at or in connection with any regulated football matches, it must make an FBO (FSA 1989, s 14A). Repetition and propensity are not required for the making of an order under s 14A, and the court is entitled to take into account and give weight to the question of deterrence (*R (on the application of White) v Crown Court at Blackfriars* [2008] EWHC 510 (Admin)). If the court is not satisfied, it must state that fact in open court and give its reasons.

Where the court is considering making an FBO on conviction, the procedure and admissibility of hearsay evidence is governed by the CPR 2015, Part 20.

An FBO can also be made on complaint under FSA 1989, s 14B on an application by the chief officer of police for the area in which the offender resides or appears to reside, if it appears to the officer that the respondent has at any time caused or contributed to any violence or disorder in the United Kingdom or elsewhere. The court must make the FBO if it is satisfied that there are reasonable grounds to believe that making the order would help to prevent violence or disorder at or in connection with any regulated football matches.

'Violence' means violence against persons or property and includes threatening violence and doing anything which endangers the life of any person, and 'disorder' includes stirring up hatred against a group of persons defined by reference to colour, race, nationality (including citizenship) or ethnic or national origins, or against an individual as a member of such a group; using threatening, abusive or insulting words or behaviour or disorderly behaviour; displaying any writing or other thing which is threatening, abusive or insulting. 'Violence' and 'disorder' are not limited to violence or disorder in connection with football. However, in the recent case of *R v Doyle* [2012] EWCA Crim 995, three defendants on their way home on the train from a football match got drunk and assaulted a passenger on the train. They were convicted of affray. They received custodial sentences and FBOs for six years were imposed. In sentencing, the judge remarked, 'watching the football match was, in my view, a direct cause of your behaving in the way you did. It is the combination of football match, drinking too much before and/or after it which led to this violent behaviour'. They appealed against the orders. On appeal the FBOs were quashed on the grounds that the evidence had shown only that the offence had arisen out of the fact that the defendants had been drunk, rather than the offences having had any connection to football and its tribal excitement.

When considering whether to make an FBO on complaint the magistrates' court may take into account any decision of a court or tribunal outside the United Kingdom, deportation or exclusion from a country outside the United Kingdom, removal or exclusion from premises used for playing football matches, whether in the United Kingdom or elsewhere and conduct recorded on video or by any other means.

An FBO prohibits the offender from attending a regulated football match in England and Wales and requires him to report to a police station when football matches are played outside England and Wales. Other requirements may also be included. The order must require the offender to surrender his passport in connection with matches played outside England and Wales.

An FBO may be made only in addition to any other sentence or in addition to a conditional discharge. On making an FBO, the court must in ordinary language explain its effect to the person subject to the order.

If the offender receives a custodial sentence, the FBO must be for at least six years but not more than ten years. Where the offender is not sentenced to a custodial sentence, the FBO must be for at least three years but not more than five years. For an FBO made on complaint the maximum is three years and the minimum is two years.

An FBO may be varied on application, in the case of where the order was made by the magistrates' court, to any magistrates' court acting for the same local justice area as that court. If an FBO has had effect for at least two-thirds of the period for which the order was made, the person subject to the order may apply to the court by which it was made to terminate it. On the application, the court may terminate the banning order as from a specified date or refuse the application. Where the application is refused, no further application in respect of the order may be made within a period of six months from the date of the refusal (FSA 1989, s 14H).

Breach

12.25   A person subject to a banning order who fails to comply with any requirement imposed by the order is guilty of an offence punishable on summary conviction to imprisonment for a term not exceeding six months, or a fine not exceeding level 5 on the standard scale, or both.

Sexual harm prevention orders

12.26   An SHPO can be made by a court in respect of an individual who has been convicted, or cautioned ('cautioned' includes those who have received a reprimand, final warning or youth caution) for a relevant offence (listed in Sch 3 or Sch 5 of the SOA 2003) including an offence committed overseas and who poses a risk of sexual harm to the public in the UK or to children or vulnerable adults abroad (SOA 2003, s 103A). SHPOs replace the previous sexual offences prevention orders (SOPOs).

An SHPO may impose any restriction the court deems necessary for the purpose of protecting the public from sexual harm and makes the offender subject to the notification requirements for the duration of the order. A prohibition contained in an SHPO has effect for a fixed period (not less than five years) specified in the order or until further order (SOA 2003, s 103C). The order may specify different periods for different prohibitions. The decision of the Court of Appeal in *R v Smith and Others* [2011] EWCA Crim 1772 reinforces the need for the terms of a SHPO to be tailored to the exact requirements of the case.

SHPOs are available to the court at the time of sentencing for a relevant offence, or on free-standing application to the magistrates' court by the police or National Crime Agency after the time of the conviction or caution. Where an application for an SHPO is made by way of complaint to the Youth Court (MCA 1980, s 53) for a child or young person, the parent or guardian should also receive a copy of the summons unless no such person is readily available.

The Home Office *Guidance on Part 2 of the Sexual Offences Act 2003* should be considered when there is an application for an SHPO in relation to a young person.

Section 103F of the SOA 2003 allows the court to make an interim order where the main application has not been determined. Such an order has effect only for a fixed period, specified in the order or ceases to have effect on the determination of the main application.

Section 103E of SOA 2003 provides details on how a person may apply to the appropriate court to vary, renew or discharge an SHPO.

A defendant may appeal against the making, renewal or refusal to vary an SHPO to the Crown Court. See also **13.06**.

Breach

12.27   If without reasonable excuse the defendant does anything which he is prohibited from doing under the SHPO, then on summary conviction he is liable to a maximum of six-month imprisonment or a fine not exceeding level 5, or both, and on indictment a maximum of five years imprisonment. Juveniles are usually dealt with in the Youth Court where the maximum custodial sentence for a young person aged 12 to 17 years (inclusive) is two years. For breach of all orders and the notification requirements, provision is made for a defence of reasonable excuse.

Enforcement of financial orders

12.28   Financial orders include fines, compensation, and costs. Where the parent has been required to pay any sum ordered by the Youth Court but fails to do so, the subsequent enforcement of that order is a matter for the adult court. In a case involving the imposition of a financial order upon a juvenile, if the court has satisfied itself that the parent or guardian cannot be found, or that it would be unreasonable to make an order for payment against the parents having regard to the circumstances of the case, the juvenile himself shall be ordered to pay (PCC(S)A 2000, s 137). If, having been ordered to pay, the juvenile then fails so to do, the court must initially enforce the order against the juvenile himself.

The Children and Young Persons Act 1933, s 46 states that '… no charge against a child or young person, and no application whereof the hearing is by rules made under this section assigned to Youth Courts, shall be heard by a court of summary jurisdiction which is not a Youth Court.' Clearly, enforcement of monetary orders is not a matter specifically assigned to the Youth Court, and as such it may be argued that the proceedings should be in the adult court. Welfare considerations should be borne in mind. In addition, it may be argued that a 'charge' preferred against a juvenile and the subsequent fine enforcement is part of the same proceedings.

The case of *Evans v Macklen* [1976] Crim LR 120, supports this argument. A defendant was convicted of an offence in her absence and a warrant issued for her arrest. She was arrested by a constable who was not in possession of the warrant at the time. The MCA 1980, s 125(3) states: 'A warrant to arrest a person charged with an offence may be executed by a constable notwithstanding that it is not in his possession at the time.' It was submitted, on appeal, that the defendant was not 'charged with an offence'. The Divisional Court held that the words in this section could be construed as referring to a person 'who had been charged with an offence' in the sense that an information had been laid, and the arrest was therefore lawful.

A juvenile who has defaulted on payment of a monetary order is in a similar position. At some stage in the proceedings he has been 'charged with an offence' and therefore may be dealt with by the Youth Court.

At the time of making an order against the juvenile the court may require the money to be paid straightaway within a certain specified period of time, ie 28 days, or by instalments (MCA 1980, s 75). Where the court has ordered payment by instalments and the juvenile defaults in the payment of any one instalment, he may be treated as being in default of the whole sum still outstanding. When a juvenile falls into default the court may issue a summons, or a warrant with or without bail for his arrest. The considerations on issuing warrants and summonses are dealt with in **Chapter 2**. Where a warrant with bail is issued, the bail is not bail as in criminal proceedings pursuant to the Bail Act 1976. Instead the person bailed has to enter into a recognisance fixed by the court which may be forfeited if he fails to attend the hearing.

12.29   The purpose of requiring the juvenile's attendance at court is to hold an inquiry into his means. Normally the court will require the defaulter to take the oath before he is questioned about his non-payment. Not every case of default is a case of wilful refusal and the following line of questioning will often assist the court in establishing the reasons for non-payment:

(a)   Can you explain why these monies have not been paid?

(b)   What is your income? Is that from a job, pocket money or other means?

(c)   Do you have any other source of income or any savings?

(d)   Do you pay rent or board to your parents? How much is that each week?

(e)   Have you any additional outgoings for household or personal necessities?

(f)   Do you have any other payments to make, for example to a mail order catalogue?

(g)   Do you have any other fines or court orders to pay?

Before the hearing the court will require a defaulter to complete a statement of means form.

The court has a wide range of powers in dealing with the juvenile defaulter. These are explained below.

Further time to pay

12.30   A magistrates' court which, after a finding of guilt, orders fines, compensation or costs to be paid may allow further time for payment or allow payment by instalments (MCA 1980, s 75(1)). The court may subsequently allow further time to pay, order payment by instalments or, if payment by instalments has already been permitted, vary such instalments (MCA 1980, s 85A). The court may adjourn and fix a further hearing to review payment.

Means inquiry

12.31   Where the court has dispensed with immediate payment and allowed time to pay or payment by instalments under MCA 1980, s 75(1), it has power, either then or later, to fix a day on which (if any instalment which has fallen due remains unpaid, or if the whole was to be paid by that date and any part remains unpaid) the offender must appear before the court for a fine default hearing and a means inquiry (MCA 1980, s 86(1)). This power is particularly useful and effective if the justices imposing the original financial order are able to return on that date fixed for the subsequent means inquiry and thereby monitor their order.

Remission

12.32   The court has the power on inquiring into a defaulter's means to remit the whole or part of the fine, if having regard to any change in his circumstances since it was imposed the court thinks it just to do so (MCA 1980, s 85). Although unusual in the Youth Court, there is also a power to remit a fine where it is imposed in the offender's absence where he later shows that his means were less than those taken in to account by the court (CJA 2003, s 165).

The court may not remit any other sum adjudged to be paid on conviction whether as a pecuniary penalty, forfeiture, or compensation. Compensation may be reviewed under the procedure found in the PCC(S)A 2000, s 133. *R v Favell* [2010] EWCA Crim 2948, confirmed that under PCC(S)A 2000, s 133 a compensation order may be reduced or discharged where a defendant against whom the order has been made 'has suffered a substantial reduction in his means which was unexpected at the time the order was made'. Where the compensation order was made by the Crown Court, the magistrates' court must obtain the consent of the Crown Court before exercising its power on this ground.

Binding over against parents

12.33   The court may make an order requiring the defaulter's parent or guardian to enter into a recognisance to ensure that the defaulter pays the outstanding sum. The court must have the parent's consent to make this order. Such an order may not be made unless the court is satisfied that the defaulter has, or has had since the date on which the sum was ordered, the means to pay the sum or any instalment of it on which he has defaulted, and refuses or neglects or has refused or has neglected to pay it (MCA 1980, s 81(1)(a)).

The court may make an order directing that the parent should take over the payment of the fine. The court must be satisfied that in all the circumstances it is reasonable to make this order (MCA 1980, s 81(1)(b)). The parent must be given the opportunity to make representations but if the parent has been required to attend and has failed so to do, this order may be made in the parent's absence (MCA 1980, s 81(5)). The court shall not make this order unless it is satisfied that the defaulter has, or has had since the date on which the sum in question was adjudged to be paid, the means to pay the sum or any instalment of it on which he has defaulted and refuses or neglects or, as the case may be, has refused or neglected to pay it (MCA 1980, s 81(4)). The court must also have considered or tried all other methods of enforcing payment and be satisfied that they are inappropriate or unsuccessful.

Once the parent has been made responsible for his child's fine it is then enforced against him as if it were his own fine, in the adult court (MCA 1980, s 81(7)).

Money payment supervision order

12.34   At the time of imposing a fine, or when dealing with a subsequent default, the court may make a juvenile defaulter the subject of a money payment supervision order. By this means the court orders the defaulter to be placed under the supervision of any person that the court may appoint. Normally the court would appoint either a social worker or a probation officer, but it may appoint any person whom it believes would be an appropriate supervisor. Some magistrates' courts employ a person specifically designated as a fine enforcement officer, and such a person will be an appropriate supervisor for the purposes of MCA 1980, s 88(1). It is the duty of the appointed supervisor to advise and befriend the offender with a view to inducing him to pay the sum adjudged to be paid. Where the court is contemplating the possibility of making a money payment supervision order to either the probation or social services, it is desirable that they request a means inquiry report from the relevant agency in order to ascertain the likely success of such an order. When a money payment supervision order has been made the court is required to consider a report about the offender's conduct and means before making any other order in respect of him (MCA 1980, s 88(6)). The order will last as long as there is an amount outstanding or until the court discharges it.

It should be noted that the function of a money payment supervision order is confined to the payment of monies and does not fulfil the same functions as a supervision order. It should however be considered on a default to pay (see *R v Exeter City Justices, ex parte Sugar* (1992) 157 JP 766).

Distress warrants/Warrants of control

12.35 Where default is made in paying a sum that has been adjudged to be paid after a finding of guilt, the court may issue a distress warrant/warrant of control (MCA 1980, s 76). This warrant authorises the bailiffs to seize goods which are then sold, the money realised being applied towards the fine. The bailiffs are entitled to seize goods to pay their costs. It would only be appropriate to issue distress warrants against juveniles in rare cases, as juveniles are unlikely to have sufficient goods. It was held in *R v German* (1891) 56 JP 358, that magistrates have a discretion to issue or refuse to issue a distress warrant, and are not bound to issue such a warrant if they are not satisfied that there would be sufficient goods to distrain upon. In this case a magistrates' court had imposed fines for non-attendance of children at school. The order was that the children would attend school or the parents would pay fines. The children did not attend school, fines were imposed, and the school board officer applied for distress warrants to enforce payments, but was not in a position to satisfy the justices that there were any goods to distrain upon. Accordingly, the justices refused to issue distress warrants. For the above reasons the issue of a distress warrant against a juvenile is a very rare occurrence, even though the court must consider them (*R v Norwich Magistrates' Court, ex parte Lilly* (1987) 151 JP 689).

Attachment of earnings order

12.36 If the juvenile defaulter is in employment, the court may make an order to his employer requiring him to take an amount out of the defaulter's wages periodically and forward that sum to the court. Such an order may only be made when the court has first conducted a means enquiry, and it must take into account the defendant's income and his outgoing. The experience of many courts is that attachment of earnings orders are not appropriate or successful where the fine is small, or where the defendant does not have a good work record with the same firm over a long period.

The school leaving age at present is 16, although young people must stay in full-time education, undertake training, apprenticeships or work (voluntary or paid). This means that few juveniles are likely to be in paid employment.

Deductions from benefits including education maintenance allowance

12.37 CJA 1991, s 24, provides that regulations may be made empowering the court to apply to the Secretary of State to deduct sums from income support to pay a fine, compensation or costs.

Deductions from benefit cannot however be made for any person under the age of 18 according to reg 7(2)(a) of the Fines (Deductions from Income Support) Regulations 1992.

Neither can deductions be made direct from education maintenance allowance (EMA). The Sentencing Council definitive guideline *Sentencing Children and Young People* states that a court should bear in mind that children and young people may have money that is specifically required for travel costs to school, college or apprenticeships and lunch expenses (para 6.18).

Attendance centre order

12.38   If the juvenile has wilfully refused to pay a financial penalty or been guilty of culpable neglect by not making it a sufficient priority then the court can make an attendance centre order. The maximum length of the order will be determined by the age of the juvenile as at the hearing date when the order is being considered.

The range of hours is:

(a)   under 14 years: 12 hours (or fewer hours if court believes 12 would be excessive);

(b)   under 16 years: 12 to 24 hours;

(c)   16 years and over: 12 to 36 hours.

The financial penalty will be considered reduced or paid in proportion to the number of hours completed. If the offender completes the attendance centre order the financial penalty will be treated as having been paid and the court will take no further action to enforce it. Alternatively, if the financial penalty is paid in full, the offender will not have to go to the attendance centre at all. Any part payments of the financial penalty will reduce the hours to be served proportionately.

Failure to comply with the attendance centre order if admitted or otherwise proved can be dealt with by way of a fine of up to £1,000 for the breach (with the order continuing) or revocation of the order and dealing with non-payment of the outstanding financial penalty in any way the court which imposed the attendance centre order could have done if that order had not been made.

Attendance centre orders can only be made where the juvenile lives within a reasonable travelling distance of a centre.

If or when youth default orders are brought into force the attendance centre requirement will supersede the attendance centre order for the purpose of the enforcement of financial penalties.

Chapter 13 Common problems in the Youth Court

Evidence

13.01 Witnesses in a court of law normally give evidence after taking the oath or affirmation. This is known as sworn evidence. However, this is not always the case where juveniles are involved. Children under 14 years will not be asked to take the oath but will give unsworn evidence. Young persons aged 14 and above will normally give sworn evidence or evidence on affirmation just as would an adult witness in an adult court (Youth Justice and Criminal Evidence Act 1999 (YJCEA 1999), s 55).

Competence to give evidence is determined by a person's ability to understand questions put to them and give answers which can be understood. In the Youth Court this will depend on the age and maturity of the child witness. There is no longer any rule of law requiring such evidence to be corroborated by other evidence once the court has adjudged that a child is competent to give testimony.

The effect of the legislation is to set a basic rule that all persons (whatever their age) are competent to give evidence in criminal proceedings (YJCEA 1999, s 53). This section sets out two exceptions to this rule. The first is that the defendant is only competent as a witness for the defence and not the prosecution. The second exception is that a witness will not be competent to give evidence if it appears to the court that he is not able to understand questions put to him and give answers to them which can be understood. If the issue is raised it is for the party calling the witness to satisfy the court that, on the balance of probabilities, the witness is competent to give evidence. Once raised, any questioning of the witness must be done by the court and not the parties and the issue is one to be determined by the court which may receive expert evidence. Any question of competence with regard to a prosecution witness should be decided at the beginning of the trial (*R v Yacob* (1981) 72 Cr App R 313, CA).

In *R v MacPherson* [2005] EWCA Crim 3605, the Court of Appeal made the following additional observations in allowing the evidence of a five-year-old child to be admitted. They emphasised that the test of competence in the 1999 Act was whether the witness could understand questions and give answers that could be understood. Clearly an infant who could communicate only in baby language with its mother would not ordinarily be competent. However, the complainant in the present case could speak and understand English with strangers and was competent. Questions of credibility and reliability were not relevant to the issue of competence. Those matters went to the weight of the evidence and might be considered when appropriate, at the end of the prosecution case by way of submission of no case to answer. A child should not be found incompetent as a witness on the basis of age alone.

This approach was affirmed in the case of *R v Barker* [2010] EWCA Crim 4, where a four-and a-half-year old witness gave evidence about the anal rape the child had suffered when the witness had been three years old. Lord Judge CJ in delivering judgment stated:

> 'There are no presumptions or preconceptions. The witness need not understand the special importance that the truth should be told in court, and the witness need not understand every single question or give a readily understood answer to every question. Many competent adult witnesses would fail such a competency test.'

The Lord Chief Justice also confirmed that the court could reconsider the competence of the witness after the witness had given evidence and, if appropriate, exclude that evidence under PACE 1984, s 78. It should be noted that the evidence of a child will not be excluded merely because it is argued that a child's evidence cannot properly be tested in cross-examination because the witness can recall some things only after viewing a video of the original ABE interview (*R v R* [2010] EWCA Crim 2469). Further in the case of *R v F* [2013] EWCA Crim 424, it was held that the competency test is not failed because the forensic techniques of the advocate or the processes of the court have to be adapted to enable a witness to give the best evidence of which they are capable.

In case of *R v W and M* [2010] EWCA Crim 1926, it was held that it was open to the jury to conclude that a child witness (aged 8) who contradicted her original allegations during cross-examination was not actually agreeing in any meaningful way with the suggestions made to her because leading questions had been asked which gave an indication of the answer sought. Although it was very difficult to tell whether the witness was truly changing her account or simply taking the line of least resistance, it was held that the judge had applied the correct test and was entitled to come to the conclusion that the jury should be allowed to make their own assessment of the whole of the victim's evidence. This was confirmed in the case of *R v R* [2012] EWCA Crim 1009, where it was held that the judge was entitled to conclude, notwithstanding the extreme youth of the children (aged 5 and 7), that they were competent to give evidence; it was a task for the jury properly directed to consider the evidence and to decide whether the prosecution had proved the case to make the jury sure of guilt.

If a witness gives unsworn evidence where he should have given evidence on oath it shall not by itself be grounds for an appeal (YJCEA 1999, s 56). If a person gives unsworn evidence in criminal proceedings under this legislation which is wilfully false, he may be guilty of a summary offence punishable in the case of an adult with imprisonment for a term not exceeding six months or a fine not exceeding £1,000 or both (£250 in the case of a person under the age of 14).

In normal circumstances a witness who is competent to give testimony is also compellable. In the context of a Youth Court, this means that a witness summons may be issued under MCA 1980, s 97 to secure the presence of a child who is a witness in the proceedings. In *Re P (minor: compellability as witness)* [1991] 2 All ER 65, the Court of Appeal, in a case involving a child who was a party in care proceedings, stated that s 97 was applicable to a child (even if they were a party to the proceedings). However, Lady Justice Butler-Sloss said that the section was an inappropriate vehicle for securing the attendance of a child in proceedings where she was a witness and had made serious allegations of sexual abuse against her stepfather, when it was he who was applying for the summons under Magistrates' Courts Act 1980, s 97. Her Ladyship went on to say that, reading the section as a whole, if the court considered at the time of an application for a summons that for reasons of the welfare of the child, the child should not be called as a witness, then it would be inappropriate to issue a summons. It may well be that this decision must be read in the knowledge of the availability of special measures for witnesses: see **13.03** to **13.05** below.

In the conduct of a criminal trial, it is for the criminal court (that is a judge in the Crown Court or magistrates in a Youth Court) to consider whether or not a ward of court should be called as a witness in those proceedings rather than the decision being made by the wardship judge. However, application for leave to interview the child is necessary and the rules and practice directions relating to applications in respect of wards of court apply in such circumstances (*Re R (a minor) (wardship: witness in criminal proceedings)* [1991] Fam 56).

It will remain good practice for a court receiving evidence from children under the age of 14 to enquire about their understanding of questions put to them, and whether in the opinion of the court they are possessed of sufficient intelligence to give answers to the questions which can be understood. The current legal position now reflects the view of the Criminal Law Commission in their *Eleventh Report* (Cmnd No 4991) which recommended that children below 14 should always give unsworn evidence and children of 14 and above should always give evidence on oath, whilst leaving with the court a discretion to exclude from consideration any evidence of a witness under 14 years of age where it appears to the court that the witness is incapable of giving intelligible testimony.

The oath

13.02 The oath taken by a juvenile witness when giving evidence, and by adults in the Youth Court, is different from that normally administered in a magistrates' court. The oath reads: 'I promise before Almighty God to tell the truth, the whole truth and nothing but the truth' (CYPA 1963, s 28).

The taking of the oath in the Youth Court should be treated as a serious matter but not made an ordeal. Every effort should be made to find out, for example, if the witness can read before he comes into court so that the oath may be repeated after a court officer without embarrassment. Holy books from different religions, and not just the New Testament, should be available.

If any person wishes to affirm, he may do so for whatever reason, and without any need to explain his reason (Oaths Act 1978, s 5(1)).

The provisions of the Oaths Act 1978, s 1, are directory only, so that where, for example, a witness fails to hold the New Testament in his hand the evidence is still admissible. In the case of *R v Chapman* [1980] Crim LR 42, CA, a juvenile witness took the oath without taking the New Testament in his hand as required. When this was brought to the judge's attention, he directed the jury to treat the boy's evidence as an unsworn statement and (as the law stood then) in need of corroboration. On appeal, the Court of Appeal held that the failure to comply with the technical requirements of the Oaths Act 1978 did not necessarily invalidate the taking of the oath.

Special measures for eligible witnesses

13.03   Many victims and witnesses find coming to court to give evidence both stressful and frightening. The Youth Justice and Criminal Evidence Act 1999 seeks to assist such witnesses in giving the best evidence they can to the court. Part II of the Act provides the criteria and test to determine eligibility for special measures provision. Most important in this context are the provisions for child witnesses (YJCEA 1999, s 16). The Act also provides a mandatory prohibition on cross-examination by defendants in person of complainants in sexual cases and certain child witnesses. See YJCEA 1999, ss 34 to 37.

A Youth Court may make a special measures direction in respect of any witness if the quality of the evidence is likely to be diminished by reason of fear or distress on the part of the witness in connection with testifying in the proceedings (YJCEA 1999, s 17). A witness will also be eligible for assistance if he is under 18 at the time of hearing; or the quality of evidence is likely to be diminished by reason of a mental disorder or significant impairment of intelligence and social functioning or a physical disability. The quality of a witness's evidence is defined in terms of its completeness, coherence and accuracy (YJCEA 1999, s 16).

Under s 17(4) the court must treat a complainant in respect of a sexual offence or an offence under ss 1 or 2 of the Modern Slavery Act 2015 (MSA 2015) and a witness in proceedings relating to a 'relevant offence' (listed in YJCEA 1999, Sch 1A) as an eligible witness for special measures unless the witness expresses the wish not to be treated as one.

It should be noted that the Act also applies to defendants as well as both defence and prosecution witnesses. Section 33A of the Youth Justice and Criminal Evidence Act 1999 provides for the use of video link evidence by the defendant if he is under 18 years of age and the following criteria are met:

(a)   the defendant's ability to participate effectively in the proceedings as a witness giving oral evidence in court is compromised by his level of intellectual ability or social functioning; and

(b)   the use of a live link would enable him to participate more effectively in the proceedings as a witness (whether by improving the quality of his evidence or otherwise); and

(c)   it is in the interests of justice for the defendant to give evidence through a live link.

If the court gives a direction for a live link to be used the defendant may not give oral evidence before the court otherwise than through that live link whilst the direction remains in force. The court must give its reasons when granting, refusing or discharging a live link direction.

Under the Act, a defendant was not considered eligible for the intermediary special measure. However, following the judicial review case of *R (on the application of OP) v Ministry of Justice* [2014] EWHC 1944 (Admin), which was brought against the Ministry of Justice, it was found that the Ministry of Justice should reconsider eligibility of defendants and carefully consider whether there should be equal provision for prosecution witnesses and defendants.

However, once s 104 of the Coroners and Justice Act 2009 (inserting ss 33BA and 33BB into YJCEA 1999) is in force then the court will be able to make a direction that any examination of the defendant is to be conducted through an intermediary, where the defendant's ability to participate effectively in the proceedings as a witness giving oral evidence is compromised by his level of intellectual ability or social functioning.

The amended Criminal Practice Directions [2015] EWCA Crim 1567 (CPD 2015) which came into force on 4 April 2016 contain a revised Practice Direction on the appointment and use of intermediaries during criminal trials (CPD 2015, para 3F). The revised Practice Direction contains a considerable shift in emphasis in relation to the recommended use of defence intermediaries. In essence it provides that:

(a)   'In light of the scarcity of intermediaries, the appropriateness of assessment must be decided with care to ensure their availability for those witnesses and defendants who are most in need.' [para 3F.5]

(b)   'The court should adapt the trial process to address a defendant's communication needs (*R v Cox* [2012] EWCA Crim 549) and will rarely exercise its inherent powers to direct appointment of an intermediary.' [para 3F.12]

(c)   'Directions to appoint an intermediary for a defendant's evidence will thus be rare, but for the entire trial extremely rare.' [para 3F.13]

(d)   'Directions for intermediaries to help defendants may be ineffective due to general unavailability, lack of suitable expertise, or non-availability for the purpose directed (for example, where the direction is for assistance during evidence, but an intermediary will only accept appointment for the entire trial).' [para 3F.19]

(e) 'A trial will not be rendered unfair because a direction to appoint an intermediary for the defendant is ineffective.' [para 3F.20]

(f) '…the appropriateness of an intermediary assessment for witnesses and defendants under 18 must be decided with care.' [para 3F.25]

For juveniles, an assessment by an intermediary should always be a consideration and decided with care given the high proportion of juveniles with recognised communication needs and each decision should be made on an individual basis in the context of the circumstances of the particular case. The revised Criminal Practice Directions further set out:

> 'Assessment by an intermediary should be considered for witnesses and defendants under 18 who seem liable to misunderstand questions or to experience difficulty expressing answers, including those who seem unlikely to be able to recognise a problematic question (such as one that is misleading or not readily understood), and those who may be reluctant to tell a questioner in a position of authority if they do not understand.' [para 3F.26]

Although the Criminal Practice Directions suggests the use of intermediaries should be discouraged for defendants it does not reflect any legislative change or guidance in recent case law (see below). Also refer to the guidance on the use of intermediaries for vulnerable defendants at paragraph 79 in the *Equal Treatment Bench Book* (November 2013) and the Law Commission's report on *Unfitness to Plead* (2016) which recommends replacing the ad hoc practice of the courts granting the use of intermediaries under its inherent jurisdiction with a statutory scheme and clear test to ensure more consistency.

In the meantime, the case of *C v Sevenoaks Youth Court* [2009] EWHC 3088 (Admin), provides that in the absence of a statutory provision to appoint an intermediary to assist the defendant (aged 12) it would be appropriate for the court to use its inherent powers to appoint an intermediary to enable the defendant, who lacked the prerequisite capacity, to participate effectively in the trial proceedings. The *Sevenoaks* decision was followed in *R (on the application of S) v Great Yarmouth Youth Court* [2011] EWHC 2059 (Admin) where it was held that the juvenile, who had been diagnosed with ADHD, 'would undoubtedly benefit from the assistance of a registered intermediary' without which there was a real risk that he might not receive a fair trial. *R v Wall* [2011] EWCA Crim 443 further supports the use of intermediaries and states that the court should use its inherent powers to appoint an intermediary where necessary before embarking on a trial of fitness to plead. Therefore, where a court is concerned that a defendant is particularly vulnerable, it must make use of its inherent jurisdiction to ensure a fair trial: *(Practice Direction) Crown Court: trial of children and young persons* [2000] 1 Cr App R 483.

However, in the more recent case of *R v Cox* [2012] EWCA Crim 549, which is referred to in the Criminal Practice Directions 2015, it was recognised that although there are occasions when the use of an intermediary would improve the trial process, it does not mean that it is mandatory for an intermediary to be made available. Judges as part and parcel of their ordinary control of the judicial process are expected to deal with specific communication problems faced by any defendant or any individual witness and where necessary, the processes have to be adapted to ensure that a particular individual is not disadvantaged as a result of those personal difficulties. In *R v Cox* it was held that despite there being no intermediary to assist the defendant, the judge conducted the proceedings with appropriate and necessary caution and therefore the defendant's conviction followed a fair trial.

Currently, the court has power to order payment of the costs of an intermediary employed for a defence witness out of central funds (Costs in Criminal Cases (General) Regulations 1986 as amended, reg 16(1)(ba). It is anticipated that this will be extended to cover the costs of an intermediary employed to assist the defendant to participate in the proceedings under the Coroners and Justice Act 2009, s 104.

Special provisions for child witnesses

13.04   Child witnesses are eligible for special measures without the court having to be satisfied of the test set out in YJCEA 1999, s 17. Children will have a video-recorded statement admitted as their evidence in chief, if one has been prepared, and be cross-examined via a video link. If no video recording has been made then they should be allowed to give all their evidence via a live video link.

YJCEA 1999, s 21(3) provides the primary rule that all child witnesses must give their evidence in chief by video recording (if one exists) and then give the remainder of their evidence on the live link unless the court is satisfied that to do so will not improve the quality of that child's evidence. A child may opt out of giving evidence by either a video-recorded interview or by evidence via a live link or both provided the court is satisfied, after taking into account certain factors, that the quality of the child's evidence will not be diminished (YJCEA 1999, s 21(4)). If as a result of opting out the child has to give evidence in court, this should be given from behind a screen so that the witness is shielded from viewing the defendant, unless the court considers that screens would not maximise the quality of the child's evidence. The child may also opt out of this subject to the agreement of the court. YJCEA 1999, s 21(4C) sets out the factors the court must consider in deciding whether the child witness may opt out of the primary rule and the secondary requirement to give evidence from behind a screen. These are:

(a)   the age and maturity of the witness;

(b)   the witness's ability to understand the consequences of giving evidence in court rather than via video recorded or live link evidence;

(c)   any relationship between the witness and the accused;

(d)   the witness's social, cultural and ethnic background;

(e)   the nature and circumstances of the offence being tried, as well as any other factors the court considers relevant.

Also see CPR 2015, r 18.9 which deals with special measures direction for a young witness.

There is nothing in the fair trial provisions which prohibits a witness from being allowed to give evidence in a way different to the accused. The court has held that these provisions do not breach Article 6 of the ECHR (*R (on the application of D) v Camberwell Youth Court* [2005] UKHL 4).

Also see: *Good Practice guidance in managing young witness cases and questioning children* (July 2009) by Joyce Plotnikoff and Richard Woolfson on www.nspcc.org. uk/measuringup and *Achieving Best Evidence: Guidance on interviewing victims and witnesses, and guidance on using special measures* (March 2011).

Procedural considerations

13.05 Applications for the use of special measures are made under the Criminal Procedure Rules 2015, Part 18. Although applications can be made by either the prosecution or the defence, defence applications are rarer.

A special measure may not be used by a court unless the Secretary of State has made the measure available to the court in which proceedings will take place. The special measures, which may be available are as follows:

(a) Screening the witness from the accused. The screen used must not prevent the witness from being seen and being able to see the magistrates, the legal representatives and any interpreter or other person appointed to assist the witness. It will be good practice for the court's legal adviser to remind the magistrates that no adverse inference should be drawn merely from the fact that the screen has been permitted to ensure the quality of the witness's evidence (*R v T* [2000] All ER (D) 1805). YJCEA 1999, s 32 covers the position of a trial on indictment with a jury.

(b) Allowing the witness to give evidence via a live video link. Such a direction may also provide for a specified person to accompany the witness while the witness is giving evidence by live link. In determining who may accompany the witness, the court must have regard to the wishes of the witness (also see CPR 2015, rr 18.23 to 18.26).

(c) Allowing the witness to give evidence in private by clearing the public from the court while the witness testifies. This applies only in sexual offence cases, Modern Slavery Act cases, or cases involving intimidation. Clearing the court will not include the accused, legal representatives, interpreters and at least one media representative.

(d) The wearing of wigs and gowns may be dispensed with in the Crown Court.

(e) A video recording of an interview of the witness may be admitted as evidence in chief of that witness and the court must consider, having regard to all the circumstances, whether it is in the interests of justice for the recording or part of it to be admitted, or not. Section 103 of the CJA 2009 has amended YJCEA 1999, s 27 to relax restrictions on a witness giving additional evidence in chief after the witness' video recorded evidence has been admitted. It was said in *R v Davies* [2011] EWCA Crim 1177 that 'giving evidence was not a memory test and the speculative possibility that a witness might say something when giving live evidence in chief which was different from what she had said in a pre-recorded interview, and thereby depriving the defence of the opportunity of cross-examining on those differences, was not in itself, an adequate reason for refusing to allow the playing of an ABE interview'.

(f) Cross-examination and re-examination of the witness may be video recorded in advance of the trial. This direction would mean that all the evidence of a child could be given and recorded pre-trial. Any such recording must be made in the hearing and sight of the magistrates and legal representatives, and the accused must be able to hear and see any such examination and communicate with his legal representatives (YJCEA 1999, s 28). It should be noted that this section is not in force except in relation to proceedings taking place before the Crown Court sitting at Kingston-upon-Thames, Leeds, or Liverpool (pilot areas).

(g) Using an interpreter or other intermediary for the purpose of examining the witness. The function of an intermediary is to communicate to the witness any questions and the answers to any person asking such questions, and to explain such questions or answers so far as necessary to enable them to be understood by the witness or person in question (YJCEA 1999, s 29(2)). It is worth noting that in cases where the defendant can speak English but the parent/guardian does not, the court may make arrangements for an interpreter to attend the Youth Court to interpret for the parent/guardian. The Costs in Criminal Cases (in General) Regulations 1986 provides authority for a court to pay for an interpreter required by a parent or guardian of the youth when the court considers the expense properly incurred. In *R v West London Youth Court, ex parte N* [1999] All ER (D) 775, it was held that although not ideal or convenient, double interpretation was justified in those cases where it proved impossible to find an interpreter who spoke fluently both English and the language in which the defendant was fluent.

(h) Allowing the witness to use an aid to communication such as a signboard.

A party to the proceedings may make an application for the court to give a direction, or the court may raise the issue of its own motion. The first step is for the court to determine that the witness is eligible. The court must examine whether any of the special measures available (or a combination of them) would be likely to improve the quality of the evidence given by the witness. In deciding whether to make a special measures direction the court must take into account all the circumstances of the case, any views expressed by the witness and whether the measure or measures proposed might tend to inhibit evidence being effectively tested by a party to the proceedings.

The application must be in writing using the form as prescribed by the Practice Direction (CPR 2015, r 18.3). CPR 2015, r 18.10 provides details of what must be included in the application for a special measures direction.

Any application should be made as soon as reasonably practicable, and in any event not more than 28 days after the date on which the defendant pleaded not guilty in the magistrates' court or 14 days after the defendant pleads not guilty in the Crown Court and the application must be served on the court officer and each other party. The time limit may be extended by the court before or after it expires and the court may allow an application or representations to be made in a different form to the one set out in the Practice Direction or to be made orally. A person who wants an extension of time must apply when serving the application or representations for which it is needed and explain the delay (CPR 2015, rr 18.3 and 18.5).

Any party who receives a copy of the application or notice of the direction must within 14 days of service or notice serve representations on the applicant and the court officer if the special measures direction is opposed and request a court hearing with an explanation of why it is required. Representations must explain:

'(a)   why the witness is not eligible for assistance;

(b)   if the witness is not eligible for assistance, why –

   (i)   no special measures would be likely to improve the quality of the witness' evidence,

   (ii)   the proposed measure or measures would not be likely to maximise, so far as practicable the quality of the witness' evidence;

   (iii)   the proposed measure or measures might tend to inhibit the effective testing of that evidence.' (CPR 2015, r 18.13)

Irrespective of representations to the contrary, where the witness is a child witness or a 'qualifying witness' the special measures that the court usually must direct must be treated as likely to maximise, so far as practicable, the quality of the witness' evidence (YJCEA 1999, ss 21 and 22).

After the expiry of 14 days from receipt of the application the court will determine whether the application may be dealt with or without a hearing, or at a hearing at which the applicant and such other party or parties as the court may direct can be represented. Where no such notice of opposition is served, a direction for special measures may be given without a court hearing. However, where the court is aware that the direction will be opposed a hearing must be held. The appropriate officer of the court shall notify the applicant and where necessary any other parties of the time and place of any such hearing.

There is nothing preventing the court from raising the issue of special measures of its own motion or giving a direction on its own initiative (YJCEA 1999, s 19(1)(b); CPR 2015, r 18.1).

Where leave to use video recorded evidence is given, the procedure at the trial is relatively straightforward, if somewhat restrictive. The child witness must be called by the party tendering the video evidence, but that witness may only be examined in chief on any matter which, in the opinion of the court, has not been dealt adequately with in his recorded testimony (YJCEA 1999, s 27(5)). Where the application for a special measures direction includes a video recording of an interview of a witness that is to be admitted as evidence in chief, the application must be accompanied by the video recording that is to be tended in evidence (CPR 2015, r 18.9(2)).

The court has power to discharge or vary the special measures direction. An application must be made in writing as soon as reasonably practicable, served on the court officer and every other party. The applicant must explain what material circumstances have changed since the direction was given or last varied; explain why the direction should be varied or discharged; and explain the request for a hearing, if required (CPR 2015, r 18.11). Whenever the court makes a direction varying or refusing an application for directions, the justices must give their reasons for so doing and those reasons must be entered in the register of proceedings (CPR 2015, r 18.4).

In addition, CPR 2015, r 18.12 provides for the situation where an application requesting a special measures direction, (or for its variation or discharge) includes information which the applicant thinks ought not be revealed to another party. The applicant must omit this information from the part of the application that is served on that other party and mark the other part to show that, unless the court otherwise directs, it is only for the court; and in that other part, explain why the applicant has withheld that information from that other party. Any hearing of this type of application must be in private, unless the court otherwise directs. The court may also direct that the hearing may be wholly or in part in the absence of a party from whom the information has been withheld. At the hearing the court will generally receive representations first from the applicant and then from each other party, in the presence of all the parties. Then further representations may be made by the applicant, in the absence of a party from whom information has been withheld. The court also has a power to direct other arrangements for the hearing.

An applicant for a defendant's evidence direction must –

'(a) explain how the proposed direction meets the conditions prescribed by the Youth Justice and Criminal Evidence Act 1999;

(b) in a case in which the applicant proposes that the defendant give evidence by live link –

(i) identify a person to accompany the defendant while the defendant gives evidence, and

(ii) explain why that person is appropriate;

(c) ask for a hearing, if the applicant wants one, and explain why it is needed' (CPR 2015, r 18.15).

According to CPR 2015, r 18.14, the court may decide whether to give, vary or discharge a defendant's evidence direction at a hearing, in public or in private, or without a hearing; in a party's absence, where a direction, variation or discharge is sought or has had at least 14 days in which to make representations. Any application to vary or discharge a defendant's evidence direction must be in writing, as soon as reasonably practicable after becoming aware of the grounds for doing so; and served application on the court officer, and each other party. The applicant must –

'(a)   on an application to discharge a live link direction, explain why it is in the interests of justice to do so;

(b)   on an application to discharge a direction for an intermediary, explain why it is no longer necessary in order to ensure that the defendant receives a fair trial;

(c)   on an application to vary a direction for an intermediary, explain why it is necessary for the direction to be varied in order to ensure that the defendant receives a fair trial; and

(d)   ask for a hearing, if the applicant wants one, and explain why it is needed' (CPR 2015, r 18.16).

Any objections and request for a hearing must be served not more than 14 days after the service of the application or notice of the direction, variation or discharge by any other party or which the court proposes of its own initiative. Representations against a direction, variation or discharge must explain why the conditions prescribed by the Youth Justice and Criminal Evidence Act 1999 are not met.

An applicant for a live link direction must –

'(a)   unless the court otherwise directs, identify the place from which the witness will give evidence;

(b)   if that place is in the United Kingdom, explain why it would be in the interests of the efficient or effective administration of justice for the witness to give evidence by live link;

(c)   if the applicant wants the witness to be accompanied by another person while giving evidence—

(i)   name that person, if possible, and

(ii)   explain why it is appropriate for the witness to be accompanied;

(d)   ask for a hearing, if the applicant wants one, and explain why it is needed' (CPR 2015, r 18.24).

Any objections and request for a hearing must be served not more than 14 days after the service of the application or notice of the direction or discharge by any other party or which the court proposes of its own initiative. Representations against a direction or discharge must explain why the conditions prescribed by the Criminal Justice Act 1988 or the Criminal Justice Act 2003 are not met.

It should be noted that these provisions only apply in the criminal jurisdiction. Civil applications for criminal behaviour orders and anti-social behaviour injunctions will not qualify for the use of special measures.

Sexual offences

13.06   Certain sexual offences in the Youth Court may be designated as grave crimes in accordance with PCC(S)A 2000, s 91. One such offence is the crime of rape or sexual penetration. The Sexual Offences Act 1993 abolished the presumption of the criminal law that a boy under the age of 14 was incapable of sexual intercourse. Consequently, if the prosecution can prove that penile penetration took place without the consent of the victim, a juvenile of 10 years or more may be convicted of rape. It follows that a juvenile may also be convicted of assault by penetration and sexual assault. Note, however, that child sex offences (Sexual Offences Act 2003 (SOA 2003), ss 9 to 15) although primarily aimed at adults, may be charged in the case of a juvenile offender by virtue of SOA 2003, s 13. The maximum penalty is reduced to five years' custody in the case of a juvenile instead of 14 years. An alternative in such a case, where the ages of the parties are similar and the acts were consensual, would be to draw the matter to the attention of the local authority with a view to care proceedings being commenced.

The age of the offender will also be significant in relation to the charging decision, venue and in the sentencing of non-consensual offences where no special sentencing provisions have been provided in the legislation. *Code for Crown Prosecutors* sets out guidance on prosecuting under the Sexual Offences Act 2003 and many other statutory provisions. It was held in *E v DPP* [2011] EWHC 1465 (Admin) that 'both the law and the guidance require a proper balancing of the interests of the defendant, of the victim and indeed of the public at large'. Its significance is particularly acute in relation to absolute offences such as 'rape of a child under 13', where the maximum penalty is life imprisonment, especially if an offender is very young and the disparity in age between the offender and the victim is very small.

Section 44(1) of the Children and Young Persons Act 1933 provides that every court dealing with a child or young person, as an offender or otherwise 'shall have regard to the welfare of the child or young person'. The youth and immaturity of an offender must always be potential mitigating factors for the courts to take into account when passing sentence. The case of *R v Marcus Petrie* [2014] EWCA Crim 2912, concerned a successful appeal against sentence and Sexual Offences Prevention Order (SOPO) imposed on a 19-year-old who had pleaded guilty to causing a 13-year-old child to engage in sexual activity and sexual activity with a child. The sentence was reduced from 30 months' detention to 12 months' detention on the grounds that the starting point for the original sentence had been too high because the young offender's social immaturity affected his culpability and there were concerns about his vulnerability. The SOPO was also quashed.

Furthermore, the Sentencing Council in its recent 'Sexual Offences Guideline' (within the *Sentencing Children and Young People* definitive guideline) provides a non-exhaustive list of factors that illustrate the type of background factors that might play a part in leading a child or young person to commit a sexual offence:

- 'Victim of neglect or abuse (sexual, physical or emotional) or has witnessed the neglect or abuse of another.

- Exposure to pornography or materials which are age inappropriate.

- Involvement in gangs.

- Associated with child sexual exploitation.

- Unstable living or educational arrangements.

- Communication or learning disabilities or mental health concerns.

- Part of a peer group, school or neighbourhood where harmful sexual norms and attitudes go unchallenged.

- A trigger event such as the death of a close relative or a family breakdown.'

Such factors need to be taken into account by the court when considering a sentence and where a sentence threshold is crossed it does not necessarily mean that that sentence should be imposed; however, if the facts of a case are particularly serious, the youth and maturity of the offender will not necessarily mitigate the appropriate sentence.

The Sentencing Council's definitive guidelines on the *Sexual Offences Act 2003* which came into force in May 2007 apply to any offence sentenced on or after that date until 1 June 2017 when the new definitive guideline *Sentencing Children and Young People* issued by the Sentencing Council comes into force (see **Appendix I**).

Where the offence of rape, assault by penetration or sexual assault is alleged to be committed against a complainant under the age of 13 (Sexual Offences Act 2003, ss 5, 6 and 7 respectively), these are punishable with life imprisonment or 14 years in the case of an adult. It is not a defence that the victim consented, nor that the defendant believed that the victim was 13 or older. The starting point for rape of a child under 13 years old is 10 years' custody in the case of an adult.

Although rape is likely to trigger the grave crimes procedure, the Sentencing Council's guidance on the *Sexual Offences Act 2003* mean that some serious sexual offences, including in exceptional cases rape or sexual penetration, may remain suitable for trial in the Youth Court (see **5.25**). In such cases the court needs to consider the Protocol for 'Sexual Offences in the Youth Court' issued by the Senior Presiding Judge with effect from 31 March 2010 and further supplementing guidance issued by the Senior District Judge on 7 December 2010 on 'Role of the Link Judges in arrangements for hearing sexual offences in the youth court, and in arranging deputy cover where appropriate'. (See **Appendix M**).

The existence of the Protocol should not however stop a court sending a serious sexual offence to the Crown Court for trial where this is justified by the likely sentence, were the defendant to be found guilty (*R (on the application of W) v Warrington Magistrates' Court* [2009] EWHC 1538 (Admin)). In that case, a 13-year-old was found guilty of the attempted rape of his eight-year-old cousin and three sexual assaults on a five-year-old boy and 13-year-old girl. The circuit judge appointed to hear the case in the Youth Court under the preceding Rape Protocol found the defendant guilty of all the charges and committed him to the Crown Court for sentence under the dangerousness provisions. The judge then imposed a sentence of detention for public protection and set a minimum of two years for the attempted rape and 12 months concurrent for the sexual assaults. The Divisional Court (Lord Justice Pill delivering the judgment) found that the magistrates' decision to retain the case could only just be defended as a proper exercise of their discretion, and noted that the true gravity of the offence of attempted rape only emerged later during the defendant's own evidence and in the pre-sentence report. The Divisional Court made it clear that the magistrates should make their decision on mode of trial based on the seriousness of the offence and not allow their decision to be affected by administrative convenience.

In *CPS v Newcastle-Upon-Tyne Youth* Court [2010] EWHC 2773 (Admin) a district judge's decision to retain jurisdiction in the Youth Court of an offence of rape was subject to criticism, where a 17-year-old defendant committed the offence on his ex-girlfriend who had fallen asleep at the side of their dying premature baby. He pleaded guilty. Although the application for judicial review was dismissed due to the CPS's delay in deciding whether to review the decision, it was said that the district judge should not have given a fifty per cent reduction from the adult guideline starting point because the defendant was nearly 18 years old. The fact that the defendant had been in a previous relationship with the victim, and the circumstances in which the offence was committed were considered to be aggravating features.

Where the victim is under 16 it is a mitigating factor if 'sexual activity between two children (one of whom is the offender) was mutually agreed and experimental'. This was echoed by the Court of Appeal in *R v C* [2009] All ER (D) 154 (Apr), which stated that the two offences of sexual activity by the defendant aged 14, with two girls (aged 13 and 14) contrary to SOA 2003, s 13, were in the context of relationships of genuine affection with there being no evidence of coercion or abusive seduction. Taking into account the sentencing guidelines and the defendant's previous good character, age and immaturity and the complainants' ages and offences being committed within the relationships, the eight-month detention and training order (DTO) was substituted with a one-year supervision order.

In the case of *R v Jason David Robert Mooney* [2010] EWCA Crim 698, a 30-month detention and training order imposed on the defendant aged 17, for two rape offences involving a 12-year-old girl was reduced to a detention and training order for 12 months. It was held that the exceptional circumstances of the case, such as the victim initiating sexual intercourse on both occasions; saying she was nearly 15 years old and the defendant not being responsible for the victim being drunk; him not ejaculating and being unaware of the law regarding consensual intercourse between a 17-year-old and a 12-year-old, permitted a radical departure from the Sentencing Council's definitive guidelines on the *Sexual Offences Act 2003*. Unfortunately the guidelines offered no practical assistance in a case of this sort.

Further in the case of *R v G* [2006] EWCA Crim 821, a 15-year-old boy pleaded guilty to the rape of a 12-year-old contrary to SOA 2003, s 5. A *Newton* hearing had been listed to decide whether the victim had in fact agreed to intercourse. The prosecution then accepted the defence basis of plea because the victim accepted that she had told the boy on a previous occasion that she was 15 years old. She was reluctant to give evidence in court. The court therefore sentenced in line with the written basis of plea. The terms of the plea were that the complainant willingly agreed to have sexual intercourse with the defendant and that the defendant believed that the complainant was 15 years old because she told him so on an earlier occasion. The Central Criminal Court imposed a 12-month DTO. The Court of Appeal noted that the juvenile had served five months in custody and varied the sentence to a 12-month conditional discharge. Lord Phillips CJ observed that the judge should have sentenced the offence as if it fell within the ambit of SOA 2003, s 13. The Lord Chief Justice also cited with approval the 'non-prescriptive guidance' in respect of the new offences created by the SOA 2003 given by the Vice President in *R v Corran* and other appeals [2005] EWCA Crim 192. The following comments were noted as being particularly pertinent:

> '6. Against that background, we turn to the offence of rape of a child under 13, contrary to section 5 of the Act. We say, at once, that no precise guidance can be given. The appropriate sentence is likely to lie within a very wide bracket, depending on all the circumstances of the particular offence. There will be very few cases in which immediate custody is not called for, even in relation to a young offender because the purpose of the legislation is to protect children under 13 from themselves, as well as from others minded to prey upon them …
>
> 8. Although absence of consent is not an ingredient of the offence, presence of consent is, in our judgment, material in relation to sentence, particularly in relation to young defendants. The age of the defendant, of itself and when compared with the age of the victim, is also an important factor. A very short period of custody is likely to suffice for a teenager where the other party consents. In exceptional cases, of which there is one before this Court, a non-custodial sentence may be appropriate for a young defendant. If the offender is much older than the victim a substantial term of imprisonment will usually be called for.'

In *R v G* [2006] EWCA Crim 821, indications were given by the Court of Appeal that where they know from the outset that the penetration was consensual, if the prosecution charge a juvenile under SOA 2003, s 5 (or even the decision to prosecute), this could be challenged as an unjustified interference with the defendant's Article 8.1 rights (right of individual to respect for private life) under ECHR.

The 'Sexual Offences Guideline' within the Sentencing Council's *Sentencing Children and Young People* provides helpful guidance in relation to the procedure which needs to be applied in determining sentences such as considering the offence seriousness (nature of the offence and aggravating and mitigating factors); personal mitigation; reduction for guilty plea; and reviewing the sentence.

A Youth Court dealing with a young offender for an offence listed in Sch 3 or Sch 5 of the SOA 2003 (including an offence committed before the commencement of the Act) either in the UK or overseas may make a sexual harm prevention order (SHPO) or a sexual risk order (SRO). These orders were introduced by the Anti-Social Behaviour, Crime and Policing Act 2014. They replace the previous sexual offences prevention orders (SOPOs), risk of sexual harm orders (RSHOs) and foreign travel orders (FTOs) which were introduced by the Sexual Offences Act 2003.

An SHPO can be made by a court in respect of an individual who has been convicted, or cautioned ('cautioned' includes those who have received a reprimand, final warning or youth caution) for a relevant offence including an offence committed overseas and who poses a risk of sexual harm to the public in the UK or to children or vulnerable adults abroad (SOA 2003, s 103A).

An SHPO may impose any restriction the court deems necessary for the purpose of protecting the public from sexual harm and makes the offender subject to the notification requirements for the duration of the order. A prohibition contained in an SHPO has effect for a fixed period (not less than five years) specified in the order or until further order (SOA 2003, s 103C). The order may specify different periods for different prohibitions. The decision of the Court of Appeal in *R v Smith and Others* [2011] EWCA Crim 1772 reinforces the need for the terms of a SHPO to be tailored to the exact requirements of the case.

SHPOs are available to the court at the time of sentencing for a relevant offence, or on free-standing application to the magistrates' court by the police or National Crime Agency after the time of the conviction or caution. Where an application for an SHPO is made by way of complaint to the Youth Court (MCA 1980, s 53) for a child or young person, the parent or guardian should also receive a copy of the summons unless no such person is readily available.

An SRO can be made by a court in respect of an individual who has done an act of a sexual nature and who, as a result, poses a risk of harm to the public in the UK or children or vulnerable adults abroad. For an SRO to be imposed the individual does not need to have committed a 'relevant offence' or any offence (SOA 2003, s 122A).

An SRO may impose any restriction the court deems necessary for the purposes of protecting the public from harm (this includes harm from the defendant outside the UK where those to be protected are children and vulnerable adults), and requires the individual to notify the police of their name and address including where this information changes. An SRO is available on free-standing application to a magistrates' court by the police or National Crime Agency. Where the court is dealing with a child or young person, the parent or guardian should also receive a copy of the summons unless no such person is readily available.

SROs prohibit the defendant from doing anything described in the order, and can include a prohibition on foreign travel, replacing foreign travel orders which were introduced by the Sexual Offences Act 2003 (SOA 2003, s 122C). A prohibition contained in an SRO has effect for a fixed period (not less than two years) specified in the order or until further order (SOA 2003, s 122A(7)). The order may specify different periods for different prohibitions.

The Home Office *Guidance on Part 2 of the Sexual Offences Act 2003* recommends the following principles when applying for an SHPO or a SRO in relation to a young person:

- 'The early consultation and participation of the Youth Offending Team in the application process.

- That 14–17 year olds made subject to civil injunctions in relation to harmful sexual behaviour are offered appropriate interventions to reduce their harmful behaviour

- That the nature and extent of that support is based on a structured assessment that takes into account the needs of the young person and the imminent risk.

- That the welfare of the child or young person is the paramount consideration, in line with local safeguarding procedures.

- That the requirements of all other orders and sentences that may already be in existence are taken into account to ensure that any requirements made by these orders to not restrict a young person's ability to complete other current orders or sentences, and the combined burden of requirements is taken into account to ensure the young person has the capacity to comply.'

A notification order (NO) can be made by the court, on application by a chief officer of police, in relation to individuals who have been convicted, cautioned or had a relevant finding made against them for specified sexual offences in a country outside the UK (SOA 2003, s 97). The effect of the order is broadly to make such offenders subject to the notification requirements of Pt 2 of the 2003 Act as if they had been convicted of or cautioned for a relevant offence in the UK.

The notification requirements of Pt 2 of the SOA 2003 are an automatic requirement under s 80 for offenders who receive a conviction or caution for certain sexual offences. For the most serious offences in Sch 3, there is no sentence threshold to registration for young offenders and adult offenders alike. The notification requirements will apply to young offenders who receive a youth caution and for those convicted by a court, regardless of the disposal that is given. The main offences requiring automatic registration in the case of the juvenile are those under ss 1, 2, 4, 5, 6 and 15 of the Act. Other sections do not automatically require registration in the case of a juvenile unless any relevant thresholds set out in it are met. For the purposes of those offences in Sch 3 that contain a threshold regarding the offender's age, it is the young offender's age at the time that the offence was committed that the court should consider when deciding whether the threshold is met.

For those under 18 when convicted or cautioned, the notification periods of 10, 7, 5 and 2 years are halved (SOA 2003, s 82). And where the statute only requires registration if there has been a 12-month sentence of imprisonment, the case of *R v Slocombe* [2005] EWCA Crim 2997, makes it clear that in relation to a juvenile this means a two-year detention and training order because only the detention part is to be regarded as imprisonment.

Section 89 of SOA 2003 provides that a court may direct a person with parental responsibility for a juvenile offender to comply with the notification requirements on behalf of the juvenile offender. Parental directions can be made at the time the court deals with the juvenile offender by recording a conviction or finding for one of the trigger offences when it makes an order which triggers the notification requirements or following an application from the police.

The effect of a direction under this section will be that the notification requirements that would otherwise have fallen on the juvenile offender will instead fall upon the parent or, in some cases, the local authority if it has parental responsibility for the juvenile offender. The parent or guardian or local authority must ensure that the juvenile offender attends the police station with him when making a notification.

Parental directions do not require the consent of the parent but the court may wish to seek the views of the parent, guardian or local authority prior to making such an order.

Breach by a parent of a parental direction is an offence and carries the same penalties (see below) as breach of the notification requirements by a sex offender.

On 30 July 2012, the Sexual Offences Act 2003 was amended by the Sexual Offences Act 2003 (Remedial) Order 2012 and introduced a mechanism for individuals to seek a review of their indefinite notification requirements. It was recognised that indefinite notification requirements were incompatible with art 8 (right to family and private life) of the ECHR as previously offenders who were on the sex offenders' register for life could not apply for a review of whether they should remain on the register: see SOA 2003, s 91F and the Home Office *Guidance on review of indefinite notification requirements* issued under the SOA 2003, s 91F.

The SOA 2003 allows the court to make an interim order in respect of SHPOs (SOA 2003, s 103F), SROs (SOA 2003, s 122E) and NOs (SOA 2003, s 100) where an application for a full order has been made or is being made at the same time but has not yet been determined. It is a matter for the courts to interpret whether or not it is just to make an interim order. If an application is properly made and supported an interim order may be granted.

SHPOs and SROs can be varied, renewed, or discharged on complaint (SOA 2003, ss 103E and 122D). However, it should be noted that it is not possible to vary, renew or discharge an NO.

A breach of any aspect of a civil order (SHPO, SRO and NO) made under Pt 2 of the Act and/or the notification requirement imposed as a result of such an order is a criminal offence. Under the 2003 Act, the maximum penalty on summary conviction (for either breach of an order or for a breach of the notification requirements) is a term not exceeding six months' imprisonment or a fine not exceeding the statutory maximum, or both. On indictment, the maximum penalty is imprisonment for five years (SOA 2003, ss 91, 103I and 122H). Juveniles are usually dealt with in the Youth Court where the maximum custodial sentence for a young person aged 12 to 17 years (inclusive) is two years. For breach of all orders and the notification requirements, provision is made for a defence of reasonable excuse.

Since being brought into force in July 2008, s 327A of the Criminal Justice Act 2003 creates a presumption in favour of releasing information to members of the public in relation to sex offenders but only where there is reasonable cause to believe that an offender poses a risk of serious harm to children or a particular child and that such disclosure is necessary to protect children from that harm.

See **J.2** at **Appendix J** for sentences in sexual offences cases.

Evidential problems

13.07   Although it will be extremely unusual for a juvenile to be unrepresented when charged with a sexual offence it is important to note that no defendant charged with a sexual offence may cross-examine *in person* a 'protected witness'. A protected witness is either the complainant in connection with that offence or in connection with any other offence charged in the proceedings, or an alleged witness to the commission of the offence who is a child or who falls to be cross-examined after giving evidence in chief either by a video recording made when he was a child or in any other way when he was a child (YJCEA 1999, ss 34 and 35). For the purposes of these sections 'child' has a special meaning and will encompass a person under the age of 14 where the offence charged is kidnapping, false imprisonment and offences under s 1 or 2 of the Child Abduction Act 1984 or an offence under s 1 of the Children and Young Persons Act 1933, or any offence involving an assault, injury or threat of injury. In respect of offences under the Protection of Children Act 1978 and Part 1 of the Sexual Offences Act 2003 the definition of child simply means a person under the age of 18.

When neither s 34 nor s 35 applies, the prosecutor may make an application to the court for a direction that the witness be protected or the court may raise the issue of its own motion. The court may give a direction prohibiting the accused from cross-examining, or further cross-examining, the witness in person but only if satisfied that it would not be contrary to the interests of justice and that the witness' evidence is likely to be diminished if the cross-examination is conducted by the accused in person and would be improved by the making of a direction (YJCEA 1999, s 36).

Before taking this step, the court must have regard to the views of the witness, the nature of the likely questions to be asked, the behaviour of the accused during the proceedings, the relationship between the witness and the accused, whether any person other than the accused has been charged in the proceedings with the sexual offence or been made subject to a direction under s 34 or s 35. Whether the court makes such a direction or refuses an application for a direction or discharges such a direction it must give its reasons for so doing and enter them in the register of the proceedings. When a direction is made preventing the accused from cross-examining the complainant or protected witness in person the court must of course ensure that the defendant is offered legal representation. If the defendant fails during a period specified by the court to arrange for legal representation the court must consider whether it is necessary in the interests of justice for the witness to be cross-examined by a legal representative appointed to represent the interests of the accused. If it is necessary the court itself will appoint a qualified legal representative to conduct the cross-examination. A person so appointed is designated an officer of the court and shall not be responsible to the accused (YJCEA 1999, s 38(5)); further the case of *Abbas v Crown Prosecution Service* [2015] EWHC 579 (Admin) provides that the aim of the legislation is simply to stop the defendant cross-examining the witness, not to prevent the person appointed to cross-examine from playing any other part in the trial. Also see Part 23 of the Criminal Procedure Rules 2015 for rules governing restrictions on cross-examination by a defendant acting in person.

The Youth Justice and Criminal Evidence Act 1999 also prohibits the introduction of evidence or the asking of questions in cross-examination by or on behalf of the accused about the sexual behaviour of the complainant. Again, the restriction applies to persons charged with a sexual offence but the definition in this case is found in YJCEA 1999, s 62. Sexual offence means any offence under Part 1 of the Sexual Offences Act 2003 (YJCEA 1999, s 41).

The court may grant leave for questions relating to the sex life of the complainant in one of four situations (as set out below), but only where a refusal of leave might result in the court reaching an unsafe conclusion on any relevant issue in the case. The court must also be satisfied that the evidence in question is relevant to one of the four issues (YJCEA 1999, s 41(3) and (5)). The first of these situations is where the issue to which the evidence is relevant is something other than the victim's consent. The second is where the issue is consent, and the evidence relates to the complainant's sexual behaviour which is alleged to have taken place at or about the same time as the event which is the subject matter of the charge. The third relates to the issue of consent where the evidence concerns earlier behaviour of the complainant that is alleged to be so similar to the accused's version of events that the similarity cannot reasonably be explained as a coincidence. The final situation is where the prosecution itself has led evidence about the complainant's sex life, and the accused wishes to explain or rebut the evidence by questioning (see *R v F* [2005] 2 All ER (D) 58 (Mar)). Part 22 of the Criminal Procedure Rules 2015, sets out the application and procedure to obtain permission to introduce evidence or cross-examine a witness about a complainant's sexual behaviour. It provides that any application must identify the issue to which the defendant says the complainant's sexual behaviour is relevant; give particulars of any evidence the defendant wants to introduce and any questions that the defendant wants to ask; identify the exception in the prohibition in YJCEA 1999, s 41 (as outlined above); and give the name and date of birth of any witnesses whose evidence regarding the complainant's sexual behaviour the defendant wants to introduce (CPR 2015, r 22.3). The court will have to be aware of any possible infringement of Article 6 of the European Convention on Human Rights when dealing with such applications. However, the court must weigh up the overall fairness of the trial and balancing the effect of such cross-examination on the victim against the need of the defendant to challenge the character or credibility of the complainant. A defendant will not be precluded by YJCEA 1999, s 41(3)(a), where his defence is a belief in consent by the complainant, from adducing evidence that they had recently taken part in sexual activity together. However, such evidence is admissible only in relation to the defendant's belief and not in relation to whether the complainant in fact consented (*R v Y* [2001] All ER (D) 66 (Jan)).

The importance of achieving an early trial date was highlighted by the case of *R v Malicki* [2009] EWCA Crim 365, where the complainant was nearly five years old and had complained of a sexual assault. The defendant's conviction was found unsafe on the grounds that there was a risk that the complainant did not have an accurate recollection of the events from 14 months previously, as she was so young. It was said that it was the responsibility of all concerned to bring the need for expedition to the attention of the court at all stages and it was the court's responsibility to ensure that such expedition was provided. This case is particularly important for those cases where the Youth Court accepts jurisdiction and applies the 'Sexual Offences in the Youth Court' Protocol. The Youth Court will need to ensure that the case is dealt with as expeditiously as possible, even if it means that a judge from outside the area has to be allocated by the Crown Court. *R v Malicki* [2009] was considered in the case of *R v MH* [2012] All ER (D) 183 (Dec) which concerned the evidence of a complainant who was three years old and had complained of a sexual assault. The defendant's conviction was upheld although his sentence of imprisonment was reduced.

Defendant's bad character

13.08   Application may be made to admit evidence that the defendant has a bad character in the sense that he has criminal convictions or has otherwise misbehaved, which is defined in CJA 2003, s 98 as 'misconduct'. The definition of bad character therefore is wide enough to apply to conduct arising out of a conviction or an acquittal. In the case of a person who has been charged with another offence for which trial is pending, the use of evidence relating to that charge in the current proceedings may also be governed by the bad character provisions. Misconduct is defined as the commission of any offence or other reprehensible behaviour. In relation to trials or hearings after August 2010, convictions under the law of any country outside England and Wales (including EU convictions) can be admitted, provided that the offence would also have been an offence in England and Wales. Reprehensible conduct must be looked at objectively, taking account whether a particular kind of behaviour could be regarded as reprehensible by the public. In *R v Hamer* [2010] EWCA Crim 2053, it was held that a fixed penalty does not impugn the good character of the defendant and he is entitled (in the absence of other evidence of bad character) to a full good character direction. Whereas in *R v Olu* [2010] EWCA Crim 2975 the judge had a discretion as to whether to give a good character direction where a caution was not challenged. In *R v McKenzie* [2008] EWCA Crim 758, it was noted that the need to call evidence to prove such misconduct might result in the trial becoming unnecessarily complex and take the focus away from the important issues. Also the lapse of time would make it difficult for the defendant to rebut the allegations causing him prejudice. For this reason these applications need to be approached with considerable caution. If a defendant does not agree with the details of the bad character, this will need to be proved by a certificate of conviction, relying on section 74 of PACE 1984 or calling witnesses to prove the bad character. Where the defendant challenges his conviction, prosecutors should follow the case management principles that follow from the judgment in *R v C* [2010] EWCA Crim 2971, which include the defendant providing a detailed defence statement, prosecution giving careful consideration as to whether the additional evidence of bad character is necessary, if witnesses will need to be called or if their evidence can be adduced via the hearsay provisions if they are reluctant to come to court for a second time.

It is important to note that the court must not convict the defendant only because he has a bad character. The court is exercising a judgment, or a determination, as to whether the defendant's bad character is relevant to an important matter in issue between him and the prosecution. In making the decision the court is allowed certain latitude, but where the judgment is plainly wrong the decision will be overturned on appeal. The appeal courts have found it difficult to give definitive guidance because the decisions will be made on the factual basis found by the lower court and, as such, that decision will be largely individual in its nature. It is important that the court gives full and detailed reasons for granting or refusing applications relating to bad character.

An exception to the rule that the court cannot convict on bad character alone is similar fact evidence where there may be no direct evidence that the defendant committed the offence charged, but the prosecution rely *solely* on evidence of bad character in the form of evidence that the defendant has committed other similar offences.

Detailed discussion of evidential points is outside the scope of this work and readers are urged to have regard to the statutory provisions, namely ss 98 to 112 of the Criminal Justice Act 2003. The following guidance does however provide a framework for the making of decisions and the giving of advice.

Evidence of bad character may be admitted through one of the following gateways:

(a)   all parties to the proceedings have agreed to it;

(b)   the defendant has given evidence of his own bad character or been asked questions by his barrister/solicitor that brought it up;

(c) it is important in order to understand other evidence in the case either in part or as a whole;

(d) it may help to resolve an important issue that has arisen between the prosecution and the defendant;

(e) the evidence has substantial probative value in that it may help to resolve an important issue that has arisen between the defendant and his co-defendant;

(f) the prosecution may adduce the evidence to correct a false impression given by the defendant;

(g) the defendant has made an attack on another's character.

Only if one or more of cases (a) to (f) above apply may the court use the evidence of the defendant's bad character for the particular purpose(s) outlined in the statute. If (f) alone applies, and it is disputed that the defendant has given a false impression, the court must decide first if a false impression has been given. If it is unsure that the defendant has given a false impression, the evidence of his bad character should be disregarded altogether.

The court may use the evidence of the defendant's bad character by taking it into account when deciding whether or not the defendant's evidence was truthful. A person with a bad character may be less likely to tell the truth, but it does not follow that he is incapable of doing so. The court may also take evidence of bad character into account when deciding whether or not the defendant committed the offence charged. In *R v D, P and U* [2011] EWCA Crim 1474, it was held that whilst evidence that a defendant possesses child pornography is not evidence that the defendant has demonstrated a practice of committing offences of sexual abuse or assault, the question for the purposes of s 101(1)(d) of CJA 2003 is whether the evidence is relevant to an important matter in issue between the defence and the Crown: namely, does it show that the defendant has exhibited a sexual interest in children? Therefore, although the evidence of the viewing and/or collection of child pornography is capable of being admissible through gateway (d) it does not follow that such evidence is automatically admissible. Admissibility requires an exercise of judgment which is case-specific in every trial. Furthermore, once the evidence is adjudged capable of admission under gateway (d), the court must then direct its attention to whether it is unfair to admit the evidence according to the various discretions applicable to the gateways set out in s 101 of CJA 2003.

Adducing a defendant's bad character is a double-edged sword; the prosecution may rely on the defendant's propensity to commit offences of a certain kind as showing that he is more likely to be guilty. The defence however may rely on the differences between his previous convictions and the offence charged as showing that he is less likely to be guilty. In the case of *R v Speed* [2013] EWCA Crim 1650 it was held that it would be inappropriate in a gateway (b) situation for a defendant to have carte blanche to make such points as he wishes about his previous record, without facing the possibility that his record does him no favours where credibility is concerned.

Detailed guidance was provided by the Court of Appeal in the case of *R v Hanson* [2005] EWCA Crim 824, which may be summarised as follows:

(a)   Parliament's intention in passing the legislation was to assist in the evidence-based conviction of the guilty, without putting those who are not guilty at risk of conviction by prejudice.

(b)   If a propensity to commit the offence is to be relied upon (ss 101(1)(d) and 103(1)(a)) there are three questions to be considered:

    (i)   whether the history of convictions establishes a propensity to commit offences of the kind charged;

    (ii)   whether that propensity makes it more likely that the defendant committed the offence charged; and

    (iii)   whether it is just to rely on convictions of the same type and, in any event, whether the proceedings would be unfair if they were admitted.

(c)   Where propensity to untruthfulness is relied upon (CJA 2003, ss 101(1) (d) and 103(1)(b)), this is not the same as propensity to dishonesty. Previous convictions (whether for dishonesty or otherwise) are only likely to show propensity to be untruthful where truthfulness is in issue, for example where the offence committed shows a propensity for untruthfulness by making false representations.

(d)   Where an attack on the character of another person is made by the defendant, s 101(1)(g) may be relied upon. The court may rely on the pre-2003 authorities and s 106 of the Act to assess whether such an attack has been made.

(e)   The Court of Appeal will generally only interfere with the court's judgment if it exercises its discretion in a manner that is plainly *Wednesbury* unreasonable.

(f)   The Crown needs to decide at the time of giving notice of the application whether it proposes to rely simply on the fact of conviction or also upon the circumstances of the conviction. It is generally expected that the relevant circumstances of previous convictions will be agreed.

(g)   In any case in which evidence of bad character is admitted to show propensity either to commit offences or to be untruthful the legal adviser should advise the magistrates that:

    (i)   they should not conclude that the defendant is guilty or untruthful merely because he has convictions;

    (ii)   although the convictions might show a propensity, this does not mean that he committed the offence or has been untruthful in this case;

(iii)   whether they in fact show a propensity is for them to decide;

(iv)   they must take into account what a defendant has said about his previous convictions; and

(v)   although they are entitled, if they find propensity is shown, to take this into account when determining guilt, propensity is only one relevant factor and they must assess its significance in the light of all the other evidence in the case.

The overriding factor for Youth Court justices to bear in mind is that bad character cannot by itself prove that the defendant is guilty. In *R v Colin Anthony Miller* [2010] EWCA Crim 1578, it was held that notwithstanding the differing ages of the victims, a judge had been justified in admitting the defendant's previous conviction as evidence of propensity for non-consensual sex with a young girl. The defendant had been convicted when he was 16 years old of the gang rape of a 15-year-old girl. The appeal related to a charge of raping an 11-year-old female relative. The court found it significant that both the conviction and the allegation involved the underlying abuse of power. In this case it was held that the Sentencing Council's *Overarching Principles – Sentencing Youths* was of no assistance and although it was recognised that the offence committed by a young person could be the consequence of immaturity, that did not alter the fact that a conviction for such an offence could be evidence of propensity.

Where an application to admit bad character is made, a defendant may apply to have such evidence excluded under CJA 2003, s 101(1)(d) or (g) (where the evidence is relevant to an issue in the case between the prosecution and the defendant or has become admissible because of the defendant's attack on another person).

In either of these circumstances the court must not admit such evidence if it appears to it that its admission would have such an adverse effect on the fairness of the proceedings that it ought to be excluded. In applying the test the court is directed to take account, in particular, of the length of time that has expired since the previous events and the current charges.

This test in CJA 2003, s 101(3) is designed to reflect the existing position under s 78 of PACE 1984, whereby the judge or magistrates assess the probative value of the evidence to the issue in the case and its prejudicial effect if admitted. Balancing these factors, evidence will be excluded if it would be unfair to allow it to be admitted.

However, the test to be applied under CJA 2003, s 101(3) is stricter than that under PACE 1984, s 78, where the court *may* refuse to admit the evidence. CJA 2003 states that the court *must* not admit such evidence if it would have an adverse effect on the fairness of the proceedings.

Where the court makes a relevant ruling it must state its reasons for doing so and, if it is a magistrates' court, it must cause the ruling and the reasons for it to be entered in the court register.

Introducing evidence of non-defendant's bad character

13.09   Evidence of the bad character of a person other than the defendant is admissible if, and only if:

(a)   it is important explanatory evidence; or

(b)   it has substantial probative value in relation to a matter which is:

   (i)   a matter in issue in the proceedings; and

   (ii)   is of substantial importance in the context of the case as a whole; or

(c)   all parties to the proceedings agree to the evidence being admissible.

The evidence may also be adduced to show the complainant had a propensity to act in the way asserted by the defendant.

According to *R v Brewster* [2010] EWCA Crim 1194, the first question for the court under CJA 2003, s 100(1)(b) is whether the creditworthiness is a matter in issue which is of substantial importance in the context of the case as a whole. It was said:

> 'Where a witness has convictions does not mean that the opposing party is entitled to attack the witness's credibility. If it is shown that creditworthiness is an issue of substantial importance, the second question is whether the bad character relied upon is of substantial probative value in relation to that issue. Whether convictions have persuasive value on the issue of creditworthiness, will, it seems to us, depend principally on the nature, number and age of the convictions. However, we do not consider that the conviction must, in order to qualify for admission in evidence, demonstrate any tendency towards dishonesty or untruthfulness. The question is whether a fair-minded tribunal would regard them as affecting the worth of the witness' evidence'.

At almost the same time as *Brewster*, the Court of Appeal in *R v Braithwaite* [2010] 2 App R 18 ruled that a police report of an allegation of an offence made against a non-defendant which remained unproven was unlikely to be of any probative value. That case was followed in *R v Dizaei* [2013] 1 Cr App R 31 where, in giving the judgment of the court, Lord Judge CJ discussed the interrelation between whether an unproven allegation was of substantial probative value and s 109 of the CJA 2003, that the bare fact of an allegation (even if assumed to be true) is not necessarily conclusive of the question whether it constitutes substantial probative evidence or evidence of substantial importance in the context of the case as a whole and therefore the pre-conditions to admissibility under s 100 cannot be satisfied without a careful examination of all the material which bears on the question. Also see *R v RW* [2017] EWCA Crim 143.

Procedural issues

13.10   A prosecutor who wants to introduce evidence of a defendant's bad character or who wants to cross-examine a witness with a view to eliciting that evidence, under s 101 of the CJA 2003, must give notice in the form set out in the Practice Direction to the court and all other parties to the proceedings at the same time as the prosecutor complies or purports to comply with s 3 of the Criminal Procedure and Investigations Act 1996 and CPR 2015, r 21.2.

A party who wants to introduce evidence of a non-defendant's bad character or who wants to cross-examine a witness with a view to eliciting that evidence must, under CJA 2003, s 100, apply in the form set out in the Practice Direction. The application must be received by the court officer and all other parties to the proceedings as soon as reasonably practicable and in any event not more than 14 days after the prosecutor has disclosed the material on which the application is based (CPR 2012, r 35.3(3)). The prosecution may oppose the application by giving notice in writing not more than 14 days after receiving the application (CPR 2015, r 21.3).

Where a party wants to introduce evidence of a defendant's bad character, the prosecutor must serve the notice not more than 28 days after the defendant pleads not guilty, in a magistrates' court. A co-defendant who wants to introduce such evidence must serve the notice as soon as reasonably practicable; and in any event not more than 14 days after the prosecutor discloses material on which the notice is based. A party who objects to the introduction of the evidence must apply to the court to determine the objection not more than 14 days after service of the notice (CPR 2015, r 21.4).

The court may allow a notice or application required under this rule to be given in a different form, or orally; or shorten a time limit under this rule or extend it even after it has expired. In (*R (on the application of Robinson) v Sutton Coldfield Magistrates* [2006] EWHC 307 (Admin), the discretion of a court to extend the time limit under the (old) CPR 2005, r 35.8 to adduce evidence of bad character was not limited to exceptional circumstances. Where a party applied for an extension of the time limit, two of the key considerations were whether there was a good explanation for the failure to give notice within the time limit and whether the opposing party had suffered any prejudice by reason of the failure to give notice within time.

The court may determine an application at a hearing, in public or in private, or without a hearing and must not determine the application unless each party other than the applicant is present, or has had at least 14 days in which to serve a notice of objection (CPR 2015, rr 21.4(6) and 21.3(5)).

The court must announce at a hearing in public the reasons for admitting or refusing bad character evidence (CPR 2015, r 21.5).

Hearsay

13.11   CJA 2003, s 114 provides the circumstances in which a statement not made in oral evidence in the proceedings is admissible in evidence of any matter. A 'statement' is defined as any representation of fact or opinion made by a person by whatever means and includes a representation made in a sketch, photo fit or other pictorial form. A 'matter stated' is one where the purpose or one of the purposes of the person making the statement appears to have been to cause another person to believe the matter or to cause another person to act or a machine to operate on the basis that the matter is as stated (CJA 2003, s 115). The effect of this definition is to enable evidence to be admitted of 'implied assertions'. The onus will be on a party to prove that the statement was not intended to cause another to believe the matter if the statement is not to be treated as hearsay. The burden on the prosecution will be beyond reasonable doubt and the burden on the defence will be the balance of probabilities.

Hearsay evidence (as defined above) is admissible in criminal proceedings only if:

(a)   any provision of the CJA 2003 or any other statutory provision makes it admissible;

(b)   any rule of law preserved by CJA 2003, s 118 makes it admissible;

(c)   all parties to the proceedings agree to it being admissible; or

(d)   the court is satisfied that it is in the interests of justice for it to be admissible.

When considering the general ground in paragraph (d) above (CJA 2003, s 114(1)(d)), the court must have regard to the following factors and to any other it considers relevant:

(a)   how much probative value the statement has (assuming it to be true) in relation to a matter in issue in the proceedings, or how valuable it is for the understanding of other evidence in the case;

(b)   what other evidence has been, or can be, given on the matter or evidence mentioned above;

(c)   how important the matter or evidence mentioned is in the context of the case as a whole;

(d)   the circumstances in which the statement was made;

(e)   how reliable the maker of the statement appears to be;

(f)   how reliable the evidence of the making of the statement appears to be;

(g)   whether oral evidence of the matter stated can be given and, if not, why it cannot;

(h)   the amount of difficulty involved in challenging the statement;

(i)   the extent to which that difficulty would be likely to prejudice the party facing it.

The test for admissibility is 'the interests of justice'. There is no obligation on the court to embark on an investigation of, and make specific findings in relation to, each of the nine factors whenever an application is made under s 114(1)(d) (*R v Taylor* [2006] EWCA Crim 260). The greatest care must be taken before admitting evidence under CJA 2003, s 114(1)(d) to ensure that the CJA 2003, s 114(2) factors are fully considered and that overall it is genuinely in the interests of justice that the court should be asked to rely on the statement without seeing its maker and without any question being addressed to the statement maker about it (*R v Y* [2008] EWCA Crim 10). Section 114(3) of the Criminal Justice Act 2003 provides that out of court statements may still be excluded even if they fulfil the requirements above, for example, confessions must meet the additional requirements of PACE 1984, ss 76 and 78 before admission.

Cases where a witness is unavailable

13.12   Section 116 of the Criminal Justice Act 2003 sets out a series of categories under which first-hand hearsay evidence, whether oral or documentary, will be admissible, provided that the witness, who is identified to the court's satisfaction, is unavailable to testify for a specified reason.

A statement will be admissible under this section (subject to the additional conditions explained below) if the person who made it is:

(a)   dead;

(b)   unfit because of bodily or mental condition;

(c)   outside the UK and it is not reasonably practicable to secure his attendance;

(d)   untraceable although such steps as are reasonably practicable have been taken to find him;

(e)   in fear and the court gives leave for the statement to be given in evidence (CJA 2003, s 116(2)).

The case of *R v Ibrahim* [2012] EWCA Crim 837 concerned hearsay statements made by an identified witness who had subsequently died before the trial. The interlocking questions for the court in order to determine whether a defendant had had a fair trial were:

(a)   was there proper justification for admitting the untested hearsay evidence in the statements; that depended on whether the conditions in CJA 2003, ss 116(1) and 116(2)(a) were satisfied, although that test was also subject to the 'counterbalancing measures' in the statutory 'code' and the common law;

(b)   how important were the untested hearsay statements in relation to the prosecution's case against the defendant; did they amount to the central corpus of evidence without which the case could not have proceeded;

(c)   how 'demonstrably reliable' were the statements; and

(d)   were the 'counterbalancing safeguards' inherent in the common law, the CJA 2003 and s 78 of PACE 1984 properly applied, so as to ensure that the defendant had a fair trial.

The court is duty bound to make an assessment of the reliability and importance of the hearsay evidence that has been admitted before making a decision on whether to let the case proceed or not. On deciding the reliability of the statement, it should be considered in the context of all the other evidence adduced. It was found in *R v Ibrahim* [2012] that the counterbalancing measures in the CJA 2003 and in the common law had not been properly applied. Accordingly, the defendant had not had a fair trial and his rights under art 6(1) of the ECHR had been infringed in relation to one of the offences. The conviction for this offence was therefore unsafe and the appeal was allowed.

In relation to the witness being unfit under CJA 2003, s 116(2)(b) it was said in *R (on the application of Meredith) v Harwich Magistrates' Court* [2006] EWHC 3336 (Admin) that:

> '... it is necessary that statements of witnesses who are indeed unfit to attend trial because of their bodily or mental condition should be able to be given, otherwise crimes may well not be brought home. But it is equally important that there is proper protection for a defendant against the admission of such statements, which may be of considerable importance in the context of proof of the offence against him unless the relevant conditions are indeed §.'

Where a witness is outside the United Kingdom, 'reasonably practicable' must be judged on the basis of the steps taken, or not taken, by the party seeking to secure the attendance of the witness and the court must also consider whether to exercise its powers under CJA 2003, s 126 or under PACE 1984, s 78 to exclude the evidence.

On an application for the admission of the statement of an absent witness formal evidence was required to prove that all reasonably practicable steps had been taken to find him, unless the relevant facts were set out in an agreed statement/section 10 admission (*R v DT* [2009] EWCA Crim 1213). In *Horncastle and others* [2009] EWCA Crim 964, Thomas LJ provided that an essential consideration in relation to an absent witness would be whether there is a justifiable reason for the absence and whether the evidence can be assessed and tested so that it is safe to rely upon.

'Fear' includes fear of death or injury, of another person, or of financial loss. Section 116(4) of the Criminal Justice Act 2003 guides the court on the exercise of this discretion by requiring the court to consider whether the statement ought to be admitted in the interests of justice, having regard to:

(a)   the statement's contents;

(b)   any risk that its admission or exclusion will result in unfairness to any party to the proceedings (and in particular to how difficult it will be to challenge the statement if the relevant person does not give oral evidence);

(c)   in appropriate cases, to the fact that special measures under the Youth Justice and Criminal Evidence Act 1999 could be made; and

(d)   any other relevant circumstances.

When deciding to admit hearsay evidence due to fear, the court is not obliged to hear evidence from the witnesses in order to 'test' that fear (*R v Davies* [2006] EWCA

Crim 2643). An application under CJA 2003, s 116(4) may be made in cases of alleged domestic violence. *R (on the application of Robinson) v Sutton Coldfield Magistrates' Court* [2006] EWHC 307 (Admin) provides additional guidance on the factors which the court may consider before deciding to admit in evidence, the original statement of the complainant.

Despite the decision reached by the ECHR in *Al-Khawaja and Tahery v UK* [2009] ECHR 26766/05, in 2009, the Court of Appeal in *R v Horncastle and others* [2009] EWCA Crim 964 reached a contrary decision stating that provided the provisions of CJA 2003 are observed, there is no breach of Article 6, even if the conviction is based solely or to a decisive degree on hearsay evidence, which the defendant has had no opportunity of challenging. Since then the Grand Chamber of the European Court of Human Rights has ruled in *Al-Khawaja and Tahery v UK (Applications nos 26766/05 and 22228/06)* in December 2011 that convictions based on statements from witnesses who could not be cross-examined in court did not violate the applicants' rights under Article 6. It has been held that the right to examine a witness contained in Article 6 (3)(d) is based on the principle that, before a defendant can be convicted, all the evidence must normally be produced in his presence at a public hearing so that it can be challenged. Two requirements follow from that principle. First, there has to be a good reason for non-attendance of a witness. Second, a conviction based solely or decisively on the statement of an absent witness is generally considered to be incompatible with the requirements of fairness under Article 6.

For the second requirement the court took the same view as the Supreme Court did in *R v Horncastle* (above) that convictions can be secured on hearsay alone and found that the sole or decisive rule should not be applied in an inflexible way, ignoring the specificities of the particular legal system concerned. It was said that 'the question in each case is whether there are sufficient counterbalancing factors in place, including measures that permit a fair and proper assessment of the reliability of that evidence to take place'. In essence the court must balance the competing interests of the defence, the victim, and witnesses, and the public interest in the effective administration of justice. All previous decisions in relation to hearsay being based solely or to a decisive degree on hearsay evidence must be read in the context of the recent decision in *Al-Khawaja and Tahery v UK*.

Procedural issues

13.13   The relevant rules governing hearsay evidence are the Criminal Procedure Rules 2015, Part 20. The rules require written notice to be given to the other party and to the court when making applications under CJA 2003, ss 114(1)(d), 116 and 121. The prosecutor must serve notice not more than 28 days after the defendant pleads not guilty in the magistrates' court and the defendant must give notice as soon as reasonably practicable. Any objection to the introduction of hearsay must be made by notice as soon as reasonably practicable and in any event not more than 14 days after the service of the hearsay notice.

The court may dispense with the requirement to give notice, or allow notice to be given in a different form or orally, or shorten a time limit or extend it. A party entitled to receive a notice of hearsay evidence may waive his entitlement by informing the court and the party who would have given the notice (CPR 2015, r 20.2(5)).

Where there is no objection to the introduction of hearsay evidence, the court will treat the evidence as if it were admissible by agreement (CPR 2015, r 20.4). Where the application is opposed, the court may determine an application at a hearing in public or in private or without a hearing and must not determine the application unless the party who served the notice is present, or has had a reasonable opportunity to respond (CPR 2012, r 20.3(3)).

Problems connected with age

Under 10 years

13.14 A child below the age of 10 years is under the age of criminal responsibility and cannot be guilty of an offence. A juvenile, whether under the age of 10 or not, may be the subject of care proceedings brought under the Children Act 1989. Alternatively, the local authority may apply to the family proceedings court for a child safety order where a child has committed an act which would have constituted an offence if the child was 10 years or over. Care proceedings and applications for child safety orders are non-criminal applications normally brought by a local authority, whenever they believe that a court order is needed to ensure the juvenile's proper care and control. Such applications are made to a family court and are therefore outside the scope of this work.

Between 10 and 14 years

13.15 A juvenile within the age group of 10 to 13 inclusive is referred to as a child (CYPA 1933, s 107).

The Crime and Disorder Act 1998, s 34 abolished the rebuttable presumption in criminal law that a child below the age of 14 years could not be guilty of a criminal offence (*doli incapax*). The Court of Appeal clarified, in *R v T* [2008] EWCA Crim 815, that there is no authority for the existence of a separate defence from the presumption abolished by Parliament.

Between 14 and 18 years

13.16 A juvenile who has attained the age of 14 but is under 18 years is referred to as a young person (CYPA 1933, s 107 as amended). However, there are specific exceptions where 'young person' means someone who has attained the age of 14 but is under 17 years. These exceptions are referred to at the appropriate parts of the text.

16- and 17-year-olds

13.17   Although 16- and 17-year-olds are not referred to as a specific group in any legislation, they are set apart from other juveniles in a number of important respects. First, they may attend court on their own without a parent. Second, a number of orders and sentences can only be made in respect of 16- and 17-year-olds.

The term 'juvenile' usually refers to any young person between the ages of 10 and 17 years to describe anyone whose case would normally be heard in the Youth Court. Note however that for the purposes of arrest, detention and charge under the Police and Criminal Evidence Act 1984 the term refers to a person of 10 to 16 years.

Attaining adulthood

13.18   The Magistrates' Courts Act 1980, s 24(1), states 'where a person under the age of 18 years appears or is brought before a magistrates' court on an information charging him with an indictable offence he shall, subject to sections 51 and 51A of the CDA 1998 and to sections 24A and 24B of the MCA 1980 below, be tried summarily'.

The initial problem with a 17-year-old is which court he is to appear in or to be brought before. This is a decision which the prosecution must take. It is submitted that the advice given by Donaldson LJ in *R v Amersham Juvenile Court, ex parte Wilson* [1981] QB 969, is still pertinent (despite the main body of that judgment being disapproved of by the House of Lords in *Re Daley* [1983] 1 AC 347, HL). He suggested that, those who arrest and charge or lay an information against persons who are in the juvenile/adult borderline age group should take all reasonable steps to find out exactly when they will attain the age of 18. If they are to be brought or summoned to appear before a court for the first time on a date when they will have attained the age of 18, the court selected or specified in the summons should be an adult court. If they have not attained the age of 18, it should be a Youth Court.

If the juvenile does not personally appear before the court at the first or subsequent hearings until he is 18 then the hearing should take place before the adult magistrates' court. The Youth Court has no jurisdiction. CYPA 1963, s 29 does not help because that section only applies if the proceedings begin when the defendant is under 18. There is no power to remit the case to the adult court in these circumstances (*R v Uxbridge Youth Court ex parte Howard* [1998] 162 JP 327, DC). CDA 1998, s 47 which allows a Youth Court to remit to the adult court only applies where the defendant has already appeared before the Youth Court when under 18 and then subsequently attains that age. In practice magistrates in a Youth Court may declare that they are sitting instead as an adult court and start to hear the case against the 18-year-old. Where this happens it is important that the court makes sure that the public are given access to that case and it is made clear that the press restrictions for juveniles do not apply.

Any charge preferred after the juvenile has attained the age of 18 should be directed to a magistrates' court. In *R v Chelsea Justices, ex parte DPP* [1963] 3 All ER 657, a 16-year-old was charged with wounding before a Youth Court. The case was adjourned and during the adjournment he attained 17 (which at that time made him an adult). He was then charged with attempted murder arising out of the same facts. It was held that the latter charge had to be heard before an adult court and subsequently, of course, the then equivalent of the Crown Court, as the charge was one triable on indictment only.

During proceedings

13.19   The attainment of 18 years of age by juveniles during the course of proceedings raises the issue of the right to trial by jury. The question is whether mode of trial (now allocation) has already been determined before the defendant attained 18 years of age. This is a question which troubled the higher courts at one time but was somewhat clarified by the case of *Re Daley* [1983] 1 AC 347, a House of Lords judgment. This was followed by *R v Lewes Juvenile Court, ex parte Turner* (1985) 149 JP 186 and *R v Nottingham Justices, ex parte Taylor* [1992] QB 557. In the latter case, it is suggested that the advice of McNeal J in the *ex parte Turner* case should be followed. McNeal J suggested that where a person under the age of 18 pleads not guilty before a Youth Court, and the circumstances set out in the Magistrates' Courts Act 1980, s 24 (relating to committal (now sending) of grave crimes to the Crown Court) do not apply, then if the Youth Court is not, there and then, able to take evidence in the trial which is to follow, the register of the court should be marked 'remanded for summary trial' [and] that would be the decisive and determinate date on which, for the purposes of the section, the defendant appeared or was brought before the court.

The position was explained thus in the *Nottingham Justices* case. If before a juvenile becomes 18, he appears before the court, whether it is for the first time or on remand, and he is charged with an indictable only offence (eg robbery) or an offence triable either way (eg theft) and:

(a)   he pleads not guilty when the charge is put directly to him; and

(b)   the mode of his trial (now allocation) is discussed with him or his legal representative, decided upon and the decision thereupon recorded in clear terms;

then whether evidence is called on that occasion or not, his becoming 18 before trial can have no effect upon the already determined mode of trial (now allocation). In other words, he must be tried as though he was still 17 years of age. It is only if the mode of trial has not been determined that his becoming 18 years of age can have any material effect whatsoever. In a case where the juvenile is charged with an indictable only offence such as robbery and his case is adjourned without a determination as to mode of trial under MCA 1980, s 24 and he then attains the age of 18 his case must go to the Crown Court and committal (now sending) proceedings must begin (*R v Vale of Glamorgan Juvenile Justices, ex parte Beattie* (1986) 82 Cr App R 1).

The issue was considered in relation to an either way offence in the case of *R v West London Justices, ex parte Siley-Winditt* [2000] Crim LR 926. The defendant was charged with violent disorder and appeared in the Youth Court when he was 17. He pleaded not guilty and the charge was adjourned to a pre-trial review but no date was fixed for the trial. At the pre-trial review the defendant attained 18. The district judge held that the Youth Court had determined the mode of trial when the plea was entered and therefore the Youth Court had jurisdiction. He declined to allow the defendant to elect trial in the Crown Court. The High Court upheld this decision even though the register of the court which took the plea and adjourned had not been marked 'remanded for summary trial'.

Adult mode of trial for either way offences

13.20 It can be seen that if a young person charged with an either way offence in a court attains the age of 18 at any time before the court has determined allocation/ mode of trial and/or entered a plea the court must give him a right to jury trial. The procedure for determining adult mode of trial is set out in MCA 1980, ss 17A to 23 as amended by CJA 2003, Sch 3.

The first step is for the legal adviser to read, and if necessary explain, the charge to the now adult defendant. The second step is to embark upon the plea before venue procedure. The procedure can be found in MCA 1980, s 17A. The legal adviser will explain to the defendant that he is to be asked to indicate a plea to the court. It must be explained that if a guilty plea is intimated that plea will normally be accepted and the case will proceed on the basis of an admission of guilt. However, if the defendant fails to intimate that plea or intimates a wish to plead not guilty the court must embark on a full mode of trial procedure. The defendant must be made aware of the court's powers to commit for sentence in the event that they find their own powers are insufficient to deal with the seriousness of the offence.

The full mode of trial procedure is a determination as to whether the offence appears more suitable to be heard by magistrates or by the Crown Court. In order to facilitate this determination, the court shall hear representations first from the prosecutor and second the defendant, as to which venue is more appropriate. At this stage the prosecutor should be allowed to refer to any previous convictions. The court is required to consider:

(a)   whether the sentence which a magistrates' court would have the power to impose for the offence would be adequate; and

(b)   any representations made by the prosecutor or the accused (as above); and

(c)   shall have regard to any definitive allocation guidelines.

If the court considers the case more suitable to be heard in the Crown Court, the court must send the defendant to that court (MCA 1980, s 21).

Where the magistrates decide that the case is suitable to be heard in the magistrates' court, the 18-year-old must be told that:

(a)   it appears to the court more suitable for him to be tried summarily for the offence, and that he can consent either to be so tried or, if he wishes, to be tried by a jury; and

(b)   if he is tried and is convicted by the court he may be committed for sentence to the Crown Court under PCC(S)A 2000, s 3, if the convicting court is of the opinion that the offence or a combination of the offence and other offences associated with it was so serious that greater punishment should be inflicted for the offence than the court has power to impose.

The 18-year-old may then ask the magistrates for an indication of whether a custodial or non custodial sentence would be more likely to be imposed if he were to be tried summarily and plead guilty. The court is not obliged to give an indication, but if it indicates that a non custodial sentence is more likely, then following an indication of a guilty plea no court will generally be able to impose a custodial sentence for that offence (MCA 1980, s 20A(1)). If the defendant asks and is given an indication then the court should ask him whether he wishes to reconsider his earlier plea indication. If the adult defendant then states that he would plead guilty, the court will then begin to consider sentence. If he does not indicate a guilty plea at this stage then the adult must be asked if he consents to trial before the magistrates or if he wishes to elect to be tried by a judge and jury at the Crown Court. If he consents to summary trial the magistrates will proceed to hear the case. If he elects trial by jury the court must send the case to the Crown Court under CDA 1998, s 51.

The mode of trial procedures described above are also applicable to the 18-year-old charged with an offence of criminal damage under the Criminal Damage Act 1971, s 1 or aggravated taking of a motor vehicle under the Theft Act 1968, s 12A.

If the adult indicates a guilty plea or is found guilty after a summary trial then he cannot be committed to the Crown Court for sentence under PCC(S)A 2000, ss 3 or 4 unless it is clear that the value involved exceeds the relevant sum (£5,000). Furthermore, in respect of criminal damage offences, if the value involved is not clearly in excess of the relevant sum then the maximum sentence in the magistrates' court is a three-month custodial sentence (MCA 1980, s 17D(2)(a)). If the accused appears charged on the same occasion with two or more offences of criminal damage etc which constitute or form part of a series of offences of the same or a similar character, then it is the aggregate value which is relevant.

The 18-year-old in the Youth Court after a finding of guilt

13.21   When an 18-year-old consents to summary trial, after hearing evidence, the Youth Court may deal with the case to finality. Where evidence has been heard and the juvenile subsequently attains the age of 18, the court may proceed to a verdict.

If the court convicts the defendant but he attains the age of 18 before an order is made, then CYPA 1963, s 29 still applies. Section 29 states that: 'Where proceedings in respect of a young person are begun for an offence and he attains the age of 18 before the conclusion of the proceedings, the court may deal with the case and make any order which it could have made if he had not attained that age.' This means that the 18-year-old may remain subject to any relevant Youth Court order.

This section applies equally in the Crown Court as it does in the Youth Court. This leaves the Crown Court with an option to sentence a young person committed to it to any of the available Youth Court orders if he attains the age of 18 during the course of the proceedings.

The main difference between the sentencing powers of the Youth Court and those of an adult court in respect of a person under 21 years of age is that the Youth Court may sentence to a DTO for up to 24 months. An adult magistrates' court is restricted in passing of a detention order in a young offenders' institute to a six-month maximum per offence or a 12-month maximum for two or more either way offences.

Reporting restorations will apply until the young person reaches the age of 18, or until the order is otherwise lifted prior to the individual's eighteenth birthday. If a young person turns 18 during the proceedings, the reporting restriction will expire at the end of the proceedings (YJCEA 1999, s 45).

The importance of age on conviction and at the sentencing hearing

13.22   Some sentencing options only become open to the court when the offender before them has attained a certain age. For example, no juvenile under the age of 15 may be sentenced to a detention and training centre order, unless the court certifies that they are a persistent offender. Similar restrictions apply to requirements imposed on a youth rehabilitation order for intensive supervision and support; fostering; residence; and an unpaid work requirement in a youth rehabilitation order may only be imposed on a 16- or 17-year-old (see **Chapter 9** for details).

Care is particularly important where a detention and training order is contemplated. The statute is clear that the order is unavailable where 'a child or young person (that is to say, any person aged under 18) is *convicted* of an offence which is punishable with imprisonment in the case of a person aged 21 or over'. In *R v T (a juvenile)* [1979] Crim LR 588, a case involving a juvenile found guilty when 14 years old and subsequently committed to the Crown Court with a view to borstal training having attained the age of 15, the Crown Court held that the word 'conviction' should be construed as meaning the finding of guilt and not the date on which the case was finally disposed of. This point was reiterated in *R v Danga* [1992] QB 476 and *R v Starkey* [1994] Crim LR 380, CA, in connection with custodial sentences. These cases confirm that as a matter of statutory construction, for the purpose of sentence, the age of the offender was his age at the date of conviction or when the plea of guilty was made and accepted.

Although PCC(S)A 2000, s 9 gives a power to remit 18-year-olds to the adult court for sentence it is of little practical application. In *R v Cassidy* [2000] All ER (D) 1200, the defendant was 17 years old at the time of his conviction. He was not sentenced until he had attained the age of 18. The court held that a detention and training centre order was valid and would not be changed to detention in a young offenders' institute. It is worth noting the effect of CYPA 1963, s 29 outlined above. Consequently, the court and advocates representing young people must pay due regard to the statute under which the court proposes to impose a particular sentence so as to ensure that the young person has attained the relevant age at the relevant time. See also *Aldis v DPP* [2002] EWHC 403 (Admin).

In terms of the approach to sentencing where a defendant crosses a relevant age threshold (ie between the date of commission of the offence and the date of conviction), the Court of Appeal have said that the starting point was the sentence the defendant would have been likely to receive if he had been sentenced at the date of the commission of the offence: *R v Ghafoor* [2002] EWCA Crim 1857, CA.

This case was followed in *R v H* [2004] All ER (D) 143 (Mar), where a defendant of previous good character who pleaded guilty when he was 15 to two offences of robbery was given concurrent 12-month DTOs. These were replaced on appeal with an intensive supervision order because the defendant had been 14 years old when the offences were committed and could not at that date have been given a DTO as he was not a persistent offender. Whilst it may be considered a 'settled principle', for sentencing purposes, that the age at the date of offence should be considered as the starting point, the Court of Appeal further considered this point in *R v Bowker* [2007] EWCA Crim 1608 and concluded that there is a need for flexibility. The defendant's age was a powerful, but not the sole, determining factor. The sentencing regime might be that relevant to the age of the defendant at the date of conviction. Thus, it might be appropriate to impose a deterrent sentence on a defendant who became 18 before conviction. In that case, it was recognised that whilst CJA 2003, s 142 expressly approved deterrence as a purpose of sentence, that section did not apply to juveniles.

In *R v B* [2011] EWCA Crim 62, a sentence of two years' detention which had been imposed on a juvenile following his plea of guilty to inflicting grievous bodily harm with intent was reduced to 18 months taking into account the fact that he was just short of his eighteenth birthday at the time of the offence. *R v Bowker* [2007] and *R v Ghafoor* [2002] were considered and it was held appropriate as a starting point to consider the sentence that would have been imposed at the time of the commission of the offence as a powerful, but not a decisive factor. Further, the case of *R v Ghafoor* [2002] was considered in *R v Burns* [2013] All ER (D) 305 (Feb), where the court failed to take into account that at the time the two offences of possession of a class A drug were committed the defendant had been 17 and therefore the sentence was manifestly excessive. 30 months' detention was substituted with 21 months' detention. See also *R v S* [2008] All ER (D) 22 (Jun).

R v Robson [2006] EWCA Crim 1414, held that where an offender attains the age of 18 between committal for sentence under the 'dangerousness' provisions and appearance before the judge, the powers of the Crown Court are those that would be applicable to a 17-year-old. In particular, the youth dangerousness provisions still applied despite the fact that the defendant was 18 at the sentencing hearing.

In summary:

(a) The likely sentence the defendant would have received if he had been dealt with on the date of the offence is the starting point.

(b) The defendant's age at the date of conviction (ie guilty plea accepted by the court, or found guilty after trial) determines the type of sentence which can be imposed (subject to the words of the relevant statute). Thus, a young person who is 18 when convicted may be given a sentence of detention in a young offenders' institute, whereas a 17-year-old should be given a detention and training order.

(c) The defendant's age as at the date of conviction determines the sentencing regime which applies. A young person is therefore subject to the adult dangerousness provisions if he is 18 when convicted, even if he was 17 when the offence was committed. Similarly, the sentencing purposes which apply to adults, including the use of deterrent sentences may be relied on when sentencing a person who was 17 when the offence was committed but 18 or older when convicted.

(d) Section 29 of the Children and Young Persons Act 1963 allows a court to sentence any defendant who is 18 or older as if he had not attained that age provided that the proceedings began at a time when he was under 18.

These issues are addressed in section 5 of the *Overarching Principles – Sentencing Youths* and in section 6 of the *Sentencing Children and Young People* published by the Sentencing Council.

The Sentencing Council's Definitive Guideline *Sentencing Children and Young People* at paragraph 6.3 provides the following guidance:

'6.1 There will be occasions when an increase in the age of a child or young person will result in the maximum sentence on the date of the *finding of guilt* being greater than that available on the date on which the offence was *committed* (primarily turning 12, 15 or 18 years old).

6.2 In such situations the court should take as its starting point the sentence likely to have been imposed on the date at which the offence was committed. This includes young people who attain the age of 18 between the commission and the *finding of guilt* of the offence but when this occurs the purpose of sentencing adult offenders has to be taken into account, which is:

- the punishment of offenders;

- the reduction of crime (including its reduction by deterrence);

- the reform and rehabilitation of offenders;

- the protection of the public; and

- the making of reparation by offenders to persons affected by their offences.

6.3 When any significant age threshold is passed it will rarely be appropriate that a more severe sentence than the maximum that the court could have imposed at the time the offence was committed should be imposed. However, a sentence at or close to that maximum may be appropriate.'

Turning 18 before breach proceedings begin

The issues

13.23 Problems arise from the many statutes which provide that young people on youth community orders must be brought before the adult court for breach if they have attained 18 years of age by the first hearing. The issue is particularly acute where the provisions give the adult court power to deal with the case either as if it had just convicted the offender of the original offence or in some other way limit the court's sentencing powers to those available to it for sentencing youths. One common question is how the adult court can deal with the offender for an indictable only offence.

Where the provision reads that the defendant can be dealt with as if just convicted by the adult court, then MCA 1980, s 24(3) might help in that it allows the court to impose a fine of £1,000 or 'exercise the same powers as it could have exercised if he had been found guilty of an offence for which but for s 89(1) of the said Act of 2000 (PCC(S)A 2000), it could have sentenced him to a term not exceeding (a) the maximum term of imprisonment for the offence on conviction on indictment; or (b) six months, whichever is the less'. This would enable the adult court to impose any adult community order or lesser sentence, and where the conditions are satisfied for custody, detention in a young offender institution up to a maximum of six months for individual offences.

Re-sentencing powers

13.24 The Criminal Justice and Immigration Act 2008 contains at least seven revocation and re-sentencing provisions for YROs in Sch 2 (paras 6, 8, 11, 12, 16, 18 and 19). They all require the re-sentencing court to deal with the offender in any way the offender could have been dealt with as at the date of the original sentencing hearing when the YRO was imposed.

Where the offender has attained 18 years of age and is before the adult court, that court will generally be able to re-sentence in any way the Youth Court could have for that offence. This may include imposing a detention and training order of up to 24 months. It would also allow the adult court to sentence offences which are indictable only in the case of an adult. The Justices' Clerks' Society has issued guidance to this effect in relation to the interpretation of paragraph 6(2)(c) of Sch 2 to the Act. This guidance is produced at **Appendix K** with the kind permission of the Society. In this Guide that approach is extended, where possible, to the rest of the re-sentencing provisions in Sch 2 to the Act.

It is notable that where a Crown Court YRO includes a direction for any subsequent proceedings to be heard in a magistrates' court, the Youth or other magistrates' court is given a power to re-sentence for the offence. This is highly unusual and may explain the different form of words used in the various statutory provisions within Sch 2. In such circumstances the sentencing powers of the magistrates' courts are generally restricted to imposing any order which a Youth Court could have imposed, or committing the offender to the Crown Court for sentence.

One possible exception to the interpretation suggested by the Justices' Clerks' Society is where application is made by the responsible officer or offender for a youth rehabilitation order to be revoked under paragraph 11 of Sch 2 to the Act. A responsible officer could seek revocation of the order and re-sentence where, for example, it later transpires that the offender is not suitable after all for the requirements imposed. If the person is 18 years or older the application will have to be made to the adult court. The powers of re-sentence are specifically those of the 'appropriate court' which in this instance is defined as 'a magistrates' court (other than a 'Youth Court'). The offender still has to be sentenced as a juvenile so that the adult court can only impose a fine or discharge, or possibly, remit the case to the Youth Court (see PCC(S)A 2000, s 8(8)).

A second exception may arise where an adult court is proposing to amend a YRO by adding a requirement which requires consent (such as a drug treatment requirement) and the offender fails to express willingness to comply. The words used in Sch 2, paragraphs 13(4) to (6) and paragraph 16 (3) or (4) are similar in effect to those in paragraph 11.

More detail about the various courts' powers to deal with breaches/applications to amend or revoke are provided in **Chapter 11**.

Reviewing the grave crime mode of trial decision

13.25   The statutory powers to change a decision on allocation now only relate to adults. They are contained in MCA 1980, s 25(1) to (2D).

Where a guilty plea has been entered

13.26 The court does not have any power to disregard the plea and send the juvenile to the Crown Court for trial. This is the case even where the court has failed to consider grave crime mode of trial (allocation) either adequately or at all. In *R v Herefordshire Youth Court, ex parte J* (1998) 142 SJLB 150 the defendant appeared in the Youth Court charged with indecent assault on a girl aged three. The defendant pleaded guilty and the prosecutor outlined the facts. The solicitor for the defendant requested an adjournment for pre-sentence reports. The clerk then raised the issue of whether, as the offence was one to which PCC(S)A 2000, s 91 could apply, the court should consider grave crime mode of trial. Eventually, the magistrates purported to treat the guilty plea as void. The Divisional Court remitted the case to the justices (with a direction to sentence the juvenile) ruling that the entering of the guilty plea meant that mode of trial had been dealt with, and the court therefore had to sentence the defendant.

In *R (on the application of D) v Sheffield Youth Court* [2008] EWHC 601 (Admin) a juvenile was charged with eight counts of supplying class 'A' drugs and three of offering to supply class 'A' drugs. He appeared in an adult court jointly charged and entered guilty pleas. The case was remitted to the Youth Court where the Crown Prosecution Service asked the proceedings to be re-opened under MCA 1980, s 142 and declared a nullity as the adult court had failed to consider venue under MCA 1980, s 24(1). The juvenile appealed against the granting of that application. The High Court, whilst accepting that the adult court had a duty to consider s 24(1) before taking pleas, held that the failure to do so did not permit a reopening under MCA 1980, s 142.

General considerations

13.27 In either case, it is not necessary for there to be any new information or change in circumstances.

There is a long line of authorities establishing the principle that grave crime mode of trial can only be reviewed under MCA 1980, s 25, and that however desirable it might be for the court to have a general discretion to reopen mode of trial this is now a matter which requires legislation. Now that MCA 1980, s 25 only applies in the adult court, it remains to be seen whether there is any development in the case law on this subject.

In the case of *R v Newham Juvenile Court, ex parte F (a minor)* [1986] 3 All ER 17 it was suggested, *obiter* that there was a power to review mode of trial where there had been a change in circumstances or there were fresh considerations. The *dicta* has been discussed in many subsequent Divisional Court cases, although rarely followed. In *R v Newham* a 16-year-old appeared before the magistrates charged with robbery and possession of a firearm. The magistrates decided to proceed summarily. No plea was taken and the case was adjourned. The defendant then appeared before a differently constituted bench which purported to change the decision of the first bench and commit the defendant for trial at the Crown Court. It was found on appeal that the second bench of magistrates had in fact not taken into account any new material and therefore the appeal by the defence was dismissed. A recent example of a Divisional Court's decision that a magistrates' court cannot review an earlier mode of trial decision except through MCA 1980, s 25 is found in *R (on the application of W) v Warrington Magistrates' Court* [2009] EWHC 1538 (Admin). See **J.2** at **Appendix J** for a summary of the case.

Juveniles appearing alone in the adult court

13.28   Where a juvenile appears alone before the adult court and the court, having no reason to believe that he is a juvenile, proceeds with the case, it is not prevented from hearing and determining the matter if it subsequently becomes known to the court that the person is in fact a juvenile. The adult court's powers on a finding of guilt are limited by PCC(S)A 2000, s 8 to a discharge, a fine, or an order binding over the parent to exercise control over the juvenile. As noted above a referral order may also be made where the mandatory conditions apply.

However, where there is a real issue about a defendant's age the case should be adjourned for an age enquiry to be conducted under the Children and Young Persons Act 1933, s 99(1) (*R v Steed* (1990) 12 Cr App R (S) 230). In the recent case of *R (on the application of M) v Hammersmith Magistrates Court* (5 May 2017, unreported), DC, the process by which a juvenile's age had been determined by a magistrates' court was deemed unlawful as no proper inquiry of the juvenile's age had been conducted under the CYPA 1933, s 99. The juvenile was arrested for theft and attempted theft and claimed to be 16 years old, spoke little English and was of Algerian ethnicity. The police did not carry out an age assessment due to the 'non-availability of qualified social workers' but he was treated as a juvenile. He was interviewed under caution in the presence of a solicitor, appropriate adult and interpreter and gave no comment to all questions asked. He was charged with two offences of theft, one of attempted theft and one of possession of an identity card with intent. The juvenile said that prior to his arrival in England he had been at school in France and that if the case was adjourned his mother could provide evidence as to his age. The court expressed doubts about his age based only on a visual assessment and deemed him to be 18. There was no evidence from the police or a local authority and no *Merton* compliant assessment. His case was sent to the Crown Court. He was remanded into custody on the basis that there were substantial grounds for believing that he would fail to attend court and/or commit further offences. It was held that where the issue of age arises much more than a superficial observation of the juvenile in the dock is required (*R v L* [2013] EWCA Crim 991). The proper course of action is to make arrangements for an age assessment to be made and in the instant case the magistrates' actions were not appropriate.

The Children and Young Persons Act 1933, s 46(1), states that a joint charge against an adult and a juvenile 'shall' be heard by the adult court. Where the adult has absconded or cannot be traced, it would be inappropriate to bring a juvenile before the adult court to stand trial alone. In such circumstances the prosecution should consider removing the joint element from the charge to allow the juvenile to appear or be brought before the Youth Court. The practice for most adult courts when faced with a juvenile charged jointly with an adult, but appearing alone, is to remand the juvenile to the Youth Court. It is important to appreciate, however, that the wording of CYPA 1933, s 46(1) is clear and unambiguous and no court could be criticised for keeping the juvenile before the adult court until it reached a stage when it was empowered to remit or deal with the juvenile.

In *R v Doncaster Justices, ex parte Langfield* (1984) 149 JP 26, a juvenile jointly charged with adults failed to attend on the day upon which the co-accused were committed for trial to the Crown Court under the provisions of MCA 1980, s 6(2). He was subsequently brought to court and committed alone to join the co-accused in the Crown Court. On appeal against the validity of the transfer, the Divisional Court held that the decision to send for trial on indictment, taken under the provisions of MCA 1980, s 24, must be taken at a time when those jointly charged were together in court. Any subsequent committal proceedings need not necessarily be held in the presence of all the accused. (See also *R v Coventry City Magistrates' Courts, ex parte M* [1992] Crim LR 810.)

Other examples of restrictions on the courts, which depend upon the age of the offender, occur relatively infrequently. They include the Contempt of Court Act 1981, s 12, which provides a general power for magistrates to commit to prison for contempt of court. The statutory restriction on the imposition of a sentence of imprisonment or the committal to prison of a person under 21 years of age applies (*R v Selby Justices, ex parte Frame* [1992] QB 72) thereby making any such committal illegal. As a result, the court's powers to deal with contempt by a young person under the age of 18 years are extremely limited (*R v Byas* [1995] Crim LR 439, CA).

Another such restriction is that placed upon the court who may wish to make an order of detention in default of payment of a fine or confiscation order. Again, due to the statutory restrictions, such an order may only be made on persons over the age of 18 years (*R v Basid* [1996] Crim LR 67).

Guilty plea by post procedure

13.29 The Magistrates' Courts Act 1980, s 12 permits a defendant to enter a plea of guilty to minor summary offences without appearing before a court. This procedure is commonly used in road traffic cases although the MCA 1980, s 12 expressly excludes the use of the plea by post procedure in the Youth Court, unless the juvenile has attained the age of 16 years.

Furthermore, if a guilty plea by letter is received by the clerk of the court in pursuance of s 12, and the offender was a child or young person, then if the court proceeds without reason or belief that the defendant is in fact a juvenile, he is deemed to have been an adult for the purpose of those proceedings (CYPA 1933, s 46(1A)).

Many 16- and 17-year-olds are now dealt with by fixed penalty ticket without court proceedings. See HOC 7/1997.

Recklessness

13.30   There has been a change of emphasis in cases involving recklessness.

In the case of *R v Caldwell* [1982] AC 341, HL, Lord Diplock gave a model direction to juries setting down an objective test for recklessness in such crimes as criminal damage and reckless driving. A different subjective test was set down in the case of *R v Cunningham* [1957] 2 QB 396, CCA for crimes of specific intent such as the Offences Against the Person Act 1861, s 18.

In a more recent case of *DPP v A* [2000] All ER (D) 1247, two boys started a game in which they agreed to shoot at each other with air pistols. They wore cricket pads for protection and agreed to aim below the knee. A had suggested they wear crash helmets but none were available. During the game A fired a shot which hit his companion in the eye. A was charged with wounding his companion.

The question for the High Court was whether the prosecution had failed to prove beyond reasonable doubt that A had foreseen that his act of firing the air pistol would cause some physical harm. The court ruled that 'maliciously' for the purposes of s 20 of the Offences against the Person Act 1861 meant either actual intention or recklessness as to whether a particular type of harm might be done. It would be sufficient that only slight harm had been foreseen. In giving judgment the High Court applied the case of *R v Parmenter* [1991] 4 All ER 698 HL.

In *R v G and Another* [2004] 4 All ER 765, the House of Lords departed from *Caldwell*, saying that it made no allowance for a defendant's youth or lack of mental capacity. The court stated that applying an objective test for recklessness to a case of arson it was offensive to justice, and to the principle that a person should not be found guilty of a serious criminal offence unless he acted with the relevant *mens rea* (ie guilty intent).

In that case, the two defendants, aged 11 and 12 respectively, set fire to some newspaper and threw it under a wheelie bin believing it would burn out on the concrete floor of the yard. In fact, the bin caught fire and then set buildings alight causing £1m worth of damage. The House of Lords said that a defendant could not be culpable under the criminal law for doing something which risked injury to another or damaging property if, due to his age or understanding, he genuinely did not perceive the risk.

Chapter 14   Criminal behaviour orders, anti-social behaviour injunctions and youth anti-gang injunctions in the Youth Court

14.01   Part 2 of the Anti-Social Behaviour, Crime and Policing Act 2014 (ASBCPA 2014) brought into force criminal behaviour orders (CBO) which replaced anti-social behaviour orders (ASBO) on 20 October 2014. And, on 23 March 2015 the new anti-social behaviour injunction (ASBI) came into force replacing the civil anti-social behaviour order (ASBO) and anti-social behaviour injunction.

Criminal behaviour orders

14.02   A CBO is designed to tackle the most serious and persistent anti-social behaviour which has brought a person before a criminal court. It is available on conviction for any criminal offence by any criminal court; although in respect of juveniles under 18 the Youth Court is the only venue which can make a CBO. Although the proceedings in which the defendant is convicted are criminal, the proceedings in which a CBO is applied for are civil. The Youth Court may only make a CBO against a juvenile on application by the prosecution. The court cannot make a CBO of its own volition. The CPS must consult the Youth Offending Team (YOT) for its views before making an application for a CBO. As a CBO is ancillary to a sentence (or conditional discharge) imposed in criminal proceedings it follows that an order may not be combined with an absolute discharge nor may it be imposed at the same time as the court defers sentence.

The criteria

14.03   The court must be satisfied, beyond reasonable doubt, that the following conditions are fulfilled:

(a)   the defendant has engaged in behaviour that caused or was likely to cause harassment, alarm or distress to any person (ASBCPA 2014, s 22(3)); and

(b)   making the order will help in preventing the defendant from engaging in such behaviour (which causes or is likely to cause harassment, alarm or distress to any person) (ASBCPA 2014, s 22(4)).

What the prosecution must prove

14.04   The CPS must prove in relation to the first condition that the defendant has engaged in behaviour 'that caused or was likely to cause harassment, alarm or distress to any person'. It is not necessary to prove a connection between the criminal behaviour which led to the conviction and the harassment, alarm or distress for the CBO. However, harassment, alarm and distress must be proved to the criminal standard of proof, ie beyond reasonable doubt.

The second condition of the test for imposing a CBO is that the court must consider that making the order will help in preventing the offender from engaging in such behaviour. No standard of proof is set out in the legislation for this condition. It is suggested that (as with ASBOs) determination of this condition will be 'an exercise of judgement or evaluation' to be made by the court (*R (on the application of McCann) v Crown Court at Manchester* [2003] 1 AC 787, HL).

When assessing whether to make an order the court may take into account conduct occurring up to one year before the commencement day. Factors which might be considered are the nature of the conduct, frequency of conduct, duration and the impact on victims or a community, likelihood of repetition, previous convictions and responses to past sentences and anti-social behaviour interventions. If the offending is more serious, even if it has not been repeated, a CBO may still be appropriate. See **14.21** below for case of *Birmingham City Council v Pardoe* [2016] EWHC 3119 (QB).

The CPS may call upon evidence to show the court why an order would help to prevent future harassment, alarm or distress.

If both conditions are fulfilled the court may make a CBO which prohibits the defendant from doing anything specified in the order or requires him to anything described (see **14.09**).

Proceedings for a CBO are civil in nature and hearsay evidence is admissible. However, whether the defendant has engaged in behaviour that caused or was likely to cause harassment, alarm or distress to any person it must be proved on the criminal standard of proof (see **14.06**). The second part of the application as to whether making the order will help in preventing the defendant from engaging in such behaviour is an exercise of judgment.

Application for a criminal behaviour order

14.05   The prosecutor must serve a notice of intention to apply for such an order as soon as practicable (without waiting for the verdict) on the court officer, the defendant against whom the prosecutor wants the court to make the order, and any person on whom the order would be likely to have a significant adverse effect (CPR 2015, r 31.3(2)). The notice must be in the form set out in the Practice Direction and must:

(a)   summarise the relevant facts;

(b)   identify the evidence on which the prosecutor relies in support;

(c)   attach any written statement that the prosecutor has not already served; and

(d)   specify the order that the prosecutor wants the court to make (CPR 2015, r 31.3(3)).

The defendant must then serve written notice, identifying the evidence and attach any written statement that has not already been served, which he intends to rely on, on the court officer and the prosecutor as soon as practicable (without waiting for the verdict) (CPR 2015, r 31.3(4)).

In the case of *R v Asfi (Nasser)* [2016] EWCA Crim 1236 it was argued on appeal that a 10-year CBO was made without notice and made at the instigation of the judge and was too wide. It was held that the lack of notice did not breach the fairness requirements of the r 31 of the CPR 2015 but the terms of the CBO were amended and its duration of 10 years was varied to seven years.

The Rules require that a party who desires to give hearsay evidence at the hearing must serve a hearsay notice on the other party and the court not less than 21 days before the hearing. Such a notice must:

(a)   state that it is a hearsay notice;

(b)   identify the hearsay evidence;

(c)   identify the person who made the statement which is to be given in evidence; and

(d)   state why that person will not be called to give oral evidence (CPR 2015, r 31.6(1)).

Such a notice may deal with hearsay evidence of more than one witness.

Failure to comply with the notice requirement will not affect the admissibility of the evidence but the court will take this into account when considering the weight which is given to that evidence. The time limits set may be altered by the court or a justices' clerk either on application or of its own motion. Where the facts of the case demand it the defendant must be given adequate time to prepare. Justices are entitled to expect that if there were a need for an adjournment an application would be made.

Rule 31.7 applies where a party wants the court's permission to cross-examine a person who made a statement which another party wants to introduce as hearsay. This could be because the party wants to challenge the credibility or consistency of the person who made the statement (CPR 2015, r 31.8). The party who wants to cross-examine that person must:

(a)   apply in writing, with reasons, not more than seven days after service of the notice of hearsay evidence; and

(b)   serve the application on the court officer, the party who served the hearsay evidence notice, and every party on whom the hearsay evidence notice was served.

Even if the court refuses permission to allow cross-examination of the person who made a statement which another party wants to introduce as hearsay, the hearsay evidence is admissible in accordance with the Civil Evidence Act 1995 but the court must carefully decide what weight to attach to it as it cannot be tested by cross-examination.

The court must disregard any act of the defendant that he shows, presumably a legal burden on the balance of probabilities, was reasonable in the circumstances (CDA 1998, s 1(5)).

See also **13.11** to **13.13** for hearsay provisions.

The prosecution must consult the YOT for its views before making an application for a CBO (ASBCPA 2014, s 22(8).

Evidential matters

14.06   As stated above, the making of a CBO is an ancillary order as part of the sentencing act.

An application for an order (Pt 31 of the CPR 2015) on conviction may be supported by the facts of the offence for which the defendant has just been convicted, the defendant's previous convictions and any other evidence. Any other evidence would include evidence of other behaviour (causing harassment, alarm or distress) by the defendant which did not lead to a conviction.

The court may consider evidence led by the prosecution and evidence led by the defendant, regardless of whether the evidence would have been admissible in the proceedings in which the defendant was convicted. The standard of proof to show that the defendant has engaged in behaviour that caused or was likely to cause harassment, alarm or distress, is to the criminal standard. It is important for the prosecution to identify the facts which constitute behaviour which caused or was likely to cause harassment, alarm or distress. If the behaviour is not accepted it must be proved to the criminal standard by the prosecution (CEA 1968, s 11).

Where the defendant's previous convictions are probative to obtaining a CBO, they will be admissible. If a defendant does not admit the existence of the previous convictions, the prosecution will need to prove them and should follow the provisions of the Civil Evidence Act 1968, s 11.

No reference should be made to convictions that are spent without the consent of the court.

Court process

14.07 The Youth Court may only make a CBO against a juvenile on application by the prosecution. The court cannot make a CBO of its own volition.

The court should first decide the appropriate sentence and then decide whether to make a CBO, whether at the sentencing hearing or a later hearing.

Under the CPR 2015, r 31.2 the court must not make a CBO unless the defendant has had an opportunity to consider what order is proposed and why; the evidence in support; and an opportunity to make representations at a hearing (whether or not he in fact attends). This restriction does not apply to interim orders (see **14.08**).

The court may adjourn any proceedings on an application for a CBO even after sentencing the defendant. Where the court adjourns the application to be heard after sentence, an interim order may be considered and could be made if the court thinks it just to do so (see **14.08**).

If the defendant does not appear for any adjourned proceedings the court may:

(a) further adjourn the proceedings; or

(b) issue a warrant for the defendant's arrest; or

(c) hear the proceedings in the defendant's absence.

The court may not issue a warrant for the defendant's arrest unless it is satisfied that the defendant has had adequate notice of the time and place of the adjourned proceedings. Also, the court may not proceed to make the order in the defendant's absence unless it is satisfied that the defendant has not only had adequate notice of the time and place of the adjourned proceedings but been informed that if he does not appear for those proceedings the court may hear the proceedings in his absence.

Where the defendant is sentenced, the court has no power to remand him in custody or on bail (with or without conditions). Therefore, it might be advisable for the court to consider/make the order at the sentencing hearing.

Although there is no requirement that the full CBO be served personally on the defendant, good practice would suggest this happens when the defendant does not appear in person otherwise the defendant not being aware of the order would amount to a reasonable excuse for any breach.

Interim orders

14.08   Where a court adjourns the hearing of an application for a CBO, the court may make an interim order that lasts until the final hearing of the application or until further order, if the court thinks it just to do so (ASBCPA 2014, s 26).

Even where an interim order is deemed just, the court as a minimum should consider all the circumstances of the case, such as the nature, seriousness and frequency of the behaviour alleged against the defendant. The court should ascertain what persons require protection from him and whether they are vulnerable, and then decide whether the need to protect them is so immediate that an interim order is justified.

The court should bear in mind the case of *R v Lawson* [2008] EWCA Crim 416 (in relation to an ASBO), which stated that where there is a need to control an individual's behaviour post-conviction but prior to sentence, bail conditions should be preferred. Interim orders may, however, be useful in a situation where the substantive CBO hearing is adjourned to a date after sentence.

The prohibitions and requirements which may be imposed in an interim order are those which may be included in a final CBO (see **14.09**).

An interim order may also be varied or discharged on the application of either the prosecution or the defendant but shall, in any event, come to an end when the full application is determined.

An interim order must be served within seven days in order for it to take effect (CPR 2015, r 2(a)(ii)) and the police will need to be in a position to effect personal service and provide evidence of that, particularly if the defendant is alleged to have breached the interim order. The penalty for a breach is up to five years' imprisonment as with the final order in the case of a juvenile in the youth court the maximum penalty on conviction is a 24-month DTO or a fine not exceeding £1,000 (£250 if under the age of 14) or both. All youth court disposals are available except a conditional discharge.

Terms of the order

14.09   A court may attach any prohibitions or requirements to an order that are necessary for the purpose of protecting any person from further behaviour which causes or is likely to cause harassment, alarm or distress by the defendant (ASBCPA 2014, s 22(5)).

Prohibitions and requirements in a CBO must, so far as practicable, be such as to avoid any interference with the times, if any, at which the child or young person normally works or attends school or any other educational establishment; and any conflict with the requirements of any other court order or injunction to which the child or young person may be subject (ASBCPA 2014, s 22(9)).

The principles supporting prohibitions on ASBOs will be relevant as to whether a prohibition can be placed on a CBO.

The terms must be proportionate to the risk and must be precise and comprehensible. Prohibition from entering a specific area, from associating with named individuals and from carrying or using a mobile phone which was not registered in the defendant's name were deemed to be necessary as the ASBOs were targeted at the nuisance, fear and intimidation that were conducive and preparatory to open drug-dealing (*R v Barclay and other appeals* [2011] EWCA Crim 32).

In *R (on the application of B) v Greenwich Magistrates'* Court [2008] EWHC 2882 (Admin), it was held that prohibition of wearing any article with a hood achieved the purpose of reducing 'swagger, menace, and fear of anti-social behaviour' was a clear, necessary and proportionate condition.

Deciding what prohibitions are necessary involves the exercise of judicial discretion and judgment and, in view of the Human Rights Act 1998, the court must act fairly and proportionately. *Lonergan v Lewes Crown Court* [2005] EWHC 457 (Admin), held that although a curfew prohibition in an ASBO is not unlawful, a curfew of two years in the life of a teenager is a considerable restriction of freedom and a shorter curfew could be proper. The test must always be what is necessary to deal with the particular anti-social behaviour of the defendant and what is proportionate in the circumstances. An ASBO may be unnecessary where a sentence has been imposed with stringent requirements, such as in *R (on the application of F) v Bolton Crown Court* [2009] EWHC 240 (Admin), where a two-year supervision order together with a curfew was imposed on a juvenile.

In *R v H* [2006] EWCA Crim 255, an anti-social behaviour order imposed on a 15-year-old was amended, where the effect of its terms would have been that, upon release from custody, his family would have had to move if he were to return home, or he would have had to find alternative accommodation outside the family home.

Courts must be vigilant to ensure that orders are clear, unequivocal and enforceable: *R v McGrath* [2005] EWCA Crim 353. In this case, the defendant was prohibited from entering any car park within three counties, trespassing on any land belonging to any person whether legal or natural, and possessing in public any window hammer, screwdriver, torch or any tool or implement that could be used for breaking into motor vehicles. These prohibitions were determined as being too wide; as an example, the phrase 'tool or implement' was difficult to determine and the prohibition on entering car parks would prohibit the defendant from accompanying someone to a supermarket for the purpose of food shopping.

R v Simsek [2015] EWCA 1268, concerned the variation of a CBO to an ASBO with only the first prohibition. The second condition, which concerned the prohibition on possession of drugs paraphernalia, was not reinstated, as the prohibition was less specific and precise than that which was found to be unnecessary in *R v Briggs* [2009] EWCA Crim 1477. The third (and final) prohibition, which prohibited the possession of herbal substances, was also not reinstated in the ASBO. The scope of this prohibition exposed the applicant to breach proceedings for being in possession of a wide range of items which are lawful and which bear no obvious relationship to the anti-social behaviour that formed the subject of the indictment. The final part of this prohibition concerning being in possession of any self-seal bags was too wide.

In *R v Browne-Morgan* [2016] EWCA Crim 1903, the defendant appealed against the imposition and terms of a CBO following his conviction for three counts of possession with intent to supply. The CBO prohibited the defendant from entering certain areas, from being with seven named associates, and from carrying a knife or bladed article in a public place. The court considered the appropriateness of prohibitions imposed and found upon consideration of the facts that the required standard to impose the order had been met and that the prohibitions imposed would in fact prevent the behaviour but amended the CBO in relation to the geographical exclusions for Southwark and was replaced with the following prohibition: the defendant must not 'congregate in a public place in a group of two or more persons in a manner causing or likely to cause any person to fear for their safety'.

The case of *R v Janes (John)* [2016] EWCA Crim 676 the defendant appealed on the grounds that the imposition of a 10-year CBO (prohibiting him from touting for business) was wrong in principle for a 'one off' offence against a single victim and against a background of him having worked in his job as a self-employed gardener for over 20 years without similar offending, and for the particular victim for a number of years. There was also a suggestion that the order would prevent him from working to provide for himself and his family in his normal occupation which infringed his rights under Article 8 of the European Convention on Human Rights. The appeal court commented that a precondition for the making of an order is not that it is 'necessary' to do so as under the former statutory provision, but rather that the court considers that the order will 'help in preventing the offender engaging in such behaviour', ie behaviour that caused or was likely to cause harassment, alarm or distress to any person and therefore the section does not require proof of a sustained course of conduct, although in the present case there were a series of dishonest demands made of this one victim over a relatively short period of time. Further the court said that although the defendant did not pursue the Article 8 point, even if that article was engaged in this case, an order of an appropriate jurisdiction would not normally fall foul of Article 8. However, the appeal court did find that a ten-year order was excessive and reduced this to three years.

Unlike an ASBO a CBO may include positive requirements that assist in preventing the offender from engaging in behaviour that could cause harassment, alarm and distress in the future. Such requirements could include attendance at a course to educate offenders on alcohol and its effects.

In *DPP v Bulmer* [2015] EWHC 2323 (Admin) the DPP appealed by way of case stated in respect of the district judge's decision. The district judge refused to make a CBO because the judge believed an order would not prevent the defendant's anti-social behaviour, partly because the proposed order did not give the defendant assistance with her chronic alcoholism. The High Court discussed the power to make CBOs under the s 22 of the Anti-Social Behaviour, Crime and Policing Act 2014, focusing on s 22(4) the second condition required before making a CBO: 'that the court considers that making the order will help in preventing the offender form engaging in such behaviour'. The High Court outlined the following considerations:

(a)　Section 22(4) of the 2014 Act does not expressly impose any burden of proof upon the prosecution. While the court hearing an application for a CBO should proceed with a proper degree of caution and circumspection because such orders are not lightly to be imposed, satisfaction to the criminal standard is not required in what is an evaluative exercise.

(b)　Whether the condition in s 22(4) of the 2014 Act has been met is not a matter of 'pure discretion'. Unless, however, the court hearing an appeal concludes that the judge has plainly erred in some way, either in his assessment of the facts or in applying the wrong test or leaving out of account matters which he was required to take into account, it should not interfere with his conclusion.

(c)　There has been no change in the emphasis of the legislation from 'necessity and protection' to 'help and prevention'.

(d)　The guidance given in decisions of the appellate courts on ASBOs is of relevance when considering whether to make a CBO.

(e)　In circumstances in which the evidence shows that a positive requirement would help prevent a person from engaging in anti-social conduct, the absence of such a requirement is a factor that can be taken into account in deciding whether to refuse to make an order. But it is impermissible to regard the absence of such a requirement as dispositive.

(f)　The fact that a person has not responded to orders and other disposals in the past is a relevant factor but is not in itself a reason for deciding not to make an order. It may indeed be a reason for varying the order or imposing a new one with different prohibitions and, if applicable, requirements.

(g)　Where a person is subject to an ASBO or a CBO, the judge considering whether to vary the order or to make a new order is entitled to take into account, as part of his evaluative exercise, the power of the police to arrest the person subject to the order where they have reasonable grounds to suspect that the person had committed the offence of breaching the order, or is about to commit the offence. However, the ordinary power of the police to arrest on reasonable suspicion may be insufficient to provide pre-emptive protection from a person with a history of anti-social behaviour to those who are or are likely to be affected by the behaviour.

This case demonstrates that the wording of s 22(4) of the ASBCPA 2014 does not mean that, where a defendant has a problem with alcohol or drugs that he will be totally unresponsive to an order and where it is not possible for the underlying cause of the behaviour to be tackled by a positive requirement, the condition in s 22(4) of the 2014 Act is not met. It was found that the judge erred by focusing on these elements.

Where an order includes a requirement, it must specify the person who is to be responsible for supervising compliance with that requirement. The person may be an individual or an organisation.

Before including a requirement, the court must receive evidence about its suitability and enforceability from the person to be specified in the order, or a person representing the organisation to be specified in the order.

The court must also consider the compatibility of the requirements and try to ensure the requirements of a CBO are not duplicated in the terms of any community or suspended sentence imposed by the court. There may be circumstances where it would be more helpful in terms of preventing criminal behaviour to have the requirements as part of a CBO, rather than a community order or suspended sentence.

In *DPP v T* [2006] All ER (D) 41 (Apr), it was held that where an ASBO lacked sufficient clarity it did not render the order invalid and its broad terms could not be raised as a defence in subsequent breach proceedings, although such vagueness could provide a reasonable excuse for non-compliance.

An order may be challenged on the ground that it is so vague that the respondent could have no certainty as to whether or not his actions would breach it (*R (on the application of M) v Sheffield Magistrates and Sheffield City Council* [2004] EWHC 1051 (Admin)).

Therefore, prohibitions and requirements in the order must be enforceable by allowing a breach to be readily identified and capable of being proved (*R v W* [2006] EWCA Crim 686). Therefore, general prohibitions and requirements should not be imposed, but provide sufficient clarity to identify the prohibition and requirement.

A CBO should not be used as a mechanism to increase the maximum sentence of imprisonment that is available for a particular offence. The purpose of a CBO is not to punish the defendant but to prevent harassment, alarm or distress, by enabling action to be taken before such behaviour takes place. A court should therefore normally refrain from imposing an order that prohibits a defendant from committing a specified criminal offence where the sentence which could be passed following conviction for the offence would be a sufficient deterrent (*R v Boness* [2005] EWCA Crim 2395).

In terms of the general principles, the whole of the procedure should take place in the presence of the defendant; to whom it must be explained; the findings of fact giving rise to the making of the order must be recorded (*R v W* [2006] EWCA Crim 686); the exact terms of the order must be pronounced in open court; and the written order must accurately reflect the order as pronounced (*R v P (Shane Tony)* [2004] EWCA

Crim 287). The terms of the order must be precise so that the defendant knows exactly what he is prohibited from doing.

Length of the order

14.10   The minimum period for a CBO is one year. The maximum is three years, but the order should only be made for as long as the court considers necessary for the protection of the community from the defendant.

A CBO comes into effect on the day it is made, save where the defendant is subject to another CBO when the new order may be made so that it takes effect on the day on which the previous order ceases to have effect.

The order must specify the period for which it has effect and may specify periods for which particular prohibitions or requirements have effect.

In the case of a CBO made before the juvenile has reached the age of 18, the order period must be a fixed period of:

(a)   not less than one year; and

(b)   not more than three years.

In the case of a CBO made after the defendant has reached the age of 18, the order period must be:

(a)   a fixed period of not less than two years; or

(b)   an indefinite period or until further order.

Either the prosecution or the defendant may apply by complaint to the court which made the order for its variation or discharge: see **14.11** below.

Variation and discharge

14.11   Applications for variation and discharge of an order on conviction may be made under s 27 of the Anti-Social Behaviour, Crime and Policing Act 2014.

A CBO (including an interim order) may be varied or discharged by the court which made it on the application of the defendant or the prosecution.

In the case of a CBO made by a magistrates' court it includes any magistrates' court acting in the same local justice area as the court that made the order.

An application for variation or discharge will be appropriate where there has been a change in the circumstances which may lead the court to think the prohibition and/or requirements can be lifted.

The procedure to follow when seeking to vary or revoke a behaviour order is set out in the Criminal Procedure Rules 2015, r 31.5. No forms for the application are specified. The application is generally made by letter setting out the variation sought and enclosing the evidence relied upon.

The prosecution must serve notice in writing on the court officer, the defendant and any other person on whom the court directed the application to be served setting out the evidence and attaching any written statement that has not already been served (CPR 2015, r 31.5(3)).

The court officer must serve the application on any person, if the court so directs; and give notice of any hearing to the applicant, and any person required to be served, by CPR 2015, r 31.5(6) or by the court.

The court must not dismiss an application under this rule unless the applicant has had an opportunity to make representations at a hearing (whether or not the applicant in fact attends); and the court must not allow an application under unless everyone required to be served has had at least 14 days in which to make representations, including representations about whether there should be a hearing (CPR 2015, r 31.5(5)).

Courts have a discretion to hear an application to vary an order in the absence of the defendant. However, to achieve a fair hearing both parties should have a proper opportunity of being heard. A court considering whether to adjourn an application would need to be careful to distinguish genuine reason for the absence of the defendant. It would only be appropriate to proceed if the reasons put forward for absence were spurious or designed to frustrate the process.

If an application by the defendant is dismissed, the defendant may make no further application without the consent of the court which made the order or the agreement of the prosecution.

If an application by the prosecution is dismissed, the prosecution may make no further application without the consent of the court which made the order or the agreement of the defendant.

The power to vary the order includes extending the term of the order or including additional prohibitions or requirements in the order. In *Leeds City Council v RG* [2007] EWHC 1612 (Admin), the court held that there is a power to extend an ASBO by way of variation. However, in such circumstances the court should examine closely why they are being asked to do so rather than make a new order. There will have to be cogent evidence adduced before the court is willing to conclude that it is necessary to extend the terms of the order and this may include evidence of further anti-social acts, but that is not necessarily so. www.justice.gov.uk/courts/procedure-rules/criminal/rulesmenu.

Review of CBOs

14.12 When an order is made in respect of a juvenile there is a requirement for an annual review where the offender is a youth (ASBCPA 2014, s 28).

The review must include consideration of:

(a) the extent to which the juvenile has complied with his order;

(b) the adequacy of any support available to help him to comply with the order; and

(c) anything else relevant to the question of whether an application should be made to vary or discharge the order.

The responsibility for carrying out the review will fall to the police with a requirement to act in co-operation with the local authority and any other person or body (such as YOT, educational establishments or other organisations who have been working with the juvenile (ASBCPA 2014, s 29)). The CPS may be asked to provide advice where, following a review, it is proposed that a CBO is varied or discharged. In such circumstances prosecutors may be asked to advice on new prohibitions and/or requirements and whether they are legally enforceable.

Breach of CBOs and sentence

14.13 A person who without reasonable excuse does anything which is prohibited or fails to do anything which is required by a CBO will commit a criminal offence. Legal representation will be available through the magistrates' court (ASBCPA 2014, s 30(1)).

Breach of the CBO will be prosecuted by the CPS and the prosecutor will need to show that the order was lawfully made, state the terms of the order and that the defendant's behaviour amounted to a breach of those terms.

It is for the prosecutor to prove that the defendant was the person made subject of the CBO in question, although the offence of breaching the order does not require proof of a mental element.

The defence may raise the defence of reasonable excuse and, if the evidential burden is satisfied, it is for the prosecution to prove, to the criminal standard, that the defendant had no reasonable excuse (*R v Nicholson* [2006] EWCA Crim 1518) (in relation to an ASBO). *JB v DPP* [2012] EWHC 72 (Admin) (in relation to an ASBO) provides that what constitutes a reasonable excuse 'is essentially a question which is dependant on the circumstances of each case in the context of the offence to which it relates' and where the issue of reasonable excuse arises a defendant can raise his state of mind at the time of the breach, as it will usually be relevant to the issue of reasonable excuse.

If, for example, a defendant fails to comply with a requirement of his CBO, the existence of a sick note that specifically excuses him from the obligation to comply is evidence of a reasonable excuse. If an investigator has any reason to doubt the authenticity or provenance of the note further enquiries should be made. Criminal Practice Directions issued on 23 July 2014 include a direction about medical certificates being submitted by defendants in criminal proceedings as justification for not answering bail. The Practice Direction may be of assistance with regard to failure to attend in respect of a requirement of a CBO.

A mistake of fact may only provide a defence if it amounts to a reasonable excuse for what the defendant did. Questions about the validity of the order cannot be raised as a defence in proceedings for its breach. However, where the prohibition that is being enforced is too vague to be enforceable, a defence of reasonable excuse may be raised (*DPP v T* [2006] All ER (D) 41 (Apr)) (in relation to an ASBO).

The absence of a term from the final CBO would not in itself affect the gravity of a breach of an interim CBO and the punishment would depend on all the circumstances including the nature and flagrancy of the breach. In *Parker v DPP* [2005] All ER (D) 98 (Jun) (in relation to an ASBO), a juvenile received a six-month DTO for breaching a condition of an interim ASBO, by associating with another young person, which did not form part of the final ASBO when made.

In sentencing a breach, the court should have regard to the nature and seriousness of the behaviour that constituted a breach, and whether that behaviour caused or could have caused harassment, alarm or distress to another person. In *R v Lamb* [2005] EWCA Crim 2487 (in relation to an ASBO), the Appeal Court drew a distinction between breaches that involved no anti-social behaviour but constituted breach, for example by the defendant entering a prohibited zone, and breaches that did not involve such behaviour but were triggered by further criminal offending.

In the Youth Court the court must of course have regard to the welfare of the juvenile, the need to prevent further offences and the seriousness of any breach before it considers its sentence. Indeed, offences of breach are dealt with following procedures in place for any criminal offence committed by a juvenile; as a consequence the CPS will normally make an assessment of the seriousness of the breach and of the juvenile's offending history. A youth caution may be deemed appropriate.

The CPS legal guidance on youth offenders states that youth cautions are intended to provide a proportionate and effective response to offending behaviour and can be used for any offence providing the statutory criteria are satisfied. Offence seriousness is determined by reference to the ACPO Gravity Matrix, which sets out the most prevalent offences, and provides them with a score of 1, 2, 3 or 4. The score may be raised or lowered by one level according to aggravating and mitigating factors which are set out in the Matrix.

The Gravity Matrix score for breach of a CBO without any aggravating factors is 3 provided the breach was not a flagrant one. Where the breach was flagrant, then the expectation would be to charge, unless there were some very unusual circumstances. Where a breach is a flagrant one, then the offender is likely to be charged unless there are some very unusual circumstances.

Breach proceedings for children or young people will be dealt with in the youth court.

The breach of a CBO is a criminal offence punishable in the adult court by a fine (maximum level 5) or imprisonment up to six months and on indictment up to five years' imprisonment. Consequently it is open to the Youth Court to impose up to a 24-month DTO. However, a fine cannot exceed £1,000 for a juvenile (£250 if under the age of 14) (ASBCPA 2014, s 30(2)).

Note that it is not open to the court to impose a conditional discharge for a breach offence and the sentence will depend on the nature of the breach; the seriousness of the breach; the reason the order was made; and whether it is the first breach or a continued breach of the order.

Appeal

14.14 A defendant has a right of appeal against a CBO made by a magistrates' court by virtue of s 108 of the Magistrates' Courts Act 1980, as 'sentence' includes any order made on conviction, (MCA 1980, s 108(3)).

Where the order is made by the Crown Court the defendant's right of appeal is the Court of Appeal Criminal Division, (Criminal Appeal Act 1968, s 9). An appeal is appropriate where the defendant seeks to argue that the order should not have been made, or the prohibitions/requirements are wrong. If the defendant seeks to argue that circumstances have changed, then an application to vary or discharge the order may be more appropriate. See **14.11** above.

Anti-social behaviour injunctions

14.15 An anti-social behaviour injunction (ASBI) is a civil power that can be applied for in respect of anyone aged 10 and above. It is designed to offer protection to victims and communities by preventing anti-social behaviour, committed by individuals, from continuing and/or escalating.

Anti-social behaviour is defined within the legislation. It is conduct:

(a)   that has caused, or is likely to cause, harassment, alarm or distress to any person (non-housing related);

(b)   capable of causing nuisance or annoyance to a person in relation to that person's occupation of residential premises, (housing-related); or

(c)   capable of causing housing related nuisance or annoyance to any person (non-housing related) (ASBCPA 2014, s 2(1)).

Despite an ASBI being a civil sanction, before making an application to the court, all other approaches should have been considered as a court injunction should be a last resort.

The criteria

14.16   An injunction can be granted against a person aged 10 or over if two conditions are met:

(a)   the court is satisfied on the balance of probabilities that the person has engaged or threatens to engage in anti-social behaviour; and

(b)   the court considers it just and convenient to grant the injunction to prevent the person engaging in anti-social behaviour (ASBCPA 2014, s 1).

The applicant

14.17   A number of agencies are entitled to make the application. They include:

(a)   a local authority;

(b)   a housing provider;

(c)   a chief officer of police for a police area;

(d)   the chief constable of the British Transport Police Force;

(e)   Transport for London;

(f)   the Environment Agency;

(g)   the Natural Resources Body for Wales;

(h)   NHS Business Services Authority (ASBCPA 2014, s 5).

The fact that an ASBI can be applied for by a range of agencies means it can be used in a wider range of circumstances than previously, such as if there is anti-social behaviour against hospital staff, shop staff and nightmare neighbours in the private rented sector.

What the applicant must prove

14.18   For anti-social behaviour in a non-housing related context the test is conduct that has caused, or is likely to cause, harassment, alarm or distress to any person. This will apply, for example, where the anti-social behaviour has occurred in a public place, such as a town or city centre, shopping mall, or local park, and where the behaviour does not affect the housing management functions of a social landlord or people in their homes.

For anti-social behaviour in a housing context the nuisance or annoyance test will apply, that is, where the conduct is capable of causing nuisance or annoyance to a person in relation to that person's occupation of residential premises or the conduct is capable of causing housing-related nuisance or annoyance to any person. Only social landlords, local councils or the police will be able to apply for an injunction under these provisions in the legislation. In the case of social landlords only, 'housing-related' means directly or indirectly relating to their housing management function.

The injunction can be applied for by the police, local councils and social landlords against perpetrators in social housing, the private-rented sector and owner-occupiers. This means that it can be used against perpetrators who are not even tenants of the social landlord who is applying for the order.

The injunction can also be used in situations where the perpetrator has allowed another person to engage in anti-social behaviour, as opposed to actively engaging in such behaviour themselves. For example, in a case where another person, such as a visitor or lodger, is or has been behaving anti-socially, the injunction could be used against the problem visitor, lodger or owner if applicable. An agency seeking to apply for the injunction must produce evidence (to the civil standard of proof, that is, 'on the balance of probabilities') and satisfy the court that it is both 'just and convenient' to grant the order.

The court will need to examine each prohibition and requirement proposed by the applicant and the applicant will need to be able to prove how each prohibition/ requirement will help stop or prevent the respondent from engaging in or threatening to engage in anti-social behaviour in the future.

The application

14.19 Applications for injunctions against respondents under the age of 18 are made to the youth court.

Before making an application to the court, all other approaches should have been considered as a court injunction should be a last resort.

An application may be made with or without notice to the respondent. Before making an application, the applicant must consult the YOT about the application and inform any other body or individual appropriate to the application (ASBCPA 2014, s 14).

The duty to consult the YOT does not apply to an ex parte application but where the court adjourns a without-notice application, before the date of the first on-notice hearing, the applicant must consult the local youth offending team about the application, if the respondent will be aged under 18 on that date and inform any other body or individual the applicant thinks appropriate of the application (ASBCPA 2014, s 14(2)).

Application without notice

14.20   An application for an injunction under s 1 of the Anti-Social Behaviour, Crime and Policing Act 2014 (ASBCPA 2014) may be made without notice being given to the respondent.

If an application is made without notice the court must either:

(a)   adjourn the proceedings and grant an interim injunction (see **14.23** below); or

(b)   adjourn the proceedings without granting an interim injunction; or

(c)   dismiss the application.

Where an interim injunction without notice is granted by the court it would be advisable to serve the injunction personally on the respondent, otherwise the respondent not being aware of the injunction would amount to a reasonable excuse for any breach.

Civil evidence

14.21   An ASBI is a civil application and the civil standard of proof ('balance of probabilities') will apply. In these proceedings, the Magistrates' Courts (Hearsay Evidence in Civil Proceedings) Rules 1999 and the Civil Evidence Act 1995 (CEA 1995) will apply. The main effect is to allow for a statement made otherwise than a person giving oral evidence to be tendered as evidence of the matters stated (CEA 1991, s 1). The Rules require that a party who desires to give hearsay evidence at the hearing must serve a hearsay notice on the other party and the court not less than 21 days before the hearing. See **13.11** to **13.13** for hearsay provisions.

Failure to comply with the notice requirement will not affect the admissibility of the evidence but the court will take this into account when considering the weight which is given to that evidence. The time limits set may be altered by the court or a justices' clerk either on application or of its own motion. Where the facts of the case demand it the respondent must be given adequate time to prepare and to meet those allegations. Justices are entitled to expect that if there were a need for an adjournment an application would be made.

In the case of *Birmingham City Council v Pardoe* [2016] EWHC 3119 (QB) the defendant appealed against the making of an ASBI on many grounds, in particular, a contention that the effect of s 21(7) of the ASBCPA 2014 is that the court is '...precluded from taking into account that conduct relied on by the claimant prior to 23 September 2014...'. The Local Authority had pleaded 49 specific allegations against one or more of the defendants and some of those allegations related to matters occurring many years ago. The High Court said the court was entitled to take into account previous behaviour and made the following observations:

(a)   Where an application for an injunction under Pt 1 of the 2014 Act is based on an allegation of actual anti-social behaviour, as opposed to an allegation of threatened anti-social behaviour, the applicant authority must satisfy the court of the first condition under s 1(2) by proving on the balance of probabilities that the respondent has engaged in anti-social behaviour which occurred after 23 September 2014. If such behaviour is not proved, the court has no jurisdiction to grant an injunction.

(b) Evidence of the respondent's conduct prior to 23 September 2014 cannot in itself satisfy the first condition. But (assuming there is no other bar to its admissibility) such evidence may be taken into account by the court at the first stage, where it is relevant (whether as similar fact evidence, or to rebut a defence, or in any other way) to the issue of whether the respondent engaged in anti-social behaviour after 23 September 2014.

(c) Evidence of the respondent's conduct prior to 23 September 2014 (again assuming there is no other bar to its admissibility) may also be taken into account by the court at the second stage, when considering whether it is just and convenient to grant an injunction.

The High Court rejected the submission that s 21(7) has the effect of preventing the court from taking into account evidence of the respondent's conduct prior to 23 September 2014.

Hearsay evidence is admissible in accordance with the Civil Evidence Act 1995 but the court must carefully decide what weight to attach to it as it cannot be tested by cross-examination. The court must disregard any act of the respondent that he shows, presumably a legal burden on the balance of probabilities, was reasonable in the circumstances (CDA 1998, s 1(5)).

Court process

14.22   For those under the age of 18 applications must be made to the youth court.

Where the application involves more than one respondent (some of whom are aged 18 or over) but at least one of those is a youth (aged under 18), the applicant may apply to the youth court to hear the cases together as a 'joint hearing'. The youth court must be satisfied that it is in the interest of justice to hear the 'mixed-aged' case together.

The court can only grant an injunction on application; it cannot do so of its own volition.

Where any application is adjourned the court has power to remand the respondent. A juvenile may only be remanded on medical grounds.

Interim injunctions

14.23   Where the court adjourns the hearing of an application (whether made with notice or without) for an injunction the court may grant an injunction lasting until the final hearing of the application or until further order if the court thinks it just to do so (ASBCPA 2014, s 7).

Where an injunction is granted ex parte the respondent cannot be required to participate in particular activities and the injunction should be served on the respondent personally otherwise the respondent not being aware of the injunction would amount to a reasonable excuse for any breach.

The court has the same powers (including powers of arrest under ASBCPA 2014, s 4) whether or not the injunction is an interim injunction.

Terms of the injunction

14.24   An injunction may prohibit the respondent from doing anything described in the injunction and/or require the respondent to do anything described in the injunction (ASBCPA 2014, s 1(4)) and any prohibitions and/or requirements must, so far as practicable, avoid any interference with times a respondent would normally work, attend school or other educational establishment and any conflict with any other court order (ASBCPA 2014, s 1(5)).

If the injunction includes a requirement, it must specify the individual or organisation that is responsible for supervising compliance with that requirement and the court must hear from them about both the suitability and enforceability of a requirement before including it in the injunction. Where there are two or more requirements the court must consider their suitability with each other.

The inclusion of positive requirements is new in comparison to the old Injunction to prevent nuisance and annoyance, employed by landlords. To include a positive requirement within the terms of an injunction, such as attendance on a drugs rehabilitation course, the agency asking for it must believe it is necessary; have the resource to make it happen; and have a named individual or organisation who will ensure compliance with this requirement. In practice, it might prove difficult to find people who will take on this management as it means they have a duty to promote compliance with the order and a duty to tell the agency that applied for the injunction if it has been breached.

For all injunctions, there is a requirement that the respondent keeps in touch with the person responsible for supervising compliance with it and notifies that person of any change of address.

Power of arrest

14.25   The court may attach a power of arrest to any prohibition or requirement.

Power of arrest may only be attached if the court thinks that:

(a)   the anti-social behaviour in which the respondent has engaged, or threatens to engage, consists of, or includes the use of, or threats to use, violence against another person; or

(b)   there is a significant risk of harm to other persons from the respondent (ASBCPA 2014, s 4).

'Significant risk' of harm is defined in the Act as including serious ill treatment or abuse, whether physical or not.

'Requirement' does not include one that has the effect of requiring the respondent to participate in particular activities.

As an injunction can only include a power of arrest if breached where the anti-social behaviour includes use or threatened use of violence or there is a significant risk of harm to others, this may well lack any real deterrent for those who are given these injunctions for incidents of anti-social behaviour that may be non-violent/non-threatening but are nevertheless causing misery to individuals and communities.

The injunction may specify a period for which the power of arrest is to have effect. This may be for a shorter period than the prohibition or requirement to which it relates.

Where a power of arrest is attached to a provision of an ASBI a constable may arrest the respondent without warrant if he or she has reasonable cause to suspect that the respondent is in breach of the provision. A constable who arrests a person under ASBCPA 2014, s 9(1) must inform the person who applied for the injunction.

The respondent must be brought before a magistrate within 24 hours of the time of arrest (excluding Sundays and Bank Holidays). The magistrate must remand the respondent to the youth court that granted the order. However, if the order was made by a youth court and the respondent is now 18 or over it will be to the county court.

Where there is no power of arrest and the person who applied for the injunction thinks the respondent is in breach of the injunction, they may apply to a magistrate for a warrant of arrest (ASBCPA 2014, s 10(1)). There must be reasonable grounds for believing the respondent is in breach before granting any warrant (ASBCPA 2014, s 10(3)). Any warrant granted will require the respondent to be brought before the youth court who granted the injunction or if the respondent is now aged 18 or above to the county court. If a constable arrests a respondent for breaching the injunction they must inform the applicant.

If a person is arrested for breach, the court may deal with the breach or adjourn proceedings for no more than 28 days. If the court does adjourn, civil bail applies.

Length of the injunction

14.26   The injunction takes effect on the day it is made and must specify the period for which it has effect. In the youth court, for those under 18, it must be no more than 12 months (ASBCPA 2014, s 1(6)).

An injunction may specify different periods for which particular prohibitions or requirements have effect within the order.

Variation and discharge

14.27   An injunction may be varied or discharged on application by the applicant or the respondent (ASBCPA 2014, s 8(1)).

A person applying for variation or discharge of an ASBI granted on that person's application must before doing so consult the local youth offending team about the application for variation or discharge, if the respondent will be aged under 18 when that application is made; and inform any other body or individual the applicant thinks appropriate of that application (ASBCPA 2014, s 14(3)).

The application to vary or discharge the injunction would be made to the court that granted the injunction, except where the injunction was granted by a youth court but the respondent is now aged 18 or over, in which case the application would be made to the county court.

The power to vary an injunction includes power to include an additional prohibition or requirement in the injunction, or to extend the period for which a prohibition or requirement has effect; and to attach a power of arrest, or to extend the period for which a power of arrest has effect.

An application may be made to amend the operative period of the supervision order, the activity requirement or the curfew requirement, or to amend the order on change of residence. An application can also be made to revoke a supervision or detention order. An application can be made to revoke a detention order if it appears it is in the interests of justice to do so, having regard to the circumstances that have arisen since the order was made.

If an application is dismissed a further application cannot be made by the same applicant unless the applicant has the consent of the court that made the order or the agreement of the other party.

Breach of ASBIs and sentence

14.28   Schedule 2 of the Anti-Social Behaviour, Crime and Policing Act 2014 deals with of breach of injunctions for under 18-year-olds. Breach of an injunction is not a criminal offence but any breach must be proved to the criminal standard of proof, beyond reasonable doubt.

If the breach is proved the court may:

(a)   take no action; or

(b)   impose a supervision order of up to six months; or

(c)   impose a detention order of up to three months (ASBCPA 2014).

According to Sch 2, para 2(1) of the Anti-Social Behaviour, Crime and Policing Act 2014 a supervision order may include one or more of the following requirements:

(a)   a supervision requirement (may not exceed six months) (ASBCPA 2014, Sch 2, para 3); or

(b)   an activity requirement (must be for not less than 12 days and not more than 24 days) (ASBCPA 2014, Sch 2, para 4); or

(c)   a curfew requirement (must be for not less than two hours but not more than eight hours) and may be electronically monitored (ASBCPA 2014, Sch 2, paras 5 and 6).

In considering whether and how to exercise its powers the court must consider any representations from YOT.

Failure to comply with a supervision order may result in the juvenile being brought back to court. The court may revoke the order and impose a new one or impose a detention order (ASBCPA 2014, Sch 2, para 12). The court must consider the representations of YOT before exercising its powers. These powers cannot be exercised after the respondent turns 18.

A detention order is only available for respondents aged 14 to 17. The court must be satisfied that the severity or extent of the breach means that no other power available is appropriate. Any detention order will be served in Youth Detention Accommodation (ASBCPA 2014, Sch 2, para 14).

Appeal

14.29 A defendant has a right of appeal against an ASBI under ASBCPA 2014, s 15. On an appeal under this section, the Crown Court may make whatever orders are necessary to give effect to its determination of the appeal; or whatever incidental or consequential orders appear to it to be just.

An order of the Crown Court made on an appeal under this section (other than one directing that an application be re-heard by the youth court) is to be treated as an order of the youth court.

Press restrictions

14.30   When a juvenile appears before the court for a CBO or for an ASBI, the usual automatic press restrictions under s 49 of the Children and Young Persons Act 1933 (restrictions on reports of proceedings in which children and young persons are concerned) do not apply.

In relation to CBOs the details of the order can be reported, ie the press could report the CBO and the prohibitions, but not the case details that led to the making of the CBO unless, of course, the court makes an order lifting the restrictions in relation to the offence. The court will need to consider whether or not to use its discretionary powers to make any order restricting publicity balancing the interests of the public to know about such cases against the welfare of the child or young person concerned.

The court may make an order preventing the reporting of the CBO or the ASBI under s 39 of Children and Young Persons Act 1933.

Section 39 states that in relation to any proceedings in any court, the court may direct that:

(a)   no newspaper report of the proceedings shall reveal the name, address, or school, or include any particulars calculated to lead to the identification of any child or young person concerned in the proceedings, either as being the person by or against or in respect of whom the proceedings are taken, or as being a witness therein;

(b)   no picture shall be published in any newspaper as being or including a picture of any child or young person so concerned in the proceedings as aforesaid; except in so far (if at all) as may be permitted by the direction of the court.

Any person who publishes any matter in contravention of any such direction shall on summary conviction be liable in respect of each offence to a fine not exceeding level 5 on the standard scale.

The court would need to have a good reason, other than age alone, for preventing the identification of any child or young person in such proceedings. The court should consider that unless the nuisance is extremely localised, enforcement of the order will normally depend on the general public being aware of the order and of the identity of the person against whom it is made.

The view that communities need to know that something is being done about disorder in their neighbourhoods needs to be balanced against the need to rehabilitate the young person and work towards their social inclusion.

Effective enforcement requires the ability to identify those subject to CBOs, which requires publication of photographs, balanced by the knowledge that much press coverage is sensationalist in its nature and may give young people a notoriety which they feel they have to live up to, thus negating the effectiveness of the order.

Where a youth is prosecuted for a breach of a CBO under s 30 of the Anti-Social Behaviour, Crime and Policing Act 2014 there are no automatic reporting restrictions on the proceedings in respect of the breach (ASBCPA 2014, s 30(5)), although any other charges heard at the same time will still be subject to s 49 of the Children and Young Persons Act 1933. Section 45 of the Youth Justice and Criminal Evidence Act 1999 (YJCEA 1999) will apply in relation to CBO breach proceedings against someone aged under 18, so the court will have the power to impose discretionary reporting restrictions. As before, care will be required when reporting breach proceedings for a CBO not inadvertently to report any previous convictions in the Youth Court to which s 49 of the CYPA 1933 continues to apply.

The guide to ASBOs published by the Home Office jointly with the Association of Chief Police Officers and Youth Justice Board in August 2006 has some relevant considerations which can be applied in CBO cases and some ASBI cases. It suggests a number of useful practice issues. For example, it notes that a sentence for breach of an ASBO should be proportionate to the behaviour that constituted the breach. On the subject of publicity, it notes the need to record considerations of the human rights implications of such publicity and, if a different court imposed reporting restrictions when the order was made, there should be a presumption in favour of their imposition in any breach hearing.

The case of *McKerry v Teesdale and Wear Valley Justices* (2000) Crim LR 594 DC (in relation to an ASBO) emphasised that the power to dispense with anonymity must be exercised with great care, caution and circumspection. The public interest criterion will rarely be satisfied and it is wholly wrong to exercise the power as an additional punishment or for 'naming and shaming'. In order to determine whether it is in the public interest to dispense with restrictions, it is entirely proper for the court to ask reporters present in court if they have any representations to make.

The application of s 39 of the Children and Young Persons Act 1933 where a juvenile was the subject of an ASBO was considered in *R v St Albans Crown Court, ex parte T* and *Chief Constable of Surrey v J H-G and D H-G* [2002] All ER (D) 308 (May). The following considerations were identified as relevant by the court when considering imposing or removing reporting restrictions:

(a)   In deciding whether to impose or thereafter to lift reporting restrictions, the court will consider whether there are good reasons for naming the defendant.

(b)   In each case there will be a wide variety of factors that have to be fully considered and, a balance has to be struck between the desirability of public disclosure on one hand and the need to protect the welfare of the juvenile on the other.

(c)   In reaching its decision, the court will give considerable weight to the age of the offender and the potential damage to any young person of public identification as a criminal before the offender has the benefit or burden of adulthood.

(d)   By virtue of CYPA 1933, s 44, the court must have regard to the welfare of the child or young person.

(e)   The prospect of being named in court with the accompanying disgrace is a powerful deterrent and the naming of a defendant in the context of his punishment serves as a deterrent to others. These deterrents are proper objectives for the court to seek.

(f)   There is strong public interest in open justice and in the public knowing as much as possible about what has happened in court, including the identity of those who have committed crime.

(g)   The weight to be attributed to the different factors may shift at different stages of the proceedings, and, in particular, after the defendant has been found, or pleads, guilty and is sentenced. It may then be appropriate to place greater weight on the interest of the public in knowing the identity of those who have committed particularly serious and detestable crimes.

(h)   The fact that an appeal has been made may be a material consideration.

(i)   Where an ASBO has been imposed, that is a factor that reinforces, and in some cases may strongly reinforce, the general public interest in the public disclosure of court proceedings.

(j)   The court should not have regard to the impact of publicity on the other members of the youth's family.

The court also has to balance any decision with its obligations under Articles 8 and 10 of ECHR. Publicity should be confined to what is reasonable and proportionate (*R (on the application of Stanley, Marshall and Kelly) v Metropolitan Police Commissioner* [2004] EWHC 2229 (Admin) (in relation to an ASBO).

In the case of *Y v Aylesbury Crown Court* [2012] EWHC 1140 (Admin) (in relation to an ASBO), there was a request from a local newspaper to vary an order under s 39 which was supported by the police. They believed that it was in the public interest to name the young person (aged 16) to act as a deterrent to others from 'committing such a grave offence' (in this case arson), to address community concerns surrounding the investigation and give potential witnesses the confidence to come forward. The judge allowed the application in part and varied the order to permit the publication of the young person's name and address but not a photograph or other description of him. On appeal the court applied the approach taken in *McKerry v Teesdale and Wear Valley Justices* (2000) Crim LR 594 DC (in relation to an ASBO) and held that on balancing the welfare of the young person with the public interest, the public interest in the facts of this case did not take precedence and the objectives sought by the police and media could be sufficiently met without naming the young person.

The case of *Medway Council v BBC* [2002] 1 FLR 104, Fam Div, suggests, as outlined above, that in most cases it would be inappropriate for the court thus to inhibit identification by the press of a child who is made the subject of such an order, for the efficacy of the order may well depend on the awareness of the local community not only of the acts that it prohibits but also of the identity of the persons against whom it is made.

Finally, the case of *R (on the application of Kenny) v Leeds Magistrates' Court* [2003] EWHC 2963 (Admin) reminds courts that when contemplating making an ASBO on someone under 18 one of their considerations must be the best interests of that child. While *DPP v Todd* [2003] EWHC 240 (Admin), is authority for the proposition that reporting restrictions in relation to the identification of a young person involved in proceedings fall away once that person reaches the age of 18, the legislation should be construed in the light of the judgment in *C v CPS* [2008] EWHC 854 (Admin) and the general freedom of the press to report proceedings in adult courts.

Anti-gang injunctions

14.31 Under s 37 of the Policing and Crime Act 2009 (PCA 2009) as amended, the police or local authorities can apply to the Youth Court for civil anti-gang injunctions (AGI) against 14- to 17-year-olds, to prevent gang related violence or drug dealing activity. Consultation with the Youth Offending Team should have taken place before an application is made.

The applicant has to show that the young person has engaged in, assisted or encouraged gang related violence or drug dealing activities. A gang is defined as a group which has at least three members and has one or more characteristic which enables others to recognise it as a group. It is also necessary to satisfy the court that the injunction is necessary to prevent the young person's involvement in, or protect them from, gang related violence or drug dealing.

If applications are made without notice to the young person (and parent/guardian) then reasons need to be given by the applicant.

Any hearing must take place at a designated Youth Court. Courts which have appropriate facilities and sufficient security have been designated. Special measures directions can be made for witnesses giving evidence provided the conditions in YJCEA 1999 are satisfied (see **13.03** to **13.05**).

If the Youth Court considers press restrictions are appropriate it will need to make an order restricting publication of the proceedings under s 39 of the Children and Young Persons Act 1933 (see **14.03** above).

Injunctions can impose both prohibitions and requirements. The prohibitions may, for example, prevent the young person from associating with gang members or going to certain areas or places. They may also require the young person to remain at certain places at particular times. Electronic monitoring can also be included. A requirement could also require participation in activities designed to help them break away from the gang. The case of *Chief Constable of Lancashire Constabulary v Wilson & Ors* [2015] EWCA Civ 907 suggests that any prohibitions and requirements should reflect the extent of involvement that the defendant is shown to have had or possibly to have had in relation to the activities of the gang; and some prohibitions would not be justified where the defendant's level of involvement in the activities of the gang was at a low level.

The Youth Court can make interim orders and vary or discharge orders.

There is a mandatory review process if any condition of the injunction lasts past the young person's eighteenth birthday, set out in PCA 2009, s 36. The purpose of this provision is to ensure that any conditions attached to the injunction remain relevant and enforceable once the young person has reached the age of 18.

Where the young person attains 18 years of age during application proceedings the Youth Court may continue to act or transfer them to the County Court (or High Court).

Appeal against the making of an order is to the Crown Court.

Breach of AGIs and sentence

14.32   Breach of an anti-gang injunction is a criminal offence for which a special menu of options is available to the Youth Court. These range from making no order, a fine, a civil supervision order, or as a last resort a Detention Order of up to three months. Under a detention order the young person can be detained at a secure training centre, young offender institution or in secure accommodation. The supervision order can be imposed for up to six months and contain a mix of supervision, activity and curfew requirements (electronically monitored). The Youth Offending Team must be consulted before any order is made and will be responsible for managing the young person under the order.

Applications can be made to vary or revoke supervision orders, and to revoke detention orders.

Chapter 15 The mentally disordered juvenile

Introduction

15.01 The number of juveniles with mental health problems or learning disabilities in the criminal justice system is significant. The Law Commission published a report on *Unfitness to Plead* on13 January 2016 following a lengthy consultation process that began in 2010. The report recommends reform of the whole unfitness to plead framework and makes specific recommendations in relation to children.

The report proposes modernising the test for unfitness to plead and widening it to encompass issues with effective participation. It is suggested that the Magistrates' Court, including the Youth Court should use the same legal test as the Crown Court and have a wider range of disposals available. Currently there is no legislative framework for fitness to plead in the Magistrates' Court /Youth Court and the range of disposals is limited. It is proposed that the new test would ask whether the defendant is able to participate effectively in his trial.

The report recommends an assessment of the defendant to ensure he is able to participate effectively in his trial. It links the higher level of issues with effective participation in the Youth Court with natural developmental immaturity and a greater prevalence of psychiatric disorders and learning disabilities or difficulties amongst children and adolescents. It recommends that all children appearing for the first time in the Youth Court should be screened for participation difficulties and that there should be mandatory specialist training for all legal practitioners and members of the judiciary dealing with cases involving juveniles in any court.

Therefore, when a mentally disordered juvenile does appear before the court there is a need for special care both in respect of the young person and the law as it applies. Where the court has an indication of a mental disorder it should call for medical reports to determine if treatment is required.

CJA 2003, s 157 specifically requires the court to obtain a medical report before passing a custodial sentence where it appears that the defendant may be mentally disordered. The court is required to consider any information before it which relates to the defendant's mental condition, whether in a medical report, a pre-sentence report or otherwise. The Youth Court may be assisted by several of the Law Commission's recommendations which also apply to those currently working with young offenders. For example, it is recommended that clinicians operating as part of Youth Offending Teams could assist in the screening process for participation difficulties. Also, the court will be assisted in finding out what facilities are available for diverting a defendant to hospital by the clinical commissioning group or the Local Health Board or the National Health Service Commissioning Board, who are under a duty to provide the said information to the court where the defendant was last resident in their area (Mental Health Act 1983, s 39).

The orders which are specifically designed for the mentally disordered juvenile are hospital orders, guardianship orders (for those aged 16 years or over) and youth rehabilitation orders with a condition of treatment by a specified medical practitioner or chartered psychologist. Hospital and guardianship orders may be appropriate where the court, having heard evidence about the juvenile's mental condition, decides that he needs to be committed to a specified hospital or placed under the guardianship of the local health authority or a person approved by the authority so that he may receive treatment to improve or stabilise his mental health. There is no absolute discharge available and where the juvenile is charged with non-imprisonable offences or is not suitable for a hospital or guardianship order the only alternative is for his legal representative to apply to the court to stay proceedings.

Definitions

15.02 A hospital order authorises the juvenile's treatment in a hospital or as an outpatient. A guardianship order allows the child to remain as an outpatient, but gives the guardian power to help them manage their affairs.

> 'The purpose of the guardianship order is primarily to ensure that the offender receives care and protection rather than medical treatment, although the guardian does have power to require the offender to attend for medical treatment. The effect of a guardianship order is to give the guardian power to require the offender to live in a specific place (this may be used to discourage the offender from sleeping rough or living with people who may exploit or mistreat him...), to attend specific places at specified times for medical treatment, occupation, education, or training, and to require access to the offender to be given at the place where the offender is living to any doctor, approved (mental health professional) or other person specified by the guardian. This power could be used for example, to ensure the offender did not neglect himself.' (Home Office Circular No 66/90, para 8(iv)(c)).

In each case, the court must comply with the provisions of the Mental Health Act 1983 (MHA 1983), s 37 as amended.

The definition of mental disorder was changed by the Mental Health Act 2007 (MHA 2007), 'Mental disorder' now means a medical determination that the person is under any disorder or disability of the mind.

Persons with learning disabilities are not mentally disordered for the purposes of most provisions of the Act by reason of that disability alone, unless the disability is associated with abnormally aggressive or seriously irresponsible conduct on the part of the person concerned.

'Learning disability' means a state of arrested or incomplete development of the mind which includes significant impairment of intelligence and social functioning (MHA 1983, s 1(2A)). Dependence on drugs or alcohol is specifically excluded from the definition of mental disorder. However, a drug or alcohol dependent person who has another mental disorder (even if that disorder is associated with alcohol or drug use) is not excluded from the definition (MHA 1983, s 1(3)).

'Place of safety' has the same meaning as in CYPA 1933, s 107 and includes inter alia a doctor's surgery, a hospital, a community home and a police station, but not a prison establishment.

'In custody' here means for juveniles aged less than 18 in local authority accommodation, unless the conditions are satisfied for remanding to youth detention accommodation.

Pre-trial considerations

15.03   The court may be faced with a number of legal issues that may best be tackled at a case management hearing, although some of the issues can only be dealt with as the trial progresses. Indeed, where it is apparent that insanity is alleged or there is potential for an order under the Mental Health Act 1983 it may be advisable to allocate the case to a district judge as in *R (on the application of Singh) v Stratford Magistrates' Courts* [2007] 4 All ER 407. The Law Commission's report on *Unfitness to Plead* also recommends that where the defendant's capacity is raised as an issue the case should be reserved to a district judge for all future hearings to achieve consistency.

The court may be faced with a suggestion that the juvenile is unfit to plead, that he is insane or that the trial should be halted on the basis that it would be an abuse of process given the juvenile's inability to take an effective part in the trial.

Insanity is a defence in law under the Criminal Procedure (Insanity) Act 1964, ss 1 and 4 and is a valid basis for an acquittal in the magistrates' courts (*R v Horseferry Road Magistrates' Court, ex parte K* [1996] 3 All ER 719).

Where the issue is not one of insanity but it is suggested that a juvenile is unfit to plead in the Youth Court he cannot be tried in the Crown Court as s 51A(3) of the CDA 1998 requires a finding of guilt; and an unfit defendant cannot be found guilty (*R (on the application of TP) v Derby Youth Court* [2015] EWHC 573 (Admin)). Instead the Youth Court may proceed to hear the evidence and determine whether they are satisfied that he did the act or made the omission charged. The Youth Court has the power to try the issues and reach a conclusion, without convicting or acquitting the accused, provided that the conditions for making a hospital or guardianship order under MHA 1983, s 37(3) are met.

The availability of this procedure was confirmed in the case of the *Crown Prosecution Service v P* [2007] 4 All ER 628 and it is worth noting that such a procedure does not infringe the defendant's rights under Article 6 to a fair trial as there is no finding of guilt (*R v H (Tyrone)* [2002] EWCA Crim 2988). The case law also explored the possibility of the court applying the doctrine of *doli incapax*, but the Court of Appeal has in a subsequent case made it clear that the defence of *doli incapax* has been abolished by s 34 of the Crime and Disorder Act 1998 (*R v JTB* [2009] All ER (D) 211 (Apr)).

The final issue that may arise is the suggestion that the case should be halted as an abuse of process on the basis that a juvenile defendant's mental impairment or lack of capacity prohibits him from taking a full part in the trial. In *C v Sevenoaks Youth Court* [2009] EWHC 3088 (Admin), it was held that although the court can interfere with the decision of the CPS to prosecute, in the absence of bad faith, such a decision would not be challenged unless the code for prosecutors has been discarded or not properly followed. Whilst the court has an inherent jurisdiction to stay proceedings as an abuse of process at any stage, it is limited to issues directly affecting the fairness of the trial of the juvenile before them, and does not extend to any sort of wider supervisory jurisdiction such as may be exercised by the High Court. In *Crown Prosecution Service v P* above, the court made it clear that only in exceptional circumstances should this power be exercised, before evidence was heard, on the ground that one or more of the capacity issues made it unlikely that the juvenile would receive a fair trial. It was pointed out that the court has a duty to keep under constant review the question of whether the trial should continue. If at any stage the court concluded that the juvenile was unable to participate effectively it can decide to halt the trial. Even then, it was pointed out that the court may consider that it is in the best interests of the child that the trial should continue if, for example, the prosecution evidence is weak and there may be no case to answer.

Medical evidence may be influential in the court's decision and the importance of it being up to date before embarking on a fact-finding was emphasised in *Blouet v Bath and Wansdyke Magistrates' Court* [2009] EWHC 759 (Admin). However medical evidence should almost always be set in the context of other evidence relating to the child, such as his understanding, mental capacity and ability to participate effectively in trial. Article 6(1) does not require that a child on trial for a criminal offence should understand or be capable of understanding every point of law or evidential detail. However, effective participation in this context presupposes that the accused has a broad understanding of the nature of the trial process, and of what is at stake for him or her, including the significance of any penalty which may be imposed. The issue as to whether the juvenile will receive a fair trial is for the court to decide. Where the court proceeds with the trial it will wish to ensure that the child understands each stage of the process. This will necessarily involve exchanges between the bench and the child. The manner in which the trial is conducted by the child's legal representative will inform the court as to whether he does or does not have adequate instructions on which to cross-examine witnesses. Therefore, in most cases medical evidence will be considered as part of the evidence in the case and not the sole evidence of a freestanding application (*R (on the application of P) v West London Youth Court* [2006] 1 All ER 477).

Again, it is the court's opinion (rather than that of a medical practitioner) of the child's level of understanding that will determine whether the trial proceeds or not (*R (on the application of P) v Barking Youth Court* [2002] EWHC 734 (Admin)). It was held in *R v Ghulam* [2009] EWCA Crim 2285, that the judge, having observed the defendant's conduct in the proceedings, was entitled to exercise his discretion and hold that the defendant was fit to plead.

In the more recent case of *G v DPP* [2012] EWHC 3174 (Admin) where a 13-year-old was charged with a sexual offence the district judge heard evidence from a doctor that the juvenile had known that what he had done was wrong, but in the way that a 5–7 year old would realise it was wrong. The doctor indicated that if the juvenile was tried, it would be appropriate to appoint an intermediary. The judge decided to appoint an intermediary and subsequently took the intermediary's advice as to how the juvenile should be assisted during the hearing. The juvenile submitted that he was not fit to plead. The judge noted that there was no express fitness to plead procedure in the magistrates' court and found that the juvenile was able to follow and understand the proceedings. The judge found the charge proved and the juvenile was convicted. The juvenile appealed by way of case stated. It was held that the questions for the determination of the court were: (i) whether the judge was bound by the opinion of the defence expert or whether the judge was able to make his own decision after hearing all the evidence in the case; and (ii) although the questions of fitness to plead was not a matter for the magistrates' court in that there was no procedure to deal with it; the fact that the juvenile's expert stated that he was not mentally ill and that the judge had on the defence's application appointed an intermediary and had conducted the trial having regard to her advice; was the judge bound to conduct an enquiry as envisaged by *R (on the application of P) v Barking Youth Court* [2002]. The appeal was dismissed on the basis that there had been no procedural irregularity. It was found that the judge had correctly followed the guidance given and there had been evidence on which he could properly have concluded that the juvenile had been fit to be tried

If the court does halt a criminal trial on the basis that the juvenile cannot take an effective part in proceedings, it may then consider switching to a fact-finding exercise as to whether the defendant did the act charged, in a procedure set out in the *Barking Youth Court* case and consequently in the *Blouet* case (which deals with the issue of up to date medical evidence). In essence, proceedings should only be stayed as an abuse of process before a fact-finding exercise if it is clear that no useful purpose at all could be served by embarking on that procedure. If the court finds that the defendant did not do the acts alleged then a finding of not guilty should be recorded and the defendant acquitted. A good deal of court time and stress to the juvenile can be avoided by good pre-court communication between the CPS and defence solicitors. The Crown always has an obligation to consider the public interest and, when faced with appropriate medical history and opinion, may take the view that a prosecution is unnecessary, especially where a treatment plan is already in existence. A defence solicitor must consider whether the best interests of the client are served by embarking on a process that could result in a hospital order following a fact-finding exercise when appropriate research and representations to the Crown may result in a more beneficial outcome.

It should be noted that staying proceedings remains an exceptional remedy (*CPS v P* [2008] 4 All ER 628) and whilst this will halt a criminal trial it offers no disposal to address the concerning behaviour which led to the commission of the offence. Significant concerns about the limited disposals available in the magistrates and Youth Court have been raised in the Law Commission's report on *Unfitness to Plead*. The report has recommended the availability of a wider range of disposals for those who lack capacity in order to improve procedures in the Magistrates' Court.

Special measures at trial

15.04   A juvenile offender may give evidence in criminal proceedings in a Youth/ magistrates' court (or Crown Court) using a live link if:

(a)   his ability to participate effectively in the proceedings as a witness giving oral evidence is compromised by his level of intellectual ability or social functioning; and

(b)   his ability to participate effectively would be improved by giving evidence over a live link (Youth Justice and Criminal Evidence Act 1999 (YJCEA 1999), s 33A(4) as inserted by the Police and Justice Act 2006 (PJA 2006), s 47); and

(c)   the court is satisfied that it is in the interests of justice for the youth to give evidence through a live link.

A live link is defined in s 33B of the Youth Justice and Criminal Evidence Act 1999 as an arrangement by which the defendant, while absent from the place where the proceedings are being held, is able to see and hear a person there, and to be seen and heard by the justices, co-accused, legal representatives and interpreters, or any other person appointed by the court to assist the accused.

The defence must apply for a live link direction, which then prevents the defendant from giving oral evidence in the proceedings in any manner other than through a live link (YJCEA 1999, s 33A(6)). The court may discharge a live link direction at any time, if it appears in the interests of justice to do so, of its own motion or on application by any party (YJCEA 1999, s 33A(7)). The court must give reasons in open court for giving or discharging a live link direction or for refusing an application for or the discharge of a live link direction. Those reasons must be recorded on the register of proceedings where the decision was made in the magistrates' court (YJCEA 1999, s 33A(8)).

The amended Criminal Practice Directions 2015 (CPD 2015) which came into force on 4 April 2016 contain a revised Practice Direction on the appointment and use of intermediaries during criminal trials (CPD 2015, para 3F). The revised Practice Direction contains a considerable shift in emphasis in relation to the recommended use of defence intermediaries. In essence it provides that:

(a)   'In light of the scarcity of intermediaries, the appropriateness of assessment must be decided with care to ensure their availability for those witnesses and defendants who are most in need.' [para 3F.5]

(b)   'The court should adapt the trial process to address a defendant's communication needs (*R v Cox* [2012] EWCA Crim 549) and will rarely exercise its inherent powers to direct appointment of an intermediary.' [para 3F.12]

(c)   'Directions to appoint an intermediary for a defendant's evidence will thus be rare, but for the entire trial extremely rare.' [para 3F.13]

(d)   'Directions for intermediaries to help defendants may be ineffective due to general unavailability, lack of suitable expertise, or non-availability for the purpose directed (for example, where the direction is for assistance during evidence, but an intermediary will only accept appointment for the entire trial).' [para 3F.19]

(e)   'A trial will not be rendered unfair because a direction to appoint an intermediary for the defendant is ineffective.' [para 3F.20]

(f)   '...the appropriateness of an intermediary assessment for witnesses and defendants under 18 must be decided with care.' [para 3F.25]

For juveniles, an assessment by an intermediary should always be a consideration and decided with care given the high proportion of juveniles with recognised communication needs and each decision should be made on an individual basis in the context of the circumstances of the particular case. The revised Criminal Practice Directions further set out:

'Assessment by an intermediary should be considered for witnesses and defendants under 18 who seem liable to misunderstand questions or to experience difficulty expressing answers, including those who seem unlikely to be able to recognise a problematic question (such as one that is misleading or not readily understood), and those who may be reluctant to tell a questioner in a position of authority if they do not understand.' [para 3F.26]

Although the Criminal Practice Directions suggests the use of intermediaries should be discouraged for defendants it does not reflect any legislative change or guidance in recent case law (see below). Also refer to the guidance on the use of intermediaries for vulnerable defendants at para 79 in the *Equal Treatment Bench Book* (November 2013) and the Law Commission's report on *Unfitness to Plead* (2016) which recommends replacing the ad hoc practice of the courts granting the use of intermediaries under its inherent jurisdiction with a statutory scheme and clear test to ensure more consistency.

In the case of *C v Sevenoaks Youth Court* [2009] EWHC 3088 (Admin), it was held that there was no statutory provision (considering YJCEA 1999, s 16(1)) to appoint an intermediary to assist a juvenile, who lacked the prerequisite capacity to participate effectively in the trial proceedings. However, it was said that it would be appropriate for the court to use its inherent powers to appoint an intermediary, to help the juvenile prepare for the trial in advance of the hearing and during the trial process so that he could have a fair trial. The *Sevenoaks* decision was followed in *R (on the application of S) v Great Yarmouth Youth Court* [2011] EWHC 2059 (Admin) where it was held that the juvenile, who had been diagnosed with ADHD, 'would undoubtedly benefit from the assistance of a registered intermediary' without which there was a real risk that he might not receive a fair trial. *R v Wall* [2011] EWCA Crim 443 further supports the use of intermediaries and states that the court should use its inherent powers to appoint an intermediary where necessary before embarking on a trial of fitness to plead. It makes it plain that the appointment of an intermediary is one mechanism which allows defendants to stand trial in circumstances where they may otherwise be unable to effectively participate and where the jury may not otherwise understand the defendant's limitations.

However, in the more recent case of R v Cox [2012] EWCA Crim 549 it was recognised that although there are occasions when the use of an intermediary would improve the trial process, it does not mean that it is mandatory for an intermediary to be made available. Judges as part and parcel of their ordinary control of the judicial process are expected to deal with specific communication problems faced by any defendant or any individual witness and where necessary, the processes have to be adapted to ensure that a particular individual is not disadvantaged as a result of personal difficulties. In R v Cox it was held that despite there being no intermediary to assist the defendant the judge conducted the proceedings with appropriate and necessary caution and therefore the defendant's conviction followed a fair trial. In *R v Yahya Rashid* [2017] EWCA Crim 2 the Court of Appeal approved the trial Judge's assessment of the defendant's mental capacity, relying on his observation of the defendant in court, on the video of the police interview and other background information about his education. It was correct to consider the need for an intermediary at different stages in the trial. The decision that the intermediary was only required when the defendant was giving evidence was upheld. It was noted that it was rare that an intermediary could be justified for a defendant and that in such cases the most common form of direction was to limit the intermediary to being present during the defendant's evidence. It was said that cases in which an order would be made for an intermediary to be present for the whole trial would be very rare.

Section 104 of the Coroners and Justice Act 2009 (inserting ss 33BA and 33BB into YJCEA 1999) has not come into force which would allow courts to make a direction that any examination of the juvenile is to be conducted through an intermediary, where the juvenile's ability to participate effectively in the proceedings as a witness giving oral evidence is compromised by his level of intellectual ability or social functioning.

The orders

Requirements for hospital and guardianship orders

15.05 In criminal proceedings, the orders may be made after the court has made a finding of guilt for an offence which carries imprisonment in the case of an adult. The power applies notwithstanding the restrictions contained in Powers of Criminal Courts (Sentencing) Act 2000, ss 110(2) to 111(2) (imposition of minimum sentences) or under s 51A(2) of the Firearms Act 1968, or under any of the provisions of ss 225 to 226B of the Criminal Justice Act 2003 (as amended by LASPOA 2012, ss 122 to 128), as nothing in those provisions shall prevent the court from making an order under MHA 1983, s 37(1) for the admission of the offender to a hospital.

The court must be satisfied, on the written or oral evidence of two registered medical practitioners that the juvenile is suffering from a mental disorder.

In addition, before detaining any person under the MHA 1983 for treatment, the court must be satisfied that medical treatment is available to that person, which is not only clinically appropriate to their condition, but also to their personal circumstances.

The court must further be satisfied that:

(a) it is of the opinion that the hospital order is the most suitable method of disposing of the case; or

(b) in the case of an offender who has attained the age of 16 years, the mental disorder is of a nature or of a degree which warrants his reception in guardianship, and the court is of the opinion, having regard to all the circumstances including the nature of the offence and the character and antecedents of the offender, and to the other available methods of dealing with him, that the most suitable method of disposing of the case is by means of an order (MHA 1983, s 37(2)(b)).

The court may make an order under MHA 1983, s 37 without making a finding of guilt if, having heard all the evidence including medical evidence, it is satisfied that the offender 'did the act or made the omission charged'. This provision allows the court to make a hospital or guardianship order in cases where the juvenile's mental condition is such that the court cannot be satisfied that the juvenile intended his action or had the necessary mental element in the criminal offence. For example, the juvenile may be charged with an offence of theft; normally the court would have to be satisfied beyond reasonable doubt that the juvenile had a dishonest intention to permanently deprive the owner of the goods in question. If the court has evidence of a mental disorder it need only be satisfied that the juvenile performed the *actus reus* of theft without regard to his intentions. In the case of *R v Lincolnshire (Kesteven) Justices, ex parte O'Connor* [1983] 1 All ER 901, it was held that this power should be exercised rarely, and usually only if those acting for the defendant consented to such an order being made.

In *R (on the application of P) v Barking Youth Court* [2002] EWHC 734 (Admin), a youth's fitness to plead was queried and the magistrates made their decision based on an expert's report and their own observations. The Divisional Court remitted the case back to the Youth Court reminding them that they were a specially constituted magistrates' court and, as such, the procedures in PCC(S)A 2000, s 11(1) applied. The court should have determined by evidence whether he did the act or omission charged (not necessarily whether he was guilty or not) and then adjourned for medical reports. The procedure may also be applicable in cases where a defendant is unable to consent to mode of trial due to a mental disorder (*R v Lincolnshire (Kersteven) Justices, ex parte O'Connor* [1983] 1 All ER 901).

Blouet v Bath and Wansdyke Magistrates' Court [2009] EWHC 759 (Admin) sets out that when dealing with a fact finding there should be up to date medical evidence before the magistrates. If there is a possibility of a hospital order being made, the issue will be tried in accordance with PCC(S)A 2000, s 11(1) (remand by magistrates for medical examination). If the obligation to adjourn for further reports arises, then that is what must happen.

Note that where this procedure is employed there can be no conviction and therefore the criminal charge provisions of Article 6 do not apply to such proceedings (*R v M* [2001] EWCA Crim 2024 and *R v H (Tyrone)* [2002] EWCA Crim 2988).

A Youth Court may only make an order without a finding of guilt in respect of a person suffering from a mental disorder as defined above. In the case of a hospital order, the court must be satisfied that arrangements have been made to admit the juvenile to a hospital within 28 days. Such evidence must be the written or oral evidence of the approved clinician who would have overall responsibility for the offender's treatment, or of some other person representing the managers of the hospital named in the order (MHA 1983, s 37(4)). Pending the juvenile's admission to the hospital which has agreed to accept him the court may, on making the hospital order, direct that he be taken and detained in a place of safety. The offender must be admitted to the specified hospital within 28 days unless it appears to the Secretary of State that an emergency or other special circumstance has arisen whereby he may give directions for admission to another hospital. Alternatively, the patient may be returned to the court for a further order to be made giving a further 28-day period in which a bed may become available.

When making a guardianship order, the court must be satisfied that either the local authority or the person under whose guardianship he is to be placed is willing to receive the juvenile into guardianship. It should be noted that a guardianship order may only be made in respect of a juvenile who has attained the age of 16 years. The Butler Committee stated that guardianship orders 'offer a useful form of control of some mentally disordered offenders who do not require hospital treatment (and are) particularly suited to the needs of offenders with (learning disabilities) including those inadequate offenders who require help in managing their affairs' (para 15.8). To date however, very little use has been made of guardianship orders in practice.

The court can request information, from the clinical commissioning group or the Local Health Board or the National Health Service Commissioning Board, about the availability of accommodation or facilities designed specially for patients under the age of 18. The purpose of this provision is to ensure that courts do not place a juvenile in a prison setting, when a suitable hospital bed would be a more appropriate option.

In April 2010 s 31 of the Mental Health Act 2007 inserted s 131A into the Mental Health Act 1983. This now places hospital managers under a duty to ensure that patients aged under 18 are accommodated in an environment that is suitable for their age (subject to their needs). In determining whether the environment is suitable, the managers must consult a person whom they consider to be suitable because of their experience in child and adolescent mental health service cases.

The court may not, at the same time as making a hospital or guardianship order in respect of an offender, make a custodial order; impose a fine, or a YRO. Nor may it make an order for the offender's parent or guardian to enter into a recognisance or an order to take proper care of and exercise proper control over him.

In the case of a hospital order the court shall not make a referral order in respect of the offence.

The fact that a court has previously held a juvenile as unfit to plead does not prevent that juvenile from being tried for subsequent criminal acts. The issue of the juvenile's ability to participate effectively must be decided afresh. A juvenile might well develop significantly over a relatively short period of time. Obtaining an addendum or new medical report would greatly assist the court in determining whether the juvenile is still unfit to plead: *DPP v P* [2007] EWHC 946 (Admin).

Medical reports

15.06   The court must be satisfied on the evidence of two approved clinicians that the juvenile is suffering from such mental disorder as to render either a hospital or guardianship order necessary. One of the approved clinicians giving evidence must be recognised by the Secretary of State as having special experience in the diagnosis or treatment of mental disorders (MHA 1983, s 12 as amended).

The medical evidence may be received for the purposes of MHA 1983, s 37 in written or oral form. Any such report in writing must be signed by an approved clinician under MHA 1983, s 12, as having special experience in the treatment or diagnosis of mental disorders (MHA 1983, s 54(2)). Request for medical reports is set out in CPR 2015, r 28.8.

Where the medical evidence is by way of written report, with a view to an order under MHA 1983, s 37, a copy must be given to an authorised person (ie the juvenile's counsel or solicitor) if he is represented. Where he is not so represented 'the substance of the report shall be disclosed' to his parent or guardian present in court (MHA 1983, s 54(3)).

Restriction orders

15.07   Where the offender is a young person over the age of 14 and the court is satisfied that the conditions under MHA 1983, s 37 exist so as to make a hospital order, but it appears to the court that there should also be an order restricting the offender's discharge, the court may commit him in custody to the Crown Court to be dealt with (MHA 1983, s 43(4)). The power to commit to the Crown Court with a view to a restriction order being made only arises on a finding of guilt, not on a finding that the accused did the act or made the omission charged.

A restriction order gives authority to detain the patient for the duration of the order, although it can be discharged by the Secretary of State.

In most circumstances, the committal will be in custody but if the court is satisfied that arrangements have been made to admit the offender to a hospital the court may order his admission pending his appearance at the Crown Court (MHA 1983, s 44).

In deciding whether to commit to the Crown Court with a view to a restriction order, the court shall take into account the nature of the offence, the antecedents of the offender and the risk of his committing further offences if released. In the case where it is necessary to protect the public from serious harm a Crown Court may order an offender to be subject to special restrictions. In doing so the court may require information from the clinical commissioning group or the Local Health Board or the National Health Service Commissioning Board, about the availability of suitable facilities for an offender under the age of 18. See (for the principles involved) *R v Birch* [1989] 11 Cr App R (S) 202, CA, and *R v Nwohia* (1996) 1 Cr App R (S) 170, CA.

Effects of a hospital order and restriction order

15.08   A hospital order only gives the responsible clinician power to detain a patient for six months in the first instance (*R v Birch* (1989) 11 Cr App R (S) 202). This period can be reviewed and extended if necessary in the interests of the patient's health or safety or for the protection of others. A patient who is 16 or over or his nearest relative can apply to a mental health review tribunal for a discharge. On the other hand, the responsible clinician can discharge the patient at any time. A patient who absents himself without leave effectively ceases to be detained.

As a consequence of this offenders who are thought to be dangerous or who do need to be detained are usually sent to the Crown Court where a restriction order can be made (see **15.07**). The authority for such a committal is contained in MHA 1983, s 43 and is restricted to juveniles of or over the age of 14 years. Guidance has been given in the case of *R v Gardiner* [1967] 1 All ER 895, CA, on the appropriateness of the two orders.

Appeal

15.09 After a finding of guilt and the making of an order under MHA 1983, s 37, a juvenile may appeal against any sentence or order. Appeals are dealt with in **Chapter 16**.

If an order has been made without a finding of guilt, that is the court has found that the juvenile did the act or made the omission charged, he has the same rights of appeal as if after a finding of guilt. The appeal may be brought by the juvenile or his parent or guardian on his behalf (MHA 1983, s 45).

Youth rehabilitation order with a requirement of medical treatment

15.10 The court may make a youth rehabilitation order that includes a requirement that the offender undertakes treatment for a mental condition.

The provisions are subject to the general requirements and restrictions on making youth rehabilitation orders found at **9.02** to **9.06**. Perhaps the most important of these is that the offence itself must be serious enough to merit the making of a YRO, which may not always be the case where the defendant is suffering from a mental condition.

Mental health treatment requirement

15.11 This requires the offender to submit, during periods specified in the order, to treatment by or under the direction of a registered medical practitioner or a chartered psychologist (or both, for different periods) with a view to the improvement of the offender's mental condition.

The treatment required must be one of the following kinds as may be specified in the relevant order:

(a) treatment as a resident patient in an independent hospital or care home within the meaning of the Care Standards Act 2000 or a hospital within the meaning of the Mental Health Act 1983, but not in hospital premises where high security psychiatric services within the meaning of that Act are provided;

(b)   treatment as a non-resident patient at such institution or place as may be specified in the order;

(c)   treatment by or under the direction of such registered medical practitioner or chartered psychologist (or both) as may be so specified.

The nature of the treatment may not be specified in the order except as mentioned in (a), (b) or (c) above.

A court may not include a mental health treatment requirement in an order unless:

(a)   the court is satisfied, on the evidence that the mental condition of the offender:

   (i)   is such as requires and may be susceptible to treatment; but

   (ii)   is not such as to warrant the making of a hospital order or guardianship order within the meaning of the Mental Health Act 1983;

(b)   the court is also satisfied that arrangements have been or can be made for the treatment intended to be specified in the order (including arrangements for the reception of the offender where he is to be required to submit to treatment as a resident patient); and

(c)   the offender has expressed his willingness to comply with such a requirement.

While the offender is under treatment as a resident patient in pursuance of a mental health requirement, his responsible officer shall carry out the supervision of the offender to such extent only as may be necessary for the purpose of the revocation or amendment of the order.

Mental health treatment at place other than that specified in order

15.12   Where the medical practitioner or chartered psychologist, treating the offender in pursuance of a mental health treatment requirement, is of the opinion that part of the treatment can be better or more conveniently given in or at an institution or place which:

(a)   is not specified in the relevant order; and

(b)   is one in or at which the treatment of the offender will be given by or under the direction of a registered medical practitioner or chartered psychologist,

he may, with the consent of the offender, make arrangements for him to be treated accordingly.

These arrangements may provide for the offender to receive part of his treatment as a resident patient in an institution or place notwithstanding that the institution or place is not one which could have been specified for that purpose in the relevant order.

Where any such arrangements are made for the treatment of an offender the medical practitioner or chartered psychologist by whom the arrangements are made shall give notice in writing to the offender's responsible officer giving details of the place and the treatment provided as it is deemed to be treatment to which the offender is required to submit to as part of the order.

Remands to hospital

15.13   The Mental Health Act 1983, ss 35 and 36, allows a court to remand an accused person to a hospital for a report on his mental condition if:

(a)   he has been convicted of an offence punishable with imprisonment in the case of an adult; or

(b)   he has been charged with such an offence and the court is satisfied that he did the act or made the omission charged; or

(c)   he has consented to the exercise by the court of this power so to remand (MHA 1983, s 35(2)(b)).

The court has to be satisfied on the written or oral evidence of one registered medical practitioner, approved by the Secretary of State as having special experience in the diagnosis or treatment of mental disorders, that there is reason to suspect that the accused person is suffering from a mental disorder. In addition to this the court has to be of the opinion that it would be impracticable for a report on the offender's mental condition to be made if he were remanded on bail. After such a remand the court may further remand the accused if it appears on evidence, either written or oral, by the doctor preparing the report that a further remand is necessary for completing the assessment of the accused's mental condition. A remand to hospital must not exceed 28 days at a time or more than 12 weeks in all.

The court shall not remand an accused person to a hospital unless satisfied on the written or oral evidence of the registered medical practitioner making the report, or a representative of the hospital management, that arrangements have been made for his admission to that hospital within a seven-day period beginning with the date of remand. If the court is so satisfied it may, pending his admission, give directions for his detention in a place of safety. The power to further remand under MHA 1983, s 36 may be exercised by the court without the juvenile patient being brought before the court, if he is represented by an authorised person who is given an opportunity of being heard. Any such further remand may only be made where the responsible medical officer warrants it as necessary. The court officer must, as soon as practicable, serve on the hospital a record of the court's order and any such information that the court has received that appears likely to assist in treating or otherwise dealing with the offender (CPR 2015, r 28.9).

Interim hospital orders

15.14   The Mental Health Act 1983, s 38 gives the court power to make interim hospital orders. The court must be satisfied on the written or oral evidence of two registered medical practitioners that:

(a)   the offender is suffering from a mental disorder;

(b)   there is reason to suppose that the mental disorder from which the offender is suffering is such that it may be appropriate for a hospital order to be made in his case.

An interim order initially may not last for more than 12 weeks, and thereafter may be renewed for further periods of 28 days at a time, but the order may not continue in force for more than 12 months in all.

The power to renew an interim hospital order may be exercised without the offender being brought before the court if he is represented by an authorised person who is given an opportunity of being heard.

An interim hospital order may be made into a full hospital order without the offender being brought before the court, subject to the relevant medical evidence being available and the authorised person for the offender being given an opportunity of being heard. Before making either a full or an interim hospital order or remanding to a hospital, the court must be satisfied on written or oral evidence that arrangements have been made for the admission of the offender to a hospital within the period of 28 days beginning with the date of the order. This evidence may be given by the approved clinician who would have overall responsibility for the offender's treatment or of preparing the report or by some other persons representing the managers of the hospital in question (MHA 1983, ss 36(3) and 38(4)).

The power to make an interim hospital order and the power to remand to hospital have significant differences. A remand will be for the purpose of obtaining information about the mental condition of an offender. To make an interim hospital order in criminal proceedings, the offender must have been found guilty (or arraigned before the court and not yet dealt with) of an offence punishable with imprisonment and there must be reason to suppose that it may be appropriate for a hospital order to be made. When remanding to hospital the court must be satisfied that provision has been made to admit the defendant to hospital.

Chapter 16   Appeals

General points

16.01   Appeals from the Youth Court may be heard either by the Crown Court, or by way of case stated by the Divisional Court. At the Crown Court, the case proceeds, except for agreed evidence, by rehearing all the evidence.

Appeal by way of case stated to the Divisional Court is reserved for appeals which involve a point of law that requires the opinion of the High Court.

Appeal against a Youth Court's decision to withhold bail and remand in custody is made in the first instance to the Crown Court.

Appeal to the Crown Court in criminal cases

Applicability

16.02   An appeal to the Crown Court is applicable in cases where the appellant is aggrieved at the magistrates' decision on questions of fact or, in the case of a juvenile, where his parent or guardian is aggrieved at a decision ordering either of them to pay a fine, costs, surcharge or compensation imposed in respect of the case involving their child (PCC(S)A 2000, s 137). A juvenile found guilty by a Youth or an adult court may appeal to the Crown Court:

(a)   if he pleaded guilty to the offence, against his sentence or order; or

(b)   if he did not plead guilty to the offence against the finding of guilt and sentence or order.

'Sentence' means any order made on a finding of guilt, including an order of conditional discharge, an order for contempt of court and orders made on breach of a YRO. Although sentence does not include an order for costs (MCA 1980, s 108), it does include a surcharge imposed under CJA 2003, s 161A.

The various routes of appeal against conviction and sentence in contempt of court cases are explored in *Haw v Westminster Magistrates' Court* [2007] EWHC 2960 (Admin). The judgment establishes that there is an appeal to the Crown Court for both conviction and sentence despite the wording of s 12(5) of the Contempt of Court Act 1981. The terms of the Magistrates' Courts Act 1980, s 111 provide for and are wide enough to encompass an appeal by way of case stated to the High Court but there is no right of appeal under s 13 of the Administration of Justice Act 1960.

A defendant may also appeal against conviction if the Youth Court treats an equivocal plea as a guilty plea. In *R v Birmingham Crown Court, ex parte Sharma* [1988] Crim LR 741, an equivocal plea was defined as a plea of guilty when the defendant had added a qualification which, if true, might have shown that he would not be guilty of the offence charged.

Notice of appeal

16.03   An appeal is commenced by the appellant's notice of appeal. Under the Criminal Procedure Rules 2015, r 34.2 the appellant has 21 days in which to serve an appeal notice, which must be in writing, on the magistrates' court officer and every other party (usually the prosecutor). In criminal proceedings, the notice must state whether the appeal is against the conviction/finding of guilt, and/or the sentence and/ or the order/failure to make an order. Details of the appeal notice and documentation can be found in CPR 2015, r 63.3.

Time limits for appeal

16.04   The time limit of 21 days is from the date of the court's order and not the date of any finding of guilt, even if the appeal is only against a finding of guilt. The period excludes the day of the decision but includes the 21st day thereafter, as held in *Stewart v Chapman* [1951] KB 792. This is a case which involved time limits in road traffic cases, although the same principles apply to all time limits. The 21-day time limit may be extended by the Crown Court on receipt of an application in writing specifying the grounds of the application (CPR 2015, r 34.2(3)(a)). The application should be sent to the appropriate officer at the Crown Court. If the extension of time is allowed then the appropriate officer at the Crown Court will notify the office for the appropriate Youth Court. The appellant must notify any other party to the appeal. Where the Crown Court refuses an extension of time, it should give a brief statement why (*Re Worth (application for judicial review)* [1979] 1 FLR 159).

Application to introduce further evidence

16.05   Rule 34.7 of CPR 2015 applies where:

(a)   a party wants to introduce evidence which was not introduced by either party in the magistrates' court; and

(b)   one of these Parts applies:

(i)   Part 18 (Measures to assist a witness or defendant to give evidence);

(ii)   Part 20 (Hearsay evidence);

(iii)   Part 21 (Evidence of bad character); or

(iv)   Part 22 (Evidence of complainant's previous sexual behaviour).

The party must serve the notice or application to introduce evidence not more than 14 days after service of the appeal notice.

Abandonment of an appeal to the Crown Court

16.06   The appellant may abandon his appeal at any time by giving notice in writing to the appropriate officer at the magistrates' court and Crown Court and every other party before the hearing of the appeal begins and may only abandon the appeal with the Crown Court's permission after the hearing begins (CPR 2015, r 34.9.). Once a notice of abandonment of appeal has been validly given the Crown Court cannot entertain an appeal: *R v Essex Quarter Sessions Appeals Committee, ex parte Larkin* [1961] 3 All ER 930, in which a defendant had been convicted by magistrates and gave notice of appeal to Quarter Sessions. He then gave notice of abandonment of appeal. Subsequently he sought to withdraw the notice of abandonment but the Quarter Sessions refused to allow him to do so. The Divisional Court upheld the Quarter Sessions decision.

Once the appeal has been abandoned by the appellant giving notice, the court against whose decision the appeal was brought may enforce that decision and issue any process necessary for enforcement subject to anything already suffered or done under it by the appellant. The costs of the appeal may be ordered against the appellant, where expenses were incurred by the other party to the appeal (MCA 1980, s 109): Pt 45 of the CPR 2015 contains rules about costs on abandoning an appeal.

If an appeal against conviction has been abandoned before a hearing of the appeal has commenced, the Crown Court has no jurisdiction to increase the sentence imposed by the justices (*R v Gloucester Crown Court, ex parte Betteridge* [1998] Crim LR 218).

The powers of the Crown Court

16.07   On hearing an appeal in criminal proceedings against conviction, the Crown Court may uphold the conviction, quash it, or remit the case to the magistrates with their opinion upon it (eg where an equivocal plea was wrongly considered to be a plea of guilty).

The hearing at the Crown Court, subject to provisions to avoid unreasonable delay, will be before the judge sitting with two Youth Court panel members (CPR 2015, r 34.11).

A Youth Court panel magistrate may not sit on the appeal of a matter upon which they adjudicated in the Youth Court (CPR 2015, r 34.11(a)(ii)).

On appeal against sentence alone or against conviction and sentence, the Crown Court may award a punishment the magistrates could have awarded whether it is more or less severe than the sentence appealed against (SCA 1981, s 48).

Appeal by way of case stated from the Youth Court

Applicability

16.08   The justices adjudicating may be asked to state a case for the opinion of the High Court by any party or any person who believes himself to be aggrieved by a conviction, order or other determination, on the ground that it was wrong in law or in excess of jurisdiction (MCA 1980, s 111).

In *James v Chief Constable of Kent* (1986) *The Times*, 7 June, Woolf LJ emphasised that an appeal by way of case stated was for an examination as to whether the justices had erred on matters of law. If the defendant was aggrieved by a decision of the justices as to matters of fact, the proper remedy was an appeal to the Crown Court, not the Queen's Bench Divisional Court.

In *R v Ealing Justices, ex parte Scrafield* [1994] RTR 195, it was made clear that the most appropriate way for an appellant to challenge a sentence imposed on him by justices was on appeal to the Crown Court, as opposed to the High Court by way of case stated. This approach was confirmed in the recent case of *Spillman v DPP* [2006] EWHC 1197 (Admin) in which it was decided that where the appellant wished to challenge findings of fact the correct course was usually to appeal to the Crown Court.

Persons who may apply

16.09   Any person or party to the proceedings may include, for example the prosecutor, victim of a crime who has not been given compensation, or a person adversely affected by an order for the restitution of stolen property, as in the case of *Moss v Hancock* [1899] 2 QB 111. A juvenile, being under 18, requires a 'litigation friend' in proceedings in the Crown Court. A 'litigation friend' will usually be the parent or guardian, or if no parent is willing to act it could be any responsible adult.

The application

16.10   The application must be made within 21 days of the justices' decision, in writing, and signed by or on behalf of the applicant.

The application must specify the decision in issue; specify the proposed question or questions of law or jurisdiction on which the opinion of the High Court will be asked; indicate the proposed grounds of appeal; and include or attach any other applications such as bail pending appeal, suspension of a driving disqualification pending appeal etc (CPR 2015, r 35.2(2)).

The submission in law for the High Court is that no reasonable tribunal, honestly applying its mind to the question, could have reached that conclusion on the facts adduced in evidence. The case stated itself should include the facts found by the court, and the question or questions of law or jurisdiction upon which the opinion of the High Court is sought. It should also include the representations of the parties, and the opinion or decision of the Youth Court. The question for the High Court should be as simple as possible reflecting the findings of fact, and seeking an answer that will decide whether the conviction or order can be upheld (CPR 2015, r 35.3).

Time limits

16.11   The application itself must be lodged with the appropriate officer within 21 days of the decision (ie the day on which the court makes its order or otherwise deals with the juvenile). In *Crown Prosecution Service v Newcastle-Upon-Tyne Youth Court* [2010] EWHC 2773 (Admin), it underlined the need for promptness in bringing judicial review proceedings, as the Crown Prosecution Service had taken five weeks to decide whether to seek judicial review of a Youth Court's decision to retain jurisdiction in respect of a juvenile, resulting in prejudice to the offender. Unless the court otherwise directs, not more than 21 days after the court's decision to state a case in a Magistrates' Court, the court officer must serve a draft case on each party which must not include an account of the evidence received by the court (CPR 2015, r 35.3(5)) except to the extent that CPR 2015, r 35.3(4)(d) requires (ie if a question is whether there was sufficient evidence on which the court reasonably could reach a finding of fact). The parties to the application then have a further 21 days in which to make representations in writing to the appropriate officer and each party concerned (CPR 2015, r 35.3(6)).

At the end of the 21-day period for representations the justices whose decision is being questioned have a further 21 days to consider the representations and make amendments to the draft case. The case itself, which may be stated on behalf of the justices by any two or more of them, shall contain a statement of facts found and the question of law or jurisdiction on which the opinion of the High Court is sought.

Unless the applicant contends that the decision was perverse, the case shall not contain a statement of evidence. The case shall be signed by the justices or, if they so direct, by their Justices' Clerk, and served on each party (CPR 2015, r 35.3).

The justices have power to require a recognisance from the appellant before they state a case, the condition of which is that he prosecutes the appeal without delay and submits to the judgment of the High Court and pays such costs as that court may award: MCA 1980, s 114.

Extensions of time

16.12   The court may shorten or extend (even if has expired) the time limit. However, a person who wants an extension of time must apply when serving the application, representations or draft case for which it is needed and explain the delay (CPR 2015, r 35.5).

Failure to state a case

16.13   Where the justices feel an application is frivolous they may refuse to state a case (MCA 1980, s 111(5)). Frivolous may be taken to mean futile, misconceived, hopeless or academic (see Lord Bingham in *R v Mildenhall Magistrates' Court, ex parte Forest Health District Council* (1997) 161 JP 401), or as having no prospect of success because the case is unarguable (*R v Betting Licensing Committee Cardiff Petty Sessions, ex parte Les Croupiers Casino Ltd* (unreported) 13 April 1992). Where such a refusal is made, the applicant may appeal to the High Court directly for an order of mandamus requiring the justices to state a case. In *Levi v North Somerset Magistrates' Courts* [2012] EWHC 1107 (Admin), the High Court allowed permission for the applicant to apply for judicial review to challenge the refusal of the magistrates' court to state a case, despite being long out of time.

The powers of the Divisional Court

16.14   The appeal to the Divisional Court by way of case stated does not proceed by a rehearing of the evidence but takes the form of legal argument before the High Court judges. The Divisional Court may reverse, affirm or amend the determination in respect of which the case had been stated, or remit the matter to the justices with the opinion of the court thereon or make such other order in relation to the matter as it sees fit (Senior Courts Act 1981, s 28A).

Upon applying to the justices to state a case an appellant loses the right to appeal to the Crown Court (MCA 1980, s 111(4)). Thus, in the case of *R v Winchester Crown Court, ex parte Lewington* (1982) 4 Cr App R (S) 224, it was held that an appellant who applied for a case stated, and subsequently withdrew the application, was debarred from appealing to the Crown Court against his conviction.

Bail pending appeal

16.15   Where a person who has given notice of appeal to the Crown Court against the decision of a Youth Court, or has applied to the Youth Court to state a case for the opinion of the High Court, is in custody the Youth Court may grant him bail (MCA 1980, s 113). The court has discretion as to whether or not to grant bail. The general right of accused persons to bail under the Bail Act 1976, s 4, does not apply.

The Youth Court will be reluctant to grant bail pending appeal when an expedited hearing of the appeal would be more appropriate. In *Re W (B) (an infant)* [1969] 1 All ER 594, CA, a respondent was committed to prison for contempt of court. He was subsequently granted bail, pending appeal, and Wimm LJ commented at the appeal hearing before the Divisional Court:

'It would be inappropriate today for this court to make any order which had the effect of returning S to prison, for it is well recognised that the court has greater reluctance in dismissing an appeal against sentence where bail has been granted during the period since sentence was imposed.'

The reasoning behind this is that bail pending appeal inevitably raises the defendant's hopes for a successful appeal, only for them to be dashed if the appeal is in fact unsuccessful. This point is illustrated by the case of *R v Lancastle* [1978] Crim LR 367, where an appellant had been released on bail pending appeal, and the Divisional Court commented: 'It was to be regretted that [the appellant] had been granted bail pending her appeal. It would have been preferable had she remained in custody and the hearing of her appeal been expedited.'

In the case of *R v Watton* [1978] 68 Cr App R 293, the Court of Appeal gave guidance as to how the court should exercise its discretion in the matter of bail pending appeal. The court indicated it only granted bail where the appeal seemed likely to succeed or where the sentence might have been served by the time the appeal was heard. Lord Lane CJ concluded that: 'the true question is, are there exceptional circumstances which would drive the court to the conclusion that justice can only be done by the granting of bail?'

A case involving a juvenile in which the question of bail pending appeal was considered is *R v Imdad Shah* (1978) 144 JP 460. Here the Crown Court sentenced a boy of 16 years to three months in a detention centre. He appealed to the Court of Appeal and was released on bail pending appeal. The result of this was that if his appeal was dismissed he would be due to go back to the detention centre for only one month, and the court was reluctant to send him back for that short period. If bail had not been granted he would, with remission, have served the full sentence.

The Court of Appeal said that bail should not be granted where the sentence appealed against was short. Instead the judge should take steps to see that the appeal was expedited. Roskill LJ again stressed that bail pending appeal should be granted only in exceptional circumstances.

Prosecution right of appeal against bail

16.16   Where bail is granted to a person charged with an offence punishable in the case of an adult with imprisonment, the prosecution may appeal to a Crown Court judge. They may only appeal if they made representations against the granting of bail. The prosecution must give oral notice at the end of the remand proceedings and written notice within two hours. The bailed juvenile must then be remanded into local authority accommodation or youth detention accommodation under the provisions of (LASPOA 2012, ss 98 or 99) until the appeal is heard and the hearing must be commenced within 48 hours from the date on which the notice was given (Bail Amendment Act 1993; CPR 2015, r 14.9). The prosecutor's notice of appeal means that the Youth Court (or if the proceedings are in the adult court), that court cannot grant bail. It is the Youth Court or adult court which decides whether the remand pending the appeal hearing will be to local authority accommodation (with or without conditions) or to youth detention accommodation. Given that bail type conditions can be added to a remand to local authority accommodation it is likely to be a rare situation where that court can justify a remand to youth detention accommodation unless there is new information.

Appeal from the Crown Court

16.17   Although strictly outside the ambit of this work it is worth noting that young people appearing in the Crown Court may also appeal. Juveniles may appear in the Crown Court as a result of being jointly charged with an adult or having been sent subject to a grave crime. An appeal from the Crown Court in these circumstances is made to the Court of Appeal. However, unlike an appeal from the Youth Court to the Crown Court an appeal may only proceed where the trial judge grants a certificate confirming that the case is a suitable one. This is known as a grant of leave to appeal. An application for leave to appeal may also be made to a High Court judge who will consider the application by reference to the papers. If he refuses leave the application may be renewed to the full Court of Appeal. Notice of application for leave to appeal must be lodged within 28 days of the decision of the court and must include the grounds of the appeal. See Pt 39 of CPR 2015 for appeals to the Court of Appeal against conviction or sentence. Also limited to young persons appearing in the Crown Court is the power given to the prosecution to appeal a sentence passed by the Crown Court which is unduly lenient. There is no such power to appeal from the case heard in the Youth Court. The Attorney-General must lodge notice of appeal to the Court of Appeal within 28 days of the decision complained of following the procedure in CJA 1988, ss 35 and 36 as amended.

Appendix A

Magistrates' Courts (Children and Young Persons) Rules 1992 (SI 1992 No 2071)

Part I
General

1 Citation and commencement

These Rules may be cited as the Magistrates' Courts (Children and Young Persons) Rules 1992 and shall come into force on 1st October 1992.

2 Interpretation

(1) In these Rules –

'the Act of 1933' means the Children and Young Persons Act 1933;

'the Act of 1969' means the Children and Young Persons Act 1969;

'the Act of 1989' means the Children Act 1989;

['the Act of 2000' means the Powers of Criminal Courts (Sentencing) Act 2000;]

'child' means a person under the age of fourteen;

'court' –

(a) in Parts II and IV and, subject to rule 13(2), in Part III, means a youth court, and

(b) in rules 26 to 29, means a magistrates' court whether a youth court or not;

['court computer system' means a computer or computer system which is used to assist to discharge and record the business of the court;]

'guardian' has the meaning given in section 107(1) of the Act of 1933;

'register' means the separate register kept for the youth court pursuant to rule 25 of these Rules; and

'young person' means a person who has attained the age of fourteen and is under the age of eighteen.

(2) In these Rules, unless the context otherwise requires, references to a parent in relation to a child or young person are references –

(a) where a local authority has parental responsibility for him under the Act of 1989, to the local authority, and

(b)   in any other case, to a parent who has parental responsibility for him under that Act.

(3) In these Rules, unless the context otherwise requires, any reference to a rule, Part or Schedule shall be construed as a reference to a rule contained in these Rules, a Part thereof or a Schedule thereto, and any reference in a rule to a paragraph shall be construed as a reference to a paragraph of that rule.

3 Revocations and savings etc

(1) Subject to paragraph (3), the Rules specified in Schedule 1 are hereby revoked to the extent specified.

(2) Subject to paragraph (3), the provisions of the Magistrates' Courts Rules 1981 shall have effect subject to these Rules.

(3) Nothing in these Rules shall apply in connection with any proceedings begun before the coming into force thereof.

Part II

. . .

4–12 . . .

. . .

Part III
Proceedings in Certain Other Matters

13 Application and interpretation of Part III

(1) This Part applies in connection with proceedings in a court in the case of any child or young person in relation to whom proceedings are brought or proposed to be brought under –

(a)   section 72 or 73 of the Social Work (Scotland) Act 1968 (persons subject to supervision requirements or orders moving from or to Scotland), or

(b)   regulations made under section 25 of the Act of 1989 (authority to retain child in secure accommodation),

except that rules 14,16(2), 20 and 21 do not apply in connection with proceedings under the enactments mentioned in sub-paragraph (a) above.

(2) In this Part –

'the applicant' means the person by whom proceedings are brought or proposed to be brought;

'court', in relation to proceedings of the kind mentioned in paragraph (1)(b), means a magistrates' court, whether a youth court or not, but does not include a family proceedings court: and

'the relevant minor' means the person in relation to whom proceedings are brought or proposed to be brought as mentioned in paragraph (1).

14 Notice by person proposing to bring proceedings

(1) The applicant shall send a notice to the [[designated officer] for] the court specifying the grounds for the proceedings and the names and addresses of the persons to whom a copy of the notice is sent in pursuance of paragraph (2).

(2) Without prejudice to section 34(2) of the Act of 1969 and regulations made under section 25 of the Act of 1989, the applicant shall –

(a)   send to each of the persons mentioned in paragraph (3) a copy of the said notice, and

(b)   notify each of those persons of the date, time and place appointed for the hearing unless a summons is issued for the purpose of securing his attendance thereat.

(3) The persons referred to in paragraph (2) are –

(a)   the relevant minor, unless it appears to the applicant inappropriate to notify him in pursuance of paragraph (2), having regard to his age and understanding,

(b)   the parent or guardian of the relevant minor if the whereabouts of such parent or guardian is known to the applicant or can readily be ascertained by him, and

[(c)   where the father and mother of the relevant minor were not married to each other at the time of his birth, any person who is known to the applicant to have made an application for an order under section 4 of the Act of 1989 (acquisition of parental responsibility by father) which has not yet been determined.

(d)   in a case where the relevant minor has a parent by virtue of section 43 of the Human Fertilisation and Embryology Act 2008, and the relevant minor is not a person to whom section 1(3) of the Family Law Reform Act 1987 applies, any person who is known to the applicant to have made an application for an order under section 4ZA of the Act of 1989 (acquisition of parental responsibility by second female parent) which has not yet been determined].

15 Rights of parents and guardians

Without prejudice to any provision of these Rules which provides for a parent or guardian to take part in proceedings, the relevant minor's parent or guardian shall be entitled to make representations to the court at any such stage after the conclusion of the evidence in the hearing as the court considers appropriate.

16 Adjournment of proceedings and procedure at hearing

(1) The court may, at any time, whether before or after the beginning of the hearing, adjourn the hearing, and, when so doing, may either fix the date, time and place at which the hearing is to be resumed or leave the date, time and place to be determined later by the court; but the hearing shall not be resumed at that date, time and place unless the court is satisfied that the applicant, the respondent and any other party to the proceedings have had adequate notice thereof.

(2) Subject to the provisions of the Act of 1969, sections 56, 57 and 123 of the Magistrates' Courts Act 1980 (non-appearance of parties and defects in process) shall apply to the proceedings as if they were by way of complaint and as if any references therein to the complainant, to the defendant and to the defence were, respectively, references to the applicant, to the relevant minor and to his case.

(3) Rules 14 and 16(1) of the Magistrates' Courts Rules 1981 (order of evidence and speeches and form of order) shall apply to the proceedings as if they were by way of complaint and as if any references therein to the complainant, to the defendant and to the defence were, respectively, references to the applicant, to the relevant minor and to his case.

17 Duty of court to explain nature of proceedings

Except where, by virtue of any enactment, the court may proceed in the absence of the relevant minor, before proceeding with the hearing the court shall inform him of the general nature both of the proceedings and of the grounds on which they are brought, in terms suitable to his age and understanding, or if by reason of his age and understanding or his absence it is impracticable so to do, shall so inform any parent or guardian of his present at the hearing.

18 Conduct of case on behalf of relevant minor

(1) Except where the relevant minor or his parent or guardian is legally represented, the court shall, unless the relevant minor otherwise requests, allow his parent or guardian to conduct the case on his behalf, subject, however, to the provisions of rule 19(2).

(2) If the court thinks it appropriate to do so it may, unless the relevant minor otherwise requests, allow a relative of his or some other responsible person to conduct the case on his behalf.

19 Power of court to hear evidence in absence of relevant minor and to require parent or guardian to withdraw

(1) Where the evidence likely to be given is such that in the opinion of the court it is in the interests of the relevant minor that the whole, or any part, of the evidence should not be given in his presence, then, unless he is conducting his own case, the court may hear the whole or part of the evidence, as it thinks appropriate, in his absence; but any evidence relating to his character or conduct shall be heard in his presence.

(2) If the court is satisfied that it is appropriate so to do, it may require a parent or guardian of the relevant minor to withdraw from the court while the relevant minor gives evidence or makes a statement; but the court shall inform the person so excluded of the substance of any allegations made against him by the relevant minor.

20 Duty of court to explain procedure to relevant minor at end of applicant's case

If it appears to the court after hearing the evidence in support of the applicant's case that he has made out *a prima facie* case it shall tell the relevant minor or the person conducting the case on his behalf under rule 18 that he may give evidence or make a statement and call witnesses.

21 Consideration of reports: secure accommodation proceedings

(1) The court shall arrange for copies of any written report before the court to be made available, so far as practicable before the hearing to –

(a)   the applicant,

(b)   the legal representative, if any, of the relevant minor,

(c)   the parent or guardian of the relevant minor, and

(d)   the relevant minor, except where the court otherwise directs on the ground that it appears to it impracticable to disclose the report having regard to his age and understanding or undesirable to do so having regard to potential serious harm which might thereby be suffered by him.

(2) In any case in which the court has determined that the relevant criteria are satisfied, the court shall, for the purpose of determining the maximum period of authorisation to be specified in the order, take into consideration such information as it considers necessary for that purpose, including such information which is provided in pursuance of section 9 of the Act of 1969.

(3) Any written report may be received and considered by the court without being read aloud.

22 Duty of court to explain manner in which it proposes to deal with case and effect of order

(1) Before finally disposing of the case, the court shall in simple language inform the relevant minor, any person conducting the case on his behalf, and his parent or guardian, if present,

of the manner in which it proposes to deal with the case and allow any of those persons so informed to make representations; but the relevant minor shall not be informed as aforesaid if the court considers it undesirable or, having regard to his age and understanding, impracticable so to inform him.

(2) On making any order, the court shall in simple language suitable to his age and understanding explain to the relevant minor the general nature and effect of the order unless it appears to it impracticable so to do having regard to his age and understanding and shall give such an explanation to the relevant minor's parent or guardian, if present.

Part IV
. . .

23–24 . . .

. . .

Part V
Miscellaneous

25–29 . . .

. . .

SCHEDULE 1
Revocations

Rule 3

Rules revoked	References	Extent of revocation
The Magistrates' Courts (Children and Young Persons) Rules 1988	SI 1988/913	The whole Rules
The Magistrates' Courts (Criminal Justice Act 1988) (Miscellaneous Amendments) Rules 1988	SI 1988/2132	Rule 4
The Family Proceedings Courts (Matrimonial Proceedings etc) Rules 1991	SI 1991/1991	Paragraph 7 of Schedule 2

SCHEDULE 2
Forms

Rule 29

Forms 1–6

. . .

Revoked by SI 2003/1236, rr 64, 71.

Date in force: 20 June 2003: see SI 2003/1236, r 1.

Form 7

. . .

Revoked, on the coming into force of the Criminal Procedure Rules 2005, SI 2005/384, by provision of r 2.1 thereof, the Courts Act 2003, the Courts Act 2003 (Commencement No 6 and Savings) Order 2004, SI 2004/2066 and the Courts Act 2003 (Consequential Amendments) Order 2004, SI 2004/2035.

Date in force: 4 April 2005: see SI 2005/384, r 2.1(3); for savings see SI 2004/2066, art 3 and SI 2005/384, r 2.1(3).

Forms 8–9

. . .

Revoked by SI 2003/1236, rr 64, 71.

Date in force: 20 June 2003: see SI 2003/1236, r 1.

Form 10

Revoked, on the coming into force of the Criminal Procedure Rules 2005, SI 2005/384, by provision of r 2.1 thereof, the Courts Act 2003, the Courts Act 2003 (Commencement No 6 and Savings) Order 2004, SI 2004/2066 and the Courts Act 2003 (Consequential Amendments) Order 2004, SI 2004/2035.

Date in force: 4 April 2005: see SI 2005/384, r 2.1(3); for savings see SI 2004/2066, art 3 and SI 2005/384, r 2.1(3).

Forms 11–54

. . .

Revoked by SI 2003/1236, rr 64, 71.

Date in force: 20 June 2003: see SI 2003/1236, r 1.

Appendix B

The Justices of the Peace Rules 2016 (Extracts relevant to Youth Courts)

Revocations and transitional provisions

2.—(1) Subject to paragraph (2)—

(c) the Youth Courts (Constitution of Committees and Right to Preside) Rules 2007 ('the Youth Courts Rules 2007') are revoked.

Interpretation

3. In these Rules—

'adult court' means a magistrates' court other than a youth court;

'JTAAAC' means a Justices' Training, Approvals, Authorisations and Appraisals Committee, and references to justices in relation to a JTAAAC mean justices assigned to the local justice area or areas in the JTAAAC area;

'JTAAAC area' means the area specified by or on behalf of the Lord Chief Justice as the area for which a JTAAAC operates;

'magistrates' court' means any court in which a justice is authorised to sit, other than a family court or a Crown Court, and

'youth justice' means a justice who is authorised by or on behalf of the Lord Chief Justice to sit as a member of a youth court.

Composition of magistrates' courts

Size of bench

4. The number of justices sitting to deal with a case as a magistrates' court must not be greater than three.

Presiding justices

5.—(1) This Rule does not apply to any justice sitting in a magistrates' court in accordance with s 16A of the Magistrates' Courts Act 1980.

(2) Subject to para (3), a magistrates' court must be presided over by—

(a)   a District Judge (Magistrates' Courts);

(b)   a justice who has been approved in accordance with these Rules, or

(c)   a justice who has completed or is undertaking approved training courses in accordance with r 19(b) or (d) (as applicable), and is under the supervision of a justice who has been approved to preside in that court.

(3) The justices present may, in the absence of a justice entitled to preside under para (2), appoint one of their number to preside in a magistrates' court to deal with any case if—

(a)   before making such an appointment, the justices present are satisfied as to the suitability for this purpose of the justice proposed, and

(b)   except as mentioned in para (4), the justice proposed has completed or is undertaking training courses in accordance with r 19(b) or (d) (as applicable) to enable that justice, if approved, to preside in that court.

(4) The condition in para (3)(b) does not apply if by reason of illness, circumstances unforeseen when the justices to sit were chosen, or other emergency, no justice who complies with that condition is present.

Elections Procedure

General provision

6. This Part sets out the election procedure for—

(a)   the offices of chairman and deputy chairman for each local justice area (and by virtue of a protocol issued by the Senior Presiding Judge the procedure is applied to Youth Court Panel Chairmen and Deputy Chairmen), and

(b)   membership of the FTAAAC and JTAAAC selection panels for each FTAAAC and JTAAAC area.

Eligibility of justices and family justices

7.—(1) A justice is eligible to stand for election and to vote in an election for the offices of chairman and deputy chairman, and membership of a JTAAAC selection panel if, on the relevant date, that justice is assigned to a local justice area to which the election relates.

(3) The relevant date in paras (1) and (2) is the day on which the justices' clerk informs the eligible justices under r 10(2).

Procedure for elections

8.—(1) The election procedure consists of a notice of candidacy procedure, and, except as provided in para (2), a secret ballot.

(2) A secret ballot is not required where the justices required to fill the available vacancies are elected under r 10(6)(a) or (b).

(3) The timetable for the election procedure must be determined by the justices' clerk and published before or at the start of the procedure.

(4) Any timetable must allow sufficient time for receipt of notices of candidacy and a secret ballot where required.

Deputy chairmen

9.—(1) The election procedure in respect of a deputy chairman must commence after the election of the chairman has been completed and the result declared.

(2) The number of deputy chairmen is determined by the justice elected as chairman for the duration of the term in which the deputy chairman or chairmen will serve.

Notice of candidacy procedure

10.—(1) Eligible justices who want to be elected in respect of a vacancy must complete a notice of candidacy.

(2) The justices' clerk must inform eligible justices that they may submit a notice of candidacy, in accordance with para (3).

(3) The justices' clerk must determine and specify:

(a)   the manner in which notices are to be submitted;

(b)   the means by which notices can be submitted, and

(c)   a closing date for receipt of notices.

(4) The justices' clerk, or anyone nominated to act on their behalf, must be satisfied that each notice has been submitted in accordance with the specifications made under para (3).

(5) A notice that has not been submitted in accordance with the specifications in para (3) must not be treated as a valid notice.

(6) Where—

(a)   a single valid notice of candidacy is received for a vacancy, the candidate who submitted that notice is elected;

(b)   the number of valid notices of candidacy received is less than or equal to the number of vacancies, those candidates are elected.

(7) As soon as practicable after an election under para (6), the justices' clerk must notify the candidates as to the result.

(8) As soon as practicable after notifying the candidates under para (7), the justices' clerk must notify the eligible justices as to the result.

Secret ballot

11.—(1) Where the valid notices of candidacy exceed the number of vacancies, the justices' clerk must arrange a secret ballot.

(2) The justices' clerk must inform the eligible justices that they may vote in the secret ballot in accordance with para (3).

(3) The justices' clerk must —

(a)   determine and specify the procedure to be followed for the ballot;

(b)   inform eligible justices of the names of the candidates and the means by which votes may be cast, and

(c)   specify a closing date by which votes must be cast if they are to be counted in the ballot.

(4) Where the election is for a single vacancy, each eligible justice may cast one vote in accordance with the specified procedure.

(5) Where the election is for more than one vacancy, each eligible justice may cast one vote per vacancy (up to but not exceeding the number of vacancies) in accordance with the specified procedure.

Determining result of secret ballot

12.—(1) Where there is a single vacancy, the candidate who receives the highest number of votes cast is elected.

(2) Where there is more than one vacancy, the requisite number of candidates (being the number equal to the number of vacancies) who have received the highest number of votes are elected.

(3) If—

(a)   two or more candidates have received an equal number of votes for a vacancy (the 'tied candidates'), and

(b)   taking into account the election of any candidate who has received a higher number of votes than the tied candidates—

    (i)   the election of one or more of the tied candidates is necessary to make up the requisite number, but

    (ii)   the election of all of the tied candidates would exceed the requisite number, the justices' clerk must decide between them by lot, and para (4) applies.

(4) Where this paragraph applies, the candidate or candidates (as applicable) on whom the lot falls is elected.

(5) As soon as practicable after an election under this Rule, the justices' clerk must notify the candidates, as to—

(a)   the result;

(b)   the number of votes cast for each candidate, and

(c)   where relevant, if a lot was required.

(6) As soon as practicable after notifying the candidates under paragraph (5), the justices' clerk must notify the eligible justices as to—

(a)   the result;

(b)   the number of votes cast for each candidate, and

(c)   where relevant, if a lot was required.

Miscellaneous provisions about secret ballots

13.—(1) Unless otherwise determined in accordance with r 16, the justices' clerk must not treat a ballot as invalidated by reason of—

(a)   information sent by the justices' clerk in accordance with the election procedure not being received by a justice,

(b)   a vote not being received by the justices' clerk.

(2) Where an eligible justice does not follow the specified procedure, any vote by that eligible justice must not be taken into account when the votes are counted.

(3) The justices' clerk and any other person carrying out the ballot procedure must not disclose how any justice voted in any ballot.

Withdrawal of notices of candidacy

14.—(1) A candidate may withdraw their notice of candidacy—

(a)   before the closing date for receipt of notices;(b) where, after the closing date, there is (or otherwise would be) a need for a ballot, before the justices' clerk has provided to the eligible justices the information under r 11 (3)(b), or

(c)   where there has been a ballot and an equality of votes requires the drawing of lots, before the lots are drawn.

(2) Where a candidate has withdrawn their notice of candidacy after the closing date for receipt of notices but before the justices' clerk has provided to the eligible justices the information under r 11(3)(b), the name of that candidate must be omitted from the ballot, save that—

(a)   where (after the withdrawal of the notice) there is only one candidate for a single vacancy, that candidate is elected, and

(b)   where (after the withdrawal of the notice) the number of candidates equals or is less than the number of vacancies, those candidates are elected.

(3) Where a candidate has withdrawn their notice after there has been a ballot and an equality of votes requires the drawing of lots, that candidate's name must not be included in the drawing of lots, save that—

(a)   where (after the withdrawal of the notice) there remains only one candidate for a single vacancy, that candidate is elected;

(b)   where (after the withdrawal of the notice) the number of candidates for the relevant vacancy equals or is less than the number of vacancies, those candidates are elected.

Absence or insufficiency of notices of candidacy

15.—(1)Where no notices of candidacy have been received within the relevant timetable, or all notices submitted are withdrawn, the justices' clerk must inform the eligible justices of that fact and inform them that they may further submit notices by a date specified by the justices' clerk.

(2) Where notices are received in accordance with para (1), the procedure set out at r 8 must be followed.

(3) If no notices are received in accordance with para (1) for the office of chairman, the justices' clerk must arrange a secret ballot, following the procedure in rr 11, 12 and 13.

(4) For the purposes of the secret ballot under para (3), all eligible justices must be treated as candidates and their names presented in alphabetical order for the vote.

(5) If no or insufficient notices are received in accordance with para (1) for the office of deputy chairman, any vacancy may remain for the duration of the term.

Material irregularity in election procedure

16.—(1) Where the justices' clerk is satisfied (either of their own motion or following representation from an eligible justice) that a material irregularity has occurred in the election procedure, the justices' clerk may revoke the result of the election and repeat the election procedure, or a part of it, in respect of the relevant vacancy or vacancies.

(2) An eligible justice must make a representation as to any material irregularity to the justices' clerk within 14 days of the notification of the result of the election under r 10(8) or 12(6).

(3) The justices' clerk must notify the eligible justice who made the representation of their decision within 14 days.

(4) If the justices' clerk does not repeat the election procedure, an eligible justice may, within 14 days of notice of such decision, request a judicial office holder, nominated for this purpose by the Lord Chief Justice, to revoke the result of the election and repeat the election procedure, or a part of it.

(5) The eligible justice making a request under para (4) must—

(a)   make the request in writing to the justices' clerk; and

(b)   specify the grounds on which the request is made.

(6) The nominated judicial office holder may—

(a)   confirm the result of the election, or

(b)   if satisfied that a material irregularity has occurred in the election procedure, revoke the result of the election and direct the justices' clerk to repeat the election procedure, or a part of it.

(7) The justices' clerk or nominated judicial office holder must give candidates and any eligible justice who has made representations under para (2), the opportunity to make representations before determining whether to repeat the election procedure, or any part of it.

Provisions specific to chairman and deputy chairmen

Duration of term in office and vacancies

17.—(1) Subject to paras (2), (5) and (6), a chairman and deputy chairman elected under rr 8 to 15 inclusive will serve a term of one year commencing on 1 April following their election and ending on 31 March of the following year (the 'normal term').

(2) The term may be less than one year if—

(a)   the chairman or deputy chairman ceases to act as such, whether by ceasing to be a justice, resignation or for any other reason, in which case the term finishes on the date the person ceases to act, or

(b)   the relevant local justice area ceases to exist, in which case the term finishes on the date the local justice area ceases to exist.

(3) Where a vacancy arises during the normal term under para (2), the justices' clerk must, as soon as possible, commence the election procedure in respect of the vacancy.

(4) Paragraph (3) does not apply if the vacancy is that of a deputy chairman and the chairman determines that the vacancy should not be filled.

(5) The term may commence on a date other than 1 April if—

(a)   there has been an election under para (3), in which case the term commences on the date of the election or such other date as may have been specified by or on behalf of the justices' clerk, or

(b)   a new local justice area is created, in which case a new term commences on the date that the new local justice area comes into existence.

(6) Subject to para (7), in respect of a justice elected to a vacancy under para (5), the term is until the end date of the normal term.

(7) If a justice is elected under para (5) in respect of a term commencing on a date between 1 January and 31 March in any given year, the term continues until 31 March of the following year.

Eligibility for re-election

18.—(1) A justice is not eligible to be elected as chairman for a local justice area for more than three terms in that local justice area, unless at least six years have elapsed since the justice last filled that vacancy.

(2) In any event, a justice is not eligible to be elected as chairman for a local justice area for more than six terms in total in any one local justice area.

(3) A justice is not eligible to be elected as a deputy chairman for a local justice area for more than five terms in any one local justice area.

Approvals, Authorisations, Training and Appraisals
Compulsory Training
Training provision for justices

19. A justice must not perform any of the following functions unless that justice has completed a training course approved by the Lord Chief Justice in respect of that function—

(c)   sitting as a youth justice;

(d)   presiding in the youth court;

Formation of JTAAAC

20.—(1)There must be one JTAAAC for each JTAAAC area.

(2) The Lord Chief Justice may amend JTAAAC areas, and in doing so shall—

(a)   specify the area that will form the new JTAAAC area, and

(b)   determine the membership of the JTAAAC for the area and the duration of the term of its members, having regard, as far as practicable, to the requirements of rr 22 and 28.

Functions of JTAAAC

21.—(1) Each JTAAAC must, as appropriate—

(a)   select justices to undertake training courses in relation to the functions set out at r 19(b) and (d);

(b)   grant and revoke approvals for justices to preside in the magistrates' courts;

(c)   grant authorisations on behalf of the Lord Chief Justice, and recommend revocations of authorisations, for justices to sit as youth justices, and

(d)   establish and operate a scheme for appraising the performance of justices within each JTAAAC area so as to satisfy itself that each justice demonstrates or continues to demonstrate the necessary competence in the role in which performance is being appraised.

(2) Each JTAAAC must, as appropriate—

(a)   identify the training needs of justices sitting in magistrates' courts in its area;

(b)   prepare a training plan to meet those needs;

(c)   specify that certain training is essential for all or certain justices, having regard to guidance issued by the Lord Chief Justice;

(d)   ensure there are arrangements in place to deliver the required training, and

(e)   monitor the training of justices in its area in relation to magistrates' courts.

(3) In undertaking the responsibilities in these Rules, each JTAAAC must have regard to—

(a)   guidance issued by the Lord Chief Justice;

(b)   the national training programme for justices;

(c)   any national minimum training provision;

(d)   any representations made to the JTAAAC concerning justices' training by any senior circuit judge in the JTAAAC area;

(e)   the budget for justices' training in the area, and

(f)   any requirements of the Lord Chief Justice to report on justices' training.

Membership of JTAAAC

23. The JTAAAC selection panel must, having regard to guidance from the Lord Chief Justice—

(a)   subject to r 22(1)(a), determine the number of justice members of the JTAAAC;

(b) consider the written applications and—

  (i) appoint the number of justice members required, and

  (ii) subject to r 28(1), determine the duration of the terms of members so appointed.

(10) The JTAAAC selection panel must ensure that sufficient members of a JTAAAC are youth justices.

(11) If insufficient youth justices have applied for membership of a JTAAAC, the JTAAAC selection panel must appoint sufficient other youth justices with their agreement.

Grant of approval or authorisation

30.—(1) In order to approve justices to preside in court or to authorise justices to sit as youth a JTAAAC must be satisfied that—

(a) each justice meets any criteria set out by the Lord Chief Justice for the relevant role;

(b) in respect of an authorisation to sit as a youth justice, the justice is suitable for that role;

(c) in respect of an approval to preside in court, the justice—

  (i) has completed training courses approved by the Lord Chief Justice for that function, and

  (ii) has been appraised as competent in that role in accordance with the appraisal scheme.

(2) Additional justices may not be authorised to sit as youth justices or approved to preside in court unless the justices' clerk advises the JTAAAC that additional justices for that role are required in the relevant local justice area.

Review of approvals and authorisations

32.—(1) This Rule applies to justices in respect of—

(a) any approval of justices to preside in the magistrates' court; and (b) any authorisation of justices to sit as a youth justice.

(2) A JTAAAC must review the approval or authorisation of a justice—

(a) if requested to do so by that justice;

(b) where a minimum sitting requirement has been laid down in directions made by the Lord Chief Justice, if the justice has not met that requirement;

(c) where no minimum sitting requirement has been laid down as in para (2)(b), if the justice has not sat in the role for which that justice is approved or authorised for a continuous period of 12 months preceding the date of the review;

(d) if it appears to the JTAAAC that a justice may not be suitable for the role for which an authorisation relates;

(e) if the justice has not completed, within a reasonable time, any training requirements specified in r 19;

(f) if the justice has not completed, within a reasonable time, one or more training requirements designated as essential pursuant to r 21(2)(c) or 25(2)(c);

(g) following an appraisal or series of appraisals carried out in accordance with this Rule or the appraisal scheme;

(h) where, following a complaint about a justices' performance or suitability to perform a particular function, the JTAAAC or FTAAAC is satisfied that the justice has failed to demonstrate the necessary competence in the role to which the approval or authorisation relates, or

(i) where, following a referral in relation to a complaint considered under the Judicial Conduct (Magistrates) Rules 2014(a), the JTAAAC is satisfied that the justice has failed to demonstrate the necessary competence in the role to which the approval or authorisation relates.

(3) A JTAAAC may review the approval or authorisation of any justice returning from absence of six months or more.

(4) Where a JTAAAC is investigating a complaint concerning the performance of a justice presiding in a magistrates' court, it may suspend the approval for that justice to preside pending the completion of its review under para (2).

(5) Following a review of an authorisation or an approval, the JTAAAC may take any action it considers appropriate, including one or more of the following—

(a) confirming the approval or authorisation;

(b) requiring the justice to undertake training or further training;

(c) requiring the justice to undertake one or more appraisal or further appraisals;

(d) revoking the approval to preside in court (either generally or in a specific role);

(e) recommending the revocation of an authorisation to sit as a youth justice;

(f) where satisfied that a justice has failed over a period of time to reach the required standard, instructing the justices' clerk to report the matter to the appropriate Lord Chancellor's advisory committee on Justices of the Peace.

Revocation of approvals and authorisations

33. A JTAAAC may revoke an approval of a justice to preside in court, or recommend to the Lord Chief Justice to revoke the authorisation to sit as a youth justice, as follows—

(a) where requested to do so by the justice who is the subject of the approval or authorisation;

(b) where the justice has not met the minimum sitting requirement as laid down in directions made by the Lord Chief Justice;

(c) if the justice has not completed, within a reasonable time, any training requirements specified in r 19;

(d) if the justice has not completed, within a reasonable time, one or more training requirements designated as essential pursuant to r 21(2)(c) or 25(2)(c);

(e) where the justice has failed to undertake training or appraisal required under r 32(5);

(f) where the JTAAAC or FTAAAC is satisfied that the justice is no longer suitable to sit in the role to which the authorisation relates, or

(g)   where the JTAAAC or FTAAAC is satisfied that the justice fails to demonstrate the necessary competence in the role to which the approval or authorisation relates.

Reconsideration and review procedure

34.—(1) This Rule applies where a justice is dissatisfied with a decision made by a JTAAAC—

(a)   not to select the justice for training in relation to the functions set out at r 19(b)(d) or (f);

(b)   following a review under r 31 or 32, or

(c)   following a revocation or recommendation of revocation under r 33.

(2) The justice concerned may—

(a)   request the JTAAAC to reconsider its decision;

(b)   where permitted by the procedure prescribed by the Lord Chief Justice or the committee, ask the chairman of the justices for the local justice area to which they are assigned, to review the decision.

(3) The chairman considering a review under para (2)(b) may—

(a)   confirm the JTAAAC's, or

(b)   direct the JTAAAC to reconsider its decision.

Review of excess authorisations

35.—(1) Where a JTAAAC is advised by the justices' clerk that the number of justices required to sit as a family or youth justice is excessive, to the extent that justices cannot sit sufficiently often to meet their minimum sitting requirements, it may—

(a)   invite authorised justices to resign their authorisation, or

(b)   recommend that the Lord Chief Justice revokes any authorisation.

(2) Any recommendation to revoke any authorisation under this Rule must be decided by lot in such a way as to retain a sufficient number of justices approved to preside to enable them to carry out their functions.

Appendix C

Criminal Procedure Rules 2015
(Current as at April 2017)

Only parts of the Rules are set out in this Appendix.

A full set of the rules together with notes can be found at www.justice. gov.uk

Part 1 The Overriding Objective

1.1 The overriding objective

(1) The overriding objective of this new code is that criminal cases be dealt with justly.

(2) Dealing with a criminal case justly includes –

(a) acquitting the innocent and convicting the guilty;

(b) dealing with the prosecution and the defence fairly;

(c) recognising the rights of a defendant, particularly those under Article 6 of the European Convention on Human Rights;

(d) respecting the interests of witnesses, victims and jurors and keeping them informed of the progress of the case;

(e) dealing with the case efficiently and expeditiously;

(f) ensuring that appropriate information is available to the court when bail and sentence are considered; and

(g) dealing with the case in ways that take into account –

　　(i)　the gravity of the offence alleged,

　　(ii)　the complexity of what is in issue,

　　(iii)　the severity of the consequences for the defendant and others affected, and

　　(iv)　the needs of other cases.

1.2 The duty of the participants in a criminal case

(1) Each participant, in the conduct of each case, must –

(a) prepare and conduct the case in accordance with the overriding objective;

(b)   comply with these Rules, practice directions and directions made by the court; and

(c)   at once inform the court and all parties of any significant failure (whether or not that participant is responsible for that failure) to take any procedural step required by these Rules, any practice direction or any direction of the court. A failure is significant if it might hinder the court in furthering the overriding objective.

(2) Anyone involved in any way with a criminal case is a participant in its conduct for the purposes of this rule.

1.3 The application by the court of the overriding objective

The court must further the overriding objective in particular when –

(a)   exercising any power given to it by legislation (including these Rules);

(b)   applying any practice direction; or

(c)   interpreting any rule or practice direction.

Part 3 Case management

3.1 The scope of this Part

This Part applies to the management of each case in a magistrates' court and in the Crown Court (including an appeal to the Crown Court) until the conclusion of that case.

3.2 The duty of the court

(1) The court must further the overriding objective by actively managing the case.

(2) Active case management includes –

(a)   the early identification of the real issues;

(b)   the early identification of the needs of witnesses;

(c)   achieving certainty as to what must be done, by whom, and when, in particular by the early setting of a timetable for the progress of the case;

(d)   monitoring the progress of the case and compliance with directions;

(e)   ensuring that evidence, whether disputed or not, is presented in the shortest and clearest way;

(f)   discouraging delay, dealing with as many aspects of the case as possible on the same occasion, and avoiding unnecessary hearings;

(g)   encouraging the participants to co-operate in the progression of the case; and

(h)   making use of technology.

(3) The court must actively manage the case by giving any direction appropriate to the needs of that case as early as possible.

(4) Where appropriate live links are available, making use of technology for the purposes of this rule includes directing the use of such facilities, whether an application for such a direction is made or not—

(a)   for the conduct of a pre-trial hearing, including a pre-trial case management hearing;

(b)   for the defendant's attendance at such a hearing—

    (i)   where the defendant is in custody, or where the defendant is not in custody and wants to attend by live link, but

    (ii)   only if the court is satisfied that the defendant can participate effectively by such means, having regard to all the circumstances including whether the defendant is represented or not; and

(c)   for receiving evidence under one of the powers to which the rules in Pt 18 apply (Measures to assist a witness or defendant to give evidence).

(5) Where appropriate telephone facilities are available, making use of technology for the purposes of this rule includes directing the use of such facilities, whether an application for such a direction is made or not, for the conduct of a pre-trial case management hearing—

(a)   if telephone facilities are more convenient for that purpose than live links;

(b)   unless at that hearing the court expects to take the defendant's plea; and

(c)   only if—

    (i)   the defendant is represented, or

    (ii)   exceptionally, the court is satisfied that the defendant can participate effectively by such means without a representative.

3.3 The duty of the parties

(1) Each party must –

(a)   actively assist the court in fulfilling its duty under r 3.2, without or if necessary with a direction; and

(b)   apply for a direction if needed to further the overriding objective.

(2) Active assistance for the purposes of this rule includes—

(a)   at the beginning of the case, communication between the prosecutor and the defendant at the first available opportunity and in any event no later than the beginning of the day of the first hearing;

(b)   after that, communication between the parties and with the court officer until the conclusion of the case;

(c)   by such communication establishing, among other things—

    (i)   whether the defendant is likely to plead guilty or not guilty,

    (ii)   what is agreed and what is likely to be disputed,

    (iii)   what information, or other material, is required by one party of another, and why, and

    (iv)   what is to be done, by whom, and when (without or if necessary with a direction);

(d)   reporting on that communication to the court—

    (i)   at the first hearing, and

    (ii)   after that, as directed by the court; and

(e) alerting the court to any reason why—

    (i) a direction should not be made in any of the circumstances listed in r 3.2(4) or (5) (the duty of the court: use of live link or telephone facilities), or

    (ii) such a direction should be varied or revoked.

3.4 Case progression officers and their duties

(1) At the beginning of the case each party must, unless the court otherwise directs –

(a) nominate an individual responsible for progressing that case; and

(b) tell other parties and the court who that person is and how to contact that person.

(2) In fulfilling its duty under r 3.2, the court must where appropriate –

(a) nominate a court officer responsible for progressing the case; and

(b) make sure the parties know who he is and how to contact that court officer.

(3) In this Part a person nominated under this rule is called a case progression officer.

(4) A case progression officer must –

(a) monitor compliance with directions;

(b) make sure that the court is kept informed of events that may affect the progress of that case;

(c) make sure that he can be contacted promptly about the case during ordinary business hours;

(d) act promptly and reasonably in response to communications about the case; and

(e) if he or she will be unavailable, appoint a substitute to fulfil his or her duties and inform the other case progression officers.

3.5 The court's case management powers

(1) In fulfilling its duty under r 3.2 the court may give any direction and take any step actively to manage a case unless that direction or step would be inconsistent with legislation, including these Rules.

(2) In particular, the court may –

(a) nominate a judge, magistrate, or justices' legal adviser to manage the case;

(b) give a direction on its own initiative or on application by a party;

(c) ask or allow a party to propose a direction;

(d) receive applications, notices, representations and information by letter, by telephone, by live link, by email or by any other means of electronic communication, and conduct a hearing by live link, telephone or other such electronic means;

(e) give a direction –

    (i) at a hearing, in public or in private, or

    (ii) without a hearing;

(f) fix, postpone, bring forward, extend, cancel or adjourn a hearing;

(g) shorten or extend (even after it has expired) a time limit fixed by a direction;

(h)   require that issues in the case should be –

    (i)   identified in writing,

    (ii)   determined separately, and decide in what order they will be determined; and

(i)   specify the consequences of failing to comply with a direction.

(3) A magistrates' court may give a direction that will apply in the Crown Court if the case is to continue there.

(4) The Crown Court may give a direction that will apply in a magistrates' court if the case is to continue there.

(5) Any power to give a direction under this Part includes a power to vary or revoke that direction.

(6) If a party fails to comply with a rule or a direction, the court may –

(a)   fix, postpone, bring forward, extend, cancel or adjourn a hearing;

(b)   exercise its powers to make a costs order; and

(c)   impose such other sanction as may be appropriate.

3.6 Application to vary a direction

(1) A party may apply to vary a direction if –

(a)   the court gave it without a hearing;

(b)   the court gave it at a hearing in his absence; or

(c)   circumstances have changed.

(2) A party who applies to vary a direction must –

(a)   apply as soon as practicable after he becomes aware of the grounds for doing so; and

(b)   give as much notice to the other parties as the nature and urgency of his application permits.

3.7 Agreement to vary a time limit fixed by a direction

(1) The parties may agree to vary a time limit fixed by a direction, but only if –

(a)   the variation will not –

    (i)   affect the date of any hearing that has been fixed, or

    (ii)   significantly affect the progress of the case in any other way;

(b)   the court has not prohibited variation by agreement; and

(c)   the court's case progression officer is promptly informed.

(2) The court's case progression officer must refer the agreement to the court if he doubts the condition in paragraph (1)(a) is satisfied.

3.8 Court's power to vary requirements under this Part

(1) The court may—

(a)   shorten or extend (even after it has expired) a time limit set by this Part; and

(b)   allow an application or representations to be made orally.

(2) A person who wants an extension of time must—

(a) apply when serving the application or representations for which it is needed; and

(b) explain the delay.

3.9 Case preparation and progression

(1) At every hearing, if a case cannot be concluded there and then the court must give directions so that it can be concluded at the next hearing or as soon as possible after that.

(2) At every hearing the court must, where relevant—

(a) if the defendant is absent, decide whether to proceed nonetheless;

(b) take the defendant's plea (unless already done) or if no plea can be taken then find out whether the defendant is likely to plead guilty or not guilty;

(c) set, follow or revise a timetable for the progress of the case, which may include a timetable for any hearing including the trial or (in the Crown Court) the appeal;

(d) in giving directions, ensure continuity in relation to the court and to the parties' representatives where that is appropriate and practicable; and

(e) where a direction has not been complied with, find out why, identify who was responsible, and take appropriate action.

(3) In order to prepare for the trial, the court must take every reasonable step—

(a) to encourage and to facilitate the attendance of witnesses when they are needed; and

(b) to facilitate the participation of any person, including the defendant.

(4) Facilitating the participation of the defendant includes finding out whether the defendant needs interpretation because—

(a) the defendant does not speak or understand English; or

(b) the defendant has a hearing or speech impediment.

(5) Where the defendant needs interpretation—

(a) the court officer must arrange for interpretation to be provided at every hearing which the defendant is due to attend;

(b) interpretation may be by an intermediary where the defendant has a speech impediment, without the need for a defendant's evidence direction;

(c) on application or on its own initiative, the court may require a written translation to be provided for the defendant of any document or part of a document, unless—

  (i)   translation of that document, or part, is not needed to explain the case against the defendant, or

  (ii) the defendant agrees to do without and the court is satisfied that the agreement is clear and voluntary and that the defendant has had legal advice or otherwise understands the consequences;

(d) on application by the defendant, the court must give any direction which the court thinks appropriate, including a direction for interpretation by a different interpreter, where—

  (i)   no interpretation is provided,

(ii) no translation is ordered or provided in response to a previous application by the defendant, or

(iii) the defendant complains about the quality of interpretation or of any translation.

(6) Facilitating the participation of any person includes giving directions for the appropriate treatment and questioning of a witness or the defendant, especially where the court directs that such questioning is to be conducted through an intermediary.

(7) Where directions for appropriate treatment and questioning are required, the court must—

(a) invite representations by the parties and by any intermediary; and

(b) set ground rules for the conduct of the questioning, rules that may include—

    (i) a direction relieving a party of any duty to put that party's case to a witness or a defendant in its entirety,

    (ii) directions about the manner of questioning,

    (iii) directions about the duration of questioning,

    (iv) if necessary, directions about the questions that may or may not be asked,

    (v) where there is more than one defendant, the allocation among them of the topics about which a witness may be asked, and

    (vi) directions about the use of models, plans, body maps or similar aids to help communicate a question or an answer.

3.10 Readiness for trial or appeal

(1) This rule applies to a party's preparation for trial or appeal, and in this rule and r 3.10 trial includes any hearing at which evidence will be introduced.

(2) In fulfilling his duty under r 3.3, each party must –

(a) comply with directions given by the court;

(b) take every reasonable step to make sure his witnesses will attend when they are needed;

(c) make appropriate arrangements to present any written or other material; and

(d) promptly inform the court and the other parties of anything that may –

    (i) affect the date or duration of the trial or appeal, or

    (ii) significantly affect the progress of the case in any other way.

(3) The court may require a party to give a certificate of readiness.

3.11 Conduct of a trial or an appeal

In order to manage a trial or an appeal, the court –

(a) must establish, with the active assistance of the parties, what are the disputed issues;

(b) must consider setting a timetable that –

    (i) takes account of those issues and of any timetable proposed by a party, and

    (ii) may limit the duration of any stage of the hearing;

(c) may require a party to identify –

    (i) which witnesses that party wants to give evidence in person,

    (ii) the order in which that party wants those witnesses to give their evidence,

    (iii) whether that party requires an order compelling the attendance of a witness,

    (iv) what arrangements are desirable to facilitate the giving of evidence by a witness,

    (v) what arrangements are desirable to facilitate the participation of any other person, including the defendant,

    (vi) what written evidence that party intends to introduce,

    (vii) what other material, if any, that person intends to make available to the court in the presentation of the case, and

    (viii) whether that party intends to raise any point of law that could affect the conduct of the trial or appeal; and

(d) may limit –

    (i) the examination, cross-examination or re-examination of a witness, and

    (ii) the duration of any stage of the hearing.

3.12 Duty of court officer

(1) The court officer must—

(a) where a person is entitled or required to attend a hearing, give as much notice as reasonably practicable to—

    (i) that person, and

    (ii) that person's custodian (if any);

(b) where the court gives directions, promptly make a record available to the parties.

Part 4 Service of documents

4.1 When this Part applies

(1) The rules in this Part apply—

(a) to the service of every document in a case to which these rules apply; and

(b) for the purposes of s 12 of the Road Traffic Offenders Act 1988, to the service of a requirement to which that section applies.

(2) The rules apply subject to any special rules in other legislation (including other Parts of these rules) or in the Practice Direction.

4.2 Methods of service

(1) A document may be served by any of the methods described in rr 4.3 to 4.6 (subject to rr 4.7 and 4.10), or in r 4.8.

(2) Where a document may be served by electronic means, the general rule is that the person serving it will use that method.

4.3 Service by handing over a document

(1) A document may be served on –

(a)   an individual by handing it to him or her;

(b)   a corporation by handing it to a person holding a senior position in that corporation;

(c)   an individual or corporation who is legally represented in the case by handing it to that representative;

(d)   the prosecution by handing it to the prosecutor or to the prosecution representative;

(e)   the court officer by handing it to a court officer with authority to accept it at the relevant court office; and

(f)   the Registrar of Criminal Appeals by handing it to a court officer with authority to accept it at the Criminal Appeal Office.

(2) If an individual is **under 18**, a copy of a document served under paragraph (1)(a) must be handed to his or her parent, or another appropriate adult, unless no such person is readily available.

4.4 Service by leaving or posting a document

(1) A document may be served by leaving it at the appropriate address for service under this rule or by sending it to that address by first class post or by the equivalent of first class post.

(2) The address for service under this rule on –

(a)   an individual is an address where it is reasonably believed that he or she will receive it;

(b)   a corporation is its principal office, and if there is no readily identifiable principal office then any place where it carries on its activities or business;

(c)   an individual or corporation who is legally represented in the case is that representative's office;

(d)   the prosecution is the prosecutor's office;

(e)   the court officer is the relevant court office; and

(f)   the Registrar of Criminal Appeals is the Criminal Appeal Office, Royal Courts of Justice, Strand, London WC2A 2LL.

4.5 Service through a document exchange

(1) A document may be served by document exchange (DX) where –

(a)   the person to be served –

  (i)   has given a DX box number, and

  (ii)   has not refused to accept service by DX; or

(b)   the person to be served is legally represented in the case and the representative has given a DX box number.

(2) A document may be served by –

(a)   addressing it to that person or representative as appropriate, at that DX box number; and

(b)   leaving it at –

> (i)   the document exchange at which the addressee has that DX box number, or
>
> (ii)   a document exchange at which the person serving it has a DX box number.

4.6 Service by electronic means

(1) A document may be served by electronic means where –

(a)   the person to be served –

> (i)   has given an electronic address, and has not refused to accept service by that method; or
>
> (ii)   is given access to an electronic address at which a document may be deposited and has not refused to accept service by the deposit of a document at that address; or

(b)   the person to be served is legally represented in the case and the legal representative –

> (i)   has given an electronic address, or
>
> (ii)   is given access to an electronic address at which a document may be deposited.

(2) A document may be served –

(a)   by sending it by electronic means to the address which the recipient has given; or

(b)   by depositing it at an address to which the recipient has been given access and –

> (i)   in every case, making it possible for the recipient to read the document, or view or listen to its content, as the case may be,
>
> (ii)   unless the court otherwise directs, making it possible for the recipient to make and keep an electronic copy of the document, and
>
> (iii)   notifying the recipient of the deposit of the document (which notice may be given by electronic means).

(3) Where a document is served under this rule the person serving it need not provide a paper copy as well.

4.7 Documents that must be served by specified methods

(1) An application or written statement, and notice, under r 48.9 alleging contempt of court may be served –

(a)   on an individual, only under r 4.3(1)(a) (by handing it to him or her);

(b)   on a corporation, only under r 4.3(1)(b) (by handing it to a person holding a senior position in that corporation).

(2) For the purposes of s 12 of the Road Traffic Offenders Act 1988, a notice of a requirement under s 172 of the Road Traffic Act 1988 or under s 112 of the Road Traffic Regulation Act 1984 to identify the driver of a vehicle may be served –

(a)   on an individual, only by post under r 4.4(1) and (2)(a);

(b)   on a corporation, only by post under r 4.4(1) and (2)(b).

4.8 *Service by person in custody*

(1) A person in custody may serve a document by handing it to the custodian addressed to the person to be served.

(2) The custodian must –

(a)   endorse it with the time and date of receipt;

(b)   record its receipt; and

(c)   forward it promptly to the addressee.

4.9 *Service by another method*

(1) The court may allow service of a document by a method –

(a)   other than those described in rr 4.3 to 4.6 and in r 4.8;

(b)   other than one specified by r 4.7, where that rule applies.

(2) An order allowing service by another method must specify –

(a)   the method to be used; and

(b)   the date on which the document will be served.

4.10 *Documents that may not be served on a legal representative*

(1) Unless the court otherwise directs, service on a party's legal representative of any of the following documents is not service of that document on that party –

(a)   a summons, requisition, single justice procedure notice or witness summons;

(b)   notice of an order under s 25 of the Road Traffic Offenders Act 1988;

(c)   a notice of registration under s 71(6) of that Act(b);

(d)   notice of a hearing to review the postponement of the issue of a warrant of detention or imprisonment under s 77(6) of the Magistrates' Courts Act 1980;

(e)   notice under s 86 of that Act of a revised date to attend a means inquiry;

(f)   any notice or document served under Pt 14 (Bail and custody time limits);

(g)   notice under r 24.16(a) of when and where an adjourned hearing will resume;

(h)   notice under r 28.5(3) of an application to vary or discharge a compensation order;

(i)   notice under r 28.10(2)(c) of the location of the sentencing or enforcing court;

(j)   a collection order, or notice requiring payment, served under r 30.2(a); or

(k)   an application or written statement, and notice, under r 48.9 alleging contempt of court.

4.11 *Date of service*

(1) A document served under r 4.3 or r 4.8 is served on the day it is handed over.

(2) Unless something different is shown, a document served on a person by any other method is served –

(a)   in the case of a document left at an address, on the next business day after the day on which it was left;

(b)   in the case of a document sent by first class post or by the equivalent of first class post, on the second business day after the day on which it was posted or dispatched;

(c)   in the case of a document served by document exchange, on the second business day after the day on which it was left at a document exchange allowed by r 4.5;

(d)   in the case of a document transmitted by electronic means,

    (i)   on the day on which it is sent under r 4.6(2)(a), if that day is a business day and if it is sent by no later than 2.30pm that day,

    (ii)   on the day on which notice of its deposit is given under r 4.6(2)(b), if that day is a business day and if that notice is given by no later than 2.30pm that day, or

    (iii)   otherwise, on the next business day after it was sent or such notice was given; and

(e)   in any case, on the day on which the addressee responds to it if that is earlier.

(3) Unless something different is shown, a document produced by a court computer system is to be taken as having been sent by first class post or by the equivalent of first class post to the addressee on the business day after the day on which it was produced, (note: 'business day' means any day except Saturday, Sunday, Christmas Day, Boxing Day, Good Friday, Easter Monday or a bank holiday – see r 2.2).

(4) Where a document is served on or by the court officer, 'business day' does not include a day on which the court office is closed.

4.12 Proof of service

The person who serves a document may prove that by signing a certificate explaining how and when it was served.

4.13 Court's power to give directions about service

(1) The court may specify the time as well as the date by which a document must be –

(a)   served under r 4.3 or r 4.8; or

(b)   sent or deposited by electronic means, if it is served under r 4.6.

(2) The court may treat a document as served if the addressee responds to it even if it was not served in accordance with the rules in this Part.

Part 5 Forms and court records

5.3 Signature of forms

(1) This rule applies where a form provides for its signature.

(2) Unless other legislation otherwise requires, or the court otherwise directs, signature may be by any written or electronic authentication of the form by, or with the authority of, the signatory.

Part 7 Starting a prosecution in a magistrates' court

7.1 When this Part applies

(1) This Part applies in a magistrates' court where –

(a)   a prosecutor wants the court to issue a summons or warrant under s1 of the Magistrates' Courts Act 1980;

(b)   a prosecutor with the power to do so issues –

  (i)   a written charge and requisition, or

  (ii)   a written charge and single justice procedure notice under s 29 of the Criminal Justice Act 2003;

(c)   a person who is in custody is charged with an offence.

(2) In this Part, 'authorised prosecutor' means a prosecutor authorised under s 29 of the Criminal Justice Act 2003 to issue a written charge and requisition or single justice procedure notice.

7.2 Information and written charge

(1) A prosecutor who wants the court to issue a summons must –

(a)   serve an information in writing on the court officer; or

(b)   unless other legislation prohibits this, present an information orally to the court, with a written record of the allegation that it contains.

(2) A prosecutor who wants the court to issue a warrant must –

(a)   serve on the court officer:

  (i)   an information in writing, or

  (ii)   a copy of a written charge that has been issued; or

(b)   present to the court either of those documents.

(3) An authorised prosecutor who issues a written charge must notify the court officer immediately.

(4) A single document may contain –

(a)   more than one information; or

(b)   more than one written charge.

(5) Where an offence can be tried only in a magistrates' court, then unless other legislation otherwise provides –

(a)   a prosecutor must serve an information on the court officer or present it to the court; or

(b)   an authorised prosecutor must issue a written charge, not more than six months after the offence alleged.

(6) Where an offence can be tried in the Crown Court then –

(a)   a prosecutor must serve an information on the court officer or present it to the court; or

(b)   an authorised prosecutor must issue a written charge, within any time limit that applies to that offence.

7.3 Allegation of offence in information or charge

(1) An allegation of an offence in an information or charge must contain –

(a)   a statement of the offence that –

     (i)   describes the offence in ordinary language, and

     (ii)   identifies any legislation that creates it; and

(b)   such particulars of the conduct constituting the commission of the offence as to make clear what the prosecutor alleges against the defendant.

(2) More than one incident of the commission of the offence may be included in the allegation if those incidents taken together amount to a course of conduct having regard to the time, place or purpose of commission.

7.4 Summons, warrant and requisition

(1) The court may issue or withdraw a summons or warrant –

(a)   without giving the parties an opportunity to make representations; and

(b)   without a hearing, or at a hearing in public or in private.

(2) A summons, warrant or requisition may be issued in respect of more than one offence.

(3) A summons or requisition must –

(a)   contain notice of when and where the defendant is required to attend the court;

(b)   specify each offence in respect of which it is issued; and

(c)   in the case of a summons, identify –

     (i)   the court that issued it, unless that is otherwise recorded by the court officer, and

     (ii)   the court office for the court that issued it; and

(d)   in the case of a requisition, identify the person under whose authority it is issued.

(4) A summons may be contained in the same document as an information.

(5) A requisition may be contained in the same document as a written charge.

(6) Where the court issues a summons –

(a)   the prosecutor must –

     (i)   serve it on the defendant, and

     (ii)   notify the court officer; or

(b)   the court officer must –

     (i)   serve it on the defendant, and

     (ii)   notify the prosecutor.

(7) Where an authorised prosecutor issues a requisition that prosecutor must –

(a)   serve on the defendant –

     (i)   the requisition, and

     (ii)   the written charge; and

(b)   serve a copy of each on the court officer.

(8) Unless it would be inconsistent with other legislation, a replacement summons or requisition may be issued without a fresh information or written charge where the one replaced –

(a) was served by leaving or posting it under r 4.7 (documents that must be served only by handing them over, leaving or posting them); but

(b) is shown not to have been received by the addressee.

(9) A summons or requisition issued to a defendant under 18 may require that defendant's parent or guardian to attend the court with the defendant, or a separate summons or requisition may be issued for that purpose.

Part 13 Warrants

13.1 When this Part applies

(1) This Part applies where the court can issue a warrant for arrest, detention or imprisonment.

(2) In this Part, 'defendant' means anyone against whom such a warrant is issued.

13.2 Terms of a warrant for arrest

A warrant for arrest must require the person(s) to whom it is directed to arrest the defendant and –

(a) bring the defendant to a court –

(i)   specified in the warrant, or

(ii)   required or allowed by law; or

(b) release the defendant on bail (with conditions or without) to attend court at a date, time and place –

(i)   specified in the warrant, or

(ii)   to be notified by the court.

13.4 Information to be included in a warrant

(1) A warrant must identify –

(a) each person to whom it is directed;

(b) the defendant against whom it was issued;

(c) the reason for its issue;

(d) the court that issued it, unless that is otherwise recorded by the court officer; and

(e) the court office for the court that issued it.

(2) A warrant for detention or imprisonment must contain a record of any decision by the court under –

(a) section 91 of the Legal Aid, Sentencing and Punishment of Offenders Act 2012 (remands of children otherwise than on bail), including in particular –

(i)   whether the defendant must be detained in local authority accommodation or youth detention accommodation,

(ii)   the local authority designated by the court,

(iii)   any requirement imposed by the court on that authority,

(iv)   any condition imposed by the court on the defendant, and

(v)   the reason for any such requirement or condition;

(b)   section 80 of the Magistrates' Courts Act 1980 (application of money found on defaulter to satisfy sum adjudged); or

(c)   section 82(1) or (4) of the 1980 Act(c) (conditions for issue of a warrant).

(3) A warrant that contains an error is not invalid, as long as –

(a)   it was issued in respect of a lawful decision by the court; and

(b)   it contains enough information to identify that decision.

Part 18 Measures to assist a witness or defendant to give evidence

18.1 When this Part applies

(1) This Part applies –

(a)   where the court can give a direction (a 'special measures direction'), under s 19 of the Youth Justice and Criminal Evidence Act 1999, on an application or on its own initiative, for any of the following measures –

    (i)   preventing a witness from seeing the defendant (s 23 of the 1999 Act),

    (ii)   allowing a witness to give evidence by live link (s 24 of the 1999 Act),

    (iii) hearing a witness' evidence in private (s 25 of the 1999 Act),

    (iv)   dispensing with the wearing of wigs and gowns (s 26 of the 1999 Act),

    (v)   admitting video recorded evidence (ss 27 and 28 of the 1999 Act),

    (vi)   questioning a witness through an intermediary (s 29 of the 1999 Act),

    (vii) using a device to help a witness communicate (s 30 of the 1999 Act);

(b)   where the court can vary or discharge such a direction, under s 20 of the 1999 Act;

(c)   where the court can give, vary or discharge a direction (a 'defendant's evidence direction') for a defendant to give evidence –

    (i)   by live link, under s 33A of the 1999 Act, or

    (ii)   through an intermediary, under ss 33BA and 33BB of the 1999 Act;

(d)   where the court can –

    (i)   make a witness anonymity order, under s 86 of the Coroners and Justice Act 2009, or

    (ii)   vary or discharge such an order, under ss 91, 92 or 93 of the 2009 Act;

(e)   where the court can give or discharge a direction (a 'live link direction'), on an application or on its own initiative, for a witness to give evidence by live link under –

    (i)   section 32 of the Criminal Justice Act 1988, or

    (ii)   sections 51 and 52 of the Criminal Justice Act 2003;

(f)   where the court can exercise any other power it has to give, vary or discharge a direction for a measure to help a witness give evidence.

18.2 Meaning of 'witness'

In this Part, 'witness' means anyone (other than a defendant) for whose benefit an application, direction or order is made.

18.3 Making an application for a direction or order

A party who wants the court to exercise its power to give or make a direction or order must –

(a)   apply in writing as soon as reasonably practicable, and in any event –

(i)   not more than 28 days after the defendant pleads not guilty; and

(b)   serve the application on –

(i)   the court officer, and

(ii)   each other party.

18.4 Decisions and reasons

(1) A party who wants to introduce the evidence of a witness who is the subject of an application, direction or order must –

(a)   inform the witness of the court's decision as soon as reasonably practicable; and

(b)   explain to the witness the arrangements that as a result will be made for him or her to give evidence.

(2) The court must –

(a)   promptly determine an application; and

(b)   allow a party sufficient time to comply with the requirements of –

(i)   paragraph (1), and

(ii)   the code of practice issued under s 32 of the Domestic Violence, Crime and Victims Act 2004.

(3) The court must announce, at a hearing in public before the witness gives evidence, the reasons for a decision –

(a)   to give, make, vary or discharge a direction or order; or

(b)   to refuse to do so.

18.5 Court's power to vary requirements under this Part

(1) The court may –

(a)   shorten or extend (even after it has expired) a time limit under this Part; and

(b)   allow an application or representations to be made in a different form to one set out in the Practice Direction, or to be made orally.

(2) A person who wants an extension of time must –

(a)   apply when serving the application or representations for which it is needed; and

(b)   explain the delay.

18.6 Custody of documents

Unless the court otherwise directs, the court officer may –

(a)   keep a written application or representations; or

(b)   arrange for the whole or any part to be kept by some other appropriate person, subject to any conditions that the court may impose.

18.7 Declaration by intermediary

(1) This rule applies where –

(a)   a video recorded interview with a witness is conducted through an intermediary;

(b)   the court directs the examination of a witness or defendant through an intermediary.

(2) An intermediary must make a declaration –

(a)   before such an interview begins;

(b)   before the examination begins (even if such an interview with the witness was conducted through the same intermediary).

(3) The declaration must be in these terms –

'I solemnly, sincerely and truly declare [*or* I swear by Almighty God] that I will well and faithfully communicate questions and answers and make true explanation of all matters and things as shall be required of me according to the best of my skill and understanding.'

SPECIAL MEASURES DIRECTIONS

18.8 Exercise of court's powers

The court may decide whether to give, vary or discharge a special measures direction –

(a)   at a hearing, in public or in private, or without a hearing;

(b)   in a party's absence, if that party –

  (i)   applied for the direction, variation or discharge, or

  (ii)   has had at least 14 days in which to make representations.

18.9 Special measures direction for a young witness

(1) This rule applies where, under s 21 or s 22 of the Youth Justice and Criminal Evidence Act 1999, the primary rule requires the court to give a direction for a special measure to assist a child witness or a qualifying witness –

(a)   on an application, if one is made; or

(b)   on the court's own initiative, in any other case.

(2) A party who wants to introduce the evidence of such a witness must as soon as reasonably practicable –

(a)   notify the court that the witness is eligible for assistance;

(b)   provide the court with any information that the court may need to assess the witness' views, if the witness does not want the primary rule to apply; and

(c)   serve any video recorded evidence on –

    (i)   the court officer, and

    (ii)   each other party.

18.10 Content of application for a special measures direction

An applicant for a special measures direction must –

(a)   explain how the witness is eligible for assistance;

(b)   explain why special measures would be likely to improve the quality of the witness' evidence;

(c)   propose the measure or measures that in the applicant's opinion would be likely to maximise so far as practicable the quality of that evidence;

(d)   report any views that the witness has expressed about –

    (i)   his or her eligibility for assistance,

    (ii)   the likelihood that special measures would improve the quality of his or her evidence, and

    (iii)   the measure or measures proposed by the applicant;

(e)   in a case in which a child witness or a qualifying witness does not want the primary rule to apply, provide any information that the court may need to assess the witness' views;

(f)   in a case in which the applicant proposes that the witness should give evidence by live link –

    (i)   identify someone to accompany the witness while the witness gives evidence,

    (ii)   name that person, if possible, and

    (iii)   explain why that person would be an appropriate companion for the witness, including the witness' own views;

(g)   in a case in which the applicant proposes the admission of video recorded evidence, identify –

    (i)   the date and duration of the recording,

    (ii)   which part the applicant wants the court to admit as evidence, if the applicant does not want the court to admit all of it;

(h)   attach any other material on which the applicant relies; and

    (i)   if the applicant wants a hearing, ask for one, and explain why it is needed.

18.11 *Application to vary or discharge a special measures direction*

(1) A party who wants the court to vary or discharge a special measures direction must –

(a)   apply in writing, as soon as reasonably practicable after becoming aware of the grounds for doing so; and

(b)   serve the application on –

    (i)   the court officer, and

    (ii)   each other party.

(2) The applicant must –

(a)   explain what material circumstances have changed since the direction was given (or last varied, if applicable);

(b)   explain why the direction should be varied or discharged; and

(c)   ask for a hearing, if the applicant wants one, and explain why it is needed.

18.12 *Application containing information withheld from another party*

(1) This rule applies where –

(a)   an applicant serves an application for a special measures direction, or for its variation or discharge; and

(b)   the application includes information that the applicant thinks ought not be revealed to another party.

(2) The applicant must –

(a)   omit that information from the part of the application that is served on that other party;

(b)   mark the other part to show that, unless the court otherwise directs, it is only for the court; and

(c)   in that other part, explain why the applicant has withheld that information from that other party.

(3) Any hearing of an application to which this rule applies –

(a)   must be in private, unless the court otherwise directs; and

(b)   if the court so directs, may be, wholly or in part, in the absence of a party from whom information has been withheld.

(4) At any hearing of an application to which this rule applies –

(a)   the general rule is that the court will receive, in the following sequence –

    (i)   representations first by the applicant and then by each other party, in all the parties' presence, and then

    (ii)   further representations by the applicant, in the absence of a party from whom information has been withheld; but

(b)   the court may direct other arrangements for the hearing.

18.13 Representations in response

(1) This rule applies where a party wants to make representations about –

(a)   an application for a special measures direction;

(b)   an application for the variation or discharge of such a direction; or

(c)   a direction, variation or discharge that the court proposes on its own initiative.

(2) Such a party must –

(a)   serve the representations on –

    (i)   the court officer, and

    (ii)   each other party;

(b)   do so not more than 14 days after, as applicable –

    (i)   service of the application, or

    (ii)   notice of the direction, variation or discharge that the court proposes; and

(c)   ask for a hearing, if that party wants one, and explain why it is needed.

(3) Where representations include information that the person making them thinks ought not be revealed to another party, that person must –

(a)   omit that information from the representations served on that other party;

(b)   mark the information to show that, unless the court otherwise directs, it is only for the court; and

(c)   with that information include an explanation of why it has been withheld from that other party.

(4) Representations against a special measures direction must explain –

(a)   why the witness is not eligible for assistance; or

(b)   if the witness is eligible for assistance, why –

    (i)   no special measure would be likely to improve the quality of the witness' evidence,

    (ii)   the proposed measure or measures would not be likely to maximise so far as practicable the quality of the witness' evidence, or

    (iii)   the proposed measure or measures might tend to inhibit the effective testing of that evidence.

(c)   in a case in which the admission of video recorded evidence is proposed, why it would not be in the interests of justice for the recording, or part of it, to be admitted as evidence.

(5) Representations against the variation or discharge of a special measures direction must explain why it should not be varied or discharged.

DEFENDANT'S EVIDENCE DIRECTIONS

18.14 Exercise of court's powers

The court may decide whether to give, vary or discharge a defendant's evidence direction –

(a)   at a hearing, in public or in private, or without a hearing;

(b) in a party's absence, if that party –

    (i) applied for the direction, variation or discharge, or

    (ii) has had at least 14 days in which to make representations.

18.15 Content of application for a defendant's evidence direction

An applicant for a defendant's evidence direction must –

(a) explain how the proposed direction meets the conditions prescribed by the Youth Justice and Criminal Evidence Act 1999;

(b) in a case in which the applicant proposes that the defendant give evidence by live link –

    (i) identify a person to accompany the defendant while the defendant gives evidence, and

    (ii) explain why that person is appropriate;

(c) ask for a hearing, if the applicant wants one, and explain why it is needed.

18.16 Application to vary or discharge a defendant's evidence direction

(1) A party who wants the court to vary or discharge a defendant's evidence direction must –

(a) apply in writing, as soon as reasonably practicable after becoming aware of the grounds for doing so; and

(b) serve the application on –

    (i) the court officer, and

    (ii) each other party.

(2) The applicant must –

(a) on an application to discharge a live link direction, explain why it is in the interests of justice to do so;

(b) on an application to discharge a direction for an intermediary, explain why it is no longer necessary in order to ensure that the defendant receives a fair trial;

(c) on an application to vary a direction for an intermediary, explain why it is necessary for the direction to be varied in order to ensure that the defendant receives a fair trial; and

(d) ask for a hearing, if the applicant wants one, and explain why it is needed.

18.17 Representations in response

(1) This rule applies where a party wants to make representations about –

(a) an application for a defendant's evidence direction;

(b) an application for the variation or discharge of such a direction; or

(c) a direction, variation or discharge that the court proposes on its own initiative.

(2) Such a party must –

(a)   serve the representations on –

    (i)   the court officer, and

    (ii)   each other party;

(b)   do so not more than 14 days after, as applicable –

    (i)   service of the application, or

    (ii)   notice of the direction, variation or discharge that the court proposes; and

(c)   ask for a hearing, if that party wants one, and explain why it is needed.

(3) Representations against a direction, variation or discharge must explain why the conditions prescribed by the Youth Justice and Criminal Evidence Act 1999 are not met.

WITNESS ANONYMITY ORDERS

18.18 Exercise of court's powers

(1) The court may decide whether to make, vary or discharge a witness anonymity order –

(a)   at a hearing (which must be in private, unless the court otherwise directs), or without a hearing (unless any party asks for one);

(b)   in the absence of a defendant.

(2) The court must not exercise its power to make, vary or discharge a witness anonymity order, or to refuse to do so –

(a)   before or during the trial, unless each party has had an opportunity to make representations;

(b)   on an appeal by the defendant to which applies Pt 34 (Appeal to the Crown Court) or Pt 39 (Appeal to the Court of Appeal about conviction or sentence), unless in each party's case –

    (i)   that party has had an opportunity to make representations, or

    (ii)   the appeal court is satisfied that it is not reasonably practicable to communicate with that party;

(c)   after the trial and any such appeal are over, unless in the case of each party and the witness –

    (i)   each has had an opportunity to make representations, or

    (ii)   the court is satisfied that it is not reasonably practicable to communicate with that party or witness.

18.19 Content and conduct of application for a witness anonymity order

(1) An applicant for a witness anonymity order must –

(a)   include in the application nothing that might reveal the witness' identity;

(b)   describe the measures proposed by the applicant;

(c)   explain how the proposed order meets the conditions prescribed by s 88 of the Coroners and Justice Act 2009;

(d)   explain why no measures other than those proposed will suffice, such as –

     (i)   an admission of the facts that would be proved by the witness,

     (ii)   an order restricting public access to the trial,

     (iii)   reporting restrictions, in particular under ss 45, 45A or 46 of the Youth Justice and Criminal Evidence Act 1999,

     (iv)   a direction for a special measure under s 19 of the Youth Justice and Criminal Evidence Act 1999,

     (v)   introduction of the witness' written statement as hearsay evidence, under s 116 of the Criminal Justice Act 2003, or

     (vi)   arrangements for the protection of the witness;

(e)   attach to the application –

     (i)   a witness statement setting out the proposed evidence, edited in such a way as not to reveal the witness' identity,

     (ii)   where the prosecutor is the applicant, any further prosecution evidence to be served, and any further prosecution material to be disclosed under the Criminal Procedure and Investigations Act 1996, similarly edited, and

     (iii)   any defence statement that has been served, or as much information as may be available to the applicant that gives particulars of the defence; and

(f)   ask for a hearing, if the applicant wants one.

(2) At any hearing of the application, the applicant must –

(a)   identify the witness to the court, unless at the prosecutor's request the court otherwise directs; and

(b)   present to the court, unless it otherwise directs –

     (i)   the unedited witness statement from which the edited version has been prepared,

     (ii)   where the prosecutor is the applicant, the unedited version of any further prosecution evidence or material from which an edited version has been prepared, and

     (iii)   such further material as the applicant relies on to establish that the proposed order meets the conditions prescribed by s 88 of the 2009 Act.

(3) At any such hearing –

(a)   the general rule is that the court must consider, in the following sequence –

     (i)   representations first by the applicant and then by each other party, in all the parties' presence, and then

     (ii)   information withheld from a defendant, and further representations by the applicant, in the absence of any (or any other) defendant; but

(b)   the court may direct other arrangements for the hearing.

(4) Before the witness gives evidence, the applicant must identify the witness to the court –

(a)   if not already done;

(b)   without revealing the witness' identity to any other party or person; and

(c)   unless at the prosecutor's request the court otherwise directs.

18.20 Duty of court officer to notify the Director of Public Prosecutions

(1) The court officer must notify the Director of Public Prosecutions of an application, unless the prosecutor is, or acts on behalf of, a public authority.

18.21 Application to vary or discharge a witness anonymity order

(1) A party who wants the court to vary or discharge a witness anonymity order, or a witness who wants the court to do so when the case is over, must –

(a)   apply in writing, as soon as reasonably practicable after becoming aware of the grounds for doing so; and

(b)   serve the application on –

   (i)   the court officer, and

   (ii)   each other party.

(2) The applicant must –

(a)   explain what material circumstances have changed since the order was made (or last varied, if applicable);

(b)   explain why the order should be varied or discharged, taking account of the conditions for making an order; and

(c)   ask for a hearing, if the applicant wants one.

(3) Where an application includes information that the applicant thinks might reveal the witness' identity, the applicant must –

(a)   omit that information from the application that is served on a defendant;

(b)   mark the information to show that it is only for the court and the prosecutor (if the prosecutor is not the applicant); and

(c)   with that information include an explanation of why it has been withheld.

(4) Where a party applies to vary or discharge a witness anonymity order after the trial and any appeal are over, the party who introduced the witness' evidence must serve the application on the witness.

Part 24 Trial and sentence in a magistrates' court

24.1 When this Part applies

(1) This Part applies in a magistrates' court where –

(a)   the court tries a case;

(b)   the defendant pleads guilty;

(c)   under s 14 or s 16E of the Magistrates' Courts Act 1980, the defendant makes a statutory declaration of not having found out about the case until after the trial began;

(d)   under s 142 of the 1980 Act, the court can –

    (i)   set aside a conviction, or

    (ii)   vary or rescind a costs order, or an order to which Pt 31 applies (Behaviour orders).

(2) Where the defendant is **under 18**, in this Part –

(a)   a reference to convicting the defendant includes a reference to finding the defendant guilty of an offence; and

(b)   a reference to sentence includes a reference to an order made on a finding of guilt.

24.2 General rules

(1) Where this Part applies –

(a)   the general rule is that the hearing must be in public; but

(b)   the court may exercise any power it has to –

    (i)   impose reporting restrictions,

    (ii)   withhold information from the public, or

    (iii)   order a hearing in private; and

(c)   unless the court otherwise directs, **only the following may attend a hearing in a youth court** –

    (i)   the parties and their legal representatives,

    (ii)   a defendant's parents, guardian or other supporting adult,

    (iii)   a witness,

    (iv)   anyone else directly concerned in the case, and

    (v)   a representative of a news-gathering or reporting organisation.

(2) Unless already done, the justices' legal adviser or the court must –

(a)   read the allegation of the offence to the defendant;

(b)   explain, in terms the defendant can understand (with help, if necessary) –

    (i)   the allegation, and

    (ii)   what the procedure at the hearing will be;

(c)   ask whether the defendant has been advised about the potential effect on sentence of a guilty plea;

(d)   ask whether the defendant pleads guilty or not guilty; and

(e)   take the defendant's plea.

(3) The court may adjourn the hearing –

(a)   at any stage, to the same or to another magistrates' court; or

(b)   to a youth court, where the court is not itself a youth court and the defendant is **under 18.**

(4) Paragraphs (1) and (2) of this rule do not apply where the court tries a case under r 24.9 (Single justice procedure: special rules).

24.3 Procedure on plea of not guilty

(1) This rule applies –

(a)   if the defendant has –

   (i)   entered a plea of not guilty, or

   (ii)   not entered a plea; or

(b)   if, in either case, it appears to the court that there may be grounds for making a hospital order without convicting the defendant.

(2) If a not guilty plea was taken on a previous occasion, the justices' legal adviser or the court must ask the defendant to confirm that plea.

(3) In the following sequence –

(a)   the prosecutor may summarise the prosecution case, concisely identifying the relevant law, outlining the facts and indicating the matters likely to be in dispute;

(b)   to help the members of the court to understand the case and resolve any issue in it, the court may invite the defendant to identify concisely what is in issue;

(c)   the prosecutor must introduce the evidence on which the prosecution case relies;

(d)   at the conclusion of the prosecution case, on the defendant's application or on its own initiative, the court –

   (i)   may acquit because the prosecution evidence is insufficient for any reasonable court properly to convict, but

   (ii)   must not do so unless the prosecutor has had an opportunity to make representations;

(e)   the justices' legal adviser or the court must explain, in terms the defendant can understand (with help, if necessary) –

   (i)   the right to give evidence, and

   (ii)   the potential effect of not doing so at all, or of refusing to answer a question while doing so;

(f)   the defendant may introduce evidence;

(g)   a party may introduce further evidence if it is then admissible (for example, because it is in rebuttal of evidence already introduced);

(h)   the prosecutor may make final representations in support of the prosecution case, where –

   (i)   the defendant is represented by a legal representative, or

   (ii)   whether represented or not, the defendant has introduced evidence other than his or her own; and

(i)   the defendant may make final representations in support of the defence case.

(4) Where a party wants to introduce evidence or make representations after that party's opportunity to do so under paragraph (3), the court –

(a)   may refuse to receive any such evidence or representations; and

(b)   must not receive any such evidence or representations after it has announced its verdict.

(5) If the court –

(a)   convicts the defendant; or

(b)   makes a hospital order instead of doing so, it must give sufficient reasons to explain its decision.

(6) If the court acquits the defendant, it may –

(a)   give an explanation of its decision; and

(b)   exercise any power it has to make –

   (i)   a behaviour order,

   (ii)   a costs order.

24.4 *Evidence of a witness in person*

(1) This rule applies where a party wants to introduce evidence by calling a witness to give that evidence in person.

(2) Unless the court otherwise directs –

(a)   a witness waiting to give evidence must not wait inside the courtroom, unless that witness is –

   (i)   a party, or

   (ii)   an expert witness;

(b)   a witness who gives evidence in the courtroom must do so from the place provided for that purpose; and

(c)   a witness' address must not be announced unless it is relevant to an issue in the case.

(3) Unless other legislation otherwise provides, before giving evidence a witness must take an oath or affirm.

(4) In the following sequence –

(a)   the party who calls a witness must ask questions in examination-in-chief;

(b)   every other party may ask questions in cross-examination;

(c)   the party who called the witness may ask questions in re-examination;

(5) If other legislation so permits, at any time while giving evidence, a witness may refer to a record of that witness' recollection of events.

(6) The justices' legal adviser or the court may –

(a)   ask a witness questions; and in particular

(b)   where the defendant is not represented, ask any question necessary in the defendant's interests.

24.5 Evidence of a witness in writing

(1) This rule applies where a party wants to introduce in evidence the written statement of a witness to which applies –

(a)   Part 16 (Written witness statements);

(b)   Part 19 (Expert evidence); or

(c)   Part 20 (Hearsay evidence).

(2) If the court admits such evidence –

(a)   the court must read the statement; and

(b)   unless the court otherwise directs, if any member of the public, including any reporter, is present, each relevant part of the statement must be read or summarised aloud.

24.6 Evidence by admission

(1) This rule applies where –

(a)   a party introduces in evidence a fact admitted by another party; or

(b)   parties jointly admit a fact.

(2) Unless the court otherwise directs, a written record must be made of the admission.

24.7 Procedure on plea of guilty

(1) This rule applies if –

(a)   the defendant pleads guilty; and

(b)   the court is satisfied that the plea represents a clear acknowledgement of guilt.

(2) The court may convict the defendant without receiving evidence.

24.8 Written guilty plea: special rules

(1) This rule applies where –

(a)   the offence alleged –

    (i)   can be tried only in a magistrates' court, and

    (ii)   is not one specified under s 12(1)(a) of the Magistrates' Courts Act 1980;

(b) the defendant is at least 16 years old;

(c)   the prosecutor has served on the defendant –

    (i)   the summons or requisition,

    (ii)   the material listed in para (2) on which the prosecutor relies to set out the facts of the offence,

    (iii)   the material listed in para (3) on which the prosecutor relies to provide the court with information relevant to sentence,

    (iv)   a notice that the procedure set out in this rule applies, and

(v)   a notice for the defendant's use if the defendant wants to plead guilty without attending court; and

(d)   the prosecutor has served on the court officer –

    (i)   copies of those documents, and

    (ii)   a certificate of service of those documents on the defendant.

(2) The material that the prosecutor must serve to set out the facts of the offence is –

(a)   a summary of the evidence on which the prosecution case is based;

(b)   any –

    (i)   written witness statement to which Pt 16 (written witness statements) applies, or

    (ii)   document or extract setting out facts; or

(c)   any combination of such a summary, statement, document or extract.

(3) The material that the prosecutor must serve to provide information relevant to sentence is –

(a)   details of any previous conviction of the defendant which the prosecutor considers relevant, other than any conviction listed in the defendant's driving record;

(b)   if applicable, a notice that the defendant's driving record will be made available to the court;

(c)   a notice containing or describing any other information about the defendant, relevant to sentence, which will be made available to the court.

(4) A defendant who wants to plead guilty without attending court must, before the hearing date specified in the summons or requisition –

(a)   serve a notice of guilty plea on the court officer; and

(b)   include with that notice –

    (i)   any representations that the defendant wants the court to consider, and

    (ii)   a statement of the defendant's assets and other financial circumstances.

(5) A defendant who wants to withdraw such a notice must notify the court officer in writing before the hearing date.

(6) If the defendant does not withdraw the notice before the hearing date, then on or after that date –

(a)   to establish the facts of the offence and other information about the defendant relevant to sentence, the court may take account only of –

    (i)   information contained in a document served by the prosecutor under para (1),

    (ii)   any previous conviction listed in the defendant's driving record, where the offence is under the Road Traffic Regulation Act 1984, the Road Traffic Act 1988, the Road Traffic (Consequential Provisions) Act 1988 or the Road Traffic (Driver Licensing and Information Systems) Act 1989,

    (iii) any other information about the defendant, relevant to sentence, of which the prosecutor served notice under para (1), and

    (iv) any representations and any other information served by the defendant under para (4) and r 24.11(3) to (9) inclusive must be read accordingly;

(b) unless the court otherwise directs, the prosecutor need not attend; and

(c) the court may accept such a guilty plea and pass sentence in the defendant's absence.

(7) With the defendant's agreement, the court may deal with the case in the same way as under para (6) where the defendant is present and –

(a) has served a notice of guilty plea under para (4); or

(b) pleads guilty there and then.

24.10 Application to withdraw a guilty plea

(1) This rule applies where the defendant wants to withdraw a guilty plea.

(2) The defendant must apply to do so –

(a) as soon as practicable after becoming aware of the reasons for doing so; and

(b) before sentence.

(3) Unless the court otherwise directs, the application must be in writing and the defendant must serve it on –

(a) the court officer; and

(b) the prosecutor.

(4) The application must –

(a) explain why it would be unjust not to allow the defendant to withdraw the guilty plea;

(b) identify –

    (i) any witness that the defendant wants to call, and

    (ii) any other proposed evidence; and

(c) say whether the defendant waives legal professional privilege, giving any relevant name and date.

24.11 Procedure if the court convicts

(1) This rule applies if the court convicts the defendant.

(2) The court –

(a) may exercise its power to require –

    (i) a statement of the defendant's assets and other financial circumstances,

    (ii) a pre-sentence report; and

(b) may (and in some circumstances must) remit the defendant to a youth court for sentence where –

    (i) **the defendant is under 18**, and

    (ii) the convicting court is not itself a youth court.

(3) The prosecutor must –

(a)   summarise the prosecution case, if the sentencing court has not heard evidence;

(b)   identify any offence to be taken into consideration in sentencing;

(c)   provide information relevant to sentence, including any statement of the effect of the offence on the victim, the victim's family or others; and

(d)   where it is likely to assist the court, identify any other matter relevant to sentence, including –

    (i)   the legislation applicable,

    (ii)   any sentencing guidelines, or guideline cases,

    (iii)   aggravating and mitigating features affecting the defendant's culpability and the harm which the offence caused, was intended to cause or might forseeably have caused, and

    (iv)   the effect of such of the information listed in para (2)(a) as the court may need to take into account.

(4) The defendant must provide details of financial circumstances –

(a)   in any form required by the court officer;

(b)   by any date directed by the court or by the court officer.

(5) Where the defendant pleads guilty but wants to be sentenced on a different basis to that disclosed by the prosecution case –

(a)   the defendant must set out that basis in writing, identifying what is in dispute;

(b)   the court may invite the parties to make representations about whether the dispute is material to sentence; and

(c)   if the court decides that it is a material dispute, the court must –

    (i)   invite such further representations or evidence as it may require, and

    (ii)   decide the dispute.

(6) Where the court has power to order the endorsement of the defendant's driving record, or power to order the defendant to be disqualified from driving –

(a)   if other legislation so permits, a defendant who wants the court not to exercise that power must introduce the evidence or information on which the defendant relies;

(b)   the prosecutor may introduce evidence; and

(c)   the parties may make representations about that evidence or information.

(7) Before the court passes sentence –

(a)   the court must –

    (i)   give the defendant an opportunity to make representations and introduce evidence relevant to sentence, and

    (ii)   **where the defendant is under 18**, give the defendant's parents, guardian or other supporting adult, if present, such an opportunity as well; and

(b)   the justices' legal adviser or the court must elicit any further information relevant to sentence that the court may require.

(8) If the court requires more information, it may exercise its power to adjourn the hearing for not more than –

(a)   three weeks at a time, if the defendant will be in custody; or

(b)   four weeks at a time.

(9) When the court has taken into account all the evidence, information and any report available, the court must –

(a)   as a general rule, pass sentence there and then;

(b)   when passing sentence, explain the reasons for deciding on that sentence, unless neither the defendant nor any member of the public, including any reporter, is present;

(c)   when passing sentence, explain to the defendant its effect, the consequences of failing to comply with any order or pay any fine, and any power that the court has to vary or review the sentence, unless –

  (i)   the defendant is absent, or

  (ii)   the defendant's ill-health or disorderly conduct makes such an explanation impracticable;

(d)   give any such explanation in terms the defendant, if present, can understand (with help, if necessary); and

(e)   consider exercising any power it has to make a costs or other order.

(10) Despite the general rule –

(a)   the court must adjourn the hearing if the defendant is absent, the case started with a summons, requisition or single justice procedure notice, and either –

  (i)   the court considers passing a custodial sentence (where it can do so), or

  (ii)   the court considers imposing a disqualification (unless it has already adjourned the hearing to give the defendant an opportunity to attend);

(b)   the court may exercise any power it has to –

  (i)   commit the defendant to the Crown Court for sentence (and in some cases it must do so), or

  (ii)   defer sentence for up to six months.

24.12 Procedure where a party is absent

(1) This rule –

(a)   applies where a party is absent; but

(b)   does not apply where –

  (i)   the defendant has served a notice of guilty plea under r 24.8 (Written guilty plea: special rules), or

  (ii)   the court tries a case under r 24.9 (Single justice procedure: special rules).

(2) Where the prosecutor is absent, the court may –

(a)   if it has received evidence, deal with the case as if the prosecutor were present; and

(b)   in any other case –

    (i)   enquire into the reasons for the prosecutor's absence, and

    (ii)   if satisfied there is no good reason, exercise its power to dismiss the allegation.

(3) Where the defendant is absent –

(a)   the general rule is that the court must proceed as if the defendant –

    (i)   were present, and

    (ii)   had pleaded not guilty (unless a plea already has been taken) and the court must give reasons if it does not do so; but

(b)   the general rule does not apply if the **defendant is under 18;**

(c)   the general rule is subject to the court being satisfied that –

    (i)   any summons or requisition was served on the defendant a reasonable time before the hearing, or

    (ii)   in a case in which the hearing has been adjourned, the defendant had reasonable notice of where and when it would resume;

(d)   the general rule is subject also to r 24.11(10)(a) (restrictions on passing sentence in the defendant's absence).

(4) Where the defendant is absent, the court –

(a)   must exercise its power to issue a warrant for the defendant's arrest, if it passes a custodial sentence; and

(b)   may exercise its power to do so in any other case, if it does not apply the general rule in para (3)(a) of this rule about proceeding in the defendant's absence.

24.13 Provision of documents for the court

(1) A party who introduces a document in evidence, or who otherwise uses a document in presenting that party's case, must provide a copy for –

(a)   each other party;

(b)   any witness that party wants to refer to that document;

(c)   the court; and

(d)   the justices' legal adviser.

(2) Unless the court otherwise directs, on application or on its own initiative, the court officer must provide for the court –

(a)   any copy received under para (1) before the hearing begins; and

(b)   a copy of the court officer's record of –

    (i)   information supplied by each party for the purposes of case management, including any revision of information previously supplied,

    (ii)   each pre-trial direction for the management of the case,

    (iii)   any pre-trial decision to admit evidence,

(iv)   any pre-trial direction about the giving of evidence, and

(v)   any admission to which r 24.6 applies.

(3) Where r 24.8 (Written guilty plea: special rules) applies, the court officer must provide for the court –

(a)   each document served by the prosecutor under r 24.8(1)(d);

(b)   the defendant's driving record, where the offence is under the Road Traffic Regulation Act 1984, the Road Traffic Act 1988, the Road Traffic (Consequential Provisions) Act 1988 or the Road Traffic (Driver Licensing and Information Systems) Act 1989;

(c)   any other information about the defendant, relevant to sentence, of which the prosecutor served notice under r 24.8(1); and

(d)   the notice of guilty plea and any representations and other information served by the defendant under r 24.8(4).

(4) Where the court tries a case under r 24.9 (Single justice procedure: special rules), the court officer must provide for the court –

(a)   each document served by the prosecutor under r 24.9(1)(d);

(b)   the defendant's driving record, where the offence is under the Road Traffic Regulation Act 1984, the Road Traffic Act 1988, the Road Traffic (Consequential Provisions) Act 1988 or the Road Traffic (Driver Licensing and Information Systems) Act 1989;

(c)   any other information about the defendant, relevant to sentence, of which the prosecutor served notice under r 24.9(1); and

(d)   any notice, representations and other information served by the defendant under r 24.9(4)(a).

24.15 Duty of justices' legal adviser

(1) A justices' legal adviser must attend the court and carry out the duties listed in this rule, as applicable, unless the court –

(a)   includes a District Judge (Magistrates' Courts); and

(b)   otherwise directs.

(2) A justices' legal adviser must –

(a)   before the hearing begins, by reference to what is provided for the court under r 24.13 (Provision of documents for the court) draw the court's attention to –

(i)   what the prosecutor alleges,

(ii)   what the parties say is agreed,

(iii)   what the parties say is in dispute, and

(iv)   what the parties say about how each expects to present the case, especially where that may affect its duration and timetabling;

(b)   whenever necessary, give the court legal advice and –

(i)   if necessary, attend the members of the court outside the courtroom to give such advice, but

(ii)   inform the parties (if present) of any such advice given outside the courtroom; and

(c)   assist the court, where appropriate, in the formulation of its reasons and the recording of those reasons.

(3) A justices' legal adviser must –

(a) assist an unrepresented defendant;

(b)   assist the court by –

(i)   making a note of the substance of any oral evidence or representations, to help the court recall that information,

(ii)   if the court rules inadmissible part of a written statement introduced in evidence, marking that statement in such a way as to make that clear,

(iii)   ensuring that an adequate record is kept of the court's decisions and the reasons for them, and

(iv)   making any announcement, other than of the verdict or sentence.

(4) Where the defendant has served a notice of guilty plea to which r 24.8 (Written guilty plea: special rules) applies, a justices' legal adviser must –

(a)   unless the court otherwise directs, if any member of the public, including any reporter, is present, read aloud to the court –

(i)   the material on which the prosecutor relies to set out the facts of the offence and to provide information relevant to sentence (or summarise any written statement included in that material, if the court so directs), and

(ii)   any written representations by the defendant;

(b)   otherwise, draw the court's attention to –

(i)   what the prosecutor alleges, and any significant features of the material listed in para (4)(a)(i), and

(ii)   any written representations by the defendant.

(5) Where the court tries a case under r 24.9 (Single justice procedure: special rules), a justices' legal adviser must draw the court's attention to –

(a)   what the prosecutor alleges, and any significant features of the material on which the prosecutor relies to prove the alleged offence and to provide information relevant to sentence; and

(b)   any representations served by the defendant.

Part 32 Breach, revocation and amendment of community and other orders in a magistrates' court

32.1 *When this Part applies*

This Part applies where –

(a)   the officer responsible for a defendant's compliance with an order to which applies –

(i)   Schedule 3, 5, 7 or 8 to the Powers of Criminal Courts (Sentencing) Act 2000,

(ii)   Schedule 8 or 12 to the Criminal Justice Act 2003, or

(iii)   Schedule 2 to the Criminal Justice and Immigration Act 2008, or

(iv)   the Schedule to the Street Offences Act 1959 wants the court to deal with that defendant for failure to comply;

(b)   one of the following wants the court to exercise any power it has to revoke or amend such an order –

(i)   the responsible officer,

(ii)   the defendant, or

(iii)   where the legislation allows, a person affected by the order; or

(c)   the court considers exercising on its own initiative any power it has to revoke or amend such an order.

32.2 Application by responsible officer or supervisor

(1) This rule applies where –

(a)   the responsible officer or supervisor wants the court to –

(i)   deal with a defendant for failure to comply with an order to which this Part applies, or

(ii)   revoke or amend such an order; or

(b)   the court considers exercising on its own initiative any power it has to –

(i)   revoke or amend such an order, and

(ii)   summon the defendant to attend for that purpose.

(2) Rules 7.2 to 7.4, which deal, among other things, with starting a prosecution in a magistrates' court by information and summons, apply –

(a)   as if –

(i)   a reference in those rules to an allegation of an offence included a reference to an allegation of failure to comply with an order to which this Part applies, and

(ii)   a reference to the prosecutor included a reference to the responsible officer or supervisor; and

(b)   with the necessary consequential modifications.

32.3 Application by defendant or person affected

(1) This rule applies where –

(a)   the defendant wants the court to exercise any power it has to revoke or amend an order to which this Part applies; or

(b)   where the legislation allows, a person affected by such an order wants the court to exercise any such power.

(2) That defendant, or person affected, must –

(a)   apply in writing, explaining why the order should be revoked or amended; and

(b) serve the application on –

    (i)   the court officer,

    (ii)   the responsible officer or supervisor, and

    (iii)   as appropriate, the defendant or the person affected.

32.4 Procedure on application by responsible officer or supervisor

(1) Except for rr 24.8 (Written guilty plea: special rules) and 24.9 (Single justice procedure: special rules), the rules in Pt 24, which deal with the procedure at a trial in a magistrates' court, apply –

(a) as if –

    (i)   a reference in those rules to an allegation of an offence included a reference to an allegation of failure to comply with an order to which this Part applies,

    (ii)   a reference to the court's verdict included a reference to the court's decision to revoke or amend such an order, or to exercise any other power it has to deal with the defendant, and

    (iii)   a reference to the court's sentence included a reference to the exercise of any such power; and

(b) with the necessary consequential modifications.

(2) The court officer must serve on each party any order revoking or amending an order to which this Part applies.

Appendix D

Code and legal guidance for Crown Prosecutors

General note: This section reflects the content of the CPS website as at 15 April 2017. The effect of the Sentencing Council's *Sentencing Children and Young People* which comes into effect on 1 June 2017 had therefore not been assimilated into the text.

Part 1

Code for Crown Prosecutors

1   Introduction

1.1 The Code for Crown Prosecutors (the Code) is issued by the Director of Public Prosecutions (DPP) under s 10 of the Prosecution of Offences Act 1985. This is the seventh edition of the Code and replaces all earlier versions.

1.2 The DPP is the head of the Crown Prosecution Service (CPS), which is the principal public prosecution service for England and Wales. The DPP operates independently, under the superintendence of the Attorney General who is accountable to Parliament for the work of the CPS.

1.3 The Code gives guidance to prosecutors on the general principles to be applied when making decisions about prosecutions. The Code is issued primarily for prosecutors in the CPS, but other prosecutors follow the Code either through convention or because they are required to do so by law.

1.4 In this Code, the term 'suspect' is used to describe a person who is not yet the subject of formal criminal proceedings; the term 'defendant' is used to describe a person who has been charged or summonsed; and the term 'offender' is used to describe a person who has admitted his or her guilt to a police officer or other investigator or prosecutor, or who has been found guilty in a court of law.

2   General principles

2.1 The decision to prosecute or to recommend an out-of-court disposal is a serious step that affects suspects, victims, witnesses, and the public at large and must be undertaken with the utmost care.

2.2 It is the duty of prosecutors to make sure that the right person is prosecuted for the right offence and to bring offenders to justice wherever possible. Casework decisions taken fairly, impartially and with integrity help to secure justice for victims, witnesses, defendants and the public. Prosecutors must ensure that the law is properly applied; that relevant evidence is put before the court; and that obligations of disclosure are complied with.

2.3 Although each case must be considered on its own facts and on its own merits, there are general principles that apply in every case.

2.4 Prosecutors must be fair, independent and objective. They must not let any personal views about the ethnic or national origin, gender, disability, age, religion or belief, political views, sexual orientation, or gender identity of the suspect, victim or any witness influence their decisions. Neither must prosecutors be affected by improper or undue pressure from any source. Prosecutors must always act in the interests of justice and not solely for the purpose of obtaining a conviction.

2.5 The CPS is a public authority for the purposes of current, relevant equality legislation. Prosecutors are bound by the duties set out in this legislation.

2.6 Prosecutors must apply the principles of the European Convention on Human Rights, in accordance with the Human Rights Act 1998, at each stage of a case. Prosecutors must also comply with any guidelines issued by the Attorney General; with the Criminal Procedure Rules currently in force; and have regard to the obligations arising from international conventions. They must follow the policies and guidance of the CPS issued on behalf of the DPP and available for the public to view on the CPS website.

3   The decision whether to prosecute

3.1 In more serious or complex cases, prosecutors decide whether a person should be charged with a criminal offence, and, if so, what that offence should be. They make their decisions in accordance with this Code and the DPP's Guidance on Charging. The police apply the same principles in deciding whether to start criminal proceedings against a person in those cases for which they are responsible.

3.2 The police and other investigators are responsible for conducting enquiries into any alleged crime and for deciding how to deploy their resources. This includes decisions to start or continue an investigation and on the scope of the investigation. Prosecutors often advise the police and other investigators about possible lines of inquiry, and evidential requirements, and assist with pre-charge procedures. In large scale investigations, the prosecutor may be asked to advise on the overall investigation strategy, including decisions to refine or narrow the scope of the criminal conduct and the number of suspects under investigation. This is to assist the police and other investigators to complete the investigation within a reasonable period of time and to build the most effective prosecution case. However, prosecutors cannot direct the police or other investigators.

3.3 Prosecutors should identify and, where possible, seek to rectify evidential weaknesses, but, subject to the Threshold Test (see **section 5**), they should swiftly stop cases which do not meet the evidential stage of the Full Code Test (see **section 4**) and which cannot be strengthened by further investigation, or where the public interest clearly does not require a prosecution (see **section 4**). Although prosecutors primarily consider the evidence and information supplied by the police and other investigators, the suspect or those acting on his or her behalf may also submit evidence or information to the prosecutor via the police or other investigators, prior to charge, to help inform the prosecutor's decision.

3.4 Prosecutors must only start or continue a prosecution when the case has passed both stages of the Full Code Test (see **section 4**). The exception is when the Threshold Test (see **section 5**) may be applied where it is proposed to apply to the court to keep the suspect in custody after charge, and the evidence required to apply the Full Code Test is not yet available.

3.5 Prosecutors should not start or continue a prosecution which would be regarded by the courts as oppressive or unfair and an abuse of the court's process.

3.6 Prosecutors review every case they receive from the police or other investigators. Review is a continuing process and prosecutors must take account of any change in circumstances that occurs as the case develops, including what becomes known of the defence case. Wherever possible, they should talk to the investigator when thinking about changing the charges or stopping the case. Prosecutors and investigators work closely together, but the final responsibility for the decision whether or not a case should go ahead rests with the CPS.

3.7 Parliament has decided that a limited number of offences should only be taken to court with the agreement of the DPP. These are called consent cases. In such cases, the DPP, or prosecutors acting on his or her behalf, apply the Code in deciding whether to give consent to a prosecution. There are also certain offences that should only be taken to court with the consent of the Attorney General. Prosecutors must follow current guidance when referring any such cases to the Attorney General. Additionally, the Attorney General will be kept informed of certain cases as part of his or her superintendence of the CPS and accountability to Parliament for its actions.

4   The Full Code Test

4.1 The Full Code Test has two stages: (i) **the evidential stage**; followed by (ii) **the public interest stage**.

4.2 In most cases, prosecutors should only decide whether to prosecute after the investigation has been completed and after all the available evidence has been reviewed. However, there will be cases where it is clear, prior to the collection and consideration of all the likely evidence, that the public interest does not require a prosecution. In these instances, prosecutors may decide that the case should not proceed further.

4.3 Prosecutors should only take such a decision when they are satisfied that the broad extent of the criminality has been determined and that they are able to make a fully informed assessment of the public interest. If prosecutors do not have sufficient information to take such a decision, the investigation should proceed and a decision taken later in accordance with the Full Code Test set out in this section.

The Evidential Stage

4.4 Prosecutors must be satisfied that there is sufficient evidence to provide a realistic prospect of conviction against each suspect on each charge. They must consider what the defence case may be, and how it is likely to affect the prospects of conviction. A case which does not pass the evidential stage must not proceed, no matter how serious or sensitive it may be.

4.5 The finding that there is a realistic prospect of conviction is based on the prosecutor's objective assessment of the evidence, including the impact of any defence, and any other information that the suspect has put forward or on which he or she might rely. It means that an objective, impartial and reasonable jury or bench of magistrates or judge hearing a case alone, properly directed and acting in accordance with the law, is more likely than not to convict the defendant of the charge alleged. This is a different test from the one that the criminal courts themselves must apply. A court may only convict if it is sure that the defendant is guilty.

4.6 When deciding whether there is sufficient evidence to prosecute, prosecutors should ask themselves the following:

Can the evidence be used in court?

Prosecutors should consider whether there is any question over the admissibility of certain evidence. In doing so, prosecutors should assess:

1. the likelihood of that evidence being held as inadmissible by the court; and
2. the importance of that evidence in relation to the evidence as a whole.

Is the evidence reliable?

Prosecutors should consider whether there are any reasons to question the reliability of the evidence, including its accuracy or integrity.

Is the evidence credible?

Prosecutors should consider whether there are any reasons to doubt the credibility of the evidence.

The public interest stage

4.7 In every case where there is sufficient evidence to justify a prosecution, prosecutors must go on to consider whether a prosecution is required in the public interest.

4.8 It has never been the rule that a prosecution will automatically take place once the evidential stage is met. A prosecution will usually take place unless the prosecutor is satisfied that there are public interest factors tending against prosecution which outweigh those tending in favour. In some cases, the prosecutor may be satisfied that the public interest can be properly served by offering the offender the opportunity to have the matter dealt with by an out-of-court disposal rather than bringing a prosecution.

4.9 When deciding the public interest, prosecutors should consider each of the questions set out below in paragraphs **4.12** 1 to 7 so as to identify and determine the relevant public interest factors tending for and against prosecution. These factors, together with any public interest factors set out in relevant guidance or policy issued by the DPP, should enable prosecutors to form an overall assessment of the public interest.

4.10 In the explanatory text below, each question in paragraphs **4.12** 1 to 7 provides guidance to prosecutors when addressing each particular question and determining whether it identifies public interest factors for or against prosecution. The questions identified are not exhaustive, and not all the questions may be relevant in every case. The weight to be attached to each of the questions, and the factors identified, will also vary according to the facts and merits of each case.

4.11 It is quite possible that one public interest factor alone may outweigh a number of other factors which tend in the opposite direction. Although there may be public interest factors tending against prosecution in a particular case, prosecutors should consider whether nonetheless a prosecution should go ahead and those factors put to the court for consideration when sentence is passed.

4.12 Prosecutors should consider each of the following questions:

1. How serious is the offence committed?

The more serious the offence, the more likely it is that a prosecution is required.

When deciding the level of seriousness of the offence committed, prosecutors should include amongst the factors for consideration the suspect's culpability and the harm to the victim by asking themselves the questions at **2** and **3**.

2. What is the level of culpability of the suspect?

Culpability is likely to be determined by the suspect's level of involvement; the extent to which the offending was premeditated and/or planned; whether they have previous criminal convictions and/or out-of-court disposals and any offending whilst on bail; or whilst subject to a court order; whether the offending was or is likely to be continued, repeated or escalated; and the suspect's age or maturity (see paragraph **4** below for suspects under 18).

Prosecutors should also have regard when considering culpability as to whether the suspect is, or was at the time of the offence, suffering from any significant mental or physical ill health as in some circumstances this may mean that it is less likely that a prosecution is required. However, prosecutors will also need to consider how serious the offence was, whether it is likely to be repeated and the need to safeguard the public or those providing care to such persons.

3. What are the circumstances of and the harm caused to the victim?

The circumstances of the victim are highly relevant. The greater the vulnerability of the victim, the more likely it is that a prosecution is required. This includes where a position of trust or authority exists between the suspect and victim.

A prosecution is also more likely if the offence has been committed against a victim who was at the time a person serving the public.

Prosecutors must also have regard to whether the offence was motivated by any form of discrimination against the victim's ethnic or national origin, gender, disability, age, religion or belief, sexual orientation or gender identity; or the suspect demonstrated hostility towards the victim based on any of those characteristics. The presence of any such motivation or hostility will mean that it is more likely that prosecution is required.

In deciding whether a prosecution is required in the public interest, prosecutors should take into account the views expressed by the victim about the impact that the offence has had. In appropriate cases, this may also include the views of the victim's family.

Prosecutors also need to consider if a prosecution is likely to have an adverse effect on the victim's physical or mental health, always bearing in mind the seriousness of the offence. If there is evidence that prosecution is likely to have an adverse impact on the victim's health it may make a prosecution less likely, taking into account the victim's views.

However, the CPS does not act for victims or their families in the same way as solicitors act for their clients, and prosecutors must form an overall view of the public interest.

4. Was the suspect under the age of 18 at the time of the offence?

The criminal justice system treats children and young people differently from adults and significant weight must be attached to the age of the suspect if they are a child or young person under 18. The best interests and welfare of the child or young person must be considered including whether a prosecution is likely to have an adverse impact on his or her future prospects that is disproportionate to the seriousness of the offending. Prosecutors must have regard to the principal aim of the youth justice system which is to prevent offending by children and young people. Prosecutors must also have regard to the obligations arising under the United Nations 1989 Convention on the Rights of the Child.

As a starting point, the younger the suspect, the less likely it is that a prosecution is required.

However, there may be circumstances which mean that notwithstanding the fact that the suspect is under 18, a prosecution is in the public interest. These include where the offence committed is serious, where the suspect's past record suggests that there are no suitable alternatives to prosecution, or where the absence of an admission means that out-of-court disposals which might have addressed the offending behaviour are not available.

5. What is the impact on the community?

The greater the impact of the offending on the community, the more likely it is that a prosecution is required. In considering this question, prosecutors should have regard to how community is an inclusive term and is not restricted to communities defined by location.

6. Is prosecution a proportionate response?

Prosecutors should also consider whether prosecution is proportionate to the likely outcome, and in so doing the following may be relevant to the case under consideration:

(a) The cost to the CPS prosecution service and the wider criminal justice system, especially where it could be regarded as excessive when weighed against any likely penalty (prosecutors should not decide the public interest on the basis of this factor alone. It is essential that regard is also given to the public interest factors identified when considering the other questions in paragraphs **4.12 1** to **7**, but cost is a relevant factor when making an overall assessment of the public interest).

(b) Cases should be capable of being prosecuted in a way that is consistent with principles of effective case management. For example, in a case involving multiple suspect offenders, prosecution might be reserved for the key main participants in order to avoid excessively long and complex proceedings.

7. Do sources of information require protecting?

In cases where public interest immunity does not apply, special care should be taken when proceeding with a prosecution where details may need to be made public that could harm sources of information, international relations or national security. It is essential that such cases are kept under continuing review.

5   The Threshold Test

5.1 The Threshold Test may only be applied where the suspect presents a substantial bail risk and not all the evidence is available at the time when he or she must be released from custody unless charged.

When the Threshold Test may be applied

5.2 Prosecutors must determine whether the following conditions are met:

1. there is insufficient evidence currently available to apply the evidential stage of the Full Code Test; and

2. there are reasonable grounds for believing that further evidence will become available within a reasonable period; and

3. the seriousness or the circumstances of the case justifies the making of an immediate charging decision; and

4. there are continuing substantial grounds to object to bail in accordance with the Bail Act 1976 and in all the circumstances of the case it is proper to do so.

5.3 Where any of the above conditions is not met, the Threshold Test cannot be applied and the suspect cannot be charged. The custody officer must determine whether the person may continue to be detained or be released on bail, with or without conditions.

5.4 There are two parts to the evidential consideration of the Threshold Test.

The first part of the Threshold Test – is there reasonable suspicion?

5.5 Prosecutors must be satisfied that there is at least a reasonable suspicion that the person to be charged has committed the offence.

5.6 In determining this, prosecutors must consider the evidence then available. This may take the form of witness statements, material or other information, provided the prosecutor is satisfied that:

1. it is relevant; and

2. it is capable of being put into an admissible format for presentation in court; and

3. it would be used in the case.

5.7 If satisfied on this, the prosecutor should then consider the second part of the Threshold Test.

The second part of the Threshold Test – can further evidence be gathered to provide a realistic prospect of conviction?

5.8 Prosecutors must be satisfied that there are reasonable grounds for believing that the continuing investigation will provide further evidence, within a reasonable period of time, so that all the evidence together is capable of establishing a realistic prospect of conviction in accordance with the Full Code Test.

5.9 The further evidence must be identifiable and not merely speculative.

5.10 In reaching this decision Prosecutors must consider:

1. the nature, extent and admissibility of any likely further evidence and the impact it will have on the case;

2. the charges that all the evidence will support;

3. the reasons why the evidence is not already available;

4. the time required to obtain the further evidence and whether any consequential delay is reasonable in all the circumstances.

5.11 If both parts of the Threshold Test are satisfied, prosecutors must apply the public interest stage of the Full Code Test based on the information available at that time.

Reviewing the Threshold Test

5.12 A decision to charge under the Threshold Test must be kept under review. The evidence must be regularly assessed to ensure that the charge is still appropriate and that continued objection to bail is justified. The Full Code Test must be applied as soon as is reasonably practicable and in any event before the expiry of any applicable custody time limit.

6 Selection of charges

6.1 Prosecutors should select charges which:

1. reflect the seriousness and extent of the offending supported by the evidence;

2. give the court adequate powers to sentence and impose appropriate post-conviction orders; and

3. enable the case to be presented in a clear and simple way.

6.2 This means that prosecutors may not always choose or continue with the most serious charge where there is a choice.

6.3 Prosecutors should never go ahead with more charges than are necessary just to encourage a defendant to plead guilty to a few. In the same way, they should never go ahead with a more serious charge just to encourage a defendant to plead guilty to a less serious one.

6.4 Prosecutors should not change the charge simply because of the decision made by the court or the defendant about where the case will be heard.

6.5 Prosecutors must take account of any relevant change in circumstances as the case progresses after charge.

7 Out-of-court disposals

7.1 An out-of-court disposal may take the place of a prosecution in court if it is an appropriate response to the offender and/or the seriousness and consequences of the offending.

7.2 Prosecutors must follow any relevant guidance when asked to advise on or authorise a simple caution, a conditional caution, any appropriate regulatory proceedings, a punitive or civil penalty, or other disposal. They should ensure that the appropriate evidential standard for the specific out-of-court disposal is met including, where required, a clear admission of guilt, and that the public interest would be properly served by such a disposal.

8 Mode of trial

8.1 Prosecutors must have regard to the current guidelines on sentencing and allocation when making submissions to the magistrates' court about where the defendant should be tried.

8.2 Speed must never be the only reason for asking for a case to stay in the magistrates' court. But prosecutors should consider the effect of any likely delay if a case is sent to the Crown Court, and the possible effect on any victim or witness if the case is delayed.

Venue for trial in cases involving youths

8.3 Prosecutors must bear in mind that youths should be tried in the youth court wherever possible. It is the court which is best designed to meet their specific needs. A trial of a youth in the Crown Court should be reserved for the most serious cases or where the interests of justice require a youth to be jointly tried with an adult.

9 Accepting guilty pleas

9.1 Defendants may want to plead guilty to some, but not all, of the charges. Alternatively, they may want to plead guilty to a different, possibly less serious, charge because they are admitting only part of the crime.

9.2 Prosecutors should only accept the defendant's plea if they think the court is able to pass a sentence that matches the seriousness of the offending, particularly where there are aggravating features. Prosecutors must never accept a guilty plea just because it is convenient.

9.3 In considering whether the pleas offered are acceptable, prosecutors should ensure that the interests and, where possible, the views of the victim, or in appropriate cases the views of the victim's family, are taken into account when deciding whether it is in the public interest to accept the plea. However, the decision rests with the prosecutor.

9.4 It must be made clear to the court on what basis any plea is advanced and accepted. In cases where a defendant pleads guilty to the charges but on the basis of facts that are different from the prosecution case, and where this may significantly affect sentence, the court should be invited to hear evidence to determine what happened, and then sentence on that basis.

9.5 Where a defendant has previously indicated that he or she will ask the court to take an offence into consideration when sentencing, but then declines to admit that offence at court, prosecutors will consider whether a prosecution is required for that offence. Prosecutors should explain to the defence advocate and the court that the prosecution of that offence may be subject to further review, in consultation with the police or other investigators wherever possible.

9.6 Particular care must be taken when considering pleas which would enable the defendant to avoid the imposition of a mandatory minimum sentence. When pleas are offered, prosecutors must also bear in mind the fact that ancillary orders can be made with some offences but not with others.

10 Reconsidering a prosecution decision

10.1 People should be able to rely on decisions taken by the CPS. Normally, if the CPS tells a suspect or defendant that there will not be a prosecution, or that the prosecution has been stopped, the case will not start again. But occasionally there are reasons why the CPS will overturn a decision not to prosecute or to deal with the case by way of an out-of-court disposal or when it will restart the prosecution, particularly if the case is serious.

10.2 These reasons include:

1. cases where a new look at the original decision shows that it was wrong and, in order to maintain confidence in the criminal justice system, a prosecution should be brought despite the earlier decision;

2. cases which are stopped so that more evidence [which is likely to become available in the fairly near future] can be collected and prepared. In these cases, the prosecutor will tell the defendant that the prosecution may well start again;

3. cases which are stopped because of a lack of evidence but where more significant evidence is discovered later; and

4. cases involving a death in which a review following the findings of an inquest concludes that a prosecution should be brought, notwithstanding any earlier decision not to prosecute.

Part 2

CPS Legal Guidance Manual

Selected extracts relating to juvenile offenders

The purpose of legal guidance

This Legal Guidance is prepared by the Crown Prosecution Service. It provides guidance to prosecutors and paralegal staff in relation to many criminal offences and procedural issues. The Legal Guidance is used as an aid to guide Crown Prosecutors and Associate Prosecutors in the use of their discretion in making decisions in cases, and is subject to the principles as set out in the Code for Crown Prosecutors.

Information which would be likely to prejudice the prevention or detection of crime, the apprehension or prosecution of offenders or the administration of justice is exempt from disclosure under the Freedom of Information Act where the public interest in maintaining the exemption outweighs the public interest in disclosing the information. Therefore, small pieces of guidance will be for use of CPS staff only and will not appear in this guidance.

Reference to the Legal Guidance does not override the need for Crown Prosecutors to consider each case on its individual merits, and to take into account special circumstances when applying the principles set out in the Code for Crown Prosecutors.

The Legal Guidance is not a substitute for any recognised legal textbook, such as *Archbold*, Blackstone's, *Stone's Justices' Manual* or Wilkinson's *Road Traffic Offences*. Crown Prosecutors and paralegal staff use these sources as well as the Legal Guidance in their work. Therefore, these are referred to at various places in the guidance. However, for contractual reasons, members of the public cannot gain access to these reference sources through this guidance. It is not intended to provide legal advice to members of the public, nor does it replace the specialised advice of lawyers or other experts.

The Legal Guidance does not create any rights enforceable at law, in any legal proceedings.

The material in the Legal Guidance may be used without seeking permission, provided it is accurately reproduced and includes an acknowledgement of the Crown Prosecution Service, as its source. The Crown Prosecution Service does not take responsibility for the accuracy or reliability of reproduced material.

Principle

The CPS is committed to ensuring that the special considerations which apply to cases involving a young offender are enshrined in its working practices and form part of the training of its prosecutors.

The key considerations governing the decisions made by Crown Prosecutors in dealing with youths are those contained in:

- Section 44 of the Children and Young Persons Act 1933 (*Archbold* 5-232), which requires the courts to have regard to the welfare of a young person;

391

- Section 37 of the Crime and Disorder Act 1998 (*Archbold* 5-231), which requires the principal aim of agencies involved in the youth justice system to be the prevention of offending by young persons; and

- The Code for Crown Prosecutors, which states that Crown Prosecutors must consider the interests of a youth, amongst other public interest factors, when deciding whether a prosecution is needed.

The Crown Prosecution Service recognises that in applying these considerations Crown Prosecutors will have regard to their obligations arising from the European Convention of Human Rights, the United Nations 1989 Convention on the Rights of the Child and the United Nations 1985 Standard Minimum Rules for the Administration of Juvenile Justice (the Beijing Rules).

Youth specialist prosecutors will have attended the youth offender specialist training course and read all its accompanying materials, which detail practice and procedure in cases involving youth suspects and offenders.

Guidance

Criminal Justice System

The CPS is one of several agencies involved within the CJS that deals with youths.

Effective partnerships within the criminal justice system will contribute to securing real improvements in the youth justice system and will help to give effect to government policy. Such partnerships require mutual cooperation and understanding.

All areas are encouraged to participate in local inter-agency groups with representatives from the Youth and Crown Courts, Youth Offending Team managers, police, CPS, appropriate defence representatives and Victim Support Service co-ordinators.

These groups should be responsible for the implementation of youth justice initiatives. For example:

- Contributing to a reduction of delay in the youth justice system;

- Monitoring of the expedited file system, ie the level of guilty pleas;

- Use of and checks with the Case Tracker Systems; and

- Developing good local practice in line with Youth Justice Board recommendations.

Area Youth Justice Co-ordinator (AYJC)

The CCP or DCCP may appoint one or more AYJCs. It will be a matter for the CCP or DCCP to decide what functions the AYJC will carry out, but they may include the following:

- Being a 'Service Ambassador' providing advice to CCPs and DCCPs on youth matters and liaising at a strategic level on behalf of the CCP/DCCP with other agencies;

- Being a focal point for advice on good practice within the Area;

- Being the point of contact for CPS Headquarters;

- Having responsibility for monitoring achievements against national and locally agreed targets in the magistrates, youth and Crown Court;

- Co-ordinating the formulation and implementation of the training of other lawyers in the Area.

The AYJC should be:

- An experienced Youth Offender Specialist; and

- Able to carry out the functions of a Youth Offender Specialist.

Youth Offender Specialist (YOS)

A YOS will be approved by the CCP/DCCP or Unit Head.

The YOS will carry out the following functions:

- Undertaking the review of files involving youth offenders and taking all major decisions in relation to those files;

- Making regular appearances in the Youth Court; and

- Together with the Area Youth Justice Co-ordinator, taking part in the formulation and implementation of the training of other lawyers.

In order to be approved as a YOS, a lawyer must:

- Be a Senior Crown Prosecutor with adequate experience and appropriate skills; and

- Have undertaken the Youth Offender Training Course.

Additionally, whenever possible, specialists should be volunteers expressing an interest in dealing with youth offender cases.

Handling of Youth Files

All cases involving youth offenders must be dealt with expeditiously and avoid delay, which has at its core the principle that there is little point in conducting a trial for a young offender long after the alleged commission of an offence when the offender will have difficulty in relating the sentence to the offence. To maximise the impact on the youth offender, the case must be dealt with as soon as possible.

All prosecutors should be able to prosecute Youth Courts and deal with youths connected with adults in the magistrates' court.

All prosecutors should be able to carry out an initial review of files prior to the first hearing to enable a youth offender to enter a guilty plea if offered.

A Youth Offender Specialist (YOS) will undertake the major reviews of files involving youth offenders and take all major decisions in relation to those files.

Whenever possible, Youth Remand Courts should be prosecuted by a YOS, who will be able to review all the files that are appearing in that court.

Prosecutors at court should liaise with the other CJS Agencies and in particular the Youth Offending Team. See Youth Justice Board: Making it Count in Court 2009.

Principles Guiding the Decision to Prosecute

Prosecutors who are not Youth Offender Specialists must refer the decision to prosecute or divert in any case to a Youth Offender Specialist.

393

A decision whether to prosecute a youth offender is open to judicial review if it can be demonstrated that the decision was made regardless of, or clearly contrary to a settled policy of the DPP. See *R v Chief Constable of Kent and Another ex parte L, R v DPP ex parte B* [1991] 93 Cr App R 416. The court held that an application for judicial review could be successful if the decision to prosecute was made without any or sufficient inquiry into the circumstances and general character of the accused. This judgment highlights the importance in appropriate cases of obtaining sufficient information about the youth's home circumstances and background from sources such as the police, youth offending service, children's services before making the decision whether to prosecute.

It is essential in all youth offender cases to ensure that all of the public interest matters which give rise to the decision are clearly identified, considered and balanced. A note of the factors identified but rejected or outweighed by other considerations should be made. This demonstrates that the decision to prosecute was taken only after a full review of the case and the background information, including that concerning the suspect provided by the youth offending service, police or local authority. Failure to show that the legal guidance has been followed and properly applied to all the information on the case may result in the decision to prosecute being quashed. See *R (on the application of E,S* and *R v DPP* [2011] EWHC 1465 (Admin).

When applying the public interest factors in the Full Code Test in a case involving a youth, paragraph 4.17 b) will always be a particularly important one. This paragraph provides that:

"A prosecution is less likely to be required if...the seriousness and the consequences of the offending can be appropriately dealt with by an out-of-court disposal which the suspect accepts and with which he or she complies."

This is a factor which will always carry a special weight in the case of youths who are at a very early stage of their offending, and can be traced back to historic police practice (as set out, for example, in Home Office Circular 18/1994) of starting from a presumption of diverting youths away from the courts where possible.

For those youths for whom formal diversion is not an option, it is still important to ensure that a prosecution is only brought in circumstances where this is a proper and proportionate response. The separate Legal Guidance chapter on Minor Offences – Prosecution Guidance and its steer towards the taking of a common-sense approach to less serious cases has direct application to a number of youth matters. Alternative options, including restorative interventions, Acceptable Behaviour Contracts and internal sanctions such as school disciplinary measures may be available, and sufficient to satisfy the public interest without a prosecution and the statutory duty to prevent offending (s 37 Crime and Disorder Act 1998).

Youth Cautions

Reprimands and warnings for youths were abolished (s 135 (1) of the Legal Aid Sentencing and Punishment of Offenders Act 2012) nationally with effect from 8 April 2013 and replaced with youth cautions (ss 66ZA and 66ZB of the Crime and Disorder Act 1998, inserted by s 135 (2) of the Legal Aid Sentencing and Punishment of Offenders Act 2012). Youth cautions are primarily administered by the police, but prosecutors should understand the principles that are applied.

A youth caution is a formal out-of-court disposal as set out in ss 66ZA and 66ZB of the Crime and Disorder Act 1998 the Ministry of Justice/Youth Justice Board Guidance on Youth Cautions (April 2013), the Ministry of Justice/YJB Youth Out-of-Court-Disposal Guide for Police and Youth Offending Services (April 2013) and ACPO Youth Offender Case Disposal Gravity Factor System (March 2013).

Youth cautions are intended to provide a proportionate and effective response to offending behaviour and can be used for any offence provided that the statutory criteria are satisfied:

- the police are satisfied that there is sufficient evidence to charge the youth with an offence;

- the youth admits the offence to the police;

- the police do not consider that the youth should be prosecuted or given a youth conditional caution for the offence.

The police cannot issue a youth caution for an offence that is indictable only in the case of an adult without the authority of the CPS.

There is no statutory restriction on the number of youth cautions that a youth can receive, and a youth may receive a youth caution even if he or she has previous convictions, reprimands, warnings, youth cautions and youth conditional cautions.

The police will take into account the offending history and the seriousness of the offence when deciding whether to issue a youth caution.

Offence seriousness is determined by reference to the ACPO Gravity Matrix, which sets out the most prevalent offences, and provides them with a score of 1, 2, 3 or 4. The score may be raised or lowered by one level according to aggravating and mitigating factors which are set out in the Matrix.

An offence that attracts a gravity score of 2 or 3 will usually result in a youth being given a youth caution. If the offending behaviour cannot be satisfactorily addressed by a youth caution, the police will consider a youth conditional caution.

The police must refer a youth who has received a youth caution to the youth offending team (s 66ZB(1) of the Crime and Disorder Act 1998).

The youth offending team:

- may assess a youth who has never had a youth caution or a youth conditional caution and may arrange a rehabilitation programme for the youth (s 66ZB(3) of the Crime and Disorder Act 1998);

- must assess a youth who has had a youth caution or a youth conditional caution and must, unless they think it inappropriate to do so, arrange a rehabilitation programme for the youth (s 66ZB(2) of the Crime and Disorder Act 1998.

Prosecutors should bear in mind that although the ACPO Guidelines are of primary relevance, they are not the final arbiter of whether to prosecute, offer an out-of-court disposal or take no formal criminal justice action. For those youths for whom formal diversion is not an option, it is still important to ensure that a prosecution is only brought in circumstances where this is a proper and proportionate response. The separate Legal Guidance chapter on Minor Offences Prosecution Guidance and its steer towards the taking of a common sense approach to less serious cases has direct application to a number of youth matters. Alternative options, including restorative interventions, Acceptable Behaviour Contracts and internal sanctions such as school disciplinary measures may be available, and sufficient to satisfy the public interest without a prosecution and the statutory duty to prevent offending (s 37 of the Crime and Disorder Act 1998). See also the legal guidance on School Bullying and Offending Behaviour in Children's Homes elsewhere in the Youth Offenders guidance.

Where a case has proceeded to court, but the prosecutor decides that a youth caution or youth conditional caution can be justified, the matter should be adjourned for consideration of that disposal. Prosecutors are reminded that an admission of guilt to the police is essential before a youth caution can be given. Once a young person has been correctly charged it is likely to be only in exceptional circumstances that a youth caution or youth conditional caution will be given.

When adjourning a case for such consideration, prosecutors should bear in mind that there may be factors unknown to the CPS that could affect the disposal of the case. Prosecutors should not raise any expectation that the case will not proceed if a youth caution or youth conditional caution is not issued.

If the offence is one covered by the Sexual Offences Act 2003, the youth may be subject to the notification requirements in s 80 (refer to notification requirements elsewhere in this guidance).

Bindovers should be rare and the reasons for their use should be fully endorsed.

Youth Conditional Cautions (YCC)

Section 48 and Sch 9 of the Criminal Justice and Immigration Act 2008 amend s 65 of the Crime and Disorder Act 1998 and insert ss 66A to H in the Crime and Disorder Act 1998 with the effect that a youth conditional caution can be given to a youth provided that the following conditions are satisfied:

- The authorised person has evidence that the youth has committed an offence;

- The prosecutor is satisfied that there is sufficient evidence to charge the youth with the offence and that a youth conditional caution should be given in respect of the offence;

- The youth admits the offence to an authorised person;

- The authorised person has explained the effect of the YCC to the youth and has warned him or her that failure to comply with any of the conditions may result in a prosecution. If the youth is 16 or under this must be done in the presence of an appropriate adult;

- The youth signs a document that contains details of the offence, an admission that he committed the offence, consent to the YCC and the conditions attached to the caution.

Youth conditional cautions are available for any offence, except an offence of hate crime or domestic violence that has a gravity core of 4, but a youth conditional caution can only be given for an indictable only offence on the authority of the CPS. The police may issue a youth conditional caution for any either way or summary offence, except an offence of hate crime or domestic violence with a gravity score of 4, without reference to the CPS.

The Youth Conditional Caution is no longer restricted to youths with no previous convictions and there is no statutory restriction on the number of youth conditional cautions that a youth can receive. However, the Director's Guidance on Youth Conditional Cautioning (2nd Edition) explains that a record of previous offending does not automatically rule out the possibility of a youth conditional caution especially where there have been no similar offences during the last two years or where it appears that the youth conditional caution is likely to change the pattern of offending behaviour and prevent reoffending. However, where a youth has been given two youth conditional cautions and continues to offend, a further youth conditional caution is unlikely to be effective in preventing offending and should not be offered as an alternative to prosecution.

When a case has proceeded to court, but the prosecutor decides that a youth caution or youth conditional caution can be justified, the matter should be adjourned for consideration of that disposal. Prosecutors are reminded that an admission of guilt to the police is essential before a youth caution or youth conditional caution can be given. Once a youth has been correctly charged it is likely to be only in exceptional circumstances that a youth caution or youth conditional caution will be given.

Public Interest and Sensitive Issues

General Issues

Guidance is given below on specific areas of work commonly raising sensitive or difficult issues. It is not intended to replace guidance given elsewhere in the Legal Guidance. For example, guidance on charging practice can be found in the chapter that covers the specific offence under consideration.

Prevalence of the Offence

If the local police force proposes from time to time to devote substantial resources to the investigation of a particularly prevalent offence, the police should be encouraged to discuss this in advance with the CPS. Every case will still finally be judged on its facts and its own merits. However, it will be appropriate to consider the police objectives and the impact on the community of the offending when reviewing the public interest factor.

Welfare Powers

Proceedings should not be taken against a youth offender solely to secure access to the welfare powers of the court.

Hostility and Hate Crime

A relatively minor incident may be more serious if there is evidence of racial or religious hostility particularly in the context of a number of incidents of violence or intimidation towards black and minority ethnic communities. Prosecutors should have regard to the availability of racially and religiously aggravated offences.

The existence of a clear racial motivation in an offence or of hostility based on the victims ethnic or national origin or religion should always be regarded as an aggravating feature pointing towards prosecution, assuming that the evidence itself justifies proceedings.

Offending Behaviour in Children's homes

The decision to prosecute looked after children for low level offences committed within a children's home is a major decision and should be taken by a youth specialist, who, wherever possible, will be a volunteer who has attended the CPS Youth Offender Specialist Course and is a Senior Crown Prosecutor.

This guidance is intended to assist youth specialists in determining where the public interest lies when it is alleged that a looked after child has committed an offence in the children's home where he or she lives. It is not intended to apply to all offences committed by looked after children; although some of the principles may be helpful when applying the public interest stage of the Full Code Test to offences committed outside the home.

Children and young people who live in children's homes are at a high risk of offending behaviour because:

- Many looked after children are between the ages of 14 and 17, which is regarded as the peak offending age range

- In some children's homes they are likely to be living with young people who have been remanded to local authority accommodation, and may be susceptible to group offending behaviour

- They may be living in accommodation far from their home, so may lack support from friends and family

- Many looked after children display challenging behaviour, which may be a reaction to past experiences of abuse and neglect; and/or have been diagnosed as experiencing Attention Deficit and Hyperactivity Disorder and Oppositional Defiant Disorder. Their offending behaviour may be caused by or otherwise linked with the disorder

- Their behaviour is likely to be more challenging and demanding because of their family experience, the breakdown of foster placements and frequent moves from other children's homes

- Living in a group with other challenging and demanding children of the same age gives rise to greater potential for conflict, bullying and peer group pressure

The police are more likely to be called to a children's home than a domestic setting to deal with an incident of offending behaviour by an adolescent. Specialists should bear this in mind when dealing with incidents that take place in a children's home. However, where offending behaviour occurs in a family context, the CPS Domestic Violence Policy would apply wherever a partner, sibling, parent or other family member experiences violence at the hands of a youth. **It is important that all people feel safe in the place that they live, whether that is in a family home or children's home and that they have confidence in the criminal justice system to intervene and protect them where this is necessary.**

A criminal justice disposal, whether a prosecution, reprimand or warning, should not be regarded as an automatic response to offending behaviour by a looked after child, irrespective of their criminal history. This applies equally to persistent offenders and youths of good character. A criminal justice disposal will only be appropriate where it is clearly required.

Informal disposals such as restorative justice conferencing, reparation, acceptable behaviour contracts and disciplinary measures by the home may be sufficient to satisfy the public interest and to reduce the risk of future offending.

Behaviour Management policies

All children's homes, whether they are run privately or by the local authority or voluntary sector must comply with the Children's Home Regulations 2001, which are mandatory, and the National Minimum Standards, which are issued by the Secretary of State under section 23 Care Standards Act 2000. These are minimum standards, not examples of good practice, and Homes should aspire to exceed them. Copies of these documents are available at:

- https://www.education.gov.uk/publications/standard/publicationDetail/Page1/DFE-00030-2011

- http://www.legislation.gov.uk/ukpga/2000/14/section/23

Each home must have a written behaviour management policy that sets out the measures of control, restraint and discipline which may be used in the children's home and the means whereby appropriate behaviour is to be promoted in the home. **A copy of this policy and a statement from the home setting out how the policy has been applied to this incident should accompany any request for advice on charging.**

Each home should have a clear written policy, procedures and guidance for staff based on a code of conduct that sets out control, discipline and restraint measures that are permitted and must reinforce positive messages to children for the achievement of acceptable behaviour. The consequences of unacceptable behaviour should be clear to staff and children and must be appropriate to the age, understanding and individual needs of the child. It must also be recognised that unacceptable or challenging behaviour may be the result of illness, bullying, disabilities such as autism, ADHD or communication difficulties.

Standard 22 National Minimum Standards for Childrens Homes requires staff to respond positively to acceptable behaviour, and where the behaviour of children is regarded as unacceptable by staff, is responded to by constructive, acceptable and known disciplinary measures approved by the registered person. Control and disciplinary measures should encourage reparation and restitution. Corporal punishment, deprivation of food and drink and punishing a group for the behaviour of an individual may not be used as a disciplinary measure, and financial penalties are restricted to the imposition of a reasonable sum, which may be paid by instalments, by way of reparation (Rule 17 CHR 2001).

Unless the registered person can show it is inappropriate, the home should also have procedures and guidance on police involvement in the home, which has been agreed with the local police. Staff should know about the agreement with the police and should be clear when the police should be involved. (para 22.15 National Minimum Standards for Children).

The Decision to Prosecute

Prosecutors are reminded of the need to consider all the circumstances surrounding the offence and the circumstances of the youth before reaching a decision and to apply all relevant CPS policies and documents. Failure to do so may result in proceedings for judicial review: *R v Chief Constable of Kent and Another ex parte L, R v DPP ex parte B (1991) 93 Cr App R 416*. Factors that should be considered include:

- The disciplinary policy of the Home

- An explanation from the Home regarding their decision to involve the police, which should refer to the procedures and guidance on police involvement.

- Information from the Home about the recent behaviour of the youth, including similar behaviour and any incidents in the youths life that could have affected their behaviour, any history between the youth and the victim, any apology or reparation by the youth, history of the incident and any action under the disciplinary policy of the Home

- The views of the victim, including their willingness to attend court to give evidence and/or participate in a restorative justice or other diversionary programme

- The views of the key worker, social worker, counsellor or CAHMS worker on the effect of criminal justice intervention on the youth, particularly where the youth suffers from an illness or disorder

Any explanation or information about the offence from the looked after child

If the looked after child wishes it to be considered, information about the local authority's assessment of his/her needs and how the placement provided by the Home is intended to address them. The local authority should be able to provide this information as it should be an integral part of the Care Plan for the looked after child.

Prosecutors should consider all of the aggravating and mitigating features when deciding on the appropriate outcome.

Aggravating features include:

- The offence is violent or induces the genuine fear of violence in the victim

- The offence is sexual

- The offence is motivated by hostility based on the gender, sexuality, disability, race, religion or ethnicity of the victim

- The victim is vulnerable

- The damage or harm caused is deliberate and cannot be described as minor

- The offence forms part of a series of offences

- Informal measures have been ineffective in preventing offending behaviour.

Mitigating features include:

- The damage or harm caused is at the lower end of the scale and has been put right

- Appropriate action has already been taken under the disciplinary procedure or other informal disposal

- Genuine remorse and apology to the victim

- The behaviour is a symptom of a disorder or illness that cannot be controlled by medication or diet. Refer also to Mentally Disordered Offenders

- Care should be taken where it appears that the youth has deliberately refused medication or deliberately consumed a substance knowing that his or her behaviour will be affected.

- Isolated incident or out of character

- The young person is under extreme stress or appears to have been provoked and has overreacted

The reasons for the charging/diversion decision should be clearly recorded and show the factors that have been considered by a youth specialist to determine how the public interest is satisfied.

Psychoactive Substances Act 2016

The Psychoactive Substances Act 2016 (Commencement) Regulations 2016 (SI 2016) brought the provisions of the Psychoactive Substances Act 2016 into force on 26 May 2016, in so far as they were not already in force.

The Psychoactive Substances Act 2016 introduces a legal definition of a psychoactive substance, which will be used to enforce a range of criminal offences and civil sanctions. The criminal offences are:

- producing a psychoactive substance;

- supplying, or offering to supply a psychoactive substance;

- possession of a psychoactive substance with intent to supply;

- importing or exporting a psychoactive substance;

- possession of a psychoactive substance in a custodial institution.

The maximum sentence, on conviction on indictment, for the production, supply, possession with intent to supply and import/export offences is seven years' imprisonment. The maximum sentence, on conviction on indictment, for the offence of possession in a custodial institution is two years' imprisonment.

A custodial institution refers to:

(a)   a prison;

(b)   a young offenders' institution, secure training centre, secure college, young offenders' centre, juvenile justice centre or remand centre;

(c)   a removal centre, a short-term holding facility or pre-departure accommodation;

(d)   service custody premises.

For full information on offences arising from the Psychoactive Substances Act 2016, advice on charging practice and factors to consider when reviewing such cases, please refer to the Legal Guidance on Psychoactive Substances.

County Lines

'County Lines' is a national issue which involves the exploitation of vulnerable young people and adults by violent gang members in order to move and sell drugs across the country.

The National Crime Agency has identified that there is growing evidence of city-based organised crime gangs extending their drug dealing activity into new areas, many of which are coastal towns. The gangs recruit vulnerable people, often children, to act as couriers and to sell drugs.

'County Lines' operate whereby gangs from cities, in particular London, introduce a telephone number in a new area to sell crack and heroin directly at street level. Potential buyers telephone the number and local runners are dispatched to make deliveries via a telephone 'relay or exchange' system. The 'runners' are invariably children, often boys aged 14 to 17 years, who are groomed with money and gifts and forced to carry out day to day dealing. Runaway and missing children are also used by gangs to expand inner city drugs empires into county towns. Children as young as 11 years of age have been reported as being recruited into the highly-sophisticated gangs.

Gang members enter into relationships with young women in order to secure a location for drugs to be stored in the new area. In addition, violence is used against drug users to coerce them to become runners, enforce debts, and use their accommodation as an operating base.

Prosecutors are encouraged to consider all available charges when considering a prosecution in connection with 'County Lines' offending.

The Modern Slavery Act 2015 may provide opportunities to consider the circumstances of 'County Line' offending, particularly where there has been deliberate targeting, recruitment and significant exploitation of young and vulnerable people. Prosecutors should, however, be alert to the challenge of securing a conviction for a Modern Slavery Act offence.

Public Order Offences

The general principles of the Code and the reprimand and final warning system should be applied. However, there are aggravating features which may increase the need to prosecute in borderline cases. These include:

•   where the incident in question is not isolated but is either prevalent within an area or is part of a wider incident or series of incidents;

- where the aggression displayed by members of the group, whether verbal or physical, is directed outside the group at members of the public (such as shopkeepers), and especially so if their attentions are directed at ethnic minorities, the elderly, or other vulnerable people

Occasionally the police locally may target a particular type of conduct for special attention in an attempt to discourage it. This will have an effect on the number of cases recommended by them for prosecution.

The police should be encouraged to discuss the implications of such a campaign in advance with the CPS. Whilst every case will be considered on its merits, the force objective should be taken into account, as a public interest factor, when deciding whether or not to institute or continue proceedings.

School Bullying

Prosecution may not be necessary because of other available alternatives, but there will be cases in which a prosecution is needed in the public interest.

In cases of serious or persistent bullying, prosecutions must be carefully considered. Such cases usually involve one pupil or a group of pupils using their strength or power to induce fear in the victimised pupil, whether or not for a particular purpose such as extortion of money or valuables. They may involve verbal persecution and abuse, physical assault or the threat of it, or even the degradation or humiliation of the victim. Such attacks tend to be systematic and persistent leading to the oppression of a fellow pupil and his or her virtual isolation from the support and friendship of others.

It is important to differentiate occasional jibes from systematic bullying of children because of ethnic origin, religion, gender, sexual orientation or disability.

In all cases relevant considerations will include:

- any background to the incident in question including any history of bullying of the same victim by the offender or generally;
- the attitude and behaviour of the offender and the offenders parent(s) or guardian(s);
- the effect of the behaviour on the victim;
- any internal remedies already taken by the school whether in connection with the incident or in the past, such as, where the victim and offender no longer attend the same school.

It is important to ensure that the seriousness of the conduct is accurately and appropriately reflected in the seriousness of the charge.

If school bullying incidents are regularly referred for prosecution (particularly if they are often appropriate for reprimands or final warning), it may well be necessary for the AYJC/local CPS to contact the local police department and the YOT responsible for youth offender cases with a view to them examining the policies of the local schools and the police.

All schools should have internal procedures and strategies for dealing with these incidents. It may be necessary to explore with the police and the YOT whether certain schools are in fact accepting their responsibility in this area fully.

In such cases the file should include information on the background of the incident, any previous incident and any disciplinary measures taken by the school.

If the incident has taken place outside school but is connected to conduct occurring at school the same information described above is relevant. Schools often feel unable to act in these circumstances.

Motoring Offences

All offences, including motoring and minor traffic offences are included in the reprimand/final warning scheme. However, under the Home Office Guidelines, Where a young person commits a minor traffic offence, a fixed penalty notice remains an appropriate response for 16 and 17 year olds.

The police deal with the majority of minor motoring offences without reference to CPS. However, when dealing with minor traffic offences a prosecutor should bear in mind the effects of the reprimand/final warning scheme and consider carefully the impact of his decision on the youth.

Some examples of the impact of the reprimand/final warning scheme are as follows:

A final warning for an offence of no insurance will prevent a youth from further statutory diversions and is likely to result in a youth being prosecuted for any other offence he or she commits.

However, a successful prosecution for no insurance is not a recordable offence and therefore will probably mean that a youth will not be prosecuted for the next offence that he commits. It will cause penalty points to be endorsed on a youths licence that could result in the licence being suspended by DVLA and the youth being required to re-take the driving test. Such a consequence may have a substantial impact on the youths employment prospects.

In adult cases, it is possible to cite previous convictions/cautions for use within the s12 procedure under the Road Traffic Act. However, the Road Traffic Act and Magistrates' Court Act procedures for citing previous convictions do not apply in the Youth Court. However, Rule 10 of the Magistrates' Court (Children and Young Persons) Rules 1992 provides that the Court should take into account the general conduct of the youth on sentence. The existence of a previous reprimand/final warning is relevant information.

The police should therefore serve a Notice of Intention to Cite Previous Reprimands and Final Warnings under the Rule 10 of the Magistrates' Court (Children and Young Persons) Rules 1992 with the summons. Failure to give such notice will mean that the Court will not be able to take into account the previous reprimand/final warning, which may materially affect the sentence.

Sexual Offences and Child Abuse by Young Offenders

This guidance expands on, and should be read in conjunction with other specific sections elsewhere in Legal Guidance, such as Sexual Offences. Also note the Notification requirements. Any decision to prosecute or not to prosecute should be free of discrimination on the grounds of sexual orientation and gender.

If an allegation of any sexual abuse committed by a youth offender has been fully investigated and there is sufficient evidence to justify instituting proceedings, the balance of the public interest must always be carefully considered before any prosecution is commenced. Positive action may need to be taken at an early stage of offending of this type. Although a reprimand or final warning may provide an acceptable alternative in some cases, in reaching any decision, the police and the CPS will have to take into account fully the view of other agencies involved in the case, in particular the Social Services. The consequences for the victim of the decision whether or not to prosecute, and any views expressed by the victim or the victims family should also be taken into account.

In child abuse cases, it will be important to have the views of the Social Services on file if at all possible, as well as any background or history of similar conduct, information about the relationship between the two and the effect a prosecution might have on the victim.

Any case referred to the CPS for advice, or in which a prosecution does proceed, must be dealt with as quickly as possible to minimise the delay before the case comes to court.

Irrespective of whether the evidence is sufficient to found a criminal prosecution, The Social Services will consider taking civil action, such as care proceedings, to protect the child. The police and the CPS may well be asked to disclose evidence to assist in this process. Great care should be taken to follow the guidance set out in the section on disclosure to third parties Refer to Disclosure of Material to Third Parties.

Rape and other offences against children under 13 (sections 5 to 8 Sexual Offences Act 2003)

CCPs or DCCPs must be notified of any such case where there are both defendants and victims under the age of 13. This includes cases which are diverted from prosecution, whether on evidential or public interest grounds.

All such cases must be reviewed by a prosecutor who is both a rape specialist and a youth specialist. All advocates conducting these cases must have a rape specialism and should also have a youth specialism.

Where the Full Code Test is satisfied in a case in which a youth is suspected of committing a sexual offence involving a child under the age of 13, the appropriate charge will be an offence contrary to sections 5 to 8 Sexual Offences Act 2003, depending on the act, and not the lesser offence contrary to section 13 Sexual Offences Act 2003.

Rape of a child under 13 (section 5), assault of a child under 13 by penetration (section 6) and causing or inciting a child under 13 to engage in sexual activity that involves penetration (section 8) are indictable only offences with a maximum sentence of life imprisonment. The offences of sexual assault of a child under 13 (section 7), causing or inciting a child under 13 to engage in sexual activity where there has been no penetration (section 8) are punishable on indictment with imprisonment for a term not exceeding 14 years. They are all grave crimes for the purposes of section 24 Magistrates' Courts Act 1980 and section 91 Powers of Criminal Courts (Sentencing) Act 2000.

A mistaken belief that the child under 13 was 16 or over and consented to intercourse is not a defence to an allegation of rape of a child under 13, assault of a child under 13 by penetration, sexual assault of a child under 13 or causing or inciting a child under 13 to engage in sexual activity contrary to sections 5 to 8 Sexual Offences Act 2003 respectively.

When reviewing a case, in which a youth under 18 is alleged to have committed an offence contrary to sections 5 to 8, prosecutors should obtain and consider:

* the views of local authority Childrens and Young Peoples Service;

* any risk assessment or report conducted by the local authority or youth offending service in respect of sexually harmful behaviour (such as AIM (Assessment, Intervention and Moving On);

- background information and history of the parties;

- the views of the families of all parties.

Careful regard should be paid to the following factors:

- the relative ages of both parties;

- the existence of and nature of any relationship;

- the sexual and emotional maturity of both parties and any emotional or physical effects as a result of the conduct;

- whether the child under 13 in fact freely consented (even though in law this is not a defence) or a genuine mistake as to her age was in fact made;

- whether any element of seduction, breach of any duty of responsibility to the girl or other exploitation is disclosed by the evidence;

- the impact of a prosecution on each child involved.

If the sexual act or activity was in fact genuinely consensual and the youth and the child under 13 concerned are fairly close in age and development, a prosecution is unlikely to be appropriate. Action falling short of prosecution may be appropriate. In such cases, the parents and/or welfare agencies may be able to deal with the situation informally.

However, if a very young child has been seduced by a youth, or a baby-sitter in a position of responsibility has taken advantage of a child under 13 in his/her care, prosecution is likely to be in the public interest. Where a child under 13 has not given ostensible consent to the activity, then a prosecution contrary to sections 5 to 8 is likely to be the appropriate course of action.

There is a fine line between sexual experimentation and offending and in general, children under the age of 13 should not be criminalised for sexual behaviour in the absence of coercion, exploitation or abuse of trust.

Child sex offences committed by children or young persons

Section 13 of the 2003 Act makes it an offence for a youth under 18 to have sexual activity with a child under 16, cause or incite a child under 16 to engage in sexual activity, engage in sexual activity in the presence of a child under or cause a child under 16 to watch a sexual act. These offences are punishable on indictment with imprisonment for a term not exceeding 5 years. They are grave crimes for the purposes of section 24 Magistrates' Courts Act 1980 and section 91 Powers of Criminal Courts (Sentencing) Act 2000. Section 13 (2) (a) purports to restrict the maximum penalty on summary conviction to a maximum of 6 months imprisonment, although this should be read in the light of section 101 (2) Powers of Criminal Courts (Sentencing) Act 2000 to allow a Detention and Training Order of up to 24 months.

An offence is not committed if the child is over 13 but is under 16 and the youth has a reasonable belief that the child is 16 or over.

It should be noted that where both parties to sexual activity are under 16, then they may both have committed a criminal offence. However, the overriding purpose of the legislation is to protect children and it was not Parliament's intention to punish children unnecessarily or for the criminal law to intervene where it was wholly in appropriate. Consensual sexual activity between, for example, a 14 or 15 year-old and a teenage partner would not normally require criminal proceedings in the absence of aggravating features. The relevant considerations include:

- the respective ages of the parties;

- the existence and nature of any relationship
- their level of maturity;
- whether any duty of care existed;
- whether there was a serious element of exploitation.

Prostitution

Youth offender prostitution, whether involving young girls or boys, can be one of the most difficult types of cases to deal with. The young people concerned are likely to be extremely vulnerable and present complex emotional problems.

When reviewing a case involving youth offender prostitution it is **essential** that you are aware of and familiar with the inter-agency guidance entitled Safeguarding Children Involved in Prostitution, published in 2000. See also Prostitution, elsewhere in the Legal Guidance.

The aim of this guidance is to both safeguard and promote the welfare of children, and to encourage the investigation and prosecution of criminal activities by those who coerce, exploit and abuse children through prostitution. One of the key purposes of the guidance is to encourage the agencies and professionals involved to treat a child (defined as a boy or girl under the age of 18) involved in prostitution as primarily a victim of abuse.

Paragraph 6.21 of the guidance states that the approach to be adopted in cases of child prostitution is one of diversion of the child from the criminal justice system and a welfare approach is to be adopted. At paragraphs 6.21–6.30, the guidance sets out the approach to be followed when deciding whether it will be appropriate to prosecute or administer a reprimand or final warning to a child involved in prostitution. This section of the Guidance replaces the Home Office Circular 109/50 insofar as the Circular dealt with the cautioning of a child, male or female, under the age of 18 involved in prostitution.

Familial Sexual Offences

Sections 25 and 26 Sexual Offences Act 2003 create the offences of sexual activity with a child family member and inciting a child family member to engage in sexual activity. These offences are punishable on indictment with imprisonment for a term not exceeding 5 years. They are grave crimes for the purposes of section 24 Magistrates' Courts Act 1980 and section 91 Powers of Criminal Courts (Sentencing) Act 2000. Section 25 (5) (b) and 26 (5) (b) purport to restrict the maximum penalty on summary conviction to a maximum of 6 months imprisonment, although this should be read in the light of section 101 (2) Powers of Criminal Courts (Sentencing) Act 2000 to allow a Detention and Training Order of up to 24 months.

Sections 64 and 65 Sexual Offences Act 2003 make it an offence for a person aged 16 or over to penetrate or consent to penetration by a family member who is aged 18 or over. The maximum penalty is imprisonment for a term not exceeding 2 years (sections 64 (5) and 65 (5)).

In cases of sexual activity between siblings, care should be taken to balance the public interest in prosecuting such conduct with the interests and welfare of the victim and the family unit. As a general rule, alternatives to prosecution should be sought where the sexual activity was wholly consensual. The welfare agencies will normally intervene.

Prosecution should be considered where there is evidence of:

- seduction;

- coercion;

- exploitation or violence;

- a significant disparity in age;

In all cases the effect of prosecution on a victim and family should be taken into account and if the views of the welfare agencies are not included with the file they should be sought.

Youths with Mental Disorders, including Learning Disabilities

A youth offender who is mentally disordered is doubly vulnerable. Prosecutors should have regard to the chapter in this manual concerning mentally disordered offenders.

The term mental disorder is used in the Mental Health Act 1983 to mean any disability or disorder of the mind. (*Archbold* 5-887). For general guidance on mentally disordered offenders refer to Mentally Disordered Offenders elsewhere in the Legal Guidance. The Mental Health Act 1983 is primarily concerned with compulsory treatment, which will be inappropriate in the majority of cases involving youth offenders.

Public Interest Considerations in relation to Mentally Disordered Offenders

Mentally disordered offenders will often commit offences that are more of a public nuisance than a danger to the public. However, in serious cases where the offender is a danger to the public, the public interest is likely to require a prosecution. In determining where the public interest lies the prosecutor should look particularly to:

- the seriousness of the offence;

- the circumstances of any previous offending;

- the nature of the youth offender's mental disability or disorder;

- the likelihood of repetition; and

- the availability of suitable alternatives to prosecution.

Reprimands and final warnings can be problematic. Both require sufficient evidence and full recognition of guilt by the offender.

Particular difficulties can arise when *mens rea* is a component of the offence. The prosecutor must be satisfied that any admissions are genuine. Particular care must be taken when considering whether to administer a reprimand or final warning in a case relying on admissions.

It may be that in a proportion of cases, which might otherwise have attracted such a disposal, that this is not an advisable option, either because of doubts about the truth of any admissions made (in cases where there is little or no supporting evidence), or because of the defendant's level of understanding. In such cases taking no further action will usually be the only appropriate way of dealing with the matter short of prosecution. Prosecutors should try and ensure the police are alert to these difficulties and guard against the inappropriate use of the reprimand and final warning system.

The file should include the opinions of the relevant welfare agencies, particularly about the offenders stage of development or understanding of the offence and the perceived likelihood of repetition, the likely effect of proceedings on his or her mental state and the available welfare options. It is particularly important in remand cases that the prosecution is furnished with as much information as possible before making representations to the court. If necessary, an application should be made for the case to be put back until information is available. Information may be obtained from a variety of sources, including criminal justice mental health teams, criminal justice liaison and diversion schemes and the youth offending team. A plea should not be accepted until the prosecutor has all the available information and has reviewed the file.

Trial Procedure for Youths with mental disorders including learning disabilities

Trial Procedure

The following trial procedure for youths with learning disabilities was laid down by the Administrative Court in *R on the application of TP v West London Youth Court* [2005] EWHC 2583 Admin.

Neither youth nor limited intellectual capacity necessarily leads to breach of the Article 6 ECHR right to effectively participate in a trial. The minimum requirements for a fair trial are that:

- The youth has to understand what he is said to have done wrong

- The court must be satisfied that the youth had the means of knowing that an act or omission was wrong at the time of the act or omission

- The youth had to understand what, if any, defences were available to him

- The youth must have a reasonable opportunity to make relevant representations if he wished to do so

- The youth must have the opportunity to consider what representations he wished to make once he had understood the issues involved.

A trial should not be abandoned before all practical steps to overcome the difficulties have been exhausted.

The youth court should take appropriate steps to enable a youth with learning difficulties or mental impairment to participate in his trial including:

- Keeping the youths cognitive functioning in mind

- Using concise and simple language

- Having regular breaks

- Taking additional time to explain court proceedings

- Being proactive in ensuring the youth has access to support

- Explaining and ensuring the claimant understands the ingredients of the charge

- Explaining the possible outcomes and sentences

- Ensuring cross examination is carefully controlled so that questions are short and clear and frustration is minimised.

The judge has a continuing jurisdiction to stay proceedings for abuse of process. If it becomes apparent during the course of the hearing that the claimant is unable effectively to participate, the judge can stay the proceedings at that point. This is better than staying the prosecution at the outset before it is known whether steps can be taken to enable a fair trial to proceed.

In *CPS v P* [2007] EWHC 946 (Admin), the Administrative Court gave guidance on the procedure to be followed in youth courts when the defence raises issues of capacity.

The Administrative Court answered the following questions posed by the District Judge:

Question: Where it is established that a person would be unfit to plead due to their mental capacity in a court of higher authority is it an abuse of process to try them thereafter for subsequent criminal acts?

Answer: The fact that a court of higher authority has previously held that a person is unfit to plead does not make it an abuse of process to try that person for subsequent criminal acts. The issue of the child's ability to participate effectively must be decided afresh. A child in early adolescence might well develop significantly over a relatively short period of time. It follows that just because the child is agreed to be unfit to plead or unable to take part in a trial on one occasion does not mean that he will still be unfit or unable on another.

Question: Where the magistrates' court establishes that a person cannot be tried in accordance with *R v Barking Youth Court* [2002] EWHC Admin 734 and then undertakes an inquiry into whether a defendant did the act alleged, is that a criminal trial?

Answer: Where the court decides to proceed to decide whether the person did the acts alleged, the proceedings are not a criminal trial.

Question: At what point in proceeding is it necessary for the court to make a decision in accordance with the procedure set out in *R v Barking Youth Court* [2002] EWHC Admin 734?

Answer: The court may consider whether to proceed to decide the facts at any stage. It may do so before hearing evidence or it may stop the criminal procedure and switch to the fact-finding procedure at any stage.

Question: Whether the District Judge erred in concluding on the evidence that the defendant did not have the mental capacity to effectively participate in the proceedings and accordingly stayed the proceedings on that basis?

Answer: The District Judge should not have stayed the proceedings at the outset as he did without considering the alternative of allowing the trial to proceed while keeping P's situation under constant review.

Question: Where it is established that a defendant is unfit to plead, to what extent is it necessary for him to participate in any trial of the facts?

Answer: If the court proceed with fact-finding only, the fact that the defendant does not or cannot take any part in the proceedings does not render them unfair or in any way improper; the defendant's Article 6 rights are not engaged by that process.

The court confirmed that it is only in exceptional cases that the youth court should exercise its power to stay proceedings before hearing any evidence on the substantive issue.

Medical opinion on the youth's capacity and ability to plead and participate in the trial is not conclusive and will not be the sole answer to the question of whether a youth should be tried for a criminal offence.

It is for the court, not the doctors to decide whether a trial should take place, because it is the court's opinion of the youth's level of understanding which must determine whether a trial takes place. The court must be willing, in appropriate cases to disagree with and reject the medical opinion, and to consider the possibility that the medical evidence might appear in a different light if and when the trial progresses. The court should take into account all relevant evidence, including:

• Medical evidence

• Evidence of what the youth is said to have done

• Evidence of the youth's behaviour on arrest and in interview

• What the youth said in interview

• Direct exchange in court between the District Judge or Chair and the youth.

If the court decides not to proceed with a criminal trial because the youth cannot take an effective part in the proceedings, it should consider whether to switch to a fact finding exercise to decide whether the child did the act or made the omission. (This procedure was set out in *R v Barking Justices* see Mentally Disordered Offenders elsewhere in this guidance.) This option may be appropriate where there is a possibility that a court will make a hospital order or guardianship order (for those aged 16 and 17).

Proceedings should be stayed as an abuse of process before the fact finding exercise only if there would be no useful purpose served by making a finding on the facts. The fact that the youth does not or cannot take any part in the proceedings does not render them unfair or in any way improper. The Article 6 ECHR right to a fair trial is not engaged by this process as it is part of the protective jurisdiction contemplated by the Mental Health Act 1983.

If the court finds that the youth did not do the act or make the omission alleged, the proceedings are terminated by way of an acquittal.

If the court finds that the youth did the acts alleged, it should consider whether to seek further medical evidence with a view to making a hospital order under section 37(3) Mental Health Act 1983. The court may also make a guardianship order if the youth is aged 16 or 17.

If a disposal under the Mental Health Act 1983 is inappropriate, it may be appropriate to alert the local authority to the position, with a view to consideration of care proceedings.

Measures to enable youth offenders to participate in their trial

The Practice Direction (Criminal Proceedings: Consolidation), para.III.30 (as inserted by Practice Direction (Criminal Proceedings: Further Directions) [2007] 1 WLR 1790) applies to trial, sentencing and appeal proceedings in the magistrate's courts (including youth courts) and the Crown Court of children under the age of 18 AND adults who suffer from a mental disorder within the meaning of the Mental Health Act 1983 or who have any other significant impairment of intelligence and social function. (Archbold 4-96b)

The overriding principle is set out at para III.30.3: A defendant may be young and immature or have a mental disorder within the meaning of the Mental Health Act 1983 or some other significant impairment of intelligence and social function such as to inhibit his understanding of and participation in the proceedings.

The purpose of criminal proceedings is to determine guilt, if that is in issue, and decide on the appropriate sentence if the defendant pleads guilty or is convicted. All possible steps should be taken to assist a vulnerable defendant to understand and participate in those proceedings. The ordinary trial process should, so far as necessary, be adapted to meet those ends. Regard should be had to the welfare of a young defendant as required by section 44 of the Children and Young

Persons Act 1933, and generally to paras 1 and 3 of the Criminal Procedure Rules (the overriding objective and the courts powers of case management).

Intermediaries for youth offenders

The court has an inherent power to appoint an intermediary to assist a youth defendant to prepare for the trial in advance of the hearing and during the trial so that he can participate effectively in the trial process. This appointment is not made pursuant to a special measures direction under the Youth Justice and Criminal Evidence Act 1999, but is part of the court's duty to take such steps as are necessary to ensure that a youth has a fair trial, not just during the proceedings, but beforehand as he and his lawyers prepare for trial: *C v Sevenoaks Youth Court* [2009] EWHC 3088 (Admin).

Live Links for youth offenders

A youth offender may give evidence in criminal proceedings in the magistrates' court and the Crown Court using a live link if:

- His ability to participate effectively in the proceedings as a witness giving oral evidence is compromised by his level of intellectual ability or social functioning; AND

- His ability to participate effectively would be improved by giving evidence over a live link (sec 33A(4) Youth Justice and Criminal Evidence Act 1999 as inserted by section 47 of the Police and Justice Act 2006.); AND

- The court is satisfied that it is in the interests of justice for the youth to give evidence through a live link.

A live link is defined in sec 33B Youth Justice and Criminal Evidence Act 1999 as an arrangement by which the accused, while absent from the place where the proceedings are being held, is able to see and hear a person there, and to be seen and heard by the judge, justices, jury, co accused, legal representatives and interpreters or any other person appointed by the court to assist the accused.

The defence must apply for a live link direction, which prevents the defendant from giving oral evidence in the proceedings in any manner other than through a live link (s33A (6). The court may discharge a live link direction at any time if it appears in the interests of justice to do so of its own motion or on application by any party. (s 33A (7) The court must give reasons in open court for giving or discharging a live link direction or for refusing an application for or the discharge of a live link direction. Those reasons must be recorded on the register of proceedings where the decision was made in the magistrates' court. (s 33A (8)).

Appendix E

Sentence Rehabilitation Periods for under 18s

Sentence Rehabilitation Periods for offenders under 18 years old at time of the conviction

SENTENCE	WHEN REHABILITATION PERIOD ENDS
Youth Restorative Disposal	Immediately after given
Youth Caution	Immediately after given
Youth Conditional Caution	At the end of the period of three months from the date on which the caution is given, or if earlier, when the caution ceases to have effect
Absolute discharge	Immediately on imposition
Conditional Discharge	The last day on which the order is to have effect
Compensation	The date on which payment is made in full
Fine	The end of the period of 6 months beginning with the date of the conviction in respect of which the sentence is imposed
Disqualification from driving	The last day on which the order is to have effect
Hospital order	The last day on which the order is to have effect
Referral Order	The last day on which the order is to have effect
Reparation Order	Immediately on imposition
Youth Rehabilitation Order	The end of the period of 6 months beginning with the day provided for by or under the order as the last day on which the order is to have effect
A custodial sentence of 6 months or less	The end of the period of 18 months beginning with the day on which the sentence (including any supervision or licence period) is completed
A custodial sentence of more than 6 months and up to, or consisting of, 30 months	The end of the period of 24months beginning with the day on which the sentence (including any supervision or licence period) is completed

A custodial sentence of more than 30months and up to, or consisting of, 48months	The end of the period of 42 months beginning with the day on which the sentence (including any licence period) is completed
A custodial sentence of more than 48 months	Never spent

Rehabilitation of Offenders Act 1974 as amended by the Legal Aid, Sentencing and Punishment of Offenders Act 2012, s 139–141, and Schs 24 & 25.

Note that if another offence is committed during the rehabilitation period this will usually extend the period by the length of the rehabilitation period for the sentence on the further offence (ROA 1974, s 6).

Where orders are subsequently varied or amended this does not usually affect the rehabilitation period.

The provisions introduced by LASPOA 2012 also apply to any sentencing orders which had been imposed before the commencement date. There is however a proviso that this must not result in a longer rehabilitation period than applied under the preceding provisions (LASPOA 2012, s 141).

Appendix F

AssetPlus

From July 2017 AssetPlus will be the only assessment tool approved by the Youth Justice Board under the National Standards. It is a sophisticated digital assessment tool. The YJB have published a number of guidance documents, including the following overview and model document:

AssetPlus

Youth Justice Board
Bwrdd Cyfiawnder Ieuenctid

AssetPlus – a new assessment and planning interventions framework for the youth justice system

What is AssetPlus?

AssetPlus is the new assessment and planning interventions framework developed by the Youth Justice Board (YJB) to replace the current framework, 'Asset', and its associated tools. The aim of the project is to provide a single framework that will span community and custody and once fully rolled out, will be shared between youth offending teams (YOTs), the YJB Placement Service and secure estate practitioners (when young people are remanded or sentenced to custody).

AssetPlus has been implemented in YOTs in a phased approach from September 2015, with the majority of YOTs planned to be live by July 2016. The indicative timescale for deployment to the YJB Placement Service and secure establishments is in the process of being confirmed.

Why have we changed the current framework?

As the number of young people entering custody has fallen, the young people within the youth justice system present with increasingly complex needs. AssetPlus has built on the successes of Asset whilst incorporating new and emerging policy areas such as speech, language and communication needs and gang affiliation. AssetPlus also incorporates areas of research such as desistance theory and the Good Lives Model.

What are the benefits?

The AssetPlus framework will make a significant improvement to the quality of assessments and intervention plans, which in turn will result in benefits of reduced offending and reoffending.

Additional benefits of the new framework have been identified and tested with YOTs and include some operational efficiency savings, potential for reduced remands and improved outcomes for young people whether they have offended, or are at risk of offending.

What do you need to know?

AssetPlus has a built-in standard Pre-Sentence Report template based on the 'Making it Count in Court' guidance produced by the YJB in collaboration with HM Courts and Tribunals Service:

A front page showing the young person's details and offence overview
Sources of information
Offence analysis
Assessment of the young person
Assessment of the need for parenting support
Assessment of the risk to the community
Conclusion and proposal for sentencing
Assessment of dangerousness

The assessment of the young person considers all circumstances where the young person could hurt/harm other people in the near future or at certain times/events as well as those circumstances that will cause serious harm

Youth justice practitioners will be assisted in their overall assessment of likelihood of offending by a Youth Offender Group Reconviction Scale (YOGRS) static calculation

Risks around vulnerability have now been redefined as risks to the **young person's safety and well-being**. Since the introduction of the Legal Aid, Sentencing and Punishment of Offenders Act (2012), there no longer exists, in law, a definition of the term 'vulnerability', as it relates to children in the youth justice system.

What do you need to do?

Youth offending teams and secure establishments will be contacting local partners such as courts in the months before they go live to ensure they are aware of changes that will affect them. At this time, it is important to be aware that AssetPlus implementation is underway and to cascade this message to the relevant staff within your organisation.

Contact

More information about AssetPlus, including an up-to-date YOT deployment list, can be found on GOV.UK:

— AssetPlus Rationale Document – outlines the research and theories included in AssetPlus
— AssetPlus Model Document – outlines what is in each section of the framework

If you have any questions about the new framework or its deployment in the youth justice system, please contact the AssetPlus team.

Youth Justice Board
Bwrdd Cyfiawnder Ieuenctid

AssetPlus Model Document

Version 1.1
Revised October 2014

Contents

Introduction

The current assessment and planning interventions framework (Asset and its associated tools) in use in youth offending teams (YOTs) and secure establishments was developed over the last decade and has adapted, where necessary, to take account of political and practice developments.

However, a number of drivers for change have emerged in recent times which have provided a mandate for the Youth Justice Board (YJB) to redesign and implement a new framework which will be known as AssetPlus.

The aim of the AssetPlus project is to deliver a nationally consistent and up to date assessment and planning interventions framework for YOTs and secure establishments in England and Wales to replace the current framework.

Who is this model document aimed at?

Although this document will be made available to all stakeholders it will be of significant importance to YOT and secure estate practitioners working directly with young people as well as their managers to help give a clear and concise overview of the new framework.

It will also be important for colleagues working in YJB Placement Service as AssetPlus incorporates all the information that is required to place young people in custody.

How should this model document be used?

This model document provides a high level overview and should be used in conjunction with AssetPlus guidance and other training and briefing materials to be of most value.

Background to AssetPlus

A comprehensive consultation exercise was carried out to inform the scope of the project. This involved:

- an online evidence gathering questionnaire to determine the strengths and weaknesses of Asset and its associated tools

- a bespoke consultation with young people and their parents and carers[1] to understand their views of the current assessment process

- consultation with the YJB Effective Practice Operational Working Group (OWG)[2]

As a result of this consultation exercise, the following drivers for change were identified and are the basis of the YJB decision to embark on a project to review and redesign Asset and its associated tools.

Emerging evidence

In order to fulfil its mandate as an evidence-based organisation, it is critical that the YJB continually adapts its approaches and the advice it provides to practitioners and Ministers in the light of the emerging evidence base in relation to assessments and interventions. The risk and protective factors paradigm, which is the foundation of Asset and its associated tools, has been the subject of increasing debate in academic literature over the past decade.

At the same time there has been growing emphasis on the development of theory and practice models based around factors which increase the likelihood of young people desisting from offending.

Changes in Policy

Asset and its associated tools are not flexible enough to allow analysis of emerging key policy areas such as speech, language and communication needs, gang affiliation and radicalisation.

End to end working

Within the secure estate there are difficulties ensuring that quality Asset documentation is received by the secure estate which can then be used effectively. This has led to concerns over the quality of sentence planning and the integration of assessments between community and custodial establishments.

---

[1] The YJB commissioned Young People in Focus to carry out a small-scale qualitative study

[2] The Operational Working Group's role is primarily to provide the YJB with a mechanism for testing and consultation in relation to the range of products and approaches which the YJB will develop and deploy to discharge its responsibilities under Effective Practice. The OWG is made up of up to 25 representatives of the youth justice sector covering community-based and secure youth justice services.

Design of Assessment tools

Asset has been considered cumbersome in its design and process, for example; the need to trigger a new assessment every time a young person goes to court led to assessments being duplicated without updates being made, which impacted on quality.

Additionally, the design has resulted in poor links between the assessment and intervention/risk management plans.

Negative feedback following serious incidents in community or custody

Asset has been implicated in a number of deaths in custody and other serious incidents as reported in coroner's reports and HMIP inspection reports.

Maintaining performance of the youth justice system

Whilst the system has had success in reducing the number of first time entrants and young people in custody there is an ongoing need to maintain performance in a context of increasing resource constraints and case complexity.

How did the YJB design AssetPlus?

Following the initial comprehensive consultation which identified the drivers for change, the YJB worked with academics and practitioners to design, develop and test the AssetPlus. This design was subject to further consultation as part of the statement of intent review which demonstrated the overall concept of AssetPlus.[3]

The design of AssetPlus reflects the latest research and academic thinking which is explore further in the Rationale document[4]

There is also an on-going change control process to allow for any changes that need to be incorporated within AssetPlus to allow it to be as flexible as possible for future shifts in policy or research.

What does AssetPlus include?

The consultation period with practitioners highlighted some of the positive features of Asset and those aspects have been retained in AssetPlus.

The Electronic Yellow Envelope (EYE) documents and other assessment and planning tools are incorporated in the new framework. Below is a list of all documents that will be covered in AssetPlus, whilst also identifying those that will not be incorporated.

---

[3] Statement of intent - http://www.justice.gov.uk/downloads/youth-justice/assessment/asessment-planning-intervention-strategy.pdf

[4] See Rationale - http://www.justice.gov.uk/downloads/youth-justice/assessment/assetplus-rationale.pdf

AssetPlus incorporates the following:

Electronic Yellow Envelope (EYE) Documents

* Asset Core Profile
* Risk of Serious Harm (RoSH)
* Bail Supervision and Support Profile
* Post Court Report (PCR)
* Vulnerability Management Plan (VMP)
* Placement Information Form (PIF)
* Pre Sentence Report (PSR)
* Risk Management Plan (RMP)
* Referral Order Report

Other assessment and planning tools:

* What do you think?
* Intervention Plan
* Final Warning Profile
* ONSET
* Secure Estate Risk Assessment and Management
* Bail package recommendation
* Remand & sentence planning forms
* CHAT screen
* SLCN screen (RCSLT)
* AUDIT (Alcohol use disorders identification test)

But excludes

* Specialist assessments and plans e.g. SIFA (Mental Health screening interview for adolescents), CHAT (Comprehensive Health Assessment Tool), SLCN assessment (Royal College Speech and Language); DUST (Drug use screening tool) and other locally used specialist assessments/ plans

---

AssetPlus is intended to identify the need for specialist assessments/plans where appropriate. The reason for excluding a number of locally used specialist assessments along with tools such as CHAT and SLCN assessment is to avoid AssetPlus becoming too unwieldy if we were to include all specialist areas.

What will AssetPlus provide?

Below are some of the key features that AssetPlus will provide:

* More emphasis on strengths and on factors which support/hinder desistance from offending.

* A clearer distinction between the identification of need and the likelihood of reoffending to help ensure appropriately targeted youth justice interventions around offending behaviour and accurate referrals to universal services to address access to mainstream services.

* Greater clarity about definitions relating to 'risk' and the use of predictive measures.

* A variety of ratings and measures, rather than one score.

* Assessments following the young person which are far more iterative and dynamic than at present. This will also contribute to a reduction in unnecessary duplication of work (for example, there will no longer be a requirement for 'start' and 'end' Assets relating to every order)

* The level of assessment reflecting the complexity of the young person's personal circumstances/behaviour representing a shift away from a one size fits all approach to assessment

* The flexibility to allow for local priorities/ challenges to be explored further

* Ability for appropriate information to be transferred at key points such as custody transitions

- Clearer relationship between assessments and intervention plans

- Plans to have a stronger focus on outcomes

- Incorporation of policy shifts that have taken place (for example, growing concern about group offending/ need to take account of a young person's speech, language and communication needs etc) and being flexible enough to adapt to future policy changes.

- Applicability to all children and young people regardless of their entry point into the youth justice system

- Improved self assessment tools and processes for young people as well as a specific tool for parents and carers.

- A holistic assessment of young people ensuring the interactions between factors in a young person's life are considered together

- Embedded screening tools such as the Speech, Language, Communication and Neuro-disability screen, Physical health screen, Emotional development and mental health screen and the Alcohol Use Disorder Identification Test (AUDIT)

- An increased focus on professional judgement

What are the benefits of AssetPlus?

As part of the development and testing of AssetPlus, the YJB, with the support of practitioners identified the following potential benefits:

- Better quality assessment leading to better quality plans and improved outcomes

- Improved identification and analysis of concerns around speech, language and communication needs and gang affiliation

- Strengthened consideration of restorative justice

- Improved quality of information and information sharing across services

- Greater confidence in the more appropriate use of breach and reduced breaches of bail

- Reduced likelihood of safeguarding and public protection incidents

- Greater confidence in the youth justice system and its assessment and screening tools

- Improved YOT operational efficiencies

AssetPlus – overview

What is AssetPlus?

The diagram below illustrates the high level structure of AssetPlus.

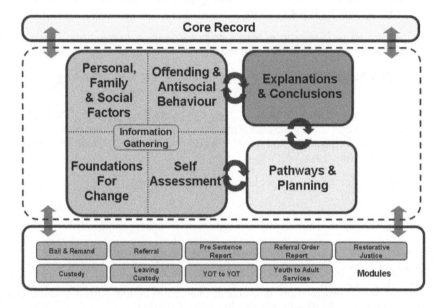

Core assessment framework - summary

Core record

The AssetPlus 'core assessment framework' will be applicable to all cases and comprises of the following key components:

- Information gathering quadrant

This section will facilitate the identification of key factors affecting a young person's life (both positive and negative).

It will include:

- o Personal, Family and Social Factors section

- o Offending/antisocial Behaviour section

- o Foundations for Change section

- o Self-assessment section

Within sections there will be minimum requirements as to the information that needs to be completed, but also additional 'further exploration' questions to allow for flexibility in the assessment process so for example, more complex cases will require more detail. It will also allow for individual YOTs to determine local areas of priority to inform areas for further exploration.

- Explanations and Conclusions

This section provides the opportunity for practitioners to review and analyse all the information gathered (i.e. drawing together all the different strands and looking at the interaction between factors) in order to explain the young person's behaviour in the context of their life situation, to make judgements about the risk of reoffending, the risk of harm and serious harm to others and themselves and also the young person's safety and well-being

- Pathways and planning

This section will be a single intervention plan and will help to identify priority pathways out of offending and ensure that the detail of intervention planning is clearly linked to achieving specified outcomes for a young person. Planning to manage risks to others and risks to the young person's safety will also be covered in this section.

- Modules

There may be specific tasks and processes that need to be carried out at particular points during a young person's involvement with the youth justice system where additional information is captured. Discrete modules have been incorporated into the framework to fulfil this purpose, but they will not be applicable to all cases.

The modules are outlined below:

- o **Bail and Remand** – the core assessment framework has been aligned to accommodate the level of assessment required for a bail assessment (therefore reducing unnecessary duplication). This information is presented in the Bail and Remand module to address the objections to bail/ recommend suitable bail packages to the court.

- o **Reports: PSRs, Referral Order Reports** – these will be a similar structure to the current reports and practitioners will have the option of auto-populating relevant sections of the report from the young person's assessment.

- o **Custody (incorporating existing YJB placement service forms)** – this module will be populated by the core framework where appropriate, to be completed when the assessment is required by the YJB Placement Service. It also includes a section for completion at the secure establishment upon the young person's arrival. It aims to provide the secure establishments with key information when a young person arrives at custody including identification of risk to the young person's safety and risk of harm and serious harm to others.

- o **Leaving custody** – this section will enable the recording of additional conditions required for the Notice of supervision/Licence and release arrangements for the young person.

- o **Other transitions (for example between YOTs or to adult services)** – this will include relevant questions in order to facilitate case transfers.

- o **Referrals to other agencies in the community and referrals to services within secure establishments** – this optional module can be populated with relevant information from the core framework in order to facilitate these referrals.

- o **Referrals to Restorative Justice opportunities** – The Restorative Justice (RJ) module will be triggered from the Pathways and Planning section of the framework when a practitioner determines that RJ intervention should be considered for a young person. The majority of the module will be pre-populated with responses from elsewhere in the framework, bringing together relevant information about the young person's attitudes to offending and response to previous RJ interventions, as well as any identified priorities for repairing harm. Additional questions within the module itself will encourage practitioners to think about any specific victim safety concerns and the young person's views about potential RJ interventions. It is intended that the RJ module will act as a precursor to more detailed, local RJ assessments undertaken by RJ workers. The module should provide information to assist decision-making regarding suitability for the full range of RJ interventions.

It is anticipated that the inclusion of these modules will:

- Enable specific additional information to be collected where needed for example, information relating to a young person's ability to cope in custody

- Be an integral part of the assessment where necessary (for example, some information can be pulled through to these specific templates) and facilitate the transfer of key information

- Help ensure that other practitioners who have contact with young people are able to make decisions/have the information they need (for example, secure estate staff have enough information at induction stage to make appropriate decisions regarding the care and safety of the young person/others in the establishment).

Outline of component parts

Core Record

Purpose

The purpose of this section is to provide a view of the essential information required about the young person (primarily pre populated from other areas of the core assessment framework). It will provide the following:

- information about critical points identified relating to needs, safeguarding and public protection

- key action points from the young person's intervention plan

- a 'one stop shop' for key information about the young person ensuring that practitioners and managers have the most up to date information to hand and are not required to spend time re-keying information that may exist elsewhere (either in the framework or the case management system)

- a summary for practitioners to quickly familiarise themselves with a case they are taking on

- a summary for managers overseeing cases to quickly identify priorities

Content

The core record will include the following areas:

- key personal information about the young person

- parent/carer details

- information relating to the young person's offending or antisocial behaviour

- information relating to the young person's *previous* offending or antisocial behaviour

- outstanding offences/matters

- alerts and flags in relation to the young person's offending, risk of serious harm to others, risk to their safety, well-being and any health concerns

- information about any contact with other services including other assessments undertaken

- summary information about the young person's personal circumstances (for example, accommodation status, ETE status and the young person's care history)

- summary of key actions from intervention planning documentation including any critical flags for intervention/ referral

Information gathering quadrant

As noted above, the focus of this section is to collect a range of information to describe the young person's situation/behaviour.

It includes:

- Personal, Family and Social factors

- Offending/antisocial Behaviour

- Foundations for Change

- Self-assessment

See below for further details on each of these sections

Within these sections, there will also be flexibility to vary the amount and detail of information recorded using further exploration[5] such that:

- for less complex cases there will a shorter, less detailed process

- for more complex cases additional information and exploration will be required.

The move onto 'further exploration' will be triggered by responses to particular questions within the assessment and will be flagged up in the assessment where it will indicate that further information is required.

There can be different reasons for going onto 'further exploration' for example due to the complexity of problems, the seriousness of the offending, the fact that a situation is unclear and needs further investigation but ultimately it will be at the discretion of the practitioner.

1. Personal, family and social factors section

Purpose

The purpose of this section is to ensure that assessments take account of a wide range of factors (both positive and negative) about a young person's current life situation. This will:

- help to ensure that needs or problems are identified (regardless of the link with offending) to allow for appropriate referrals

- provide information which can be used in the later Explanations and Conclusions section to help understand a young person's behaviour

- help to identify strengths and factors for desistance which can be used later in the process of planning interventions

---

[5] See Appendix A for further exploration detail

Content

Personal, Family and Social factors will include the following areas:

- Living arrangements and Environmental factors
    - living arrangements, housing and financial considerations
    - social and community/neighbourhood factors
- Parenting, family and relationships
    - Parenting, care and supervision
    - Care history and Children's Services involvement
    - Family and wider networks
    - How the young person relates to others
- Young person's development
    - health (general health and physical developments; speech language and communication needs; emotional development and mental health)
    - lifestyle, identity and behaviour (including substance/ alcohol use; young person as a parent; young person's self identity; thinking and behaviour)
- Learning, education, training and employment

How will this section be rated/ scored?

The only area that will use numerical scores will be in AUDIT (Alcohol use disorders identification test). Otherwise practitioners will be able to identify key desistance factors. This will focus practitioners' thinking when it comes to the Explanations and Conclusions section and Pathways and Planning by identifying priority areas of concern.

Basis for inclusion

One of the key aims of AssetPlus is to have clearer distinction between the identification of need and the likelihood of reoffending to help ensure that youth justice interventions are appropriately targeted to address offending behaviour and that appropriate referrals are made to universal services.

This section of AssetPlus will make it easier for practitioners to record concerns about needs or problems in a young person's life (for example, it should resolve the issue of assessors artificially manipulating offending-related scores in order to trigger a referral to a specialist services, as sometimes happens at the moment). The removal of offending-related scores will also make it easier for practitioners to see details about health needs in their own terms rather than filtered through an offending-related score.

Further, by recognising that there are a wide range of factors impacting on a young person's life, this section will help to retain one of the benefits of the current Asset i.e. comprehensive coverage of issues. In addition, the design of this section will also have the extra benefit of helping assessors to set young people's lives in context, rather than seeing identified factors as individual isolated issues.

AssetPlus has also included new policy areas such as Speech, Language and Communication Needs, radicalisation and exploitation which were not addressed in Asset.

2. Offending/antisocial behaviour section

Purpose
The purpose of this section is to focus specifically on describing characteristics and patterns of a young person's antisocial and/or offending behaviour. It will therefore provide a more concentrated overview of a young person's behaviour and more detailed descriptions (where relevant) of behaviour.

Content
As with other sections of information gathering, there will be flexibility here so that different levels of detail can be recorded depending on the seriousness and complexity of a young person's behaviour.

Offending/antisocial behaviour section will include the following areas:

- Current offending episodes including:

  o   key details of offending – Location, Involvement of others, Behaviours involved and whether the victim was deliberately targeted

  o   what happened including the young person's account and CPS account

  o   attitudes to offences

- Patterns of offending over time including attitudes to offending

- Other behaviours of concern that have not been formally dealt with through the criminal justice system but may indicate future offending

How will this section be rated/ scored?
This section will not be scored. Practitioners will also have the opportunity to identify any key areas of concern about the young person's behaviour and will use their professional judgement to contribute to the final likelihood of reoffending rating which will be addressed in the Explanations and Conclusions section.

Basis for inclusion
At the moment, accounts of a young person's offending/antisocial behaviour tend to be spread across different sections of the assessment tools which can make it more difficult to see patterns and themes. This was raised as an area for suggested improvement through consultation with stakeholders.

3. Foundations for Change section

Purpose

The purpose of this section is to identify and explore areas of the young person's life that may promote or prevent behavioural change. This section puts a sharper focus than the current tools on factors which might affect a young person's willingness to participate in interventions, and affect the prospect of achieving positive change. It increases the emphasis in the assessment process on identifying strengths. Information from this section will be important for planning pathways out of offending and for developing the intervention plan.

Content

Foundations for Change will include the following areas:

- the young person's resilience (including when faced with opportunities to offend), goals and attitudes

- opportunities to help the young person achieve positive outcomes

- the young person's engagement and participation

- factors affecting desistance (including the related category such as substance misuse)

How will this section be rated/ scored?

This section will not use numerical scores but will allow practitioners to highlight issues which may be critical in either supporting or preventing positive change, by identifying factors for and against desistance.

4. Self-assessment section

Purpose

Ensuring young people and their parents/carers feel engaged in the assessment and planning intervention process is important in securing participation and achieving the desired outcomes of each young person's intervention plan. This section will help to facilitate this engagement and participation.

Content

The self-assessment for young people will be available in both first and third person and will be tailored to the various stages the young person may be at in the youth justice system. Self-assessment questionnaires will also be available for parents/carers.

There will be a greater opportunity for the young person to reflect on their offence; greater focus on the young person's perception of the consequences of offending and a greater focus on future aspirations and identifying steps needed to achieve these.

Explanations and Conclusions section

Purpose

The purpose of this section is to pull together and analyse key information from the information gathering quadrants, draw some conclusions in order to reach judgements about future behaviour and to inform an outcome-focussed intervention plan for the young person.

Content

In Explanations and Conclusions, practitioners will consider the evidence they have gathered in the information gathering quadrant to make judgements in three key areas:

- Understanding offending behaviour:
  - significant life events
  - putting into context the interplay between a young person's life events, offending and interventions received
  - understanding the interconnections and interaction between a young person's past behaviour
  - understanding the factors affecting/preventing desistance
- Making judgements about the likelihood and impact of future behaviour:
  - identifying the type of behaviour and potential impact on others
  - the circumstances and context in which this may happen
  - identifying the likelihood of the behaviour happening
  - dangerousness assessment (where relevant, will only apply to a small number of cases)
  - summary of likelihood of reoffending and risk of serious harm to others based on the judgements made
- Making judgements about the likelihood and impact of concerns in relation to the young person's safety and well-being
  - identifying the causes and the adverse outcomes on the young person
  - the circumstances and context in which this may happen
  - identifying the likelihood of the adverse outcome happening
  - summary of safety and well-being concerns including an overall safety and well-being concern judgement

This section reflects a number of themes from literature and research, including:

- pathways into offending
- desistance
- contingency planning for complex/high risk of serious harm to others cases

- obstacles to change

- need for clarity in definitions/risk terminology

How will this section be rated/ scored?

There will be a number of key ratings used in this section of AssetPlus. These ratings are listed below:

- Desistance factor ratings

    o A list of factors based on the assessment of the young person either for or against desistance. Each factor will be associated to a category (e.g. substance misuse) and rated as Potential, Weak, Moderate or Strong.

- YOGRS (Youth Offender Group Reconviction Score)

- Reconviction rate of a sample group with similar factors/offending histories to the young person including gender, offence category, offence history status and age at time of sentence.

- Indicative Likelihood of Reoffending

    o Indicative LoR will be automatically calculated based on thresholds set against the YOGRS Score (either High, Medium or Low)

- Likelihood of Re-offending

    o Final Likelihood of Reoffending rating where professional judgement is applied against the Indicative LoR (either High, Medium or Low)

- RoSH (Risk of Serious Harm)

    o The RoSH is set by the practitioner as currently (either Very High, High, Medium or Low rating)

- Overall safety and well-being concerns judgement

- The overall safety and well-being judgement based on the concerns identified and is set by the practitioner (either Very High, High, Medium or Low)

Basis for inclusion

Desistance factor ratings have been included as part of Desistance Theory which is now incorporated into AssetPlus.

Pathways and Planning

Purpose

Based on the Explanations and Conclusions section, and depending on what decisions have been made for example, by courts/panels, this section focuses on desired outcomes for a young person and the priority actions required to achieve them.

The plan format will allow for:

- interventions in relation to reducing offending, building desistance, ensuring safety and well being, managing risks to others and repairing harm to be recorded in one place.

- recording of interventions delivered directly by the YOT (for example, in relation to offending) and recording of plans for interventions to be delivered by other services (for example, addressing health needs).

- prioritising and review of targets in relation to interventions.

- the relevant objectives in the intervention plan to be reflected in secure estate sentence planning processes.

- space to record in one place actions and measures relating to external and internal controls, as well as interventions to address offending/behaviour.

- additional scope to incorporate details relating to other work being undertaken for example, MAPPA plans, care plans, education plans etc.

- easier to see distinction between actions that the practitioner/agency will take and the actions that young person will take and the actions the parent/carer will take.

- intervention plans using young person friendly terminology to be shared with the young person

Content

Pathways and Planning will include the following areas:

- Intervention Indicators including Scaled Approach and recording of other plans in place

- Key areas of intervention where priorities are identified under five key outcomes areas:

1. Goals and life opportunities

2. Not Offending

3. Not hurting others

4. Keeping safe

5. Repairing harm

- Resources and Proposals to record areas for further action and referrals

- Tailoring Interventions including considerations of learning styles and suitability for interventions

- Our Intervention Plan

  o Targets/actions needed to achieve the outcomes

  o Other actions to be taken by parents/carers and staff/agency (for example, referrals, information sharing or disclosure)

  o Additional controls

- Mobility and ROTL (for custodial cases only)

- Dealing with changing circumstances

Basis for inclusion

One of the main aims of AssetPlus is to facilitate a more streamlined and coherent relationship between intervention plans and intended outcomes.

The requirement to specify outcomes more clearly should ensure more appropriate use and targeting of interventions. It will be easier than the current format to show that some interventions can help to achieve several different targets at once.

Further, this section will rationalise the current documentation (intervention plan, RMP, VMP, remand plan and sentence plan where appropriate) into one place, thus reducing duplication.

Reviewing/updating assessments

The AssetPlus framework will provide a single assessment and plan for a young person, which will be dynamic and iterative in nature, making it easier to update assessments on an ongoing basis and therefore always presenting the latest information. It will allow for specific sections, or questions within sections, to be updated without requiring revisions to all sections. This should encourage practitioners to maintain an up-to-date assessment and plan throughout. Historical information and an audit trail will be accessible for practitioners to refer to.

The common structure will also facilitate more effective use of information when young people move through the youth justice system (i.e. from prevention through to pre-court through to community) making the process of updating assessments much more straightforward.

Process for completion

AssetPlus is not designed to be an interview schedule (a separate 'prompt sheet' has been developed for this) or a fixed template for data collection but instead provides a structure for recording a range of relevant information.

There is no defined order for completing the different parts of the AssetPlus and practitioners can use their discretion to decide on the most useful order of completion for any individual case.

However, it is recommended that the Speech, Language, Communication and Neuro-disability screening section is completed first to understand how best to engage with the young person followed by the Self-Assessment section to gain his/her input into the assessment process.

Young people in custody

AssetPlus will be an end to end framework. Home YOT practitioners will retain overall case management responsibility, supported by practitioners in the secure estate who undertake case work with young people. This means that when young people are in custody, secure estate practitioners will review and update relevant sections of the assessment and intervention plan based on their work with the young person in custody. These updates will then be sent to the YOT.

There are some areas of the assessment that are specific to YOT practitioners and these areas will be viewable by secure estate practitioners but will not be changed by them.

Appendix A – AssetPlus excerpts

In order to illustrate some of the AssetPlus design concepts and content, excerpts from a demonstration tool are contained within this Appendix. The excerpts as shown below will demonstrate:

- how areas from Asset are being carried forward into AssetPlus

- how the framework addresses both simple and complex cases through the application of further exploration

- how the latest research and policy has been incorporated into AssetPlus

- how greater emphasis is being placed on positive factors

- how information gathering is linked through to Explanations and Conclusions and Pathways and Planning

1. Personal Family Social Factors: Living arrangements and Environmental Factors: Living arrangements, housing and financial considerations

---

Living arrangements, housing and financial considerations

Please select the young person's current accommodation: `Family home`

Please state who the young person is currently living with, and outline any positives or strengths relating to the young person's current living arrangements *(e.g. stability, location etc)*

Do you have any concerns about the young person's current accommodation situation? `Yes`

Further exploration:

Instability ☐ Over-crowded ☐ Living with known offenders ☑
Absconding/staying away ☐ Unhealthy or unsafe ☐ Other ☑
Short-term/temporary ☐ Offending in family/residential home ☐

Please provide as much detail as possible here:

Give details of the young person's financial circumstances eg money from parents/carers, regular income, benefits, debt problems, casual income, no legitimate income etc:

Provide an outline/overview of the financial situation for the young person's family (where relevant) – employment, benefits, income, deprivation etc.

Possible further action required:
Click to record key life events:

437

The above excerpt demonstrates the way in which AssetPlus will use further exploration to address any areas of the assessment that may need further exploration such as living arrangements, housing and financial considerations shown above.

It also demonstrates the feature 'possible further action required' which will allow the practitioner to capture areas for potential referral which will then be presented for consideration in the Pathways and Planning area of the framework.

2. Foundations for Change: Resilience, goals and attitudes

Resilience, goals and attitudes
What does the young person do to cope with problems and difficulties in his/her life?   *Give specific examples where possible, positive and negative*
To what extent does the young person understand the potentially negative consequences of further ASB/offending for his/her future? — Please select
To what extent does the young person think it is possible to achieve positive change / avoid further ASB/offending? — Please select
Does the young person have some positive goals and aspirations?
Details *(for example, reasons for his/her fatalistic attitude about inevitability of further offending, reasons for his/her optimism about change) Where possible, give examples of the young person taking action/showing interest in achieving positive goals.*

The above demonstrates the way in which AssetPlus places greater emphasis on positive factors in the young persons life

3. Foundations for Change: Engagement and Participation

Engagement and Participation

Does he/she have experience of previous YOT supervision/contact? `Yes`

Please provide as much detail as possible here:
e.g. extent of compliance, how well did s/he engage with interventions, any particular actions taken by the YOT to assist him/her with compliance and participation, anything which the YOT did/didn't do that made engagement more

What is the young person's attitude at the moment towards supervision/contact with the YOT? `Please select`

	Motivated to work on	Resistant to work on
What is the young person motivated to work on/change and which things s/he does not want to address?		

Where known, provide information about the young person's preferred learning style.
Note any specific tools used, preferred types of activity, other learning preferences.

Have particular barriers to engagement and participation been identified? `No`

Where the young person is, or has been, involved with other services, please comment on any particular positives or problems with regards to their engagement:

This excerpt from the Foundations for Change area of AssetPlus demonstrates the way in which information gathering is linked to Explanations and Conclusions and Pathways and Planning

Appendix G

Maximum fines

Juveniles

Offender under 14 (a child). Maximum fine is the amount in the statute creating the offence or £250, whichever is less.*

Offender 14 – under 18 (young person). Maximum fine is the amount in the statute creating the offence or £1,000, whichever is the less.*

* Note that the maximum fine for breach of a Youth Rehabilitation Order is £2,500 (CJA 03, Sch 8, para 9(1)(aa)). Also, the maximum fine for breach of a referral order is £2,500. (PCC(S)A 2000, Sch 1).

Appendix H

Sentencing orders guide

Sentencing principles – the Youth Court

- To determine the seriousness of the offence and make any restriction on liberty (a court order) proportionate to its seriousness.

- A custodial sentence should only be imposed as a last resort or where necessary to protect the public from serious harm and such a sentence would be the most effective way of achieving that objective.

- To have regard to the aim of preventing further offences.

- To have regard to the welfare of the child or young person.

A Discharges: absolute/conditional

- Absolute: technically guilty but morally blameless.

- Conditional: inexpedient to inflict further punishment; not to commit further offences during a period up to three years after the order. A victim surcharge of £15 for offences committed on or after 8 April 2016, (before that date it is £10) must be imposed.

- May *not* be made within two years of a second youth caution without exceptional circumstances.

B Fines

- Must enquire into offender's circumstances or if the parent or guardian is going to pay them.

- Normally parents of offenders under 16 years old will pay unless they cannot be found or it would be unreasonable in the circumstances of the case. Parents of 16- and 17-year-olds *may* be directed to pay if the court believes it is reasonable and after giving the parents an opportunity to address the court. A collection order can be made if an adult is to pay.

- A victim surcharge (£20 or £15 for offences committed before 8 April 2016) must be imposed on the occasion that any fines are imposed.

Maximum fine	10–13	£250
	14–17	£1,000

C Referral order

Period of order: 3 to 12 months. A victim surcharge of £20 or £15 for offences committed before 8 April 2016) must also be imposed. [The order may not be combined with a youth rehabilitation order, fine, reparation, conditional discharge, bind over or parental bind over.]

Mandatory

- Custodial sentence or absolute/conditional discharge or hospital order not proposed.
- Offender has pleaded guilty to all offences.
- No previous conviction in UK or EU (but note that absolute or conditional discharges do not count as previous convictions for these purposes).
- The offence is imprisonable.

Discretionary

- Defendant pleaded guilty to at least one offence and the mandatory conditions above do not apply.

Further convictions

If the court intends to impose any of the following sentences for the further offence: absolute discharge, conditional discharge, a hospital order, a custodial sentence or any sentence fixed by law then it cannot extend the existing referral order. Otherwise it can extend the referral order provided this does not extend the overall referral compliance period to more than 12 months.

If the court imposes an absolute or conditional discharge for the further conviction, or extends an existing referral order then it cannot revoke the referral order. In other cases, it may revoke the referral order and resentence the juvenile in any way the court which imposed the order could have (other than making a new referral order).

The court can leave the existing referral order in place and impose a new referral order in relation to the further conviction. The court can direct that the new referral order does not take effect until the old order is completed/revoked.

Applications to extend

A referral order may be extended by up to 3 months on the application of YOT or the offender, where this would be in the interests of justice. The overall maximum length of 12 months for referral orders must not be exceeded.

D Reparation order

- Written report required.
- Not to be combined with custody, or youth rehabilitation order. Maximum of 24 hours' work to be completed within a three-month period.
- No conflict with religious beliefs, any other community order or attendance at school or work.
- Recipient of reparation consulted and consents.
- Reparation commensurate with the seriousness of offence(s).
- *[Reasons required where reparation order available but not made.]*
- *[Compensation order remains available.]*

'Serious enough?'

E Youth rehabilitation order

The following requirements may be attached to a youth rehabilitation order. The details are found in CJIA 2008, Sch 1 and the relevant paragraph of the schedule is in brackets next to each of the requirements. A £15 victim surcharge must also be imposed.

(a) an activity requirement (paras 6 to 8),

(b) a supervision requirement (para 9),

(c) an unpaid work requirement (in a case where the offender is aged 16 or 17 at the time of conviction) (para 10),

(d) a programme requirement (para 11),

(e) an attendance centre requirement (para 12),

(f) a prohibited activity requirement (para 13),

(g) a curfew requirement (para 14),

(h) an exclusion requirement (para 15),

(i) a residence requirement (in a case where the offender is aged 16 or 17 at the time of conviction) (para 16),

(j) a local authority residence requirement (paras 17 and 19),

(k) a mental health treatment requirement (para 20),

(l) a drug treatment/drug testing requirement (paras 22 and 23),

(m) an intoxicating substance treatment requirement (para 24),

(n) an education requirement (para 25), and

(o) an electronic monitoring requirement (para 26).

'So serious?'

F YRO with intensive supervision and surveillance or fostering

- Refer to CJIA 2008, Sch 1, paras 4, 8 and 19 for fostering requirement and para 3 for intensive supervision and surveillance requirement.

- Can only be made for an offence punishable with imprisonment (except where the offender has wilfully and persistently breached a standard YRO.)

- The offence (or combination of offences) crosses the custody threshold, and custody would otherwise be an appropriate sentence.

- *Fostering requirement:*

    (i) The offender should be legally represented unless he has failed to apply despite being given the opportunity or after the granting of such representation the right is withdrawn because of his conduct;

(ii) The court must be satisfied the offence was due to a significant extent to the circumstances in which the offender was living, and the imposition of a fostering requirement would assist in the offender's rehabilitation; and

(iii) Offender's parents must be consulted.

- If offender aged under 15 at time of conviction, must be a persistent offender for such orders to be imposed.

- Written pre-sentence report received.

G Detention and training order

- Grounds: either 'so serious' or (violent or sexual offence) only custody adequate to protect public from serious harm from offender (or falls within criteria in CJA 2003, s 152(3)).

- Custody must only be used as a last resort. Must explain why a YRO with ISS requirement (or a fostering requirement where available) cannot be justified instead.

- Offender aged 12 to 17 inclusive and convicted of imprisonable offence.

- No order permissible for offenders aged 10 or 11, but in exceptionally serious cases offender may be sent to the Crown Court for trial pursuant to CDA 1998, s 51A and MCA 1980, s 24A as a grave crime. If a guilty plea is indicated then the child can be committed to the Crown Court for sentence under PCC(S)A 2000, ss 3B (grave crime) or 3C (dangerousness).

- Offender legally represented or offered legal aid.

- Written pre-sentence report received (the court may rely on a recent report).

- If offender aged under 15 at time of conviction, must be a persistent offender (reasons required).

- Order of at least four months required after discount for guilty plea and taking account of time spent on remand (either in a secure unit, remand centre/prison, or half of time spent on a tagged curfew of at least 9 hours' duration). Cannot apply an exact mathematical formula when reducing length due to the prescribed lengths for DTOs but where the appropriate reduction would place the length of sentence between two prescribed lengths the court must select the lower when applying guilty plea credit, and the nearest when applying credit for time spent on remand.

- Individual DTOs must be either 4, 6, 8, 10, 12, 18 or 24 months long. Such orders can be made consecutive provided the aggregate maximum 24 months is not exceeded.

Ancillary orders for parents

Parenting order

- If offender under 16 family circumstances report obtained (otherwise discretionary).

- Order desirable to prevent the commission of further offences.

- Reasons must be given if order not made in case of offender under 16 years old, unless a referral order is made.

- Order may be made where a parent/guardian fails to attend youth offender panel meetings in respect of a referral order.

Parental bind over

- Child or young person convicted of offence. Parent or guardian can be bound over to ensure the juvenile behaves or complies with a youth rehabilitation order.

- Bind over desirable in the interests of preventing the commission of further offences by the offender.

- Bind over must be made in case of offender aged under 16 or reasons given.

- Discretionary for 16- or 17-year-old.

Appendix I

Sentencing Council: Sentencing Children and Young People

I. 1 Application and Overarching Principles

The Sentencing Council issues this definitive guideline in accordance with section 120 of the Coroners and Justice Act 2009.

It applies to all children or young people, who are sentenced on or after 1 June 2017, regardless of the date of the offence.

Section 125(1) of the Coroners and Justice Act 2009 provides that when sentencing offences committed after 6 April 2010:

"Every court –

(a) must, in sentencing an offender, follow any sentencing guidelines which are relevant to the offender's case, and
(b) must, in exercising any other function relating to the sentencing of offenders, follow any sentencing guidelines which are relevant to the exercise of the function,

unless the court is satisfied that it would be contrary to the interests of justice to do so."

Guidance for sentencing children and young people set out in the 2006 robbery guideline and the 2007 sexual offences guideline, both produced by the Sentencing Guidelines Council, are replaced by this guideline.

Guilty plea section only
Section 144 of the Criminal Justice Act 2003 provides:
(1) In determining what sentence to pass on an offender who has pleaded guilty to an offence[1] in proceedings before that court or another court, a court must take into account:
   (a) the stage in the proceedings for the offence at which the offender indicated his intention to plead guilty, and
   (b) the circumstances in which this indication was given.

This section of the guideline applies regardless of the date of the offence to all children or young people where the **first hearing** is on or after 1 June 2017. It applies equally in youth courts, magistrates' courts and the Crown Court.

---

1   'Offence' includes breach of an order where this constitutes a separate criminal offence but not breach of terms of a sentence or licence.

Effective from 1 June 2017

Section one: General approach

Sentencing principles

1.1 When sentencing children or young people (those aged under 18 at the date of the finding of guilt) a court must[2] have regard to:
- the principal aim of the youth justice system (to prevent offending by children and young people);[3] and
- the welfare of the child or young person.[4]

1.2 While the seriousness of the offence will be the starting point, the approach to sentencing should be individualistic and focused on the child or young person, as opposed to offence focused. For a child or young person the sentence should focus on rehabilitation where possible. A court should also consider the effect the sentence is likely to have on the child or young person (both positive and negative) as well as any underlying factors contributing to the offending behaviour.

1.3 Domestic and international laws dictate that a custodial sentence should always be a measure of last resort for children and young people and statute provides that a custodial sentence may only be imposed when the offence is so serious that no other sanction is appropriate (see section six for more information on custodial sentences).

1.4 It is important to avoid "criminalising" children and young people unnecessarily; the primary purpose of the youth justice system is to encourage children and young people to take responsibility for their own actions and promote re-integration into society rather than to punish. Restorative justice disposals may be of particular value for children and young people as they can encourage them to take responsibility for their actions and understand the impact their offence may have had on others.

1.5 It is important to bear in mind any factors that may diminish the culpability of a child or young person. Children and young people are not fully developed and they have not attained full maturity. As such, this can impact on their decision making and risk taking behaviour. It is important to consider the extent to which the child or young person has been acting impulsively and whether their conduct has been affected by inexperience, emotional volatility or negative influences. They may not fully appreciate the effect their actions can have on other people and may not be capable of fully understanding the distress and pain they cause to the victims of their crimes. Children and young people are also likely to be susceptible to peer pressure and other external influences and changes taking place during adolescence can lead to experimentation, resulting in criminal behaviour. When considering a child or young person's age their emotional and developmental age is of at least equal importance to their chronological age (if not greater).

1.6 For these reasons, children and young people are likely to benefit from being given an opportunity to address their behaviour and may be receptive to changing their conduct. They should, if possible, be given the opportunity to learn from their mistakes without undue penalisation or stigma, especially as a court sanction might have a significant effect on the

---

2 This section does not apply when imposing a mandatory life sentence, when imposing a statutory minimum custodial sentence, when imposing detention for life under the dangerous offender provisions or when making certain orders under the Mental Health Act 1983
3 s.37(1) Crime and Disorder Act 1998
4 s.44(1) Children and Young Persons Act 1933

prospects and opportunities of the child or young person and hinder their re-integration into society.

1.7 Offending by a child or young person is often a phase which passes fairly rapidly and so the sentence should not result in the alienation of the child or young person from society if that can be avoided.

1.8 The impact of punishment is likely to be felt more heavily by a child or young person in comparison to an adult as any sentence will seem longer due to their young age. In addition penal interventions may interfere with a child or young person's education and this should be considered by a court at sentencing.

1.9 Any restriction on liberty must be commensurate with the seriousness of the offence. In considering the seriousness of any offence, the court must consider the child or young person's culpability in committing the offence and any harm which the offence caused, was intended to cause or might foreseeably have caused.[5]

1.10 Section 142 of the Criminal Justice Act 2003 sets out the purposes of sentencing for offenders who are over 18 on the date of conviction. That Act was amended in 2008 to add section 142A which sets out the purposes of sentencing for children and young people, subject to a commencement order being made. The difference between the purposes of sentencing for those under and over 18 is that section 142A does not include as a purpose of sentencing 'the reduction of crime (including its reduction by deterrence)'. Section 142A has not been brought into effect. Unless and until that happens, deterrence can be a factor in sentencing children and young people although normally it should be restricted to serious offences and can, and often will, be outweighed by considerations of the child or young person's welfare.

For more information on assessing the seriousness of the offence see section four.

Welfare

1.11 The statutory obligation to have regard to the welfare of a child or young person includes the obligation to secure proper provision for education and training,[6] to remove the child or young person from undesirable surroundings where appropriate[7] and the need to choose the best option for the child or young person taking account of the circumstances of the offence.

1.12 **In having regard to the welfare of the child or young person, a court should ensure that it is alert to:**
   - **any mental health problems or learning difficulties/disabilities;**
   - **any experiences of brain injury or traumatic life experience (including exposure to drug and alcohol abuse) and the developmental impact this may have had;**
   - **any speech and language difficulties and the effect this may have on the ability of the child or young person (or any accompanying adult) to communicate with the court, to understand the sanction imposed or to fulfil the obligations resulting from that sanction;**

---

5   s.143(1) Criminal Justice Act 2003
6   s.44 Children and Young Persons Act 1933
7   ibid.

- the vulnerability of children and young people to self harm, particularly within a custodial environment; and
- the effect on children and young people of experiences of loss and neglect and/or abuse.

1.13 Factors regularly present in the background of children and young people that come before the court include deprived homes, poor parental employment records, low educational attainment, early experience of offending by other family members, experience of abuse and/or neglect, negative influences from peer associates and the misuse of drugs and/or alcohol.

1.14 The court should always seek to ensure that it has access to information about how best to identify and respond to these factors and, where necessary, that a proper assessment has taken place in order to enable the most appropriate sentence to be imposed.

1.15 The court should consider the reasons why, on some occasions, a child or young person may conduct themselves inappropriately in court (e.g. due to nervousness, a lack of understanding of the system, a belief that they will be discriminated against, peer pressure to behave in a certain way because of others present, a lack of maturity etc) and take this into account.

1.16 Evidence shows that looked after children and young people are over-represented in the criminal justice system.[8] When dealing with a child or young person who is looked after the court should also bear in mind the additional complex vulnerabilities that are likely to be present in their background. For example, looked after children and young people may have no or little contact with their family and/or friends, they may have special educational needs and/or emotional and behavioural problems, they may be heavily exposed to peers who have committed crime and they are likely to have accessed the care system as a result of abuse, neglect or parental absence due to bereavement, imprisonment or desertion. The court should also bear in mind that the level of parental-type support that a looked after child or young person receives throughout the criminal justice process may vary, and may be limited. For example, while parents are required to attend court hearings, this is not the case for social workers responsible for looked after children and young people. In some instances a looked after child or young person (including those placed in foster homes and independent accommodation, as well as in care homes) may be before the court for a low level offence that the police would not have been involved in, if it had occurred in an ordinary family setting.

1.17 For looked after children and young people who have committed an offence that crosses the custody threshold sentencers will need to consider any impact a custodial sentence may have on their leaving care rights and whether this impact is proportionate to the seriousness of the offence. For other young people who are in the process of leaving care or have recently left care then sentencers should bear in mind any effect this often difficult transition may have had on the young person's behaviour.

1.18 There is also evidence to suggest that black and minority ethnic children and young people are over-represented in the youth justice system.[9] The factors contributing to this are complex. One factor is that a significant proportion of looked after children and young people are from a black

---

8 Department for Education (2014) Outcomes for Children Looked After by Local Authorities in England, as at 31 March 2014. Statistical First Release 49/2014. [accessed via: https://www.gov.uk/government/statistics/outcomes-for-children-looked-after-by-local-authorities]
9 https://www.gov.uk/government/uploads/system/uploads/attachment_data/file/568680/bame-disproportionality-in-the-cjs.pdf

and minority ethnic background.[10] A further factor may be the experience of such children and young people in terms of discrimination and negative experiences of authority. When having regard to the welfare of the child or young person to be sentenced, the particular factors which arise in the case of black and minority ethnic children and young people need to be taken into account.

1.19 The requirement to have regard to the welfare of a child or young person is subject to the obligation to impose only those restrictions on liberty that are commensurate with the seriousness of the offence; accordingly, a court should not impose greater restrictions because of other factors in the child or young person's life.

1.20 When considering a child or young person who may be particularly vulnerable, sentencers should consider which available disposal is best able to support the child or young person and which disposals could potentially exacerbate any underlying issues. This is particularly important when considering custodial sentences as there are concerns about the effect on vulnerable children and young people of being in closed conditions, with significant risks of self harm, including suicide.

1.21 The vulnerability factors that are often present in the background of children and young people should also be considered in light of the offending behaviour itself. Although they do not alone cause offending behaviour – there are many children and young people who have experienced these circumstances but do not commit crime – there is a correlation and any response to criminal activity amongst children and young people will need to recognise the presence of such factors in order to be effective.

These principles do not undermine the fact that the sentence should reflect the seriousness of the offence. Further guidance on assessing the seriousness of an offence can be found at section four.

Section two: Allocation
(See also the allocation charts at pages 11 – 13 when reading this section.)

2.1 **Subject to the exceptions noted below, cases involving children and young people should be tried in the youth court.** It is the court which is best designed to meet their specific needs. A trial in the Crown Court with the inevitably greater formality and greatly increased number of people involved (including a jury and the public) should be reserved for the most serious cases.[11] The welfare principles in this guideline apply to all cases, including those tried or sentenced in the Crown Court.

This section covers the exceptions to this requirement.[12]

2.2 A child or young person must always appear in the Crown Court for trial if:
  • charged with homicide;
  • charged with a firearms offence subject to a mandatory minimum sentence of three years (and is over 16 years of age at the time of the offence); or

---

10   https://www.gov.uk/government/statistics/children-looked-after-in-england-including-adoption-2015-to-2016 (National table, figure B1)
11   *R on the application of H, A and O v Southampton Youth Court [2004]* EWHC 2912 Admin
12   s.24 Magistrates' Courts Act 1980

- notice has been given to the court (under section 51B or 51C of the Crime and Disorder Act 1998) in a serious or complex fraud or child case.

Dangerousness

2.3 A case should be sent to the Crown Court for trial if the offence charged is a specified offence[13] **and** it seems to the court that if found guilty the child or young person would meet the criteria for a sentence under the dangerous offender provisions.

2.4 A sentence under the dangerous offender provisions can only be imposed if:
- the child or young person is found guilty of a specified violent or sexual offence; **and**
- the court is of the opinion that there is a significant risk to the public of serious harm caused by the child or young person committing further specified offences; **and**
- a custodial term of at least four years would be imposed for the offence.

2.5 A 'significant risk' is more than a mere possibility of occurrence. The assessment of dangerousness should take into account all the available information relating to the circumstances of the offence and **may** also take into account any information regarding previous patterns of behaviour relating to this offence and any other relevant information relating to the child or young person. In making this assessment it will be essential to obtain a pre-sentence report.

2.6 Children and young people may change and develop within a shorter time than adults and this factor, along with their level of maturity, may be highly relevant when assessing probable future conduct and whether it may cause a significant risk of serious harm.[14]

2.7 In anything but the most serious cases it may be impossible for the court to form a view as to whether the child or young person would meet the criteria of the dangerous offender provisions without greater knowledge of the circumstances of the offence and the child or young person. In those circumstances jurisdiction for the case should be retained in the youth court. If, following a guilty plea or a finding of guilt, the dangerousness criteria appear to be met then the child or young person should be committed **for sentence**.

Grave crimes

2.8 Where a child or young person is before the court for an offence to which section 91(1) of the Powers of Criminal Courts (Sentencing) Act 2000 applies and the court considers that it ought to be possible to sentence them to more than two years' detention if found guilty of the offence, then they should be sent to the Crown Court. The test to be applied by the court is whether there is a **real prospect** that a sentence in excess of two years' detention will be imposed.

2.9 An offence comes within section 91 where:
- it is punishable with 14 years imprisonment or more for an adult (but is not a sentence fixed by law);
- it is an offence of sexual assault, a child sex offence committed by a child or young person, sexual activity with a child family member or inciting a child family member to engage in sexual activity; or

---

13 As listed in the Criminal Justice Act 2003 Sch.15
14 *R v Lang* [2005] EWCA Crim 2864, [2006] 1 WLR 2509

- it is one of a number of specified offences in relation to firearms, ammunition and weapons which are subject to a minimum term but, in respect of which, a court has found exceptional circumstances justifying a lesser sentence.

2.10 Before deciding whether to send the case to the Crown Court or retain jurisdiction in the youth court, the court should hear submissions from the prosecution and defence. As there is now a power to commit grave crimes for sentence[15] the court should no longer take the prosecution case at its highest when deciding whether to retain jurisdiction.[16] In most cases it is likely to be impossible to decide whether there is a real prospect that a sentence in excess of two years' detention will be imposed without knowing more about the facts of the case and the circumstances of the child or young person. In those circumstances the youth court should retain jurisdiction and commit for sentence if it is of the view, having heard more about the facts and the circumstances of the child or young person, that its powers of sentence are insufficient.

Where the court decides that the case is suitable to be dealt with in the youth court it must warn the child or young person that all available sentencing options remain open and, if found guilty, the child or young person may be committed to the Crown Court for sentence.

Children and young people should only be sent for trial or committed for sentence to the Crown Court when charged with or found guilty of an offence of such gravity that a custodial sentence substantially exceeding two years is a realistic possibility. For children aged 10 or 11, and children/young people aged 12 – 14 who are not persistent offenders, the court should take into account the normal prohibition on imposing custodial sentences.

Charged alongside an adult

2.11 The proper venue for the trial of any child or young person is normally the youth court. Subject to statutory restrictions, that remains the case where a child or young person is jointly charged with an adult. If the adult is sent for trial to the Crown Court, the court should conclude that the child or young person must be tried separately in the youth court unless it is in the interests of justice for the child or young person and the adult to be tried jointly.

2.12 Examples of factors that should be considered when deciding whether to send the child or young person to the Crown Court (rather than having a trial in the youth court) include:
- whether separate trials will cause injustice to witnesses or to the case as a whole (consideration should be given to the provisions of sections 27 and 28 of the Youth Justice and Criminal Evidence Act 1999);
- the age of the child or young person; the younger the child or young person, the greater the desirability that the child or young person be tried in the youth court;
- the age gap between the child or young person and the adult; a substantial gap in age militates in favour of the child or young person being tried in the youth court;
- the lack of maturity of the child or young person;
- the relative culpability of the child or young person compared with the adult and whether the alleged role played by the child or young person was minor; and/or
- the lack of previous findings of guilt on the part of the child or young person.

15 s.3(b) Powers of Criminal Courts (Sentencing) Act 2000, (as amended)
16 *R (DPP) v South Tyneside Youth Court* [2015] EWHC 1455 (Admin)

2.13 The court should bear in mind that the youth court now has a general power to commit for sentence (as discussed at paragraph 2.9); in appropriate cases this will permit a sentence to be imposed by the same court on adults and children and young people who have been tried separately.

2.14 The court should follow the plea before venue procedure (see flowcharts on pages 11 – 13) prior to considering whether it is in the interests of justice for the child or young person and the adult to be tried jointly.

Remittal from the Crown Court for sentence

2.15 If a child or young person is found guilty before the Crown Court of an offence other than homicide the court must remit the case to the youth court, unless it would be undesirable to do so.[17] In considering whether remittal is undesirable a court should balance the need for expertise in the sentencing of children and young people with the benefits of the sentence being imposed by the court which determined guilt.

2.16 Particular attention should be given to children and young people who are appearing before the Crown Court only because they have been charged with an adult offender; referral orders are generally not available in the Crown Court but may be the most appropriate sentence.

Child or young person charged alone or with other children and young people

(This is intended to be a reference tool only; for full guidance on allocation, particularly for grave crimes, please see pages 7 – 10.)

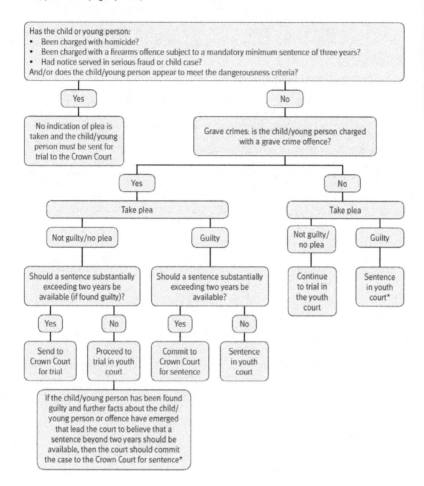

Has the child or young person:
- Been charged with homicide?
- Been charged with a firearms offence subject to a mandatory minimum sentence of three years?
- Had notice served in serious fraud or child case?
And/or does the child/young person appear to meet the dangerousness criteria?

Yes → No indication of plea is taken and the child/young person must be sent for trial to the Crown Court

No → Grave crimes: is the child/young person charged with a grave crime offence?

Yes → Take plea
- **Not guilty/no plea** → Should a sentence substantially exceeding two years be available (if found guilty)?
  - **Yes** → Send to Crown Court for trial
  - **No** → Proceed to trial in youth court
- **Guilty** → Should a sentence substantially exceeding two years be available?
  - **Yes** → Commit to Crown Court for sentence
  - **No** → Sentence in youth court

If the child/young person has been found guilty and further facts about the child/young person or offence have emerged that lead the court to believe that a sentence beyond two years should be available, then the court should commit the case to the Crown Court for sentence*

No → Take plea
- **Not guilty/ no plea** → Continue to trial in the youth court
- **Guilty** → Sentence in youth court*

OVERARCHING PRINCIPLES

* If the dangerousness provisions appear to be satisfied the court must commit for sentence

Child or young person and adult charged as co-defendants where the adult is charged with either way offence

(This is intended to be a reference tool only; for full guidance on allocation, particularly for grave crimes, please see pages 7 – 10.)

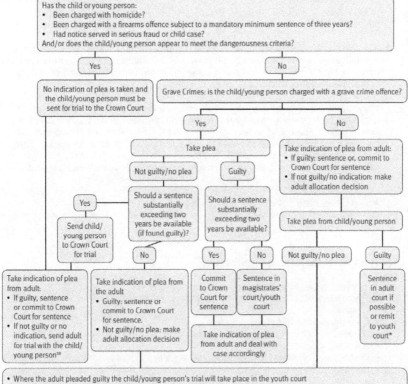

Has the child or young person:
- Been charged with homicide?
- Been charged with a firearms offence subject to a mandatory minimum sentence of three years?
- Had notice served in serious fraud or child case?

And/or does the child/young person appear to meet the dangerousness criteria?

Yes

No indication of plea is taken and the child/young person must be sent for trial to the Crown Court

No

Grave Crimes: is the child/young person charged with a grave crime offence?

Yes

Take plea

No

Take indication of plea from adult:
- If guilty: sentence or, commit to Crown Court for sentence
- If not guilty/no indication: make adult allocation decision

Not guilty/no plea — Guilty

Take plea from child/young person

Yes — Should a sentence substantially exceeding two years be available (if found guilty)?

Send child/young person to Crown Court for trial

Should a sentence substantially exceeding two years be available?

Not guilty/no plea — Guilty

No

Yes — **No**

Commit to Crown Court for sentence

Sentence in magistrates' court/youth court

Sentence in adult court if possible or remit to youth court*

Take indication of plea from adult:
- If guilty, sentence or commit to Crown Court for sentence
- If not guilty or no indication, send adult for trial with the child/young person[18]

Take indication of plea from the adult
- Guilty: sentence or commit to Crown Court for sentence.
- Not guilty/no plea: make adult allocation decision

Take indication of plea from adult and deal with case accordingly

- Where the adult pleaded guilty the child/young person's trial will take place in the youth court
- Where the adult is being tried summarily then a joint trial will take place in the magistrates' court
- Where the adult is to be sent for trial in the Crown Court then the court should consider whether it is in the interests of justice to send the child/young person to the Crown Court for a joint trial with the adult, if not proceed with summary trial in youth court

If the child/young person has been found guilty after a summary trial and further facts about the child/young person or offence have emerged that lead the court to believe that a sentence substantially beyond two years should be available, then the court should commit the case to the Crown Court for sentence*

* If the dangerousness provisions appear to be satisfied the court must commit for sentence

18   s.51A(6) Crime & Disorder Act 1998

Section three: Parental responsibilities

3.1 For any child or young person aged under 16 appearing before court there is a statutory requirement that parents/guardians attend during all stages of proceedings, unless the court is satisfied that this would be unreasonable having regard to the circumstances of the case.[19] The court may also enforce this requirement for a young person aged 16 and above if it deems it desirable to do so.

3.2 Although this requirement can cause a delay in the case before the court it is important it is adhered to. If a court does find exception to proceed in the absence of a responsible adult then extra care must be taken to ensure the outcomes are clearly communicated to and understood by the child or young person.

3.3 In addition to this responsibility there are also orders that can be imposed on parents. If the child or young person is aged under 16 then the court has a duty to make a **parental bind over** or impose a **parenting order**, if it would be desirable in the interest of preventing the commission of further offences.[20] There is a discretionary power to make these orders where the young person is aged 16 or 17. If the court chooses not to impose a parental bind over or parenting order it must state its reasons for not doing so in open court. In most circumstances a parenting order is likely to be more appropriate than a parental bind over.

3.4 A court cannot make a bind over alongside a referral order. If the court makes a referral order the duty on the court to impose a parenting order in respect of a child or young person under 16 years old is replaced by a discretion.[21]

Section four: Determining the sentence

4.1 In determining the sentence, the key elements to consider are:
- the principal aim of the youth justice system (to prevent re-offending by children and young people);
- the welfare of the child or young person;
- the age of the child or young person (chronological, developmental and emotional);
- the seriousness of the offence;
- the likelihood of further offences being committed; and
- the extent of harm likely to result from those further offences.

The seriousness of the offence
(This applies to all offences; when offence specific guidance for children and young people is available this should be referred to.)

4.2 The seriousness of the offence is the starting point for determining the appropriate sentence; the sentence imposed and any restriction on liberty must be commensurate with the seriousness of the offence.

---

19 s.34A Children and Young Persons Act 1933
20 s.150 Powers of Criminal Courts (Sentencing) Act 2000 & s.8 Crime and Disorder Act 1998
21 s.9(1A) Crime and Disorder Act 1998

4.3 The approach to sentencing children and young people should always be individualistic and the court should always have in mind the principal aims of the youth justice system.

4.4 In order to determine the seriousness of the offence the court should assess the culpability of the child or young person and the harm that was caused, intended to be caused or could foreseeably have been caused.

4.5 In assessing **culpability** the court will wish to consider the extent to which the offence was planned, the role of the child or young person (if the offence was committed as part of a group), the level of force that was used in the commission of the offence and the awareness that the child or young person had of their actions and its possible consequences. There is an expectation that in general a child or young person will be dealt with less severely than an adult offender. In part, this is because children and young people are unlikely to have the same experience and capacity as an adult to understand the effect of their actions on other people or to appreciate the pain and distress caused and because a child or young person may be less able to resist temptation, especially where peer pressure is exerted. Children and young people are inherently more vulnerable than adults due to their age and the court will need to consider any mental health problems and/or learning disabilities they may have, as well as their emotional and developmental age. Any external factors that may have affected the child or young person's behaviour should be taken into account.

4.6 In assessing **harm** the court should consider the level of physical and psychological harm caused to the victim, the degree of any loss caused to the victim and the extent of any damage caused to property. (This assessment should also include a consideration of any harm that was intended to be caused or could foreseeably have been caused in the committal of the offence.)

4.7 The court should also consider any aggravating or mitigating factors that may increase or reduce the overall seriousness of the offence. **If any of these factors are included in the definition of the committed offence they should not be taken into account when considering the relative seriousness of the offence before the court.**

Aggravating factors
Statutory aggravating factors:
Previous findings of guilt, having regard to a) the **nature** of the offence to which the finding of guilt relates and its **relevance** to the current offence; and b) the **time** that has elapsed since the finding of guilt
Offence committed whilst on bail
Offence motivated by, or demonstrating hostility based on any of the following characteristics or presumed characteristics of the victim: religion, race, disability, sexual orientation or transgender identity
Other aggravating factors (non-exhaustive):
Steps taken to prevent the victim reporting or obtaining assistance
Steps taken to prevent the victim from assisting or supporting the prosecution
Victim is particularly vulnerable due to factors including but not limited to age, mental or physical disability
Restraint, detention or additional degradation of the victim

OVERARCHING PRINCIPLES

Prolonged nature of offence

Attempts to conceal/dispose of evidence

Established evidence of community/wider impact

Failure to comply with current court orders

Attempt to conceal identity

Involvement of others through peer pressure, bullying, coercion or manipulation

Commission of offence whilst under the influence of alcohol or drugs

History of antagonising or bullying the victim

Deliberate humiliation of victim, including but not limited to filming of the offence, deliberately committing the offence before a group of peers with the intention of causing additional distress or circulating details/photos/videos etc of the offence on social media or within peer groups

Factors reducing seriousness or reflecting personal mitigation (non-exhaustive)

No previous findings of guilt **or** no relevant/recent findings of guilt

Remorse, particularly where evidenced by voluntary reparation to the victim

Good character and/or exemplary conduct

Unstable upbringing including but not limited to:
• time spent looked after
• lack of familial presence or support
• disrupted experiences in accommodation or education
• exposure to drug/alcohol abuse, familial criminal behaviour or domestic abuse
• victim of neglect or abuse, or exposure to neglect or abuse of others
• experiences of trauma or loss

Participated in offence due to bullying, peer pressure, coercion or manipulation

Limited understanding of effect on victim

Serious medical condition requiring urgent, intensive or long-term treatment

Communication or learning disabilities or mental health concerns

In education, work or training

Particularly young or immature child or young person (where it affects their responsibility)

Determination and/or demonstration of steps taken to address addiction or offending behaviour

Age and maturity of the child or young person

4.8 There is a statutory presumption that no child under the age of 10 can be guilty of an offence.[22]

4.9 With a child or young person, the consideration of age requires a different approach to that which would be adopted in relation to the age of an adult. Even within the category of child or young person the response of a court to an offence is likely to be very different depending on whether the child or young person is at the lower end of the age bracket, in the middle or towards the top end.

22 s.50 Children and Young Persons Act 1933

4.10 Although chronological age dictates in some instances what sentence can be imposed (see section six for more information) the developmental and emotional age of the child or young person should always be considered and it is of at least equal importance as their chronological age. It is important to consider whether the child or young person has the necessary maturity to appreciate fully the consequences of their conduct, the extent to which the child or young person has been acting on an impulsive basis and whether their conduct has been affected by inexperience, emotional volatility or negative influences.

Section five: Guilty plea

This section of the guideline applies regardless of the date of the offence to all children or young people where the **first hearing** is on or after 1 June 2017. It applies equally in youth courts, magistrates' courts and the Crown Court.

Key principles

5.1 The purpose of this section of the guideline is to encourage those who are going to plead guilty to do so as early in the court process as possible. Nothing in this section should be used to put pressure on a child or young person to plead guilty.

5.2 Although a guilty person is entitled not to admit the offence and to put the prosecution to proof of its case, an acceptance of guilt:
 a) normally reduces the impact of the crime upon victims;
 b) saves victims and witnesses from having to testify; and
 c) is in the public interest in that it saves public time and money on investigations and trials.

5.3 A guilty plea produces greater benefits the earlier the plea is made. In order to maximise the above benefits and to provide an incentive to those who are guilty to indicate a guilty plea as early as possible, this section of the guideline makes a clear distinction between a reduction in the sentence available at the first stage of the proceedings and a reduction in the sentence available at a later stage of the proceedings.

5.4 The purpose of reducing the sentence for a guilty plea is to yield the benefits described above and the guilty plea should be considered by the court to be independent of the child or young person's mitigation.
 • Factors such as admissions at interview, co-operation with the investigation and demonstrations of remorse should **not** be taken into account in determining the level of reduction. Rather, they should be considered separately and prior to any guilty plea reduction, as potential mitigating factors.
 • The benefits apply regardless of the strength of the evidence against a child or young person. The strength of the evidence should **not** be taken into account when determining the level of reduction.
 • This section applies only to the punitive elements of the sentence and has no impact on ancillary orders including orders of disqualification from driving.

OVERARCHING PRINCIPLES

The approach

Stage 1: Determine the appropriate sentence for the offence(s) in accordance with any offence specific sentencing guideline or using this *Overarching Principles* guideline.
Stage 2: Determine the level of reduction for a guilty plea in accordance with this guideline.
Stage 3: State the amount of that reduction.
Stage 4: Apply the reduction to the appropriate sentence.
Stage 5: Follow any further steps in the offence specific guideline to determine the final sentence.

Nothing in this guideline affects the duty of the parties to progress cases (including the service of material) and identify any issues in dispute in compliance with the Criminal Procedure Rules and Criminal Practice Directions.

Determining the level of reduction

The maximum level of reduction for a guilty plea is one-third.

5.5 **Plea indicated at the first stage of the proceedings**
Where a guilty plea is indicated at the first stage of proceedings a reduction of **one-third** should be made (subject to the exceptions below). The first stage will normally be the first hearing in the magistrates' or youth court at which a plea is sought and recorded by the court.[23]

5.6 **Plea indicated after the first stage of proceedings – maximum one quarter – sliding scale of reduction thereafter**
After the first stage of the proceedings the maximum level of reduction is **one-quarter** (subject to the exceptions below).

5.7 The reduction should be decreased from **one-quarter** to a maximum of **one-tenth** on the first day of trial having regard to the time when the guilty plea is first indicated relative to the progress of the case and the trial date (subject to the exceptions below). The reduction should normally be decreased further, even to zero, if the guilty plea is entered during the course of the trial.

5.8 For the purposes of this guideline a trial will be deemed to have started when pre-recorded cross-examination has begun.

Applying the reduction

Detention and training orders

5.9 A detention and training order (DTO) can only be imposed for the periods prescribed – 4, 6, 8, 10, 12, 18 or 24 months. If the reduction in sentence for a guilty plea results in a sentence that falls between two prescribed periods the court must impose the lesser of those two periods. This may result in a reduction greater than a third, in order that the full reduction is given and a lawful sentence imposed.

---

23 In cases where (in accordance with the Criminal Procedure Rules) a child/young person is given the opportunity to enter a guilty plea without attending a court hearing, doing so within the required time limits will constitute a plea at the first stage of proceedings.

Imposing one type of sentence rather than another

5.10 The reduction in sentence for a guilty plea can be taken into account by imposing one type of sentence rather than another, for example:
- by reducing a custodial sentence to a community sentence; or
- by reducing a community sentence to a different means of disposal.

Alternatively the court could reduce the length or severity of any punitive requirements attached to a community sentence.

5.11 The court must always have regard to the principal aim of the youth justice system, which is to prevent offending by children and young people. It is, therefore, important that the court ensures that any sentence imposed is an effective disposal.

5.12 Where a court has imposed one sentence rather than another to reflect the guilty plea there should normally be no further reduction on account of the guilty plea. Where, however, the less severe type of sentence is justified by other factors, the appropriate reduction for the plea should be applied in the normal way.

More than one summary offence

5.13 When dealing with more than one summary offence, the aggregate sentence is limited to a maximum of six months. Allowing for a reduction for each guilty plea, consecutive sentences might result in the imposition of the maximum six month sentence. Where this is the case, the court **may** make a modest *additional* reduction to the *overall* sentence to reflect the benefits derived from the guilty plea.

Sentencing up to 24 months DTO for offences committed by children and young people

5.14 A DTO of up to 24 months may be imposed on a child or young person if the offence is one which, but for the plea, would have attracted a sentence of detention in excess of 24 months under section 91 of the Powers of Criminal Courts (Sentencing) Act 2000.

Exceptions

Referral order

5.15 As a referral order is a sentence that is only available upon pleading guilty there should be no further reduction of the sentence to reflect the guilty plea.

Further information, assistance or advice necessary before indicating plea

5.16 Where the sentencing court is satisfied that there were particular circumstances which significantly reduced the child or young person's ability to understand what was alleged, or otherwise made it unreasonable to expect the child or young person to indicate a guilty plea **sooner than was done**, a reduction of one-third should still be made.

5.17 In considering whether this exception applies, sentencers should distinguish between cases in which it is necessary to receive advice and/or have sight of evidence in order to understand whether the child or young person is, in fact and law, guilty of the offence(s) charged, and cases

OVERARCHING PRINCIPLES

461

in which a child or young person merely delays guilty plea(s) in order to assess the strength of the prosecution evidence and the prospects of a finding of guilt or acquittal.

Newton hearings and special reasons hearings

5.18 In circumstances where a child or young person's version of events is rejected at a Newton hearing[24] or special reasons hearing,[25] the reduction which would have been available at the stage of proceedings the plea was indicated should normally be halved. Where witnesses are called during such a hearing, it may be appropriate further to decrease the reduction.

Child or young person found guilty of a lesser or different offence

5.19 If a child or young person is found guilty of a lesser or different offence from that originally charged, and has earlier made an unequivocal indication of a guilty plea to this lesser or different offence to the prosecution and the court, the court should give the level of reduction that is appropriate to the stage in the proceedings at which this indication of plea (to the lesser or different offence) was made taking into account any other of these exceptions that apply. In the Crown Court where the offered plea is a permissible alternative on the indictment as charged, the child or young person will not be treated as having made an unequivocal indication unless the defendant has entered that plea.

Minimum sentence under section 51A of the Firearms Act 1968

5.20 There can be no reduction for a guilty plea if the effect of doing so would be to reduce the length of sentence below the required minimum term.

Appropriate custodial sentences for young persons aged at least 16 but under 18 when found guilty under the Prevention of Crime Act 1953 and Criminal Justice Act 1988

5.21 In circumstances where an appropriate custodial sentence of a DTO of at least four months falls to be imposed on a young person who is aged at least 16 but under 18, who has been found guilty under sections 1 or 1A of the Prevention of Crime Act 1953; or section 139, 139AA or 139A of the Criminal Justice Act 1988 (certain possession of knives or offensive weapon offences) the court may impose any sentence that it considers appropriate, having taken into consideration the general principles set out above.

Mandatory life sentences for murder

5.22 Murder is the most serious criminal offence and the sentence prescribed is different from all other sentences. By law, the sentence for murder is detention for life and the child or young person will remain subject to the sentence for the rest of their life.

5.23 Given the special characteristic of the offence of murder and the unique statutory provision in Schedule 21 of the Criminal Justice Act 2003 of starting points for the minimum term to be

24 A Newton hearing is held when a child/young person pleads guilty but disputes the case as put forward by the prosecution and the dispute would make a difference to the sentence. The judge will normally hear evidence from witnesses to decide which version of the disputed facts to base the sentence on.

25 A special reasons hearing occurs when a child/young person is found guilty of an offence carrying a mandatory licence endorsement or disqualification from driving and seeks to persuade the court that there are extenuating circumstances relating to the offence that the court should take into account by reducing or avoiding endorsement or disqualification. This may involve calling witnesses to give evidence.

served by a child or young person, careful consideration has to be given to the extent of any reduction for a guilty plea and to the need to ensure that the minimum term properly reflects the seriousness of the offence.

5.24 Whilst the general principles continue to apply (both that a guilty plea should be encouraged and that the extent of any reduction should reduce if the indication of plea is later than the first stage of the proceedings) the process of determining the level of reduction will be different.

Determining the level of reduction

5.25 In other circumstances:
- the court will weigh carefully the overall length of the minimum term taking into account other reductions for which the child or young person may be eligible so as to avoid a combination leading to an inappropriately short sentence;
- where it is appropriate to reduce the minimum term having regard to a plea of guilty, the reduction will not exceed one-sixth and will never exceed five years; and
- the maximum reduction of one-sixth or five years (whichever is less) should only be given when a guilty plea has been indicated at the first stage of the proceedings. Lesser reductions should be given for guilty pleas after that point, with a maximum of one-twentieth being given for a guilty plea on the day of trial.

The exceptions outlined at 5.16 – 5.18 apply to murder cases.

Section six: Available sentences

Crossing a significant age threshold between commission of offence and sentence

6.1 There will be occasions when an increase in the age of a child or young person will result in the maximum sentence on the date of *the finding of guilt* being greater than that available on the date on which the offence was *committed* (primarily turning 12, 15 or 18 years old).

6.2 In such situations the court should take as its starting point the sentence likely to have been imposed on the date at which the offence was committed. This includes young people who attain the age of 18 between the *commission* and the *the finding of guilt* of the offence[26] but when this occurs the purpose of sentencing adult offenders[27] has to be taken into account, which is:
- the punishment of offenders;
- the reduction of crime (including its reduction by deterrence);
- the reform and rehabilitation of offenders;
- the protection of the public; and
- the making of reparation by offenders to persons affected by their offences.

6.3 When any significant age threshold is passed it will rarely be appropriate that a more severe sentence than the maximum that the court could have imposed at the time the offence was committed should be imposed. However, a sentence at or close to that maximum may be appropriate.

---

26 *R v Ghafoor* [2002] EWCA Crim 1857, [2003] 1 Cr App R (S) 428
27 s.142 Criminal Justice Act 2003

Persistent offenders

6.4 Some sentences can only be imposed on children and young people if they are deemed a persistent offender. A child or young person **must** be classed as such for one of the following to be imposed:
- a youth rehabilitation order (YRO) with intensive supervision and surveillance when aged under 15;
- a YRO with fostering when aged under 15; and
- a detention and training order (DTO) when aged 12 – 14.

6.5 The term persistent offender is not defined in statute but has been considered by the Court of Appeal. In general it is expected that the child or young person would have had previous contact with authority as a result of criminal behaviour. This includes previous findings of guilt as well as admissions of guilt such as restorative justice disposals and conditional cautions.

6.6 A child or young person who has committed one previous offence cannot reasonably be classed as a persistent offender, and a child or young person who has committed two or more previous offences should not necessarily be assumed to be one. To determine if the behaviour is persistent the nature of the previous offences and the lapse of time between the offences would need to be considered.[28]

6.7 If there have been three findings of guilt in the past 12 months for imprisonable offences of a comparable nature (or the child or young person has been made the subject of orders as detailed above in relation to an imprisonable offence) then the court could certainly justify classing the child or young person as a persistent offender.

6.8 When a child or young person is being sentenced in a single appearance for a series of separate, comparable offences committed over a short space of time then the court could justifiably consider the child or young person to be a persistent offender, despite the fact that there may be no previous findings of guilt.[29] In these cases the court should consider whether the child or young person has had prior opportunity to address their offending behaviour before imposing one of the optional sentences available for persistent offenders only; if the court determines that the child or young person has not had an opportunity to address their behaviour and believes that an alternative sentence has a reasonable prospect of preventing re-offending then this alternative sentence should be imposed.

6.9 The court may also wish to consider any evidence of a reduction in the level of offending when taking into account previous offending behaviour. Children and young people may be unlikely to desist from committing crime in a clear cut manner but there may be changes in patterns of criminal behaviour (e.g. committing fewer and/or less serious offences or there being longer lengths of time between offences) that indicate that the child or young person is attempting to desist from crime.

6.10 Even where a child or young person is found to be a persistent offender, a court is not obliged to impose one of the optional sentences. The approach should still be individualistic and all other considerations still apply. **Custodial sentences must be a last resort for all children and**

28 *R v M* [2008] EWCA Crim 3329
29 *R v S* [2000] 1 Cr App R (S)18

young people and there is an expectation that they will be particularly rare for children and young people aged 14 or under.

Sentences available by age:

Sentence	Age of child or young person 10 – 11	12 – 14	15 – 17	Rehabilitation period
Absolute or conditional discharge or reparation order	✓	✓	✓	Absolute discharge and reparation: spent on day of sentence Conditional discharge: spent on last day of the period of discharge
Financial order	✓	✓	✓	Spent 6 months after the finding of guilt
Referral order	✓	✓	✓	Spent on day of completion
Youth rehabilitation order (YRO)	✓	✓	✓	Spent 6 months after the last day the order is to have effect
YRO with intensive supervision and surveillance or fostering	✗	✓ For persistent offenders **only**	✓	Spent 6 months after the last day the order is to have effect
Detention and training order	✗	✓ For persistent offenders **only**	✓	6 months or under: spent 18 months after the sentence is completed (including supervision period) More than 6 months: spent 24 months after the sentence is completed (including supervision period)
s.91 PCC(S) Act detention (grave crime)	✓	✓	✓	More than 6 months – 30 months: spent 24 months after sentence completed (including licence period) More than 30 months – 48 months: spent 42 months after sentence completed (including licence period) More than 48 months: never spent
Extended sentence of detention*	✓	✓	✓	Never spent

* If found guilty of a specified violent or sexual offence and the court is of the opinion that there is a significant risk to the public of serious harm caused by the child or young person committing further specified offences.

6.11 Some sentences have longer rehabilitation periods than others, for example referral orders are spent on the last day on which the order is to have effect.[30] Sentences can also have varying impacts on the future of children and young people; for example absolute or conditional discharges are not deemed to be treated as convictions other than for the purposes of criminal proceedings[31] and therefore may have a lesser impact on the child or young person's future prospects than other sentences. The length of the rehabilitation periods and any likely effects on the child or young person's future prospects should be taken into account when considering if the sentence is commensurate to the seriousness of the offence.

Breaches and the commission of further offences during the period of an order

6.12 If a child or young person is found guilty of breaching an order, or commits a further offence during the period of an order, the court will have various options available depending upon the nature of the order **(see Appendix one at page 32)**. The primary aim of the court should be to encourage compliance and seek to support the rehabilitation of the child or young person.

30 s.139 Legal Aid, Sentencing and Punishment of Offenders Act 2012
31 s.14 (1) Powers of Criminal Courts (Sentencing) Act 2000

Absolute or conditional discharge and reparation orders

6.13 An absolute discharge is appropriate in the least serious cases when, despite a finding of guilt, the court considers that no punishment should be imposed.

6.14 A conditional discharge is appropriate when, despite a finding of guilt, the offence is not serious enough to warrant an immediate punishment. The fixed period of conditional discharge must not exceed three years. Unless exceptional circumstances are found, a conditional discharge cannot be imposed if the child or young person has received one of the following in the previous 24 months: two or more cautions; or a conditional caution followed by a caution.[32]

6.15 A reparation order can require a child or young person to make reparation to the victim of the offence, where a victim wishes it, or to the community as a whole. Before making an order the court must consider a written report from a relevant authority, e.g. a youth offending team (YOT), and the order must be commensurate with the seriousness of the offence.

6.16 If the court has the power to make a reparation order but chooses not to do so, it must give its reasons.

Financial order

6.17 The court may impose a fine for any offence (unless the criteria for a mandatory referral order are met). In accordance with statutory requirements, where financial orders are being considered, priority must be given to compensation orders and, when an order for costs is to be made alongside a fine, the amount of the cost must not exceed the amount of the fine. If the child or young person is under 16 then the court has a duty to order parents or guardians to pay the fine; if the young person is 16 or over this duty is discretionary. In practice, many children and young people will have limited financial resources and the court will need to determine whether imposing a fine will be the most effective disposal.

6.18 A court should bear in mind that children and young people may have money that is specifically required for travel costs to school, college or apprenticeships and lunch expenses.

Referral orders

6.19 A referral order is the mandatory sentence in a youth court or magistrates' court for most children and young people who have committed an offence for the first time and have pleaded guilty to an imprisonable offence. Exceptions are for offences where a sentence is fixed by law or if the court deems a custodial sentence, an absolute or conditional discharge or a hospital order to be more appropriate.

6.20 A discretionary referral order can also be imposed for any offence where there has been a plea of guilty regardless of previous offending history. It should be remembered that they are not community orders and in general terms may be regarded as orders which fall between community disposals and fines. However, bearing in mind that the principal aim of the youth justice system is to prevent children and young people offending, second or subsequent referral orders should be considered in those cases where:

---

32 s.66ZB Crime & Disorder Act 1998

(a) the offence is not serious enough for a YRO but the child or young person does appear to require some intervention OR

(b) the offence is serious enough for a YRO but it is felt that a referral order would be the best way to prevent further offending (as an example, this may be because the child or young person has responded well in the past to such an order and the offence now before the court is dissimilar to that for which a referral order was previously imposed).

Referral orders are the main sentence for delivering restorative justice and all panel members are trained Restorative Conference Facilitators; as such they can be an effective sentence in encouraging children and young people to take responsibility for their actions and understand the effect their offence may have had on their victim.

6.21 In cases where children or young people have offended for the first time and have pleaded guilty to committing an offence which is on the cusp of the custody threshold, YOTs should be encouraged to convene a Youth Offender Panel prior to sentence (sometimes referred to as a "pseudo-panel" or "pre-panel") where the child or young person is asked to attend before a panel and agree an intensive contract. If that contract is placed before the sentencing youth court, the court can then decide whether it is sufficient to move below custody on this occasion. The proposed contract is not something the court can alter in any way; the court will still have to make a decision between referral order and custody but can do so on the basis that if it makes a referral order it can have confidence in what that will entail in the particular case.

6.22 The court determines the length of the order but a Referral Order Panel determines the requirements of the order.

Offence seriousness	Suggested length of referral order
Low	• 3 – 5 months
Medium	• 5 – 7 months
High	• 7 – 9 months
Very high	• 10 – 12 months

The YOT may propose certain requirements and the length of these requirements may not correspond to the above table; if the court feels these requirements will best achieve the aims of the youth justice system then they may still be imposed.

Youth rehabilitation orders (YRO)

6.23 A YRO is a community sentence within which a court may include one or more requirements designed to provide for punishment, protection of the public, reducing re-offending and reparation.

6.24 When imposing a YRO, the court must fix a period within which the requirements of the order are to be completed; this must not be more than three years from the date on which the order comes into effect.

6.25 The offence must be 'serious enough' in order to impose a YRO, but it does not need to be an imprisonable offence. Even if an offence is deemed 'serious enough' the court is not obliged to make a YRO.

6.26 The requirements included within the order (and the subsequent restriction on liberty) and the length of the order must be proportionate to the seriousness of the offence and suitable for the child or young person. The court should take care to ensure that the requirements imposed are not too onerous so as to make breach of the order almost inevitable.

6.27 The available requirements within a YRO are:
- activity requirement (maximum 90 days);
- supervision requirement;
- unpaid work requirement (between 40 and 240 hours);*
- programme requirement;
- attendance centre requirement (maximum 12 hours for children aged 10–13, between 12 and 24 hours for young people aged 14 or 15 and between 12 and 36 hours for young people aged 16 or over (all ages refer to age at date of the finding of guilt);
- prohibited activity requirement;
- curfew requirement (maximum 12 months and between 2 and 16 hours a day);
- exclusion requirement (maximum 3 months);
- electronic monitoring requirement;
- residence requirement;*
- local authority residence requirement (maximum 6 months but not for any period after young person attains age of 18);
- fostering requirement (maximum 12 months but not for any period after young person attains age of 18);**
- mental health treatment requirement;
- drug treatment requirement (with or without drug testing);
- intoxicating substance requirement;
- education requirement; and
- intensive supervision and surveillance requirement.**

* These requirements are only available for young people aged 16 or 17 years old on the date of the finding of guilt.

** These requirements can only be imposed if the offence is an imprisonable one AND the custody threshold has been passed. For children and young people aged under 15 they must be deemed a persistent offender.

Many of the above requirements have additional restrictions. Always consult your legal adviser before imposing a YRO.

6.28 When determining the nature and extent of the requirements the court should primarily consider the likelihood of the child or young person re-offending and the risk of the child or young person causing serious harm. A higher risk of re-offending does not in itself justify a greater restriction on liberty than is warranted by the seriousness of the offence; any requirements should still be commensurate with the seriousness of the offence and regard must still be had for the welfare of the child or young person.

6.29 The YOT will assess this as part of their report and recommend an intervention level to the court for consideration. It is possible for the court to ask the YOT to consider a particular requirement.

	Child or young person profile	Requirements of order[33]
Standard	Low likelihood of re-offending **and** a low risk of serious harm	Primarily seek to repair harm caused through, for example: • reparation; • unpaid work; • supervision; and/or • attendance centre.
Enhanced	Medium likelihood of re-offending **or** a medium risk of serious harm	Seek to repair harm caused and to enable help or change through, for example: • supervision; • reparation; • requirement to address behaviour e.g. drug treatment, offending behaviour programme, education programme; and/or • a combination of the above.
Intensive	High likelihood of re-offending **or** a very high risk of serious harm	Seek to ensure the control of and enable help or change for the child or young person through, for example: • supervision; • reparation; • requirement to address behaviour; • requirement to monitor or restrict movement, e.g. prohibited activity, curfew, exclusion or electronic monitoring; and/or • a combination of the above.

6.30 If a child or young person is assessed as presenting a high risk of re-offending or of causing serious harm but the offence that was committed is of relatively low seriousness then the appropriate requirements are likely to be primarily rehabilitative or for the protection of the public.

6.31 Likewise if a child or young person is assessed as presenting a low risk of re-offending or of causing serious harm but the offence was of relatively high seriousness then the appropriate requirements are likely to be primarily punitive.

Orders with intensive supervision and surveillance or with fostering

6.32 An intensive supervision and surveillance requirement and a fostering requirement are both community alternatives to custody.

6.33 The offence must be punishable by imprisonment, cross the custody threshold and a custodial sentence must be merited before one of these requirements can be imposed.

6.34 An order of this nature may only be imposed on a child or young person aged below 15 (at the time of the finding of guilt) if they are a persistent offender.

With intensive supervision and surveillance:

6.35 An order of this nature must include an extended activity requirement of between 90 and 180 days, a supervision requirement and a curfew requirement. Where appropriate, a YRO with intensive supervision and surveillance may also include additional requirements (other than a fostering requirement), although the order as a whole must comply with the obligation that the requirements must be those most suitable for the child or young person and that any restrictions on liberty are commensurate with the seriousness of the offence.

---

33 The examples provided here are not exclusive; the YOT will make recommendations based upon their assessment of the young offender which may vary from some of the examples given.

6.36 When imposing such an order, the court must ensure that the requirements are not so onerous as to make the likelihood of breach almost inevitable.

With fostering:

6.37 Where a fostering requirement is included within a YRO, it will require the child or young person to reside with a local authority foster parent for a specified period that must not exceed 12 months.

6.38 In order to impose this requirement the court must be satisfied that the behaviour which constituted the offence was due to a significant extent to the circumstances in which the child or young person was living, and that the imposition of fostering requirement would assist in the child or young person's rehabilitation. It is likely that other rights will be engaged (such as those under Article 8 of the European Convention on Human Rights)[34] and any interference with such rights must be proportionate.

6.39 The court must consult the child or young person's parent or guardian (unless impracticable) and the local authority before including this requirement. It can only be included if the child or young person was legally represented in court when consideration was being given to imposing such a requirement unless the child or young person, having had the opportunity to do so, did not apply for representation or that right was withdrawn because of the child or young person's conduct. **This requirement may be included only where the court has been notified that arrangements are available in the area of the relevant authority.**

6.40 A YRO with a fostering requirement must include a supervision requirement and can include other requirements when appropriate (except an intensive supervision and surveillance requirement). The order as a whole must comply with the obligation that the requirements must be those most suitable for the child or young person and that any restrictions on liberty are commensurate with the seriousness of the offence.

6.41 It is unlikely that the statutory criteria[35] will be met in many cases; where they are met and the court is considering making an order, care should be taken to ensure that there is a well developed plan for the care and support of the child or young person throughout the period of the order and following conclusion of the order. The court will need to be provided with sufficient information, including proposals for education and training during the order and plans for the child or young person on completion of the order.

Custodial sentences

A custodial sentence should always be used as a last resort. If offence specific guidelines for children and young people are available then the court should consult them in the first instance to asses whether custody is the most appropriate disposal.
The available custodial sentences for children and young people are:

---

34 Right to respect for family and private life
35 See paragraphs 5.28-30

Youth Court	Crown Court

• Detention and training order for the following periods:
  • 4 months;
  • 6 months;
  • 8 months;
  • 10 months;
  • 12 months;
  • 18 months; or
  • 24 months.
	• Detention and training order (the same periods are available as in the youth court)
	• Long-term detention (under section 91 of the Powers of Criminal Courts (Sentencing) Act 2000)
	• Extended sentence of detention or detention for life (if dangerousness criteria are met)
	• Detention at Her Majesty's pleasure (for offences of murder)

6.42 Under both domestic and international law, a custodial sentence must only be imposed as a **'measure of last resort;'** statute provides that such a sentence may be imposed only where an offence is "so serious that neither a fine alone nor a community sentence can be justified."[36] If a custodial sentence is imposed, a court must state its reasons for being satisfied that the offence is so serious that no other sanction would be appropriate and, in particular, why a YRO with intensive supervision and surveillance or fostering could not be justified.

6.43 The term of a custodial sentence must be the shortest commensurate with the seriousness of the offence; any case that warrants a DTO of less than four months must result in a non-custodial sentence. The court should take account of the circumstances, age and maturity of the child or young person.

6.44 In determining whether an offence has crossed the custody threshold the court will need to assess the seriousness of the offence, in particular the level of harm that was caused, or was likely to have been caused, by the offence. The risk of serious harm in the future must also be assessed. The pre-sentence report will assess this criterion and must be considered before a custodial sentence is imposed. A custodial sentence is most likely to be unavoidable where it is necessary to protect the public from serious harm.

6.45 Only if the court is satisfied that the offence crosses the custody threshold, and that no other sentence is appropriate, the court may, as a preliminary consideration, consult the equivalent adult guideline in order to decide upon the appropriate length of the sentence.

6.46 When considering the relevant adult guideline, the court **may** feel it appropriate to apply a sentence broadly within the region of half to two thirds of the adult sentence for those aged 15 – 17 and allow a greater reduction for those aged under 15. This is only a rough guide and must not be applied mechanistically. In most cases when considering the appropriate reduction from the adult sentence **the emotional and developmental age and maturity of the child or young person is of at least equal importance as their chronological age**.

6.47 The individual factors relating to the offence and the child or young person are of the greatest importance and may present good reason to impose a sentence outside of this range. The court should bear in mind the negative effects a short custodial sentence can have; short sentences disrupt education and/or training and family relationships and support which are crucial stabilising factors to prevent re-offending.

---

36 s.152(2) Criminal Justice Act 2003

OVERARCHING PRINCIPLES

6.48 There is an expectation that custodial sentences will be particularly rare for a child or young person aged 14 or under. If custody is imposed, it should be for a shorter length of time than that which a young person aged 15 – 17 would receive if found guilty of the same offence. For a child or young person aged 14 or under the sentence should normally be imposed in a youth court (except in cases of homicide or when the dangerous offender criteria are met).

6.49 The welfare of the child or young person must be considered when imposing any sentence but is especially important when a custodial sentence is being considered. A custodial sentence could have a significant effect on the prospects and opportunities of the child or young person and a child or young person is likely to be more susceptible than an adult to the contaminating influences that can be expected within a custodial setting. There is a high reconviction rate for children and young people that have had custodial sentences and there have been many studies profiling the effect on vulnerable children and young people, particularly the risk of self harm and suicide and so it is of utmost importance that custody is a last resort.

Detention and training order (DTO)

6.50 A court can only impose a DTO if the child or young person is legally represented unless they have refused to apply for legal aid or it has been withdrawn as a result of their conduct.

6.51 If it is determined that the offence is of such seriousness that a custodial sentence is unavoidable then the length of this sentence must be considered on an individual basis. The court must take into account the chronological age of the child or young person, as well as their maturity, emotional and developmental age and other relevant factors, such as their mental health or any learning disabilities.

6.52 A DTO cannot be imposed on any child under the age of 12 at the time of the finding of guilt and is only applicable to children aged 12 – 14 if they are deemed to be a persistent offender. (See section on persistent offenders on page 22.)

6.53 A DTO can be made only for the periods prescribed – 4, 6, 8, 10, 12, 18 or 24 months. Any time spent on remand in custody or on bail subject to a qualifying curfew condition should be taken into account when calculating the length of the order. The accepted approach is to double the time spent on remand before deciding the appropriate period of detention, in order to ensure that the regime is in line with that applied to adult offenders.[37] After doubling the time spent on remand the court should then adopt the nearest prescribed period available for a DTO.

Long-term detention

6.54 A child or young person may be sentenced by the Crown Court to long-term detention under section 91 of the Powers of Criminal Courts (Sentencing) Act 2000 if found guilty of a grave crime and neither a community order nor a DTO is suitable.

6.55 These cases may be sent for trial to the Crown Court or committed for sentence only[38] (see section two for further information).

---

37 *R v Eagles* [2006] EWCA Crim 2368
38 s.3(b) Powers of Criminal Courts (Sentencing) Act 2000, (as amended)

6.56 It is possible that, following a guilty plea, a two year detention order may be appropriate as opposed to a sentence of section 91 detention, to account for the reduction.

Dangerous offenders

6.57 If a child or young person is found to be a dangerous offender they can be sentenced to **extended detention** or **detention for life**.

6.58 A sentence of extended detention may be imposed only where the appropriate custodial term would be 4 years or more. The extension period must not exceed 5 years in the case of a specified violent offence and 8 years in the case of a specified sexual offence. The term of the extended sentence of detention must not exceed the maximum term of imprisonment for an adult offender convicted of that offence.

6.59 A sentence of detention for life should be used as a last resort when an extended sentence is not able to provide the level of public protection that is necessary. In order to determine this, the court should consider the following factors in the order given:
- the seriousness of the offence;
- the child or young person's previous findings of guilt;
- the level of danger posed to the public and whether there is a reliable estimate of the length of time the child or young person will remain a danger; and
- the alternative sentences available.

The court is required to set a minimum term which must be served in custody before parole can be considered.

Detention at Her Majesty's pleasure

6.60 This is the mandatory sentence for any child or young person found guilty of committing a murder. The starting point for the minimum term is 12 years.

OVERARCHING PRINCIPLES

Appendix one: Breach of orders

Breach of a conditional discharge

7.1 If a child or young person commits an offence during the period of conditional discharge then the court has the power to re-sentence the original offence. The child or young person should be dealt with on the basis of their current age and not the age at the time of the finding of guilt and the court can deal with the original offence(s) in any way which it could have if the child or young person had just been found guilty.

7.2 There is no requirement to re-sentence; if a court deems it appropriate to do so they can sentence the child or young person for the new offence and leave the conditional discharge in place. If the order was made by the Crown Court then the youth court can commit the child or young person in custody or release them on bail until they can be brought or appear before the Crown Court. The court shall also send to the Crown Court a memorandum of conviction.

7.3 If the offender is convicted of committing a new offence after attaining the age of 18 but during the period of a conditional discharge made by a youth court then they may be re-sentenced for the original offence by the convicting adult magistrates' court. If the adult magistrates' court decides to take no action then the youth court that imposed the conditional discharge may summon the offender for the breach to be dealt with.

Breach of a reparation order

7.4 If it is proved to the appropriate court that the child or young person has failed to comply with any requirement of a reparation order that is currently in force then the court can:
- order the child or young person to pay a fine not exceeding £1,000; or
- revoke the order and re-sentence the child or young person in any way which they could have been dealt with for that offence.

If re-sentencing the child or young person the court must take into account the extent to which the child or young person has complied with the requirements of this order.

7.5 If the order was made by the Crown Court then the youth court can commit the child or young person in custody or release them on bail until they can be brought or appear before the Crown Court.

7.6 The child or young person or a Youth Offending Team (YOT) officer can also apply for the order to be revoked or amended but any new provisions must be ones that the court would have been able to include when the original reparation order was given. There is no power to re-sentence in this situation as the child or young person has not been found to be in breach of requirements.

Even when an offender has attained the age of 18 breach of a reparation order must be dealt with in the youth court.

Breach of a referral order (referral back to court)

7.7 If a child or young person is found to have breached the conditions of their referral order the court can revoke the referral order and re-sentence the child or young person using the range of sentencing options (other than a referral order) that would have been available to the court that originally sentenced them. If the court chooses not to revoke the referral order then it is possible to:
- allow the referral order to continue with the existing contract;
- extend the length of the referral order up to a maximum of 12 months (in total); or
- impose a fine up to a maximum of £2,500.

7.8 If an offender has attained the age of 18 by the first court hearing then breach proceedings must be dealt with by the adult magistrates' court. If the court chooses to revoke the order then its powers are limited to those available to the court at the time of the original sentence.

Commission of further offences whilst on a referral order

7.9 The court has the power to extend a referral order in respect of additional or further offences. This applies to not only a first referral order but also to any subsequent referral orders. Any period of extension must not exceed the total 12 month limit for a referral order.

7.10 If the court chooses not to extend the existing referral order or impose a discharge they have the power to impose a new referral order (where the discretionary referral order conditions are satisfied) in respect of the new offences only. This order can remain or run alongside the new order or the court may direct that the contract under the new order is not to take effect until the earlier order is revoked or discharged. Alternatively, the court may impose an absolute or conditional discharge.

7.11 If the court sentences in any other way they have a discretionary power to revoke the referral order. Where an order is revoked, if it appears to be in the interests of justice, the court may deal with the original offence(s) in any way that the original court could have done, but may not make a new referral order. Where the referral contract has taken effect, the court shall have regard to the extent of the child or young person's compliance with the terms of the contract.

Breach of a youth rehabilitation order (YRO)

7.12 Where a child or young person is in breach of a YRO the following options are available to the court:
- take no action and allow the order to continue in its original form;
- impose a fine (up to £2,500)(and allow the order to continue in its original form);
- amend the terms of the order; or
- revoke the order and re-sentence the child or young person.

7.13 If the terms of the order are amended the new requirements must be capable of being complied with before the expiry of the overall period. The court may impose any requirement that it could have imposed when making the order and this may be in addition to, or in substitution for, any requirements contained in the order. If the YRO did not contain an unpaid work requirement and the court includes such a requirement using this power, the minimum period of unpaid work is 20 hours; this will give greater flexibility when responding to less serious breaches or where there are significant other requirements to be complied with.

7.14 A court may not amend the terms of a YRO that did not include an extended activity requirement or a fostering requirement by inserting them at this stage; should these requirements be considered appropriate following breach, the child or young person must be re-sentenced and the original YRO revoked.

7.15 A court must ensure that it has sufficient information to enable it to understand why the order has been breached and should be satisfied that the YOT and other local authority services have taken all steps necessary to ensure that the child or young person has been given appropriate opportunity and the support necessary for compliance. This is particularly important if the court is considering imposing a custodial sentence as a result of the breach.

7.16 Where the failure arises primarily from non-compliance with reporting or other similar obligations and a sanction is necessary, the most appropriate response is likely to be the inclusion of (or increase in) a primarily punitive requirement such as the curfew requirement, unpaid work, the exclusion requirement and the prohibited activity requirement or the imposition of a fine. However, continuing failure to comply with the order is likely to lead to revocation of the order and re-sentencing for the original offence.

7.17 Where the child or young person has 'wilfully and persistently' failed to comply with the order, and the court proposes to sentence again for the offence(s) in respect of which the order was made, additional powers are available.

A child or young person will almost certainly be considered to have 'wilfully and persistently' breached a YRO where there have been three breaches that have demonstrated a lack of willingness to comply with the order that have resulted in an appearance before court.

7.18 The additional powers available to the court when re-sentencing a child or young person who has 'wilfully and persistently' breached their order are:
- the making of a YRO with intensive supervision and surveillance even though the offence is non-imprisonable;
- a custodial sentence if the YRO that is breached is one with an intensive supervision and surveillance requirement, which was imposed for an offence that was imprisonable; and
- the imposition of a DTO for four months for breach of a YRO with intensive supervision and surveillance which was imposed following wilful and persistent breach of an order made for a non-imprisonable offence.

The primary objective when sentencing for breach of a YRO is to ensure that the child or young person completes the requirements imposed by the court.

7.19 If an offender has attained the age of 18 by the first court hearing then breach proceedings must be dealt with by the adult magistrates' court. If the court chooses to revoke the order then its powers are limited to those available to the court at the time of the original sentence.

Commission of further offences during a YRO

7.20 If a child or young person commits an offence whilst subject to a YRO the court can impose any sentence for the new matter, but can only impose a new YRO if they revoke the existing order. Where the court revokes the original order they may re-sentence that matter at the same time as sentencing the new offence.

Breach of a detention and training order (DTO)

7.21 If a child or young person is found to have breached a supervision requirement after release from custody then the court may:
- impose a further period of custody of up to three months or the length of time from the date the breach was committed until the end of the order, **whichever is shorter;**
- impose a further period of supervision of up to three months or the length of time from the date the breach was committed until the end of the order, **whichever is shorter;**
- impose a fine of up to £1,000; or
- take no action.

Even if the offender has attained the age of 18 proceedings for breach of the supervision requirements must be dealt with in the youth court.

Commission of further offences during a DTO

7.22 If a child or young person is found guilty of a further imprisonable offence committed during the currency of the order then the court can impose a further period of detention. This period of detention cannot exceed the period between the date of the new offence and the date of when the original order would have expired.

7.23 This period can be served consecutively or concurrently with any sentence imposed for the new offence and this period should not be taken into account when determining the appropriate length of the sentence for the new offence.

I.2 Robbery

Robbery Guideline

ROBBERY GUIDELINE

> This guideline should be read alongside the *Overarching Principles – Sentencing Children and Young People* definitive guideline which provides comprehensive guidance on the sentencing principles and welfare considerations that the court should have in mind when sentencing children and young people.

The first step in determining the sentence is to assess the seriousness of the offence. This assessment is made by considering the nature of the offence and any aggravating and mitigating factors relating to the offence itself. **The fact that a sentence threshold is crossed does not necessarily mean that that sentence should be imposed.**

STEP ONE
Offence Seriousness – Nature of the offence

The boxes below give **examples** of the type of culpability and harm factors that may indicate that a particular threshold of sentence has been crossed.

A non-custodial sentence* may be the most suitable disposal where one or more of the following factors apply:
Threat or use of minimal force
Little or no physical or psychological harm caused to the victim
Involved through coercion, intimidation or exploitation

A custodial sentence or youth rehabilitation order with intensive supervision and surveillance* or fostering* may be justified where one or more of the following factors apply:
Use of very significant force
Threat or use of a bladed article, firearm or imitation firearm (where produced)
Significant physical or psychological harm caused to the victim

* Where the child or young person appears in the magistrates' court, and the conditions for a compulsory referral order apply, a referral order must be imposed unless the court is considering imposing a discharge, hospital order or custody.

STEP TWO
Offence Seriousness – Aggravating and mitigating factors

To complete the assessment of seriousness the court should consider the aggravating and mitigating factors relevant to the offence.

Aggravating factors

Statutory aggravating factors:

Previous findings of guilt, having regard to a) the **nature** of the offence to which the finding of guilt relates and its **relevance** to the current offence; and b) the **time** that has elapsed since the finding of guilt

Offence committed whilst on bail

Offence motivated by, or demonstrating hostility based on any of the following characteristics or presumed characteristics of the victim: religion, race, disability, sexual orientation or transgender identity

Other aggravating factors (non-exhaustive):

Significant degree of planning

Deliberate humiliation of victim, including but not limited to filming of the offence, deliberately committing the offence before a group of peers with the intention of causing additional distress or circulating details/photos/videos etc of the offence on social media or within peer groups

Threat or use of a weapon other than a bladed article, firearm or imitation firearm (whether produced or not)

Threat to use a bladed article, firearm or imitation firearm (not produced)

Victim is particularly vulnerable due to factors including but not limited to age, mental or physical disability

A leading role where offending is part of a group

Attempt to conceal identity (for example, wearing a balaclava or hood)

Any steps taken to prevent reporting the incident/seeking assistance

High value goods or sums targeted or obtained (includes economic, personal or sentimental)

Restraint, detention or additional degradation of the victim

Mitigating factors (non-exhaustive)

No previous findings of guilt **or** no relevant/recent findings of guilt

Good character and/or exemplary conduct

Participated in offence due to bullying, peer pressure, coercion or manipulation

Remorse, particularly where evidenced by voluntary reparation to the victim

Little or no planning

STEP THREE
Personal mitigation

Having assessed the offence seriousness, the court should then consider the mitigation personal to the child or young person to determine whether a custodial sentence or a community sentence is necessary. The effect of personal mitigation may reduce what would otherwise be a custodial sentence to a non-custodial one, or a community sentence to a different means of disposal.

Personal mitigating factors (non-exhaustive)
Particularly young or immature child or young person (where it affects their responsibility)
Communication or learning disabilities or mental health concerns
Unstable upbringing including but not limited to: • time spent looked after • lack of familial presence or support • disrupted experiences in accommodation or education • exposure to drug/alcohol abuse, familial criminal behaviour or domestic abuse • victim of neglect or abuse, or exposure to neglect or abuse of others • experiences of trauma or loss
Determination and/or demonstration of steps taken to address offending behaviour
Child or young person in education, training or employment

STEP FOUR
Reduction for guilty plea

The court should take account of any potential reduction for a guilty plea in accordance with section 144 of the Criminal Justice Act 2003 and part one, section five of the *Overarching Principles – Sentencing Children and Young People* definitive guideline.

The reduction in sentence for a guilty plea can be taken into account by imposing one type of sentence rather than another; for example:
• by reducing a custodial sentence to a community sentence; or
• by reducing a community sentence to a different means of disposal.
Alternatively the court could reduce the length or severity of any punitive requirements attached to a community sentence.

See the *Overarching Principles – Sentencing Children and Young People* definitive guideline for details of other available sentences including Referral Orders and Reparation Orders.

ROBBERY GUIDELINE

STEP FIVE
Review the sentence

The court must now review the sentence to ensure it is the most appropriate one for the child or young person. This will include an assessment of the likelihood of reoffending and the risk of causing serious harm. A report from the Youth Offending Team may assist.

See the *Overarching Principles – Sentencing Children and Young People* definitive guideline for comprehensive guidance on the sentencing principles and welfare considerations that the court should have in mind when sentencing children and young people, and for the full range of the sentences available to the court.

Referral Orders
In cases where children or young people have offended for the first time and have pleaded guilty to committing an offence which is on the cusp of the custody threshold, YOTs should be encouraged to convene a Youth Offender Panel prior to sentence (sometimes referred to as a "pseudo-panel" or "pre-panel") where the child or young person is asked to attend before a panel and agree an intensive contract. If that contract is placed before the sentencing youth court, the court can then decide whether it is sufficient to move below custody on this occasion. The proposed contract is not something the court can alter in any way; the court will still have to make a decision between referral order and custody but can do so on the basis that if it makes a referral order it can have confidence in what that will entail in the particular case.

The court determines the length of the order but a Referral Order Panel determines the requirements of the order.

Offence seriousness	Suggested length of referral order
Low	• 3 – 5 months
Medium	• 5 – 7 months
High	• 7 – 9 months
Very high	• 10 – 12 months

The YOT may propose certain requirements and the length of these requirements may not correspond to the above table; if the court feels these requirements will best achieve the aims of the youth justice system then they may still be imposed.

Youth Rehabilitation Order (YRO)
The following table sets out the different levels of intensity that are available under a YRO. The level of intensity and the content of the order will depend upon the court's assessment of seriousness.

		Requirements of order
Standard	Low likelihood of re-offending **and** a low risk of serious harm	Primarily seek to repair harm caused through, for example: • reparation; • unpaid work; • supervision; and/or • attendance centre.

		Requirements of order
Enhanced	Medium likelihood of re-offending **or** a medium risk of serious harm	Seek to repair harm caused and to enable help or change through, for example: • supervision; • reparation; • requirement to address behaviour e.g. drug treatment, offending behaviour programme, education programme; and/or • a combination of the above.
Intensive	High likelihood of re-offending **or** a very high risk of serious harm	Seek to ensure the control of and enable help or change for the child or young person through, for example: • supervision; • reparation; • requirement to address behaviour; • requirement to monitor or restrict movement, e.g. prohibited activity, curfew, exclusion or electronic monitoring; and/or • a combination of the above.

YRO with Intensive Supervision and Surveillance (ISS) or YRO with fostering

A YRO with an ISS or fostering requirement can only be imposed where the court is of the opinion that the offence has crossed the custody threshold, and custody is merited.

The YRO with ISS includes an extended activity requirement, a supervision requirement and curfew. The YRO with fostering requires the child or young person to reside with a local authority foster parent for a specified period of up to 12 months.

Custodial Sentences

If a custodial sentence is imposed, the court must state its reasons for being satisfied that the offence is so serious that no other sanction would be appropriate and, in particular, why a YRO with ISS or fostering could not be justified.

Where a custodial sentence is **unavoidable** the length of custody imposed must be the shortest commensurate with the seriousness of the offence. The court may want to consider the equivalent adult guideline in order to determine the appropriate length of the sentence.

If considering the adult guideline, the court may feel it appropriate to apply a sentence broadly within the region of half to two thirds of the appropriate adult sentence for those aged 15 – 17 and allow a greater reduction for those aged under 15. This is only a rough guide and must not be applied mechanistically. The individual factors relating to the offence and the child or young person are of the greatest importance and may present good reason to impose a sentence outside of this range.

I.3 Sexual Offences Act 2003

Sexual Offences Guideline

Sentencing a child or young person for sexual offences involves a number of different considerations from adults. The primary difference is the age and level of maturity. Children and young people are less emotionally developed than adults; offending can arise through inappropriate sexual experimentation; gang or peer group pressure to engage in sexual activity; or a lack of understanding regarding consent, exploitation, coercion and appropriate sexual behaviour.

Below is a non-exhaustive list of factors that illustrate the type of background factors that may have played a part in leading a child or young person to commit an offence of this kind.
- Victim of neglect or abuse (sexual, physical or emotional) or has witnessed the neglect or abuse of another.
- Exposure to pornography or materials which are age inappropriate.
- Involvement in gangs.
- Associated with child sexual exploitation.
- Unstable living or educational arrangements.
- Communication or learning disabilities or mental health concerns.
- Part of a peer group, school or neighbourhood where harmful sexual norms and attitudes go unchallenged.
- A trigger event such as the death of a close relative or a family breakdown.

> This guideline should be read alongside the *Overarching Principles – Sentencing Children and Young People* definitive guideline which provides comprehensive guidance on the sentencing principles and welfare considerations that the court should have in mind when sentencing children and young people.

The first step in determining the sentence is to assess the seriousness of the offence. This assessment is made by considering the nature of the offence and any aggravating and mitigating factors relating to the offence itself. **The fact that a sentence threshold is crossed does not necessarily mean that that sentence should be imposed.**

STEP ONE
Offence Seriousness – Nature of the offence

The boxes below give **examples** of the type of culpability and harm factors that may indicate that a particular threshold of sentence has been crossed.

A non-custodial sentence* may be the most suitable disposal where one or more of the following factors apply:
Any form of non-penetrative sexual activity
Any form of sexual activity (including penetration) without coercion, exploitation or pressure except where there is a significant disparity in age or maturity
Minimal psychological or physical harm caused to the victim

A custodial sentence or youth rehabilitation order with intensive supervision and surveillance* or fostering* may be justified where one or more of the following factors apply:
Any penetrative activity involving coercion, exploitation or pressure
Use or threats of violence against the victim or someone known to the victim
Prolonged detention/sustained incident
Severe psychological or physical harm caused to the victim

* Where the child or young person appears in the magistrates' court, and the conditions for a compulsory referral order apply, a referral order must be imposed unless the court is considering imposing a discharge, hospital order or custody.

STEP TWO
Offence Seriousness – Aggravating and mitigating factors

To complete the assessment of seriousness the court should consider the aggravating and mitigating factors relevant to the offence.

Aggravating factors

Statutory aggravating factors:

Previous findings of guilt, having regard to a) the **nature** of the offence to which the finding of guilt relates and its **relevance** to the current offence; and b) the **time** that has elapsed since the finding of guilt

Offence committed whilst on bail

Offence motivated by, or demonstrating hostility based on any of the following characteristics or presumed characteristics of the victim: religion, race, disability, sexual orientation or transgender identity

Other aggravating factors (non-exhaustive):

Significant degree of planning

Child or young person acts together with others to commit the offence

Use of alcohol/drugs on victim to facilitate the offence

Abuse of trust

Deliberate humiliation of victim, including but not limited to filming of the offence, deliberately committing the offence before a group of peers with the intention of causing additional distress or circulating details/photos/videos etc of the offence on social media or within peer groups

Grooming

Significant disparity of age between the child or young person and the victim (measured chronologically or with reference to level of maturity) (where not taken into account at step one)

Victim is particularly vulnerable due to factors including but not limited to age, mental or physical disability

Any steps taken to prevent reporting the incident/seeking assistance

Pregnancy or STI as a consequence of offence

Blackmail

Use of weapon

Mitigating factors (non-exhaustive)

No previous findings of guilt **or** no relevant/recent findings of guilt

Good character and/or exemplary conduct

Participated in offence due to bullying, peer pressure, coercion or manipulation

Genuine belief that activity was lawful

STEP THREE
Personal mitigation

Having assessed the offence seriousness, the court should then consider the mitigation personal to the child or young person to determine whether a custodial sentence or a community sentence is necessary. The effect of personal mitigation may reduce what would otherwise be a custodial sentence to a non-custodial one, or a community sentence to a different means of disposal.

Personal mitigating factors (non-exhaustive)

Particularly young or immature child or young person (where it affects their responsibility)

Communication or learning disabilities or mental health concerns

Unstable upbringing including but not limited to:-
- time spent looked after
- lack of familial presence or support
- disrupted experiences in accommodation or education
- exposure to drug/alcohol abuse, familial criminal behaviour or domestic abuse
- exposure by others to pornography or sexually explicit materials
- victim of neglect or abuse, or exposure to neglect or abuse of others
- experiences of trauma or loss

Determination and/or demonstration of steps taken to address offending behaviour

Strong prospect of rehabilitation

Child or young person in education, training or employment

STEP FOUR
Reduction for guilty plea

The court should take account of any potential reduction for a guilty plea in accordance with section 144 of the Criminal Justice Act 2003 and part one, section five of the *Overarching Principles – Sentencing Children and Young People* definitive guideline.

The reduction in sentence for a guilty plea can be taken into account by imposing one type of sentence rather than another; for example:
- by reducing a custodial sentence to a community sentence; or
- by reducing a community sentence to a different means of disposal.

Alternatively the court could reduce the length or severity of any punitive requirements attached to a community sentence.

See the *Overarching Principles – Sentencing Children and Young People* definitive guideline for details of other available sentences including Referral Orders and Reparation Orders.

STEP FIVE
Review the sentence

The court must now review the sentence to ensure it is the most appropriate one for the child or young person. This will include an assessment of the likelihood of reoffending and the risk of causing serious harm. A report from the Youth Offending Team may assist.

See the *Overarching Principles – Sentencing Children and Young People* definitive guideline for comprehensive guidance on the sentencing principles and welfare considerations that the court should have in mind when sentencing children and young people, and for the full range of the sentences available to the court.

Referral Orders

In cases where children or young people have offended for the first time and have pleaded guilty to committing an offence which is on the cusp of the custody threshold, YOTs should be encouraged to convene a Youth Offender Panel prior to sentence (sometimes referred to as a "pseudo-panel" or "pre-panel") where the child or young person is asked to attend before a panel and agree an intensive contract. If that contract is placed before the sentencing youth court, the court can then decide whether it is sufficient to move below custody on this occasion. The proposed contract is not something the court can alter in any way; the court will still have to make a decision between referral order and custody but can do so on the basis that if it makes a referral order it can have confidence in what that will entail in the particular case.

The court determines the length of the order but a Referral Order Panel determines the requirements of the order.

Offence seriousness	Suggested length of referral order
Low	• 3 – 5 months
Medium	• 5 – 7 months
High	• 7 – 9 months
Very high	• 10 – 12 months

The YOT may propose certain requirements and the length of these requirements may not correspond to the above table; if the court feels these requirements will best achieve the aims of the youth justice system then they may still be imposed.

Youth Rehabilitation Order (YRO)

The following table sets out the different levels of intensity that are available under a Youth Rehabilitation Order. The level of intensity and the content of the order will depend upon the court's assessment of seriousness.

		Requirements of order
Standard	Low likelihood of re-offending **and** a low risk of serious harm	Primarily seek to repair harm caused through, for example: • reparation; • unpaid work; • supervision; and/or • attendance centre.

		Requirements of order
Enhanced	Medium likelihood of re-offending **or** a medium risk of serious harm	Seek to repair harm caused and to enable help or change through, for example: • supervision; • reparation; • requirement to address behaviour e.g. drug treatment, offending behaviour programme, education programme; and/or • a combination of the above.
Intensive	High likelihood of re-offending **or** a very high risk of serious harm	Seek to ensure the control of and enable help or change for the child or young person through, for example: • supervision; • reparation; • requirement to address behaviour; • requirement to monitor or restrict movement, e.g. prohibited activity, curfew, exclusion or electronic monitoring; and/or • a combination of the above.

YRO with Intensive Supervision and Surveillance (ISS) or YRO with Fostering
A YRO with an ISS or fostering requirement can only be imposed where the court is of the opinion that the offence has crossed the custody threshold and custody is merited.

The YRO with ISS includes an extended activity requirement, a supervision requirement and curfew. The YRO with fostering requires the child or young person to reside with a local authority foster parent for a specified period of up to 12 months.

Custodial Sentences
If a custodial sentence is imposed, the court must state its reasons for being satisfied that the offence is so serious that no other sanction would be appropriate and, in particular, why a YRO with ISS or fostering could not be justified.

Where a custodial sentence is **unavoidable** the length of custody imposed must be the shortest commensurate with the seriousness of the offence. The court may want to consider the equivalent adult guideline in order to determine the appropriate length of the sentence.

If considering the adult guideline, the court may feel it appropriate to apply a sentence broadly within the region of half to two thirds of the appropriate adult sentence for those aged 15 – 17 and allow a greater reduction for those aged under 15. This is only a rough guide and must not be applied mechanistically. The individual factors relating to the offence and the child or young person are of the greatest importance and may present good reason to impose a sentence outside of this range.

SEXUAL OFFENCES GUIDELINE

Appendix J

Sentencing cases compendium

J.1 Robbery (also see Appendix I.2)

R v H (R) [2016] EWCA Crim 2064, CA

The defendant was 15 at the time of the offence. The victim was on his way home after attending a local public house when he came across three males, including the defendant and his co-defendant (S) and a female. He had some beer with them. The victim invited them back to his home to drink the beer. They all went to the victim's home and continued to drink for a few hours. S went into the kitchen and returned, carrying the victim's medicine box, which he put under his coat and then left the property and passed the medicine box to someone in the car before returning. They all carried on drinking for another hour or so. S then unplugged the television. The victim asked what he was doing and told him to put it back. The defendant and an unknown individual who was there punched the victim to the eye and the jaw area. The defendant went into the kitchen and returned with a black handled knife which he brandished at the victim. All three males then left the property with the co-defendant S carrying the television. Just before leaving, the defendant picked up the victim's house keys and snatched a mobile phone out of his hand. The victim suffered bruising to his eyes and his cheek and a cut on his nose. In sentencing the defendant, the judge said that the aggravating features of the case were the vulnerability of the victim, who was left even more exposed after his necessary medication was taken away by the co-defendant (S). The defendant had applied actual violence and produced a knife. The judge considered the Sentencing Council's Guidelines and particularly the new sentencing guidelines which applied only to those of 18 years and over. So, although the new guidelines did not apply, the court took note that for those aged 18 or over the sentence for what is plainly a Category 2A case involving a knife had a starting point of eight years' custody with a range of six to ten years, before any aggravating features and the vulnerability of the victim were taken into account. The old guideline, as it applied to those under 18, was very different. It proposed for offences in which a weapon is produced, used to threaten and results in injury, the starting point of only three years' detention, with a range of one to six years. But it was not, said the learned judge, that straightforward. The heading to page 14 of that guideline, he observed, listed the types of robberies to which it applied, and they did not include robbery in a dwelling, which of course this was. The judge said that the aggravating features of this robbery were similar to those listed for the adult co-defendant (S). The defendant's role was worse than S's because he had punched the vulnerable victim and produced a knife. Furthermore, the judge took into account his previous findings of guilt for dishonesty and violence and the fact that he had served a custodial sentence previously. The defendant's mitigation, youth, genuine remorse, difficult early life and guilty pleas were taken into account. The PSR said that his previous convictions would indicate that he was at a high risk of re-offending but the frequency of his offending had reduced indicating that the risk was also reducing. The PSR recommended a youth rehabilitation order, with a supervision requirement, together with an electronically monitored curfew. He was also suitable for an intensive supervision and surveillance disposal. The judge imposed four years' detention under PCC(S)A 2000, s 91 for the offence of robbery. The defendant appealed against his sentence. The Court of Appeal found the sentence of four years' detention manifestly excessive, particularly in view of the defendant's age and circumstances. It was said that the sentencing judge took too high a starting point thereby arriving at an excessive sentence. The sentence of four years' detention was quashed and replaced with a two-year detention and training order.

R v JB [2016] EWCA Crim 1350, CA

The defendant was 14 years old at the time of the offences and was charged with two offences of attempted robbery and an offence of robbery, possession of a bladed article and theft. In relation to attempted robbery the defendant and another youth entered a shop with hoods pulled over their heads. The owner asked them to put their hoods down; they did not. They approached the counter and one of the youths (not the defendant) pulled out a knife with a five-inch blade from his coat and pointed it at the shop owner. They demanded that he gave them money and cigarettes. The shop owner then produced an axe from behind the counter and chased them out of the shop, during which time, still within the shop, the defendant also produced a smaller knife before leaving the shop. The shop owner followed them outside and then the police were notified. The defendant was apprehended nearby after trying to escape from the officers. Whilst on bail the defendant stole an I-Pad belonging to the brother of a friend of the defendant into whose house he had been invited. He sold that I-Pad for £20. The next offence was the second attempted robbery and the possession of a bladed article. The victim (WM) who was 15 years old and his 14-year-old friend were sitting at bus stop when the defendant walked past with his hood up. He stared at them. He then approached them and accused them of laughing at him. The victim said that they were laughing at something that had happened at school but he did not accept that. He told them: 'Do you know who I am? I am a big hard lad'. He told them his name. He asked for their names and said: 'Give me your money and nothing will happen.' They said they had no money, to which he replied: 'Second choice. Two choices then.' He produced a knife with a 3 to 4-inch blade which he pointed at the boys. He said he was either going to stab them there or pull them into the bushes, search them and beat them up. They were terrified and the 14-year-old decided to go with the defendant but WM noticed some adults in a car nearby and went to ask for help. The defendant ran off and the police were called. The final offence of robbery was also committed by the defendant when he was on bail. The victim (RB) was a young person. He was in a basement car park. The defendant was also there with others and called him over using his nickname. The group appeared to RB to be friendly at first. He was offered a smoke. He felt obliged to accept and then he went with the defendant and another of the group to a quiet place behind the bus station. The defendant told him to hand over his tobacco. He complied, being frightened. The defendant then told him to hand over his I-Phone. He refused and the defendant snatched the phone. He and his companion then ran off and RB approached some passing members of the public for help. The police were called. When interviewed the defendant said that another youth was responsible for stealing the phone. The defendant had no previous convictions. He had, however, a caution for offences which were committed about six months before the first offence. The caution was for resisting or obstructing a police officer for an offence of threatening or abusive words or behaviour and failing to comply with a direction excluding him from a certain area. The defendant entered early guilty pleas before the Youth Court in relation to one of the attempted robberies and to the charge of robbery but subsequently pleaded guilty to the other attempted robbery on the day of trial. The Youth Court said that the Crown Court should have the power to sentence the defendant to detention under PCC(S)A 2000, s 91 and committed him for sentence under PCC(S)A 2000, s 3(b). They also committed an offence of a possession of a bladed article and theft under s 3(b) in error. The PSR indicated that he showed remorse for some offences and that he limited his responsibility in some of the offences. His offending behaviour was linked to his drug use and peer group. The report indicated that his behaviour had become more problematic as his sister's health had deteriorated. She was at the time suffering from terminal cancer (and died two days after the sentence was imposed). The defendant also had had a problematic childhood and had been exposed to significant domestic violence. He was assessed as posing a high risk of offending and a high risk of serious harm. He showed limited victim empathy. The author of the report invited the sentencing court to consider dangerousness, but gave as an alternative to a custodial sentence a youth rehabilitation order. The defendant received a total of three years' detention under PCC(S) 2000, s 91 for the two offences of attempted robbery and one offence of robbery. No separate penalty was imposed for offences of having an article with a blade in a public place and theft. A victim surcharge order in the sum of £20 was also made. The defendant appealed the sentence. The Court of Appeal said there were two sentencing guidelines which were relevant – the Sentencing Council's Guideline *Overarching Principle for Sentencing Youths* and the *Robbery Guideline* with specific reference to young offenders. It was accepted that the attempted robbery and robbery in which knives were produced and used to threaten both came within the middle category with a starting point for an offender aged 17 pleading not guilty of three years' detention with a range of one to six years. It was said that for the judge to pass a custodial sentence he would have had to have found that the defendant was a persistent offender within the meaning of that term PCC(S) 2000, s 100(2). Consideration was given to the guidance on persistent offenders in the *Overarching Principles for Sentencing Youths* and *R v AS* [2001] 1 Cr App R (S) and it was said that there was no doubt that the custody threshold was comfortably passed. The Court of Appeal said the real issue was whether having regard to the number and seriousness of the offences a term of detention of three years gave sufficient weight to the age, the relative good character of the defendant and to the personal mitigation advanced on his behalf. The aggravating factors were that some of the offences were committed whilst on bail; pre-planned; and a knife was used. However, it was held that a sentence of three years' detention was manifestly excessive having regard to the defendant's age and lack of previous convictions and in the light of the mitigation set out in the pre-sentence report. The three-year DTO was substituted with a two-year DTO for each offence to run concurrently.

R v Gibson (Robert) [2016] EWCA Crim 1261, CA

This was an offence which was committed at night against a victim who was alone, by a group of three young people. The victim had been working late in London and caught a late train home intending to go to Canterbury where he lived. He fell asleep on the train and woke up in Margate, which is where the defendant (who was 17 years old) and his associates were. They saw him in the railway station and they observed that he had gone to a cash machine because he needed to get some money to pay for a taxi to take him from Margate back to his home. They followed him for some distance. He became aware of the fact that he was being followed and rapidly appreciated that he was in danger of being assaulted. The defendant's younger brother pushed past him, striking him with his elbow but not causing any serious injury and then the group of three frisked the victim, relieving him of his wallet, which contained £85 which was never recovered. The victim was afraid and co-operated because he feared that otherwise violence would be used against him. The offence fell under the 2006 *Robbery* Guideline in the lowest category, as indeed it did in the new guideline published by the Sentencing Council which applied to offenders of 18 and over sentenced on or after 1 April 2016. It was the new guideline which the judge was required to follow rather than the 2006 Guideline in the case of the defendant, but the old guideline continued to apply to his brother. The 2006 Guideline contains a category for an offence which includes the threat or use of minimal force and removal of property. The starting point was a community order, the sentence range was a community order up to a 12 months' detention and training order. The defendant was 17 years old and of previous good character at the time. He and his brother pleaded guilty and were entitled to full credit. The defendant was sentenced to 10 months' detention in a young offender institution. His younger brother was sentenced to a detention and training order of 10 months'. Those sentences were calculated on the basis of a starting point in the case of the defendant of 15 months and a starting point in the case of his brother of 12 months. Full credit for the plea in each case was allowed of one third. In the case of defendant, a period of 30 days spent under a qualifying curfew was ordered to count against that sentence under the provisions of the Criminal Justice Act 2003, s 240A. The defendant appealed against his sentence. The Court of Appeal said that new guidelines for the lowest category of street robbery (category 3C) had a starting point of one year's custody and a range of a high-level community order to three years' custody in the case of an adult and the sentence should have reflected the youth of the offender at the time of the offence. It was said that the judge should have approached the category in the guidelines with that principle in mind. The Appeal Court found that it appeared the judge did not have a copy of the new guideline, at least at the start of the hearing, and his comment that custodial sentences must follow in all cases of this kind suggests he failed to follow it. The Court of Appeal found the sentence imposed on the defendant to be manifestly excessive and said the appropriate starting point in this case would have been one of nine months' detention in a young offender institution which should have been discounted by one third to reflect the early plea and an appropriate sentence would therefore have been one of six months' detention in a young offender institution. The original sentence was quashed and six months' detention was substituted with 32 days of the qualifying curfew to count towards that.

R v W [2014] EWCA Crim 718, CA

The defendant was 16 years old at the time of the offence and his co-defendant (Benjamin Grimshaw) was aged 23. The defendant and the victim resided at hostel accommodation. The victim telephoned the defendant. He had paid him £25 for some cannabis and wanted to know if he could collect what had been ordered. They arranged to meet at a nearby cycle track. The victim cycled to the agreed location. The defendant arrived with Grimshaw. The defendant told him to go to a nearby alleyway, where the victim presumed the drugs would be handed over. When he arrived in the alleyway the victim was told by the defendant to get off his bicycle. His jacket was grabbed and he was pushed backwards and pinned up against a nearby fence by Grimshaw. Grimshaw told him to empty his pockets and to pass their contents to the defendant. He did so. His BlackBerry and his wallet were taken. The defendant then punched him on the left cheek and the victim fell to the ground. Grimshaw punched him twice to the face, causing him significant pain. He tried to protect himself while he was on the ground by covering his head with his arms, but the defendant punched him a further three times. The victim heard Grimshaw tell the defendant that he wanted to leave. The victim went to a friend's house. He was bleeding at the nose and mouth. He had a deep cut on his forehead and the left side of his face was blackened and swollen. His right eye and cheekbone were also swollen. He told the friend that he had been kicked in the stomach as he lay on the ground. The matter was reported to the police and he was taken to hospital. The defendant went to a pre-booked appointment with a charitable organisation and began to brag about beating up the victim. The defendant was arrested the day after the offence. He denied having committed it. Grimshaw was also arrested. He, too, denied the offence and indicated an alibi of having been with the defendant somewhere else. The defendant continued to deny the offence until he attended an identification procedure and was duly identified. The defendant had been before the courts on two previous occasions for six offences, including burglary of a dwelling-house and criminal damage offences. The defendant pleaded guilty to one charge of robbery and his co-defendant also pleaded guilty to the same offence. The reports (which included an addendum pre-sentence report) indicated that the defendant's offending behaviour began when he became estranged from his family following his parents' separation and his father's diagnosis with a serious illness. He became homeless. He was housed by the Children's Services authorities in accommodation of last resort used predominantly to house adult offenders. His co-defendant was also living at the same property. The report recognised an emerging pattern of offending as well and an escalation in its seriousness. The previous sentence imposed on 16 August 2013 was recorded, and the Youth Offending Team Officer who had supervised the order then imposed, said that the defendant had complied fully and that his engagement with it had been exemplary. It stated that the defendant recognised the link between his offending and the peer influence to which he had become subject. YOT attributed all these events to the influence of others, the defendant's youth, his immaturity, his low self-esteem, and some involvement with unlawful substances. The defendant had expressed remorse and regret, and wanted to apologise to the victim for what had happened. It was reported that he had since learnt how to manage cannabis misuse. His mother, who the officer was told had received him back into her home, reported an improvement in his overall demeanour and behaviour following his return. He was assessed to be at 'medium' risk of re-offending and of causing serious harm to others and it was said he could be appropriately managed in the community, enabling the Youth Offending Team to continue to manage his sentence and to motivate him positively. YOT recommended a 12-month Youth Rehabilitation Order with requirements of intensive supervision and surveillance, extended activity and curfew. The addendum report informed the court that, shortly before sentence, the defendant had obtained full-time employment. The judge sentence the defendant to an 18-month Detention and Training order and his co-defendant to two and a half years' imprisonment. The defendant appealed against his sentence on the basis it was excessive as the judge had failed to recognise the defendant's particular mitigation and insufficient regard was paid to the particular requirements of the *Robbery* guideline that requires a court to consider the welfare of a child offender and the aim of preventing re-offending. The Court of Appeal held that although the judge had correctly addressed the general tenor of the guideline on sentences for robbery of this kind, as they appeared in the grid on page 14 of the Sentencing Council's Guideline document, inadequate regard was paid to the points made in paragraphs 5 and 6 and 13 and 14 on pages 12 and 13 of the guideline document. The Appeal Court allowed the appeal by quashing the sentence imposed in the Crown Court and substituting in its place a Youth Rehabilitation Order.

R v M [2011] EWCA Crim 2897, CA

The defendant was 15 at time of the offence. The victim was using her mobile to text a friend when the defendant put his hand on her left shoulder and took her phone. She tried to hold onto it but was unable to do so. The defendant and his co-defendant sold the phone. The defendant was charged with robbery. The defendant accepted the prosecution version of events and the PSR noted that although he had a good relationship with both parents, his mother had been very ill over the previous year and had been in and out of hospital. His father spent a lot of time looking after his mother, resulting in him lacking boundaries and associating with pro criminal peers. He was polite and respectful and was in mainstream education preparing for his GCSEs. His teachers were aware of his vulnerability and were willing to put in extra levels of support to ensure he reached his potential. The defendant expressed remorse for his behaviour and empathy for his victim. A youth rehabilitation order or referral order was recommended, with requirements, as a custodial sentence might mean that he would be unable to take his GCSEs. The judge in passing sentence said the fact that the phone was sold within a short period of time and the defendant committed the offence to be thought of as one of the 'big boys' were aggravating factors. The defendant was given credit for a guilty plea and his age and the fact there had been no physical injury, but concluded that there was no alternative to a custodial sentence. The defendant was sentenced to a 6-month DTO. The co-defendant (aged 18) received a 12-month community order with a requirement of 120 hours' unpaid work for an offence of handling stolen goods. The two defendants were initially jointly charged with robbery. The defendant appealed against his sentence. The Court of Appeal disagreed with the sentencing judge in that there was minimal force used for the removal of property. Consideration was also given to the Sentencing Council's guidelines on *Robbery* and *Overarching Principles – Sentencing Youths*, which at paragraph 11.5 suggests that a custodial sentence must only be imposed as a measure of last resort. Pending this appeal, the defendant appeared at Brent Youth Court who sentenced him to a further 6-month DTO. The Court of Appeal deemed the initial sentence as wrong in principle as a non-custodial sentence should have been passed. The fact that the defendant served 2 months of the custodial term was taken into account and a youth rehabilitation order with 4 months' supervision was imposed in order to get the defendant's life back on track and to prevent him from further harming the public. In relation to the subsequent sentence passed by the Youth Court it was said that the fact that the appeal had been allowed to the extent indicated was a matter which could bear significantly on either an appeal or a review of the Youth Court's sentence.

R v S [2011] EWCA Crim 2860, CA

The defendant was 15 years old when one evening, in the company of two older young people, aged 21 and 19, he approached another group, asked to borrow a mobile phone to make a call and, when refused, started a fight with them, in the course of which he kneed the victim in the face and punched him. Forty-minutes later the defendant and his group approached a lone youth. They took his mobile phone from his pocket and then punched him twice in the face. They then stole his wallet, earphones and a house key. The two older defendants each received a sentence of 32 months' imprisonment. The defendant pleaded guilty to attempted robbery and robbery and was sentenced to an 8-month DTO, for each offence, to run consecutively (16 months in total). The defendant appealed against his sentence. It was argued that he was remorseful, came from a decent and supportive home and his parents had grounded him since the offence. He had not been in trouble before. The PSR had recommended a referral order and the defendant was assessed as constituting a low risk of re-offending. It was pointed out by the Court of Appeal that the SC's guidelines on *Robbery* have a separate section on young offenders. The robbery seemed to be towards the top of 'level 1' (threat or use of minimal force and removal of property) or at the borderline with 'level 2' (force is used which results in injury to the victim). The range for 'level 1' being 'community order – 12 months DTO' and the range for 'level 2' being '1–6 years' detention'. These figures assumed a 17-year-old pleading not guilty, and S was a 15-year-old who pleaded guilty and was presumably under the influence of the older two offenders. However, there was also the attempted robbery which had to be taken into account. The Court of Appeal said that a custodial sentence was inevitable, but in view of the circumstances the two terms of detention would be ordered to run concurrently rather than consecutively, making 8-months in all.

R v REJF [2011] EWCA Crim 2812, CA

The defendant was 16 years old at the date of the offence. She was out with two other girls at night and had been drinking. The victim who was out alone had not been drinking. She was attacked by the three girls, one of them wielded a broken bottle, and one of them shouted that the victim was a 'Paki'. The victim's handbag was snatched and abuse was shouted. The victim was threatened with a bottle and knocked to the ground. She was kicked, and the three defendants ran off laughing. The defendant came from a good family and had no previous convictions. It was said she had changed her ways and had stopped drinking. The defendant pleaded guilty at the first opportunity to robbery and was sentenced to an 18-month DTO. Her co-defendant who was of the same age received the same sentence and the third female was never apprehended. The defendant appealed against her sentence. The Court of Appeal said that: 'The price has to be paid. Contrition is a start but it is also wholly right that there should be proper punishment. The wickedness of what was done can be brought home by serving the sentence. The sentence cannot be faulted'. The appeal was dismissed.

R v PF [2010] EWCA Crim 2624, CA

The defendant (aged 17 at the time of the offences) committed eleven street robberies with others, but was largely charged on his own for the majority of them. He admitted the offences in interview, which mainly consisted of young vulnerable white males being targeted. Items such as jewellery, iPods and mobile phones were taken. In respect of ten of those robberies he entered guilty pleas and was remanded for a PSR. Subsequently he came before the judge at the Crown Court with others and pleaded guilty to robbery. In relation to this offence the defendant with others approached the victim (aged 18), who was walking home from school, listening to his iPod. From the group the defendant and his co-defendant, Lafta, (aged 18) stood in front of the victim and one of the others took the headphones. Lafta stood in front of the victim, demanded to be shown the iPod, and threatened to punch him in the face if he did not do so. The victim was extremely scared and did not resist when Lafta grabbed the iPod from his hand. The victim told the defendant that he would do anything to get the iPod back. The defendant said he would give him his iPod back if he gave him his chain. The victim gave the chain to the defendant but his iPod was not returned. The defendant had no previous convictions, although he had received cautions for a number of significant matters: two for using racially abusive threatening or insulting words or behaviour, and for criminal damage. The PSR described the defendant as reserved and quiet, the defendant's father having a terminal illness, frank admissions about his involvement in the offence, remorse, that he profited little from them, and that following his arrest he abruptly realised the enormity of what he had become involved in. In passing sentence the judge identified the wickedness of the offences: the targeting of lone white individuals on a racial basis; it was a group robbery; the robbery contained a number of aggravating factors, particularly to do with the level of threat and the number involved. The judge did make the point that the magistrates should if at all possible commit the remaining offences to the Crown Court so that all offences could be dealt with together. Unfortunately, this did not happen and the Youth Court sentenced the defendant to various terms of DTO, some concurrent and some consecutive, which resulted in a total of 18 months' DTO. At the Crown Court the defendant with his co-defendant was sentenced to an 8-month DTO to be served consecutively to the 18-month DTO already passed by the Youth Court, totalling a 26-month DTO. The co-defendants included Rohaan Lafta, who was sentenced to 9 months' detention in a young offender institution for the same robbery; a juvenile, O, who was given a 6-month DTO; another juvenile, B, who was given a Youth Rehabilitation Order with 18 months' supervision and a curfew; and another in respect of whom no evidence was offered. The judge referred to the defendant's father's illness but observed that that was no excuse for what he did and was satisfied that a consecutive sentence was appropriate. The defendant appealed against his sentence on the basis that it should have been concurrent and not consecutive, having regard to totality and no previous convictions. The Appeal Court held that the judge passed a consecutive 8-month DTO, which added to the pre-existing sentence of 18 months, gave a total a 26-month DTO, which was beyond the possible maximum DTO as per PCC(S)A 2000, s 101(1). The Court of

Appeal by operation of statute, remitted the extra 2 months. The Court of Appeal agreed that the robbery was one of a series and should have been dealt with together with the others. There was no good reason for the magistrates not to follow the indication of the judge in suggesting that the matter should be remitted to the Crown Court. The Court of Appeal held that for a 17-year-old with some personal mitigation and with no previous convictions a sentence of 18 months DTO would be sufficient. Accordingly, the existing sentence was quashed and a 6-month DTO was substituted which was to be served concurrently with the other sentence being served by the defendant.

R v Raithley [2009] EWCA Crim 1854, CA

The defendant was 17 years old at the time of the offence and 18 when he was sentenced. The victim was walking through the city centre at night when he was accosted by two men wearing crash helmets. One ran up behind him and pressed what he thought to be a blade to his neck. He was told to hand over his stuff and was threatened with being stabbed if he did not do so. The victim thought that a knife was being held to his neck throughout the incident, which left a red mark. One of the men searched his pockets. A camera and a mobile phone were taken. Their value was about £400 in total. One of the robbers dropped a mobile phone. This was traced back to the defendant who was also the owner of a motor scooter which had been observed in the area. He was later confronted by the police who accused him of being one of the robbers. He burst into tears and admitted the offence. A Stanley knife was recovered from his bedroom. The defendant pleaded guilty at the first opportunity to the charge of robbery. He had no previous convictions. There were positive testimonials to his good character, including a petition signed by over 50 local people. He had a troubled family life, his mother and grandfather had died and he had a difficult relationship with his father. The defendant had no problems with alcohol or drugs, gained some GCSEs and an apprenticeship in carpentry and had completed a two-year college course. He claimed that he had severed his links with the gang. The PSR assessed him as posing a low risk of re-offending. The judge took into account the Sentencing Guidelines Council's guideline that where a weapon is used to threaten the victim the recommended starting point for a 17-year-old pleading not guilty is 3 years' detention. The judge gave full credit for the early guilty plea but took a very serious view of those who carry knives, still more when they go on to use them to commit robbery and therefore imposed detention for 2 years. The Court of Appeal reaffirmed that this was a serious offence and that custody was inevitable but taking into account the substantial amount of personal mitigation in this case (the defendant cutting ties to his former associates, the personal references and his commitment to education and training) and substituted a sentence of 15 months' detention.

R v Richard Brown [2008] EWCA Crim 2451, CA

The defendant who was aged 17 on sentence and another two offenders approached the victim and asked him what type of phone he had. The victim showed them his phone at which point the defendant noticed the victim's wallet. He said he only had a couple of pounds in it. This was challenged until it became apparent that he was in possession of £50. The defendant tried to rob the victim, who resisted. He told the victim that if he did not let go that he would stab him and appeared to fiddle in his pockets as if to demonstrate that he had a knife in his possession. The defendant then threatened to head butt the victim, at which point he stopped struggling and the wallet was snatched from him. All three offenders then ran off. The defendant and one other were arrested and they pleaded guilty at the first opportunity to robbery. The defendant had previous convictions which included a robbery and an attempted robbery when he was aged 11 years. The PSR brought to the court's attention a deprived, neglected and abusive childhood.

His recent record, however, revealed significant and, in the author's view, quite impressive steps to improve himself and to avoid offending. The defendant received a 12-month DTO. The co-defendant appeared on a different occasion and received a suspended sentence of 8 months' detention for robbery and 4 months' detention consecutive for the offence of witness intimidation, together with an unpaid work requirement. On appeal reference was made to the definitive guideline for sentencing in the case of robbery and pointed out that this was a low-level mugging ('level 1') and therefore the starting point would be a community order and the sentencing range up to 12 months' detention and training. The Appeal Court acknowledged that there were two aggravating features in particular, the threat to use a weapon and the offence being committed by more than one offender. The co-defendant was two years older and he too had significant previous convictions but his record was not quite as bad as the defendant. Having regard to the positive features of the defendant's recent history and the co-defendant's sentence, an 8-month DTO was substituted.

R v B and Another [2008] All ER (D) 347 (Jul), CA

The defendants drove around at night and robbed two teenage victims (aged 16 and 18) of a mobile telephone and some cash. The defendants were charged with and pleaded guilty to, two offences of robbery. The defendants were effectively of good character. The judge gave them full credit for their guilty pleas and they both received 16 months' detention concurrent on each charge. The Court of Appeal upheld the appeals and substituted 12 months' detention in a young offender institution in respect of the first defendant and the second defendant who was 17 years old received a 12-month DTO. The court said that the offences fell within 'level 1' of the relevant definitive Sentencing Guidelines Council's guideline so that the starting point was one year, with a third off for a guilty plea. Robbery was a violent offence and community penalties were not deemed appropriate.

R (on the application of M) v Burnley and Pendle Magistrates' Court [2007] All ER (D) 357 (Oct), Div Court

The defendant who was 15 years old, with two others robbed a 17-year-old victim with learning difficulties of his mobile phone at knifepoint late one evening. The defendants had been wearing hoods or disguises. The defendant was charged with robbery and was of previous good character. The justices had regard to the test set out in previous authorities, and to the criteria set out in the Sentencing Guidelines Council's definitive guidelines. They considered the offence to be a 'level 2' robbery for the purposes of those guidelines, and determined that there was a real prospect that the defendant would receive a sentence of 2 years' detention or more. They committed the defendant for trial, and he applied for judicial review. It was held that the decision to decline jurisdiction was not wrong, as this was a 'level 2' robbery so there was a real prospect that the defendant would receive a sentence in excess of 2 years.

R v M [2007] All ER (D) 331 (Mar), CA

The defendant, who was a 15-year-old girl, jointly with another girl (aged 17), tried to steal two 16-year-old girls' handbags and threatened one of the victims with a lock knife. The defendant was arrested and pleaded guilty to two charges of robbery. She had previous convictions and a difficult background. She had responded positively to an intensive surveillance and supervision programme, which had been a condition of her bail for a previous offence. She was sentenced to an 18-month DTO on each charge to run concurrently. Her co-defendant, who also pleaded guilty to two charges of robbery and had no previous convictions, was sentenced to an 8-month DTO.

The defendant appealed against her sentence due to the disparity between her sentence and that of her co-defendant. The Court of Appeal looked at the mitigating factors, such as her youth, her difficult family background; her positive response to the intensive surveillance and supervision programme; and her good progress in detention. It followed that, in the light of all of the circumstances, and the fact that the defendant and co-defendant had been charged jointly, and had both taken part in a pre-meditated joint enterprise, the difference of 10 months between the sentences for the defendant and her co-defendant, was greater than could be justified. Accordingly, the sentence passed on the defendant was too long. The sentence of an 18-month DTO was quashed and substituted by a 12-month DTO.

R v J [2006] All ER (D) 151 (Oct), CA

The 17-year-old defendant was with two others. They pushed the 16-year-old victim into an alley, kicked and punched her and stole an MP3 player, a mobile phone and £20. Although the defendant at one stage did tell the others to stop, after the attack she put the victim into an arm lock and warned her not to talk about the incident. The victim was very distressed, and sustained a fractured jaw, cuts and scratches. Defendant pleaded guilty to robbery on the basis that she had been the look-out and support but had not herself used violence against the victim. The defendant was of previous good character. The PSR assessed the defendant as posing a low risk of offending and stated that the defendant was remorseful having acted out of a misguided loyalty to the co-defendants. Her personality had been affected by alcohol and occasional cannabis misuse. She was otherwise a caring, but easily led person. The defendant was sentenced to a 6-month DTO. She appealed against sentence. The Court of Appeal said that the offence was very nasty and a custodial sentence could not be avoided but bearing in mind the defendant's previous good character, the limited nature of her involvement, and her personality, a sentence of a minimum term would have been appropriate; a 4-month DTO was substituted.

R v M [2006] All ER (D) 21 (Oct), CA

The 15-year-old defendant and two others approached two males and robbed them of cash and their mobile telephones. He twice punched one of the victims in the face. He pleaded guilty to two charges of robbery and had previous convictions for violence. The PSR reported that the defendant felt no empathy towards the victim, believed stealing 'was no big thing' and hit the victim because he resisted. The report assessed him as presenting a high risk of harm and a high risk of re-offending. The judge imposed a sentence of detention for public protection with a minimum term of 22 months, taking into account the time spent on remand. On appeal against sentence, the Court of Appeal said that the judge had rightly held that the defendant posed a significant risk of harm to members of the public occasioned by the commission by him of further specified offences, by exhibiting pride in his violent behaviour. Although the sentence of detention for public protection remained, the minimum term was reduced from 22 months to 16 months.

R (on the application of S) v Central Herts Youth Court; R (on the application of C) v Croydon Youth Court; R (on the application of S) v Croydon Youth Court [2006] All ER (D) 49 (Oct), Div Court

Defendant (S1) was 17 years old. The defendants pulled their hats down and pulled their scarves over their faces and approached the victims. They demanded bikes and mobile telephones. The defendant (S1) was carrying a claw hammer but apart from the grabbing of one person's wrist no physical violence was used. S1 was said to have taken telephones from the hands of the two victims. He was charged with two offences of robbery and two offences of assault with intent to rob. The defendant, S1, was also charged with possession of an offensive weapon (the claw hammer). The Youth Court found that the offences amounted to grave crimes so as to justify committal to the Crown Court for trial. S1 applied for judicial review. Defendant (C) was 15 years old and defendant (S2) was 16 years old. They were jointly charged with assault with intent to rob. They approached the victim who was 14 years old and asked if she had any money. C then asked some boys who were watching whether they wanted to see some blood before taking the victim's walkman and £5. When they all got on a bus S2 sat beside the victim and asked her for her mobile telephone, which she refused so S2 her hit her about the head. The victim was also detained on the bus. C did not use violence but she waved an iron bar around. The Youth Court committed C and S2 to the Crown Court for trial. They applied for judicial review. None of the defendants had previous convictions. The Divisional Court dismissed the applications on the grounds that each offence was within 'level 2' in the Sentencing Guidelines Council's sentencing guidelines. The starting point was 3 to 6 years' DTO due to a weapon being produced or use of force and injury to the victim. Targeting a vulnerable victim and joint enterprise were also aggravating factors which meant that the justices' could treat the offences as falling within a higher level.

Attorney General's References Nos 102 and 103 of 2006 [2006] EWCA Crim 3247, CA

The defendant was 16 years old. He approached the victim in the street, produced small knife and demanded money. He pressed the knife against the victim's throat and another offender (31 years old) then joined in. They forced the victim to take them to his home, where they ransacked the premises and stole items (DVDs, CDs, a mobile telephone and a PlayStation). The victim was punched twice in the mouth, causing a cut lip. Some of the stolen property was recovered. The defendant entered a guilty plea but on a basis and after a *Newton* hearing the judge accepted the victim's account. The defendant had four previous convictions for burglary and theft and was subject to a supervision order at the time of the offence. The judge imposed an 18-month DTO. It was submitted on behalf of the Attorney General that the aggravating features of this offence were that a knife was used to threaten the victim, he was assaulted and his home was violated. The offenders took advantage of the fact that he was drunk. The robbery lasted for a significant period and was clearly a very frightening experience for the victim. Due to the *Newton* hearing it was submitted that the defendant should either have no credit for his plea or such credit should be limited. It was acknowledged that his age meant that the sentence must reflect the fact that he was a young man and should not be treated as if he was an adult. Also the judge when considering sentence was unable to take into account the 87 days which the defendant spent on remand. It was held that there should be some credit for his plea, albeit small, due to the concessions which he made. It was also recognised that the offence was serious and that the defendant despite his age was the instigator. An 18-month DTO was considered to be unduly lenient and a 4-year DTO was imposed under PCC(S)A 2000, s 91.

The cases below on robbery must now be read subject to the Sentencing Guidelines Council's (http://www.sentencing-guidelines.gov.uk/docs/robberyguidelines.pdf): **See Appendix I.2 for relevant extract.**

Attorney General's References Nos 16, 17 and 18 of 2006 [2006] All ER (D) 230 (Apr), CA

The defendants, who were 16 when sentenced, were charged with robbery and attempting to choke, strangle or suffocate with intent to rob. Defendant 1 believed that the victim had stolen jewellery from her, and the attack was in revenge for that. The defendants punched and kicked the victim, liquid was poured into her hair, and an attempt was made to set her hair alight. While on the ground, the victim was stripped, and her belt was taken and used to beat and throttle her. She lost consciousness for a short time and her clothes were thrown over a fence. Defendant 1 pleaded guilty on the day of trial but the basis upon which she pleaded was not accepted by the judge and he treated the trial as a *Newton* hearing on the issue. Both defendants 1 and 2 had no previous convictions but defendant 3 had a previous conviction for robbery. The defendants were sentenced to 24 months', 18 months' and 24 months' DTO respectively. However, in relation to defendant 1 (who was the ringleader) the judge subsequently reduced the period of DTO to 10 months in light of her pregnancy and intention to keep the child. The Attorney General sought leave to refer the sentences to the Court of Appeal as being unduly lenient, which was granted. The Court of Appeal ruled that the sentences were unduly lenient and failed adequately to reflect the seriousness of the offences. This involved a group action, victim was vulnerable and was subjected to deliberate degradation, the offence was pre-planned and there was deliberate infliction of injury beyond that which was necessary to carry out the robbery. It was recognised the defendant 1 had been the ringleader and that defendant 3 had previous convictions for robbery. The sentences were quashed and periods of detention of 3 ½ years, 2 ½ years and 3 ½ years were respectively substituted.

R v FA and Others [2003] EWCA Crim 508, CA

Three defendants aged 13 years intimidated and robbed boys of the same age who were pupils at the same school. The victims complained that the defendants had threatened them with violence and stolen items of property and small sums of money. All three pleaded guilty to one charge of theft and two charges of robbery. Defendants F and S also pleaded guilty to common assault. The PSR on F said that he had had no previous contact with the criminal justice system and came from a good family. He was assessed as not posing any danger to the public but the writer remained uncertain if F fully comprehended the serious nature of the offences. Defendant M repeatedly denied his involvement in the offences to the author of the PSR and said that he had only pleaded guilty on advice from his barrister. He also told the writer that he felt pressured by F to be involved in the offences and was fearful of the consequences if he refused. The report noted that he had expressed regret for his behaviour, but demonstrated very little victim empathy. He was assessed as posing a medium-level risk of re-offending and presented a low risk to the public. The PSR on S assessed the risk posed to the public as low due to the remorse and victim empathy shown by him and his willingness to accept guilt by association. All defendants were of previous good character. F was treated as the ringleader. They were sentenced to DTOs, in the case of F of eight months and in the case of the other defendants, six months. On appeal, the Court of Appeal said that it was wrong for the judge to treat F as the ringleader without hearing evidence to determine whether or not that was the case. The Appeal Court reduced the sentence on F from an 8-month DTO to a 6-month DTO. It was also said that pupils at school who indulged in campaigns of intimidation and violence, terrifying their fellow pupils, could expect to be dealt with severely. Only in this way could courts assist teachers in stamping out the real evil which such bullying represented.

J.2 Sexual offences (also see Appendix I.3)

R v E(R) [2016] EWCA Crim 1028, CA

The defendant was aged 14 years old when he began a relationship with the victim who was also aged 14. It soon became a consensual sexual relationship. The victim had not long turned

15 when the defendant who was still 14 anticipated that the sexual activity would lead to full sexual intercourse but the victim asked him to stop. He continued and inserted his penis into her vagina whilst holding her neck. After five to ten minutes he stopped and then apologised. Since that occasion their relationship continued and they continued to have consensual sexual intercourse. The victim's father contacted the police after becoming increasingly concerned about his daughter. The victim was video interviewed by the police and made the complaint of rape. The defendant in police interview denied the offence but pleaded guilty on a basis (as per the facts set out above). The sentencing judge took into account the pre-sentence report and psychological reports. The defendant had special needs and his general intellectual function was described as lower than 99.7% of people of his age. That had a detrimental effect on his social function, particularly maturity and social interaction. He was vulnerable and easily manipulated by others. The pre-sentence report argued on the basis of the defendant's immaturity and his other needs that an 18-month youth rehabilitation order should be imposed. The judge referring to that recommendation concluded that it was most important to bear in mind that the defendant was only 14 at the time of the offence and emotionally probably rather less mature than that; however, the only appropriate sentence was one of immediate custody. He added the starting point was six years for an adult in a similar situation and that was reduced by a third to reflect age and maturity, bringing it to four years. He then gave a further full one third reduction for the guilty plea, leaving a sentence of 32 months. He said that this could not be reduced further to fit into the detention and training order range. Sentence was therefore 32 months' detention under PCC(S)A 2000, s 91. The defendant appealed on the grounds that the sentence was wrong in principle and manifestly excessive. The Court of Appeal said it was difficult to assess the impact that a lengthy period of detention must have on a 16-year-old boy with no previous convictions or cautions and with the background and difficulties that this particular defendant had. It was said that the sentencing regime requires the court to have regard to paragraph 1.2 of the Sentencing Council's *Overarching Principles – Sentencing Youths*: '(a) the principal aim of the youth justice system (to prevent offending by children and young persons); and (b) the welfare of the offender.' Reference was also made to paragraphs 1.3 and 3.3 to 3.5 in the *Overarching Principles – Sentencing Youths* guidance. It was held that there was no minimum term of custody for the offence of rape and this was an exceptional case as to allow a non-custodial option to be considered. The sentence of 32 months' detention was quashed and substituted with an 18-month youth rehabilitation order which included an 18-month period of supervision, a period of 91 days' activity requirement, a three month electronically monitored curfew requirement and a four month programme requirement. The period of registration under the Sexual Offences Act 2003 was reduced to run in line with the youth rehabilitation order. The sexual harm prevention order was quashed and replaced with a restraining order prohibiting the defendant from contacting the victim and her family for a similar period of five years.

R v H [2015] EWCA Crim 1579, CA

The defendant was aged 15 years old when he entered into a relationship with the victim who was 12. Initially the defendant thought that the victim was 14 but soon discovered that she was only 12. However, he continued to tell his parents throughout the relationship that the girl was 14. When the defendant turned 16 a sexual relationship started involving oral and vaginal intercourse. The victim subsequently alleged to the police that she had been 'forced' to have intercourse with the defendant. In interview, the defendant freely admitted both oral and vaginal intercourse but said that it was all consensual. The police investigations revealed messages from the victim to the defendant demonstrating there had been consensual sexual activity and the victim herself subsequently acknowledged that that was the case. The defendant was charged with three vaginal rapes and one oral rape. He pleaded guilty at the first opportunity in the

Youth Court on a basis which was accepted. The basis was that the offences had commenced shortly after he had turned 16. Further if the victim had had the capacity to consent, then everything which took place was on a consensual basis. There was a specific denial of the use of force at any time. In passing sentence the judge accepted that basis of the plea, but said that it was important to emphasise that everything which had occurred took place when the defendant was 16 and the victim was 12. The judge referred to the number of occasions on which offences had been committed, the gap in age between the parties and the defendant's misleading of his parents as to the girl's age. The Crown Court judge imposed an 18-month detention and training order concurrent on each count. The defendant appealed on the basis that the sentence passed did not properly reflect the facts of the case and the available mitigation and 18 months was manifestly excessive. The Court of Appeal said there was no doubt that there were many mitigating factors available to the defendant. It was accepted that what took place was not forced and that the victim appeared to have assented to it. The defendant was of previous good character. His behaviour and family circumstances had otherwise given no cause for concern. He had educational ambitions. Whilst in custody he has shown a readiness to engage with rehabilitative and preventative work. He had been frank and remorseful and he had pleaded guilty at the earliest possible opportunity. He represented a low risk of re-offending. In addition, at the time of his offending he was aged 16 and had been described as emotionally immature. Those considerations were balanced by the disparity in the age between the parties and the evidence that the defendant knew that what he was doing was wrong and the sexual activity was a settled and relatively frequent course of conduct which took place over several months in circumstances where the defendant knew that what he was doing was wrong. The Sentencing Guidelines concerned single offences and not multiple offences as in this case. It was held that although the judge had made very considerable reductions in the term which he imposed, he had not made sufficient allowance for the mitigation available to the defendant and the need to keep custody, if justified, to a minimum. The 18-month DTO was reduced to a 12-month DTO to run concurrently on each count.

R v D (R) [2015] EWCA Crim 2228, CA

The defendant pleaded guilty to three counts of sexual activity with his sister and one count of rape. The sexual activity occurred over several years and started when the victim, who was the defendant's half-sister and three years younger than him, was six years old and the defendant nine years old and it culminated in a rape offence when the victim was 12 and the defendant 15 years old. The defendant had suffered a troubled childhood and was seen by a psychiatrist at an early age. During one of the sessions he disclosed the sexual activity with his sister and someone spoke to the victim who disclosed the offences but did not support a prosecution; however, three years later she changed her mind. The sexual activity had started as childish experimentation (looking at each other's naked bodies) but eventually led to the defendant demanding she perform oral sex on him and when she was seven years old and the defendant ejaculated in her mouth. The abuse stopped for a period when they were no longer sharing a bed and the opportunity did not arise. However, when the victim was 12 and the defendant 15 the defendant raped her vaginally. The defendant in an interview with the police indicated that some of the offences were known within the family for some considerable time before the victim had made a formal complaint to the police and therefore could have been addressed a good deal earlier. This assertion was confirmed by the medical records. The basis of plea, which the Crown chose not to dispute, was that starting at the age of eight he had sexually experimented with his half-sister. At that time he had no idea anything was wrong. The experimentation continued, usually when they shared a bed. He insisted he did not force her physically but admitted he sometimes used verbal pressure to persuade her. Oral sex occurred. Sometimes his sister seemed willing.

He admitted he knew she was too young to consent but claimed he did not know that oral sex was wrong. He attempted digitally to penetrate her but stopped when she said no. It was said that his behaviour was influenced by early exposure to pornographic material and a difficult childhood as described in the psychiatric report. The defendant had no previous convictions but three cautions for possessing drugs of class B and C and one for criminal damage. On sentence the court considered a number of character references, reports from the YOT and from a psychiatrist instructed to assess the defendant. The reports disclosed that the defendant had had a very troubled childhood including being excluded from nursery school. He continued being excluded from school during his primary and secondary education and at 13 was diagnosed as suffering from a conduct disorder and probably ADHD. The psychiatrist also noted that the defendant's problems continued into his adolescence when he misused drugs including ketamine. The author of the probation report considered that the defendant's fractured and difficult childhood and the exposure to pornography' had had a profound effect on his behaviour. There remained concerns about suicide and self-harm. The defendant was now living with his father in a close and supported family unit and had not committed any further offences and had made significant progress. The court imposed 12 months' imprisonment for the offence of indecent assault; nine month's imprisonment for the offence of attempted indecent assault; two years' imprisonment for the offence of rape. All the sentences were ordered to run concurrently. A sexual harm prevention order was made for ten years. The defendant appealed against his sentence on the basis that he should have been treated as if he was appearing before the court to be sentenced at the age he was when the last offence was committed. He would have been no older than 15 and had he been prosecuted as a child for this offence committed as a child and had he been dealt with at the youth court and the court would most probably have made him the subject of a referral order and at most the courts would have imposed a detention and training order the maximum term of which is two years. The Court of Appeal found that the sentencing judge significantly reduced the sentence to reflect the fact that the defendant was a child at the time the offence was committed and also took account of very extensive mitigation available to him. He followed the approach suggested in *R v H and Others* [2012] 2 Cr App R (S) 21 which provides guidance for sentencing historic sexual offences. The Court of Appeal dismissed the appeal as the sentence was not manifestly excessive.

R (on the application of BH) v Llandudno Youth Court [2014] EWHC 1833 (Admin), Div Court

The defendant (BH) was aged 11 at the time of the offence and his co-defendant (TL) was also aged 11 and the victim (TB) was aged 10. All three of them were Year 6 pupils at the same primary school. BH and TL had asked the victim to go with them into the school toilets where TL and BH had pretended to kiss each other, pretending that they were homosexual. Both of them then exposed their penises. BH is said to have said to TB: 'suck on the one you think is best' before grabbing his head and trying to force his mouth towards his penis, causing his penis to touch the outside of the victim's mouth. The victim managed to escape and reported the incident to a teacher. The defendant BH was charged with a single offence of causing or inciting a boy under the age of 13 to engage in sexual activity of a non-penetrative nature, contrary to ss 8(1) and (3) of the Sexual Offences Act 2003. His co-defendant TL was committed to the Crown Court in respect of this offence and another more serious offence (anal rape) of the victim which was said to have taken place the week before this offence. The District Judge in the Youth Court sent the defendant for trial to the Crown Court under CDA 1988, s 51A(3)(b). The defendant sought judicial review of the decision to send him for trial to the Crown Court. The Divisional Court examined the approach the District Judge had taken. He took as his starting point the range of sentences that an adult offender might have received for like behaviour and then applied a reduction for the age of the child and came to the conclusion that however great the reduction a custodial sentence was inevitable. The Divisional Court held that the District Judge had plainly approached the matter from the wrong direction. The tariff that an adult offender might receive for an offence of this nature afforded no guidance to the sentence that a child, especially a child who was 11 at the time of the offence, was likely to receive. The question that the Judge should have asked himself is on an assumption that the child is convicted of the offence is there a 'real prospect' that the Crown Court would exercise its powers under PCC(S)A 2000, s 91 to impose a custodial sentence bearing in mind the mitigating (age of the defendant and previous good character) and aggravating features (joint enterprise, element of pre-planning, force used). The Divisional Court said the venue for trial of this defendant should have been the Youth Court and the decision to send him to the Crown Court was plainly wrong. On this basis, the decision to send to the Crown Court was quashed.

R v K and Others [2013] EWCA Crim 649, CA

The four defendants were K who was 14 years of age at the date of the offences, D 15, JR 16 and M 15. At the date of conviction and sentence the boys' ages were as follows: K was 15, D 16, JR 18 and M 16. The four defendants and the victim who was a girl then 14 years of age and some other teenagers gathered in a park. D was a friend of the victim. Previously there had been some sexual contact between them. Afterwards there was a lot of text messaging between them, some of which was of a flirtatious and sexually-suggestive nature. The messages also indicated a degree of fondness and attraction between the two of them. The park where they gathered was a usual place for teenagers to congregate and to drink alcohol. The victim was very drunk and for a while she sat on D's lap. K called the victim over to a wooded area and she followed him. There he started to kiss her and undid her trousers and pulled her trousers and underwear down, pushed her forward and penetrated her from behind. He withdrew after a few moments. Due to her intoxication, the victim could not remember everything about the incident except D penetrating her vaginally. At the same time the co-accused, JR, penetrated her mouth with his penis. M filmed what was happening on a mobile phone and the film showed K gripping the victim while D had sexual intercourse with her. The victim had said that she could not tell whether there had been any ejaculation by any of the three, but they each stopped after a relatively short time. A few days later at school, rumours started to circulate about what had happened and a teacher spoke to the victim who disclosed what had happened to her. All four defendants were arrested. They declined to comment when interviewed. However, K and D pleaded guilty to three offences of sexual activity with a child, contrary to ss 9 and 13 of the Sexual Offences Act 2003. M pleaded guilty to one such offence and to an offence of making indecent photographs of a child, contrary to s 1(1)(a) of the Protection of Children Act 1978. JR also pleaded guilty to three offences of sexual activity with a child. K had no previous convictions and showed limited victim empathy and was adamant that the victim had consented to what had occurred. His parents were supportive of him. K had been permanently excluded from school after a further complaint from a female student. The PSR recommended a two-year Youth Rehabilitation Order. D also had no convictions and he also asserted consent on the part of the victim but said that he now felt 'awful' for her. Again, his family were supportive and there were no major problems at school. A similar recommendation of a two-year Youth Rehabilitation Order was made. Although M had no previous convictions, he had had two reprimands for battery. He told the YOT that if he had not been drunk he would never have filmed the incident. He said that he had been a friend of the victim and had previously been concerned about her behaviour. He acknowledged an alcohol problem on his own part and said that he was anxious to engage with the YOT and not to offend again. A similar order for a rehabilitation disposal was proposed in his case. The judge, when passing sentence, said these offences were aggravated by: group activity; joint enterprise of penetration by three offenders in a public place; impact on the victim; victim exploited and degraded; victim vulnerable through self-induced intoxication; boasting afterwards; and report of film seen by a third party. The judge said that the offending came at the top end of the bracket of offences of sexual activity with a child and the starting point in the Sentencing Guidelines was a range of 6 to 24 months' custody. Making allowance for mitigation and the pleas of guilty, he found that the appropriate sentence in each case was a 12-month detention and training order. K appealed against his sentence on the basis that if he had been charged initially with a sexual activity offence rather than rape, his case would have been before the Youth Court where, as a person without previous convictions, that court would have been compelled to make a referral order. D applied for leave to appeal on the basis that his case should be considered in parallel with that of K and that if any reduction in K's sentence was granted then a parallel reduction should be made in his case. Similar points are raised on behalf of M to those advanced by D and that no penetrative act was committed by M, and that he was to be sentenced only on the basis of one count of sexual activity with regard to the act which he was responsible for filming. The Court of Appeal considered several authorities including *R v Ghafoor* [2002] EWCA Crim 1857; *R v Jahmal Thomas* [2004] EWCA Crim 2199; *R v Q, W and C* [2012] EWCA Crim 296 and *R(W) v Thetford Youth Court* [2002] EWHC 1252 (Admin) and found this was a most unusual case. It found the aggravating features were clear even if the contentious issue of the alleged exploitation was ignored. This case involved a series of group acts in a public place committed on a very young girl. The acts were in fact not consensual on the part of victim, whatever the position as to the reasonable belief of the accused as to her consent. Part of the incident was filmed. There was much boasting about the matter after the event. The impact of the incident on C has been significant, as attested to by two Victim Personal Statements. These features in the Court of Appeals' judgment were amply sufficient to indicate that these offences passed the custody threshold even after taking into account the young ages of the defendants and guilty pleas. It was found that the sentences were not excessive. K's appeal against sentence was dismissed and leave to appeal outside of time was refused for D and M.

R v Jason David Robert Mooney [2010] EWCA Crim 698, CA

The defendant was aged 17 at the time of the offence. The victim (aged 12) and some of her friends went out for the evening and became drunk. The girls went back to a friend's house but were asked to leave in the early hours of the morning. The defendant, who was present at the house, said the girls could stay at his aunt's house not far away, and three of the girls went there with him. At the aunt's house the defendant showed the girls where to sleep in one room and went to bed in another room. During the course of the night the victim joined the defendant in bed and eventually initiated sexual intercourse with him. The girls stayed in the house the next day and sexual intercourse happened the following night in similar circumstances. The girl subsequently told her mother what had happened and the police were informed. The defendant admitted immediately that sexual intercourse had taken place. He was charged with two counts of rape of a child under 13. He pleaded guilty and was sentenced to 30 months' detention, under PCC(S)A 2000, s 91, concurrent on each count. The defendant appealed against the sentence, on the basis that he had not invited the girls to stay with the intention that sexual activity would take place; the victim initiated sexual intercourse on both occasions; she said she was nearly 15; the defendant was not responsible for the victim being drunk; he did not ejaculate and was unaware of the law regarding consensual intercourse between a 17-year-old and an under-14-year-old. It was said that although consent was not relevant to the offence itself, it was relevant to mitigation. It was held that this case did not fall within the guidelines in relation to rape and therefore the exceptional circumstances of the case meant that a more radical departure was called for. It was held that although a custodial sentence could not be regarded as wrong in principle, the sentence passed was considerably too long. A 12-month DTO would meet the offending behaviour and recognise the purpose for which legislation had been passed.

R v C [2009] EWCA Crim 2231, CA

The defendant, aged 14, asked his 8-year-old male cousin to suck the defendant's penis, to touch his anus and to put his finger in the defendant's anus. The defendant attempted to insert his penis into the child's anus and the defendant asked the child to masturbate him. The sexual episodes grew out of the practice of challenging to 'dares'. No overt force was used but the 8-year-old was an unwilling participant and he did what he was asked to do only because the defendant was in a position of influence over him as his older and bigger cousin. The defendant pleaded guilty to four counts of causing a child under 13 to engage in sexual activity, one count of attempted rape of a child under 13 and one count of rape of a child under 13. He was sentenced to a 2-year DTO. The defendant appealed against his sentence. The Court of Appeal agreed that the defendant did not fall within the statutory provisions relating to dangerous offenders but that the offences were serious and the gravity of the offences lay in the disparity in the age between the defendant and victim. The Court of Appeal considered the statutory provisions imposed by CDA 1998, s 37(1) and the CYPA Act 1933, s 44(1), which required the court to have regard to the welfare of the defendant. It was held that the case was not one in which a sentence of detention was necessary. The residual risk the defendant might pose was best addressed by a community sentence. It was not believed that the offences were so serious that the interest of the defendant's own welfare and of preventing further offending must come second to the need to punish him. The DTO was quashed and replaced with a supervision order with a specified activities requirement.

R v S [2009] EWCA Crim 2808, CA

The defendant (S) was aged 15 at the time of the offence. The defendant, his co-defendant, SP, (aged 15) and the victim had been friends for some time. All three of them were at the defendant's house when they found a vibrator in the defendant's stepsister's drawer. SP grabbed the victim and shouted to the defendant to help hold him down. The defendant held the victim's arms and SP sat on his legs. SP then pulled down the victim's trousers and inserted the vibrator into his anus. Shortly after they let him go and the victim went home. The incident came to light some months later when the victim told a teacher at his school about it. The defendant was asked by two teachers about it and accepted that there had been an incident with a vibrator but asserted that it had happened two years previously. The defendant was arrested and in interview accepted that a vibrator was found but denied inserting it into the victim's anus. The defendant was of previous good character and SP had one previous conviction for theft for which he received an absolute discharge. They were charged with sexual assault by penetration. SP pleaded guilty on the day of the trial. The defendant (S) entered a not guilty plea and was convicted after trial. The judge concluded that the assault was not inherently sexual in nature; it was more a bullying offence than a sexual one. Nonetheless, it was a highly unpleasant experience for the young man and the effects psychologically were still with him. She made reference to the pain, injury, distress and humiliation that the victim had suffered. She gave SP full credit of one-third for his plea, notwithstanding the fact that his change of plea only took place on the day of the trial. SP received a DTO for 12 months and the defendant (S) received an 18-month DTO. The defendant (S) appealed against sentence. The Court of Appeal agreed with the defendant that the overall sentence was too long for what was described in reality as an assault occasioning actual bodily harm. Secondly, there was an element of disparity in the sentence in comparison to the co-defendant, bearing in mind the fact that SP had taken the major role, that he was almost a year older and that his change of plea was very late. A DTO of 12 months was substituted.

Attorney General's Reference No 67 of 2009 [2009] All ER (D) 129 (Oct), CA

The defendant was aged between 14 and 16 when he committed a variety of sexual offences against his younger sister over a three-year period. She had been aged 11 to 13 when the offences were committed. Early on in the offences, the offender had raped her vaginally; albeit the penetration was minimal and the offender did not ejaculate. That was the only incident of rape which had occurred. The remaining conduct consisted of digital penetration of the victim's vagina, the defendant performing oral sex upon her, masturbation and ejaculation in front of her. On one occasion the defendant ejaculated on the victim. The offences came to light when the mother of the defendant and victim noticed that the victim had been harming herself. By that time, the defendant had been ejected from the family home. The police were contacted. The defendant gave full and frank admissions in interview and pleaded guilty at the first available opportunity on a basis of plea which was accepted by the prosecution. The basis of plea included the fact that the rape had involved minimal penetration and that the defendant had stopped when he had thought better of it; that the victim, whilst not suggested to have been enthusiastic nor to have instigated the offences, had not physically resisted; that the defendant had stopped when asked. The offences had not escalated in seriousness over the period of offending. The defendant himself had been sexually assaulted after the offences. He had no previous convictions. There was some history of infliction of self-harm and eating disorders on his part. The defendant pleaded guilty at the first opportunity to rape and engaging in sexual activity with a family member under the age of 13. In sentencing the offender, the judge took into account the relevant sentencing guideline and a starting point of 3 years' detention in a young offender institution. He gave the offender credit for his guilty plea, frank admissions and his young age, and imposed a total term of 12 months' detention in a young offender institution. The Attorney General applied for leave to refer the sentence to the Court of Appeal as being unduly lenient. The Court of Appeal said that the defendant was, at most, aged 16 at the time of the offences and accordingly the maximum sentence would have been 5 years' detention. In that context, a sentencing range was suggested by the Sentencing Guidelines Council of 6 to 24 months' detention. There were none of the specific aggravating features referred to in the guideline, for example, there had been no coercion, no use of alcohol or drugs and no threats. On the other hand, the victim was an innocent girl who had been subjected to persistent and systematic abuse. A custodial sentence had been inevitable and appropriate. However, there were circumstances which had to be taken into account. On the evidence in the instant case, justice had not required the offence of rape to have been treated more seriously than the other offences. The mitigating elements included: the background of horseplay and fun which had gradually developed into sexual activity; the age and lack of maturity of the offender; the ending of the offences of the offender's own volition; the candid and frank admissions in interview; and the early guilty plea. In the light of all the material, the sentence was not increased.

R v S [2009] EWCA Crim 1969, CA

The defendant was 15 and a half years old at time of the offence. The victim was a girl, B, who was 11 years and 8 months old at the time. She hung around with a group of youngsters who congregated in a lane near her home. That group included the defendant. On the evening of the offence the group was playing a game of truth or dare. In due course in a lane behind a shop when the defendant and B were alone, as part of the game the defendant asked B to perform oral sex upon him. This lasted for a few minutes and was only interrupted when B's mobile phone rang and she was summoned home. She told her mother about what had happened and in turn her mother called the police. The defendant was arrested and interviewed. Initially he denied the allegation but later admitted that sexual contact had taken place. He also candidly accepted that he knew it was illegal because B was under age. The reason the defendant knew that fact was because he had been undergoing intensive work under a supervision order in an attempt to deal with his inappropriate sexual conduct. The defendant pleaded guilty on the basis that there was no force or threats used against the victim and also there was no ejaculation. The judge took into account: the defendant's young age, that he was taking medication for ADHD, the basis of plea, and the very disturbing picture which emerged from the reports dealing with the defendant's background and home circumstances. The judge referred to the Sentencing Guidelines Council guideline for rape and also to the guideline for sexual activity with a child. He noted that the guideline, when dealing with an adult with no previous convictions, but having contested the charge, suggested a starting point of 10 years. He considered that the defendant's previous conviction of rape in connection with the boy of eight substantially aggravated the offence. The judge's conclusion was that absent a guilty plea, the notional determinate sentence would have been 8 years. The defendant entered a guilty plea to rape of a child under the age of 13, contrary to SOA 2003, s 5. Full credit for the plea was given and the defendant was sentenced to detention for public protection, imposing a minimum term of 32 months, less time spent on remand. The defendant appealed against his sentence. The Court of Appeal were persuaded that the starting point should have been lower, having regard in particular to the defendant's youth and immaturity. The Appeal Court was of the view that the notional equivalent determinative sentence in this case should have been one of 7 years before reduction for the plea. Allowing a full discount for the plea would result in a notional equivalent determinate sentence of 4 years and 8 months. That in turn resulted in a minimum term of 28 months. A term of 28 months' detention was substituted.

R v C [2009] All ER (D) 154 (Apr), CA

The defendant, when he was 14, had a sexual relationship with a girl of the same age, and then with a girl aged 13. He was originally charged with rape but eventually pleaded guilty to two charges of sexual activity with a child, contrary to SOA 2003, s 13. A report stated that he came from a supportive and respectable family, was a good student and presented a low risk of re-offending. It said that he would struggle if he received a custodial sentence and recommended a referral order. The defendant had no previous matters of any kind. The judge imposed a DTO for eight months. The defendant appealed against his sentence. The Court of Appeal held that although the offences involved two different girls, the defendant had been in an affectionate relationship with each of them and there had been no abusive seduction or evidence of coercion. Applying the sentencing guidelines the correct starting point was a community order with a range of 'an appropriate non-custodial sentence'. The DTO was replaced with a supervision order for 1 year.

R v G [2009] EWCA Crim 265, CA

The defendant was aged 14 at the time of the offences and the victim was only 10 years old. The defendant and the victim lived in the same street. Following disclosures made first to her grandmother and then her mother, the victim give a video interview to the police making a number of allegations against the defendant. On several occasions the defendant made the victim perform oral sex on him, including him ejaculating into her mouth on one occasion. The judge in passing sentence had regard to the guidance of the Sentencing Guidelines Council that the defendant was an immature young man, still only 15 years of age and had no previous convictions, warnings or reprimands and many people had come forward to speak highly of him as a well-mannered and thoughtful young man. The defendant also suffered from ADHD and was a naïve, fragile and unsophisticated young man. The defendant pleaded not guilty and was convicted after trial. The PSR described the defendant as immature and unable to comprehend the consequences of his actions on the victim. The judge imposed concurrent sentences of 4 years' detention in respect of each of the three charges of rape of a child under 13 and 2 years in respect of each of the charges of sexual assault of a child under 13, making a total sentence of 4 years' detention. The Court of Appeal substituted a sentence of 3 years' detention due to the defendant being only 14 years old at the time of the offences and being of previous good character.

R (on the application of W) v Warrington Magistrates' Court [2009] EWHC 1538 (Admin), Div Court

The defendant was 13 years of age when he was charged with the offence of attempted rape. He was subsequently charged with the commission of three additional sexual assaults. The attempted rape was oral and vaginal. The victim was his cousin, aged eight years. The victims of the sexual assaults were a 5-year-old boy and a 13-year-old girl. When the defendant appeared before the Youth Court on the charge of attempted rape, both prosecution and defence counsel sought his committal to the Crown Court for trial. The justices refused to do so and a date was set for the trial. The prosecution applied, unsuccessfully, for the joinder of the four charges. The cases were assigned to a circuit court judge who was requested to exercise his powers as a district judge pursuant to the Courts Act 2003, s 66. That procedure was advised in a protocol issued by the Senior Presiding Judge in 2007 entitled *Rape Cases in the Youth Court*. At neither trial was a renewed application made to commit the cases to the Crown Court. During the course of the hearing it became apparent that the defendant had succeeded in vaginal intercourse with the victim. Having found the defendant guilty of all offences, the judge committed him to the Crown Court for sentence, reserving the case for himself. The defendant was of previous good character. He was sentenced to detention for public protection. A minimum term of 2 years was ordered for the offence of attempted rape. Sentences of 12 months' detention for the sexual assaults were ordered to run concurrently with each other and with the sentences for attempted rape. The defendant sought judicial review on the basis that: (i) the judge ought not to have heard the cases of sexual assault, having previously heard the case of attempted rape; (ii) that he ought to have been committed to the Crown Court for trial either at the Youth Court hearing or before the close of the prosecution case for attempted rape under MCA 1980, s 24(1)(a). The application was dismissed. The Divisional Court said that the judge was entitled to hear the cases of indecent assault and accepted that he could have heard all four charges together. Hearing them one after the other did not render the second trial unfair on that ground. The court also said that there was no power to reverse the original decision not to commit to the Crown Court. MCA 1980, s 24 provided for a single decision on the mode of trial and did not permit serial reconsideration of the same question, whether or not new material had emerged. The general policy of the legislature was that those below 18 years of age and in particular children under 15 years of age should, whenever possible, be tried in the Youth Court. It was held that the decision of the Youth Court not to commit for trial could just be considered a proper exercise of their discretion under MCA 1980, s 24. At the time of the offences the claimant was 13 years old and without previous convictions. The full seriousness of the offences, which justified the sentence in the event imposed, only fully emerged at a later stage. When the relevant decisions were taken, the court had been entitled to conclude that the test for committal had not been satisfied. Valuable though the procedure encouraged by the protocol might be, the court had to apply the statutory test in MCA 1980, s 24(1)(a) and not be diverted from it. Parliament had seen fit to grant a right to a Crown Court hearing to young offenders in certain circumstances and that could not be defeated administratively. There were alleged sexual offences involving very young defendants where committal to the Crown Court was the correct decision. The decision not to commit to the Crown Court was upheld. The Rape Protocol has now been superseded by the 'Sexual Offences in the Youth Court' Protocol (see Appendix M).

R v G and Others [2008] EWCA Crim 2112, CA

The victim was a 14-year-old girl in year 11 at a school which was also attended by each of the defendants G, M and A who were 15 years old, and P was 13 years old. M walked up to the girl and took her mobile telephone and said that he would only give it back to her if she performed oral sex on him. G, A and P and another youth, L, arrived and together with M made explicit sexual remarks, asking the victim what she was going to do to get the telephone back, with M and L being the most insistent. The victim refused and was dragged to the floor, the door was shut and lights were turned off. The boys would not let the victim get up and some of them removed their trousers and boxer shorts. G stood in front of her with his penis exposed and repeatedly said: 'Come on, do it'. P and A thrust their exposed penises towards her face, whereupon the victim said 'no' and she held her hand over her mouth. The boys continued behaving in this way for about five or six minutes until someone said that a teacher was coming, whereupon the boys ran out of the room. Before the victim could get up and leave, the boys returned and crowded round her again. The victim was pushed face down on the floor. Two of the boys got on top of her and simulated sexual intercourse. The victim followed asking for her mobile telephone to be returned. The boys only returned the telephone when another boy told them to give it back. The victim reported the incident to the teacher and the police were called. They all pleaded guilty at the Inner London Youth Court to causing or inciting a child to engage in sexual activity, contrary to SOA 2003, s 13(1). The PSR in relation to G explained that he was a mature young man, fully admitted his part in the offence and expressed a great deal of remorse. He had a good relationship with his parents and had become reclusive since the offence. He was assessed as posing a low risk of re-offending and causing harm. In the case of M the PSR recorded that his involvement was attributed to a sexual immaturity and his susceptibility to negative peer influence. These factors heightened his sexual tension and his willingness to exert control, as was shown by the fact that he seized and obtained the victim's mobile telephone. M expressed some remorse but he demonstrated limited insight. He was assessed as posing a medium risk of re-offending and a medium to high risk of harm. He hoped to focus on his education and his football. A presented a high level of general remorse but limited understanding of sexual offending. He posed a low to medium risk of re-offending and a low risk of harm. In the case of P his PSR said that he minimised his involvement and failed to take responsibility. He was regarded as naive and easily led, who failed to recognise the consequences and the enormity of his actions. He demonstrated, according to the writer of the report, a good level of victim awareness. He was assessed as posing a medium risk of harm and a low risk of re-offending. The report proposed a medium length supervision order. There were also before the judge nine character references in respect of G, one in respect of M and one in respect of A. The judge gave the defendants credit for their youth and their pleas and said there was no reason to distinguish between the defendants based on their involvement, save that in the case of G's exceptional testimonials and remorse centring on the victim enabled the judge to impose a slightly shorter sentence on him. M and A received sentences of 10 months' DTO, while G received a sentence of eight months' DTO; P, who was aged 14, received a sentence of 10 months' detention pursuant to the provisions of PCC(S)A 2000, s 91. On appeal, it held that the custody threshold was met due to the seriousness of the offence and impact on the victim. The Court of Appeal accepted that this was not a premeditated offence and that all the defendants M, A and G were young, and had no previous convictions. Although the offence was serious, the lengths of the sentences, were considered to be too high. A 6-month DTO was substituted in respect of M and A. The Appeal Court also decided that due to the prominent role that G played he should receive the same period of 6 months' DTO as

M and A, regardless of the impressive references and his remorse in respect of the victim. In the case of P the important distinguishing feature was that he was 13 years of age at the time of the offence and still only 14 years of age when the appeal was determined. P was of previous good character and therefore not suitable for a DTO, under PCC(S)A, s 100(2)(A) as he could not be described as a persistent offender. A community sentence was suitable and desirable for P, and therefore it was not permissible to impose a sentence under PCC(S)A 2000, s 91. A supervision order for 2 years was substituted.

Attorney General's Reference No 12 of 2008 [2008] All ER (D) 424 (Apr), CA

The defendant was 16 years old and living with his aunt. On numerous occasions he caused one of his cousins, aged eight or nine, to engage in sexual activity with him. Later he was staying with another family and engaged in sexual activity with some young boys. He pleaded guilty on the day of his trial to offences of sexual assault and causing a child to engage in sexual activity. He had no previous convictions and it was common ground that he had a disturbed background. The judge concluded that a custodial sentence would not offer the intervention required to protect the public. The defendant was by now aged 17 and the judge imposed a community sentence with requirements related to treatment for sexual offending. The Attorney General was given leave to refer the case as unduly lenient. Aggravating features included: sexual abuse over several months in the victim's home; sexual penetration of one boy by another, at the defendant's instigation; the youth of the victims and the effect on them. Mitigation included: defendant had been 16; he had been seriously emotionally deprived and was of below-average intelligence; his mother had died and his father had physically abused him; there had been no substantial intervention or support although he had been on the 'at risk' register. The Court of Appeal said that the case presented an acute sentencing dilemma. The offences were serious and the defendant had known that what he was doing was wrong. The judge might have imposed a custodial term to 'see what happened and hope for the best'. The defendant would have had no intervention for a year and perhaps none after that. If given a 2-year DTO, there would have been no intervention, no obligation on him to undergo follow-up treatment, and he would emerge probably more damaged, and possibly more dangerous, than when he went in. Long-term protection of the public was an important consideration and the judge had been entitled to bear that in mind when balancing the difficult and conflicting factors. There was no basis for interfering with the order.

R v B [2007] All ER (D) 364 (Nov), CA

The defendant who was aged 14 had started to talk to a girl (aged 13) and suggested they go to the park. He grabbed her by the wrist and started to touch her inappropriately. Eventually he pushed her to the ground, she told him to stop and he told her to be quiet or he would hit her and hurt her. He lay on top of her, pulled down his trousers and penetrated her with his penis. In police interview, he denied the offence of rape, alleging that the victim had consented. He denied rape but pleaded guilty to sexual assault by touching contrary to SOA 2003, s 3. He had no previous convictions for sexual offences but did have convictions for theft, robbery and possession of a bladed article in a public place. The PSR stated that he was unable to appreciate that what he had done was wrong. He was given an extended sentence of 7 ½ years. His appeal was dismissed. When considering dangerousness it was not necessary for the danger to arise from the same sort of offending as the court was dealing with. Thus if danger arose from possible future offences of robbery, the fact that the defendant was being sentenced for a sexual offence did not prevent the judge from imposing an extended sentence. The key question was whether there was a substantial risk of serious harm if the defendant were to be allowed his liberty without the necessary safeguards. The judge in this case could properly conclude that the conditions for such a sentence existed.

All cases below on sexual activity with a child; causing or inciting a child to engage in sexual activity; engaging in sexual activity in the presence of a child; causing a child to watch a sexual act must now be read subject to the guidance on Sexual Offences Act 2003 by the Sentencing Guidelines Council (http://www.sentencingguidelines.gov.uk/docs/82083-COI-SCG_final.pdf): See Appendix I.3 for relevant extracts.

R (on the application of G) v Burnley Magistrates' Court [2007] EWHC 1033 (Admin), Div Court

Five defendants (aged 13 and 14 at the time of the offence) were at a party when they followed the victim (aged 13), who had consumed a substantial quantity of alcohol, to the lavatory. They sexually assaulted the girl by fondling her breasts, and inserted a vibrator into her vagina. The incident lasted five minutes. The defendants were charged with sexual activity contrary to SOA 2003, s 13. They were of previous good character. The Youth Court declined jurisdiction and committed the defendants to the Crown Court for trial. Judicial review was sought in respect of the justices' decision. The Divisional Court held that whilst incident was unpleasant and reprehensible, it lasted a short time, the defendants were young offenders of previous good character and therefore there was no real prospect of sentences in excess of 2 years' detention, and therefore the decision of Youth Court to commit for trial was wrong.

R (on the application of H) v South and South East Hants Youth Court [2006] EWHC 1147 (Admin), Div Court

H was an immature boy of 14, of previous good character. He was accused of putting his finger into the vagina of an 8-year-old girl, who was a friend of his sister and whom he knew well. The victim complained that the claimant asked if he could do it a second time. She also claimed that he had 'snogged' her. He came before the Youth Court charged with sexual assault on a girl under the age of 13, contrary to SOA 2003, s 6, and two further offences of sexual assault by touching, contrary to SOA 2003, s 7. The CPS suggested to the court that the offences were grave offences. The Youth Court declined jurisdiction in favour of the Crown Court. The Divisional Court held that in the circumstances, the justices in the Youth Court reached a conclusion that was erroneous in law. Although the offences appeared to be very serious, on the facts, the imposition of a sentence in excess of 2 years would have been so disproportionate as to amount to an error of law.

R (on the application of B) v Richmond-on-Thames Youth Court and the Crown Prosecution Service (Interested party) [2006] EWHC 95 (Admin), Div Court

The defendant (B) was charged with two offences of rape when he was almost 13 years of age. The victim of the alleged rapes was a girl, aged 13 years at the time (LS). The rapes were alleged to have taken place at B's home in his bedroom. LS had decided to stay the night at B's home. With the connivance of B's parents, LS told lies to her mother on the telephone claiming that she was staying at the home of a girlfriend. LS claimed that some time later B made a sexual approach to her in his bedroom which she rejected. She said that B had then suddenly got on top of her and pushed her down. He had pulled down her trousers and had intercourse with her. She objected verbally and tried to knock him off. She claimed that afterwards she felt unable to tell B's parents or to leave the house because the [downstairs] doors were locked. She claimed that some time later B raped her again. She objected and did not consent as B claimed. The following morning she left and went home. She immediately complained of rape to her mother. The magistrates declined jurisdiction on the grounds that having regard to the gravity of the charges and the facts, the Crown Court would pass a sentence in excess of 2 years if B was convicted. Judicial review was sought of the Youth Court's decision to decline jurisdiction. It was held that the conclusion of the Youth Court could not be criticised. It was stated, *obiter* that in the case of very young defendants it may be appropriate to accept jurisdiction.

R v H [2004] All ER (D) 349 (Oct), CA

Defendant was 14 years old (15 years old when sentenced). The victim (aged 18 with learning disabilities) was subjected to a serious indecent assault by a group of boys, involving each of the four boys placing his penis in her mouth and touching her breasts, and one boy touching her vagina. The defendant admitted to having oral sex with her but contended that she had consented. The defendant was charged and pleaded guilty to indecent assault on a female on the basis that he had not known about her learning disabilities, had been reckless as to consent and had not been involved in the initial incident when she was forced to perform oral sex on the other boys. He had two cautions and was sentenced to a 12-month DTO. On appeal against sentence, the Appeal Court substituted a supervision order of 12 months taking into account the defendant's age, background and absence of relevant convictions. The court followed the approach in *R v Ghafoor* [2002] EWCA Crim 1857; at the time of the offence he had been only 14 years old and was not a persistent offender. See Appendix M for the 'Sexual Offences in the Youth Court' Protocol.

J.3 Section 18 wounding/GBH with intent

Attorney General's Reference No 36 of 2011 [2011] EWCA Crim 1814, CA

The defendant was 17 years old at the time of the offence. The victim was out with friends in the evening when he entered the public house and saw the defendant, the boyfriend of his ex-girlfriend. The defendant gestured to the victim, who left as he did not want any trouble. When walking on the street the victim felt a blow to the back of his head that made him crouch down. He tried to cover himself with his arms for protection. He sustained a number of injuries from the incident including a broken jaw on the left side, a tender swelling over the right side of his forehead including deep grazing, tender swelling of his left cheek, swelling and bruising to both eyes, abrasions to his right cheek and chin, abrasions to his right hand and grazes on his right arm and scratches to his upper left arm and lumps on his head within the hairline. The defendant made full and frank admissions and said that he had been drinking and that after he had broken up with his girlfriend she had gone out with the victim and complained to him about the victim harassing her. The defendant pleaded guilty when he was 18 years old to an offence of causing grievous bodily harm with intent. The defendant was 2 months short of his 18th birthday at the time of this offence and save for a single reprimand for criminal damage, committed when he was 13, which the judge made clear that he ignored, was of good character. The PSR said the defendant demonstrated genuine remorse for his actions and concluded that there was nothing to suggest that the defendant held an anti-social attitude generally and there was no pattern of violent or aggressive behaviour. He represented a low likelihood of further conviction although the report writer noted that he had clearly evidenced his ability to cause serious harm to others in the commission of this offence. He was sentenced to a term of 15 months' detention. The Attorney General referred the case to the Court of Appeal as an unduly lenient sentence. It was submitted that the aggravating features were the premeditation; the attack came from behind, without warning or provocation; the defendant kicking the victim in the face and stamping on his head with a shod foot; leaving the victim isolated and alone in a dark deserted park; and making no attempt whatsoever to call for help. The mitigating features were also recognised that the defendant made full and frank admissions; entered a guilty plea at the first opportunity; was of previous good character; 17 years of age at the time of the commission of the offence; showed genuine remorse and had not caused lasting physical injury. The defendant submitted that if there had not been a delay in the charging him, he would have appeared before the Youth Court whereupon it is at least arguable that jurisdiction would have been retained, giving the court a maximum possible penalty of 2 years' DTO, which would have to be reduced to reflect his guilty plea. The Appeal Court said that although *R v Ghafoor* [2002] EWCA Crim 1857 had been followed and approved in *R v Bowker* [2007] EWCA Crim 1608 it was not deemed relevant as this case was serious and it was right to have been before the Crown Court for sentence. The 15-month DTO was deemed to be unduly lenient, especially as the sentencing judge had adopted the wrong starting point. The starting point for an adult in relation to this offence would have been one of 5 years' custody, on the basis that injury was caused following a premeditated attack, thus the category within the guidance issued by the Sentencing Council was not the fourth but the third level. The sentence was replaced with 2 ½ years in a young offender institution.

R v SP [2010] EWCA Crim 1064, CA

The defendant was 17 years old at the time of the offence, when a dispute culminated in him hitting the victim (aged 19) who was a neighbour, in relation to a debt. He hit the victim three times with a hammer to the head causing him serious injuries. He pleaded guilty to wounding with intent and was sentenced to a community punishment and rehabilitation order. The Attorney General referred the case to the Court of Appeal as an unduly lenient sentence. The Court of Appeal said that although the defendant had pleaded guilty, he was young, genuinely remorseful and had served 4 months in detention before being sentenced, he had carried out a premeditated and serious attack, which involved the use of a weapon, targeting the head of his victim and inflicting serious injuries. It was also noted that the victim had made a reasonable recovery from his physical injuries but there remained some psychological effects. The sentence was replaced with a DTO of 18 months.

Attorney General's Reference Nos 74 and 75 of 2009 [2009] EWCA Crim 2934, CA

The defendants, M and V, were both aged 15 at the time of the offence. M, V and a third defendant (X) had been involved in a revenge attack against the victim. The victim had been at home and answered his door to V, and then saw that M and X were with her. X stabbed him with a knife procured by V, inflicting two serious stab wounds, one of them life-threatening. During the attack, M verbally encouraged X. M had previously received a caution for actual bodily harm and had convictions for battery, drunk and disorderly behaviour, and robbery. For the latter offence M had received a 12-month DTO, and the instant offence was committed whilst he was on licence. V had no previous convictions. Following their convictions for wounding with intent to do grievous bodily harm M received a 2-year DTO and V received a community order for 2 years with a condition of attending an intensive supervision and surveillance programme. The Attorney General referred the case to the Court of Appeal as unduly lenient. The Court of Appeal found that the sentences passed were unduly lenient. They found the offence to be very serious and one which an adult offender would have received a sentence in excess of 10 years' imprisonment. M's participation in the offence marked a step change in his offending, and was aggravated by the fact that it was committed whilst he was on licence and were it not for the encouraging report from the young offender institution he would have been deemed a dangerous offender. The proper sentence for M was 8 years' custody but due to the progress he had made and the principle of double jeopardy, M's original sentence was quashed and replaced with a determinate term of 7 years' detention pursuant PCC(S)A 2000, s 91. As regards the sentence imposed on V, in a number of recent judgments the Lord Chief Justice had made it very clear that those who used knives should expect custodial sentences. The public had to be protected against violence involving knives, and judges wholly failed in their public duty if they did not impose a custodial sentence in such circumstances, whatever the reason might be. V had no previous convictions and had done her utmost to try to put her life in order. However, she did not have the mitigation of a guilty plea, she had provided the knife and must have appreciated that it would be used, and she had lured the victim out of his home. It was held that despite V's immaturity and good character, the judge should have imposed a sentence of 4 years' detention under PCC(S)A 2000, s 91. The Court of Appeal said it would not be doing its public duty if it did not mark the gravity of the matter with a custodial sentence to deter others. However, taking in account the principle of double jeopardy and the progress V had made to date, the exceptional circumstances of the case permitted the Appeal Court to take the merciful course of quashing the original sentencing and replacing it with a DTO for 6 months.

Attorney General's Reference No 6 of 2009 [2009] EWCA Crim 1132, CA

The defendant was 17 at the time of the offence and 19 at the time of sentence. The defendant and the victim had been participating in a game of football in a public space. They became involved in a confrontation, during which defendant stabbed the victim in the chest using a penknife with a three-to-four-inch blade. The defendant ran off, but was subsequently arrested. During police interview he admitted the stabbing, expressed remorse, and stated that he had carried the knife for self-defence. The defendant pleaded guilty to wounding with intent and possession of an offensive weapon in a public place. A PSR concluded that the risk that the defendant would re-offend was low. At the sentencing hearing, a medical report was produced, which stated that the defendant was suffering from severe depression, anxiety and post-traumatic stress disorder arising from his experience after having been remanded in custody and from worrying about what he had done. The report also made clear his extreme vulnerability if given a custodial sentence. The defendant was of previous good character, with excellent school reports, and there was evidence suggesting that he had a bright future in sports. When passing sentence the Recorder who was unaware of the decision in *Attorney General's Reference No 49 of 2008* [2008] EWCA Crim 2304 imposed a community sentence comprising 18 months' supervision, 100 hours' unpaid work and a 6-month curfew. The Attorney General referred the case to the Court of Appeal as an unduly lenient sentence. The Court of Appeal held that there was the strongest possible personal mitigation in defendant's case, namely his youth, his immediate admission to the police, his plea, his positive good character, his remorse and his medical condition. However, regard also had to be had to the circumstances of the offence and its prevalence today. The problems of knife crime were well known, and the words of the Lord Chief Justice in *Attorney General's Reference No 49 of 2008*, namely 'no ifs, no buts, no perhaps – we must do what we can to eradicate this dreadful knife problem' had to apply to the defendant's case. The defendant had admitted to carrying the knife as an offensive weapon, he became involved in a confrontation, and the very vice to which the prohibition of carrying knives was directed had occurred, namely that when irritated or angry the defendant had taken the knife out and stabbed the victim. It was fortunate that very serious injury was not caused. Custody was inevitable; if the authority of *Attorney General's Reference No 49 of 2008* was not sufficient, then the Sentencing Guidelines Council guidelines in relation to the offence of wounding with intent also made it clear that a custodial sentence with a starting point of 4 years and a range of 3 to 5 years was the appropriate sentence for an adult on a not guilty plea. A message had to be conveyed to all that if a person took a knife out into the streets and used it, they would go to prison. As the defendant had been on a curfew, for 67 days and he had performed 30 hours of the unpaid work requirement, the court substituted a 24-month detention and training order, concurrent on each charge.

Attorney General's Reference No 48 of 2008 [2008] EWCA Crim 2514, CA

The defendant (G) was aged 15 at the time of the offence. G had been on a bus, waiting by the door to alight, when the driver braked forcefully, causing a boy (V) to fall against him. The boys got off the bus and verbal abuse and gestures were exchanged. G went home, picked up a knife and with his older brother returned to V, who was walking home. The defendant ran at V, grabbed him by his blazer and threw him to the ground. Realising that the defendant had a knife, V curled himself up into a ball. The defendant leaned over V and struck him once with the knife to the left thigh in a punching motion. The knife went straight through V's leg near the groin and narrowly missed his femoral artery. V's mother arrived and found him in a very serious condition. The injury caused damage to V's nerves and to the sensation in his left foot. He was away from school for two months and was unable to play sport for some time. Shortly before the instant offence, the defendant was convicted of an offence contrary to the OAPA 1861, s 18, but appealed successfully against the conviction. The defendant pleaded guilty to wounding with intent. The PSR stated that the defendant had come from a stable background and decent home, with supportive parents. The PSR concluded that a supervision order would be appropriate. The judge took the view that this crime was far too serious for such an outcome and imposed a 2-year DTO. The Attorney General asked the court to review the sentence on the ground that it was unduly lenient. The Court of Appeal found that the defendant was not out and about carrying a knife; he went home on the basis of a perceived insult, returned to the scene with a weapon and attacked the victim, stabbing him whilst he lay defenceless. Although G was only 15 years old at the time of the offence and of previous good character, he knew what he was doing and acted deliberately just two weeks after he had appeared in court for an earlier incident. It was held that even allowing for G's youth, it was a very grave crime and, notwithstanding G's guilty plea, a sentence of four years' detention was substituted.

Attorney General's Reference No 49 of 2008 [2008] EWCA Crim 2304, CA

The defendant, who was 16 at the time, went with two friends to a fast-food restaurant, where they had an altercation about the quality of the chips. They were escorted from the premises and one of the friends punched the victim. A little while later the defendant produced a kitchen knife which was about four inches long. He stabbed the victim six times, causing a collapsed lung, which necessitated 25 stitches and a blood transfusion. The victim did make a good recovery from his physical injuries. The victim suffered considerable psychological damage as a result of the incident. The defendant pleaded guilty at the first opportunity to wounding with intent (OAPA 1861, s 18). He had a previous conviction from when he was aged 14 to an assault occasioning actual bodily harm. The PSR stated that the defendant had experienced a troubled upbringing and that he had a tendency to outbursts of anger. The defendant had expressed remorse and wrote a letter to the court in which he described how sorry he was. The defendant was assessed as presenting a high risk of harm and a medium risk of re-offending. The judge said that 2 years' custody was appropriate, but considering the mitigation, in particular his youth, he would be sentenced to a 12-month DTO. His friends were sentenced to eight months' YOI and a 6-month DTO for affray. The Attorney General appealed against the defendant's sentence on the ground that it was unduly lenient. He submitted that: (i) the injuries had been serious with a significant risk of death; (ii) the assault had been sustained; (iii) the defendant had acted as part of a group;

(iv) the victim had been providing a service to the public; (v) the defendant had armed himself with a weapon prior to leaving home and had used it; and (vi) the defendant had a previous conviction for a violent offence. The appeal was allowed. The court considered the case of *R v Blizard and Povey* [2008] EWCA Crim 126, which said that every weapon carried on the streets, even if concealed or out of sight, or not likely or intended to be used, or unused, represented a threat to public safety and public order. That was because, even if the item was carried only for bravado or some misguided sense that it would be used for possible self-defence, there might arise a moment of irritation, drunkenness, anger, perceived insult or something utterly trivial like a look, where the weapon was then produced, and mayhem would follow, including offences of the greatest seriousness, such as murder, manslaughter, causing grievous bodily harm and wounding. Offences involving knife crime had recently escalated into epidemic proportions. Courts would do what they could to reduce or, if possible, eradicate it. Those who carried knives in the street then used them to wound others had to expect severe punishment. The judge had attached too much weight to the mitigating factors. The defendant had carried a knife and had drawn it and used it, causing very serious injuries. The sentence was increased to 3 years' detention.

Attorney General's Reference No 47 of 2003 [2003] EWCA Crim 3078, CA

The defendant was aged 14 and with other youths he congregated outside a takeaway and caused a nuisance. The owner of the takeaway went outside and asked a youth, R (who appeared to be under the influence of drugs or alcohol), to get off the delivery moped. R approached one of the workers at the takeaway (the victim) and asked him why he had sworn at him. The worker was apprehensive that he might be assaulted. At that point the defendant behaved sensibly, intervened and told R to stop. Another worker also intervened and put his arm between R and the victim. R started to throw punches at the worker and the defendant took from his pocket a flick knife and he held it above the victim's head and then stabbed him in the chest with significant force. The defendant continued to throw punches at the victim, who had not realised that he been stabbed. The victim's lung had been penetrated by the knife close to his heart and had collapsed. He was given stitches to his lower lip. He was in hospital for six days and was in great discomfort. When he was interviewed, the defendant said that he had been carrying a flick knife which had a four-inch blade for protection, although he had never been threatened, attacked or robbed. He pleaded guilty to wounding with intent contrary to OAPA 1861, s 18. The judge imposed a 3-year supervision order, due to there being no medical evidence as to the nature of the victim's injury, nor a prognosis. The Attorney General referred the sentence to the court as being unduly lenient. It was submitted that were a number of aggravating features present: (i) the defendant was in possession of a flick knife which he regularly carried for protection and which he used offensively; (ii) the defendant stabbed his victim in the chest and thereby put at risk the victim's life; (iii) the victim suffered significant injuries; (iv) the victim was himself unarmed. The mitigating factors were also recognised such as the defendant's early guilty plea, that he had taken steps to surrender before he was apprehended, his youth, previous good character, people spoke well of him, and his genuine remorse. A custodial sentence was however inevitable and 3 years' detention would be appropriate. The welfare of the defendant was only one factor and others were the need to punish the defendant, the interests of the victim and the requirement to deter others from committing such offences. Due to the fact that the defendant had to be re-sentenced which would be a 'very real blow', an 18-months' DTO was substituted.

R v W [2002] EWCA Crim 2106, CA

The defendant (W), who had been aged 10 at the time of the offence with others, had assaulted a 6-year-old child (E), with a piece of concrete, leaving E with injuries to the face, cuts and bruises particularly around his right eye, and burns to his back from a burning stick which had been applied to his body. After trial he was convicted for an offence of causing grievous bodily harm with intent. W suffered from attention deficit hyperactivity disorder, and the medication which W was taking at the time of the offence was not appropriate and had produced some side effects. These could have resulted in loss of control. In addition, W had moderate learning difficulties and a reading age of about half his actual age. His mother had done her best to look after him and he had shown some progress. The judge imposed detention for 4 years pursuant to PCC(S)A 2000, s 91. The defendant appealed against the sentence. Reports from the institution in which W had been detained since the trial were encouraging. It was recognised that when dealing with a very young person, the court had to have regard to the length of sentence and the child's perception of that length. A sentence which might have been appropriate for someone older may be crushing for someone who was very young. Four years represented a third of this defendant's life, therefore 3 years' detention was substituted.

J.4 Drugs supply

R v C (C) [2015] EWCA Crim 2040, CA

The defendant was 17 years old at the time of the offences. He was stopped by the police for the purposes of a drug search. At the police station, he was found to have 20 wraps of cocaine and 20 wraps of heroin (both Class A drugs) hidden between his buttocks. He claimed at that time in interview that these were for his personal use. He was charged with to two offences of possession of a Class A drug with intent to supply, contrary to s 5(3) of the Misuse of Drugs Act 1971. The Youth Court sent him to the Crown Court under s 91 of the Powers of Criminal Courts (Sentencing) Act 2000. He pleaded guilty on the basis that he had been given the wraps containing drugs by a man whom he knew to be a drugs dealer who asked him to hold the wraps until he returned. He did not wish to name the male as he was fearful of repercussions. He was not acting under duress but was fearful as he had been stabbed some time the month before. He accepted that he would have been paid on returning the drugs. His basis of plea was not accepted by the prosecution. However, there was no *Newton* hearing to determine any issue arising from the basis of plea. The prosecution did not seek one and the judge decided such a hearing was unnecessary. This was because the defendant had accepted that there was a financial element to the offending, making this, had he been over 18 years of age, within the Sentencing Council Guidelines a category 3 case with the defendant playing a significant role. This would result for an adult in a starting point of four and a half years' imprisonment, with a range of three and a half to seven years. The defendant had previous convictions for 23 offences; mostly for offences of violence with one offence of burglary. He had one previous conviction for possession of cannabis. The defendant had never received a custodial sentence before, each offence in the past had resulted in a youth rehabilitation order. He was subject to such an order at the time of these offences. In coming to the sentence the judge decided that the quantity of drugs found in the defendant's possession put him 'well above' the starting point but because of the defendant's age he expressly reduced the sentence, having stated in the course of the prosecution opening that he should reduce it by 'somewhere between half and two thirds of what an adult would get'. In deciding the extent of the reduction, he assessed the defendant as 'sufficiently mature enough to know better who must have been a trusted servant to be allowed to carry such a quantity which he had to make money'. The judge acknowledged the Sentencing Council's Guideline *Definitive Guideline on Overarching Principles of Sentencing Youths* that required a court in sentencing a youth aged 15, 16, or 17 years to consider the maturity of the offender as well as his chronological age. The judge sentenced the defendant and assessed his maturity without ordering a pre-sentence report. The defendant was sentenced to three years' detention for each offence to run concurrently. The defendant appealed against the sentence on the grounds that the judge failed to take proper account of his age, the basis of plea and his early guilty plea. The Court of Appeal ordered such a report to assist it in its consideration of whether the judge's assessment of the defendant's maturity was correct. However, the YOT was unable to interview the defendant because he was moved from one Young Offender Institution to another because of his poor behaviour and she was unable to interview him by way of telephone conference as arranged as he was confined to his cell due his behaviour. The author relied on her case records, her previous knowledge of the defendant and information provided by his family and youth offending team manager in writing a detailed report. The report stated that the start of the defendant's offending coincided with his first admission to local authority care. As a result of poor behaviour he had been placed in 16 different placements. His offending was said to be in part due to his willingness to prove himself amongst his peers. In the past, he had viewed his offending as comical and exciting and had failed to appreciate the seriousness of his actions. His attitude was said to be indicative of a lack of maturity. Although he was 17 years of age his coping mechanisms when dealing with stressful situations was said to be poor and he continued to demonstrate a low level of maturity even within custodial settings. He had been diagnosed as suffering from attention deficit and hyperactivity disorder although he had not taken medication for some time as he felt he had outgrown it. The Appeal Court accepted this case crossed the custody threshold and fell into category 3 of the Sentencing Guidelines and that by reason of the defendant's financial gain he had a significant role but considering his basis of plea the defendant would have fallen towards the bottom end of the category of significant role. The basis put forward was not manifestly absurd. The only aggravating factor which was identified by the Court of Appeal was the defendant being subject to a youth rehabilitation order at the time of the offence. His age and/or lack of maturity where it affects the responsibility of the offender would be a mitigating factor and the defendant had only just turned 17 years of age. The Court was of the view that the offences were serious and should not have remained within the Youth Court. However, the sentence was manifestly excessive as the judge had adopted too high a starting point and failed to have sufficient regard to the basis of plea. The sentence of three years' detention was substituted with a sentence of 24 months' detention and training order on each count concurrent, taking into account the days served on remand prior to sentence and the defendant's early guilty pleas.

R v Vickers [2013] EWCA Crim 831, CA

At the time of the offences the defendant was aged 17 years and eight months. He was arrested and a search was carried out at his home address where police found a small amount of skunk cannabis weighing 6.8 grams and valued at £68. Typical dealer paraphernalia were also found: dealer bags, digital scales and two cannabis grinders. When the defendant was arrested, he was found to be in possession of a BlackBerry mobile telephone. During the course of his interview, he openly accepted possession of the 6.8 grams of cannabis, but when asked about text messages recorded on the mobile telephone he remained silent. Subsequent interrogation of the mobile phone revealed dozens of text messages over a month period, demonstrating that during that period the defendant had been acting as a cannabis dealer. He was charged with supplying a controlled drug of Class B and possession of a controlled drug of Class B with intent to supply. The defendant pleaded guilty in the Crown Court. He had been before the courts on two previous occasions for a total of three offences, respectively handling stolen goods, burglary of a dwelling and assault. The pre-sentence report indicated that the defendant did not view his activity as drug dealing, as he claimed that he was only supplying to his friends. He nevertheless was recorded in the report as taking responsibility for his actions and recognising the consequences of his behaviour on the community, in consequence of which he had stopped selling drugs after his arrest. He had been out of work since leaving school, doing odd jobs for his family for money and had not claimed income support. The author of the report noted that the defendant lacked motivation and confidence. His cannabis use was, in the author's view, perhaps out of boredom and because the defendant felt that it helped him to deal with depression. He wanted to stop and was aware of the long-term effects on his mental health. He presented himself in interview as being polite and respectful. The author of the report observed that a custodial sentence might affect his current motivation to change his offending lifestyle. He was assessed as posing a low risk of harm and a medium risk of reconviction. The author of the report pointed out that, if sentenced to custody, the defendant would be placed in an environment where he would be vulnerable given that he would be in the company of other more entrenched and experienced offenders. Against that background, a community order with an unpaid work requirement was proposed as he was now 18 years old. The sentencing judge took into account the defendant's age, said it would be his first time in custody, early guilty plea and dissimilar previous offences. The judge said the defendant's role was somewhere between significant and leading and fell within category 3. The defendant was sentenced to eight months' detention in a young offender institution concurrent on each count. The defendant appealed against the sentence on the grounds that it was manifestly excessive or wrong in principle. He argued that if he had been charged promptly and dealt with in the Youth Court a non-custodial sentence would have been likely. The principles in the Definitive Guideline entitled *Overarching Principles Sentencing Youths* were referred to, particularly paragraphs 5.2 and 11.6. The Court of Appeal held that the sentence was not manifestly excessive and the sentence of eight months' detention was within the appropriate range. The appeal was therefore dismissed.

R v Burns [2013] All ER (D) 305 (Feb), CA

The defendant who was 17 years old was charged with two drug offences: (i) possessing a controlled drug of class A (diamorphine); and (ii) possessing a controlled drug of class A (crack cocaine). The heroin weighed 84.23g with a purity of between 11–17% and the crack cocaine weighed 12.9g with a purity of 26%. The street values for the heroin and crack cocaine were £5,560 and £645 respectively. The defendant denied any wrongdoing and was subsequently convicted of the offences after a contested trial. In the preparation of the pre-sentence report (PSR) the defendant had disclosed to the probation officer that he had committed the offence and had intended on hiding the drugs for a short period for someone else. He had been coerced into hiding the drugs and not been paid to do so. The PSR also stated that the defendant had showed genuine remorse and his behaviour whilst on bail had been exemplary. The PSR recommended a sentence which consisted of a youth rehabilitation order. The sentencing judge referred to the guidelines regarding drug offences and stated that the court's hands were tied by those guidelines and that the sentence could not be suspended. The judge further stated that the starting point for someone convicted after trial in category three of the relevant guidelines with a lesser role, as had been the case with the defendant, was three years' detention. Taking into account the defendant's lack of previous convictions and his remorse, the sentence was reduced to 30 months' detention in a young offender institution for each count to run concurrently, giving the total sentence of 30 months' detention. The defendant was aged 18 at the time of sentencing. The defendant appealed against sentence. The Court of Appeal held the sentence had been manifestly excessive as the defendant's youth at the time of the commission of the offences had not been reflected in the sentence. The sentence was quashed and a sentence of 21 months' detention in a young offender institution was substitute, with the period served on remand and on curfew set off against the sentence.

R v Antoine Nathaniel Joseph and Ritchie Nelson [2011] EWCA Crim 1392, CA

The defendants in the early hours of the morning were riding their bicycles when they were stopped by police officers, to carry out a drugs search. Joseph (aged 17 at the time) had to be chased by the police officer and when he briefly went out of sight of the chasing officer, he disposed of the jacket he had been wearing. The discarded jacket was found by the police and in the pockets there were 40 wraps of cocaine powder, a total weight of 8.68 grams (that was the first count), and 59 wraps of heroin powder, total weight of 10.88 grams (the second count), with a total street value just short of £1,700. There also was £70 in cash in the jacket. Close to where the jacket had been discarded, the police found a mobile telephone. Joseph also had £55 in cash in his possession when he was caught. Nelson (aged 16) had no drugs in his possession, but he had £55 in cash and two mobile telephones and subsequent examination of one of those telephones in particular disclosed (a) significant contact between the two defendants and (b) text messages that were plainly in relation to the sale of drugs. Both defendants denied the offences and were released pending the outcome of scientific examination of the drugs/jacket and other investigations. Joseph was charged and whilst on bail was found to be in possession of a number of wraps of heroin powder, a small quantity of cannabis and a set of scales at his home. There were 29 wraps in total on that occasion, street value of £300. Joseph tendered a basis of plea that the drugs in his possession were being held by him for someone else. He said that after their seizure that person had told him that he owed £500 for the drugs. He was told to supply more drugs in order to repay the debt and then, when he lost the second lot of drugs, the same person used a hot iron to burn him to the top of his leg. Joseph pleaded guilty to possession of cocaine with intent to supply and possession of diamorphine (heroin) with intent to supply and guilty to possession of diamorphine (heroin) with intent to supply and possession of cannabis. He was sentenced to 2 years' and 8 months' detention under PCC(A)A 2000, s 91 in respect of each count relating to class A drugs, the sentences to run concurrently. No separate penalty was imposed in relation to the cannabis offence. Nelson, having been convicted of the offences of possession with intent to supply, was sentenced to 4 years' detention under PCC(S)A 20001, s 91. Joseph had previously appeared in the Youth Court for possession of crack cocaine and for threatening behaviour, when a referral order was made. Joseph appealed on the grounds that he should have been made the subject of a non-custodial sentence because of the progress (educationally, improvement in his behaviour at home, compliance with his bail package curfew) made since his second arrest in May 2010 and his appearance at the Crown Court in August of 2010. The Court of Appeal found that the SC's *Overarching Principles – Sentencing Youths* was applied and that the sentencing judge considered the matter for about an hour before imposing the sentence he did, which demonstrated a very significant reflection on the need for a custodial sentence and its proper length. The sentence reflected the damage done to the community by the sale of such drugs and the motivation of the defendant in being involved in such a sale. Those factors wholly outweighed the matters advanced by the defendant to support the imposition of a non-custodial sentence. According to *Overarching Principles – Sentencing Youths* the sentence of 2 years and 8 months was not manifestly excessive. The appeal of Joseph was dismissed. Nelson began offending when he was just 13 and had a previous conviction for possession of a substantial amount of heroin with intent to supply. He was previously made the subject of a community sentence involving an intensive supervision package, which he breached and received a sentence of 2 years' detention and was on licence at the time of this offence. Nelson appeal was in relation to the length of the custodial sentence. It was argued that, because of his age, a sentence of four years' detention under PCC(S)A 2000, s 91 was manifestly excessive and wrong in principle. The only mitigating factor was the defendant's age and from the PSR it was apparent that although the defendant was young he was not particularly immature and did not appear to recognise the need for a change in his behaviour and attitude. He had received a one third discount. The Court of Appeal found that a sentence of 4 years' detention was neither manifestly excessive nor wrong in principle and Nelson's appeal was also dismissed.

R v P [2010] EWCA Crim 2875, CA

The defendant, aged 17, had 72 wraps of crack cocaine found on him at the time of his arrest and which were estimated to have a street value of £3,520. The drugs were forfeited, as was £415 which was also on him at the time of his arrest. He pleaded guilty to possession of crack cocaine with intent to supply and being concerned in supplying crack cocaine. He was sentenced to an 18-month DTO for each offence concurrent. A man named Sbuiti (aged 17), was charged with being concerned in the supply of those drugs. The Crown's case was that the defendant and Subuiti had brought their respective drugs down to Portsmouth for the supply of the local drugs market. Subuiti pleaded not guilty at first but changed his plea to guilty on the first day of his trial. He received a 12-month DTO. The defendant pleaded guilty on a basis that he owed money which he was unable to pay and therefore agreed to work off the debt by delivering a quantity of drugs to a man in Portsmouth. The defendant had previous convictions for theft, assault with intent to resist arrest and possessing an offensive weapon, all of which had been dealt with by community penalties. He had however been given an 18 months' DTO for violent disorder, where the offence had involved a gang fight, which resulted in the death of one person. The DTO still had 4 months to run at the time of the present offences. The defendant had also been a victim of a group assault when he was on board a bus and was stabbed seven times in the back, arms and legs and spent two days in hospital. The defendant was relocated to a hostel, away from his family home due to a gun being fired outside his house, connected to the people that he owed money to. The PSR assessed the defendant as posing a medium risk of re-offending and a high risk of serious harm to the public because of his connection with gangs. However, it also said that the defendant now recognised that he needed and wanted to distance himself from these gangs. The defendant spent about 7 ½ months in custody before sentence. On appeal, it was said that on the defendant's basis of plea he was not a street dealer, but had been given a very specific task by Psycho (the person to whom he owed money) and had agreed to make that particular delivery only because of duress. Following the timely plea, charge not being contested, taking into account the time spend on remand (*R v Eagles* [2007] 1 Cr App Rep (S) 18), doubling the 7 ½ months spent on remand would be 15 months and then deducted from 24 months would leave 9 months. Applying the case of *Eagles* it would be 8 months in this case. As the defendant had already served over 4 months after sentence, this had the effect that he would be entitled to be released on licence for the remainder of the term (PCC(S)A 2000, s 102). The appeal was allowed to the extent that that the sentence of an 18-month DTO on each count was quashed and substituted, with an 8-month DTO on each count.

R v H [2010] EWCA Crim 1839, CA

The defendant, aged 16, went as a visitor to a prison with 16 rocks of crack cocaine with a weight of 2,41 grams at 17 per cent purity; 13.5 grams of heroin at 45 per cent purity; 6.64 grams of cannabis and 65.1 grams of cannabis resin hidden inside his trainers. The prison value of such a cache of drugs is substantially larger than the street value, which was placed at approximately £12,000. During his visit the defendant attempted to transfer one of his trainers to the inmate he was visiting, but a prison officer intervened and the drugs were discovered. The defendant pleaded guilty on the day of his trial to two counts of possession of Class A drugs with intent to supply and two counts of possession of Class B drugs with intent to supply. He pleaded guilty on the basis that that he had been introduced to drugs when he was aged 15 by a group of males who were associates of drug dealers and became a user and owed debts (£4,000) to his suppliers, which he could not pay. His parents, who had assisted him with debts in the past, could not afford to help him and it was made plain to him that he could either face the consequences of non-payment or he could clear the debt by swapping trainers with an inmate at the prison. While he did not know what was in the trainers, he frankly conceded that he suspected it must have been drugs. He had quite an extensive criminal record largely for offences of dishonesty and driving matters. He had never, however, received a custodial sentence but had been dealt with by way of supervision, reparation orders and attendance centre orders until July 2009 (after the commission of the index offences) when he was sent to a detention centre for 4 months for breaching a community order imposed for an offence of taking a conveyance without authority. The sentencing judge recognised the pressure that the defendant was put under to smuggle drugs into the prison, his age and vulnerability and referred to the Sentencing Council's *Overarching Principles – Sentencing Youths* guidelines. The PSR referred to the progress the defendant had made when he went into custody, good attendance record at college and improved relationship with his family. The likelihood of further offending was assessed as medium and the likelihood of causing serious harm was described as low. Nevertheless, it was recognised that given the gravity of these offences, a custodial sentence of some length was the most likely outcome. The defendant was sentenced on each of the 2 counts alleging possession of Class A drugs with intent to supply to 4 years' detention, the sentences to run concurrently. No separate penalty was imposed on the counts alleging possession of Class B drugs. He appealed against sentence. The Court of Appeal found that the judge's starting point of 7 years in this case, reduced further for plea, age and vulnerability, seemed to more than adequately reflect the mitigation but also the considerations expressed in the guideline. The 4-years detention was not deemed to be open to criticism as it was clear from the judge's sentencing remarks that he was at great pains to ensure that the sentence was not only appropriate, but also that he had regard to all the relevant considerations, including the guidelines. The sentence was not deemed to be manifestly excessive and the appeal was dismissed.

R v Akinyemi [2007] EWCA Crim 1921, CA

Defendant, who was 17, supplied drugs to undercover police officers. He pleaded guilty to nine charges of supplying heroin, and six of supplying cocaine. He was of previous good character. The PSR acknowledged that he had acted stupidly. He said to the writer that he had given little thought to the consequences of his actions and had focused on financial gain for himself. The judge sentenced him to three years' detention. His appeal was allowed. A starting point of four and a half years would be appropriate for an adult. However, since the defendant had been a youth at the time the offences were committed, and had been of good character, that was too long a period. Sentence reduced to 2 years and 3 months.

R v Hunter [2007] EWCA Crim 2361, CA

Defendant when she was 17, lodged with two others who were involved in the supply of class A drugs. At the request of her co-defendant, she supplied drugs to a person who happened to be an undercover police officer. She pleaded guilty to six charges of supplying a class A drug and two charges of offering to supply a class A drug. On arrest the defendant made full admissions and had two previous convictions of little relevance. The PSR noted her genuine remorse, her tragically unhappy and neglected family background, her own drug and alcohol misuse and homelessness. A community penalty was recommended but the judge said that a custodial sentence must be imposed because of the harm caused to others, although he noted that the defendant had made considerable progress while on bail. He made a DTO for 12-months. The defendant's appeal against sentence was allowed. The message must go out that custody would almost inevitably result from the supply of class A drugs, although an exception could be made in rare cases. The defendant was a young girl and she had had truly appalling childhood experiences. The court also took into account the circumstances in which she had become involved with drugs, how she had come under the controlling influence of the co-accused who had told her to supply the wraps, her guilty plea and remorse. The DTO was quashed and a 2-year community sentence was substituted.

R v H [2004] All ER (D) 23 (May), CA

The defendant was 17 years old (18 years when he pleaded guilty) and supplied 20/160 mg heroin and crack cocaine (with a purity of between 9% and 14%) to undercover police in a city. It was organised supply in an area known as a 'drug supermarket'. He was of previous good character, with learning difficulties. He pleaded guilty to four offences of supplying class A drugs and was sentenced to 5 years' detention in YOI. On appeal it was held that the judge had taken insufficient account of the defendant's mitigation and consequently the sentence was manifestly excessive. The judge had correctly considered that the defendant had required a sentence of detention to take into account the necessity for deterrence and parity of sentence. However, the fact that the defendant had crossed into a new sentencing range between the date he had committed the offence and the date of sentence was a powerful factor. Moreover, the defendant had been of previous good character and had learning difficulties. Accordingly, the sentence was quashed and a sentence of 4 years' detention was substituted.

R v Mitchell [2004] All ER (D) 145 (Nov), CA

The defendant was 17 and had no previous convictions. She pleaded guilty to importation of 13.8 kg of cannabis resin. She had agreed to import the drugs for £2,000. The PSR recommended a supervision order of 2 years' duration. The report stated that she was vulnerable, had been influenced by an older man, that she had suffered an abusive, chaotic and troubled childhood, and that the exposure to the criminal justice system had been a sobering experience for her. She had shown remorse and had accepted full responsibility for her actions. On the evening following the imposition of the sentence, she had discovered that she was pregnant. At three to four months of the pregnancy she suffered a miscarriage. The defendant was sentenced to an 18-month DTO. She had submitted on appeal that insufficient account had been taken of her age, plea and unfortunate background. Moreover, she contended that had the judge known that she was pregnant he might have concluded that a shorter period would have been appropriate. Her appeal was allowed. Insufficient weight had been given to defendant's circumstances, previous good character and early guilty plea although immediate and substantial custodial terms were warranted for such offences 12 months' custody was adequate.

R v Simon Coudjoe [2001] EWCA Crim 3015, CA

The defendant was 15 years old and was seen by a police officer acting suspiciously in a street. When the police officer searched he found a plastic bag containing nine packages with 913mg of heroin powder at 44% purity and seven packages with 801mg crack cocaine at 56% purity. A further bag was found in his coat pocket which contained 118mg of heroin at 46% purity. The street value of the heroin was estimated at £100, and of the cocaine at £140. He pleaded guilty to possessing heroin and cocaine with intent to supply, on the basis that he had found the drugs concerned in an alleyway and was taking them to his father; that basis of plea was rejected by the sentencing judge following a *Newton* hearing. He had two previous convictions resulting in non-custodial sentences, neither of which involved drug offences. The PSR indicated that the defendant did not himself use hard drugs and showed that he had a blasé attitude towards the dangers of supplying drugs. The offences were committed whilst he was on bail. It was said that there was a significant risk of re-offending until the defendant was prepared to accept responsibility for his own actions and behaviour. He was sentenced to 30 months' detention under PCC(S)A 2000, s 91, concurrently on each charge. The judge gave as much credit for guilty plea as he could having rejected the basis of plea following the *Newton* hearing. The judge took the view that the defendant was going to supply drugs to friends but accepted that there was no evidence that he was going to trade drugs on the street. On appeal against sentence, it was held that the judge had considered the case carefully, given the public concern about the proliferation of class A drugs, but had concluded that the sentence passed failed adequately to take into account the mitigating factors, in particular of the youth of the defendant. An 18-month DTO was substituted, concurrently on each charge.

R v JM [2001] 1 Cr App R (S) 29, CA

The defendant was 16 years old and was found by a police officer to be in possession of two bags of heroin containing 55g at 28% purity. His home was searched and a further 13g of heroin at 30% purity were uncovered. The police also seized £9,170 in cash; the defendant entered guilty pleas to two charges of possession with intent to supply. The defendant was of previous good character. The PSR referred to the defendant's desire to have money irrespective of the consequences but also said that his naivety regarding the seriousness of the offence had also played a part, as indeed had the bad company into which he had fallen. It was acknowledged that a custodial sentence was inevitable and the defendant appeared genuine in his desire not to continue with his lifestyle and to demonstrate to his family that he truly regretted his actions. He was keen to pursue his education and to make something positive of his life. The judge imposed 3 years' detention under CYPA 1933, 53(3) (now s 91), with a confiscation order in the amount of £9,170. The appeal against the defendant's sentence was dismissed on the basis that this was a serious offence of its kind; the quantity of drugs and cash recovered pointed to drug trafficking for substantial profit. The sentence passed was not manifestly excessive.

J.5 Burglary

R v H [2014] EWCA Crim 2292, CA

The defendant was 14 years old at the time of the offence when one night with a group of up to between 15 and 20 youths, he forced his way into a dwelling. One or more of the youths brandished meat cleavers, knives or other weapons. They had their faces covered with scarves and hoods. They threatened the occupants with violence. They forced their way into the occupants' rooms and they stole whatever came to hand. This included games consoles, money, tobacco, fishing rods and other items. Only the defendant was at that point in time identified; later others were also arrested. The defendant was 15 years old at the time of sentence. He was sent to the Crown Court by the Youth Court on a charge of domestic burglary. The prosecution initially included a count of aggravated burglary but in the event accepted a guilty plea to burglary. The judge observed that the defendant was only 14 when he committed the offence and 15 at the time of sentence; it was a serious burglary; group action; at night; and weapons were used to put people in fear. The judge took into account the defendant had entered a guilty plea at the earliest opportunity; did not have a particularly bad record and the pre-sentence report was positive about the defendant. The judge was of the view that anyone who participated in mob violence, going armed into the homes of others, out of necessity had to face an immediate custodial sentence and imposed a 12-month detention and training order. The defendant appealed against his sentence. He submitted that a noncustodial sentence should have been imposed and that a 12-month order was manifestly excessive given that before the plea this would amounted to a period of 18 months' detention and given the defendant's age and the policy of seeking to avoid the detention of children. The Court of Appeal held that in light of the defendant's age a noncustodial sentence was the appropriate one and the sentence of 12 months' detention was substituted with a 12-month youth rehabilitation order.

R v W [2010] EWCA Crim 393, CA

The defendant, who was 13 at the time of the offence, was seen by police officers seeking to force entry into a dwelling house via a rear patio door and a kitchen window. He pleaded guilty to the attempted burglary at the first available opportunity and admitted the breach of a community order (imposed for a previous offence of an attempted burglary). The defendant was sentenced to a 10-month DTO. His co-defendants were sentenced to an 18 month DTO and a suspended sentence of 6 months. He appealed against the sentence. The defendant had previously appeared before the courts for four burglaries, one of a dwelling house. He was a persistent offender. There was no alternative to a custodial sentence, bearing in mind the breach of the community order and previous orders not addressing the defendant's offending. The PSR stated that there was some progress with his education but there was also a list of examples of unacceptable behaviour. The Court of Appeal took into account the Sentencing Council's Definitive Guidelines *Overarching Principles – Sentencing Youths*, which stresses the basic and important proposition, that the 'The length of a custodial sentence must be the shortest commensurate with the seriousness of the offence'; the guilty plea and admissions; the extreme youth of the defendant' the fact that here sentencing was for an attempt and not the substantive offence; and the fact that this was a first custodial sentence. The 10-month DTO was thereby quashed and substituted by a sentence of a 6-month DTO.

R v D [2009] EWCA Crim 2426, CA

The defendant was 17 years old. He had been drinking heavily with his two friends before he broke into one of the flats in a block in the middle of the night. They threatened the occupant and demanded money from him and the defendant's friend punched the victim in the face. They took money, a laptop, computer games and DVDs. This was the defendant's first conviction, although he had been previously reprimanded and given a warning. He pleaded guilty to burglary and the court was asked to take into consideration one offence of vehicle interference. The PSR stated that the defendant was under the influence of drink and drugs at the time of the offence and was remorseful. He accepted that he had behaved in an unacceptable way and was ashamed of himself. He was assessed as being of a low to medium risk of re-offending and that he posed a low risk of causing physical harm. It was recommended that a community sentence should be imposed. The judge imposed an 18-month DTO due the victim's vulnerability and the premeditated group violence in which the three men had 'steamed into' the flat. On appeal the sentence was upheld due to the defendant being part of a dangerous gang and breaking into the victim's flat at night. The sentence reflected his level of participation.

R (on the application of R) v Manchester City Youth Court [2006] EWHC 564 (Admin), Div Court

The defendant (R) was aged 15 years and of previous good character. The defendant climbed into unoccupied domestic premises, opened the door of the property and let two other persons in. They left the house in some turmoil, having stolen property valued at almost £6,000. They took some of the goods to the home of R's father, which was close by. That house was searched the same morning and R was arrested at his home address. Some of the stolen property was recovered. When interviewed, R made full admissions and provided the police with the names of the others who had taken part in the burglary. R signified his intention to plead guilty at the earliest opportunity. He was charged with a single offence of burglary. The Youth Court declined jurisdiction despite the Crown and the solicitor representing R submitting that the case was suitable for summary trial. Counsel appearing for R sought later to persuade the justices to exercise their powers under MCA 1980, s 25 and to review the decision on mode of trial. The justices declined to do so. R sought judicial review of their refusal. It was held that it could not be said that there was a real possibility of R being sentenced to a custodial term in excess of 2 years. Therefore, it was clear that the justices' previous decision was wrong. The examination of the facts should have led the examining justices to conclude, as the case evolved before them, that summary trial was appropriate.

R v Peel [2005] All ER (D) 119 (Aug), CA

The defendant when aged 17, with another forced entry into an unoccupied home of an elderly lady. They took a lot of property, leaving when the house caught fire. The total value of damage and property stolen was about £300,000. One of defendant's fingerprints was found in the house. He at first denied being involved in the burglary but later said that it was the co-defendant's idea and he pleaded guilty to burglary. He showed little remorse and his risk of re-offending was assessed as high. He was sentenced to three years' detention in a young offenders' institute. On appeal it held that the defendant had been under 18 at the time of conviction and should have been sentenced to a DTO. Taking into account the time he had spent in custody, a DTO of 10 months was substituted.

R v Frota [2004] All ER (D) 166 (Jul), CA

The defendant committed two dwelling-house burglaries at night, stealing goods worth £1,800 none of which were recovered. On the second occasion the occupants were awoken. The defendant said that he had been threatened by a drug dealer to whom he owed money. The defendant pleaded guilty to the first offence in the Youth Court and was sentenced to an 8-month DTO. Two months later he was sentenced in the Crown Court to a 12-month DTO for the second offence, to run consecutively. The judge took into account the fact that the defendant had a number of previous convictions, the effect on the occupants of waking up to find a burglar in their home, and that the second offence was within days of the first. On appeal, it was said that the totality of the sentence was too great, although the matters were serious. A period of 8 months, consecutive, was substituted.

R (on the application of C) v Sussex Central Magistrates' Court [2003] EWHC 1157 (Admin), Div Court

The defendant (C) was 14 years old at the time of the offence, when together with three others he entered an empty dwelling at night. They stole property worth £125, caused substantial damage, defecated on fittings and killed a goldfish. The defendant was of previous good character. He was charged with dwelling burglary and criminal damage. The Youth Court declined jurisdiction under MCA 1980, s 24(1)(a). C sought judicial review of the Youth Court's decision. It was held that the Youth Court should have asked itself whether there had been a more than theoretical or vague possibility that the Crown Court would impose a sentence approaching 2 years' detention or more. C was 15 and of good character, and it was highly unlikely that the Crown Court would have sentenced him to a period of detention under the PCC(S)A 2000, s 91. In the circumstances, the Youth Court should not have declined jurisdiction and committed him for trial in the Crown Court.

R v M [2001] All ER (D) 11 (Jul), CA

The defendant was aged 15, went into a family home whilst members of the family were in residence and stole some clothing and demanded money from one of the occupants. The defendant had a previous conviction for assault occasioning actual bodily harm and was subject to a supervision order at the time the offence was committed. He made full admissions, indicating that he had been drunk, and that he had sent a letter of apology to the victim. He pleaded guilty to aggravated burglary and was sentenced to 3 years' detention under PCC(S)A 2000, s 91. The Court of Appeal substituted a DTO for 24 months and considered that the defendant would benefit from a DTO, given the element of supervision involved.

J.6 Arson

R v Iles [2012] EWCA Crim 1610, CA

The defendant was 16 years old at the time of the offence. Late one evening the police attended a school following a report that someone was smashing windows there. They found the defendant running from the scene and arrested him. The defendant had smashed 22 windows with a crowbar and by kicking. One of the windows had been prised open, and within the English block an attempt had been made to start a fire. That block was found to be full of smoke. A deodorant can was found in the corridor. It was wrapped in some kind of material and set alight. In interview the defendant admitted causing the damage and attempting to set fire to the school because he had been banned from attending the school prom. He was given police bail with a curfew. At the time of the attack on the school the defendant was living with his aunt and her husband. They were acting as foster carers for the defendant after his mother had died. He continued to live with Mr and Mrs Jones after the attack on the school and while on police bail. During that period, the defendant committed further offences which were dealt with by the Youth Court. Whilst on bail the defendant had damaged the tyres on his aunt's car by stabbing them with a knife and kicked her wing mirror and assaulted her husband, causing a cut to his head which bled. He then made threats against him whilst holding a pool cue. When the police officers tried to arrest him he made threatening gestures towards the officers. In interview, he eventually admitted that he was going to use the pool cue on his aunt's husband. He was bailed again. During a meeting with his youth worker, the youth worker became concerned about the defendant's obsession with knives. The defendant also threatened to kill his cousin. Further, the defendant went to the home of his aunt and her husband with others. He was armed with a pool cue and was wearing a Halloween mask. He made threats and the police were called. When they realised the police had been called he and the others ran off. The defendant was charged with arson and criminal damage relating to the school. When he first appeared for these offences before the justices they concluded that the arson was a grave crime and was so serious that it could not be dealt with in the Youth Court. Jurisdiction was declined under s 24 of the Magistrate's Courts Act 1980 and the matter was adjourned for committal for trial to the Crown Court (this was in 2010). The defendant was in custody on the date of the committal hearing. The defendant appeared before the justices in relation to the criminal damage (to the tyres), possession of a bladed article in a public place, assault occasioning actual bodily harm, possession of an offensive weapon and threatening behaviour. He pleaded guilty to these matters and these were adjourned for sentence. The defendant further appeared before the justices and pleaded guilty to the offence of making threats to kill and the offence of affray. Those matters, too, were adjourned for sentence. At the Crown Court the defendant pleaded guilty to the offences of arson and criminal damage to the school. The indictments made no mention of the value of damage to property on either count. The defendant had previously been convicted for assault on a constable and had also received reprimands for affray and possessing alcohol in a sports ground. The pre-sentence report said his offending began when he discovered his aunt had contact with his father and kept it from him. He was angry that she had not told him. The defendant showed very little empathy and no remorse. Social Care had been involved with his family since 2005 and the defendant was subject to a care order. The defendant admitted that he drank to intoxication and said he had tried various drugs. The opinion of the author was that he required a lot of work on his anger management. The defendant was likely to re-offend and the risk of harm was very high. Nevertheless, the report writer recommended a youth rehabilitation order with a supervision requirement, a curfew requirement and an electronic monitoring requirement. The court also had reports from a psychiatrist and a psychologist. The main points made by the psychiatrist were that the defendant was not suffering from a mental illness and did not suffer from a psychotic or mood disorder. There was nothing to suggest a hospital disposal. However, he did fulfil the criteria for a conduct disorder. The opinion was expressed that since the death of his mother his difficulties had been exacerbated. His lack of concern for the well-being of others was of some concern. The psychologist said that the defendant presented with delinquent predisposition and was at risk of behavioural disorder diagnosis. His aggressive behaviour had been present for a number of years. This had increased since the death of his mother. He presented a risk of re-offending due to his experiences, distorted beliefs and attitude. However, he was motivated to engage with intervention and treatment. The Judge passed a sentence of four years' detention with an extended licence of three years. He then sat with two Justices as a Youth Court and imposed concurrent sentences of detention for the other offences. The Definitive Guideline *Overarching Principles – Sentencing Youths* was considered when deciding the sentence. It was noted that the arson did not cause substantial monetary damage but it was nevertheless a grave offence carrying obvious dangers not merely to property but also to human life. The Appeal Court quashed the Crown Court's sentence and imposed a two years and six months detention and training order for the arson and no separate penalty in relation to the criminal damage. The Divisional Court considered the dangers as well as the benefits of a Crown Court Judge sitting as a Youth Court to sentence other offences which had not been committed to the Crown Court. In this case, the Judge sitting with Magistrates as a Youth Court had wrongly imposed sentences of detention under PCC(S)A 2000, s 91. These were replaced by concurrent detention and training orders or where the offence carried less than four months' custody, no separate penalty. The sentences for the other offences did not extend the main sentence of 30 months imposed for the arson. The Court said it was unnecessary in this case to decide whether the other offences should have been taken into account when assessing whether a term of more than four years was justified for the purposes of the dangerousness provisions – 'even taking account of all the other offending, a custodial term of 4 years would in our view have been manifestly excessive. The offences involved alarming violence and threats of violence. Bearing in mind the appellant's age, however, they were not in such a category as would warrant a custodial term of 4 years'.

R v H [2011] EWCA Crim 1913, CA

The defendant was aged 13 at the time of the offence and his co-defendant (K), was aged 14. The premises were a business which operated a rescue, recovery and repair service for commercial vehicles and cars from their site near a town centre. The premises were subject to two arson attacks, the first in the early hours of the morning and the second later in the evening on the same day. The first fire caused fire damage to five vehicles, two cherry pickers vehicles, a cement mixer and two cars. The second fire was more extensive and caused damage, estimated to be between £500,000 and £750,000 involving twenty-two fire damaged vehicles. The fire necessitated the setting up of an exclusion zone for twenty-four hours of several hundred metres owing to the risk of further gas cylinders present on the site. In relation to the second fire an unsuccessful attempt had been made to start the fire in one vehicle, but a second fire had then spread from vehicle to vehicle. Accelerant present in the yard had been used to set the fire. H had been part of the group responsible for starting the second fire. H and co-defendant (K) were arrested in the area. When interviewed he stated he was walking to a friend's house when he came across his co-defendant and others. He admitted entering the yard through a hole in the fencing to see damage caused by the first fire and stated that at the encouragement of his co-defendant he had participated in the offence. He had made the unsuccessful attempt to light a fire in the van. K had then lit the successful fire and he helped that to take hold by adding paper. He expressed remorse for his actions. The PSR recommended a youth rehabilitation order. The judge deemed the offence to be a grave crime and imposed 2 years' detention on the basis that although K had been the leader H had been a willing follower and that H had every opportunity not to join in but had not taken those opportunities. The sentence reflected H's credit for a guilty plea and early admissions to the police, his age (13 at the time of the offence) and previous good character. The co-defendant received 4 years' detention under PCC(S)A 2001, s 91. The Court of Appeal said despite H's remorse; family problems; his vulnerability in a custodial setting; the lack of premeditation and peer pressure from a more sophisticated and older boy; his frank admissions about his and his co-defendant's roles; and the salutary effect of the court proceedings, the offence deserved a custodial punishment to reflect the gravity of criminality and obvious danger of the act. However, the Court of Appeal substituted an 18-month DTO in light of the defendant's continuing progress since not only being sentenced but the lengthy period before sentence.

R v B [2010] EWCA Crim 401, CA

The defendant, who was 15 at the time of the offence, set fire to a discarded armchair which had been left outside the door of a flat. No accelerant was used but the chair was burnt out, the flat door scorched and the life of a sleeping shift worker placed at risk when smoke entered his home. The shift worker sustained minor burns to his hand and thigh in the course of his escape. The fire was able to be extinguished by the landlord of a nearby public house with a fire extinguisher. The defendant pleaded guilty to an offence of arson, being reckless as to whether life was endangered, and received an 18-month DTO. He appealed against his sentence. Despite the defendant's age and immaturity; good character save a caution for criminal damage; being affected by a bereavement; and remorse it was said that a custodial sentence was inevitable. However, since this case was not a case in which detention for public protection or a sentence of detention pursuant to PCC(S)A 2000, s 91 was necessary, the maximum term available was a 24-month DTO. Taking into account the defendant's guilty plea and time spent on remand the sentence of an 18 months' DTO was quashed and substituted with a 12-month DTO.

R v Ryder [2008] EWCA Crim 3328, CA

The defendant was aged 16 at the time of the offence; she had been suffering from post-natal depression following the birth of her child. She had consumed alcohol following an argument with her partner, flipped a lit cigarette causing a fire in her home. She refused to leave and had to be removed by the fire service. There were young children in the houses to each side of the house she occupied. The fire caused £17,000 worth of damage. The defendant had a previous conviction for robbery. She pleaded guilty to arson being reckless as to whether life was endangered. The PSR suggested a possible non-custodial sentence but concluded that there was a high risk of re-offending and harm to the public. The defendant was sentenced to 18 months' detention. This was upheld on appeal.

Attorney General's Reference No 58 of 2007 [2007] EWCA Crim 2057, CA

The defendant was 14 years old. He climbed onto the roof of a school drama block after school finished and set fire to a piece of paper. This resulted in an extensive blaze which took 80 fire fighters to tackle. The blaze also destroyed a significant amount of pupils' course work and caused damage valued at approximately £3 million. Some people had to be evacuated from the premises. The defendant had previous convictions for offences of theft and failure to surrender, for which he had received a referral order and supervision orders. The defendant pleaded guilty on the day of trial to arson being reckless as to whether life was endangered. The judge imposed a supervision order with conditions attached including a 6-month intensive supervision programme and a 5-year anti-social behaviour order (ASBO). The Attorney General submitted that the sentence imposed failed adequately to reflect the gravity of defendant's offending and that a custodial sentence was required. The Court of Appeal took into account that the defendant had deliberately set fire to a building when there were people inside, caused the school substantial costs including loss to those students whose course work had been destroyed, the defendant had entered a late guilty plea, the defendant was out of control and had breached various orders on a number of occasions. Further since the instant sentence had been passed the defendant had been arrested on suspicion of committing other offences, had removed his electronic tagging device and broken the terms of his curfew order. The Court of Appeal held that it was clear that the defendant required a structured and controlled environment and it was not in the public interest to allow him to continue to commit crimes without punishment. The sentence was plainly unduly lenient and a sentence of 4 years' detention was substituted. The Court of Appeal commented that had the defendant previously received a custodial term and had he not been so young, the period of detention would have been substantially longer. The ASBO was quashed due to the lengthy custodial sentence imposed which would include relevant conditions on his licence following release.

R v N [2007] EWCA Crim 2524, CA

The defendant was a very vulnerable 13-year-old girl. She suffered from ADHD and had lacked parental support throughout her life. She had consumed alcohol in the early hours of the morning and set fire to some cardboard boxes in a shop doorway causing over £1million in damage. The defendant was of previous good character and pleaded guilty to arson, but said that she had not expected the fire to spread nor intended to damage the shop. It was recognised by the sentencing judge that the defendant was a victim of her circumstances, that her parents had inadequately discharged their parental duties, including failing to provide her with even basic health care. Also, the defendant had developed a tendency to alcohol addiction that her parents had not addressed. The YOT and a psychiatrist strongly suggested a lengthy supervision order, as she had responded well to a bail package whilst awaiting sentence. The judge however, was concerned about the extent of the supervision which would in reality be available for the defendant. He took the view that the defendant would not receive the vital support that she needed from her parents to manage the high risk that she posed and therefore a 3-year sentence of detention was imposed. The Court of Appeal substituted a 2-year DTO in light of the defendant's age, lack of foresight, guilty plea and lack of intention to destroy the shop.

R v C (Shaun) [2001] EWCA Crim 2007, CA

The defendant was a 14-year-old boy. On two occasions, he pushed burning material through the house letterbox of the 73-year-old victim. On each occasion the fire was extinguished. The defendant was of previous good character and suffered from ADHD. He pleaded guilty to two charges of arson being reckless as to whether life was endangered. The sentence of 3 years' detention was upheld by the Court of Appeal, despite the defendant's young age, given the serious nature of the offences and the defendant's apparent indifference to the distress caused to the elderly victim.

R v David Letham [2000] 1 Cr App R (S) 185, CA

The defendant was 16 years old at the time of the offence. He was a former student of the school where he broke some windows. Some weeks later he returned with another youth and started a fire in an art block, causing £400,000 damage. The defendant had no previous convictions and entered a guilty plea to simple arson on the basis of recklessness. He was sentenced to two years' detention for arson, with 3 months concurrent for criminal damage. The Court of Appeal accepted that there was no pre-planning and that no accelerant had been used. Also there was evidence that at the time of the offence the defendant was suffering from a depressive illness for which he could be treated. If the defendant had not been young and of good character, a significantly longer sentence would have been justified. It was said that apart from the damage done to the school, the work of many students had been destroyed and therefore a sentence of less than 2 years could not be justified.

J.7 Violent disorder

R v B [2012] EWCA Crim 2596, CA

The defendant was aged 14 at the time of the offence of violent disorder. The defendant was a 'looked after child', being looked after by the local authority and had lived with his aunt for a period of three weeks at a temporary address which was in the heart of the area where the riots took place. The defendant participated in those disturbances to the extent that he was present with other youths who tipped over bins and attempted to set them on fire. He was with a group of youths moving towards police lines, and CCTV footage showed him making gestures to the police which he told the Probation Service were motivated both by his immaturity and his having felt hemmed in by the police tactics. Beyond his gestures to the police, he did not participate in any acquisitive crime; nor was there any evidence that he committed any violence, but he plainly had a 'wonderful time' (as it was described by the sentencing judge). The defendant had two previous convictions, both for battery: one in April 2010 and the other in October 2011 (after the date of the violent disorder). He entered a guilty plea to the offence of violent disorder. The judge sentenced him to a one year Youth Rehabilitation Order and reserved the breaches of the order to him. The Youth Rehabilitation Order had a number of conditions attached to it. There was a supervision requirement for twelve months which would expire with the order on 12 April 2013. The defendant was subsequently sentenced for a significant breach of the Youth Rehabilitation Order. The defendant had gone missing for a period of 24 days, had failed to provide an address or to attend any appointments with his case manager during that time. He was in touch by telephone on two occasions but he would not say where he was and it was plain that he had disabled his electronic curfew equipment. The breach report made it clear that his unstable living arrangements were a main factor for the breach. He had been living at his mother's home. His mother had her own personal problems. Their relationship was unstable and the defendant had apparently been thrown out of that residence. The recommendation of the author of the report was that a robust community sentence should address any risks presented by the defendant and proposed that the Youth Rehabilitation Order should continue, but that there should be an addition of a fresh three-month exclusion requirement, a three-month prohibited activity requirement and a further curfew period of six months to be reinforced by the use of the electronic 'Buddi' system. The judge decided to impose a Detention and Training Order for eight months, having taken into account the fact that the defendant accepted the breach, he had admitted the violent disorder (the trigger offence), the fact that he had already spent some time in custody, and the fact that he was only 15 years old. The defendant appealed against the sentence on the grounds that the judge had failed to have regard to many of the principles set out in the Sentencing Council's Guideline *Overarching Principles for Sentencing Youths*. The Court of Appeal found that the defendant had been given a chance to demonstrate his ability properly to be managed within the community and to slough off the malevolent influence of the gang of which he was a part when he committed the offence of violent disorder. Although the Appeal Court did not find the sentence imposed to be manifestly excessive, it decided in light of the recommendation of the author of the report about the longer-term management of the defendant within the community to quash the Detention and Training Order and substitute it for a 15 month Youth Rehabilitation Order in different terms from the original one imposed.

R v L; Graham Lee Smith; Charles Michael Clark [2011] EWCA Crim 129, CA

The defendants, L (aged 15); Clark and another (Simpson) were part of a group of 12 to 15 people in the early hours of the morning when they came across four Polish nationals who were walking home from a public house. The defendant, Smith, appeared at the scene after receiving a text message and almost immediately started acting aggressively towards one of the Polish people. Tempers rose and the Polish people removed themselves from the area. They were followed by the group. Bottles and large planks of wood were thrown towards the Polish men. The group caught up with one of the men and he was struck by a bottle by one of the group (but not the defendants). He fell to the ground; he pulled himself up and was kicked by members of the group. Clarke encouraged a member of the group to attack the man and L appeared to be one of those who joined in the attack. Members of the public contacted the police. However the abuse continued with Smith throwing a plank at one of the other Polish men who had started to run off. The pursuit continued. One of the Polish men hid in a garden, another was caught and kicked and punched after having been knocked to the ground. The other Polish person was also knocked to the ground. He was punched and kicked as well as being struck with a piece of wood several times. The three Polish people were taken to hospital. One had sustained a cut to his forehead and another sustained serious head injuries requiring 41 stitches. The third received relatively minor injuries. The defendants were charged with violent disorder to which they entered guilty pleas at the retrial. Due to the very serious nature of the offence, a sustained attack on a group of people due to their nationality, use of weapons, serious injury being caused to one of the victims, L was sentenced to 18 months' DTO, Clark to 15 months' in YOI and Smith to 15 months' imprisonment. Due to the late guilty pleas the discount was only ten percent. L had previous numerous racially aggravated offences and the offence was committed when he was in a breach of a supervision order and a curfew order. On appeal it was argued that the maximum that could be imposed was a 2-year DTO taking into account the SC's *Overarching Principles – Sentencing Youths* paragraph 11.16 that for a 15 to 17 year old the starting point should be half to three-quarters of that which would have been identified for an adult offender. It was held that the judge had borne this in mind when he imposed the sentence. The appeals were dismissed.

R v N; Andrew Steven Rees; Joshua Reece Davies; Michael Thomas Paul
[2010] EWCA Crim 1515, CA

The defendants left a football match and went to a public house in Southampton city centre where they consumed alcohol, after which they committed the offence of violent disorder. CCTV captured the incident which showed N (juvenile) going into the public house and running out with others towards the area where the violence took place. As one person was being restrained N ran in and pushed out at that person. Paul was seen running out of the area near the public house and then punching out twice, with one of punches making contact. Davies was seen running from the area near the public house and pushing out twice and chasing others away. Rees chased others away and then walked towards where the violence was going on. There were also other defendants. The defendants all pleaded guilty. N was sentenced to 8 months DTO; Paul, 12 months' detention in a YOI; Davies 14 months' imprisonment. Football banning orders were imposed on all defendants for a period of 6 years. The Court of Appeal said that the Recorder was entitled to reach the conclusion that only an immediate custodial sentence could be justified. However N's sentence was reduced to a 4-month DTO taking into account the statutory provisions and guidelines which relate to youth sentencing (SC's *Overarching Principles – Sentencing Youths*). In each of the cases of the other defendants 6 months was substituted for the sentence imposed. The football banning orders were to remain in force.

R v H [2009] EWCA Crim 1453, CA

The defendants (H and N) had been part of a group of youths who had caused a disturbance outside a residential address. It was alleged that in the course of the disturbance H had abused and assaulted three people (K, B and C) and that N had been at the forefront of the disturbance, having punched K and kicked his front door. H and N admitted their presence at the disturbance but no more. They were charged with offences of violent disorder. The issue at trial was one of identification. H and N were convicted after trial and were sentenced, respectively, to 14 months' detention and to a 12-month DTO. H appealed against his conviction and N appealed against his sentence. It was held that the H's conviction was unsafe and N's sentence was quashed and replaced with a 12-month supervision order with a condition of 25 days of specified activities as he possessed a good school record and was studying for professional qualifications and A-levels.

R v C [2004] All ER (D) 345, CA

Defendant was 15 years old and part of a group of 20 to 30 men sharing an interest in football hooliganism. He became involved in an attack on a rival group. His participation lasted for 52 seconds during which he struck and kicked a window. The damage caused by the incident amounted to about £1,000. The defendant was of previous good character. He pleaded guilty to violent disorder. A DTO for 6 months was upheld due to the defendant being fully involved in a serious incident of mob violence.

J.8 Perverting the course of justice

R v O [2008] All ER (D) 246 (Jun), CA

When the defendant was aged 11, she made an allegation that her brother and another boy indecently assaulted her when she was aged nine. They were convicted and required to sign the sex offender register and the girl's brother thereafter spent two years in care. When challenged by her mother about the allegations, the defendant admitted that she had lied because she was fed up with her brother's behaviour at home. The defendant pleaded guilty to perverting the course of justice. PSR stated that the defendant had not appreciated the serious nature of what she had done. She expressed remorse, but did not fully understand the extent of hurt and distress which she had caused. A curfew and supervision order was recommended. The judge was condemnatory of the defendant and sentenced her to 18 months' detention, pursuant to PCC(S)A 2000, s 91. The Court of Appeal substituted an 18-month supervision order, as it was recognised that despite the dreadful act done by the defendant the effects could not have been imagined or understood by a child of her age (11). She had lacked the maturity to understand the enormity of what she had done. The sentence of detention should never have been passed. Whilst the judge had rightly been condemnatory, the defendant was a child and was still only 14. The defendant and her family required support rather than the sort of punishment which had been visited on her.

R (on the application of S) v Folkestone Youth Court [2007] All ER (D) 76 (May), Div Court

The defendant was 16 years old. He told the police that he had been robbed by a young man who had a knife, and he signed a witness statement. He admitted that the allegation was untrue after the young man had spent nine days in custody. The defendant had no previous convictions and was charged with perverting the course of justice. The Youth Court committed him to the Crown Court pursuant to MCA 1980, s 24(1)(a). On judicial review the Divisional Court said that even if an adult had been convicted of an offence of perverting the course of justice, it was unlikely that a sentence of 2 years or more would be imposed. Accordingly, there was no possibility that the Crown Court would have imposed a sentence in excess of 2 years and therefore the decision to commit the defendant to the Crown Court for trial had been manifestly wrong.

J.9 Driving offences resulting in death

R v M (Shabaaz) [2016] EWCA Crim 1323, CA

The defendant was 15 years old at the time when he killed a 68-year-old grandmother, a pedestrian crossing a single carriageway in a residential area which has maximum speed of 30 miles per hour. That afternoon it had been raining and there was light drizzle at the time of the accident. The defendant despite his age had been driving the vehicle on a daily basis and did not have a driving licence nor did he had any formal instruction on driving. He also had no third-party insurance for the vehicle. He had two passengers in the car and the accident investigation report assessed the average speed of the vehicle as it was driving towards the point where it killed the victim was 42 mph. The report also said had the defendant been travelling at the maximum permissible speed of 30 mph he would have had ample time to brake and stop and he would not have hit the victim. The defendant admitted seeing the victim and sounded his horn for some time and the victim was seen on the CCTV to quicken her steps on hearing the horn. He eventually applied his brakes but only after he had sounded the horn for some five to six seconds but by then it was too late. The vehicle went into a skid and its front nearside struck the victim just as she was reaching the pavement. The impact speed was assessed at 31 mph. The defendant did not stop at the scene despite having significant impact damage to his windscreen. The following day the defendant turned himself in. During the police investigations, a Youtube video was discovered showing the defendant driving a vehicle on a public highway in a busy residential area of Birmingham with cars parked on either side of narrow roads. He was driving aggressively around cars and travelling at speeds of up to 50 mph including on streets covered by a 20 mph restriction. He would have been aged 14 at the time. The defendant pleaded guilty to causing death by dangerous driving on the basis that he was travelling at about 40 mph prior to the accident. He saw the deceased crossing, sounded his horn but was surprised that she continued to cross the road. The basis of plea continued that he braked, the vehicle skidded and she made contact with the front nearside of the vehicle. At the point of impact he was travelling at about 30 mph. It was wet at the time. The basis of plea was that he slowed down but panicked and drove off. He continued for a short while since the nearside of the windscreen was cracked and impaired his vision. On the whole the prosecution accepted the basis of plea. The pre-sentence report explained that his mother had left his father because of trouble in the home. She was working full time and the defendant refused to comply with the boundaries that she had set. So he returned to live in his grandmother's home where his uncle took responsibility for him. He had been excluded from school for fighting. He was studying to be a motor mechanic. He had struggled to come to terms with his actions but demonstrated remorse. The pre-sentence report stated that he was loved and cared for by the family and they had put in place strategies to ensure that he would not repeat his behaviour. The pre-sentence report assessed him as a medium risk until work could be done on the impact of his offending, his propensity to attempt to impress his peers and their influence on him. A custodial sentence was warranted, said the report writer, but she expressed concerns about the defendant's naivety, vulnerability and susceptibility to negative peer influence. There was no evidence in a medical report prepared about a development delay, learning difficulties, ADHD or autism spectrum. There were very positive character references before the judge from the defendant's mother and uncle, from family friends, from an employer for whom he worked part-time and from a local councillor who had known the defendant since birth. The report from the young offender institution where the defendant was detained was equally positive. The defendant's behaviour was very good and he had received excellent reports for his educational and recreational activities. The report added that his family were offering support which was a very positive element for change. The judge accepted the offence fell into category 3 for causing death by dangerous driving and said the defendant's offending was significantly aggravated in three ways. First, said the judge, he was driving without any driving licence, training or insurance. Further, he had driven away rather than remain in the vicinity after the accident. Secondly, his offending was aggravated significantly by the fact that he was no doubt showing off to passengers in the car. Thirdly, he had been regularly driving the vehicle in the weeks before the accident. Given the YouTube video this was not a momentary lapse but a habit of driving in ways to show off to friends in a dangerous fashion. The judge said that the defendant's lack of experience was not a mitigating factor. That could only be appropriate where he had driven with a licence and had faced a sudden situation which he did not have the experience to handle. The judge said that with those aggravating features the starting point for an adult would be above that envisaged by the third category in the guideline. After trial the sentence would have been six years. The judge reduced that by 25% for the defendant's age, which was 15 at the time of the accident, 16 at sentencing. It was not a momentary lapse case but a case where the defendant had decided regularly to flout the laws of driving. Therefore the reduction was limited. The judge imposed a sentence of three years' detention under s 91 of the Powers of Criminal Courts (Sentencing) Act 2000. No separate penalty was imposed on related offences, namely driving without a licence, using a motor vehicle on a road without third-party insurance, failing to stop after a road accident and failing to report a road accident. The defendant was also disqualified from driving for five-and-a-half years and until he passed an extended driving test. The defendant appealed against the sentence on the grounds that the judge took too high a starting point, even having regard to the aggravating features. He said it was not an appropriate case to take a starting point for an adult of six years' imprisonment and that the judge had not properly reduced the sentence in light of his age. The reduction given was only 25% to take into account his age, lack of foresight and immaturity which was too little given that he had no previous convictions and all the indications were that he was very remorseful, had learnt his lesson and would not re-offend. In terms of the disqualification for driving the defendant submitted that a disqualification of five-and-a-half years was counter-productive and did not assist his rehabilitation. The Court of Appeal agreed that the five-and-a-half year disqualification was inappropriate, especially since the defendant was training in motor mechanics. The Appeal Court substituted a three-year period of disqualification but found the judge was correct in placing the offending in the guidelines in the way that he did and was entitled to limit the youth discount to 25%. The appeal was dismissed except with regards to the length of the disqualification.

R v Landon [2011] EWCA Crim 1755, CA

The defendant, who was 17 at the time of the offence, drove in excess of 66 mph in a 40 mph limit when it was raining, with large puddles and the road being poorly lit. He overtook another friend's vehicle, attempted to negotiate a bend, drove into a large puddle, lost control and collided with a wall, killing his two passengers. He pleaded guilty to two counts of causing death by careless driving and was sentenced to 20 months' detention in a young offender institution on both counts concurrent. He had passed his driving test a month prior to the offences. The aggravating factors were the standard of driving in the conditions, the excessive speed and the fact that two people had died, and the judge found that the offences fell just short of dangerous driving. The defendant on appeal argued that the starting point was too high for what had been a freak accident. His appeal was dismissed on the basis that the judge's approach had been unimpeachable, and he had regard to all the mitigating circumstances, including the defendant's age and remorse.

R v Fearn Theaker [2009] EWCA Crim 620, CA

When the defendant was aged 17, she was drinking with a group of friends and subsequently left with a friend whose car she later drove. The car collided with a wall and the friend who was the passenger suffered injuries from which two weeks later he died. There was no sure evidence of bad driving prior to the car leaving the road or of the defendant being over the legal limit. The defendant had only recently passed her driving test and was an inexperienced driver. The PSR reported that the defendant had a rebellious nature in the past; twice in 2006 she was cautioned by the police for ABH and she received a referral order for 6 months for criminal damage in October 2006. However, the PSR also said that she had developed into a sensible and stable young woman who spoke responsibly about drinking and driving but had too much to drink on the night in question and was behaving out of character. She also had been very affected by the consequences of the incident. The defendant pleaded guilty to causing death by careless driving when under the influence of drink or drugs and received a sentence of 2 years' detention (starting point 3 years prior to plea). She was disqualified from driving for 4 years and until she passed an extended driving test. The Court of Appeal said that the starting point of 3 years' custody which the judge took was too long. Balancing the real concern that the defendant may have been over the legal limit against the mitigating features (driving inexperience and youth as per the Sentencing Guidelines Council's guidelines) the appropriate starting point would have been 18 months' custody. Giving one-third discount for the early plea of guilty, the appropriate sentence would be one of 12 months' detention.

R v Charles William Bennett [2009] EWCA Crim 591, CA

The defendant (aged 17) had spent the evening drinking with his best friend. He had passed his driving test over three months before. They were both drunk before they left in the defendant's car and during the journey the car mounted a mini island in the centre of the road and knocked down a bollard. The impact damaged the rear nearside tyre of the car. The defendant continued to drive and within 75 metres or so the damaged tyre had deflated completely, making the car difficult to steer. The car veered onto the nearside grass verge before, at a point about 370 metres from the traffic island, travelling onto the wrong side of the road and colliding with a tree, causing the death of the defendant's friend. The defendant pleaded guilty to causing death by dangerous driving. The PSR recognised the likelihood of a custodial sentence and stated that the defendant accepted responsibility for his friend's death and wished to be punished for it. He was assessed as presenting a low risk of re-offending provided that he moderated his alcohol consumption. There were 12 character references which spoke highly of the defendant's capacity for work, his sporting abilities and his personality. The offence fell into the highest level according to the Sentencing Council's definitive guideline on *Causing Death by Driving*. The starting point for the sentence was eight years' detention after trial, but that starting point was increased to take account of three factors. First, that just two weeks before this offence the defendant had received a fixed penalty for being drunk and disorderly. The second factor was the extremely high level of alcohol in his blood and the third factor were the two warnings (collision with the bollard and losing control when the tyre deflated) which the defendant had disregarded. Mitigating factors taken into account were the defendant's good character, his age and his lack of driving experience, early guilty plea, the fact that the victim was his best friend, his genuine remorse and that in every other respect he was a caring, hard working honest youth. Defendant was sentenced to five years and four months' detention, disqualified from driving for seven years and ordered to take an extended re-test. The Court of Appeal reduced the detention to four years having regard in particular to the defendant's age and the mitigating factors. The starting point used by the judge was excessive and should have been six years, which after credit for guilty plea would result in four years' detention. It was also considered that the judge was entitled, to the limited extent that he did, to take account of the recent fixed penalty for being drunk and disorderly which should have alerted the defendant to the fact that the consumption of alcohol to excess was liable to involve him in serious trouble.

J.10 Possession of prohibited weapon

R v Gomes-Monteiro and Others [2014] EWCA Crim 747, CA

The Court of Appeal ordered these six appeals and applications to be heard together so that it could review whether the guidance given in *R v Povey* [2008] EWCA Crim 1261 by Sir Igor Judge CJ (as he then was) was being followed and applied, and so that it could decide whether any further guidance was required. In *R v Povey* Sir Igor Judge made clear the dangers caused by carrying knives and the escalation in the number of offences involving knives and in particular the carrying of knives in public places. It was made clear that sentences passed by courts had to focus on the reduction of crime, including its reduction by deterrence and the protection of the public. Further judgments of the Court of Appeal and the subsequent guidelines issued by the Sentencing Council emphasised the seriousness with which the use of a knife or similar weapon in any crime must be treated. Whilst it may be deduced from the six appeals from decisions of the Crown Court heard together before the Court of Appeal in the instant case that in the Crown Court the guidance given *R v Povey*, and repeated by Sir Igor Judge in other cases, is being followed and that no further guidance is required, it needs to be borne in mind that there are also offences that either do not come to court, where cautions are administered or which are dealt with in the magistrates' court and the Youth Court. In magistrates' courts and the Youth Court the position is more complex, particularly in relation to offenders between 10 and 15 and to those aged 16 and 17. The Guidance for magistrates was updated and strengthened to take account of *R v Povey* and changes in practice and legislation in 2014. It is essential that magistrates' courts strictly apply the new Guidance in relation to knife crime and the starting point of 12 weeks' custody for the lowest level of offence involving the use of knives. The principles governing sentencing for knife crime in the Youth Court are set out in the Guideline of the Sentencing Council entitled: *Overarching Principles – Sentencing Youths*. It is important that the Youth Court plays the closest attention to the guidance given in *R v Povey*. Given the prevalence of knife crime among young persons, the Youth Court must keep a very sharp focus, if necessary through the use of more severe sentences, on preventing further offending by anyone apprehended for carrying a knife in a public place and to securing a reduction in the carrying of knives. It is also important, particularly in relation to knife crime, that the guidance given in respect of cautions is aligned to the sentencing practice in the Youth Court, the magistrates' court and the Crown Court. The reader is referred to this judgment which deals with six appeals concerning offensive weapons.

Attorney General's Reference No 45 of 2008 [2008] EWCA Crim 2019, CA

The defendant was 16 years old when during the execution of a search warrant at his property under Drugs Act 1971, s 23 a prohibited weapon in the form of a converted blank-firing pistol capable of discharging lethal projectiles was found beneath the floor boards. In addition, a set of body armour was recovered from the defendant's wardrobe. The defendant told the police that he had the gun for his own protection due to a previous attack on his family but was considering returning the weapon to the person who gave it to him and had not considered taking it to a police station. He also told the police that he bought the body armour for his own protection. The defendant had previous convictions for offences, including violence and robberies, possession of an offensive weapon, a bladed article, on school premises, and common assault. The defendant pleaded guilty to possession of a prohibited weapon (handgun) contrary to the Firearms Act 1968 (FA 1968), s 5(1)(aba) and possession of ammunition without a firearm certificate contrary to the FA 1968, s 1(1)(b). The PSR indicated that the defendant was in contact with more criminally entrenched, sophisticated offenders than himself. He was described as a naive and immature young person who would struggle with leading a law abiding life on his release and was therefore assessed as presenting a high risk of re-offending and high risk of serious harm. The judge was aware that the offence attracted a minimum of 3 years' detention in the absence of exceptional circumstances. He found that the defendant's possession of the firearm in the light of the previous attack on his family members, together with his age and immaturity, amounted to exceptional circumstances. The defendant was sentenced to a 12-month DTO on each charge concurrently taking into account the time spent on remand. The Attorney General asked the Court to review the sentence on the grounds that it was unduly lenient. The Court of Appeal said that according to the case of *R v Lucas* [2007] EWCA Crim 708 the youth of a defendant would not provide an exceptional circumstance and in *R v Blackall* [2005] EWCA Crim 1128 the fact that the defendant had a firearm for the purposes of protecting himself was held not to amount to exceptional circumstances. Therefore the court could not agree that the facts of the present case justified a finding of exceptional circumstances. On the facts of the offences, and bearing in mind the defendant's previous convictions and PSR assessment a sentence of 3 years' detention under PCC(S)A 2000, s 91 was substituted The time spent on remand was taken into account.

J.11 Aggravated criminal damage

R v Alan T [2009] EWCA Crim 1441, CA

The defendants aged 16, 15 and 13 threw stones and bricks at vehicles travelling on a busy road, as a result of which a fatal accident occurred. They pleaded guilty to damaging property, being reckless as to whether life would be endangered. Eleven vehicles were damaged by having windscreens smashed or body work dented. One motorist suffered fatal injuries when taking evasive action and another motorist suffered a broken arm. The defendants were sentenced to 4 years', 3 years' and 2 years' detention respectively under PCC(S)A 2000, s 91. The Court of Appeal's view was that the sentencing judge was perfectly entitled to conclude that it was the defendants' acts that caused the vehicle to stop in the carriageway and that the defendants had set in train a sequence of events that ultimately led to the death of the motorist. The offence was extremely serious; the defendants engaged and persisted in a course of conduct on a busy road carrying fast-moving traffic which led indirectly to death, serious injury and substantial damage. The appeals were dismissed.

J.12 Section 20 inflicting bodily injury/ABH

R v M (J) [2015] EWCA Crim 2324, CA

The defendant was aged 14 at the time of the offence and his co-defendant was 15. The defendant got involved in a fight at school. The boy he fought asked for help from his 20-year-old cousin (GW). The following day the defendant was at a McDonald's restaurant with his girlfriend when GW went with his younger cousin to 'speak to him'. An argument started which also involved the co-defendant, in the course of which GW was asked why he was picking on someone younger than him. The argument continued and GW told the defendant to go outside. GW, the defendant, the co-defendant and others, including someone who was to film what happened on a mobile phone, went outside. There was plainly an expectation of a fight. Outside the co-defendant swung a punch at the side of the head of GW which was followed by a punch to GW's head from the defendant causing GW to fall to the floor. Both the defendant and co-defendant kicked GW to the arms and body. GW got up and further punches were exchanged before the fight concluded. GW left the scene. He did not report the matter to the police, and it was a week later that he went to hospital, when what he had thought was bruising was not healing. He was found to have sustained a depressed fracture of the right cheekbone. The bone was lifted and plated. Three months after the event GW continued to complain of some numbness and a vague symptom of blurred vision. The injury was likely to have resulted from a punch; there was no allegation of kicking to the head. The defendant and co-defendant were charged with causing grievously bodily harm with intent contrary to OAPA 1861, s 18. They appeared in the Youth Court and were sent to the Crown Court where they pleaded guilty to the alternative count of assault occasioning actual bodily harm (under OAPA 1861, s 20). The defendant had no previous convictions and his school attendance and behaviour had been good up to the date of the incident. There were references before the court from his headmistress and from family and friends who spoke highly of him. The report from the Youth Offending Team indicated that the defendant felt shocked and disgusted when he realised the result of the extent of the injuries sustained in the attack. The pre-sentence report acknowledged the risk of a custodial sentence but put forward other options including a Youth Rehabilitation Order with or without an intensive supervision and surveillance requirement. The sentencing judge viewed the mobile phone footage which had been shared through social media. The judge reviewed the Sentencing Council's Guideline on

Assault and took the view that the offence was within the highest category, expressing the view that there was greater harm: resulting from a sustained attack and injury that was serious in the context of the offence. It was said there was higher culpability because of the use of weapons in the form of a shod foot, and it was in essence a group attack. The judge expressed the view that, for an adult, the appropriate starting point after a trial would have been a sentence of two years' imprisonment, but that the sentence should be halved because of the youth of the defendant. The defendant was given full credit for the early guilty plea which reduced the sentence to a six-month DTO. The co-defendant (KL) who had delivered the first blow, was a year older at 16 and had a previous conviction for assault and one for criminal damage, he was also sentenced to a six-month Detention and Training Order. The defendant appealed against the sentence on the basis that judge referred at the sentencing hearing to the Guideline on Assault but made no specific reference to the Guideline *Overarching Principles – Sentencing Youths*. The Court of Appeal said that the defendant had been invited to go outside before he went on to use unlawful violence. He was at the date of the offence 14 years of age and without convictions, and there was no history of him being involved in trouble at school. He had expressed remorse for his actions, and his mother expressly was willing to co-operate with the Youth Offending Team and there was reason to believe that the defendant could best be prevented from further offending by the imposition of a community penalty. There was nothing in the report from the place in which he was now detained to change that view. A six-month DTO was quashed and substituted with a Youth Rehabilitation Order and an intensive supervision and surveillance requirement was not attached in light of the work that the defendant had done over the previous six weeks whilst he had been in custody at Rainsbrook.

R v A [2015] EWCA Crim 700, CA

The circumstances of the offence were that the victim was waiting at a bus stop to catch a bus to her sixth form college one morning. She was with her boyfriend. The defendant arrived and she was aware of his presence. He was somebody that she knew, although not well. She asked him how he was and he said that he was all right. A few minutes later the defendant stabbed her between the shoulder blades with a kitchen knife. When asked why he had done it, he said: 'I'm angry because I got kicked off the IT course at my college.' The victim's boyfriend tended to her, applying pressure to the wound. The defendant remained on the scene and made no attempt to run or to hide the knife and when the police arrived he showed them where it was. He was arrested. The victim was taken to hospital. She had a one centimetre superficial laceration to her back. She had three stitches. She was released later the same day and the stitches were removed. He pleaded guilty to unlawful wounding, contrary to s 20 of the Offences Against the Person Act 1861 and having an offensive weapon, contrary to s 1(1) of the Prevention of Crime Act 1953. The maximum sentence available to the judge under s 20 and in view of the defendant's age was a 24 months' DTO. To the extent that the sentencing guidelines were applicable, this was a category 2 case within those guidelines, that was to say a case of higher culpability and lesser harm, and in the case of an adult offender the starting point in the guidelines would have been one of 18 months with a range of one to three years. In view of the circumstances of the offence, including the premeditation and the use of a knife, there were aggravating features which would have been likely to result in a sentence somewhat higher than the 18-month starting point. However, given the defendant's age, the sentencing exercise for the judge was complicated by a number of factors. These included the restrictions applicable to a sentence of detention and training, the need to take account of the guilty plea tendered by the defendant and the fact that by the time the sentence came to be imposed the defendant had served four months on remand which in the case of a detention and training order would not count automatically against the detention element of whatever sentence was imposed, but would need to be taken into account in fixing the term of any detention and training order. There was a pre-sentence and a psychiatric report. Those reports expressed considerable concern at the defendant's wholly disproportionate reaction to failing his IT course and being excluded from it which resulted in the use of serious violence. He was assessed as being someone who was unlikely to re-offend, although it was also noted that he had failed to manage his emotions on that particular occasion and both report writers agreed that it was critical that he addressed emotional management and coping strategies and that until that was done there would be continuing concern. His behaviour at these secure training centres was described as 'impeccable' and he was making good progress with his sentence. The judge imposed a sentence of 18 months' detention and training concurrent on both counts. The defendant appealed against the sentence. The Court of Appeal said the judge could not be criticised for starting at or about the maximum available within the scope of a detention and training order but it did appear that he did not take sufficiently into account the combination of the defendant's guilty plea and the fact that he had by the time of sentence already served four months on remand. The Appeal Court reduced the sentence to one of 12 months' detention and training concurrent on each count.

R v C(H) [2012] EWCA Crim 2801, CA

The defendant was 16 at the time of the offence. The victim who was 14 years old was staying, on a temporary basis at the home of someone called Natalie (17 years old at the time). Natalie had bought food for the victim while she was staying there and she expected to be paid. There had been an exchange of views and an argument on a Blackberry messenger between the victim and Natalie. After the victim had entered the property Natalie locked the front door and the gate behind her. The victim finished packing and asked to be allowed to leave. At that point Natalie told her she could not. She said that the victim had to wait 10 minutes and told her to go into the lounge. Within 10 minutes or so the defendant and another person called Tanysha (18 years old at the time) arrived and came into the flat. They were known to the victim as being from the area. At that point, Natalie became aggressive. She confronted the victim over the insults on the Blackberry messenger. Natalie slapped the victim around the face, pulled the victim's hair and dragged her to the ground. All three girls then kicked and punched the victim after she had been dragged to the ground. Natalie then took a mop and a bucket filled with dirty water and poured it over the victim's face. As well as dirty water, there was also evidence that cleaning fluid, not bleach, was thrown into the victim's face. Tanysha then threw the remainder of the bucket's contents over the victim. There was some continuing violence. Then Natalie got sellotape and wrapped it around the victim's mouth and head. Natalie told Tanysha to take the victim's hands. Natalie held the victim's hands whilst Tanysha taped them. There was a man present who eventually persuaded them all to stop. The victim was allowed to go to the bathroom to wash and change her clothes. The defendant and Tanysha left the premises. The victim remained locked in the premises but was allowed to leave the next day when Natalie went to college. Natalie pleaded guilty to the assault occasioning actual bodily harm and also to another count of false imprisonment and was sentenced to 16 months in a young offender institution. Tanysha pleaded guilty to assault occasioning actual bodily harm and was sentenced to eight months' detention in a young offenders' institution suspended for two years with 12 months' supervision. The defendant pleaded guilty to one count of assault occasioning actual bodily harm. The pre-sentence report stated that the defendant had resided with her grandparents since the age of one after a serious domestic violence incident between her mother and her father. Her mother suffered post-natal depression which resulted in alcohol problems and her father died of a heroin and alcohol overdose when she was a baby. The family were known to social services. It was stated that the defendant was vulnerable and had a history of excessive alcohol abuse. The recommendation in that report was to make a referral order for 12 months.

The alternative was to make a youth rehabilitation order. The judge sentenced the defendant to an eight-month detention and training order. The defendant appealed against the sentence on the basis that the judge did not have regard to parity between the three defendants, failed to apply the necessary principles in the sentencing guidelines in sentencing the defendant who was a young offender and failed to take account of the mitigating circumstances. In addition, there had been further developments since the judge imposed the sentence. At the time of sentencing the defendant was pregnant and the length of sentence took account of the fact that it was expected the defendant would not be in custody at the time of the birth. However, post the sentence the defendant miscarried which had had a very serious effect on her wellbeing. The Court of Appeal held that applying the sentencing guidelines for assault and for sentencing youths, a sentence of eight months' detention and training order was manifestly excessive. The eight-month DTO was quashed and substituted with a 12-month referral order.

Appendix K

Justices' Clerks' Society guidance on breach of YRO

J C S

News Sheet
No:12/2009

Justices' Clerks' Society

England and Wales

2nd Floor, Port of Liverpool Building
Pier Head, Liverpool L3 1BY

Tel: 0151 255 0790 **Fax:** 0151 236 4458
E-Mail: Secretariat@jc-society.co.uk
Website: www.jc-society.co.uk

3rd December 2009

Ref: 51.0098

CIRCULATED DIRECT TO ALL MEMBERS OF THE JUSTICES' CLERKS' SOCIETY

Dear Colleague

NATIONAL LEGAL FORUM: YOUTH REHABILITATION ORDER QUERY - REVISED

Q: What power does the adult court have when re-sentencing an offender for breach of a youth rehabilitation order under Schedule 2 Part 2 Para 6(2)(c) Criminal Justice and Immigration Act 2008?

The Society has been considering the issue contained in the question regarding the interpretation of the following provisions of the Criminal Justice and Immigration Act 2008 when a person aged 18 years appears before an adult court for breach of a Youth Rehabilitation Order.

Schedule 2 Part 2 Para 6 (2) (c) states that the court may deal with the offender "by dealing with the offender, for the offence in respect of which the order was made, in any way in which the court could have dealt with the offender for that offence (had the offender been before that court to be dealt with for it)"

A youth may be sentenced by a Youth Court to a YRO for an offence which could not be tried in an adult magistrates' court because the offence is triable only on indictment in the case of an adult. A Youth Court may also sentence an offender to a YRO for an offence which, had it not made a YRO, would have justified a sentence of more than six months' custody.

Council has recognised that there are two possible interpretations of the statute, the first, which would mean the adult court before which a person brought for breach of a YRO can re-sentence using only the powers of an adult court, the second, that its powers are those of a youth court. The interpretation rests on the meaning of the words "the court" in para 6 (2) (c) of schedule 2 of the Act.

Council concluded that it must have been Parliament's intention that the latter meaning be given to the words of the statute, namely, that the words "the court" refer to the Youth Court which passed the sentence, not to the "appropriate court" which is defined earlier in the provision which gives the adult court jurisdiction to deal with the breach.

Council took account of the case of *R v Ghafoor* [2002] EWCA Crim 1857 and the general principle that courts should sentence with reference to the age of the offender at the time of the offence rather than when the offender falls to be sentenced.

Schedule 2 Part 2 para. 5 (3)(b) provides that when an offender who breaches a YRO has reached the age of 18 years or over the appropriate court before which he should appear is a magistrates' court (other than a youth court). This provision, in the opinion of Council, determines only the venue before which the offender appears to be dealt with and does not determine the powers of that court.

The powers of the court are determined by para. 6(2)(c), which states that the court may deal with the offender, for the offence in respect of which the order was made, in any way in which the court could have dealt with the offender for that offence (had the offender been before that court to be dealt with for it)". The use of the words "had the offender been before the court to be dealt with" implies that the phrase "the court" in para. 6(2)(c) means a court having jurisdiction to deal with the offender when originally sentenced and must be read to mean a youth court. To read "the court" as meaning an adult court could have the result of depriving the court of the power to deal with indictable offences and of giving a Youth Court the power to impose a longer period of custody on breach than the adult court would have in respect of other offences. Furthermore, if the legislation were intended to mean that the court's powers in such circumstances were those of the adult court the words in parentheses in that paragraph would be otiose.

Council also noted that the draftsman had chosen to use different language to that in paragraph 4 of schedule 3 of the Powers of Criminal Courts (Sentencing) Act 2000. That provision unambiguously states that the powers of a magistrates' court on breach are to deal with an offender "in any way in which it could deal with him if he had just been convicted by the court of the offence". The words which appear in parentheses in para 6(2)(c) of the 2008 Act are not used. Council noted also that the draftsman had not included in the 2008 Act an equivalent provision to that of sched 3 para 9(3) of 2000 Act which specifically provides that an adult court may impose a fine not exceeding £5,000, and/or deal with the offender "in any way a magistrates' court could deal with him if it had just convicted him of an offence punishable with imprisonment for a term not exceeding six months". Council was not persuaded this omission was an oversight but one which Parliament regarded as unnecessary as it intended the legislation to be interpreted in the manner already described.

A: *The adult court has the same powers that a Youth Court would have when dealing with a breach of a YRO. The court should sentence the offender as if he were a youth, notwithstanding the fact he has since attained the age of 18.*

Sid Brighton
Chief Executive

"Putting Justice First"

Appendix L

Allocation: Sending for Trial and Committal for Sentence Suggested step by step approach

A Youths not linked with Adults

1. Determine offences which are related (ie if indictable can be included in the same indictment or if summary only arise out of the same circumstances).

2. For each set of related offences

(i)   First identify whether any must be sent to the Crown Court for trial:

    (a)   homicide

    (b)   serious/complex fraud where notice served by prosecution under CDA 1998, s 51B

    (c)   child witness case where notice served by prosecution under CDA 1998, s 51C

    (d)   Firearms offences which attract minimum three-year custodial sentence for a youth (see Firearms Act 1968, s 51A or Violent Crime Reduction Act 2006, s 29)

    (e)   specified sexual or violent offences where the court is satisfied that the defendant is dangerous and the offence merits a custodial sentence with an equivalent fixed term of at least 4 years

(ii)   Secondly deal with potential grave crime offences. Note that *Sentencing Children and Young People* suggests that it is likely to be impossible to decide whether there is a real prospect that a sentence in excess of two years' detention will be imposed without knowing more about the facts of the case and the circumstances of the child or young person. In those circumstances the youth court should retain jurisdiction and commit for sentence if it is of the view, having heard more about the facts and the circumstances of the child or young person, that its powers of sentence are insufficient.

(iii) Thirdly deal with all other related offences.

If the court needs to adjourn the main offences (those which might be sent for trial) then the Court should adjourn possible related offences to tie (general principles and s 4A(3) PCC(S)A 2000).

If at least 1 related offence is to be sent to the Crown Court for trial then the youth plea before venue procedure must be followed with all offences which are related. Where a not guilty plea is indicated then consider whether the offence should also be sent for trial under CDA 1998, s 51A (4) or (5). Where a guilty plea is indicated the only power to commit for sentence is in

PCC(S)A 2000, s 6 which is dependent on other offences being committed for sentence in their own right (see step (ii) above).

If there is no related offence which is to be sent then the youth plea before venue procedure does not apply so that pleas may be taken in the usual way.

(iv) Finally take pleas in respect of any unrelated offences. Note that even unrelated convicted offences can be committed for sentence under s 6 PCC(S)A 2000, provided that at least one other offence has been committed for sentence under a different provision (such as sections 3B, 3C or 4A of the PCC(S)A 2000) (grave crimes, dangerous offenders, potential grave crimes)

Where there are some offences which must remain in the Youth Court because guilty pleas have been indicated under the youth plea before venue process and committal for sentence is not available then only sentence if satisfied this will not tie the hands of the Crown Court.

B Youths linked with Adults

1. If youth is sent for trial then adult on a related either way offence shall also be sent for trial if at same hearing. If adult appears at later hearing after youth has been sent then court may send the adult. (CDA 1998, s 51A (6))

2. If adult sent for trial then youth jointly charged/has related indictable charge and is indicating a not guilty plea (or no plea) should only be sent if in interests of justice. (CDA 1998, s 51(7) and MCA 1980, s 24A). See SC's definitive guideline *Sentencing Children and Young People* paras 2.12–2.14.

3. However youth sent, all related offences may also be sent whether on same or subsequent occasion provided that not guilty pleas (or no pleas) are indicated. (CDA 1998, s 51(7) & (8) and MCA 1980, s 24A)

General point: CJA 1988, s 40 can still be used to add certain summary only offences (assault on (prisoner custody officer/secure training centre custody officer/secure college custody officer/other person), damage, drive disqualified, taking a vehicle without consent Theft Act 1968, s 12(1)) provided that they are disclosed within the material served on the defendant under CDA 1998, ss 51 and 51A.

C. Youth Plea Before Venue Procedure

1. **Plea before venue does not apply:**

Youth Indictable only offences:

(a) Homicide;

(b) Firearms offences which carry a minimum three-year sentence for youths;

(c) Serious/complex fraud cases where Notice given under s 51B CDA 1998;

(d) Child witness cases where Notice given under s 51C CDA 1998;

(e) Dangerous offenders where the criteria is met.

2. Plea before venue does apply:

Youth Grave Crimes CDA 1998 (3)(b); MCA 1980, s 24A(1)

Offences related* to a sent offence: CDA 1998, s 51A(4) & (5); s 51 (7) & (8); MCA 1980, s 24A(1).

* related means:

if indictable that it can be joined in the same indictment

if summary only that it is punishable with imprisonment or disqualification and it arises out of circumstances which are the same as or connected with those giving rise to the indictable offence.

3. Youth Plea before venue:

Where the offence is a grave crime (or specified violent/sexual offence) defendants should be warned before an indication of plea is taken that the Youth Court/Magistrates' Court does have a power to send them to the Crown Court for a sentence of long term detention for that type of offence.

In other case simply take an indication of plea.

4. Committal for sentence:

PCCSA 2000, s 4A only allows the court to commit a potential grave crime for sentence where another offence is being sent for trial. This only applies if the defendant indicates a guilty plea. The provision is particularly useful for those offences which are unlikely to attract a custodial sentence of more than 2 years DTO but are better dealt with by the Crown Court because they are related to an offence which is to be tried at the Crown Court. Grave crimes which justify more than 2 years can be committed for sentence under PCCSA 2000, s 3B.

Appendix M

Sexual Offences in the Youth Court

The sexual offences protocol issued by the senior presiding Judge has now been incorporated into the Criminal Practice Direction:

CPD XIII Annex 2

SEXUAL OFFENCES IN THE YOUTH COURT

1. This annex sets out the procedure to be applied in the Youth Court in all cases involving allegations of sexual offences which are capable of being sent for trial at the Crown Court under the grave crime provisions.

2. This applies to all cases involving such charges, irrespective of the gravity of the allegation, the age of the defendant and/or the antecedent history of the defendant.

3. This does not alter the test that the Youth Court must apply when determining whether a case is a 'grave crime'.

4. In the Crown Court, cases involving allegations of sexual offences frequently involve complex and sensitive issues and only those Circuit Judges and Recorders who have been specifically authorised and who have attended the appropriate Judicial College course may try this type of work.

5. A number of District Judges (Magistrates' Courts) have now undertaken training in dealing with these difficult cases and have been specifically authorised to hear cases involving serious sexual offences which fall short of requiring to be sent to the Crown Court ('an authorised DJ (MC)'). As such, a procedure similar to that of the Crown Court will now apply to allegations of sexual offences in the Youth Court.

Procedure

6. The determination of venue in the Youth Court is governed by s 51 Crime and Disorder Act 1998, which provides that the youth must be tried summarily unless charged with such a grave crime that long term detention is a realistic possibility, or that one of the other exceptions to this presumption arises.

7. Wherever possible such cases should be listed before an authorised DJ (MC), to decide whether the case falls within the grave crime provisions and should therefore be sent for trial. If jurisdiction is retained and the allegation involves actual, or attempted, penetrative activity, the case must be tried by an authorised DJ (MC). In all other cases, the authorised DJ (MC) must consider whether the case is so serious and/or complex that it must be tried

by an authorised DJ (MC), or whether the case can be heard by any DJ (MC) or any Youth Court Bench.

8. If it is not practicable for an authorised DJ(MC) to determine venue, any DJ(MC) or any Youth Court Bench may consider that issue. If jurisdiction is retained, appropriate directions may be given but the case papers, including a detailed case summary and a note of any representations made by the parties, must be sent to an authorised DJ(MC) to consider. As soon as possible the authorised DJ(MC) must decide whether the case must be tried by an authorised DJ(MC) or whether the case is suitable to be heard by any DJ(MC) or any Youth Court Bench; however, if the case involves actual, or alleged, penetrative activity, the trial must be heard by an authorised DJ(MC).

9. Once an authorised DJ(MC) has decided that the case is one which must be tried by an authorised DJ(MC), and in all cases involving actual or alleged penetrative activity, all further procedural hearings should, so far as practicable, be heard by an authorised DJ(MC).

Cases remitted for sentence

10. All cases which are remitted for sentence from the Crown Court to the Youth Court should be listed for sentence before an authorised DJ(MC).

Arrangements for an authorised DJ(MC) to be appointed

11. Where a case is to be tried by an authorised DJ(MC) but no such Judge is available, the Bench Legal Adviser should contact the Chief Magistrates Office for an authorised DJ(MC) to be assigned.

Index

[all references are to paragraph number]